Speech, Image, and Language Processing for Human Computer Interaction:

Multi–Modal Advancements

Uma Shanker Tiwary
Indian Institute of Information Technology Allahabad, India

Tanveer J. Siddiqui
University of Allahabad, India

Information Science
REFERENCE

Managing Director:	Lindsay Johnston
Senior Editorial Director:	Heather A. Probst
Book Production Manager:	Sean Woznicki
Development Manager:	Joel Gamon
Development Editor:	Myla Harty
Acquisitions Editor:	Erika Gallagher
Typesetter:	Jennifer Romanchak
Cover Design:	Nick Newcomer, Lisandro Gonzalez

Published in the United States of America by
Information Science Reference (an imprint of IGI Global)
701 E. Chocolate Avenue
Hershey PA 17033
Tel: 717-533-8845
Fax: 717-533-8661
E-mail: cust@igi-global.com
Web site: http://www.igi-global.com

Library of Congress Cataloging-in-Publication Data

Speech, image, and language processing for human computer interaction : multi-modal advancements / Uma Shanker Tiwary and Tanveer J. Siddiqui, editors.
      p. cm.
   Includes bibliographical references and index.
   Summary: "This book identifies the emerging research areas in Human Computer Interaction and discusses the current state of the art in these areas"--Provided by publisher.
   ISBN 978-1-4666-0954-9 (hardcover) -- ISBN 978-1-4666-0955-6 (ebook) -- ISBN 978-1-4666-0956-3 (print & perpetual access) 1. Human-computer interaction. I. Tiwary, Uma Shanker, 1960- II. Siddiqui, Tanveer.
   QA76.9.H85S654 2012
   004.01'9--dc23
                                 2011047364

British Cataloguing in Publication Data
A Cataloguing in Publication record for this book is available from the British Library.

All work contributed to this book is new, previously-unpublished material. The views expressed in this book are those of the authors, but not necessarily of the publisher.

Table of Contents

Section 3
Multimodal Developments

Detailed Table of Contents

Section 1
Modeling Interaction

Chapter 1

Pradipta Biswas, University of Cambridge, UK

This chapter presents a brief survey of different user modelling techniques used in human computer interaction. It investigates history of development of user modelling techniques and classifies the existing models into different categories. In the context of existing modelling approaches it presents a new user model and its deployment through a simulator to help designers in developing accessible systems for people with a wide range of abilities. This chapter will help system analysts and developers to select and use appropriate type of user models for their applications.

Chapter 2

Uma Shanker Tiwary, Indian Institute of Information Technology Allahabad, India
Tanveer J. Siddiqui, University of Allahabad, India

This chapter views human-computer interaction as a cognitive process and underlines the representations and mechanisms which are required to develop a general framework for a collaborative human-computer interaction. The authors argue that the separation of specific problem solving skills and problem related knowledge from the general skills and knowledge will lead to separate interaction layer consisting of many cognitive processes. A three layer architecture has been suggested for designing collaborative HCI systems with multiple humans and computational agents. Some important characteristics of existing architectures useful for HCI are outlined. The representations and mechanisms used in these architectures help in exploring the process of design and development of collaborative interaction. An attempt has been made to outline the requirements of a general framework for collaborative HCI.

Chapter 3

Hung-Pin Hsu, National Chiao Tung University, Taiwan

The Metaverse describes a future virtual-reality based iteration of the Internet. It provides an interactive design environment to users using which they can design artifacts and cooperate with each other. This chapter describes features of Metaverse and compares it with two other interactive design environments.

Chapter 4

Ilham N. Huseyinov, European University of Lefke, Turkey

This chapter explores fuzzy logic based methodology of computing an adaptive interface in an environment of imperfect, vague, multimodal, complex nonlinear hyper information space.

Section 2
Speech, Image and Language-Based Interaction

Chapter 5

Navarun Gupta, University of Bridgeport, USA
Armando Barreto, Florida International University, USA

The role of binaural and immersive sound is becoming crucial in virtual reality and HCI related systems. This chapter proposes a structural model for the pinna, to be used as a block within structural models for the synthesis of Head-Related Transfer Functions, needed for digital audio spatialization.

Chapter 6

R. K. Aggarwal, National Institute of Technology Kurukshetra, India
M. Dave, National Institute of Technology Kurukshetra, India

This chapter reviews classical and recent approaches of Markov modeling, and also presents an empirical study of few well known methods in the context of Hindi speech recognition system.

Chapter 7

Tanveer J. Siddiqui, University of Allahabad, India
Uma Shanker Tiwary, Indian Institute of Information Technology Allahabad, India

Spoken dialogue systems are a step forward towards realizing human-like interaction. This chapter discusses issues related to spoken dialogue systems and presents a general architecture in which knowledge sources and models are separated from control information. This decoupling helps in achieving generality. The chapter identifies the key research challenges and gives a brief overview of some of the existing evaluation methods.

The area of speech recognition has been thoroughly researched upon during the past fifty years, ; however, robustness is still an important challenge to overcome. It has been established that there exists a correlation between speech produced and lip motion which is helpful in the adverse background conditions to improve the recognition performance. This chapter presents main components used in audio-visual speech recognition systems. Results of a prototype experiment conducted on audio-visual corpora for Hindi speech have been reported of simple phoneme recognition task. The chapter also addresses some of the issues related to visual feature extraction and the integration of audio-visual and finally present future research directions.

Describing the shape of an object is a well-studied, yet ever-engrossing problem, because an appropriate description can improve the efficiency of a shape matching algorithm, thereby enriching subsequent applications. This chapter proposes a novel boundary-based shape description using the Farey sequence to capture an object shape represented as a sequence of discrete straight line segments. The method would be computationally attractive for polygonal approximation and shape description of a large database of gray-scale images.

This chapter presents a new approach to multi finger gesture recognition in order to facilitate a direct graphical interaction with mobile computing devices equipped with mini projectors instead of conventional displays.

Metasearching is the process of combining search results of different search systems into a single set of ranked results which, in turn, is expected to provide us the collective benefit of using each of the participating search systems. Since, user is the direct beneficiary of the search results; this motivates the researchers in the field of Human Computer Interaction (HCI) to measure user satisfaction. . To measure user satisfaction, we the authors need to obtain feedback from user. This feedback might also be used to improve the quality of metasearching. This chapter discusses the design of a metasearch system that is based on human computer interaction.

Michal Ptaszynski, Hokkai-Gakuen University, Japan
Jacek Maciejewski, Independent Researcher, Poland
Pawel Dybala, Kotoken Language Laboratory, Poland
Rafal Rzepka, Hokkaido University, Japan
Kenji Araki, Hokkaido University, Japan
Yoshio Momouchi, Hokkai-Gakuen University, Japan

Text-based messages were the first online communication media. Emoticons are an extension to them which compensate for its limitations. They attempt to imitate /communicate body language in text. Emoticons are being heavily used in online communications. However, they have found little interest in natural language processing. This chapter focuses on the analysis of Japanese emoticons. The authors argue that emoticons represent multimodal information and propose a general framework for research on emoticons. They also present a prototype system, CAO (emotiCon Analysis & decOding), for affect analysis of Eastern style emoticon and experimentally demonstrate that their system provides nearly ideal results in different aspects of emoticon analysis.

Section 3
Multimodal Developments

David Griol, Carlos III University of Madrid, Spain
Zoraida Callejas, University of Granada, CITIC-UGR, Spain
Ramón López-Cózar, University of Granada, CITIC-UGR, Spain
Gonzalo Espejo, University of Granada, CITIC-UGR, Spain
Nieves Ábalos, University of Granada, CITIC-UGR, Spain

Multimodal systems have attained increased attention in recent years, which has made possible important improvements in the technologies for recognition, processing and generation of multimodal information. However, there are still many issues related to multimodality which are not clear, for example, the principles that make it possible to resemble human-human multimodal communication. This chapter focuses on some of the most important challenges that researchers have recently envisioned for future multimodal interfaces. It also describes current efforts to develop intelligent, adaptive, proactive, portable and affective multimodal interfaces.

Andrew Molineux, Lancaster University, UK

Keith Cheverst, Lancaster University, UK

In recent years, vision recognition applications have made the transition from desktop computers to mobile phones. This has allowed a new range of mobile interactions and applications to be realised. However, this shift has unearthed new issues in mobile hardware, interactions and usability. As such the authors present a survey into mobile vision recognition, outlining a number of academic and commercial applications, analysing what tasks they are able to perform and how they achieve them. The authors conclude with a discussion on the issues and trends found in the survey.

Khaled Necibi, University of Annaba, Algeria

Halima Bahi, University of Annaba, Algeria

Toufik Sari, University of Annaba, Algeria

Human Computer Technology has found applications in healthcare domain also. One such application is covered in this chapter. The chapter focuses on the use of automatic speech recognition technology for evaluating speech disorder. It discusses different types of speech disorders, reviews existing systems that can be used to detect such disorders, presents the main innovations in the field and discusses the available resources that can be used to develop such systems.

Preface

Human Computer interaction (HCI) deals with the relationships among people and computers. As the digital world is getting multi-modal, the information space is getting more and more complex. In order to navigate this information space and to capture and apply the implicit and explicit knowledge to appropriate use an effective interaction is required. Such an effective interaction is only possible if computers can understand and respond to important modalities of human perception and cognition, i.e., speech, image and language, including other modalities, e.g., haptic, olfactory and brain signals. HCI researchers have to respond to these challenges by developing innovative concepts, models and techniques. There have been efforts in the areas of language, speech, vision and signal processing. However, the general techniques may not be applicable to or may degrade in HCI environment. This book attempts to bring all relevant technologies (for Language, Speech, Image and other signal processing) at one place in an interaction framework.

The signal processing community and HCI researchers can refer the book to improve their understanding of the state-of-the-art in HCI and broaden their research spheres. It will help postgraduate and doctoral students in identifying new and challenging research problems in the HCI areas.

We invited chapter proposals for *Speech, Image and Language Processing for Human Computer Interaction: Multimodal Advancements* and received around forty proposals. After three rounds of reviews, revisions, suggestions and editing we are herewith fifteen chapters in this book. The book is neither a handbook consisting of numerous research papers nor a textbook describing each aspect of HCI coherently. It is not possible to cover all the aspects of HCI in a single book, especially when HCI is still not a matured area. The 15 chapters in the book provide contribution on models, techniques and applications of HCI and are organized in three sections which are as follows: 1) Modeling Interaction 2) Interaction based on Speech, Image and Language, and 3) Multimodal Developments. We had to include the first section, which describes cognitive user models and underlines the need of a general framework for effective interaction. Chapters contained in the second section present methods of audio, visual and lingual processing for multimodal interaction. The third section introduces issues related to multimodal interfaces and conversational systems. It describes current efforts to develop intelligent, adaptive, proactive, portable and affective multimodal interfaces and discusses mobile vision and health-care applications.

The book opens with a brief summary of different user modeling techniques in HCI in the first chapter. This chapter is useful for system analysts and developers who find it difficult to choose an appropriate user model for their applications. The models discussed in the chapter include GOMS family of models, cognitive models and application specific models. Chapter 2 emphasizes on the separation of specific problem solving skills and problem related knowledge from the general skills and knowledge. In this line of argument the chapter proposes a general three layer architecture of HCI, consisting of the human layer, the interaction layer and the computer layer. The authors categorize existing architectures for HCI based on the use of no cognition, individual cognition and social cognition, highlight their main features and outline a framework for collaborative HCI. The next chapter (chapter 3) analyzes the cognitive and interactive behavior of users in the collaborative design activities. The chapter presents features of Metaverse and compares it with two other cooperative design environments. The first section ends with chapter 4 presenting a fuzzy logic-based methodology for designing an adaptive user interface in imperfect, vague and multimodal environment.

The second section of the book collects methods for speech, Image and language processing for multimodal interaction. To improve human computer interaction, it is necessary to create immersive audio environments where the user feels like a part of the system. For this, chapter 5 presents a structural model for the pinna for the synthesis of head related transfer functions. Chapter 6 offers a brief review of classical and recent approaches of Markov modeling for speech recognition while chapter 7 gives an overview of spoken dialog systems. In chapter 8, the authors give a broad introduction to audio-visual speech recognition systems and address some of the issues related to visual feature extraction and integration of audio-visual information for speech recognition. Shape analysis and recognition is a well known problem in the areas of HCI and computer vision. Chapter 9 presents a novel idea of using Farey sequence to represent the edge slopes, and the vertex angles to get an efficient description in integer domain. In chapter 10, the authors report their work on gesture recognition by finding fingertip point locations aiming at the development of an 'accessory-free' or 'minimum accessory' interface for communication and computation. Considering the importance of HCI aspects of web search we have a chapter (chapter 11) focusing on effective meta-searching. An interesting extension to text-based messages is emoticons which have been almost overlooked in the area of HCI. The last chapter of this section describes a prototype system, CAO (emotiCon Analysis & decOding), for affect analysis of Eastern style emoticon.

The three chapters contained in the third section of the book discuss the applications and research issues involved in the multimodal development of interfaces and interactive systems. The section begins with an overview of architectures and toolkits for the development of multimodal interface in chapter 13. The revolutionary changes in communication led to the development of vision recognition applications on mobile phones. Chapter 14 identifies a number of such applications. Human Computer Technology has found applications in healthcare domain also. A number of gadgets are being used to monitor health of patients automatically. One such application is covered in the final chapter of the book. This chapter focuses on the use of automatic speech recognition technology for evaluating speech disorder. It reviews existing systems and discusses different types of speech disorders, the main innovations in the field, and the available resources that can be used to develop such systems.

We would like to thank all the authors for their contributions. We would also like to thank the members of the advisory board for extending their support and suggestions. Special thanks go to reviewers for providing thoughtful and valuable comments on the initial and revised chapters. Their comments and suggestions helped in improving the quality of the book.

Finally, we are deeply indebted to our family members for their patience and understanding while we were busy with this book.

We wish you happy reading.

Uma Shanker Tiwary
Indian Institute of Information Technology Allahabad, India

Tanveer J. Siddiqui
University of Allahabad, India

Section 1
Modeling Interaction

Chapter 1
A Brief Survey on User Modelling in Human Computer Interaction

Pradipta Biswas
University of Cambridge, UK

ABSTRACT

This chapter presents a brief survey of different user modelling techniques used in human computer interaction. It investigates history of development of user modelling techniques and classified the existing models into different categories. In the context of existing modelling approaches it presents a new user model and its deployment through a simulator to help designers in developing accessible systems for people with a wide range of abilities. This chapter will help system analysts and developers to select and use appropriate type of user models for their applications.

INTRODUCTION

A model can be defined as "a simplified representation of a system or phenomenon with any hypotheses required to describe the system or explain the phenomenon, often mathematically". The concept of modelling is widely used in different disciplines of science and engineering ranging from models of neurons or different brain regions in neurology to construction model in architecture or model of universe in theoretical physics. Modelling human or human systems is widely used in different branches of physiology, psychology and

ergonomics. A few of these models are termed as user models when their purpose is to design better consumer products. By definition a user model is a representation of the knowledge and preferences of users (Benyon & Murray, 1993).

Research on simulating user behaviour to predict machine performance was originally started during the Second World War. Researchers tried to simulate operators' performance to explore their limitations while operating different military hardware. During the same time, computational psychologists were trying to model the mind by considering it as an ensemble of processes or pro-

DOI: 10.4018/978-1-4666-0954-9.ch001

grams. McCulloch and Pitts' model of the neuron and subsequent models of neural networks, and Marr's model of vision are two influential works in this discipline. Boden (1985) presents a detailed discussion of such computational mental models. In the late 70s, as interactive computer systems became cheaper and accessible to more people, modelling human computer interaction (HCI) also gained much attention. However, models like Hick's Law (Hick, 1952) or Fitts' Law (Fitts, 1954) which predict visual search time and movement time respectively were individually not enough to simulate a whole interaction.

The Command Language Grammar (Moran, 1981) developed by Moran at Xerox PARC could be considered as the first HCI model. It took a top down approach to decompose an interaction task and gave a conceptual view of the interface before its implementation. However it completely ignored the human aspect of the interaction and did not model the capabilities and limitations of users. Card, Moran and Newell's Model Human Processor (MHP) (Card, Moran, & Newell, 1983) was an important milestone in modelling HCI since it introduced the concept of simulating HCI from the perspective of users. It gave birth to the GOMS family of models (Card, Moran, & Newell, 1983) that are still the most popular modelling tools in HCI.

There is another kind of model for simulating human behaviour that not only works for HCI but also aims to establish a unified theory of cognition. These types of models originated from the earlier work of computational psychologists. Allen Newell pioneered the idea of unifying existing theories in cognition in his famous paper "You can't play 20 questions with nature and win" at the 1973 Carnegie Symposium (Newell, 1973). Since then, a plethora of systems have been developed that are termed as cognitive architectures and they simulate the results of different experiments conducted in psychological laboratories. Since these models are capable (or at least demanded to be

capable) of simulating any type of user behaviour, they are also often used to simulate the behaviour of users while interacting with a computer. Gray et al. (1997) assert that cognitive architectures ensure the development of consistent models over a range of behavioural phenomena due to their rigorous theoretical basis.

So there are two main approaches of user modelling: the GOMS family of models was developed only for HCI while the models involving cognitive architectures took a more detailed view of human cognition. Based on the accuracy, detail and completeness of these models, Kieras (2005) classified them as low fidelity and high fidelity models respectively. These two types of model can be roughly mapped to two different types of knowledge representation. The GOMS family of models is based on goal-action pairs and corresponds to the Sequence/Method representation while cognitive architectures aim to represent the users' mental model (Carroll & Olson, 1990). The Sequence/Method representation assumes that all interactions consist of a sequence of operations or generalized methods, while the mental model representation assumes that users have an underlying model of the whole system.

There is a third kind of model in HCI that evaluates an interface by predicting users' expectations, rather than their performance, e.g., Task Action Language (Reisner, 1981), Task Action Grammar (Payne and Green, 1986) etc.). These models represent an interaction by using formal grammar where each action is modelled by a sentence. They can be used to compare users' performance based on standard sentence complexity measures; however, they have not yet been used and tested extensively for simulating users' behaviour (Carroll & Olson, 1990).

Finally, there was a plethora of systems developed during the last three decades that are claimed to be user models. Many of them modelled users for certain applications - most notably for online recommendation and e-learning systems.

However most of these models are closely tied with an application limiting their scalability to different projects.

In the following sections, I briefly describe these four different types of user models:

- GOMS family of models
- Cognitive architectures
- Grammar based models and
- Application specific model

The description is followed by a critical review of existing models and a new user modelling system that aims to strike a balance among different kinds of models with practical implications.

THE GOMS FAMILY OF MODELS

GOMS stands for Goals, Operators, Method and Selection. It was inspired by the GPS system (Newell & Simon, 1995) developed by Newell. It assumes that people interact with a computer to achieve a goal by selecting a method, which consists of a sequence of basic operations. The GOMS model enables a designer to simulate the sequence of actions of a user while undertaking a task by decomposing the task into goals and sub goals (John & Kieras, 1996). There are many variations of the original GOMS model.

The KLM model (Keystroke Level Model, Card, Moran, & Newell, 1983) simplifies the GOMS model by eliminating the goals, methods, and selection rules, leaving only six primitive operators. They are:

1. Pressing a key
2. Moving the pointing device to a specific location
3. Making pointer drag movements
4. Performing mental preparation
5. Moving hands to appropriate locations, and
6. Waiting for the computer to execute a command.

The durations of these six operations have been empirically determined. The task completion time is predicted by the number of times each type of operation must occur to accomplish the task.

Kieras developed a structured language representation of GOMS model, called NGOMSL (Natural GOMS Language) (Kieras, 1994). Originally, it was an attempt to represent the content of a CCT model (Johnson, 1992) at a higher level of notation. CCT is a rule-based system developed by Bovaria et al. (1990) to model the knowledge of users of an interactive computer system. In NGOMSL, the methods of the original GOMS model are represented in terms of production rules of the CCT model. Kieras et al. (1995) also developed a modelling tool, GLEAN (GOMS Language Evaluation and Analysis), to execute NGOMSL. It simulates the interaction between a simulated user with a simulated device for undertaking a task. John and Kieras (1996) proposed a new version of the GOMS model, called CPMGOMS, to explore the parallelism in users' actions. This model decomposes a task into an activity network (instead of a serial stream) of basic operations (as defined by KLM) and predicts the task completion time based on the Critical Path Method.

COGNITIVE ARCHITECTURES

Allen Newell (1990) developed the SOAR (State Operator and Result) architecture as a possible candidate for his unified theories of cognition. According to Newell (1990) and Johnson-Laird (1988), the vast variety of human response functions for different stimuli in the environment can be explained by a symbolic system. So the SOAR system models human cognition as a rule-based system and any task is carried out by a search in a problem space. The heart of the SOAR system is its chunking mechanism. Chunking is "a way of converting goal-based problem solving into accessible long-term memory (productions)" (Newell, 1990). It operates in the following way. During a problem solving task, whenever the system cannot determine a single operator for achieving a task and thus cannot move to a new state, an impasse is said to occur. An impasse models a situation where a user does not have sufficient knowledge to carry out a task. At this stage SOAR explores all possible operators and selects the one that brings it nearest to the goal. It then learns a rule that can solve a similar situation in future. Laird and colleagues successfully explained the power law of practice through the chunking mechanism (Laird, Rosenbloom, & Newell, 1984).

However, there are certain aspects of human cognition (such as perception, recognition, motor action) that can better be explained by a connectionist approach than a symbolic one (Oka, 1991). It is believed that initially conscious processes control our responses to any situation while after sufficient practice; automatic processes are in charge for the same set of responses (Hampson & Morris, 1996). Lallement and Alexandre (1997) have classified all cognitive processes into synthetic or analytical processes. Synthetic operations are concerned with low level, non decomposable, unconscious, perceptual tasks. In contrast, analytical operations signify high level, conscious, decomposable, reasoning tasks. From the modelling point of view, synthetic operations can be mapped on to connectionist models while analytic operations correspond to symbolic models. Considering these facts, the ACTR system (Adaptive Control of Thought-Rational) (Anderson & Lebiere, 1998) does not follow the pure symbolic modelling strategy of the SOAR, rather it was developed as a hybrid model, which has both symbolic and sub symbolic levels of processing. At the symbolic level, ACT-R operates as a rule-based system. It divides the long-term memory into declarative and procedural memory. Declarative memory is used to store facts in the form of 'chunks' and the procedural memory stores production rules.

The system works to achieve a goal by firing appropriate productions from the production memory and retrieving relevant facts from the declarative memory. However the variability of human behaviour is modelled at the sub-symbolic level. The long-term memory is implemented as a semantic network. Calculation of the retrieval time of a fact and conflict resolution among rules is done based on the activation values of the nodes and links of the semantic network.

The EPIC (Executive-Process/Interactive Control) (Kieras & Meyer, 1990) architecture pioneers to incorporate separate perception and motor behaviour modules in a cognitive architecture. It mainly concentrates on modelling the capability of simultaneous multiple task performance of users. It also inspired the ACT-R architecture to install separate perception and motor modules and developing the ACT-R/PM system. A few examples of their usage in HCI are the modelling of menu searching and icon searching tasks (Hornof & Kieras, 1997; Byrne, 2001).

The CORE system (Constraint-based Optimizing Reasoning Engine) (Howes, Vera, & Lewis, 2004; Tollinger et al., 2005; Eng et al., 2006,) takes a different approach to model cognition. Instead of a rule-based system, it models cognition as a set of constraints and an objective function. Constraints are specified in terms of the relationship between events in the environment, tasks and psychological processes. Unlike the other systems, it does not execute a task hierarchy; rather prediction is obtained by solving a constraint satisfaction problem. The objective function of the problem can be tuned to simulate the flexibility in human behaviour.

There exist additional cognitive architectures (such as Interactive Cognitive Subsystems) (Barnard, 2007), Apex, DUAL, CLARION (Wikipedia, n.d.) etc., but they are not yet as extensively used as the previously discussed systems.

GRAMMAR BASED MODELS

The grammar based model, such as Task action grammar (Payne & Green, 1986) and Task action language (Reisner, 1981) simulates an interaction in the form of grammatical rules. As for example, Task Action Language models

- Operations by Terminal symbols
- Interaction by a Set of rules
- Knowledge by Sentences

This type of modelling is quite useful to compare different interaction techniques. However, they are more relevant to model knowledge and competence of a user than performance.

APPLICATION SPECIFIC MODELS

A lot of work has been done on user modelling for developing customizable applications. These models have the following generic structure (Figure 1). They maintain a user profile and use different types of Artificial Intelligence (AI) systems to predict performance. The user profile section stores detail about user relevant for a particular application and inference machine use this information to personalize the system. A plethora of examples of such models can be found at the User Modelling and User-Adapted Interaction journal and proceedings of User Modelling, Adaptation and Personalization conference. This type of models is particularly popular in online recommender or help systems. A few representative applications of such models are as follows.

The Generative User Model (Motomura, Yoshida, & Fujimoto, 2000) was developed for personalized information retrieval. In this model input query words are related to user's mental state and retrieved object using latent probabilistic variables. Norcio (1989) used fuzzy logic to classify users of an intelligent tutoring system. The fuzzy groups are used to derive certain characteristic of the user and thus deriving new rules for each class of user. Norcio and Chen (1992) also used an artificial neural network for the same purpose as their previous work (Norcio, 1989). In their model, users' characteristics are stored as an image and neural networks are used to find patterns in users' knowledge, goals and so on.

The Lumiere convenience project (Horovitz et al., 2008) used influence diagram in modelling users. Lumiere project is the background theory of the Office Assistant shipped with Microsoft Office application. The influence diagram models the relationships among users' needs, goals, user background etc. However all these models are developed by keeping only a single application in mind and so they are hardly usable to model human performance in general.

Figure 1. Application specific user models

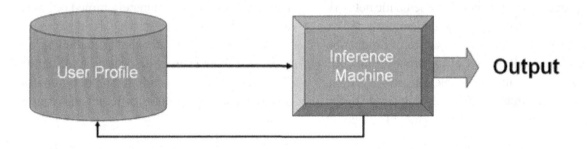

REVIEW

The GOMS family of models is mainly suitable for modelling the optimal behaviour (skilled behaviour) of users (John & Kieras, 1996). These models assume that for each instance of a task execution, the goal and the plan of a user are determined before the execution is started. During execution of a task, a novice first time user or a knowledgeable intermittent user may not have a fixed plan beforehand and can even change goals (or subgoals) during execution of the task. Even expert users do not follow a fixed sequence of actions every time. So the assumptions of the GOMS model may not hold true for many real life interactions. In actuality, these models do not have probabilistic components beyond the feature of selecting the execution time of primitive operators from a statistical distribution in order to model the uncertainty involved in the sub-optimal behaviour of users. As it fails to model the sub-optimal behaviour, it cannot be used to predict the occurrences of different errors during interaction. These problems are common for any Sequence/Method representations since these ways of representations overlook the underlying mental models of users (Carroll & Olson, 1990).

On the other hand, cognitive architectures model the uncertainty of human behaviour in detail but they are not easily accessible to non psychologists and this causes problem as interface designers are rarely psychologist as well. For example, the ACTR architecture models the content of a long-term memory in the form of a semantic network, but it is very difficult for an interface designer to develop a semantic network of the related concepts of a moderately complex interface. Developing a sequence of production rules for SOAR or a set of constraints for CORE is equally difficult. The problem in usability issues of cognitive architectures is also supported by the development of the X-PRT system (Tollinger et al., 2005) for the CORE architecture. Additionally, Kieras (2005) has shown that a high fidelity model cannot always outperform a low fidelity one though it is expected to do so.

Researchers have already attempted to combine the GOMS family of models and cognitive architectures to develop more usable and accurate models. Salvucci and Lee (2003) developed the ACT-Simple model by translating basic GOMS operations (such as move hand, move mouse, press key) into ACT-R production rules. However, they do not model the 'think' operator in detail, which corresponds to the thinking action of users and differentiates novices from experts. The model works well in predicting expert performance but does not work for novices.

Blandford et al. (2004) implemented the Programmable User Model (PUM) (Young, Green, & Simon, 1989) by using the SOAR architecture. They developed a program, STILE (SOAR Translation from Instruction Language made Easy), to convert the PUM Instruction Language into SOAR productions. However, this approach also demands good knowledge of SOAR on the part of an interface designer. Later, the PUM team identified additional problems with runnable user models and they are now investigating abstract mathematical models (Butterworth & Blandford, 2007).

There also exist some application specific models that combine GOMS models with a cognitive architecture. For example, Gray and Sabnani (1994) combined GOMS with ACT-R to model a VCR programming task, while Peck and John (1992) used SOAR to model interaction with a help-browser, which ultimately turned out to be a GOMS model.

Another problem of existing modelling approaches stems from issues related to disability. Researchers have concentrated on designing assistive interfaces for many different applications including

- Web Browsers (Stephanidis, 1998; IBM Web Adaptation Technology, 2008)
- Augmentative and alternative communication aids (Alm, Arnott, & Newell, 1992; Pasero, Richardet, & Sabatier, 1994; Mccoy, 1997; Stephanidis, 2003) etc.
- New interaction techniques
  - Scanning interfaces (Moynahan & Mahoney, 1996; Steriadis & Constantnou, 2002; Ntoa, Savidis, & Stephanidis, 2004)
  - Gravity wells (Hwang et al., 2002)
- Novel hardware interfaces
  - Head mounted switches
  - Eye gaze trackers
  - Brain-computer interfaces (Kennedy et al., 2000; Majaranta & Raiha, 2002; Gnanayutham et al., 2005; Abledata Products, 2007).

Most of these works concentrate on a particular application or a set of users, which reduces the scalability of the overall approach. Furthermore, developing systems for a small segment of market often makes the system very costly (Stephanidis et al., 1997).

There is not much reported work on systematic modelling of assistive interfaces. McMillan (1992) felt the need to use HCI models to unify different research streams in assistive technology, but his work aimed to model the system rather than the user.

The AVANTI project (Stephanidis et al., 1998, 2003) modelled an assistive interface for a web browser based on static and dynamic characteristics of users. The interface is initialised according to static characteristics (such as age, expertise, type of disability and so on) of the user. During interaction, the interface records users' interaction and adapts itself based on dynamic characteristics (such as idle time, error rate and so on) of the user. This model works based on a rule based system and does not address the basic perceptual, cognitive and motor behaviour of users and so it is hard to generalize to other applications.

The EASE tool (Mankoff, 2005) simulates effects of interaction for a few visual and mobility impairments. However the model is demonstrated for a sample application of using a word prediction software but not yet validated for basic pointing or visual search tasks performed by people with disabilities.

Keates et al. (2000) measured the difference between able-bodied and motor impaired users with respect to the Model Human Processor (MHP) (Card, Moran, & Newell, 1983) and motor impaired users were found to have a greater motor action time than their able-bodied counterparts. The finding is obviously important, but the KLM model itself is too primitive to model complex interaction and especially the performance of novice users.

Serna et al. (2007) used ACT-R cognitive architecture (Anderson & Lebiere, 1998) to model progress of Dementia in Alzheimer's patient. They simulated the loss of memory and increase in error for a representative task at kitchen by changing different ACT-R parameters (Anderson & Lebiere, 1998). The technique is interesting but their model still needs rigorous validation through other tasks and user communities.

Our previous user model (Biswas et al., 2005) also took a more generalized approach than the AVANTI project. It broke down the task of user modelling into several steps that included clustering users based on their physical and cognitive ability, customizing interfaces based on user characteristics and logging user interactions to update the model itself. However the objective of this model was to design adaptable interfaces and not to simulate users' performance.

Gajos, Wobbrock, and Weld (2007) developed a model to predict pointing time of users with mobility impairment and adapt interfaces based on the prediction. They estimated the movement time by selecting a set of features from a pool of seven functions of movement amplitude and target width, and then using the selected features in a linear regression model. This model shows interesting characteristics of movement patterns among different users but fails to develop a single model for all. Movement patterns of different users are found to be inclined to different functions of distance and width of targets.

THE SIMULATOR

Existing user modelling systems either work for a specific application or specific type of users, mainly expert users. Cognitive architectures do consider a wide variety of users and applications, but they are neither easy to program nor consider users with disabilities.

Figure 2 plots the existing general purpose HCI models in a space defined by the skill and physical ability of users. To cover most of the blank spaces in the diagram, we need models that can:

- Simulate HCI of both able-bodied and disabled users.
- Work for users with different levels of skill.
- Be easy to use and comprehend for an interface designer.

To address the limitations of existing user modelling systems, we have developed the simulator (Biswas, Robinson, & Langdon, 2010) as shown in Figure 3. It consists of the following modules:

The Environment model contains a representation of an application and context of use. It consists of:

- **The Application model** containing a representation of interface layout and application states.
- **The Task model** representing the current task undertaken by a user that will be simulated by breaking it up into a set of simple atomic tasks following the KLM model.

Figure 2. Existing HCI models w.r.t. skill and physical ability of users

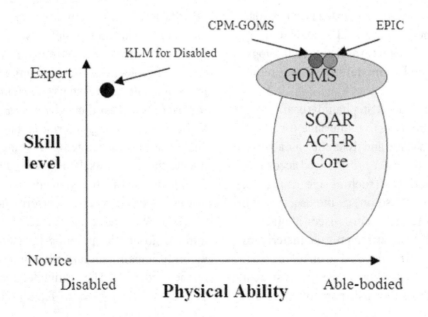

Figure 3. Architecture of the simulator

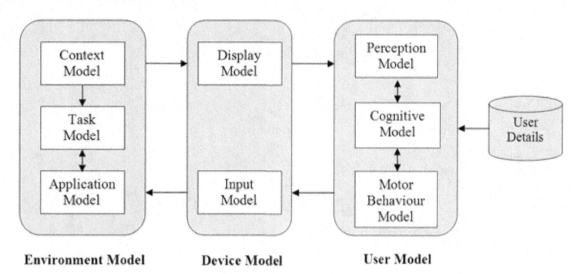

- **The Context model** representing the context of use like background noise, illumination and so on.

The Device model decides the type of input and output devices to be used by a particular user and sets parameters for an interface.

The User model simulates the interaction patterns of users for undertaking a task analysed by the task model under the configuration set by the interface model. It uses the sequence of phases defined by Model Human Processor.

- **The Perception model** simulates the visual perception of interface objects. It is based on the theories of visual attention.
- **The Cognitive model** determines an action to accomplish the current task. It is more detailed than the GOMS model but not as complex as other cognitive architectures.
- **The Motor behaviour** model predicts the completion time and possible interaction patterns for performing that action. It is based on statistical analysis of screen navigation paths of disabled users.

The details about users are store in xml format in the user profile following the ontology shown in Figure 4. The ontology stores demographic detail of users like age and sex and divide the functional abilities in perception, cognition and motor action. The perception, cognitive and motor behaviour models takes input from the respective functional abilities of users.

STM: Short Term Memory, IQ: Intelligent Quotient, EIQ: Emotional Intelligent Quotient

The visual perception model (Biswas & Robinson, 2009) simulates the phenomenon of visual perception (like focussing and shifting attention). We have investigated eye gaze patterns (using a Tobii X120 eye tracker) of people with and without visual impairment. The model uses a backpropagation neural network to predict eye gaze fixation points and can also simulate the effects of different visual impairments (like Maccular Degeneration, colour blindness, Diabetic Retinopathy and so on) using image processing algorithms. Figure 5 shows the actual and predicted eye movement paths (green line for actual, black line for predicted) and points of eye gaze fixations (overlapping green circles) during a visual search

Figure 4. User ontology

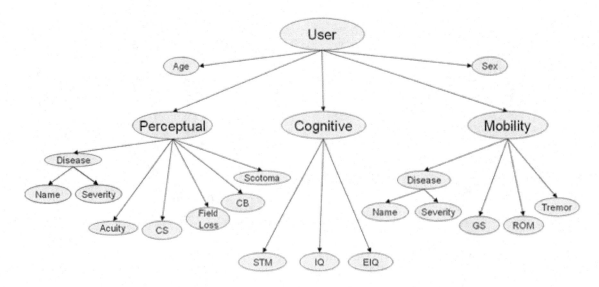

task. The figure shows the prediction for a protanope (a type of colour blindness) participant and so the right hand figure is different from the left hand one as the effect of protanopia was simulated on the input image.

The auditory perception model is under development. It will simulate effect of both conductive (outer ear problem) and sensorineural (inner ear problem) hearing impairment. The models will be developed using frequence smearing al-gorithm (Nejime & Moore, 1997) and will be calibrated through audiogram tests.

The cognitive model (Biswas & Robinson, 2008) breaks up a high level task specification into a set of atomic tasks to be performed on the application in question. The operation of it is illustrated in Figure 6. At any stage, users have a fixed policy based on the current task in hand. The policy produces an action, which in turn is converted into a device operation (e.g., clicking on

Figure 5. Eye movement trajectory for a user with colour blindness

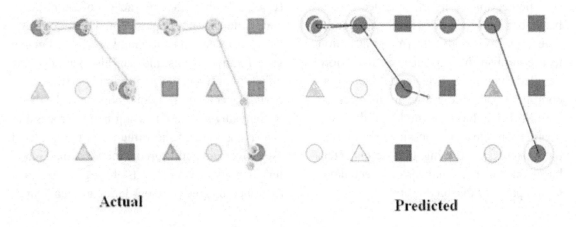

Actual   **Predicted**

a button, selecting a menu item and so on). After application of the operation, the device moves to a new state. Users have to map this state to one of the state in the user space. Then they again decide a new action until the goal state is achieved.

Besides performance simulation, the model also has the ability to learn new techniques for interactions. Learning can occur either offline or online. The offline learning takes place when the user of the model (such as an interface designer) adds new states or operations to the user space. The model can also learn new states and operations itself. During execution, whenever the model cannot map the intended action of the user into an operation permissible by the device, it tries to learn a new operation. To do so, it first asks for instructions from outside. The interface designer is provided with the information about previous, current and future states and he can choose an operation on behalf of the model. If the model does not get any external instructions then it searches the state transition matrix of the device space and selects an operation according to the

label matching principle (Rieman & Young, 1996). If the label matching principle cannot return a prospective operation, it randomly selects an operation that can change the device state in a favourable way. It then adds this new operation to the user space and updates the state transition matrix of the user space accordingly. In the same way, the model can also learn a new device state. Whenever it arrives in a device state unknown to the user space, it adds this new state to the user space. It then selects or learns an operation that can bring the device into a state desirable to the user. If it cannot reach a desirable state, it simply selects or learns an operation that can bring the device into a state known to the user.

The model can also simulate the practice effect of users. Initially the mapping between the user space and the device space remains uncertain. It means that the probabilities for each pair of state/action in the user space and state/operation in the device space are less than 1. After each successful completion of a task the model increases the probabilities of those mappings that lead to the

Figure 6. Sequence of events in an interaction

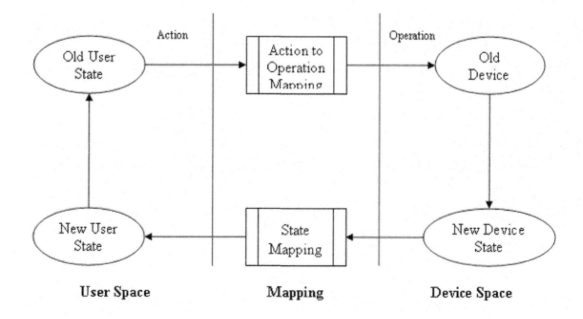

successful completion of the task and after sufficient practice the probability values of certain mappings reach one. At this stage the user can map his space unambiguously to the device space and thus behave optimally.

The motor behaviour model (Biswas & Robinson, 2009) is developed by statistical analysis of cursor traces from motor impaired users. We have evaluated hand strength (using a Baseline 7-pc Hand Evaluation Kit) of able-bodied and motor impaired people and investigated how hand strength affects human computer interaction. Based on the analysis, we have developed a regression model to predict pointing time. Figure 7 shows an example of the output from the model. The thin purple line shows a sample trajectory of mouse movement of a motor impaired user. It can be seen that the trajectory contains random movements near the source and the target. The thick red and black lines encircle the contour of these random movements. The area under the contour

has a high probability of missed clicks as the movement is random there and thus lacks control.

Each of the perception, cognitive and motor behaviour models were calibrated and validated separately involving people with and without visual and mobility impairment (Biswas, 2010).

The perception model was validated through an eye gaze tracking study for a visual search task. We compared the correlation between actual and predicted visual search time, eye gaze and also investigated the error in prediction. The actual and predicted visual search time correlated statistically significantly with less than 40% error rate for more than half of the trials (Biswas & Robinson, 2009a).

The cognitive model was used to simulate interaction for first time users and it can simulate the effect of learning as well (Biswas & Robinson, 2008).

The motor behaviour model was validated through ISO 9241 pointing task. The actual and

Figure 7. Mouse movement trajectory for a user with cerebral palsy

predicted movement time correlated statistically significantly with less than 40% error rate for more than half of the trials (Biswas & Robinson, 2009b).

These models do not need detailed knowledge of psychology or programming to operate. They have graphical user interfaces to provide input parameters and showing output of simulation. Figure 8 shows a few interfaces of the simulator.

At present it supports a few types of visual and mobility impairments. For both visual and mobility impairment, we have developed the user interfaces in three different levels:

- In the first level (Figure 8a) the system simulates different diseases.

- In the next level (Figure 8b) the system simulates the effect of change in different visual functions (like Visual acuity, Contrast sensitivity, Visual field loss and so on.) hand strength metrics (like Grip Strength, Range of Motion of forearm, wrist and so on) and auditory parameters (like audiogram, loudness and so on).

- In the third level (Figure 8c), the system allows different image processing and digital filtering algorithms to be run (such as high/low/band pass filtering, blurring etc.) on input images and to set demographic detail of users.

Figure 8. A few interfaces of a prototype of the toolbox

a. Interfaces to simulate the effects of different diseases

b. Interfaces to simulate the effects of different visual functions and hand strength metrics

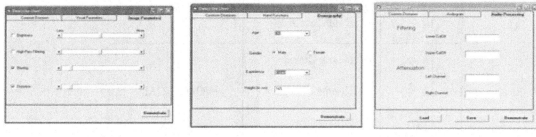

c. Interfaces to run image processing algorithms and set demographic detail of users

The simulator can show the effects of a particular disease on visual functions and hand strength metrics and in turn their effect on interaction. For example, it can demonstrate how the progress of dry macular degeneration increases the number and sizes of scotoma (dark spots in eyes) and converts a slight peripheral visual field loss into total central vision loss. Similarly it can show the perception of an elderly colourblind user, or in other words the combined effect of visual acuity loss and colour blindness. We have modelled the effects of age and gender on hand strength and the system can show the effects of Cerebral Palsy or Parkinson's disease for different age group and gender. A few sample screenshots can be found at http://www.cl.cam.ac.uk/~pb400/Demo.htm.

The simulator works in the following three steps.

1. While a task is undertaken by participants, a monitor program records the interaction. This monitor program records
   a. A list of key presses and mouse clicks (operations),

Figure 9. Timescale of human action (taken from Newell, 1990)

TIME SCALE OF HUMAN ACTION		
SCALE (sec)	SYSTEM	STRATUM
10^7 10^6 10^5		SOCIAL
10^4 10^3 10^2	Task Task Task	RATIONAL
10^1 10^0 10^{-1}	Unit Task Operations Deliberate Act	COGNITIVE
10^{-2} 10^{-3} 10^{-4}	Neural Circuit Neuron Organelle	BIOLOGICAL

b. A sequence of bitmap images of the interfaces (low-level snapshot)
c. Locations of windows, icons, buttons and other controls in the screen (high-level snapshot).

2. Initially, the cognitive model analyzes the task and produces a list of atomic tasks (detailed task specification).

3. If an atomic task involves perception, the perception model operates on the event list and the sequence of bitmap images. Similarly, if an atomic task involves movement, the motor behaviour model operates on the event list and the high-level snapshot

A demonstration version of the simulator can be downloaded from http://www.cl.cam. ac.uk/~pb400/CambridgeSimulator.zip

IMPLICATIONS AND LIMITATIONS

User trials are always expensive in terms of both time and cost. A design evolves through an iteration of prototypes and if each prototype is to be evaluated by a user trial, the whole design process will be slowed down. Buxton (2010) has also noted that *"While we believe strongly in user testing and iterative design……….. each iteration of a design is expensive. The effective use of such models means that we get the most out of each iteration that we do implement"*. Additionally, user trials are not representative in certain cases, especially for designing inclusive interfaces for people with special needs. A good simulation with a principled theoretical foundation can be more useful than a user trial in such cases. Exploratory use of modelling can also help designers to understand the problems and requirements of users, which may not always easily be found through user trials or controlled experiments.

I have shown that it is possible to develop engineering models to simulate human computer interaction of people with a wide range of abilities

and that the prediction is useful in designing and evaluating interfaces. According to Allen Newell's time scale of human action (Figure 9) (Newell, 1990), our model works in the cognitive band and predicts activity in millisecond to second range. It can not model activities outside the cognitive band like micro-saccadic eye gaze movements, response characteristics of different brain regions in biological band (Newell, 1990), affective state, social interaction, consciousness in rational and social band (Newell, 1990) and so on.

Simulations of each individual band have their own implications and limitations. However the cognitive band is particularly important since models working in this band are technically feasible, experimentally verifiable and practically usable. Research in computational psychology and more recently in cognitive architectures supports this claim. I have added a new dimension in cognitive modelling by including users with special needs.

CONCLUSION

This chapter presents a literature survey on human behaviour simulation and their applications on modelling users in human computer interaction. The review of the current state-of-the-art work shows a deficiency of modelling tools for users with disabilities. This chapter describes a simulator to address the problems in existing modelling techniques that proposes a set of models to simulate basic visual and auditory perception, cognition and motor action considering people with a wide range of abilities. It should be evident that the use of modelling and the type of model to be used depend on many factors like the application, the designers, availability of time and cost for design and so on. However, I hope this chapter will give system analysts an understanding of different modelling paradigms, which in turn may help them to select the proper type of model for their applications.

REFERENCES

Anderson, J. R., & Lebiere, C. (1998). *The atomic components of thought*. Mahwah, NJ: Lawrence Erlbaum.

Barnard, P. (2007). *The Emotion Research Group Website: MRC Cognition and Brain Sciences Unit*. Retrieved from http://www.mrc-cbu.cam. ac.uk/~philb

Benyon, D., & Murray, D. (1993). Applying user modeling to human computer interaction design. *Artificial Intelligence Review*, *7*(3-4), 199–225. doi:10.1007/BF00849555

Biswas, P., Bhattacharyya, S., & Samanta, D. (2005). User model to design adaptable interfaces for motor-impaired users. In *Proceedings of the IEEE TENCON Region 10 Conferences* (pp. 1801-1844).

Biswas, P., & Robinson, P. (2008a). A new screen scanning system based on clustering screen objects. *Journal of Assistive Technologies*, *2*(3). doi:10.1108/17549450200800023

Biswas, P., & Robinson, P. (2008b). Automatic evaluation of assistive interfaces. In *Proceedings of the 13th ACM International Conference on Intelligent User Interfaces* (pp. 247-256).

Biswas, P., & Robinson, P. (2009a). Modelling perception using image processing algorithms. In *Proceedings of the 23rd British HCI Group Annual Conference on People and Computers: Celebrating People and Technology* (pp. 494-503).

Biswas, P., & Robinson, P. (2009b). Predicting pointing time from hand strength. In A. Holzinger & K. Miesenberger (Eds.), *Proceedings of the 5th Symposium of the Workgroup Human-Computer Interaction and Usability on HCI and Usability for e-Inclusion* (LNCS 5889, pp. 428-447).

Blandford, A., Butterworthb, R., & Curzonb, P. (2004). Models of interactive systems: a case study on programmable user modelling. *International Journal of Human-Computer Studies*, *60*, 149–200. doi:10.1016/j.ijhcs.2003.08.004

Boden, M. A. (1985). *Computer models of mind: Computational approaches in theoretical psychology*. Cambridge, UK: Cambridge University Press.

Bovair, S., Kieras, D. E., & Polson, P. G. (1990). The acquisition and performance of text-editing skill: A cognitive complexity analysis. *Human-Computer Interaction*, *5*, 1–48. doi:10.1207/s15327051hci0501_1

Butterworth, R., & Blandford, A. (1997). *Programmable user models: The story so far*. Retrieved June 30, 2007, from http://www.cs.mdx. ac.uk/puma/wp8.pdf

Buxton, W. (2009). (2010). *Human input to computer systems: Theories, techniques and technology*. Retrieved October 27, 2009, from http://www. billbuxton.com/inputManuscript.html

Byrne, M. D. (2001). ACT-R/PM and menu selection: Applying a cognitive architecture to HCI. *International Journal of Human-Computer Studies*, *55*, 41–84. doi:10.1006/ijhc.2001.0469

Card, S., Moran, T., & Newell, A. (1983). *The psychology of human-computer interaction*. Mahwah, NJ: Lawrence Erlbaum.

Carroll, J. M., & Olson, J. M. (1990). Mental models in human-computer interaction. In Helander, M. (Ed.), *Handbook of human-computer interaction* (pp. 135–158). Amsterdam, The Netherlands: Elsevier.

Duffy, V. G. (2008). *Handbook of digital human modeling: Research for applied ergonomics and human factors engineering*. Boca Raton, FL: CRC Press.

Eng, K., Lewis, R. L., Tollinger, I., Chu, A., Howes, A., & Vera, A. (2006). Generating automated predictions of behavior strategically adapted to specific performance objectives. In *Proceedings of the ACM/SIGCHI Conference on Human Factors in Computing Systems* (pp. 621-630).

Fitts, P. M. (1954). The information capacity of the human motor system in controlling the amplitude of movement. *Journal of Experimental Psychology, 47*, 381–391. doi:10.1037/h0055392

Gajos, K. Z., Wobbrock, J. O., & Weld, D. S. (2007). Automatically generating user interfaces adapted to users' motor and vision capabilities. In *Proceedings of the ACM Symposium on User Interface Software and Technology* (pp. 231-240).

Gray, W., Young, R. M., & Kirschenbaum, S. (1997). Introduction to this special issue on cognitive architectures and human-computer interaction. *Human-Computer Interaction, 12*, 301–309. doi:10.1207/s15327051hci1204_1

Gray, W. D., & Sabnani, H. (1994). Why you can't program your VCR, or, predicting errors and performance with production system models of display-based action. In *Proceedings of the Conference Companion on Human Factors in Computing Systems in ACM/SIGCHI Conference on Human Factors in Computing Systems* (pp. 79-80).

Griffiths, T. L., Kemp, C., & Tenenbaum, J. B. (2008). *Bayesian models of inductive learning.* Tutorial presented at the Annual Meeting of the Cognitive Science Society.

Hampson, P. J., & Moris, P. E. (1996). *Understanding cognition.* Oxford, UK: Blackwell.

Hick, W. E. (1952). On the rate of gain of information. *Journal of Experimental Psychology, 4*, 11–26.

Hornof, A. J., & Kieras, D. E. (1997). Cognitive modeling reveals menu search is both random and systematic. In *Proceedings of the ACM/SIGCHI Conference on Human Factors in Computing Systems* (pp. 107-114).

Horvitz, E., Breese, J., Heckerman, D., Hovel, D., & Rommelse, K. (1995). *The Lumiere Project: Bayesian user modeling for inferring the goals and needs of software users.* Redmond, WA: Microsoft Research. Retrieved from http://research.microsoft.com/en-us/um/people/horvitz/lumiere.HTM

Howes, A., Vera, A., Lewis, R. L., & Mccurdy, M. (2004). Cognitive constraint modeling: A formal approach to reasoning about behavior. In *Proceedings of the 26th Annual Meeting of the Cognitive Science Society.*

John, B. E., & Kieras, D. (1996). The GOMS family of user interface analysis techniques: Comparison and contrast. *ACM Transactions on Computer-Human Interaction, 3*, 320–351. doi:10.1145/235833.236054

Johnson, P. (1992). *Human computer interaction: psychology, task analysis and software engineering.* New York, NY: McGraw-Hill.

Johnson-Laird, P. A. (1988). *The computer and the mind.* Cambridge, MA: Harvard University Press.

Keates, S., Clarkson, J., & Robinson, P. (2000). Investigating the applicability of user models for motion impaired users. In *Proceedings of the ACM/SIGACCESS Conference on Computers and Accessibility* (pp. 129-136).

Kieras, D. E. (1994). GOMS modeling of user interfaces using NGOMSL. In *Proceedings of the Conference Companion on Human Factors in Computing Systems*, Boston, MA (pp. 371-372).

Kieras, D. E. (2005). Fidelity issues in cognitive architectures for HCI Modelling: Be careful what you wish for. In *Proceedings of the International Conference on Human Computer Interaction.*

Kieras, D. E., & Meyer, D. E. (1990). An overview of the EPIC architecture for cognition and performance with application to human-computer interaction. *Human-Computer Interaction, 12,* 391–438.

Kieras, D. E., Wood, S. D., Abotel, K., & Hornof, A. (1995). GLEAN: A computer-based tool for rapid GOMS model usability evaluation of user interface designs. In *Proceedings of the ACM Symposium on User Interface and Software Technology* (pp. 91-100).

Laird, J. E., Rosenbloom, P. S., & Newell, A. (1984). Towards chunking as a general learning mechanism. In *Proceedings of the National Conference on Artificial Intelligence,* Austin, TX (pp. 188-192).

Lallement, Y., & Alexandre, F. (1997). Cognitive aspects of neurosymbolic integration. In Sun, R., & Alexandre, F. (Eds.), *Connectionist-symbolic integration.* London, UK: Lawrence Erlbaum.

Mankoff, J., Fait, H., & Juang, R. (2005). Evaluating accessibility through simulating the experiences of users with vision or motor impairments. *IBM Systems Journal, 44*(3), 505–518. doi:10.1147/sj.443.0505

Mcmillan, W. W. (1992). Computing for users with special needs and models of computer-human interaction. In *Proceedings of the ACM/SIGCHI Conference on Human Factors in Computing Systems* (pp. 143-148).

Moran, T. P. (1981). Command language grammar: A representation for the user interface of interactive computer systems. *International Journal of Man-Machine Studies, 15*(1), 3–50. doi:10.1016/S0020-7373(81)80022-3

Motomura, Y., Yoshida, K., & Fujimoto, K. (2000). Generative user models for adaptive information retrieval. In *Proceedings of the IEEE International Conference on Systems, Man and Cybernetics* (pp. 665-670).

Nejime, Y., & Moore, B. C. J. (1997). Simulation of the effect of threshold elevation and loudness recruitment combined with reduced frequency selectivity on the intelligibility of speech in noise. *The Journal of the Acoustical Society of America, 102,* 603–615. doi:10.1121/1.419733

Newell, A. (1973). *You can't play 20 questions with nature and win: Projective comments on the papers of this symposium.* Pittsburgh, PA: Carnegie Mellon University.

Newell, A. (1990). *Unified theories of cognition.* Cambridge, MA: Harvard University Press.

Newell, A., & Simon, H. A. (1995). *GPS: A program that simulates human thought.* Cambridge, MA: MIT Press.

Norcio, F. (1989). Adaptive interfaces: Modelling tasks and users. *IEEE Transactions on Systems, Man, and Cybernetics, 19*(2), 399–408. doi:10.1109/21.31042

Norcio, F., & Chen, Q. (1992). Modeling user's with neural architecture. In *Proceedings of the International Joint Conference on Neural Networks* (pp. 547-552).

Oka, N. (1991). Hybrid cognitive model of conscious level processing and unconscious level processing. In *Proceedings of the IEEE International Joint Conference on Neural Networks* (pp. 485-490).

Payne, S. J., & Green, T. R. G. (1986). Task-action grammars: A model of mental representation of task languages. *Human-Computer Interaction, 2,* 93–133. doi:10.1207/s15327051hci0202_1

Peck, V. A., & John, B. E. (1992). Browser-Soar: a computational model of a highly interactive task. In *Proceedings of the ACM/SIGCHI Conference on Human Factors in Computing Systems* (pp. 165-172).

Phillips, N. (2009). *Graphical modification for partially sighted gamer accessibility (Tripos Part II)*. Cambridge, UK: University of Cambridge.

Reisner, P. (1981). Formal grammar and human factors design of an interactive graphics system. *IEEE Transactions on Software Engineering, 7*, 229–240. doi:10.1109/TSE.1981.234520

Rieman, J., & Young, R. M. (1996). A dual-space model of iteratively deepening exploratory learning. *International Journal of Human-Computer Studies, 44*, 743–775. doi:10.1006/ijhc.1996.0032

Salvucci, D. D., & Lee, F. J. (2003). Simple cognitive modelling in a complex cognitive architecture. In *Proceedings of the ACM/SIGCHI Conference on Human Factors in Computing Systems* (pp. 265-272).

Serna, A., Pigot, H., & Rialle, V. (2007). Modeling the progression of Alzheimer's disease for cognitive assistance in smart homes. *User Modeling and User-Adapted Interaction, 17*, 415–438. doi:10.1007/s11257-007-9032-y

Stephanidis, C., & Constantinou, P. (2003). Designing human computer interfaces for quadriplegic people. *ACM Transactions on Computer-Human Interaction, 10*(2), 87–118. doi:10.1145/772047.772049

Stephanidis, C., Paramythis, A., Sfyrakis, M., Stergiou, A., Maou, N., & Leventis, A. …Karagiannidis C. (1998). Adaptable and adaptive user interfaces for disabled users in the AVANTI Project. In S. Trigila, A. Mullery, M. Campolargo, H. Vanderstraeten, & M. Mampaey (Eds.), *Proceedings of the 5th International Conference on Intelligence in Services and Networks* (LNCS 1430, pp. 153-166).

Tollinger, I., Lewis, R. L., McCurdy, M., Tollinger, P., Vera, A., Howes, A., & Pelton, L. (2005). Supporting efficient development of cognitive models at multiple skill levels: Exploring recent advances in constraint-based modeling. In *Proceedings of the ACM/SIGCHI Conference on Human Factors in Computing Systems* (pp. 411-420).

Wang, H. C. (2008). Modeling idea generation sequences using hidden Markov models. In *Proceedings of the Annual Meeting of the Cognitive Science Society* (pp. 107-112).

Wikipedia. (n.d.). *Cognitive architectures*. Retrieved July 1, 2007, from http://en.wikipedia.org/wiki/Cognitive_architecture

Young, R. M., Green, T. R. G., & Simon, T. (1989). Programmable user models for predictive evaluation of interface designs. In *Proceedings of the ACM/SIGCHI Conference on Human Factors in Computing Systems* (pp. 15-19).

Chapter 2
Working Together with Computers:
Towards a General Framework for Collaborative Human Computer Interaction

Uma Shanker Tiwary
Indian Institute of Information Technology Allahabad, India

Tanveer J. Siddiqui
University of Allahabad, India

ABSTRACT

The objective of this chapter is twofold. On one hand, it tries to introduce and present various components of Human Computer Interaction (HCI), if HCI is modeled as a process of cognition; on the other hand, it tries to underline those representations and mechanisms which are required to develop a general framework for a collaborative HCI. One must try to separate the specific problem solving skills and specific problem related knowledge from the general skills and knowledge acquired in interactive agents for future use. This separation leads to a distributed deep interaction layer consisting of many cognitive processes. A three layer architecture has been suggested for designing collaborative HCI with multiple human and computational agents.

1. INTRODUCTION

Human Computer Interaction (HCI) tends to include every development taking place in the field of computing, together with those in the areas of Cognitive Science, Multimedia Signal Processing, Ergonomics, etc., in its own domain. Right from the appearance of the first display device or time-sharing system, to any form of ubiquitous computing through an ordinary daily use device, or social network based systems or automated sensor-based monitoring of environments can be part of HCI. However, our purpose here is to discuss the architecture of interactive systems where human agents and the computational agents interact frequently to design or solve some tasks and use their

DOI: 10.4018/978-1-4666-0954-9.ch002

experiences to improve further interactions. The objective here is to create a general framework which can include the basic underlying processes of collaborative HCI. Although a technological development may add a new dimension to the whole framework, e.g., advent of web technologies for connecting millions of people in a virtual community, but we restrict ourselves to basic core processes. However, let us put a disclaimer at the beginning itself that there are many such attempts with different viewpoints (Gluck & Pew, 2005; Taatgen & Anderson, 2009; Chong et al., 2007; Sun, 2006). This effort is also one such attempt where collaboration among many humans and computers forms the basis of the framework and hence distances itself from the traditional or other specific frameworks, e.g., UAN or RASCALLI.

HCI includes processes (computational as well as human processes) which interact in a meaningful manner to solve a complex problem or problems on an appropriate time scale. However, it should be noted that the goal of the interaction is not just to solve one or the other problem, but to enhance the interaction itself, say, by gaining experience for solving problems in a better way in future. Hence, the definition of HCI as given by Dix and Finlay (1998), as "a field of study related to design, evaluation and implementation of interactive computer systems used by humans, which also includes research of the main phenomena that surround it" may not be sufficient. In this definition, human beings are considered as users of the interactive system; they are not part of the system, although, the human processes, e.g., collecting expert knowledge or human-like visual system, etc. may be simulated on computers. Also, the role of environment (context) needs to be analysed. The interaction takes place in an environment (real-life or synthetic) which provides the context for interaction. In dynamic environments the result of interaction can change the environment, which in turn, can affect the interaction, and so on. The problem solving process has a specific goal at that

moment, which may not be the long term goal of interaction process. Thus, solving one problem does not necessarily kill the interaction process; rather it can provide important information to improve further interaction. However, in real practice, the interaction-process is designed to fulfill a goal, although learning (long term) has now become an important component of HCI systems.

Existing framework of HCI (interactive) systems talks about a two layer system, one representing the computer and the other a user (human). The thin line that separates the two is the interface level, which provides various mechanisms for input/output exchange between the two. Various types of GUIs, movement of cursors through mouse or keyboards and various other input / output devices have been analyzed to enhance the efficiency or effectiveness of such systems. Recently, some human like processes, such as visual or speech based perceptual processes based on camera or microphone inputs are also being considered, which of course will lead to automatic natural interaction for systems based on gesture recognition, eye or head tracking or speech recognition, etc. However, the interaction is not a surface level small event which stops once the information exchange takes place. Interaction may take place in a deep manner and on a continuous basis, cycle by cycle, where it will acquire knowledge, learn and modify its mechanisms and select one or more appropriate choice. Hence the interaction processes, including the knowledge acquisition and deployment, implicit and explicit learning, representing and handling various types of memories, propagating information within and outside the system, evaluation and modification of processes, etc., require to be running and getting updated regularly and must be represented as a separate layer between human and computer layers. This three layer architecture is the key to the present work.

It must be noted that humans and systems are very different in their modus- operandi. The various paradigms for problem solving or for planning, reasoning, learning, knowledge acquisition, representation and retrieval are very much different. Even the language they speak and work in, are very different. Thus, the development of an interaction platform to facilitate real-life complex problem solving in a collaborative manner poses numerous challenges. The interaction layer must facilitate on one side the 'human faces' to collaborate with human beings naturally at various levels, and on the other 'computer faces' for collaboration with computational agents. It should also keep track of various applications and systems connected at the computer end, as well as humans - their thinking, knowledge and actions.

A number of HCI models based on different architectures and paradigms have been implemented and used, e.g., GOMS (Card et al., 1983), SOAR (Newell, 1990; Laird et al., 1987; Laird, 2008), ACT-R (Anderson, 2005), RASCALLI (Krenn & Schollum, 2008), CLARION (Sun, 2006, 2007), etc. All these models claim to represent HCI as cognitive processes. However, many cognitive processes run inside our brains and hence they are highly interdependent and cooperate with each other. HCI is collaborative in nature as it must collaborate at least between one human and one computer agents. Thus the interaction process must be distributed as in distributed cognition (Hollan, 2000) and the processes in it should be loosely coupled. Our purpose in this chapter is not to describe the implementation details of various selected architectures or models, but to introduce and investigate various logical components they include (Section 2), and paradigms, representations and mechanisms employed in those architectures (Section 3). In Section 4, some suggestions, based on the reviews of various architectures described in Section 3, are given to develop a loose framework for collaborative HCI. Conclusion is added as Section 5. The final task of developing a practical architecture for collaborative HCI has been left to the readers themselves.

2. BASIC COMPONENTS OF HCI

The basic Norman's model of an interactive system consists of four components: the user, the system, the input and the output. The input and output together is the interactive part of the system, where the user gives or modifies the input to the system based on the evaluation of the system's observed output. The system executes the task based on the user's present input and presents the output to the user for further evaluation, and this interaction cycle continues [Norman's Model]. This model is based on the user's view of the system (a desktop computer) and the main goal is to enhance the system's performance, providing easy to use interface based on WIMP (Windows, Icons, Menus and Pointers) on command line. User Action Model (UAN) (Harrison & Duke, 1995) was an attempt to understand the complexity of interactions with respect to the system, rather than the user. UAN mixed graphical and text notation for efficiently expressing temporal relations and constraints for interaction. XUAN (eXecutable User Action Notation) (Gray et al., 1994) is a further extension of UAN adding more features on temporal constraints so that one can evaluate multimodal and distributed interfaces.

However, these frameworks only capture the interfacing task and facilitate human beings to provide inputs to the computer in an efficient and systematic way. They consider the modeling of interaction as appropriate interface design. Let us consider the fact that interactions are long term processes and is independent of applications. They run in parallel to the application development, execution and maintenance. In this sense, these frameworks do not capture the true nature of interaction and the collaborative (human and computer) knowledge acquisition, learning and decision making aspects, which, in our view, forms the core of interactive processes. As the new technologies are making the concerns for computational time and memory more and more irrelevant, the focus is shifting towards solving more real-life complex problems, e.g., knowledge discovery, virtual/augmented reality based gaming, need based online tutorial systems, etc. These problems demand solutions which may require joint effort of multiple human beings and multiple computers. In such a framework interaction is no longer a passive input/output window, where user just clicks the button and the system provides the expected output in the predefined format. In the extended framework (Figure 1), the human, the computer and the interaction can be represented by a set of processes. The human processes may involve various perceptual, attentional or cognitive processes, or some actions, which are the outcome of motor processes. It is to be noted here that interaction processes may run in parallel to both computational and human processes, which imply that the problem solving tasks require to be differentiated from interaction tasks. They may intermingle to complete a task, but their purposes are different. Interaction must include knowledge, a mechanism to acquire it and apply it at appropriate moments. This means that interaction can also have its own intention (can be implemented through software agents). Interaction processes, e.g., gaining experience and updating its knowledge for future applications and sharing it or discussing it with other experts, require

that they have their own cognitive, physical and environmental resources and should manage these resources independently.

It is important to note in Figure 1, that environment is a part of the whole interactive system. Humans have their own social and natural environment, which will have impact on the interaction and one may have to simulate these environments also, e.g., in training for airplane driving or war games, etc. However, the scope of this chapter, does not allow going into the details of this aspect. One may study Hutchins (1995) and Tambe et al. (1995) (Wargame Simulation, etc.) or many other literature available on this. The computational processes also have their own environment, specially the digital space created for the action oriented processes (e.g., robots) or the internet environment. However, the interaction processes can also have their own environment, which can be a hybrid of human and computer environments and can change the way (perspective or viewpoint) the interaction will take place. One example can be playing games, where the strategy can change, if two or more players collaborate against one or more players.

The Human Computer Interaction is a group behavior and any model must provide the mechanism to extend it to multiple agents (humans or computers). The Garrido's (Garrido & Gea, 2001)

Figure 1. Extension of basic Norman's Model of HCI

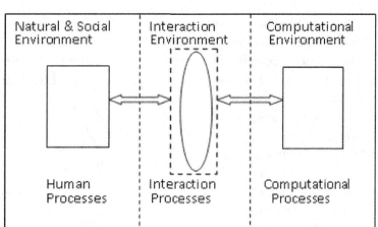

approach of using UML notations for group behavior of interactive systems is only useful for scheduling tasks and input events at the computer's interface level. There can be a problem in abstracting a group of users as their temporal behavior (or response time) may change. In the extended model, we have not specified any limit on the number of processes and their multiple instances, therefore, in the abstract sense it can include any number of human or computational agents. But, one must realize that the interaction processes should include mechanisms for shared, group-wise or independent interactions, e.g., for social network based interactions or game-playing on the internet. Here the environment may be common or it may be different for different groups or individuals.

3. PARADIGMS FOR HCI ARCHITECTURE

Initially the interaction was modeled more as a behavior. Understanding the input stimulus and making a flexible decision based on the stimulus and expertise is considered as internal to human beings. What is visible is the stimulus-response behavior and therefore the initial HCI models are basically behaviorist in nature, where human beings are external to the system and the computer responds to given stimuli.

When cognitive theories of mind were discovered, HCI was also largely modeled as the process of cognition. As human beings gains experience, acquire knowledge, learns and modifies their skill for future use, the interactive system should also do so. Hence, it has to incorporate those cognitive processes which give rise to acquiring and utilizing knowledge and experience.

There are various kinds of cognitive architectures which model cognition at various levels. Say for example, there are cognitive architectures (like SOAR and ACT-R) explaining and constructing individual level of cognition. They assume

that the process of cognition takes place in each individual mind. However, the social cognition theory defines cognition as a social process which takes place while interacting with others and the environment. The relationship of mind with the outside world poses a challenge to the cognitive theorists in understanding cognition only on the basis of internal processes in one human mind. The physical tools employed for actions and the objects of actions or in other words, the human-object relationship (the physical environment), as well as the human-human relationship (socio-cultural environment) must be included in order to understand the processes of cognition. Hence, there is a paradigm shift in the design of collaborative HCI system (Hollan, 2000).

Three Categories of HCI Architecture

Based on the above three paradigms (a) where no cognitive process is taken into account and HCI is modeled as a set of actions, (b) where individual cognition is taken into account and (c) where social cognition is applied, we have grouped HCI models in three categories. Let us first investigate the basic model of one cycle interaction as shown in Figure 2.

In this process, the decision making should be taken in a broader sense. It requires the knowledge of goals and the actions, the present state of the

Figure 2. Model of one cycle of interaction for each agent

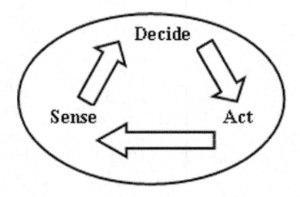

problem and the environment. It also requires the knowledge of the procedure or mechanism for implementation of actions. However, in a multi-cycle interaction, the agent should acquire knowledge and skill for future use and therefore knowledge acquisition, learning, memory and deployment of knowledge or information, etc. also become the part of the interaction process. Similarly sensing and evaluating the output of series of actions are all complex processes. Thus, emotion, attention and many other cognitive processes may become a part of interactive systems.

In HCI systems both human and computer agents coordinate and participate together. Acquisition and deployment of knowledge has remained the main concern for HCI system designers. The three categories we have defined, differ mainly in terms of the representations of knowledge and its deployment mechanisms.

In the first category, the system does not acquire or memorize any such knowledge, but it is the burden of human being to get such knowledge apriori and use it for sensing and decision. However, the various options for decisions at various stages and their immediate implications (results) can be displayed to assist the human. In the second category there are a range of architectures which

represent and learn knowledge, both declarative and procedural, in varying degrees and hence the computational system takes decision up to various extent. Although these architectures have provisions for sensing modules, but actual implementation of the sensing module and its integration has been done recently. We can have a third category where there are multiple human and computational agents situated in the same or different environments and collaborate with each other for interaction. Here various agents may sense, decide and act individually or partially or collaborate and share the knowledge at any or all stages.

A. First Category: Architectures based on Series of Actions Only (No Cognition)

The basic Norman's model, UAN or XUAN (Figure 3) and many of their variants can be put in this category. The Computer is modeled as a basic stimulus (input) receiving system and presents appropriate response (output through action). Decisions regarding the sequence of actions and providing appropriate feedback at each step to enhance the performance of the system is

Figure 3. XUAN/t model of a typical activity on the Interface ($t_1, t_2, ..., t_5$ indicates the time-slots and the layers where the sub-activities takes place)(adapted from Dordevic et al., 2007)

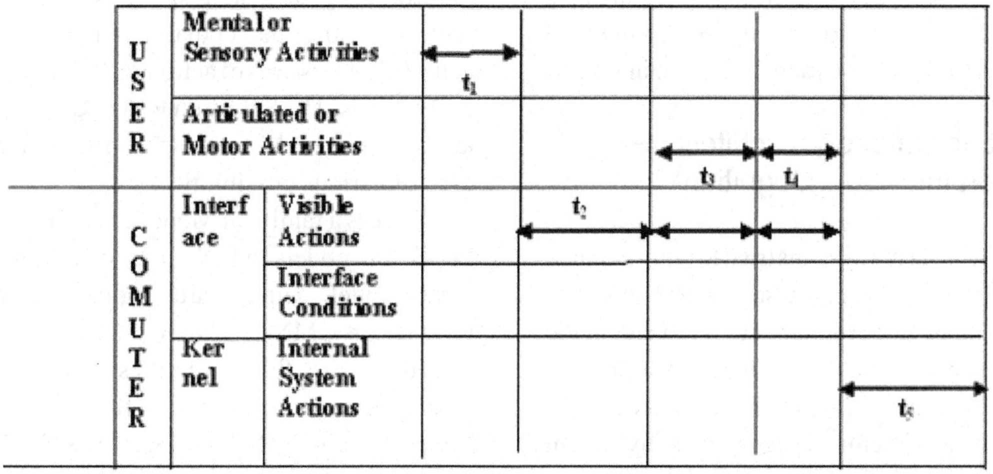

USER	Mental or Sensory Activities		t_1				
	Articulated or Motor Activities					t_3 t_4	
COMPUTER	Interface	Visible Actions		t_2			
		Interface Conditions					
	Kernel	Internal System Actions					t_5

the main task of the human or designers of the system. The user's actions were systematically analyzed and divided into basic actions. A notation system was developed for these basic actions and their average time durations were measured. The interactive system provides a platform on which users can design and implement any interactive task efficiently by decomposing the task into a series of basic actions and taking into account their time durations.

A1. XUAN Model

The User Action Notation (UAN) Model treats interaction (and evaluates performance) with respect to system only, whereas Extended UAN (XUAN) treats interaction with respect to user as well as system and hence for performance evaluation it calculates also the time required by users for articulated or motor activities and Mental or sensory activities (Dordevic et al., 2007).

It is to be noted that the user's action (physical or motor) takes place on the interface provided by the computer, however, one additional layer each for user's mental actions (on top of motor actions) and computer's internal or core actions (below the interface level) has been considered to effectively account for interactive behavior timings. Although the model is valid for graphics or text based interfaces, the deep nature of interaction processes which may include non visible actions cannot be captured with it. It requires the knowledge of expert to decompose and map the task into simpler actions and design the interface.

B. Second Category: Architectures based on Individual Cognition

Second level of HCI systems tried to mimic human sensing and decision processes on the computers so that human can program and intervene in the interaction process at various levels. The "Model Human Processor' (Card et al., 1986) provided a plethora of architecture designs, specially known

as GOMS family of HCI Models. Other attempts to provide a working model of artificial intelligence gave rise to 'Cognitive Architectures' which also became a part of HCI architectures, such as SOAR (Card et al., 1983), ACT-R (Anderson, 2005), EPIC (Kieras et al., 2000), etc. These models have used the memory (Short Term, Long Term and Episodic), learning (Rule based and Statistical), knowledge representation (Declarative and Procedural), knowledge acquisition, knowledge deployment, and other human-like processes and their variants. Let us discuss here some basic features of these architectures to highlight their important features and their limitations.

B1. GOMS Family of Architectures

GOMS (Goals, Operators, Methods, and Selection Rules) is the widely known model in HCI, originally proposed by Card et al. (1983). Enhancing the approach of analyzing human (user's) task to enhance the user's performance, as in XUAN, it is the first significant attempt to simulate high level human tasks based on Model Human Processor (MHP). The MHP model represents user as a set of perceptual, cognitive and motor processors and perceptual and working memories. Goals and Operators are the basic representations of the task and action, respectively in GOMS. The application has to be represented in terms of goals and subgoals and operators will accomplish the action to fulfill the goal or subgoal. These operators can represent either perceptual, cognitive, or motor activities. The series of actions can be represented by Methods. The Selection Rules can provide the knowledge to select one appropriate Method in case of various possibilities.

There is a family of Models, known as GOMS family of models, which are the variants of the basic model, called Card, Moran and Newell GOMS or CMN-GOMS (Card et al., 1983). The details of the similarities and differences among these models, such as KLM (Keystroke-Level Model), CMN-GOMS, NGOMSL (Natural

GOMS Language), CPM-GOMS (Cognitive-Perceptual-Motor GOMS), etc. can be read in John and Kieras (1996).

There are two basic principles of GOMS (John & Kieras, 1996): (a) The Problem Space Principle says that a user's activity can be characterized by a sequence of actions (operators which can transform states) and with user's experience this sequence (Methods) can be recalled (without inferencing them again); and (b) The Rationality Principle, which says that a user develops methods that are efficient, given the task-environment and his abilities. The NGOMSL refines GOMS by including methods based on an architecture known as Cognitive Complexity Theory (CCT) (Kieras & Polson 1985). CCT representation assumes a set of production rules which can be triggered through a simple serial architecture of working memory. These rules can be learnt. CCT also provides a good prediction of Execution time, Learning time and Transfer of procedure learning (Bovair et al., 1988, 1990).

The rationality principle claims that the user only develops an efficient method. This may be true for experts, but not for beginners or common users. Hence the GOMS architecture does not provide room for trial and error or for experimentation. In fact, there is no built-in mechanism to evaluate the performance error. This is one of the main drawbacks of GOMS which restricted its widespread use.

GOMS family of models, although was the beginning of the inclusion of cognitive processes in interaction, they were basically motivated by the 'Model-Human Processor', which represents mind as a cognitive processor. These models do not consider the details of many related cognitive processes going-on during the interaction. They have no consideration for experience, or knowledge acquisition and deployment. They do not take into account of the context or environment in which the tool or the system is used. In short, GOMS provides a technique through which one

can design an application based on human behavior analysis and the computer can learn through past user behavior, with respect to the task in hand.

B2. SOAR (State, Operator and Result)

Although SOAR was developed as an example to realize a general model of intelligence, its architecture can be used for HCI systems. Newell (1990) has proposed SOAR as a candidate of 'Unified Theory of Cognition'. It was a huge attempt to model, develop and explore a general theory of intelligence onto computers, taking clues from human cognitive processes. The basic assumption is that a system with general intelligence (which can solve a large number of human -like tasks) can be created with a large knowledge memory consisting of a large number of production rules. One research demonstrating that it can even handle one million rules without significant degradation (Doorenbos, 1994). Thus, like any other symbolic intelligent system, SOAR takes a system's view point to simulate some mental tasks on computers.

Unlike human being, it represents memory in three parts: (i) Production memory (ii) Blackboard memory or working memory and (iii) Preference memory. The production memory consists of mainly hand-coded production rules in predicate logic. Active memory objects are maintained in blackboard memory, These active objects trigger all rules in production memory for which the condition part is satisfied, which in turn, results in more active objects given by the action part of the rules.. The preference memory is used to express preference of operators, when more than one operator is applicable.

Soar has a unique concept of operator, representing the concept of a 'procedure' consisting of many productions distributed over many memory objects. The operators has preconditions represented by one or more proposed production rules and postconditions represented by the outcomes of the productions triggered by the operator. These operators are applied on a 'state' to change it to a new 'state', and so on. The failure to associate any operator or availability of multiple operators to the current state (which is not the goal state) gives rise to an 'impasse' for that state's problem space. In this manner soar combines the production rule approach to state space approach. The reasoning in soar is not through rule-to-rule execution but through an operator which encompass several rules. Thus the problem solving by state space search is applied by transforming individual states with an operator defined by a set of production rules. In this sense, soar extracts many features of the BDI (Belief-Desire-Intention) framework but actually implements SDA (Sense-Decide-Act) cycles by replacing 'Sense' by 'Input' phase and expanding the 'Decide' phase into 'Elaborate & Compare', 'Select' and 'Apply' phases. Like any other rule based system it has also pattern-directed control, as only those rules are elaborated whose conditions match with objects in the working memory. Then the preference semantics in the preference memory selects a particular operator. In case of an impasse either sub-goaling and task decomposition can be done or a comparison and evaluation procedure is applied to select one operator or it may go for conflict resolution, depending on the type of impasse. Hence soar is a combination of reactive as well as goal-driven approach.

The only learning mechanism built-in to the soar architecture is the chunking mechanism. Whenever an impasse is resolved, the results of the resolution process (the experience obtained in the problem search) is cached and memorized in its knowledge base at the architecture level. Thus, soar has a built-in mechanism at the architecture level to generalize its experience and memorize the situation and results of the impasse for future applications.

Soar responds to the dynamic changes in the environment by introducing the concept of persistent and non-persistent objects in the blackboard memory. Persistent objects are those objects which are asserted through operator application, while all other objects, say, through individual elaboration of states or resolution of impasse, etc., are non-persistent. The justification – based truth maintenance system (JTMS) of soar requires that any changes made to non-persistent objects in the blackboard memory will remain as long as the production rule which created those objects continues to match the conditions. As soon as the condition changes, the justification is invalidated and the object is retracted.

Although soar is a cognitive architecture, it is more focused to implement a computational model of general intelligence. The goal driven state-space search and production rule (which may require to be hand coded for acquisition) biases its simple architecture to make it machine-friendly. Online human collaboration is a difficult task and must go in a predefined way. The learning mechanism is very weak and the system fails if a slightly changed context appears.

B3. ACT-R (Adaptive Control of Thought – Rational)

ACT-R, developed by Anderson and Lebiere (1998) is another effort for realizing complex cognition taking human experience as a guiding principle. Unlike SOAR, it has attempted to go beyond the symbolic level of processing. Some of the concepts and mechanisms introduced in ACT-R, such as differentiating declarative and procedural knowledge, learning through experience at both the symbolic and sub-symbolic levels, and knowledge acquisition, can be helpful in designing collaborative models of HCI. The basic ACT-R paradigm is that the rational complex cognition can be generated if the system knows or learns the procedural knowledge (represented as Productions) to combine or transform some simple relevant declarative facts (represented structurally as Chunks) and given the intension (goal) to solve that problem. Hence the basic cognition arises due to interaction between the declarative knowledge and the procedural knowledge. The basic unit of knowledge is the Chunk which has few elements in it and for a complex cognition, like in humans; there should be a large number of such units. Human beings initially start with few given instructions to solve some simple problems, but as one continues to gather experience by solving many problems, one acquires the new procedural knowledge. ACT-R proceeds in a similar fashion to acquire new knowledge and enhance its utility value based on its performance evaluation mechanism, and hence the structures get tuned to the environment. One of the characteristics of ACT-R, unlike SOAR, is that it always refers to human mind. It has the modules which correspond to various human brain regions. It is based on the analysis of results of tasks performed by human subjects and various parameters of the model are adjusted accordingly. The performance of the simulated model is also validated by comparing it to the performance of human subjects on a similar task.

Architecture

In ACT-R, like SOAR, the Production System Module takes the centre stage, which interacts with other modules, and is responsible for achieving the goal. There are some internal modules, which represent the internal interactions of various brain modules, such as the Declarative Module, the Goal Module, and the Problem State Module (in earlier versions the last two modules exist as a single Intensional Module), together with the Production System Module as depicted in Figure 4 The peripheral modules, such as the Visual System Module and the Manual Module, provide interface with the external world (which is a reimplementation of the EPIC's (Executive – Process Interactive Control) (Kieras & Meyer 1997) perceptual – motor system (Anderson, 2005).

The production system module has procedural knowledge in the form of production rules, which typically can be represented as:

```
If the Goal is To solve the
equation   (*/ request the control
buffer/*)
        and the equation is of the
form  Expression + Num1 = Num2 (*/
request the problem state buffer/*)
        and Num2 – Num1 is Num3
(*/ request retrieval buffer/*)
    Then transform the equation to
Expression = Num3 (*/ write to the
problem state buffer/*)
```

Note that the comments are added to indicate the interaction of the production module with the appropriate buffer. Other modules represent knowledge in the form of Chunks. A typical chunk in the declarative module for representing the fact of subtraction expressed in line 3 of the production rule above

ACT-R has no working memory module, but it has buffers connected to each module through which the Production module interacts (Figure 4), getting the information required at the moment. The Production module performs pattern matching, selection and execution and controls the interaction with each module. Each module works asynchronously and in parallel, but the interaction of Production module with other modules is done through buffers and is strictly serial and it is done chunk by chunk in both the directions, thus enforcing coordination among modules. The model can incorporate many perceptual modules other than the Visual Module (Figure 4). Similarly, there can be other output modules than Manual Module, for interaction with the external world. One such effort is the inclusion of Language Comprehension Module (see CMU website) in the extended ACT-R versions.

Figure 4. Architecture of ACT-R

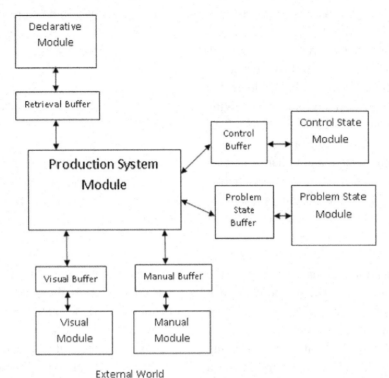

Learning, Knowledge Acquisition, and Knowledge Deployment in ACT-R

ACT-R allows both symbolic and sub-symbolic level of knowledge representations allowing fine-graded quantitative models of learning and performance evaluation. Its unique feature (unlike SOAR) is its strong learning and knowledge acquisition capability. It has built-in mechanisms through which its performance gets enhanced as the system gets more and more experience, as is the case for human minds. The rational analysis assumes that the knowledge is made available according to its odds of being used in a particular context. Modelling it as a Bayesian process the log posterior odds is the sum of log prior odds (usefulness in the past) and log likelihood ratio representing its usefulness in the current context (Anderson, 1996).

ACT-R has come up with a mechanism in which those knowledge structures (Chunks and Production Rules) which are used frequently and has been used recently has more chances of selection. It also allows forgetting and error-making by introducing a noise-factor in the process. Each chunk I is associated with a quantity called activation, given as (Taatgen et al., 2006)

Activation$_i$ = Base-level activation$_i$ + Associative activation$_i$

where Base-level activation$_i$ = ln $((\sum_{j=1}^{n} t_j^{-d}),)$, and Associative activation$_i$ = $\sum_j w_j S_{ji.}$

Hence, the base-level activation depends on the frequency of use (n) of a particular chunk, but inversely proportional to the time-interval since its jth use (d is the decay parameter, usually taken as 0.5 for many applications). The associative activation depends on the attentional weighting (w_j) of the elements that are part of the current goal, together with the association strength of elements j to the chunk i (S_{ji}). Similarly, each production rule I is associated with a utility value, $U_i = P(i) G - C_i$, where P(i) is the probability of achieving goal if the ith production is chosen and C_i is the associated cost (in time), G being an architectural parameter.

Both these performance functions provide the basis for learning through experience. Hence, ACT-R has both instance learning based on the usefulness of chunks and the competitive strategies learning and evaluation for selecting a valuable strategy (rule) out of many possible ones. In the model various system level parameters are involved and different values can be put for different degrees of competences (say the value of the parameter w_i above), as in different individuals. In the evaluation process, the element level details of each chunk are taken into consideration, signifying that the sub-symbolic level interactions also decide the activation. The effect of forgetting (decay) and interference can also be simulated in ACT-R. As the utility value is probability based, there is always a chance factor to allow suboptimal strategies. In other words, the system allows for error to be made which can get corrected with more number of trials and also allows for selection of few evolving strategies.

The model can create new chunks by action of production rules automatically, each time a goal is completed. It can also create new chunks directly through environment encoding when a perceptual/motor event is registered. This new chunk is added in the declarative module, if it is already present there, then they are merged combining their activation values. The new production rules can originate through production compilation, which merges two rules that fire in sequence. Once they

are there, their future use will depend on their activation or utility values.

In summary, ACT-R provides a very comprehensive and useful architecture, which may be used for HCI systems or applications. Actually, the simulation of human problem – solving behavior has been used as validation of the model. Even the various regions of the human brain corresponding to various modules have been identified, representing that the model can complete tasks in a similar way as it is solved by humans and therefore providing opportunities for interaction at many levels.

While ACT-R take an overall view of the organization of mental processes, there is little effort on issues related to Executive Processes, as say in EPIC (Kieras et al., 2000), which implements executive processes that coordinate multiple processes and is consistent with several resource allocation strategies. Although ACT-R can implement planning, but not resource conflict and allocation processes as in EPIC (Cooper, 2002).

C. Third Category: Architectures based on Social and Distributed Cognition (Collaborative Processing)

With the formation of the Social Networks and large scale interactive processes through Internet, the necessity of modeling a multi-agent human computer interaction instead of one-to-one interaction is being felt by the HCI community. Collaborative interaction requires representations that help us understand, analyze, explain and predict patterns of group behavior, including mental behavior. It demands for development of computational models that can handle different aspects involved in collaborative interaction, such as defining and discussing tasks, identifying roles of group members, knowledge sharing or cognitive conflict, social factors, motivations, contextual and domain specific information, group dynamics, explaining ways to perform the task and collaborating to get it done etc. This is unlike other architectures which model interaction as a series of commands or individual cognition. Instead, the interactions need to be contextually interpreted with respect to the interactions performed so far. The system has to anticipate the user's need and provide responses at best, to further the user's goals. Such systems will create a new paradigm for human computer interaction. Theories such as distributed cognition (Hollan et al., 2000) and cognitive architectures such as CLARION have been proposed to support such interactions. Extensions to existing architectures have also been proposed (Sun, 2006).

C1. CLARION (Connectionist Learning with Adaptive Rule Induction ON-line)

There are many platforms which can be used for HCI system, but CLARION is a recent cognitive architecture suitable for social simulation. Unlike SOAR and ACT-R, CLARION has the unique feature of integrating bottom-up and top-down, implicit and explicit learning implemented through connectionist and rule formation approach (as indicated by its name) (Sun & Peterson, 1996; Sun et al., 2007). This architecture provides functional modules so that it can interact with its physical and social environments and can take into account their regularities and structures. It can be used to simulate social agents. Here we will not discuss its implementation details, but will try to emphasize those features which will be helpful in the development of collaborative HCI architecture.

The basic philosophy of CLARION is the integration of implicit and explicit processes instead of studying each type in isolation. Further, it uses both top-down and bottom-up approach for learning which was radically different from the then existing models (Sun & Zhang, 2004). Other distinguishing characteristics include provision of Cognitive -- Meta-cognitive and Cognitive — Motivational interactions, which distinguish

CLARION architecture from other well-known architectures, like SOAR, ACT-R, etc., and make it suitable for social simulation.

Architecture

CLARION has four functional subsystems: the Action-Centered Subsystem (ACS), the Non-Action-Centered Subsystem (NACS), the Meta-Cognitive Subsystem (MCS), and the Motivational Subsystem (MS) as shown in Figure 1. In Figure 5 the action centered subsystem (ACS) and the Non-Action Centered Subsystem (NACS) have been functionally separated to learn, acquire knowledge and reason about the actions and its implications on the world, respectively. ACS is mainly used for action decision making. The implicit and explicit processes make their separate decisions.

Their results are then combined to decide the action. If the resulting action is successful, then a rule is extracted at the top level. Based on subsequent interactions this rule will be either generalized or made more specific. The NACS maintains general world knowledge, both implicit and explicit, and is responsible for reasoning about the world. The MS and MCS supervise the operations of ACS and NACS. The MS provides "the context in which the goal and the reinforcement of ACS are determined" (Sun et al., 2006). The main task of MCS is cognitive monitoring and parameter setting of ACS and NACS. The main features of this architecture can be summarized as follows:

1. **Use of dual representational structure:** Each subsystem in CLARION uses dual representational structure: separate connectionist (neural network) representation for implicit knowledge and symbolic representation (rules and chunks) for explicit knowledge. The top level corresponds to explicit knowledge (easily accessible) whereas the bottom level corresponds to implicit knowledge (less accessible and more "holistic).

Figure 5. A typical chunk representation (a) graphical (b) textual

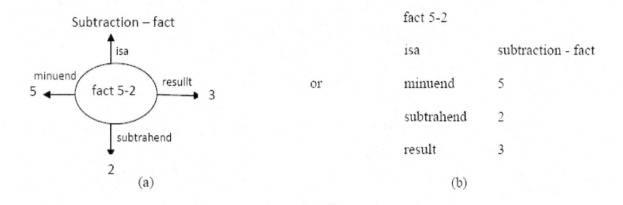

2. **Top-down and bottom-up learning:** Traditional cognitive architectures (e.g., SOAR) focuses mainly on top-down learning. However, several lines of research demonstrate that individuals may learn to perform complex skills without first obtaining a large amount of explicit declarative knowledge. We can learn explicit knowledge through trial and error, without necessarily using a priori knowledge. Following these lines, CLARION also supports bottom-up learning in which procedural knowledge develops first and declarative knowledge develops later. An agent in CLARION can learn on its own, i.e., in the absence of externally supplied knowledge, explicit knowledge may be developed gradually through a trial and error basis.

3. **Cognitive-Meta-Cognitive Interaction:** Meta-cognition is an essential part of cognition. meta-cognitive mechanism should be an integral part of a cognitive architecture(Sun et al, 2006). The subsystems in this architecture interact constantly to accomplish cognitive processing. This interaction may be executive control of some sub-systems or meta-cognitive control and monitoring of some processes. Such interaction is not fully supported in SOAR and ACT-R.

4. **Use of motivational structures:** CLARION includes motivational structures using which agents can understand and appreciate each others' motivation and find ways to cooperate. This helps in social interaction.

Action Centered Subsystem

The bottom level of ACS consists of a number of small neural networks (NNs) each of which is adapted to a specific task, modality, or group of stimuli. These networks enable CLARION to handle very complex situations that cannot be handled by simple rules. The Q-learning (a variant of reinforcement learning) algorithm is used at this level.

The top level of ACS captures explicit symbolic knowledge in terms of explicit symbolic rules. It can acquire explicit knowledge using bottom-up learning. If an action implicitly decided by the bottom level is successful then the agent extracts a rule and adds it to the top level. In subsequent interaction with the world the rule is verified. If the result of application of rule is successful then the rule is generalized otherwise it is made specific to the case.

Figure 6. CLARION architecture

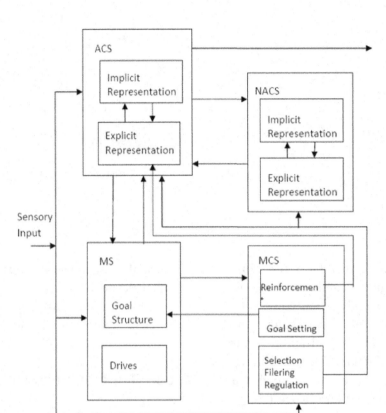

Non-Action Centered Subsystem

The NACS works under the control of ACS. It maintains general world knowledge, both explicit and implicit, and performs various kinds of memory retrievals and inferences. The bottom level uses "associative memory" to encode non-action centered implicit knowledge. The associations are formed by mapping input to output. A regular back propagation learning algorithm can be used for creating such associations. At the top level of the non-action centered subsystem, a general knowledge store (the GKS) encodes explicit non-action-centered knowledge (Sun, 2004).

NACS also supports bottom-up and top-down learning. It uses bottom up learning to extract explicit knowledge in the top level from the implicit knowledge whereas top-down learning is used to assimilate explicit knowledge of the top-level into implicit knowledge in the bottom level.

Motivational Subsystem

Motivational dynamics is considered to be an essential part of human (or animal) behavior. CLARION attempts to bring this characteristic in cognitive agents through a two level (explicit and implicit) motivational representation. The top level in MS encodes explicit knowledge whereas bottom level represents implicit knowledge. Implicit level is the most fundamental part of MS. It consists of basic drives, basic needs, basic desires, intrinsic motives, etc. The explicit level corresponds to goals. The drives provide the context within which explicit goals are set and carried out. CLARION uses these representations to handle issues related to purpose and focus. This dual representation is in line with human cognition. The theories of human skill learning emphasize explicit representation of goal whereas the internal process of drives, needs and desires are definitely not explicit and are hard to characterize cognitively. Explicit knowledge is encoded using symbolic representation whereas implicit knowledge uses distributed representation. The two levels interact by cooperating in action decision making and in learning. Goal structure is an integral part of MS and ACS and is closely tied to MCS. It is at the centre of the whole architecture. MS maintains a goal list consisting of potential goals which compete to be the current goal. It interacts with MCS for goal setting. The current goal is used in action decision making by ACS. CLARION also support top-down learning so that it can use externally supplied knowledge when it is available.

Meta Cognitive Subsystem (MCS)

The MCS is a unique concept in CLARION introduced to facilitate some executive control and monitoring of all other functional subsystems. In other words, this subsystem provides the cognitive agent to reflect upon its own processes and adjust and collaborate effectively with other agents and the environment, say for example, to avoid social impasse. The Cognitive – Metacognitive interaction in CLARION is facilitated through many metacognitive processes which sets (through networks at the bottom level) many parameters, such as parameters of the ACS and NACS, select learning methods, reasoning methods, input and output dimensions, reinforcement function, etc. It interacts closely with MS for setting goals.

CLARION Features for Social Interaction

Separation of knowledge related module (NACS) from the action centred module will facilitate the use of implicit and explicit knowledge to and from other agents. This is the model which can be placed in the middle (interaction) layer of the three layer collaborative architecture as suggested in Figure 1. It is to be noted that the implicit knowledge can still remain as individual experiences, whereas the

general knowledge store can be shared frequently with other agents. One may have to implement an additional sharing mechanism.

It should be noted that the simple reward and penalty mechanism, based on the measurement of appropriateness of the actions for goal achievement, is not sufficient for HCI. There can be complex and multiple goals and complex social motivations which may drive human and social agents, e.g., social recognition, drive for exploration, desire for reciprocation and many more social and cultural norms and values. It will be difficult to realize these motivations with the help of the simple reward-penalty schemes. The MS module can learn to provide such group based complex motivations.

The executive control lying with meta – cognitive module is the key component for collaborative interaction. It does not only self reflect and has the knowledge of its own performance, but can adapt to changes in the physical and social environment to the extent that it can interrupt and change the ongoing processes in ACS and NACS (say in the case of social conflict). It will be useful when a collaborative task will be divided among participants and individual goals will be set up accordingly. It can dynamically include or exclude agents when the process is in progress and change the cognitive load.

It is to be noted that the MS – MCS interaction is not one way, but MCS provides a feedback to the individual goal structure in MS, which reflects the true spirit of collaboration.

It is to be noted that in social interaction each agent should not have only the knowledge about self, but also about others (Anderson & Chen, 2002). This knowledge about others may be stored in ACS. If the system faces a new person, then his/her features are compared with that of an underlying significant other. This model of deciding her behaviour with a totally new person can be implemented easily in the CLARION architecture.

In collaborative interaction not only the non-human agents are required to be simulated but similar modules, corresponding to each human agent may be required. Other agents can derive information about the human agent through these modules. However, the human may have direct access to many of his own explicit information and can be developed and changed through direct intervention.

4. TOWARDS A NEW FRAMEWORK FOR DISTRIBUTED COLLABORATIVE HCI

It is interesting to note that, in all collaborative tasks the computer is not just to help human agents in processing and communication but it is an integral part of the framework. Many theories have been proposed (Susi, 2000), for social cognitive process in human cooperative work, such as, Activity Theory (Vygotsky, 1978; Kaptlenin et al., 1999), Situated Cognition (Ziemke, 2002) and Distributed Cognition (Hollan et al., 2000; Wright et al., 2000) which can provide the basis for this framework. However, as far as we know, no widely acceptable collaborative HCI (CHCI) framework exists. Here, we will present a broad outline and few comments on such a possible collaborative framework.

One must note that the framework of Computer Supported Collaborative Work (CSCW) can be seen as extension of social cognition, where many computers facilitate many human agents to cooperate by providing a shared workspace (with many services) and mechanisms for communication and synchronization. They are not appropriate for CHCI, as here individuals complete their tasks independently and share the solution. For CHCI the cognition emerges in group interaction (Stahl et al., 2006).

No one kind of architectures discussed is sufficient for CHCI. Taking a clue from individual-social paradox – i.e., individual determines social or the social determines individual (Hollan et al., 2000), we assume that a general framework of

collaborative HCI will require a kind of hybrid of many/various architectures described in this chapter.

Three Layer Architecture of Collaborative HCI

As discussed in Figure 1, the general logical architecture of HCI, should be a three layer architecture –one layer for facilitating, monitoring, tracking and controlling human processes, one for computational agents and the most important one for the interaction. It is very important to note that this is a logical view of CHCI architecture. The whole system is distributed in time and space and hence its implementation on computers is also distributed, may be through distributed agents.

The Human Layer

The general collaborative HCI should help to execute tasks which require various range of human interactions at various levels. There can be a task which involves human agents completely from the beginning to the end or there may be other tasks which require human intervention only if there is a contingency. Some require at the control or decision level, some at perception level only, and so on. The human interacts naturally at all appropriate levels. It is to be noted that most of the initial models, such as UAN, XUAN, and GOMS, as described in Section 3 have tried to implement processes, where humans can interfere directly at the input level or some predefined decision points. Applications of ACT-R model requires that initially some parameters are learnt from human practice and it provides a manual level of interaction, where human agents may have to perform some tasks. CLARION has some implicit learning methods which can give rise to explicit learning and some routine human tasks can be learnt from human practices.

In collaborative HCI, this layer should have processes to analyze human practices or perceptual data and learn them. It should also have access to data, information and past experiences to support human agents to take decisions and perform her tasks. Providing a natural interface to communicate efficiently to /from the human agents is also one of the prime tasks of processes in this layer. Hence, handling multimodal information and converting from human consumable form to computational form, is the primary functionality of this layer. Hence, this layer tries to bridge the gap between the human and computer asymmetries. However, one should not consider this layer as only performing morphological changes to information as the distributed cognitive theory recognizes physical and social resources as an integral part of cognition; this layer extends the interaction layer to physical and social environment. Adapting the system parameters to include subjective factors can also be best performed in this layer, say changing acoustic parameters or the domain of the conversation as per the mood of the human.

The Computer Layer

One of the important criticisms of the distributed cognition theory is that it considers human beings and computers equally, whereas there are lots of asymmetries between the two. Therefore, human and computer layers should be separated, although there can be lot of commonalities. As described in Section 1 each computational agent can have an architecture based on social cognition, say CLARION, but with lot of competencies, to take input from or to give input to other agents through interaction layer.

However, on one side it can give its output to the external world (systems or users) and should perceive the stimulus from the external world. Developing such competencies for inputting and outputting in different modalities is the active area of research in HCI and integrating such technologies and devices into the collaborative HCI framework will always be one of the important

considerations. But one must note that perception, attention and cognition are both bottom-up and top-down processes and can continue for long in cycles. This posses a major challenge in developing such a cognitive computational self sufficient agent. One can have various types of expert agents and can be called into action at the appropriate time. It is to be noted that many extensions of SOAR and ACT-R are trying to simulate agents with emotions and motivations which can talk to human beings in natural language (Linch et al., 2011) or even looks like a real human being.

The Interaction Layer

Although, the actual interaction (activity) takes place in the environment, the interaction layer, we are talking about, consists of the processes for representing planning, executing, modifying, exploring, analyzing, evaluating, experiencing, learning, and so on for collaborative interaction. As we will see, many of these processes are also taking place on many individual computational agents or in the head of human agents. But interaction is not just concerning two nodes (humans or computers) but to provide faithful representations of the external world on which one or more agents can act to transform it meaningfully to fulfill the overall task in many cycles. Coordination, synchronization, and memorization are some of the important tasks to be implemented.

As pointed out in the distributed cognition, activity theory or situated action the unit of representation for interaction is not simply the information in our head but must represent the way in which the information is organized in the material and social world (Hollan et al., 2000) including the artifacts that participate in the process, delimited by functional relationships. The unit can be a socio-technical system, say pilots in the cockpit (Hutchins, 1995). It is to be noted that there can be multiple agents, but the collaboration is realized through these structures, modifying them through series of activities and propagating them through place to place, where dynamically agents can drop in and out completing their respective tasks, It is important to note that the artifacts also put constraints on agents and may force them to adapt or change their course of action.

This layer should also take into consideration the knowledge, representation and transformations of the relationships of the material and social world involving coordination of internal resources of mind, such as, memory, attention, executive function to external resources, such as, the objects, artifacts and materials surrounding us (Hollan et al., 2000). As human agents live in cultural set up and one can simulate computational agents embedded in cultural setup, its impact on information and control flow as well as on the process of collaboration itself needs to be considered. It is also very important that the actions in this layer are mental activities, which may not have a resulting physical activity in the environment; in such cases the abstract conceptual structures (e.g., language structures) can play the role of artifacts. All these activities do require the simulation of cognitive processes described earlier, but in a distributed sense.

Components of Knowledge and Memory

At this stage it is very difficult to fix-up the exact forms of knowledge representations and the memory modules, but the rich experience of ACT-R implementations and experiments in CLARION can help in representing both the language and the imagery concepts in the form of sub-symbolic chunks or subgraphs with association weights or scores as well as in implicit feature vectors in connectionist framework. Procedural knowledge in production rule form either as individual rules (as in ACT-R) or as combined multiple rules (as operators in SOAR) should be included.

However, as stated earlier the unit of knowledge representation, in general, should be a scene, consisting of one or many information chunks and objects together, say for e.g., pilot in a cockpit

or a tutor in a classroom. It is important to mention that the collaborative cognitive processes involved in a classroom teaching –learning or in a distant education setup are not same and hence should be designed differently. The tools and objects involved in the process, say chairs and blackboards, or cameras and speakers in the tutor-classroom scene, should be part of the representation schemes. Many other knowledge representation schemes, such as word-mesh and sentence-mesh (Srivastava et al., 2011), ontology etc. can be tried.

Learning and Knowledge Deployment Approaches

As in CLARION, top-down and bottom-up learning; implicit to explicit knowledge mapping and use of explicit knowledge to guide or monitor implicit information analysis: both approaches are needed here. The explicit knowledge can also be used for perspective modification or removing impasse or putting social constraints on the learning process. However, both the statistical methods (as in ACT-R or ideas of belief networks used elsewhere) and connectionists method (as in CLARION) should be utilized. Rule based approaches, like rule-compilation in ACT-R or Rule Induction in CLARION, can also help in formation of new rules. One of the main challenges in automatic knowledge acquisition is the conversion of an implicit knowledge to explicit one. Various methods of reinforcement learning in an ANN framework has been tried (Nasson & Laird, 2004) and can be utilized in this framework also.

To summarize the new hybrid framework will be a distributed general purpose human computer interaction framework which will be based on the principles of the distributed cognition. It is not simply the models of humans and computers and the communication among them but it is a complex cognitive process in which complex structures consisting of mind, objects, and other minds connected functionally participate in a collaborative fashion distributed in space and time.

5. CONCLUSION

In this chapter an outline of various cognitive architectures which may be used to model human-computer interaction is presented. This underlines the challenges involved in designing a framework for collaborative human computer interaction. It is emphasized that collaborative HCI can be modeled as a distributed social cognition process and hence should include the components and mechanisms experimented in the design of distributed and social cognition. The relevant details of some representations and mechanisms involved in SOAR, ACT-R and CLARION opens up the possibilities of inclusion or non-inclusion of these representations and mechanisms or creating a new or hybrid ones in the new collaborative HCI framework. A new basis of classification of architectures for HCI and the proposed three layer architecture for HCI models add a new dimension in the investigation and design of collaborative HCI systems.

REFERENCES

Anderson, J. R. (1996). ACT – A simple theory of complex cognition. *The American Psychologist*, *51*, 355–365. doi:10.1037/0003-066X.51.4.355

Anderson, J. R. (2005). Human symbol manipulation within an integrated cognitive architecture. *Cognitive Science*, *29*, 313–341. doi:10.1207/s15516709cog0000_22

Anderson, J. R., & Lebiere, C. (1998). *The atomic components of thought*. Mahwah, NJ: Lawrence Erlbaum.

Bovair, S., Kieras, D. E., & Poison, P. G. (1988). *The acquisition and performance of text editing skill: A production system analysis* (Tech. Rep. No. 28). Ann Arbor, MI: University of Michigan.

Bovair, S., Kieras, D. E., & Polson, P. G. (1990). The acquisition and performance of text-editing skill: A cognitive complexity analysis. *Human-Computer Interaction*, *5*, 1–48. doi:10.1207/s1532705lhci0501_1

Card, S. K., Moran, T. P., & Newell, A. (1983). *The psychology of human computer interaction*. Mahwah, NJ: Lawrence Erlbaum.

Card, S. K., Moran, T. P., & Newell, A. (1986). The model human processor: An engineering model of human performance. In K. R. Boff, L. Kaufman, & J. P. Thomas (Eds.), *Handbook of perception and human performance. Vol. 2: Cognitive processes and performance* (pp. 1-35). Wright-Patterson AFB, OH: Harry G. Armstrong Aerospace Medical Research Lab.

Chong, H.-Q., Tan, A.-H., & Ng, G.-W. (2007). Integrated cognitive architectures: a survey. *Artificial Intelligence Review*, *28*, 103–130. doi:10.1007/s10462-009-9094-9

Cooper, R. P. (2002). *Modeling high - Level cognitive processes*. Mahwah, NJ: Lawrence Erlbaum.

Dix, A., Finlay, J., Abowd, G., & Beale, R. (1998). *Human-computer interaction* (2nd ed.). London, UK: Prentice Hall.

Doorenbos, R. B. (1994). Combining left and right unlinking for matching a large number of learned rules. In *Proceedings of the Twelfth National Conference on Artificial Intelligence*, Seattle, WA.

Dordevic, N., Rančic, D., & Dimitrijevic, A. (2007, July). Evaluation of user cognitive ability. In *Proceedings of the 11ᵗʰ WSEAS International Conference on Computers*, Agios Nikolaos, Crete Island, Greece (pp. 469-474).

Garrido, J. L., & Gea, M. (2001). Modelling dynamic group behaviours. In C. Johnson (Ed.), *Proceedings of the 8ᵗʰ International Workshop on Interactive Systems: Design, Specification and Verification* (LNCS 2220, pp. 128-143).

Gluck, K. A., & Pew, R. W. (Eds.). (2005). *Modeling human behavior with integrated cognitive architectures: Comparison, evaluation, and validation*. London, UK: Psychology Press.

Gray, P., England, D., & McGowan, S. (1994). XUAN: Enhancing the UAN to capture temporal relationships among actions. In *Proceedings of the 9th Conference on People and Computers* (pp. 301-312).

Harrison, M. D., & Duke, D. J. (1995). A review of formalisms for describing interactive behavior. In R. N. Taylor & J. Coutaz (Eds.), *Proceedings of the Workshop on Software Engineering and Human-Computer Interaction* (LNCS 896, pp. 49-75).

Hollan, J., Hutchins, E., & Kirsh, D. (2000). Distributed cognition: Toward a new foundation for human computer interaction research. *ACM Transactions on Computer-Human Interaction, 7*(2), 174–196. doi:10.1145/353485.353487

Hutchins, E. (1995). How a cockpit remembers its speeds. *Cognitive Science, 19*, 265–288. doi:10.1207/s15516709cog1903_1

John, B. E., & Kieras, D. E. (1996). The GOMS family of user interface analysis techniques: Comparison and contrast. *ACM Transactions on Computer-Human Interaction, 3*(4), 320–351. doi:10.1145/235833.236054

Kaptelinin, V., Nardi, B. A., & Macaulay, C. (1999). The activity checklist: a tool for representing the space of context. *Interactions Magazine, 6*(4), 27–39.

Kieras, D. E., & Meyer, D. E. (1997). An overview of the EPIC architecture for cognition and performance with application to human-computer interaction. *Human-Computer Interaction, 4*(12), 391–438.

Kieras, D. E., Meyer, D. E., Ballas, J. A., & Lauber, E. J. (2000). Modern computational perspectives on executive mental processes and cognitive control: Where to from here? In Monsell, S., & Driver, J. (Eds.), *Attention and performance, XVIII: Control of cognitive processes* (pp. 681–712). Cambridge, MA: MIT Press.

Kieras, D. E., & Polson, P. G. (1985). An approach to the formal analysis of user complexity. *International Journal of Man-Machine Studies, 22*, 365–394. doi:10.1016/S0020-7373(85)80045-6

Krenn, B., & Schollum, C. (2008, April 2-4). The RASCALLI platform for a flexible and distributed development of virtual systems augmented with cognition. In *Proceedings of the International Conference on Cognitive Systems*, Karlsruhe, Germany.

Laird, J. E. (2008). Extending the soar cognitive architecture. In *Proceedings of the First Conference on Artificial General Intelligence* (pp. 224-235).

Laird, R., Newell, J., & Paul, A. (1987). Soar: An architecture for general intelligence. *Artificial Intelligence, 33*, 1–64. doi:10.1016/0004-3702(87)90050-6

Nason, S., & Laird, J. E. (2004, July 30-August 1). Soar-RL: Integrating reinforcement learning with soar. In *Proceedings of the International Conference on Computing and Mission* (pp. 208-211).

Newell, A. (1990). *Unified theories of cognition*. Cambridge, MA: Harvard University Press.

Srivastava, A., Vaidya, D., Singh, M., Singh, P., & Tiwary, U. S. (2011, August 29-31). A cognitive interactive framework for multi-document summarizer. In *Proceedings of the Third International Conference on Intelligent Human Computer Interaction*, Prague, Czech Republic.

Stahl, G., Koschmann, T., & Suthers, D. (2006). Computer-supported collaborative learning: An historical perspective. In Sawyer, R. K. (Ed.), *Cambridge handbook of the learning sciences* (pp. 409–426). Cambridge, UK: Cambridge University Press.

Sun, R. (2006). The CLARION cognitive architecture: Extending cognitive modeling to social simulation. In Sun, R. (Ed.), *Cognition and multi-agent interaction*. New York, NY: Cambridge University Press. doi:10.1017/CBO9780511610721.005

Sun, R. (2007). The importance of cognitive architectures: An analysis based on CLARION. *Journal of Experimental & Theoretical Artificial Intelligence, 19*(2), 159–193. doi:10.1080/09528130701191560

Sun, R., & Peterson, T. (1996). Learning in reactive sequential decision tasks: The CLARION Model. In *Proceedings of the IEEE International Conference on Neural Networks* (Vol. 2, pp. 1073-1078).

Sun, R., & Zhang, X. (2004). Top-down versus bottom-up learning in cognitive skill acquisition. *Cognitive Systems Research, 5*(1), 63–89. doi:10.1016/j.cogsys.2003.07.001

Sun, R., Zhang, X., & Mathews, R. (2006). Modeling meta-cognition in a cognitive architecture. *Cognitive Systems Research, 7*(4), 327–338. doi:10.1016/j.cogsys.2005.09.001

Sun, R., Zhang, X., Slusarz, P., & Mathews, R. (2007). The interaction of implicit learning, explicit hypothesis testing learning, and implicit-to-explicit knowledge extraction. *Neural Networks, 20*(1), 34–47. doi:10.1016/j.neunet.2006.07.002

Susi, T., & Ziemke, T. (2001). Social cognition, artefacts, and stigmergy: A comparative analysis of theoretical frameworks for the understanding of artefact-mediated collaborative activity. *Cognitive Systems Research, 2*(4), 273–290. doi:10.1016/S1389-0417(01)00053-5

Taatgen, N., Lebiere, C., & Anderson, J. (2006). Modeling paradigms in ACT-R. In Sun, R. (Ed.), *Cognition and multi-agent interaction: From cognitive modeling to social simulation* (pp. 29–52). Cambridge, UK: Cambridge University Press.

Taatgen, N. A., & Anderson, J. R. (2009). The past, present, and future of cognitive architectures. *Topics in Cognitive Science, 2*(4), 1–12.

Tambe, M., Johnson, W. L., Jones, R. M., Koss, F., Laird, J. E., Rosenbloom, P. S., & Schwamb, K. (1995). Intelligent agents for interactive simulation environments. *AI Magazine, 16*(1).

Urban, C. (2001). *PECS: A reference model for human-like agents* (Tech. Rep. No. FS-01-02) (pp. 206-216). Palo Alto, CA: AAAI.

Vygotsky, L. S. (1978). *Mind and society*. Cambridge, MA: Harvard University Press.

Wright, P., Fields, R., & Harrison, M. (2000). Analyzing human-computer interaction as distributed cognition: The resources model. *Human Computer Interaction Journal, 51*(1), 1–41. doi:10.1207/S15327051HCI1501_01

Ziemke, T. (2002). Introduction to the special issue on situated and embodied cognition. *Cognitive Systems Research, 3*(3), 271–274. doi:10.1016/S1389-0417(02)00068-2

Chapter 3
Interactive and Cognitive Models in the Social Network Environment for Designing

Hung-Pin Hsu
National Chiao Tung University, Taiwan

ABSTRACT

In recent years, Metaverse has become a new type of social network. It provides an integrated platform and interactive environment for users to design artifacts and cooperate with each other. Facing this new type of social network, this chapter focuses on the cognitive and interactive behavior of users in the collaborative design activities. The chapter consists of three stages. In stage one the chapter introduces related theories and previous studies in order to present the Metaverse features. In stage two, the author chooses two different design and interactive environments to compare with Metaverse, which are, a normal face to face environment and a regular distance environment. Then the author executes three experiments in these different environments. In stage three, the author analyzes the retrospective data of three experiments with qualitative analysis by undertaking contextual inquiries in order to structure cognitive and interactive models of three environments. Furthermore, the author also executes an in-depth interview to get the qualitative data of subjects' opinion. Finally, the affinity diagrams could be established with these models and the interview to provide knowledge of Metaverse for readers who research or develop social network environment.

INTRODUCTION

According to the target, which users interacted with, there are two kinds of interaction in the design activities. The first one is Cognitive Interaction, the inner-communication, which means users communicate with themselves through the interface between them and the environment. This kind of interface could be products, buildings, and computer interfaces in the Metaverse. The second one is Multipersonal Interaction, the inter-communication, which means users communicate with each other through the interface between themselves (not through environment).

DOI: 10.4018/978-1-4666-0954-9.ch003

The interfaces could be speech, image and language, etc.

The cognitive interaction is often referred to as design thinking, and the concept generation is one of the important action types in design thinking field (Dorst & Dijkhuis, 1995). The behavior oriented studies of design thinking focus on the information processing of designers in the design activities (Akin, 1986; Gero, 1990). Moreover, the concept oriented studies of design thinking focus on what the designers saw, made, thought in the design process, as well as the ideas stimulated from memory (Mckim, 1980; Larkin & Simon, 1987; Laseau, 1993). So it attracted many researchers to study about the influences of sketches on vision thinking (Goldschmidt, 1991, 1992, 1994; Dorst & Dijkhuis, 1995; Suwa & Tversky, 1997; Suwa et al., 1998).

The multi-personal interaction in the design field is highly focused to study that the designers interacted with others through what they design (Koenig, 1974; Nelson, 1979; Pile, 1979; Eco, 1980). Moreover, the verbal speech is the most natural media to interact with others directly. Thus, using verbal speech in the descriptive, explanatory, or representative stages plays very important roles (Lawson & Loke, 1997; Tomas et al., 1998). Besides, designers often execute the multi-personal interactions with images, prototypes, texts (Schrage, 2003; Forslund et al., 2006). In conclusion, studying the multi-personal interactions in the cooperative work becomes an important issue.

Following the impact of digital technology, the interactive media and environment are facing a great transformation. Because users exist in the environment full of stimulations, it also impacts the opportunities that the users develop creatively in the design process (Bennett, 2006). Users begin to use digital media in speech, image, and language processing to generate concepts in the cognitive interaction (Fish & Scrivener, 1990; Goldschmidt, 1991; Goal, 1995). Moreover, due to the popularity of computers and network, it has already

broken through the limitations of time and space to execute the multi-personal interaction. The Computer Supported Cooperative Work systems are also developed and connected by internet. More importantly, there are many kinds of distributed work environments constructed by these factors (Maher et al., 1997; Chiu, 1998). Thus, more and more studies are focusing on the multi-personal interaction in these new types of environments (Maher et al., 1997; Hoog et al., 2007).

COMPUTER SUPPORTED COOPERATIVE WORK

With the enhancement of functions of computer and the progress as well as popularization of internet technology, the applications of computer systems are getting transformed from individualized into distributed type gradually. Due to the multitudinous semi-structured and unstructured problems, users must rely on collaborative communication to look for the solutions. Therefore, users pay more and more attention to the computer supported cooperative system.

The concept and structure of Computer Supported Cooperative Work (CSCW) were brought in as the basic theory to develop groupwares. Ellis and Keddara (1995) defined the groupware as an interface to provide resources for sharing. A computer software system can support members of a group to execute the same work or reach the same goal. According to the definition of groupware, we know that the purpose is to support the members to execute communicative, collaborative and coordinative activities to make the group-work proceed smoothly to enhance the efficiency and productivity. In the case of cooperative design, the designers consider the internet as the communicative media to transmit the design concepts. The content of design concept consists of text, image, video and 3D model. In the network space, the text is regarded as a media to transmit messages. As verbal communication is one of the most natural communicative methods in real world, the text definitely is not less important than vision media (Hoog & Seifried, 2007).

The design researchers must consider if the new design environment would destroy the design process and the cooperative activities (Bannon & Schmidt, 1991). Facing to the new cooperative design tool, users must consider the resources, the method of work, and the obstacle of communication (Finholt et al., 1990). A successful computer supported cooperative design system does not necessarily mean to imitate the real environment (Gabriel & Maher, 2002). Despite the slightly different way of communication, Gabriel and Maher found that the designers still could cooperate and communicate their design ideas effectively. The designers could still proceed with the design work successfully without those media. They also point out that the multi-personal communication in the computer supported cooperative design would be influenced by communicative control, communicative technology, social communication, and design communication. Among those factors, the design communication could be subdivided into several sub-factors which include design idea, task, scope, etc.

The synchronous distributed communication technology is applied in the computer supported cooperative work. Various other distributed design environments are also used for design, such as Cooperative Pen-Based Environment and Virtual Design Studio (VDS) (Maher et al., 1997; Chiu, 1998). The virtual design studio is a digital environment and procedure which is established through the computer connected with the internet. The goal of virtual design studio in the early stages is to investigate the design application education. These early studies could help users to understand the creative possibilities which are produced by applying information technology into the scope of design. Mitchell (1995) points out that the virtual design studio not only builds up a new paragon of computer aided design, but also manifests design to be intrinsically related to social behavior.

In recent years, the purpose of the studies on virtual design studio is that the designer would attempt to use new communicative technology to execute the design project. Most of these studies investigate the distance cooperative design projects and observe the phenomena of the designer using network space to execute the design communication (Schnabel et al., 2001; Kvan, 2001; Broadfoot & Bennett, 2003). Through virtual design studio, a number of groups could work in the distributed environment synchronously or asynchronously. Thus, around the world, lots of organizations have been established through the use of new computing and communicative technology (Wojtowicz, 1994; Branko et al., 2000; Kvan, 2000).

METAVERSE

According to users' need, cyberspace has been transformed into BBS and chat room in 80s, MUD and MMORPG in 90s, and Metaverse in 21st century. The features of Metaverse are that users could interact with each other immediately through the 3D avatars in the virtual environment on the internet. The best representative of the Metaverse is Second Life, which was created by Linden Lab in 2003. This platform supports users to create their avatars' faces, artifacts, buildings, even the landscape of cities with Linden Script Language and 3D modeling design tools.

In the Second Life, users could build virtual artifacts with not only 3D virtual modeling function provided inside, but also other softwares not included in the Metaverse, such as Autodesk 3D Max. Moreover, users could communicate with each other through avatars they built by typing, mailing, or speaking. Second Life also inserts searching function on internet. This function would narrow down the gap between different interfaces. Due to these creations in the Second Life, the Metaverse becomes friendlier to communicate and cooperate with other users (Hsu, 2010).

Second Life has become a platform of distance virtual class in many universities, and it is useful for shrinking the gap between students and teachers (Nesson, 2007). Due to the development of these educative organizations in the Second Life, it attracts many researchers to study related interactive issues inside (Abdellatif & Calderon, 2007; Hoog et al., 2007, 2008; Kathryn et al., 2008; Antonieta et al., 2009; Tan & Lim, 2009; Hsu, 2010). Through modeling and comparing the cognitive and interactive design behavior of users, this chapter would introduce the phenomena of collaborative design activities in a new type of cooperative web based environment, the Metaverse.

The technology of Metaverse, through a signal interface, allows users to do productive, consuming, and communicative activities in the virtual environment. The Metaverse builds up a virtual online world on different scales of culture, society, and economy (Hsu, 2010). Use of Metaverse as the cooperative work environment has become an essential issue and it has begun to attract many researchers to pay attention to this issue. Abdellatif and Calderon (2007) studied the way to use Second Life as a computer mediated environment of distance learning in the architectural education. Hoog's research team (2008) also designed an architectural course in the Second Life. The point of Hoog's research emphasizes that the course participator must manipulate the role of architect as an avatar and design architectures for the users who manipulate the role of proprietor as an avatar in the Metaverse. The result of this research shows that students who manipulate their avatars easily project their thoughts of the real world upon the virtual world. Hsu (2010) analyzed the phenomena of behaviors of designers who implemented the cooperative design both in the normal distance environment and the Metaverse. Nowadays, more and more users execute the cooperative work in the Metaverse, and many other related issues are still required to be investigated.

METHODOLOGY

To study the design behavior in the Metaverse, two kinds of environments of design and interaction were chosen to compare with Metaverse. Those two environments were normal face to face environment and regular distance environment. In these three different environments, users executed cooperative design on the same topic with the media that was used. The processes in these experiments were also recorded on the camera.

Experiment Design

In the method of protocol analysis, Video/Audio Retrospective Protocols were designed to solve the problem of the lack of synchronous protocol data and retrospective data (Suwa & Tversky, 1997; Suwa et al., 1998). Subjects were asked to watch and control the video/audio data from experiments and retrospect their thinking process. Meanwhile, researchers could ask questions or request subjects to interpret their descriptions. The protocol analysis in this method emphasized the response of cognitive behavior (Dorst & Dijkhuis, 1995; Suwa et al., 1998), but less interference in the design and communicative processes. Therefore, in this study, Video/Audio Retrospective Protocols were chosen to collect cognitive behavior data.

To execute three kinds of cognitive experiments, two architectural designers were invited as the subjects in the experiments. Each subject has had five years of architecture design experience and knowledge of cooperative design in these three kinds of environment. On the other hand in this study, the Second Life, which was the most representative platform as mentioned in the introduction, was chosen to be the target environment of Metaverse.

The cooperative design could be divided into three kinds of communicative types which include mutual, dictator and exclusive cooperative design (Maher et al., 1997). First of all, the mutual cooperative design means that cooperators deal with the same design problem through communication and coordination. Secondly, the dictator cooperative design emphasizes the relation of primary and secondary between designers. This approach is a way that some designers direct the design activity and others execute the design work. However, in both the mutual and dictator cooperative designs, designers usually communicate with each other through voice and drawings, so it is much harder to record the cognitive behavior.

The third kind of cooperative design methodology is the exclusive cooperative design, which means that co-designers divide the design problems into several sub-problems. Then the co-designers solve their own sub-problems which are distributed, and discuss the result of design when all sub-problems have been solved. The feature of this method is that designers belong to their own cognitive activities in the design process and they execute the design communication activities after a part of design has been completed. The structure of design activities in the exclusive cooperative design is so much clear that it is easier to record the design behavior at each stage. Due to this advantage, the exclusive cooperative design methodology was chosen.

For choosing the design site, this study picked a site which was totally open to design behavior. This site could support designers to execute land-mark creating, flying, objects inputting, object creating, and storyboard setting. In addition, this site could also allow anyone to take or revise all the objects on it, so that designer could manipulate their design mutually. In the part of designing communication, all kinds of communicative functions in Second Life were also open on this site. Thus, designers could execute the cooperative design by exchanging text, voice, and objects. And then subjects were asked to design with the same topic and site in these three experiments respectively. The materials of design were given as those shown in Figure 1.

The proprietor in this design case is a female ocean biologist. She plans to build her own house for living with her husband in this island. Because they both love to live near the ocean, they choose the site in the plain on the south of this island. This house not only means a building, but also means a space to live, work and enjoy in.

Since this study was using the design communication environments of both normal face to face and regular distance to compare with Metaverse and get the models of interactive and cognitive design in Metaverse, this study first executed those two design communication environments and then Metaverse at last.

Before these three experiments, the subjects were asked to choose the design and communicative tools they were used to in the cooperative design activity. And there was no limitation on design sequence and timing. Subjects could decide when they would finish their work in any situation. Furthermore, to make sure that their thoughts, operations and communication were not interfered, each experiment was separated by more than two weeks.

Experiments and Results

The purpose of the experiment one is to observe the interactive and cognitive behavior of designers, who execute cooperative design in the normal face to face design and communication environment. The subjects participated in the interview before the experiment and picked the design media and communicative interface which they were used to. The methods of using media and interface were decided by subjects in the experiment. In the part of design media, the subjects chose paper, pen, digital camera, and moreover, Sketch UP for model building, Photoshop for image processing, PowerPoint for brief editing, and notebook. All these softwares were installed. Besides, in the part of communicative media, the subjects only chose USB flash disk for data exchanging.

Figure 1. The materials of design

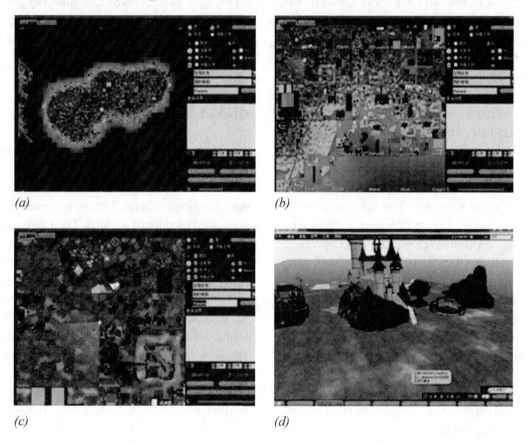

(a)

(b)

(c)

(d)

The design activities in experiment one could be separated into six stages. First of all, stage one is to conceive the concept of design. And then, stage two is to search the design cases on the internet. Stage three is the design developing stage, which discusses the design concepts and cases with cooperators. Furthermore, stage four is to actually execute the result of initial discussion, while stage five discusses the result of initial design. Finally, stage six executes the final revision of overall design and discussion at the same time.

The second experiment was conducted in the regular distance design and communication environment. Subjects could also pick up the design media and communicative interface and then determine how to use as the way in the first experiment. In the part of design media, both subjects chose the software, such as Sketch UP, Photoshop, PowerPoint, and the notebooks (in-stalled these softwares). Furthermore, one of the subjects could choose the tablet to replace the mouse and to draw sketches on the notebook. On the other hand, in the part of communicative media both subjects chose the function of video conferencing on Skype and conversed to each other on the internet.

The design activities in the second experiment were arranged in a similar way as the first experiment. The only difference was that subjects had one more stage to revise design work individually before the final cooperative revision stage. In this additional stage, the subjects individually executed their work which they were allotted in the stage of discussion. And finally, subjects at the same time opened the function of video conferencing in the stage of cooperative revision to understand the current status of implementation of other subjects.

The goal of the third experiment was to understand the behavior of interaction and cognition when designers executed the cooperative design in the Metaverse. The method of choosing and using the design media and communicative interface was the same as the previous experiment. Although the options of media and interface were not limited to Second Life, both subjects merely chose the media and interface provided by Second Life.

The demarcation line between each stage of design activities in the third experiment was much more indistinct relatively. The third experiment comprised three stages, which were concept generating and concept developing for the cooperative stage, and concept revising for the individual stage as shown in Figure 4. The first three stages of experiment one and experiment two plus the design activities of discussion stage were integrated into the cooperative stage of experiment three. The difference was that subjects through the avatar immediately discussed and revised the design work with the cooperator. Comparing with the first and second experiments, subjects spent more time discussing the feature of the site and its relation with neighbor environment. These discussions about the site replaced the case searching on the internet. Besides, subjects directly executed design on the site in the Metaverse and these models and figures for discussing and explaining were also parts of the final design work, so both discussion and execution of design synchronously proceeded with the development of design.

In the individual stage of design revision, subjects according to the result of previous discussion executed the design work which they were allotted. And they continued to develop the design project until the whole project was finished. This individual stage consisted of design execution stage and revision stage just as those in the first and second experiments. In the final revision stage of the first two experiments, the subjects would make briefing to their proprietor about design concept and artifact. However, subjects thought they could directly introduce their design work to the avatar of the proprietor with the architecture models in the Metaverse, so they would omit briefing in the final revision stage.

ANALYSIS AND DISCUSSION

This study applies user experience based research method which is qualitative analysis through the use of contextual inquiries to analyze the human data from experiments. Firstly, the researcher records the behavior of subjects. Then, the recorded data is established as the affinity diagram. This action is essentially meaningful because the affinity diagram helps the researchers to arrange the considerable data of behavior. Secondly, the researcher builds work models according to affinity diagrams and the records of subjects' behavior in the experiments. These models can help researchers to easily analyze the interactive and cognitive behaviors of subjects. Through analyzing these work models, this study gets the interactive and cognitive phenomena of subjects in the experiments.

Affinity Diagram from Experiments

Affinity diagram is a kind of qualitative methodology that is frequently used to analyze data in the human-computer interaction domain. It is a qualitative method to generalize data that effectively streamlines the numerous and complicated data into a few main points. Affinity diagram can also help researcher to find out the behavior mode and potential demand of subject (Kuniavsky, 2003).

In order to establish affinity diagram, researchers first wrote down the qualitative contents which were observed on the notes in two or three sentences during the experiment. Then all the notes were spread and pasted on the same table or wall to help the researcher read and organize these notes conveniently. After reading all content of these

Figure 2. The flow model from the experiment one: normal face to face environment

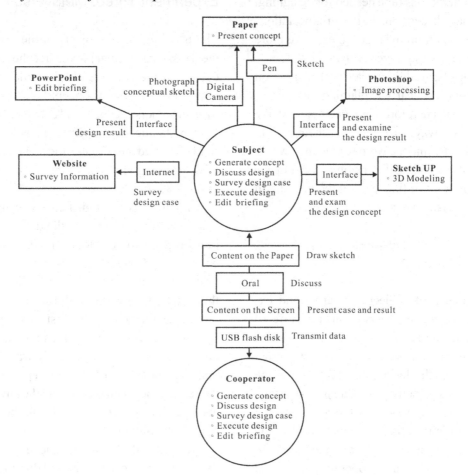

notes, researchers stack the notes with relevant content together into a small group. Then, they find common phenomena of this small group and write a new label representing this small group. When researchers established affinity diagram, the numbers of notes of one small group is controlled in two to four pieces. Following the same rules, the researchers built a middle group with these labelled small groups and create a label representing the middle group. Similarly, the big/large? group is built by the labels of middle groups. Finally, the phenomena of the interactive and cognitive behavior of subjects are built by the labels of big/large groups. Through this qualitative methodology, the three experiments in this study had such phenomena of behavior as given.

Experiment One: Normal Face to Face Environment

The phenomena of subjects in the first experiment were that designers spent more time to execute design communication work with their cooperators in the face to face environment. This communication helps designers to execute their distributed design work more efficiently. The main goal of all design work was to make a perfect briefing of their architecture design to the proprietor.

The subjects did not plan the stages and schedules of design activities. Most of the time, the subjects discussed the design concepts and the method to execute their design work. Discussion and design were inseparable. The more time spent in discussion, the less time needed for designing. With adequate discussion, the gap in expectations is reduced. And moreover, designers have more time to develop design creatively.

The subjects, in addition, paid a lot of attention to proprietors for clearly explaining their architecture design. Therefore, they decided to make a briefing as a way for presenting their design. They also left behind the words or pictures which were suitable to put into the briefing. The subjects finally spent a lot of time editing the briefing in the design revision stage.

Experiment Two: Regular Distance Environment

The phenomena of subjects in the second experiment were that designers frequently suffered difficulties in the regular distance environment due to the restriction of the computer and internet devices. It urged the designer to decide to plan the schedule of design activities in the primary stage of cooperative design. Because the designer spent less time communicating about design idea, the design results were easy to be accepted directly.

The subjects shared the operating screen of computers to communicate about design work with the cooperator. Thus the cooperator could see the browsed web pages and the windows of application software. However, this sharing overloads the computer calculation and network transmission. So, the subjects were usually in the situations that video and audio was delayed or even disconnected.

Due to these reasons, subjects could not discuss their design fluently. They tended to plan the schedule of the design activities in advance. But the discussion time is restricted so that they only discuss the distribution of the works on the schedule of design activities. The details of design work were forced to be surrendered during discussion, and instead, to be decided by subjects. On the contrary, this phenomenon, allows subjects to have more freedom to create their design concept.

Experiment Three: Metaverse

The phenomena of subjects in the third experiment were that designers executed the architecture design on the site directly. It could deepen the importance of design concept for the site. Moreover, designers executed and discussed the design work by facing the cooperator in the same virtual field. It could also make the designer capable of distributing and discussing the design works immediately.

Undoubtedly, through their avatar, the subjects could visit the site and get the detailed information directly. So even though, there was a function contained in the interface of Second Life to browse on the internet, the subjects still did not choose this function to search for the design cases on the internet as they did in the first two experiments. Instead, the detailed and easy to get information on the site let subjects directly transform their understandings into a design concept. For example, the relation between the site and the environment, and the relation between style and height of the neighbor building.

Besides, in the Metaverse, the subjects, through their avatar, faced to the site and directly executed the design work. It was clear and instant for subjects to understand the design models built by cooperators. The subjects also could revise the design models together during the process of discussion. So, the subjects did not advisedly plan the schedule of the design activities.

In the front part of design activities, the subjects got together to generate the design concepts, to discuss the design work, and to build the design models. When the design models were almost over, the subjects were separated to execute the design works in the back part of design activities.

Design Behavior Modeling

Beyer and Holtzblatt (1998) thought that the researchers can establish five kinds of work models by observing the qualitative human data in the experiment and the affinity diagram. The categories of work models consist of Flow Model, Sequence Model, Artifact Model, Cultural Model, and Physical Model. Each model stands for different meaning of human behavior. And these work models can replace a large number of textual data. These models, moreover, led researchers to understand the interactive and cognitive behavior of subject in the field.

Thus, in this stage of analysis, researcher uses the recorded data in the experiment as well as the affinity diagram to establish five categories of work models for each experiment. The recorded data include video and audio recording, the behavior data on the notes, the design sketch and article, the temporary file and locations of website. After observing those data of subjects' behavior, the researcher draws the following five categories of work models.

Model 1. Flow Model

The flow model represents the behavior of communicative and cooperative processes in the activities. This model describes five important factors: The first factor is communicative object.

Figure 3. The flow model from the experiment two: regular distance environment

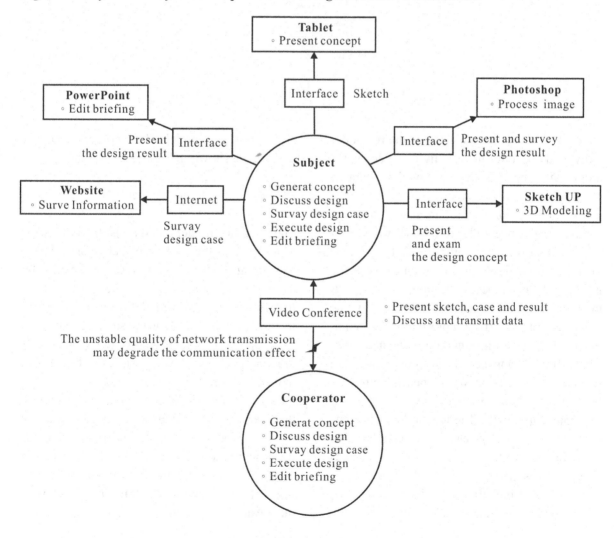

Figure 4. The flow model from the experiment three: Metaverse

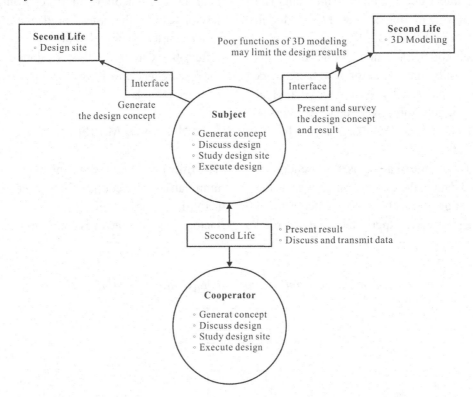

Object represents the subjects and the relational individual or groups in the activities. Each communicative object in the flow model is drawn as a bubble and the behaviors of object are also marked in the bubble icon. The second factor is communicative place. Place is the one-way pattern to provide or receive information in the process of information flow. The communicative place is presented as a block in the flow model. Then, the third factor is communicative flow which is drawn as an arrow. Arrow represents the direction of flow to transmit information in the activities. If something happened during communicative process, this situation would be embalmed as lightning on the arrow with words of problem and handicap nearby. The fourth factor is communicative artifact, which means the tool used to communicate in the activities. The communicative artifact is marked in shape of a block on the arrow. Finally, the fifth factor is the content of communication. The content is written near the arrow. The flow models of experiment from one to three are shown in Figures 2, 3, and 4.

Model 2. Sequence Model

The sequence model could assist the researcher to understand the process of behavior which is happening during the activities. It can also be used to redesign and regulate the process of activities. The sequence model is made up of four factors. The first factor is the steps of sequence. The steps express each action and the process of thinking that the subjects manifest. The steps in the sequence model are drawn as a block with the meaning inside. In the steps of sequence model, the researcher could find the purpose and strategy of each action, as well as the specific behavior or the basic purpose of action. The second factor is trigger. Trigger means the original point of a string of evens and behavior. It is drawn as a block with the meaning inside, too.

The third factor is the intent of action, which is the written next step of sequence. The sequence model includes the main intent, and in the after process, there are second or third intent to let the sequence of action keeps going. Then, the fourth factor is the flow of sequence, which describes the happening direction of steps of sequence through the arrow symbol. The flow in the sequence model could be order, loop, or branch. It could assist the researcher to understand clearly how the steps are connected. As the flow model, the lightning symbol is used to express the breakdown situation during the process of sequence.

In the sequence model, researcher could get each step after the beginning of trigger and the different intents included in the process. Besides, the sequence model also provides with the deeper information for understanding the actual process of activities. Thus, it could allow the designer to plan the more detailed design activities. The sequence models of experiments from one to three are shown in Figures 5, 6, and 7.

Model 3. Artifact Model

According to the artifact model, researchers can find out what the subject's intent is and how the subject uses the tools to finish their particular task. The artifact model reveals a kind of situation, concept, structure, or strategy. It could also assist the researcher in knowing what point the subject focuses on.

The artifact model exhibits some important features. The first one is the content of message, which could display the intent of a part of tasks. The second feature explains who, when, where, and how to use the artifact. The third feature is the structure of artifact which presents how the work is to be organized and arranged. The fourth feature is the informal annotation which is additional information. It could inform the researcher about the method of using the artifact and the intent of subject's thought.

There is no specific method to establish the artifact model, but the main goal is to clearly display how the tool is to be used. As with the previous two models, the lightning symbol is used to mark the difficulty that the subject encounters when using the tool. The artifact models of experiments from one to three are shown in Figures 8, 9, and 10.

Model 4. Cultural Model

Through establishing the cultural model, researchers could define the cultural factors of the subjects in the activities. The factors, for example, are expectancy, standard, or values, etc. The purpose of the cultural model is to present the behavior and the influence of social environment on the subject, but not to describe the formal framework of the organization.

The cultural model consists of two main units: The first unit is the influencer, which is represented as an ellipse. The ellipse is labeled with certain factors that influence the activities, such as a person, group, event, or artifact. The second unit is the influence, which is represented as an arrow symbol. Along the direction of arrow, the researcher could know the direction of the influence. The arrow is marked by words about the method and content of influence. In the cultural model, the lightning symbol represents the obstructive factor and the content of factor is presented in form of words.

If the ellipse overlaps in the cultural model, the overlapping would reveal the degree of influence that influencer affects the subject in the activities. Meanwhile, the auxiliary arrow also assists to point out the direction of influence between influencers. The cultural models of experiments from one to three are shown in Figures 11, 12, and 13.

Model 5. Physical Model

The physical model describes the environment where the subject executes the activities. The influential factors of environment consist of the

Figure 5. The sequence model from the experiment one: normal face to face environment

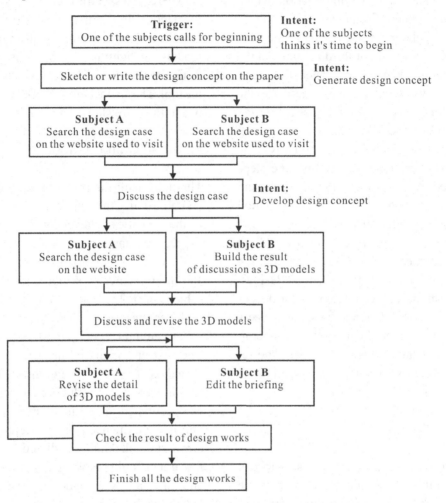

framework of space, the purpose and method of being used, the location of article, and the route of activities. Most importantly, the physical model depicts the influence of the physical environment on the activities.

The main point of the physical model is to clearly describe the physical environment, but there is no specific method to establish. The difficulties that the subject encounters when they are executing the activities in the environment are presented as a lightning symbol and explained with auxiliary text. On the other hand, because this study arranges subjects to execute the design activities in the specific experiment environment, we will get less information from physical model

relatively. The physical model of experiment one is shown in Figure 14. Moreover the physical model of experiments two and three is also shown in Figure 15.

DISCUSSION

After using the qualitative method to analyze and compare the work models in these experiments, the affinity diagrams can be established to infer the phenomena of cooperative behaviors in the Metaverse. This study finds that parts of distant problems during design process have been improved in the Metaverse. Metaverse provides a

Figure 6. The sequence model from the experiment two: regular distance environment

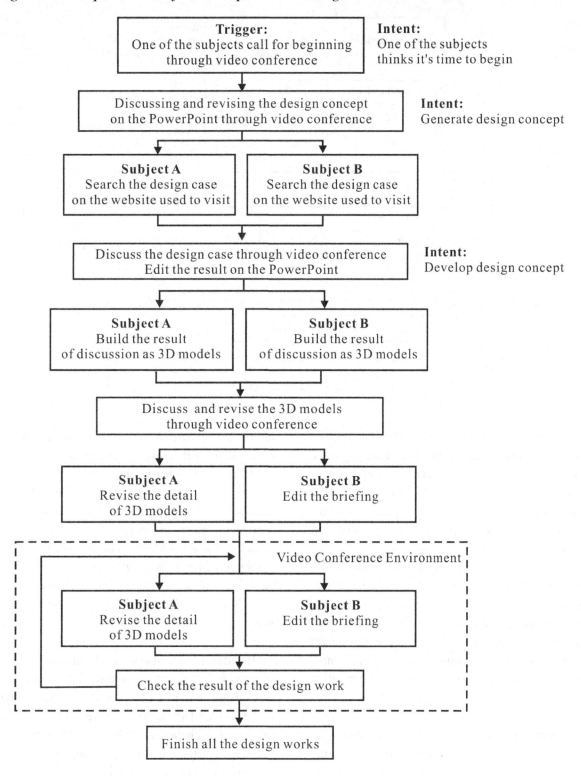

Figure 7. The sequence model from the experiment three: Metaverse

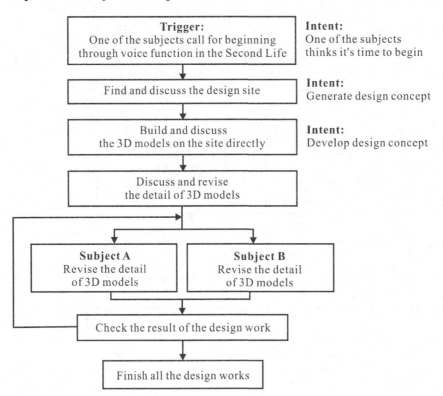

communicative environment better than regular distance environment to ensure that the cognitive process will not be interfered by the collaborators during design process. And it is much closer to the status in the face to face environment for designers to understand the response and presentation from others.

As a result of the integration of communication and design media, the cognitive burden of crossing interfaces has been decreased, and the communicative effect on the distance has been improved. Moreover, because the environment is more similar to an on-line game, it could provide more interesting design and communicative process:

...I think that the avatar actually adds much interest when I am cooperating with others in the Second Life. This feeling is something like making physical models with other designers face to face.

However, there are still details to be implemented. In the Second Life, using the avator to build the 3D models resembles to discuss with sketching in the face to face environment or discuss with 3D CAD software in the regular distance environment. It is hard to categorize this cooperative method, but it is an interesting method to cooperate the design work with others. The most advantage of building models in the Second Life is that it's easy for me to know others' thoughts...(Quote from in-depth interview of subject B, translated from Chinese)

Besides, the distribution of design tasks in the Metaverse is much closer to the habit of cooperation design in the face to face environment than in the regular distance environment. However, in the Second Life there are limitations of active and facial communication on the avatar, so the effect of confirmation and response in the Metaverse still cannot compare to the face to face environment:

Figure 8. The artifact model from the experiment one: normal face to face environment

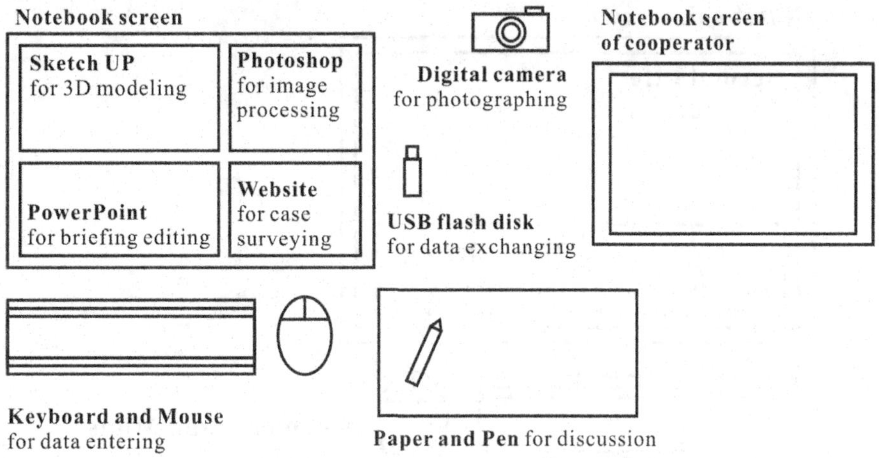

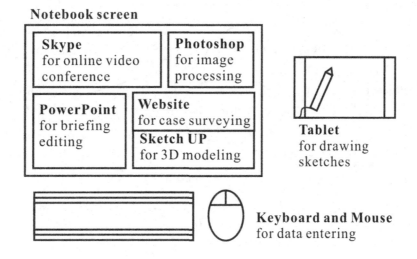

... *I used to communicate our design work with my partner through speaking because I think typewriting might interfere with thinking when I am in the design work. As usual, I do not write words when I am designing. On the other hand, I think the movement and facial expression are just fun of the Second Life, and nothing to do for designing. It is more like the graphics made up by texts and symbols in the email... (Quote from in-depth interview of subject A, translated from Chinese)*

In the Metaverse, another phenomenon is that the designers have more respect to the conceptual generation and discussion in the initial design stage. This phenomenon could be obtained by observing the result of experiments that the subjects have more respect to the understanding of the design site than to the design or case experience in the past. Besides, designers spend more time to distribute their work in the initial design process, and therein, the communicative content is more influential for the design result. Comparatively, the communicative content in the latter stage is more like social talking. Designers adopt more

Figure 9. The artifact model from the experiment two: regular distance environment

Figure 10. The artifact model from the experiment three: Metaverse

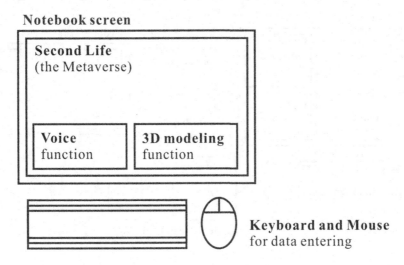

clear strategies in the initial stage of Metaverse than in other environments, and this action also makes the communicative effect much clearer than in the regular distance environment.

...Usually, I would look for more information on the internet or magazines when I need more inspiration or data to understand the design topic. But, in the Second Life, I think the best way to get more information is looking from the site directly. I could discuss the design concept and distribute works at the same time when analyzing the de-

sign site with my partner. Furthermore, because the avatar of my partner is right next my avatar during the process of executing design work, it is easy and relaxes to talk to each other and check the design progress and result anytime... (Quote from in-depth interview of subject A, translated from Chinese)

In this study, we also find out that the designers manifest new design methods and habits in the Metaverse. During the cooperation design activity, designers communicate with each other through

Figure 11. The cultural model from the experiment one: normal face to face environment

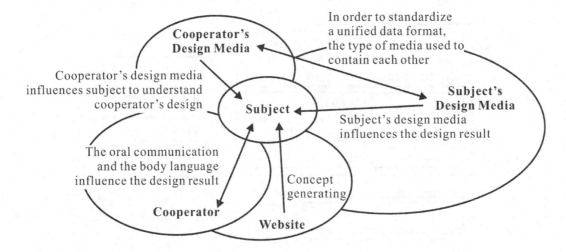

Figure 12. The cultural model from the experiment two: regular distance environment

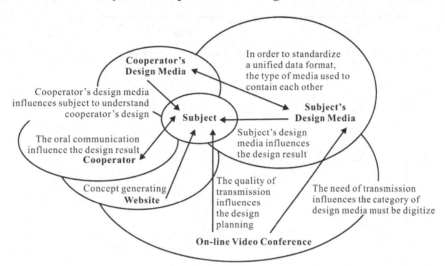

avatar and create actual digital 3D models in the virtual world. As the result of integrating multiple design media into the communicative environment, the need for the different media is less and Metaverse is more; tallies with the habits and expectations of generating concept than regular distance environment.

On the other hand, the designers in the Metaverse care about less reference of generating concept but more discussion in the initial design stage. The phenomenon shows that their design ideas are very elastic in Metaverse because they just discuss the outline of the design content. However, the design result and behavior are still limited due to the poor design tools.

Figure 13. The cultural model from the experiment three: Metaverse

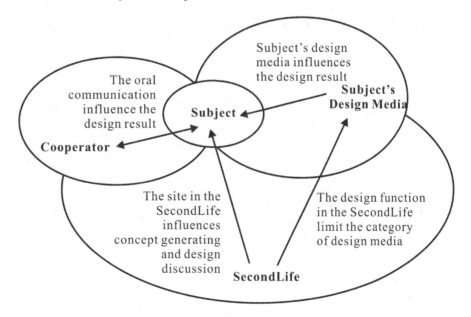

Figure 14. The physical model from the experiment one: normal face to face environment

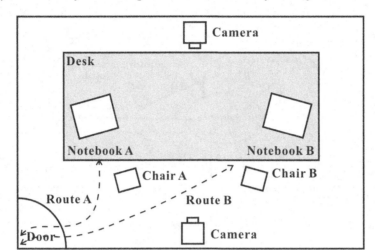

CONCLUSION

The results of this study show that designers depend more on the discussion and exposition of design concept, and to the distribution of design work. It not only decreases the influence of distance in the design process and improves effective communication, but also lets designers discuss and determine the design concept and cooperative method in the initial stage of Metaverse.

Due to the integration of design media and communication environment provided in the Metaverse, it not only maintains the conveniences of distance communication, but also approaches to the face to face environment. The communication through avatar reduces the information error for distance and overcomes the difficulty that designers communicate with each other through different interfaces. Therefore, comparing with the regular distance environment, Metaverse is much closer to the users' need.

Figure 15. The physical model from the experiment two and three: regular distance environment and Metaverse

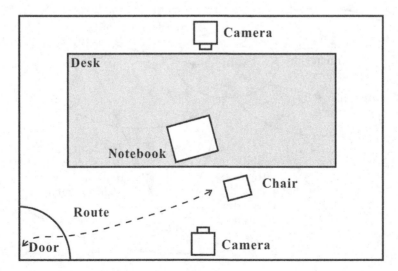

This study has already presented the interactive cognitive models of Metaverse and the other two cooperative environments. However, due to the limitation of resources, this study concentrates the subjects on the designers. This compromise may influence the cognitive models of communication. Besides, the design topic in the experiment may also generate special effects on design thinking. Even so, the findings in this study still provide us with a systematic understanding about the interactive and cognitive behavior of the designer who cooperates in the Metaverse.

This understanding could be directly applied to the communicative phenomena in the Metaverse. More importantly, the structure of this study could be extended to further investigate interactive and cognitive phenomena in other communication environment.

REFERENCES

Abdellatif, R., & Calderon, C. (2007). SecondLife: A computer-mediated tool for distance-learning in architecture education? In *Proceedings of Em'body'ing Virtual Architecture: The Third International Conference of the Arab Society for Computer Aided Architectural Design* (pp. 17-34).

Akin, O. (1986). *Psychology of architectural design*. London, UK: Pion.

Antonieta, A., Fillwalk, J., & Vásquez, G. V. (2009). Collaborating in a virtual architectural environment: The Las Americas Virtual Design Studio (LAVDS) populates Second Life. In *Proceedings of Anais do XIII Congresso da Sociedade Ibero Americana de Gráfica Digital*.

Bannon, L. J., & Schmidt, K. (1991). CSCW: four characters in search of a context. In Bowers, J. M., & Bendford, S. D. (Eds.), *Studies in computer supported cooperative work*. Amsterdam, The Netherlands: North Holland.

Bennett, A. (2006). *Design studies: theory and research in graphic design*. New York, NY: Princeton Architectural Press.

Beyer, H., & Holtzblatt, K. (1998). *Contextual design: Defining customer-centered systems*. San Francisco, CA: Morgan Kaufmann.

Branko, K., Schmitt, G., Hirschberg, U., Kurmann, D., & Johnson, B. (2000). An experiment in design collaboration. *Automation in Construction*, *9*, 73–81. doi:10.1016/S0926-5805(99)00050-3

Broadfoot, O., & Bennett, R. (2003). Design studios: Online? Comparing traditional face to face design studio education with modern Internet-based design studios. In *Proceedings of the Apple University Consortium Conference: Digital Voyages*.

Chiu, M. L. (1998). The design guidance of CSCW: learning from collaborative design studios' in Sasada. In *Proceedings of the 3rd International Conference of the Association for Computer-Aided Architectural Design Research in Asia* (pp. 261-270).

Dorst, K., & Dijkhuis, J. (1995). Comparing paradigms for describing design activity. *Design Studies*, *16*(2), 261–274. doi:10.1016/0142-694X(94)00012-3

Eco, U. (1980). Function and sign: the semiotics of architecture. In Broadbent, G., Bunt, R., & Jencks, C. (Eds.), *Signs, symbols and architecture* (pp. 11–69). Chichester, UK: John Wiley & Sons.

Ellis, C. A., & Keddara, K. (1995). *Dynamic change within workflow systems (Tech. Rep.)* (pp. 1–20). Boulder, CO: University of Colorado.

Finholt, T., Sproull, L., & Kiesler, S. (1990). Communication and performance in ad hoc task groups. In Galegher, J., Kraut, R. E., & Egido, C. (Eds.), *Intellectual teamwork: Social and technological foundations of cooperative work* (pp. 291–325). Mahwah, NJ: Lawrence Erlbaum.

Fish, J., & Scrivener, S. (1990). Amplifying the mind's eye: sketching and visual cognition. *Leonardo, 23*, 117–126. doi:10.2307/1578475

Forslund, K., Dagman, A., & Söderberg, R. (2006). Visual sensitivity: communicating poor quality. In *Proceedings of the International Design Conference* (pp. 713-720).

Gabriel, G. C., & Maher, M. L. (2002). Coding and modeling communication in architectural collaborative design. *Automation in Construction, 11*, 199–211. doi:10.1016/S0926-5805(00)00098-4

Gero, J. S. (1990). Design prototypes: A knowledge representation schema for design. *AI Magazine, 2009*, 27–36.

Goel, V. (1995). *Sketches of thought*. Cambridge, MA: MIT Press.

Goldschmidt, G. (1991). The dialectics of sketching. *Creativity Research Journal, 4*(2), 123–143. doi:10.1080/10400419109534381

Goldschmidt, G. (1992). Serial sketching: visual problem solving in designing. *Cybernetics and Systems: An International Journal, 23*, 191–219. doi:10.1080/01969729208927457

Goldschmidt, G. (1994). On visual design thinking: the via kids of architecture. *Design Studies, 15*(2), 158–174. doi:10.1016/0142-694X(94)90022-1

Hoog, J., Falkner, C., & Seifried, P. (2007). Collaborative spaces as learning environments. In *Proceedings of the Conference of the Arab Society for Computer Aided Architectural Design* (pp. 357-364).

Hoog, J., Falkner, C., & Seifried, P. (2008). Second City: A three-dimensional city model as interdisciplinary platform for research. In *Proceedings of the Conference on Education and Research in Computer Aided Architectural Design in Europe* (pp. 359-366).

Hsu, H. P. (2010). Design behavior in the interactive virtual environment on the network space. In *Proceedings of the Second IEEE International Conference on Intelligent Human Computer Interaction* (pp. 320-327).

Kathryn, M., Lou, M. M., & Saunders, R. (2008). Achieving adaptable behavior in intelligent rooms using curious supervised learning agents. In *Proceedings of the 13th International Conference of the Association for Computer-Aided Architectural Design Research in Asia* (pp. 185-192).

Koenig, G. K. (1974). *Architettura e comunicazione Seconda edizione accresciutia da un saggio su Schindler e Neutra*. Florence, Italia: Liberia Editrice Fiorentina.

Kuniavsky, M. (2003). *Observing the user experience: A practitioner's guide to user research*. San Francisco, CA: Morgan Kaufmann.

Kvan, T. (2000). Collaborative design: what is it? *Automation in Construction, 9*, 409–415. doi:10.1016/S0926-5805(99)00025-4

Kvan, T. (2001). The pedagogy of virtual design studio. *Automation in Construction, 10*, 345–354. doi:10.1016/S0926-5805(00)00051-0

Larkin, J. H., & Simon, H. A. (1987). Why a diagram is (sometimes) worth ten thousand words. *Cognitive Science, 11*, 65–99. doi:10.1111/j.1551-6708.1987.tb00863.x

Laseau, P. (1993). *Graphic thinking for architects and designers*. New York, NY: Van Nostrand Reinhold.

Lawson, B., & Loke, S. (1997). Computers, words and pictures. *Design Studies, 18*(7), 171–183. doi:10.1016/S0142-694X(97)85459-2

Maher, M. L., Simoff, S. J., & Cicognani, A. (1997). Observations from an experimental study of computer-mediated collaborative design. In *Proceedings of the Third International IFIP WG 5.2 Workshop on Formal Design Methods for CAD* (pp. 165-186).

Mckim, R. H. (1980). *Experiences in visual thinking*. Florence, KY: Brooks/Cole Press.

Mitchell, W. J. (1995). *City of Bits: Space, Place, and the Infobahn*. Cambridge, MA: MIT Press.

Nelson, G. (1979). *Problems of design*. New York, NY: Whitney Library of Design.

Nesson, R. (2007). *A Harvard Law school lecture in Second Life*. New York, NY: Christine Lagorio.

Pile, J. F. (1979). *Design: purpose, form and meaning*. Amherst, MA: University of Massachusetts Press.

Schnabel, M. A., Kvan, T., Kruijff, E., & Donath, D. (2001). The first virtual environment design studio. In *Proceedings of the Conference on Education and Research in Computer Aided Architectural Design in Europe* (pp.394-400).

Schrage, M. (2003). *Serious play: how the world's best companies simulate to innovate*. Cambridge, MA: Harvard Business School Press.

Suwa, M., Purcell, T., & Gero, J. (1998). Macroscopic analysis of design processes based on a scheme for coding designer's cognitive actions. *Design Studies, 19*(4), 455–483. doi:10.1016/S0142-694X(98)00016-7

Suwa, M., & Tversky, B. (1997). What do architects and students perceive in their design sketches? A protocol analysis. *Design Studies, 18*(4), 385–403. doi:10.1016/S0142-694X(97)00008-2

Tan, B. K., & Lim, T. Y. (2009). Place-making in online virtual environment: The case of Second Life. In *Proceedings of the CAAD Futures Conference on Joining Languages Cultures and Visions* (pp. 31-32).

Tomes, A., Oates, C., & Armstrong, P. (1998). Talking design: Negotiating the verbal-visual translation. *Design Studies, 19*, 127–142. doi:10.1016/S0142-694X(97)00027-6

Wojtowicz, J. (1994). *Virtual design studio*. Hong Kong: Hong Kong University Press.

Chapter 4

Fuzzy Linguistic Modelling in Multi Modal Human Computer Interaction:
Adaptation to Cognitive Styles using Multi Level Fuzzy Granulation Method

Ilham N. Huseyinov
European University of Lefke, Turkey

ABSTRACT

The purpose of this chapter is to explore fuzzy logic based methodology for computing an adaptive interface in an environment of imperfect, vague, multimodal, complex nonlinear hyper information space. To this end, based on fuzzy linguistic modelling and fuzzy multi level granulation an adaptation strategy to cognitive/learning styles is presented. The granulated fuzzy if-then rules are utilized to adaptively map cognitive/learning styles of users to their information navigation and presentation preferences through natural language expressions. The important implications of this approach are that, first, uncertain and vague information is handled; second, a mechanism for approximate adaptation at a variety of granulation levels is provided; third, a qualitative linguistic model of adaptation is presented. The proposed approach is close to human reasoning and thereby lowers the cost of solution, and facilitates the design of human computer interaction systems with high level intelligence capability.

INTRODUCTION

The growing amount of information on the WEB and the heterogeneous characteristics of Web users have lead to a considerable attention to web-based adaptive hypermedia systems (WAHS) by the research community (Brusilovsky, 1996, 2001). The power of hypermedia of web technology is in its capability to support non-linear navigation in hyperspace and multimedia presentation of the web content. WAHS offers an alternative to the traditional "one-size-fits-all" hypermedia and Web systems by adapting to the goals, interests, and knowledge of individual

DOI: 10.4018/978-1-4666-0954-9.ch004

users represented in the individual user models (Brusilovsky, 2001). WAHS aims to minimize cognitive overload faced by users, to alleviate the disorientation problem of users, to enhance the usability and the utility of the system by applying intelligent information adaptation (personalization) techniques for user/system interactions that take into account individual differences of users (Mobasher & Anand, 2010). Adaptation involves two key activities: (i) a user modelling activity to develop a user model and (ii) an adaptation activity that leverages a 'rich' user-model to personalize the information content, the information presentation style and the navigation path of the system to the user (Brusilovsky, 1996). One of the ways to enhance the efficiency of WAHS is to build accurate user models. It can be achieved by taking into account human factors (or individual differences) that have significant effects on human computer interaction and on the learning process (Nikos, Panagiotis, Zacharias, Constantinous, & George, 2009; Triantafillou, Pomportsis, & Demetriadis, 2003). Research into individual differences suggests cognitive/learning styles have significant effects on student learning in hypermedia systems (Triantafillou, Pomportsis, & Demetriadis, 2003; Chen, 2002; Mitchell, Chen, & Macredie, 2010; Nikos, Panagiotis, Zacharias, & Costas, 2009).

Information imperfection, that is, information used in one or more respects is imprecise, uncertain, incomplete, unreliable, vague or partially true, is an inherent characteristics of WAHS (Garcia, & Sicilia, 2010). Imprecision of WAHS is rooted in imprecision of its input information. Sources of input information to build a user model are either the explicit information provided by subjective judgments of users/experts or the implicit information inferred by monitoring and measurement of a user behaviour, or combination of both. This imprecision is passed on user model and then on adaptation strategy that is guided by heuristics, hypotheses, or approximate decisions.

The purpose of this chapter is to explore fuzzy logic based methodology of computing an adaptive interface in an environment of imperfect, vague, multimodal, complex nonlinear hyper information space. To this end, based on fuzzy linguistic modelling and fuzzy multi-level granulation an adaptation strategy to cognitive/learning styles is presented. The granulated fuzzy if-then rules are utilized to create a fuzzy inference system (FIS) to adaptively map cognitive/learning styles of users to their information navigation/presentation preferences through natural language expressions. The important implications of this approach are that, first, uncertain and vague information used is handled; second, a mechanism for approximate adaptation at a variety of granulation levels is provided; third, a qualitative linguistic model of adaptation is presented. The proposed approach is close to human reasoning and thereby lowers the cost of solution, and facilitates the design of human computer interaction systems with high level intelligence capability.

The chapter is organized as follows. First I present a brief description of WAHS and fuzzy logic theory in WAHS. The description of cognitive and learning styles is given. Navigation and presentation preferences of users are presented. The adaptation process, examples of fuzzy granulation of input and output linguistic variables, and an inference mechanism of adaptation are presented. The next section is devoted to description of a simulation example to illustrate the proposed approach. Finally, we present conclusions and future work.

WEB-BASED ADAPTIVE HYPERMEDIA SYSTEMS AND FUZZY LOGIC THEORY

WAHS can be defined as the technology that allows personalization for each individual user of hypermedia application. The process of personalization customizes the content and structure of a web site to meet the specific needs of individual users, without requiring them to ask for it explicitly (Mobasher & Anand, 2010). For example, in educational AHS, personalization allows to dynamically adapt the instructional sequence to the individual user knowledge level, goals, preferences and etc. A typical architecture of WAHS is shown in Figure 1. It consists of two parts: client side and server side.

The client side provides interface to user/ system interactions. Certain parameters of the user interface can be adjusted either by users manually or by the system automatically. In the first case, the user interface is said to be adaptable, in the second case, it is said to be adaptive. The server side is composed of three modules: the user module, the domain module and the adaptation module. The user module builds user model through a user modelling process. This process is divided into two sub processes: acquisition information about the user and representation of this information in database. The user model is a key source of information for the adaptation module. It contains basic features of an individual user, such as user's goals, state of knowledge about the subject, background, hyperspace experience and preferences. This data can be collected explicitly from the user by querying, tests, during registration process with the system, or can be inferred implicitly by the system recording user interactions with the system. An accurate user

model would include all features of the user behaviour and knowledge that affect his/her learning process, performance and efficiency. The domain module contains information about the knowledge of the domain and the knowledge about domain structure expressed by navigation paths. The adaptation module selects the content and restricts the hyperspace of navigation links according to user needs. A first taxonomy of adaptation is defined at three levels, namely the information (or content), hyperlinks (or navigation) and presentation level (Brusilovsky, 1996).

Fuzzy modelling techniques have been previously applied with success to user modelling for information (or content) adaptation purposes. FIS based on a rule-based representation of user profiles is given in Nasraoui and Petenes (2003) for web recommendation system. These rules are automatically derived from prediscovered user profiles. In the educational AHS, the work (Kavcic, 2004) employs fuzzy logic for modelling user knowledge of domain. The results of this work have shown that fuzzy logic based modelling provides a valuable, easy-to-use tool, which positively affects user knowledge acquisition and, therefore, leads to better learning results. The work Garcia and Sicilia (2010) proposed a model named MAZE to capture imprecise behaviours of users. The neural network-based fuzzy modelling approach to assess aspects of students' learning style is presented in Stathaco-

Figure 1. General architecture of WAHS

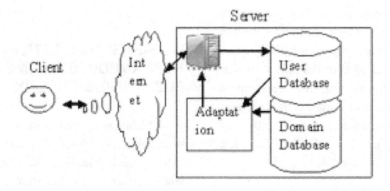

poulou, Grigoriadou, Samarakou, and Mitropoulos (2007). The results of this work have shown the potential of neuro-fuzzy diagnostic model in managing uncertain and conflicting situations. The work Huseyinov and Akin (2010) proposes an algorithm of adaptation to psychological factors using multi utility attribute theory and fuzzy set theoretic similarity measure. A survey of application of soft computing methods to modelling user behaviour is presented in Frias-Martinez, Magoulas, Chen, and Macredie (2005). The neuro-fuzzy based web recommendation system is examined in Castellano, Fanelli, and Torsello (2006). A recommendation strategy based on users' qualitative preference is suggested in Huseyinov and Akin (2009). However, there is little research on applying fuzzy logic techniques to issues of designing adaptive multimodal interfaces. The work Huseyinov (2011) proposed the linguistic FIS for the adaptation presentation style based on multi level information granulation technique. Xu, John, and Boucouvalas (2008) have demonstrated that fuzzy logic is theoretically ideal for emotion modelling in communication of human machine interaction. An idea of developing brain computer interface using fuzzy logic is proposed in Kaur and Tanwar (2010), but no experimental results are reported. This chapter proposes fuzzy linguistic model of multi modal interaction between user modalities, cognitive/learning styles, and computer modalities, presentation media and navigation preferences. The key idea is to use fuzzy granulation method to model modalities. Fuzzy information granulation was first introduced in 1979 Yao (2007) and Zadeh (1979). Later, in the context of human cognition, the term `information granulation` was described as follows: "Among the basic concepts which underlie human cognition there are three that stand out in importance. The three are: granulation, organization and causation. In a broad sense, granulation involves decomposition of whole into parts; organization involves integration of parts into whole; and causation relates to association

of causes with effects. Inspired by the ways in which humans granulate human concepts we can proceed to granulate conceptual structures in various fields of science" (Zadeh, 1997). For example, using fuzzy granulation method, the degree of control of human-computer interaction can be presented as shown in Figure 2.

Where μ_c is membership function representing the degree of control of human-computer interaction, CC is computer control granule, FC is federated control granule, and HC is human control granule.

The degree of control depends on user's characteristics. For example, computer control option can be beneficial for novice users, federated control option for intermediate users, and human control option for advance users.

COGNITIVE/LEARNING STYLES

The nature of cognitive styles (CL) is studied by cognitive psychology. CS deal with the form of cognitive activity (thinking, perceiving, remembering), not its content. Learning styles (LS), on the other hand, is seen as a broader construct, which includes cognitive along with affective and physiological styles. A key factor in determining cognitive styles with respect to learning is the field dependency factor. Field dependency refers to an individual's ability to perceive a local field as discrete form of its surrounding field. It is a single bi-polar dimension ranging from Field dependent (FD) individuals at one extreme to Field

Figure 2. Granulation of control of human-computer interaction

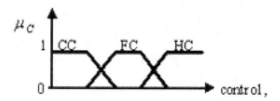

independent (FI) individuals at the other (Witkin, Moore, Goodenough, & Cox, 1977).Some cognitive abilities are highly coupled to perceptual abilities because they are sensitive to acquisition modalities (view, hearing, touch, taste, smell) (Franck, & Halima, 2005). Characteristics of users in respect to CS are described in Mitchell, Chen, and Macredie (2010) and can be modelled by a hierarchy type tree structure given in Figure 3.

Where FD – field dependent, PA – passive approach, GT – global tendency, ED – externally directed, FI – field independent, AA – active approach, AT – analytical tendency, ID – internally directed.

The LS dimension *visual/verbal* of the model developed by Felder-Silverman (Felder & Silverman, 1988) is used to reflect the learning modalities. However, cognitive/learning styles (CLS) are disputable concepts that are not fully accepted by the whole community.

In most of the systems CLS is assessed through psychological questionnaires and psychometric tests or in the form of self-report. This kind of measures of CLS is based on subjective judgment users make about themselves. Furthermore, not all characteristics they measure are stable and invariable across different subject domains. It is often the case when the mixed result for the same person is obtained, that is a user may have preference for one particular style, preference for more than one style and different levels of preferences for the different styles (Coffield, Moseley, Hall, & Ecclestone, 2010; Stash, 2007).For example, a learner may be attributed to the visual style at the

high level, but also to verbal style up to a certain extent, at the medium level. For that reason, CLS characteristics of users are intrinsically imprecise and consist of overlapping classes of styles one cannot draw a line between them. Fuzzy logic and granulation methods are suggested to handle this conflict situation.

NAVIGATION AND PRESENTATION PREFERENCES

Navigation preferences of users in respect to cognitive styles characteristics presented in Mitchell, Chen, and Macredie (2010) can be shown in Figure 4.

Where NP – navigation preference, LO – link ordering, LH – link hiding, AL – adaptive layout, DF – depth firth path, FI – field independent, BF – breadth-firth path, FD – field dependent, RL – rich links, DL – disabled links, AI – alphabetical index, HM – hierarchical map.

Presentation preferences are modes of delivering the content using a variety of multimedia techniques such as text, graphics, image, audio, video and etc. (Alejandro & Nicu, 2007; Frankie & Rama, 2009).

ADAPTATION TO COGNITIVE/ LEARNING STYLES

Two types of adaptation are distinguished in WAHS, namely adaptive presentation support and adaptive navigation support. The aim of adaptive navigation is to support users to find their learning paths in hyperspace by editing links. For example,

Figure 3. Hierarchical type tree structure of CS

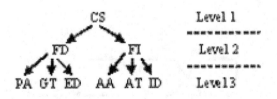

Figure 4. Navigation preferences

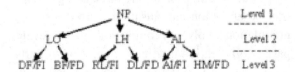

a link can be added, removed, or edited to change its format and presentation. The adaptive presentation supports users in selecting the content of the current node of course structure and the content presentation style or mode (Brusilovsky, 1996). In this study, the basic source of the adaptation information is CLS that is to be adapted to navigation and presentation preferences (NPP) of users. We interpret the process of adaptation as an inference mechanism that maps a set of input variables to a set of output variables. FIS provides the formalism that maps one family of fuzzy sets to another family of fuzzy sets. This formalism serves as a means of precision of imprecise information through graduated (or fuzzy) granulation (Zadeh, 1975a, 1975b, 1975c, 2008).

Fuzzy Multilevel Granulation of Input Linguistic Variables

Let us introduce linguistic variables **CS, FD, PA, GT, ED, FI, AA, AT, ID,** associated with the concepts CS, FD, PA, GT, ED, FI, AA, AT, ID, respectively, which are described in Figure 3. Initial membership functions of fuzzy sets of these linguistic variables are supposed to be in the trapezoidal form. The first level of granulation applied to the root **CS** of the tree yields that shown in Figure 5 and Figure 6.

The second level of granulation is applied to the nodes of the tree that are in the second level, for example, for **FD** we have that shown in Figure 7 and Figure 8.

Finally, we granulate the nodes from the third level through linguistic qualifiers **poor, good,** and **excellent** as shown in Figure 9.

Next, we can use *hedges* for the next granularity level. Hedges are linguistic modifiers operated on membership functions. They are expressed by adjectives and/or adverbs such as *very, somewhat, slightly, more or less, quite, extremely, fairly, below* and etc. For example, hedge *very* applied to qualifier *poor* modifies its membership function as follows: $\mu_{verypoor}=(\mu_{poor})^2$.

The *visual/verbal* dimension of LS modelled by linguistic variables **VI/VB**, respectively, can also be granulated in the similar way.

Fuzzy Multilevel Granulation of Output Linguistic Variables

Based on Figure 4 we introduce output linguistic variables **NP, LO, LH, AL, DF, BF, RL, DL, AI,** and **HM** associated with the concepts NP, LO, LH, AL, DF, BF, RL, DL, AI, and HM, respectively. Applying multi level granulation method, similar to the one described, we can form output membership functions for output linguistic variables **LO, LH,** and **AL** in the form shown in Figure 8, where the linguistic variable **LO - A** stands for **DF, B** stands for **BF;** for the linguistic variable **LH − A** stands for **RL, B** stands for **DL**; and finally, for the linguistic variable **AL − A** stands for **AI**, B stands for **HM** (Figure 10).

Finally, *we* create one more output linguistic variable **MMM** associated with the concept *presentation preferences* and relate it with the input linguistic variables **VI/VB**. The multimedia mode

Figure 5. Crisp sets for linguistic variable **CS**

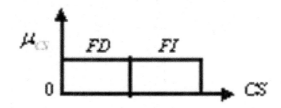

Figure 6. Granulation of **CS**

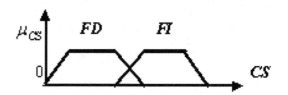

Figure 7. Crisp sets for FD

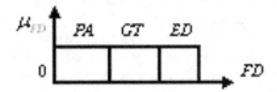

Figure 8. Granulation of FD

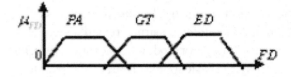

of presentation includes text, image, audio, video, graphics, games, animation and any combination of these elements. One granulation option of linguistic variable **MMM** can be shown as in Figure 11.

Again, we can use linguistic qualifiers and modifiers, as we did with input linguistic variables, for the next granulation levels. The linguistic qualifiers *low, medium, high* are used for output linguistic variables and shown in Table 1.

Inference

Fuzzy inference is a method that interprets the values in the input vector and, based on some set of if-then rules, assigns values to the output

vector. Fuzzy if - then rules capture the expert knowledge in the form of fuzzy predicates that establishes relations between input and output linguistic variables. The fuzzy predicates are associated with linguistic terms, and the proposed model is, in fact, a qualitative description of the system using rules like: IF input linguistic variable **CLS** is *poor* THEN output linguistic variable **NPP** is *high*. Such models are often called linguistic models (Zimmerman, 2001; Siler & Buckley, 2005).

More formally, let **CLS** and **NPP** are linguistic variables defined by fuzzy sets on the universes of discourse that contain granular values described in the previous section. Denote membership functions of linguistic variables **CLS** and **NPP** by μ_{CLS} and μ_{NPP}, respectively. Then the

Table 1. FIS for adaptation cognitive/learning styles to navigation/presentation preferences with a variety of granulation levels

Input linguistic variables			terms	hedges	rules	hedges	terms	Output linguistic variables		
Granular levels								Granular levels		
1	2	3						3	2	1
CLS	VI		*poor*	*Very*	r1	*very*	*low*	*text*	MMM	NPP
					r2			*graphics*		
			good	*slightly*	-	*slightly*	*medium*	*image*		
					-			*audio*		
			excellent	*somewhat*	-	*somewhat*	high	*video*		
	VB				rn					
	FD	PA		*more or less*		*more or less*		*DF*	LO	
		GT						*BF*		
		ED		*quite*		*quite*		*RL*	LH	
	FI	AA		extremely		extremely		*DL*		
		AT						*AI*	AL	
		ID						*HM*		

Figure 9. Granulation of linguistic variable **PA**

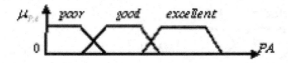

Figure 10. Granulation of linguistic variables LO, LH, and AL

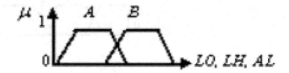

adaptation process can be characterized by a mapping $f : \mu_{CLS} \to \mu_{NPP}$. Granulation of function f is a fuzzy graph that is described as a collection of if-then rules. A fuzzy if-then rule can be defined as a binary fuzzy relation R considered as a fuzzy set with membership function: $\mu_R = f(\mu_{CLS}, \mu_{NPP})$. Using the compositional rule of inference, we can formulate the inference procedure in fuzzy reasoning in the form: ***NPP=CLS*** $\circ R$, where the sign $\circ$ denotes a fuzzy composition operator, consisting of a t-norm operator, followed by a t-conorm operator. The FIS for the adaptation of CLS to NPP is shown in Table 1. Some examples of rules at a variety of granulation level are presented.

Level 1: IF *CLS* is *FD*, THEN *NPP* is *DL*; IF *CLS* is *AA,* THEN *NPP* is *DF;* IF *CLS* is *poor,* THEN *NPP* is *high*; IF *CLS* is *very poor,* THEN *NPP* is *extremely high.*

Level 2: IF *FD* is *good,* THEN *DL* is *medium*; IF *FI* is *quite good,* THEN *AI* is *somewhat medium;* IF *VI* is *excellent,* THEN *MMM* is *video;* IF *VI* is *good* and *VB* is *good,* THEN *MMM* is *video* and *audio.* Level 3: IF *PA* is *good* and *AA* is *good,* THEN *DF* is *medium* and *BF* is *medium;* IF *AA* is *very good,* THEN *AI* is *quite high.*

The number of rules increases exponentially with the number of inputs, but some rules may rarely or never occur. So, fewer rules may be predefined by experts in the domain. Moreover, one can switch between granules at different levels. It can be done using a meta rule. For example, if *X* is a set of granules *FD, FI, VI* and *VB* then the following two step rule can be written: IF *CLS* is *X* THEN *select the rule associated with the value of X.* Here the first rule serves as a meta rule and is used to control the order of firing rules from Level 2.

SIMULATION EXAMPLE

To illustrate the proposed methodology, we consider constructing fuzzy linguistic models using MATLAB simulation software. Mamdani-type FIS is used, which is well suited to human input, has widespread acceptance and is intuitive. Let us have a case study in the form shown in Table 2.

Sample knowledge rule base is:

1. IF (Visual is excellent) OR (Verbal is poor), THEN (Multimodal is video)
2. IF (Visual is good) OR (Verbal is good), THEN (Multimodal is mixed)

Table 2. MATLAB simulation example

Linguistic variables	Type	Terms	Range
Visual	Input	Poor Good Excellent	$0 - 10$
Verbal	Input	Poor Good Excellent	$0 - 10$
Cognitive style	Input	FD Mixed FI	$0 - 10$
Multimodal	Output	Audio Mixed Video	$0 - 30$
Link ordering	Output	Depth-first Mixed Breadth-first	$0 - 30$

Figure 11. Granulation of the linguistic variable MMM

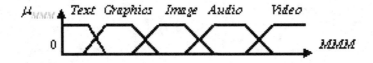

3. IF (Visual is poor) OR (Verbal is excellent), THEN (Multimodal is video)
4. IF (Cognitive style is FD), THEN (Link ordering is breadth-firth)
5. IF (Cognitive style is FI), THEN (Link ordering is depth-firth)
6. IF (Cognitive style is mixed), THEN (Link ordering is mixed)

Simulation of this case study in MATLAB generates the fuzzy linguistic model with the following characteristics. The FIS structure information obtained by *getfis ()* function from command line is as follows:

```
>>getfis (a)
    Name       = multimodal
    Type       = mamdani
    NumInputs = 3
InLabels =
Visual
Verbal
Cognitive style
    NumOutputs = 2
    OutLabels =
Multimodal
Link Ordering
    NumRules = 6
    AndMethod = min
    OrMethod = max
    ImpMethod = min
    AggMethod = max
    DefuzzMethod = centroid
```

Figures 12 through 19 show screenshots of FIS information structure, membership functions of input/output linguistic variables, behaviour of the model by rule viewer, and interaction of variables of visual and verbal for surface view of variable of multimodal.

More complex models may incorporate a higher level of granularities, and yet the nature of the methodology does not change.

CONCLUSION AND FUTURE WORK

The proposed fuzzy logic based methodology of computing navigation/presentation adaptation strategies to cognitive/learning styles can be tested and validated using Fuzzy Logic Toolbox in MATLAB. The aim is to observe the behaviour of the proposed model and tune its parameters such as: input and output linguistic terms and their membership function shapes; relevance and weights of rules; the type of inference mechanism – Mamdani type max-min composition (Mamdani, 1974) or Takagi-Sugeno type linear bounded-sum (Takagi & Sugeno, 1985); the type of defuzzification (centroid, middle of maximum, largest of maximum, and smallest of minimum). The Mamdani type FIS expects the membership functions of output linguistic variables to be fuzzy sets and requires the defuzzification step while Takagi-Sugeno type FIS expects output membership functions to be singletons. A simulation example using Fuzzy Logic Toolbox in MATLAB is presented to illustrate the proposed methodology, which is based on Mamdani type FIS. As a future work, a prototype of the model shall be developed to validate the proposed linguistic model within the efficiency of user/system interactions in terms of the usability and the utility of the system. Next, fuzzy clustering method can be employed to

Figure 12. FIS structure information diagram

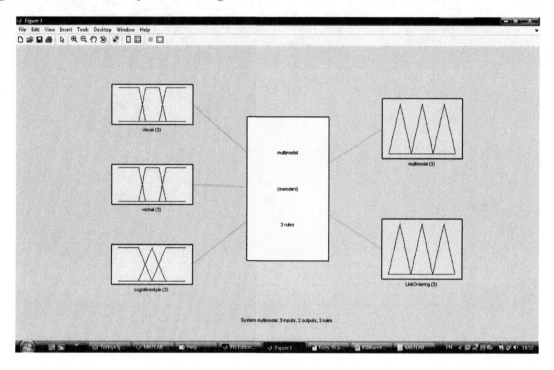

Figure 13. Membership function for linguistic variable visual

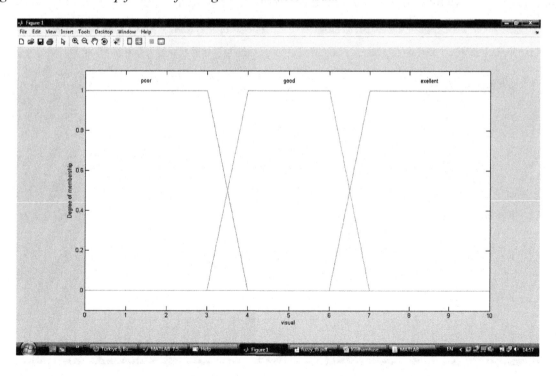

Figure 14. Membership function for linguistic variable verbal

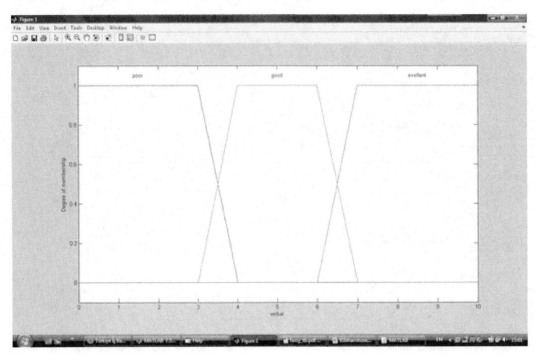

Figure 15. Membership function for linguistic variable cognitive style

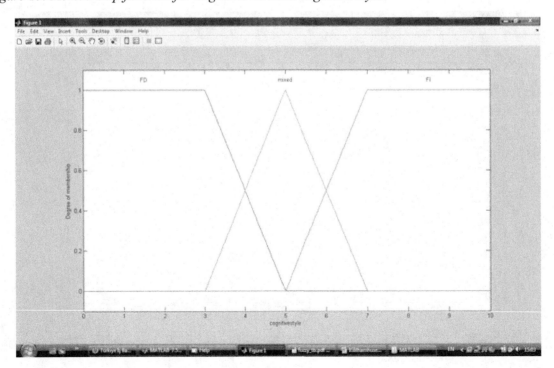

Figure 16. Membership function for linguistic variable multimodal

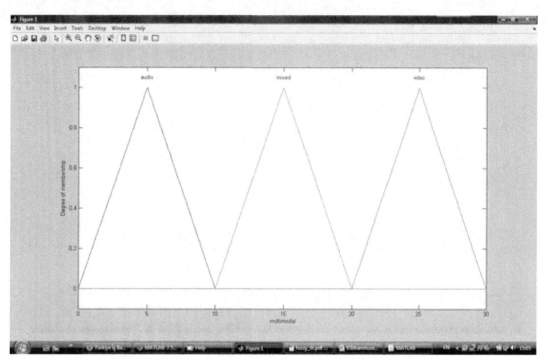

Figure 17. Membership function for linguistic variable link ordering

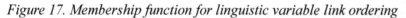

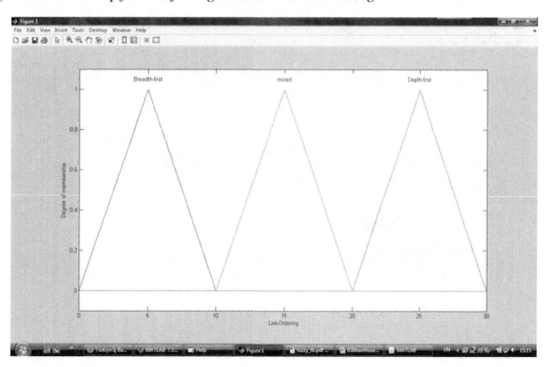

Figure 18. Behaviour of model with rule viewer

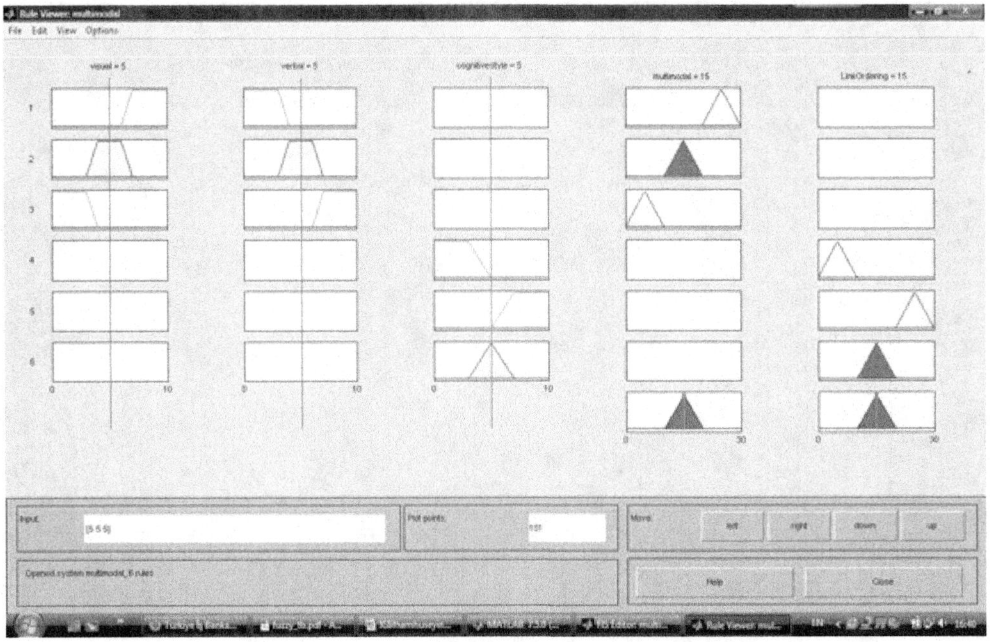

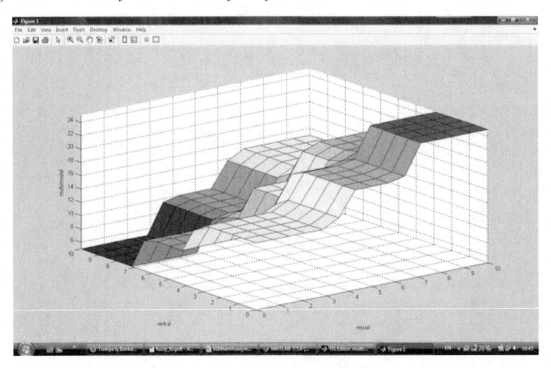

Figure 19. Interaction of visual and verbal for surface view multimodal

reduce the number of if – then rules, since some rules may occur similar in the sense that their corresponding outputs cannot be distinguished. Fuzzy logic is inherently suitable for coping with linguistic domain knowledge and producing more interpretable solutions. Future trend is the further investigation of other modalities of human computer interaction based on fuzzy logic based methodology to develop a system that will provide well structured adaptation rules satisfying users' individual needs and preferences. This paper has proposed a fuzzy linguistic model for adaptation of NPP to CLS based on multi level granulation method. The implication of this approach for designing adaptive user interfaces is introducing more natural language expressions. The qualitative description of the adaptation process is close to human reasoning and thus facilitates the design of the adaptive interface, increases the interpretability, usability of the system and utility of information, saves memory space and cost expenses by computation with words instead of numbers.

REFERENCES

Alejandro, J., & Nicu, S. (2007). Multimodal human-computer interaction. *Computer Vision and Image Understanding*, *108*(1-2), 116–134. doi:10.1016/j.cviu.2006.10.019

Brusilovsky, P. (1996). Methods and techniques of adaptive hypermedia. *User Modeling and User-Adapted Interaction*, *6*(2), 87–129. doi:10.1007/BF00143964

Brusilovsky, P. (2001). Adaptive hypermedia. *User Modeling and User-Adapted Interaction*, *11*(1-2), 87–110. doi:10.1023/A:1011143116306

Castellano, G., Fanelli, A. M., & Torsello, M. A. (2006). Dynamic link suggestion by a neuro-fuzzy web recommendation system. In *Proceedings of the IADIS International Conference on World Wide Web/Internet* (pp. 219-225).

Chen, S. (2002). A cognitive model for non-linear learning in hypermedia programmes. *British Journal of Educational Technology*, *33*(4). doi:10.1111/1467-8535.00281

Coffield, F., Moseley, D., Hall, E., & Ecclestone, K. (2010). *Learning styles and pedagogy in Post-16 Learning: a systematic and critical review*. UK: Learning and Skills Research Centre. Retrieved November 20, 2010, from http://www.lsda.org.uk/files/pdf/1543.pdf

Felder, R. M., & Silverman, L. K. (1988). Learning and teaching styles in engineering education. *English Education*, *78*(7), 674–681.

Franck, T., & Halima, H. M. (2005). Modelling elementary cognitive abilities for adaptive hypermedia presentation. *User Modeling and User-Adapted Interaction*, *15*, 459–495. doi:10.1007/s11257-005-2529-3

Frankie, J., & Rama, G. (2009). Multimodal and federated interaction. In Chen, S., & Magoulas, G. (Eds.), *Adaptable and adaptive hypermedia systems* (pp. 102–122). Hershey, PA: IRM Press.

Frias-Martinez, E., Magoulas, G., Chen, S., & Macredie, R. (2005). Modelling human behaviour in user adaptive systems: Recent advances using soft computing techniques. *Expert Systems with Applications*, *29*, 320–329. doi:10.1016/j.eswa.2005.04.005

Garcia, E., & Sicilia, M. A. (2010). Information imperfection as inherent characteristics of adaptive hypermedia: imprecise models of users and interactions. In Chen, S., & Magoulas, G. (Eds.), *Adaptable and adaptive hypermedia systems* (pp. 150–167). Hershey, PA: IRM Press.

Huseyinov, I. N. (2011, July 9-14). Fuzzy linguistic modelling cognitive styles/learning styles for adaptation through multi-level granulation. In J. A. Jacko (Ed.), *Proceedings of the 14th International Conference on Human Computer Interaction: Users and Applications*, Orlando, FL (LNCS 6764, pp. 39-47).

Huseyinov, I. N., & Akin, C. (2009) Collaborative filtering recommender systems with fuzzy set theory. In *Proceedings of the International Conference on e-Learning, e-Business, EIS, and e-Government*, Las Vegas, NV (pp. 397-400).

Huseyinov, I. N., & Akin, C. (2010). Adaptation based on psychological factors using fuzzy logic. In *Proceedings of the International Conference on e-Learning, e-Business, EIS, and e-Government*, Las Vegas, NV (pp. 297-303).

Kaur, M., & Tanwar, P. (2010). Developing brain computer interface using fuzzy logic. *International Journal of Information Technology and Knowledge Management, 2*(2), 429–434.

Kavcic, A. (2004). Fuzzy user modelling for adaptation in educational hypermedia. *IEEE Transactions on Systems, Man and Cybernetics. Part C, Applications and Reviews, 34*(4), 439–449. doi:10.1109/TSMCC.2004.833294

Mamdani, E. M. (1974). Applications of fuzzy algorithms for simple dynamic plants. *Proceedings of the IEEE, 21*(2), 1585–1588.

Mitchell, T. J., Chen, S., & Macredie, R. D. (2010). *Cognitive styles and adaptive Web-based learning*. Retrieved October 12, 2010, from http://bura.brunel.ac.uk/handle/2438/388

Mobasher, B., & Anand, S. S. (2010). *Intelligent techniques for Web personalization*. Retrieved November 3, 2010, from http://www.inf.unibz.it/~ricci/ATIS/papers/itwp-v5.pdf

Nasraoui, O., & Petenes, C. (2003). Combining web usage mining and fuzzy inference for web personalization. In *Proceedings of the WEBKDD Conference on Web Mining as Premise to Effective Web Applications* (pp. 37-46).

Nikos, T., Panagiotis, G., Zacharias, L., Constantinous, M., & George, S. (2009). An assessment of human factors in adaptive hypermedia environments. In Chen, S., & Magoulas, G. (Eds.), *Adaptable and adaptive hypermedia systems* (pp. 1–34). Hershey, PA: IRM Press.

Nikos, T., Panagiotis, G., Zacharias, L., & Costas, M. (2009). Individual differences in adaptive educational hypermedia: the effect of cognitive style and visual working memory. In Chen, S., & Magoulas, G. (Eds.), *Adaptable and adaptive hypermedia systems* (pp. 147–163). Hershey, PA: IRM Press.

Siler, W., & Buckley, J. J. (2005). *Fuzzy expert systems and fuzzy reasoning*. New York, NY: John Wiley & Sons.

Stash, N. (2007). *Incorporating cognitive/learning styles in a general-purpose adaptive hypermedia system*. Eindhoven, The Netherlands: Technische Universiteit Eindhoven, Proefschrift. Retrieved November 18, 2010, from http://alexandria.tue.nl/extra2/200710975.pdf

Stathacopoulou, R., Grigoriadou, M., Samarakou, M., & Mitropoulos, D. (2007). Monitoring student's action and using teacher's expertise in implementing and evaluating the neural networked-based fuzzy diagnostic model. *Expert Systems with Applications, 32*, 955–975. doi:10.1016/j.eswa.2006.02.023

Takagi, T., & Sugeno, M. (1985). Fuzzy identification of systems and its applications to modelling and control. *IEEE Transactions on Systems, Man, and Cybernetics, 15*, 116–132.

Triantafillou, E., Pomportsis, A., & Demetriadis, S. (2003). The design and the formative evaluation of an adaptive educational system based on cognitive styles. *Computers & Education, 41*, 87–103. doi:10.1016/S0360-1315(03)00031-9

Witkin, H. A., Moore, C. A., Goodenough, D. R., & Cox, P. W. (1977). Field-dependent and field independent cognitive styles and their educational implications. *Review of Educational Research, 47*, 164.

Xu, Z., John, D., & Boucouvalas, A. C. (2008). Fuzzy logic usage in emotion communication of human machine interaction. In Sugumaran, V. (Ed.), *Intelligent information technologies: Concepts, methodologies, tools, and applications* (pp. 147–163). Hershey, PA: IGI Global. doi:10.4018/978-1-59140-562-7.ch036

Yao, Y. (2007) Granular computing: Past, present and future. In *Proceedings of the IEEE International Conference on Granular Computing* (pp. 72-77).

Zadeh, L. (1975a). The concept of a linguistic variable and its applications to approximate reasoning. *Information Sciences, 8*(Part 1), 199–249. doi:10.1016/0020-0255(75)90036-5

Zadeh, L. (1975b). The concept of a linguistic variable and its applications to approximate reasoning. *Information Sciences, 8*(Part 2), 301–357. doi:10.1016/0020-0255(75)90046-8

Zadeh, L. (1975c). The concept of a linguistic variable and its applications to approximate reasoning. *Information Sciences, 9*(Part 3), 43–80. doi:10.1016/0020-0255(75)90017-1

Zadeh, L. (1979). Fuzzy sets and information granularity. In Gupta, N., Ragade, R., & Yager, R. (Eds.), *Advances in fuzzy set theory and applications* (pp. 3–18). Amsterdam, The Netherlands: North-Holland.

Zadeh, L. (1997). Towards a theory of fuzzy information granulation and its centrality in human reasoning and fuzzy logic. *Fuzzy Sets and Systems, 19*, 111–127. doi:10.1016/S0165-0114(97)00077-8

Zadeh, L. (2008). Is there a need for fuzzy logic? *Information Sciences, 178*, 2751–2779. doi:10.1016/j.ins.2008.02.012

Zimmerman, H.-J. (2001). *Fuzzy set theory and its applications*. Boston, MA: Kluwer Academic. doi:10.1007/978-94-010-0646-0

KEY TERMS AND DEFINITIONS

Cognitive Styles: Characterize thinking, perceiving, remembering abilities of a human.

Fuzzy Granulation: A technique for decomposition of the whole into modalities in a graduated manner.

Fuzzy Inference System: A collection of if – then rules in the form of fuzzy predicates that establishes relations between antecedent and consequent parts.

Fuzzy Logic: A mathematical tool to manage uncertain, imperfect, vague, imprecise, partially true information.

Linguistic Model: A model expressed in human natural language.

Multi Modal Human Computer Interaction: The communication between human and computer modalities.

Navigation Preferences: Link ordering, link hiding and adaptive layout.

Presentation Preferences: Modes of delivering the content using a variety of multimedia techniques such as text, graphics, image, audio, video and etc.

Web-Based Adaptive Systems: Select the web content and restrict the hyperspace of navigation links according to user needs.

Section 2
Speech, Image and Language–Based Interaction

Chapter 5
Improving Audio Spatialization Using Customizable Pinna Based Anthropometric Model of Head–Related Transfer Functions

Navarun Gupta
University of Bridgeport, USA

Armando Barreto
Florida International University, USA

ABSTRACT

The role of binaural and immersive sound is becoming crucial in virtual reality and HCI related systems. This chapter proposes a structural model for the pinna, to be used as a block within structural models for the synthesis of Head-Related Transfer Functions, needed for digital audio spatialization. An anthropometrically plausible pinna model is presented, justified and verified by comparison with measured Head-Related Impulse Responses (HRIRs). Similarity levels better than 90% are found in this comparison. Further, the relationships between key anthropometric features of the listener and the parameters of the model are established, as sets of predictive equations. Modeled HRIRs are obtained substituting anthropometric features measured from 10 volunteers into the predictive equations to find the model parameters. These modeled HRIRs are used in listening tests by the subjects to assess the elevation of spatialized sound sources. The modeled HRIRs yielded a smaller average elevation error (29.9°) than "generic" HRIRs (31.4°), but higher than the individually measured HRIRs for the subjects (23.7°).

INTRODUCTION

Immersive sound systems are an essential part of any modern virtual reality system. Computer games, navigation systems, and teleconferencing – all require a life like reproduction of sound that surrounds the user and makes human computer interaction effortless and authentic.

Audio spatialization, the ability to impart a virtual originating location to digital sounds, is gaining increasing relevance due to its continuously expanding applications in the entertainment

DOI: 10.4018/978-1-4666-0954-9.ch005

industry, computer gaming, and also in the broader fields of Virtual Reality (VR) and Human-Computer Interaction (HCI). Current advances in this field are ultimately predicated on an inextricable interplay between physics, signal processing, audiology, cognitive neuroscience and anthropometry.

It is known that we are able to discern the location of the source of a sound, around us, by exploiting localization clues that are part of the sounds that reach our eardrums. If a well-defined sound, such as the buzzer of an alarm clock is originated at a given location relative to the position of a static listener who faces North (e.g., two meters away from the listener, at ear level, from the NE direction), the deflections of the listener's right eardrum will not be the same as those of the buzzer's diaphragm. The acoustic signal originated in the buzzer will be transformed as it is propagated to the listener's right ear, due to multi-path reflections involving the torso, head and (right) outer ear of the listener. Furthermore, the acoustic signal reaching the listener's left ear will be affected by the same effects and, in addition, it may be affected by diffraction, as the listener's head is interposed between the buzzer and the his/her left eardrum. From a dynamic system's point of view, the transformation of sound from source (buzzer) to the destination (e.g., right eardrum) can be modeled as a transfer function, which describes how each frequency component of the buzzer sound (and any other sound originated at the same source location, for that matter), is modified in magnitude and phase, as it travels from source to destination. Evidently, the transfer function that mediates between the buzzer and the left eardrum will be different from that associated with the right eardrum. We can expect a more dramatic attenuation of high frequencies in the sound reaching the left ear, for the situation described. Because these pairs of transfer functions have been known to depend on the shape and size of the listener's anthropometric features, particularly head measurements, they are termed "Head-Related Transfer Functions",

HRTFs. Evidently, the HRTF pair changes as we consider different sound source locations around the listener. Consider, for example, that the buzzer is now placed two meters away from the static listener, but in a position west from his/her location. Clearly, now the right HRTF will indicate a more severe attenuation of high frequencies than the left HRTF. Perceptually, our brains are capable of discerning the location of a sound source by comparing the transformation suffered by the sound from its origin to each one of our eardrums ("binaural localization clues"), or by learned recognition of characteristic features present in even the sounds reaching a single one of our eardrums ("monoaural localization clues").

Clearly, if the HRTF pair corresponding to a given source location around a listener can be specified and, later implemented by engineering means, we could process a single-channel sound signal (e.g., a monoaural recording of the buzzer sound collected right next to the buzzer), and process it by both HRTFs in the pair, resulting in a binaural sound that, when delivered through headphones to a listener, should produce a similar sound localization perception to the one experienced when the buzzer was physically placed there. If HRTF pairs are defined for many locations around the listener, one could change the HRTF pair used for the sound spatialization process described and, therefore re-assign the buzzer sound to a different "virtual source location".

Even the highly simplified overview of the foundations of most contemporary sound spatialization approaches, summarized above, highlights the critical role played by the "correct" specification of the HRTF pairs for locations around the listener and its proper implementation, toward the generation of convincing spatialized binaural sounds. The description given also implies that the required HRTF pairs should be defined individually for the prospective listener, since the physical elements cited as their defining factors (torso, head and outer ears) are clearly individual and must match the localization clues that each individual learns to extract form real world sounds. Currently, some sound spatialization systems will make use of HRTFs that are empirically measured for each prospective user. These "custom" HRTFs are "anthropometrically correct" for each user, but the equipment, facilities and expertise required to obtain these "measured HRTF pairs" (see next section for details of the process), constrain their application to high-end, purpose-specific sound spatialization systems only. The most common alternative is the use of "generic" HRTFs, originally recorded from a manikin shaped according to "average" anthropometric data, expected to be representative of a pool of prospective listeners. While this solution has proved practical and useful for consumer-grade sound spatialization applications, it should be recognized that it is fundamentally limited by its disregard for the individual aspect of the anthropomorphic nature of the signal processing challenge being addressed.

This chapter reports on our work to advance an alternative approach to sound spatialization, based on the postulation of anthropometrically-related "structural models" that will transform a single-channel audio signal into a Left/Right binaural spatialized pair, according to the sound source simulation. Specifically, the work reported here proposes linkages between the parameters of the HRTF model and key anthropometric features of the intended listener, so that the model, and consequently the resulting HRTF's are easily "customizable" according to a small set of anthropometric measurements.

MEASUREMENT AND IMPLEMENTATION OF HRTFS

The effective empirical measurement of HRTF pairs is carried out essentially as described in the examples proposed in the previous section. A speaker is placed at known relative positions with respect to the subject for whom the HRTFs are being determined, and a known, broad-band audio signal is used as excitation. In our laboratory, we use the Ausim3D's HeadZap HRTF Measurement System (AuSIM3D HRTF Measurement System Manual, 2000). This system measures a 256-point impulse response for both the left and the right ear using a sampling frequency of 96 KHz. Golay codes are used to generate a broad-spectrum stimulus signal delivered through a Bose Acoustimass speaker. The response is measured using miniature blocked meatus microphones placed at the entrance to the ear canal on each side of the head. Under control of the system, the excitation sound is issued and both responses (left and right ear) are captured. Since the Golay code sequences played are meant to represent a broad-band excitation equivalent to an impulse, the sequences captured in each ear are the impulse responses corresponding to the HRTFs. Therefore these responses are called Head-Related Impulse Responses (HRIRs). The system provides these measured HRIRs as a pair of 256-point minimum-phase vectors, and an additional delay value that represents the Interaural Time Difference (ITD), i.e., the additional delay observed before the onset of the response collected from the ear that is farthest from the speaker position. In addition to the longer onset delay of the response from the "far" or "contralateral" ear (with respect to the sound source), this response will typically be smaller in amplitude than the response collected in the "near" or "ipsilateral" ear. The difference in amplitude between HRIRs in a pair is referred to as the Interaural Intensity Difference (IID).

The measurement sequence must be completed for each of the source locations for which an HRIR pair is desired. The different sound source positions are characterized by two descriptive angles. The azimuth angle (θ) sweeps the horizontal plane. If the subject is facing North ($\theta = 0°$), the East direction would be associated with $\theta = -90°$, West would be associated with $\theta = 90°$, and sound coming from the South would be assigned $\theta = +/- 180°$. The elevation angle (ϕ) is the angle between the horizontal plane that intersects the head of the subject at ear level and a straight line that connects the center of the subject's head to the sound source location (locations above ear level are assigned positive elevation values). Our protocol records HRIR pairs from source locations at the 72 possible combinations of $\phi = \{-36°, -18°, 0°, 18°, 36°, 54°\}$ and $\theta = \{0°, 30°, 60°, 90°, 120°, 150°, 180°, -150°, -120°, -90°, -60°, -30°\}$. The left (L) and right (R) HRIRs collected for a source location at azimuth θ and elevation ϕ will be symbolized by $h_{L,\theta,\phi}$ and $h_{R,\theta,\phi}$, respectively. The corresponding HRTFs would be $H_{L,\theta,\phi}$ and $H_{R,\theta,\phi}$.

The creation of a spatialized binaural sound (left and right channels) involves convolving the single-channel digital sound to be spatialized, s(n), with the HRIR pair corresponding to the azimuth and elevation of the intended virtual source location:

$$y_{L,\theta,\varphi}(n) = \sum_{k=-\infty}^{\infty} h_{L,\theta,\varphi}(k) \cdot s(n-k), \text{ and}$$

$$y_{R,\theta,\varphi}(n) = \sum_{k=-\infty}^{\infty} h_{R,\theta,\varphi}(k) \cdot s(n-k). \quad (1)$$

These convolutions can be implemented in real-time, constraining the values of the summation index, k, to the interval [0,255], to correspond with the numerical HRIRs obtained from the recording experiments. The real-time convolution required for spatialization does not directly employ the complex frequency Head-Relate Transfer Functions, $H(z)_{L,\theta,\phi}$ and $H(z)_{R,\theta,\phi}$, instead the discrete-time counterparts, $h(n)_{L,\theta,\phi}$ and $h(n)_{R,\theta,\phi}$ are used. Nonetheless, the proper correspondence of the HRTFs, H(z), or equivalently, the corresponding HRIRs, h(n), to the anthropometric features of the intended listener is necessary to achieve a convincing spatialization effect. In summary, most current sound spatialization systems require the availability of a library of HRIR pairs, indexed by azimuth and elevation, which can be retrieved and used for the convolution process outlined.

The distance to the sound source is emulated by making the amplitude of the binaural spatialized channels inversely proportional to some power (typically second power) of the distance emulated.

In this framework of operation, the costly individualized spatialization requires the measurement of a library of HRIRs for each intended listener. It should be noted, however, that the algorithm for real-time rendering of spatialized sounds is completely dissociated from the anthropometric characteristics of the user. The morphological features of the user have been involved (in an indistinguishable way) in the recording of the "personalized" HRIRs of the subject's library. Guidelines for the adaptation of a subject's HRIRs to fit a second subject are not available, in spite of observations such as those by (Middlebrooks, 1999), who associated the size of the listener's head with a "stretching factor" in the frequency scale of the frequency response of the listener's HRTFs.

SOUND SPATIALIZATION BASED ON ANTHROPOMETRIC MODELS

A radically different approach to the generation of binaural spatialized sounds has been proposed recently. The basic premise of this alternative approach is that, since the transformation of sound from source to destination (eardrum) is dictated by known physical phenomena involving the head, torso and outer ears of the listener (which are also known entities), a mathematical model of the interactions can be developed for the transformation of sounds that reach both the left and right eardrums. This would require a model with two symmetrical branches (left and right), fed with a common input signal (the sound at the source), to yield two output signals: the two channels of a binaural spatialized sound. Processing of the input signal by each of the two branches of the model replaces the convolution of that input signal with the corresponding HRIR. Instead of complete substitution of the HRIR pairs to simulate a different sound location, this approach would only require the update of the parameters in both branches of the model. Because such model has its origin in the physical characteristics of the entities involved in the phenomenon, it should be possible to derive the value of its parameters (for a given source location), from the sizes of those entities, i.e., the anthropometric features of the intended listener. Proper identification of such parameters, and adequate association of their numerical values with the anthropometric features of the intended listener may provide a mechanism to interactively adjust a generic base model to the specific characteristics of an individual. In other words, a structural HRTF model with anthropometric parameters may lead to the development of an interactively customizable sound spatialization system, which seemed unachievable in the context of spatialization based on empirically measured custom HRIRs.

Traditionally, it has been considered that certain aspects of localization performance, such as the ability to resolve a location along a particular "cone of confusion" (Mills, 1972) are distorted by a synthesis process that uses non-individualized HRTFs (Wenzel et al., 1993), particularly for the spatialization of broadband sounds (e.g., clicks or noise) (Begault, et al., 2001). Therefore, the goal of "customizing" the HRTFs or HRIRs measured from a prototypical subject or a manikin remains of interest (Tan & Gan, 1998). This interest has fueled the development of anthropometric or "structural" models (Brown & Duda, 1998) for the synthesis of binaural spatial sounds.

EVOLUTION OF STRUCTURAL SOUND SPATIALIZATION MODELS

One of the earliest analytical models for spatial hearing was Lord Rayleigh's study of the diffraction of a plane wave by a rigid sphere (Strutt, 1945). His analysis revealed that frequencies above a cutoff point (approximately 6204 Hz, for a sphere radius of 8.75 cm., which is similar to the "average" head radius (Kuhn, 1977) are attenuated if the sound comes from the side of the sphere that is opposite to the measurement point. On the other hand, when the sound originates on the same side as the measuring point these high frequencies are actually boosted by about 6 dB. This effect has been labeled the "Head Shadow" effect (Brown & Duda, 1998) and, when considered simultaneously for the two positions on the sphere that would correspond to human ears, it gives rise to the Interaural Intensity Differences (IID) (sometimes also identified as Interaural Level Differences, ILD), which partially characterize the location of the sound source with respect to the subject's head, roughly modeled by the rigid sphere. This head shadow effect has been verified experimentally by Duda and Martens (1998).

A simple one-pole / one-zero model has been developed to approximate the results obtained by Lord Rayleigh, and represent the IID. In one of its simplest formats (Brown & Duda, 1997), the head shadow effect is implemented by the continuous time transfer function (The azimuth variable used in this expressions, ψ increases in the clockwise direction, i.e., $\psi = -\theta$):

$$H(s, \psi) = [\alpha(\psi) s + \beta] / [s + \beta] \qquad (2)$$

In this model, the pole is fixed at $s = -\beta$, where β is determined by the speed of sound, c, and the customizable parameter a, representing the head radius:

$$\beta = (2 c) / a \qquad (3)$$

On the other hand, as the azimuth, θ, varies, the zero is shifted to location $s = -\beta / \alpha(\theta)$, which are calculated using different azimuth-dependent parameters α for each ear:

$$\alpha_L(\psi) = 1 - \sin(\psi) \qquad (4)$$

$$\alpha_R(\psi) = 1 + \sin(\psi) \qquad (5)$$

Similarly, the formulas derived by Woodworth and Schlosberg (Woodworth & Schlosberg, 1962), can be used to determine the different times of arrival of an acoustic wave front to two diametrically placed "ears" on the sphere model. For a sound approaching the sphere from a direction $0° <= \psi <= 90°$, (where, again $\psi = -\theta$) the times of arrival of the sound to each ear, with respect to the time when it first strikes the sphere, are (Brown & Duda, 1997):

$$T_L(\psi) = [a + a\,\psi\,] / c \text{ (for the LEFT ear), and} \qquad (6)$$

$$T_R(\psi) = [a - a\sin\psi] / c \text{ (for the RIGHT ear)} \qquad (7)$$

where a is the head radius and c is the propagation speed of sound. These equations are valid for $0° < \psi < 90°$. For the range $0° > \psi > -90°$ the formulas for $T_L(\psi)$ and $T_R(\psi)$ must be swapped.

The difference in time of arrival between $T_L(\psi)$ and $T_R(\psi)$ yields the Interaural Time Difference

$$\text{ITD} = \Delta T(\psi) = T_L(\psi) - T_R(\psi), \qquad (8)$$

which is also partially specific of certain locations around the subject.

Recently, there has been a re-emergence of interest in the use of simple dynamical models for the different physical elements that are responsible for the transformation of sound from its spatial source to the listener's eardrums. The composition of all the sub-models that are necessary to account for the full interaction of the sound with the body of the listener has been termed a "Structural HRTF Model" (Algazi et al., 2001).

The interest in the development of these models is propelled by the prospective advantages of this approach to sound spatialization, such as:

1. The possibility of establishing a direct correspondence between the parameters of the model (e.g., the parameter "β" in Equation 2) and the anthropometric features of the intended listener (e.g., the head radius, a), allowing for practical customization of the structural model for each individual. This feature may allow the development of interactively customizable sound spatialization systems.

2. Continuous description/modeling of the phenomenon across azimuth and elevation, which would remove the current need to interpolate experimentally measured HRTFs in the spatialization process.

Most current comprehensive structural models connect the sub-models, like the ones discussed above, for each ear in series (Algazi et al., 2001). One of the most practical models has been proposed by Brown and Duda (1998). Their model is illustrated in Figure 1.

This model involves the representation of three main physical components:

1. The HEAD MODEL, representing the diffraction of the sound by the head, resulting in the IIDs, modeled through the Head Shadow block (Equation 2), and the ITDs modeled through the delays indicated in the corresponding blocks (Eqsuations. 6, 7 and 8).

2. The SHOULDER REFLECTION, which is meant to represent a secondary path taken by the acoustic waves, in which they bounce off the ipsilateral shoulder of the subject before reaching the outer ear. This longer path would be modeled by a delay and a reflection coefficient.

3. The PINNA or OUTER EAR MODEL, which represents the way in which sounds diffracted by the head or bounced off the

Figure 1. Right Channel half for Brown & Duda's Structural HRTF Model. The model comprises a symmetric Left half (not shown) (Brown & Duda, 1998).

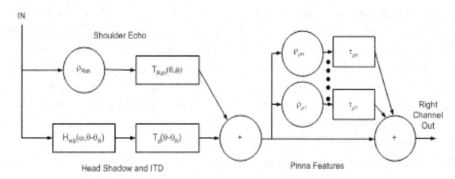

shoulder, are processed by the structures of the outer ear before they reach the ear canal and then the eardrum. The specifics of this block model will be discussed.

In spite of having this initial layout for the complete structural HRTF model, Brown and Duda (Carlile, 1996) concur with other researchers (e.g., Han, 1994) in estimating that the shoulder reflections do not play a primary role in localization, particularly within the horizontal plane, and discard the shoulder component in the basic consideration of the model. So, the simplified block diagram for a single-side (Left OR Right) structural model is as shown in Figure 2. For illustration this figure shows the generation of the RIGHT binaural channel.

It is important to acknowledge that the HEAD MODEL alone, incorporating the IID and ITD effects, can account for an approximate localization, particularly in the horizontal plane (elevation,

$\phi = 0$). However, it should also be noted that, by construction, the diametrically placed "ears" make the spherical head model symmetric around the inter-aural axis, the imaginary straight line that connects both ears. So, by construction, sources located on any radial vector which makes the same angle with the inter-aural axis will have the same head shadow and ITD effects. This geometric locus was called the "Cone of Confusion" by Mills (1972). In the horizontal plane this creates perceptual reversals between a source in the front hemisphere and one placed symmetrically (with respect to the inter-aural axis) in the back hemisphere. Evidently, the Pinna Model must transform sound in a way that does not have the same symmetry as observed in the Head Model, so that the ambiguity introduced by the cone of confusion can be resolved. In his study of the auditory localization properties of the outer ear, or pinna, Mills distinguishes two types of effects:

Figure 2. Simplified Structural HRTF model. Only Right half shown.

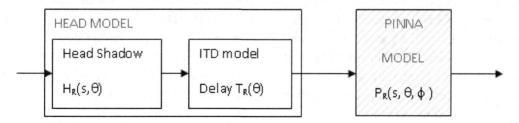

1. **Pinna Shadows**, representing the fact that the structural anterior-posterior asymmetries of the pinna "distinguish front from back for high frequency sounds." He cites the localization experiments of Stevens and Newman (1936) who noted a marked reduction in perceptual reversals for tone pulses at frequencies above 3000 Hz, where the outer ear shadow effect can be expected to be most significant (Gupta et al., 2001).
2. **Pinna Reflections**, representing the indirect paths followed by sound into the entrance of the ear canal. Mills refers to the initial model proposed by Batteau (1967), including a direct path (unity gain) in parallel with two delayed paths. In each of these delayed paths sound is affected by a reflection coefficient, ρ and lags by a delay τ.

Parameter Customization in Structural Models

The applicability of structural HRTF models, on a customizable basis, is predicated on the feasibility of assigning their internal parameters from anthropometric data easily obtained from the intended user.

Customizable Head Model

Since the HEAD MODEL component of the structural model proposed depends exclusively on the "equivalent head radius", a, that best approximates the head of a subject to a sphere, results published by Algazi (2001), may provide the key to instantiating this part of the overall model. These researchers first identified the best equivalent head radius, a_e, for each of 25 subjects, by minimizing the error between Woodworth's ITD (Equations 6, 7 and 8), and the measured ITDs (from experimentally acquired HRIRs), at 25 values of azimuth. Next, they set up 25 equations (one per subject) proposing the definition of a_e on the basis of three measurable head radii:

$$a_e = w_1 X_1 + w_2 X_2 + w_3 X_3 + b \qquad (9)$$

where X_1, X_2, and X_3 are halves ("radii") of the ear-to-ear, vertex-to-chin, and nasion-to-inion head diameters, determined from high-resolution digital photographs of the subjects. Solving the set of 25 equations and 4 unknowns through regression analysis yielded the values: $w_1 = 0.51$, $w_2 = 0.019$, $w_3 = 0.18$, and $b = 32$ mm. So, the "best" equivalent radius, a_e, for a subject can now be readily determined by measuring X_1, X_2 and X_3 in the subject, and using Equation 9. These authors also verified that estimates of this type for the 25 subjects in their experiment are much closer to the head radius derived from ITD measurements than the average of X_1, X_2 and X_3, and the "generic" head radius considered by Kuhn (1977), of 87.5 mm.

Customizable Pinna Model

The definition and anthropometric characterization of the PINNA MODEL has remained an open question, so far, and it is the objective of our work. Carlile (1996), divides pinna models according to the main phenomenon that they address: Resonating, diffractive and reflective. From these, reflective models have attracted the most attention in the literature. Originally, Batteau (1967) proposed that sound entering the ear would reach the entrance of the ear canal through a direct path and also through an indirect path because it is reflected by one of the projecting parts of the pinna. He postulated two pinna reflectors: one that would reflect sounds approaching the ear mainly along the horizontal plane, and a second one that would reflect waves approaching the ear along trajectories with significant vertical component. Due to the fixed pinna geometry, the relative delays between the direct and indirect paths (τ_1 and τ_2) would vary as the azimuth of the source (for reflector 1) and its elevation (for reflector 2) changed. Figure 3 illustrates Batteau's pinna model.

Using a 5x model of a human pinna, Batteau recorded the responses measured in the ear canal for impulses at various azimuths (θ) an elevations (ϕ), and "identified a waveform peak that was delayed by amounts that varied systematically with azimuth; another feature varied, although less distinctly, with elevation" (Mills, 1972). Scaled back to the normal size ear, "the delay of the first reflection dropped from 80 to 10 μs as the azimuth angle of the source increased from 10° to 100°. The delay of the second reflection increased from 100 to over 300 μs when the source moved from above via the side to below" (Han, 1994). Batteau developed a three-path acoustic coupler to simulate his proposed pinna model, in which the delays were such that the shorter delay τ_1, encoded azimuth (θ) as:

$$\tau_1 = (s_1/c)(1 + \cos\theta) \tag{10}$$

and the longer delay, τ_2, encoded elevation (ϕ) as:

$$\tau_2 = (2\,s_1/c) + (s_2/c)(1 + \sin\phi) \tag{11}$$

In these equations s_1 and s_2 are the separations between two holes in the coupler and a third, reference hole.

Watkins (1978) was able to verify the perception of vertical displacement of a sound source when he implemented Batteau's model, assigning unity value to all the gains in the system ($\rho_1 = \rho_2 = 1$), and keeping the shorter delay, supposed to encode azimuth, constant, ($\tau_1 = 15\ \mu$s), while varying the second delay, τ_2, between, 100 and 300 μs. Most importantly, he performed experiments confirming the existence of a relationship between delay and perceived elevation in both cases.

Recently, Brown and Duda (1998) used a model inspired in Batteau's, augmented to comprise not two but five delay-and-add branches, for which the delays where determined according to an equation that mixes both of Batteau's equations:

$$\tau_k(\theta, \phi) = A_k \cos(\theta/2)\sin(D_k(90° - \phi)) + B_k,$$
$$k = 1,\ldots,5 \tag{12}$$

In these expressions A_k, B_k and D_k are constants, which, along with the five values of the reflective coefficients, ρ_k, were set in the model in an *ad hoc* fashion. In fact, all the constants in this model were kept the same when performing localization tests with two subjects, but the five D_k parameters had to undergo *ad hoc* adjustment for a third subject. It is also noteworthy that they used 3 reflective coefficients with positive values and assigned negative values to the other 2.

Anthropometric Characterization of the Pinna Model

The intent of our work is to define a functional pinna sub-model that has anthropometric plausibility and then associate its parameters to anthropometric features of the listener's pinna, in a way similar to the linkage established by Algazi et al. (2001) between the three measured "radii"

Figure 3. Original reflective pinna model, by Batteau

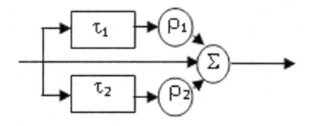

of the head and the ITD and Head Shadowing effect for given θ and ϕ values (through the "effective head radius," a_e). Our work has been limited to the development of models for $\theta = 90°$ and $\theta = -90°$, where the pinna effects are known to be more accentuated and most critical for the establishment of monoaural elevation clues. This research involved the assessment of the HRTFs and critical anthropometric features of 15 volunteers. Because of the range of positions selected for the study, the equations that define the head shadow model (Equation 2) and the ITD values (Equations 6, 7, and 8) will have the elevation angle (ϕ) and not the azimuth angle (θ or ψ) as independent variable.

Functional Pinna Model

According to the block diagram in Figure 2, experimentally measured HRIRs for the right ear represent the impulse response of the series connection of three functional blocks. However, the first two blocks have very limited dynamics, and are not, therefore, responsible for the bulk of the transformation of the hypothetical impulse excitation to the system into the more complex waveform typically observed in the measured HRIRs (e.g., Figure 5). The one-pole / one-zero head shadow model has very fast dynamics for all the operating range of its $\alpha(\phi)$ parameter. In essence this block only re-scales the impulse input, by different factors, depending on the elevation of the source. The second sub-block, the ITD model, is clearly just a delay, which also

depends on elevation. Therefore, the input to the proposed Pinna sub-model can be approximated as a re-scaled, delayed delta function. Since the re-scaling factor and delay length can already be calculated using the head shadow and ITD models, our focus here is in the waveform transformation in the pinna, from an approximated delta function (which we will assume not affected by delay) into the complex HRIR configurations observed, by means of reflective and resonant effects.

Taking into account the information available about the existence of a resonant effect implemented by the ear's concha (Shaw & Teranishi, 1996), and according to the reflective pinna models discussed in the previous paragraphs, we proposed that the pinna may, in turn, be modeled as the series connection of an equivalent second-order resonator and a series of characteristic echoes, representing the delayed and attenuated secondary paths taken by the incoming sound, in addition to a "direct path". A block diagram representation of this model is shown in Figure 4.

According to this model, the impulse input will project the underdamped oscillatory impulse response of the resonator, $h_r(n)$, as the intermediate output, $y_r(n)$, which will then be convolved with the impulse response of the block of echoes, $h_e(n)$, to yield the overall output, $y(n)$. Since $h_e(n)$ is expected to consist only of a few non-zero values, the output sequence can be interpreted as the superposition of several copies of the resonant response, $y_r(n)$, re-sized and delayed according to the several non-zero values of $h_e(n)$, as shown in the figure. The re-sizing factors and latencies

Figure 4. Block diagram of the proposed pinna model

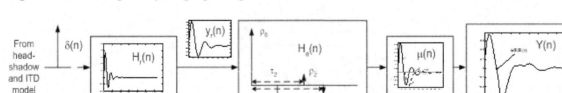

Figure 5. Comparison of an original (measured) HRIR, and the corresponding reconstructed R(n)

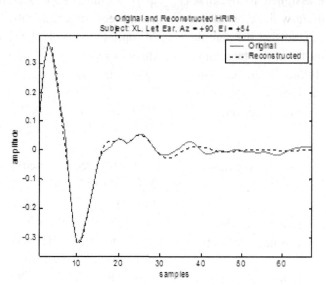

for each "echo" have been assigned the variable names ρ_k and τ_k, where k is the number of the echo ($\tau_0 = 0$). In turn, the second-order resonant block can be defined by the frequency, f, and damping factor, σ, for its impulse response.

Thus, the instantiation of this proposed model will require the identification of f, σ, and the several ρ and τ values, to characterize the parameters of the model that successfully approximates an HRIR collected for a given azimuth and elevation, through the y(n) provided by the pinna model. The main challenge in this operation is the fact that the several replicas of the damped oscillation are irreversibly mixed together, partially overlapping in time, in the measured HRIR. This problem was addressed by the sequential application of Prony's modeling algorithm (Kahn et al., 1992) to partial segments of the response. Prony's method approximates a given signal $\mu(t)$ as the superposition of p damped sinusoidals:

$$\mu(t) = \sum_{j=1}^{p} \rho_j e^{(\sigma_j t)} Sin(2\pi f_j t + \xi_j) \qquad (13)$$

However, Prony's method assumes that all p components start at the same instant (the beginning of the segment under modeling). So, the overall model had to be obtained in an iterative process that involved (starting with $t_0 = 0$):

a. Apply Prony's method for the fitting of a single damped sinusoidal to progressively larger windows of observation, which extend from the beginning of the current modeling segment (t_m). Monitor the average residual error as the window is increased in size.

b. When a sudden increase in modeling error becomes apparent, reduce the window size to the value that yielded the minimum in the modeling error prior to its sudden increase. Label that latency as t_{m+1}.

c. Extrapolate the single damped sinusoidal modeled by Prony's method between t_m and t_{m+1}, to extend for 256 points. This sequence will model the m-th replica of the resonant response, $\mu_m(n)$. Assign $\rho_m =$ as the peak amplitude of $\mu_m(n)$.

d. Subtract $\mu_m(n)$ from the current modeling segment. Shift the resulting difference sequence t_{m+1} samples to the left (discarding samples that are re-assigned to negative time indices, and filling with zeros on the right of the sequence), so that the sample labeled t_{m+1} will now be at the beginning of the 256-sample shifted difference. This sequence will be the new modeling segment that will be used in the next iteration.

e. Repeat from step a).

Each completion of the iteration indicated above yields:

- A damped sinusoidal sequence, which is the m-th replica of the resonator response, $\mu_m(n)$
- The intensity of one of the echoes in the pinna model, ρ_m,
- The overall latency of that same echo, as $\tau_m = t_0 + t1 \ldots + t_m$.

Corresponding to the physical situation being modeled, it is observed the every new echo found is less and less significant to the overall composition of the HRIR under modeling. In order to keep the number the parameters in the model low, it was decided to include only the first four components (m = 0, 1, 2, 3) in the modeling process. This decision was based on the average value of the τ_3 latencies found, which was approximately 300 μs, coincident with the upper bound of elevation-related delays observed by Mills (1972) and Han (1994). To verify the adequacy of the sequential decomposition described, a reconstructed waveform, R(n), can be synthesized by the superposition of the shifted sinusoidals obtained from each Prony stage:

$$R(n) = \mu_0(n) + \mu_1(n - \tau_1) + \mu_2(n - \tau_2) + \mu_3(n - \tau_3)$$

(14)

Figure 5 shows the superposition of the original HRIR(n) and its corresponding reconstructed signal R(n), for the left HRIR measured in one of the experimental subjects with the source position

at $\theta = 90°$ and $\phi = 54°$. The similarity achieved can be appreciated graphically. To quantify this level of similarity we calculate the "%Match" between the two sequence as follows, where "SS{}" represents the sum of squares of the series:

%Match = {1 - [SS{HRIR(n) – R(n)} / SS{HRIR(n)}]} x 100%   (15)

For the reconstructed sequence shown in Figure 5 the %Match is 97.8%. It should be noticed that most of the significant departures of R(n) from HRIR(n) occur at the long latencies. This section of the original HRIR is not being fully modeled, since we only performed the first 4 iterations indicated in the algorithm described above (m = 0, 1, 2, 3).

Although the iterative application of Prony's method indicated above independently identifies a new damped sinusoid, $\mu_m(n)$ in each iteration m, the model presumes the existence of a single damped sinusoidal response from an equivalent resonator for the ear. It was, in fact, confirmed that most of the independently found damped responses were similar to each other. Therefore, so as to adhere to the model proposed, and in order to keep the number of parameters to adjust to the minimum necessary, properly resized copies of $\mu_0(n)$ were used also to represent the last 3 replicas of the resonator response in the "modeled" approximation to the measured HRIRs, M(n):

$$M(n) = \mu_0(n) + (\rho1/\rho0) [\mu_0(n - \tau_1)] + (\rho2/\rho0) [\mu_0(n - \tau_2)] + (\rho3/\rho0) [\mu_0(n - \tau_3)]$$ (16)

The $\mu_0(n)$ response was selected as the most representative one, since only the very first modeling segment addressed in the iterations (m = 0) is known to be free of potential distortion by the trailer of a previous replica. In addition it is in this first segment that the Prony modeling process is executed at the most advantageous signal-to-noise level.

The second goal of our research is to establish empirical relationships that will define the values of the nine parameters required to create M(n), as an approximation of HRIR(n), i.e., f_0, σ_0, ρ_0, ρ_1, τ_1, ρ_2, τ_2, ρ_3 and τ_3, from anthropometric features can be obtained from the prospective user of the spatialization system, as described.

Measurement of Anthropometric Features

Key anthropometric features of the ears of the 15 experimental subjects in the study (same 15 subjects for whom the HRIRs were empirically measured with the Ausim 3D system) were captured by means of digital photography (including a distance reference), and laser 3-D scanning, using a Polhemus FastScan handheld scanner. Figure 6 shows a sample digital photograph, a sample 3-D reconstruction from a 3-D scanned file, and a schematic drawing identifying some of the key

anthropometric features estimated for each of the 30 ears involved in this study.

Table 1 provides the names of the anthropometric features indicated in Figure 6, indicating also the average values calculated for the 30 ears measured in this study and the average values for those same parameters from the ears studied in the development of the CIPIC HRTF Database (Algazi et al., 2001). Measurement of parameters such as Concha Area, Concha Depth and Concha Volume required the use of 3-D modeling programs, such as 3D Studio Max and Autocad.

Association between Model Parameters and Anthropometric Measurements

Following the procedure described in the two preceding sections two independent sets of data were available for each pinna of each of the 15 subjects in the study:

Figure 6. Anthropometric characterization of subject ears: a) Sample high resolution 2-D photograph; b) Sample rendering of a 3-D laser scan; c) Definition of key anthropometric features

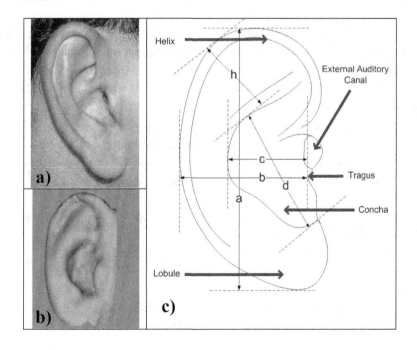

Table 1. Average and identifiers for the key anthropometric features of the ear used

Identifier in Schematic	Abbreviation Equations	Feature Name	Average This Study	CIPIC average
a	E_L	Ear Length	6.90 cm	6.41 cm
b	E_W	Ear Width	3.25 cm	2.92 cm
d	C_H	Concha Height	2.75 cm	2.59 cm
c	C_W	Concha Width	1.89 cm	1.58 cm
No ID	C_A	Concha Area	3.41 cm²	Not available
No ID	C_V	Concha Volume	2.72 cm³	Not available
No ID	C_D	Concha Depth	0.82 cm	1.02 cm
h	H_L	Helix Length	2.40 cm	1.51 cm

Estimated Model Parameters

$r_{0\phi}$, $\alpha_{0\phi}$, $\rho_{0\phi}$, $\rho_{1\phi}$, $\tau_{1\phi}$, $\rho_{2\phi}$, $\tau_{2\phi}$, $\rho_{3\phi}$ and $\tau_{3\phi}$, for ϕ = −36°, −18°, 0°, 18°, 36°, and 54°

(Note, here r_0 and α_0 are the magnitude and angle of the poles of the resonator, which define the resonator response $\mu_0(n)$, in terms of its frequency f_0 and its damping factor σ_0)

Measured Anthropometric Features

E_L, E_W, C_H, C_W, C_A, C_V, C_D and H_L

Under the assumption that the model parameters depend of the anthropometric features, a general dependency equation may be set, for each model parameter. For example, for the amplitude of the first replica in the pinna model, ρ_0, at ϕ = 54°, the following equation may be set up:

$$\rho_{0\,\phi=54} = KEL(E_L) + KEW(E_W) + KCH(C_H) + KCW(C_W) + KCA(C_A) + KCV(C_V) + KCD(C_D) + KHL(H_L) + B \qquad (17)$$

Coalescing the data from both ears, at the same elevation, (under the assumption of symmetry), 30 equations like the one above can be set up, for each model parameter, at each elevation. Each group of 30 equations can then be analyzed through multiple regression to estimate the values of the constants (KEL, KEW, …KHL, B), that represent the relative importance of the different anthropometric features in defining this model parameter (for this elevation). Once the estimated values of the constants are known, this same equation can be used to predict the value of parameter ρ_0, at ϕ = 54°.

The multiple regression analysis was carried out using the Statistical Package for the Social Sciences (SPSS) (Field, 2000), to estimate the constants. Several of them were found to be much smaller than others and therefore their corresponding terms in the equation were dropped, so that, for example, the final predictive equation for this particular parameter was:

$$\rho_0 = -0.0304*C_V + 0.006302*H_L + 0.311$$

The same process was performed for all the model parameters, at all the elevations studied. An example of a full set of simplified predictive equations (for ϕ = 54°) is:

$$\rho_0 = -0.0304*C_V + 0.006302*H_L + 0.311; \quad (18)$$

$$\rho_1 = 0.03088*C_V + 0.0128*C_D - 0.365; \tau_1 = round(-0.1547*C_D + 7.895);$$

$$\rho_2 = -0.00642*C_W + 0.136; \tau_2 = round(-0.196*E_W + 23.36);$$

$\rho_3 = 0.000886 * E_L + 0.003112 * H_L - 0.106; \tau_3 =$ round($-4.967 * C_V + 43.349$);

$\alpha_0 = 0.0002504 * C_A + 0.02361 * C_V + 0.361; r_0 = -0.000304 * C_A + 0.922;$

With this type of set of predictive equations available for all six elevations studied, the 9 model parameters can be found by simply entering the anthropometric features in them. In turn, the parameters can be substituted in Equation 16, to define M(n), the "modeled" HRIR for the given ear and elevation corresponding to the set of predictive equations used.

The next section describes the performance comparisons established between the original, empirically measured HRIRs, which are denoted by HRIR(n), and the reconstructed, R(n) and modeled, M(n), impulse response sequences.

MODEL EVALUATION: PROCEDURE, RESULTS AND DISCUSSION

The adequacy with which the model provides representative HRIRs for binaural sound spatialization was evaluated with 10 subjects (7 male, 3 female). The evaluation involved two processes:

a. The "%Match" of the reconstructed sequences, R(n), with respect to their "original" measured HRIRs, from the 10 subjects, at all six elevations under analysis, was calculated. This part of the evaluation investigated the plausibility of the model itself.

b. The second part of the evaluation addresses the efficiency of the predictive equations found, in providing the model parameters to create a "modeled" HRIR, M(n), given the anthropometric data of a subject. This was assessed by evaluating the "%Match" of the modeled sequences, M(n), with respect to their "original" measured HRIRs, and also by recording the amount of source localiza-

tion (elevation) error in listening tests with these 10 subjects.

Table 2 indicates the percentages of match found, as an average over all 30 ears, between the reconstructed sequence R(n) and the originally measured sequence, HRIR(n), by elevation angle.

The percentages of match in this table range between 91% and 95%. This indicates that the proposed model is, in fact, capable of creating modeled HRIR sequences that closely resemble the ones that would be obtained by empirical measurement, provided it is set with the proper model parameters. It should also be recalled that the model reconstruction process is being limited to involve only the first four components, which may leave some later features of the HRIR unrepresented. Overall, this suggests that the model proposed is, in fact, a viable one.

When the model is not set up with the parameters directly obtained from the deconstruction of the original HRIRs, but instead the parameters values are found substituting the anthropometric data of a given subject in the predictive equations, the resulting modeled sequences have a lower percentage of match, with respect to the original HRIRs. The average values for these "%Match" figures are shown, by elevation angle in Table 3.

In spite of the smaller "%Match" values in Table 3, the modeled sequences still retain the basic amplitude and timing features of the original HRIRs. An example of this is illustrated in Figure 7, which shows the modeled sequence, M(n), for the same case introduced in Figure 5 (Subject XL, left ear, $\theta = 90°$, $\phi = 54°$), along with the corresponding original HRIR(n).

Ultimately, the efficiency of the modeled sequences obtained by predicting the model parameters from the anthropometric measurements of the subjects was gauged in listening tests. In these tests, white noise bursts were spatialized using the modeled sequences, M(n), that had been obtained based on the ear measurements of the subject under test, for the six elevations under

Table 2. Average match between reconstructed and original HRIRs

Elevation	54°	36°	18°	0°	-18°	-36°
% Match	95%	95%	92%	93%	93%	91%

Table 3. Average match between model and original HRIRs

Eleva-tion	54°	36°	18°	0°	-18°	-36°
% Match	68%	63%	57%	58%	59%	49%

study. The order in which these elevations where used for the spatialization was randomized. Each elevation was simulated four times (i.e., there were 24 trials for each side of the head.) In each trial the subject would listen to each spatialized sound and then use a graphic user interface to indicate the perceived elevation. Since the spatialization was performed to emulate six specific locations, the absolute value of the angular dif-

ference between the perceived elevation and the emulated one would be considered as the elevation error for the trial. Each subject was asked to complete six sets of 24 trials:

- θ = +90° (source on left side), left ORIGINAL HRIRs
- θ = +90° (source on left side), left MODELED HRIRs
- θ = +90° (source on left side), left "GENERIC" HRIRs
- θ = -90° (source on right side), right ORIGINAL HRIRs
- θ = -90° (source on right side), right MODELED HRIRs
- θ = -90° (source on right side), right "GENERIC" HRIRs

The order in which the subject completed these six 24-trial sets was also randomized. The "Generic" HRIRs used were those obtained from a B&K acoustic manikin and made available courtesy of Drs. Elizabeth Wenzel and Durand Begault (NASA Ames Research Center) and Agnieszka

Figure 7. Comparison of an original (measured) HRIR, and the corresponding modeled M(n)

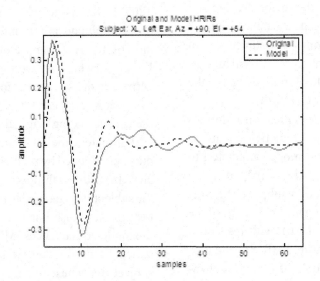

Roginska (AuSIM Engineering Solutions). In all cases the binaural pair was completed with original (measured) HRIRs in the contralateral side.

Figure 8 illustrates the average angular error (across all 10 subjects) experienced in the perception of the different emulated elevations, when the spatialization was based on the modeled sequences. For reference the average angular errors observed when the spatialization was based on "original", custom (measured) HRIRs and when the generic (measure from the B&K manikin) HRIRs. The global average error (across all subjects and all elevations) with the "original", custom HRIRs, which can be considered a golden standard of performance, was 23.7°. The corresponding global average error with modeled HRIRs was 29.9°. Finally, the global average error when the subjects used the generic HRIRs, collected from the B&K manikin, was 31.4°. Therefore, in an average, the HRIRs created by the proposed model, based on individual anthropometric measurements from the subjects performed better than the "generic" HRIRs from the B&K manikin, but not as well as the individual HRIRs measured specifically for each subject.

It should be noted, however, that near the horizontal plane (e.g., between $\phi = -18°$ and $\phi =$ 36°), the performance of the modeled HRIRs was very close to, and sometimes even slightly better than, that of the individually measured HRIRs. Furthermore, it may be speculated that the deterioration in the performance of the modeled HRIRs at very low ($\phi = -36°$) and very high ($\phi = 54°$) elevations may be linked to the decision we made to limit the echoes in the model to the four earliest components found by the iterative Prony deconstruction of the HRIRs. It is possible that echoes occurring at longer latencies, which were not represented in the model, may play important roles in the accuracy of source localization of very high or very low sources, for which the delays involved are expected to be the longest (Watkins, 1978).

CONCLUSION

To improve human computer interaction, it is necessary to create immersive audio environments where the user feels like a part of the system.

This chapter has presented a proposed functional model of the pinna, to be used as the output block in a structural HRTF model. The definition of the model, containing a second order resonance

Figure 8. Localization performance using 3 different types of HRIRs

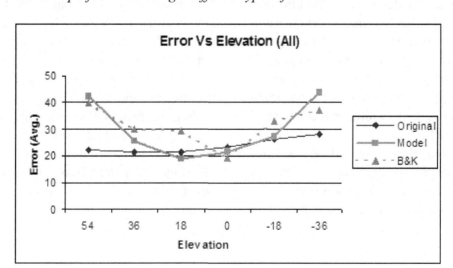

and non-recursive filter representing a number of "echoes" at varied latencies, was introduced and justified in terms of the sequential Prony deconvolution of the damped oscillatory response of the resonator, from the measured HRIRs of 15 subjects, at 6 different elevations. The values of the model parameters that emerge of this process were used to confirm that HRIRs reconstructed by instantiating the model with those recovered parameter values yielded high ("%Match" > 90%) levels of agreement with the corresponding measured HRIRs. This verified the plausibility of the model. Further, an attempt was made to develop predictive equations that would yield model parameter values when individual anthropometric features of the prospective listener are substituted in them. This method of instantiation of the model parameters represents a step forward towards the development of customizable audio spatialization systems that can involve individual anthropometric features from the user, to enhance the realism of the spatialization effects, without requiring the costly and cumbersome measurement of an HRTF (or HRIR) database for each user of the system.

Modeled HRIRs obtained by substitution of the anthropometric features of 10 volunteers were instantiated using the predictive equations found in this study and listening test were conducted with those 10 volunteers. The listening tests confirmed that the modeled HRIRs obtained from the proposed model helped the volunteers perform better (29.9° average error) than "generic" HRIRs from a manikin (31.4° average error), in localizing broadband sounds spatialized to 6 different elevations on the frontal plane. However, the performance of the volunteers was better with their own individual (measured) HRIRs (23.7° average error).

Examination of the error levels by elevation revealed that near the horizontal plane (e.g., between $\phi = -18°$ and $\phi = 36°$), the performance of the modeled HRIRs was significantly better and close to the individually measured HRIRs. It is speculated that the deterioration in the performance of the modeled HRIRs at very low ($\phi = -36°$) and very high ($\phi = 54°$) elevations may be linked to the decision we made to limit number of Prony components retained from the deconstruction of the HRIRs. It is possible that echoes occurring at longer latencies, which were not represented in the model, may play important roles in the accuracy of source localization of very high or very low sources, for which the delays involved are expected to be the longest. Future studies will expand the number of Prony components retained for the model, to test this hypothesis.

Although this study resorted to the sue of a relatively expensive 3-D laser scanner and specialized software to determine some of the anthropometric features of our subjects, which is a prerequisite to the use of the predictive equations developed in this research, it is likely that empirical relationships can be found to obtain these feature values from two-dimensional high-resolution photographs (commonly available) and a few direct physical measurements in the subject.

FUTURE RESEARCH DIRECTIONS

Further research is needed to explore the complex relationship between the pinna structure and the HRTFs (particularly azimuth). This chapter only explores the elevations and how they relate to the pinna. Further research will need more subjects and more measurements of HRTFs in various azimuths and elevations.

Improvement in 3D measurement and imaging techniques will lead to improved accuracies and better models. Customization using other algorithms (other than Prony's) may also provide better models.

ACKNOWLEDGMENT

This work was sponsored by NSF grants EIA-9906600 and HRD-0317692, and ONR grant N00014-99-1-0952. The authors wish to thank Drs. Elizabeth Wenzel and Durand Begault from NASA Ames Research Center, and Agnieszka Roginska, from AuSIM Engineering Solutions, for providing the B&K manikin HRTF data.

REFERENCES

Algazi, V. R., Avendano, C., & Duda, R. O. (2001). Estimation of a spherical-head model from anthropometry. *Journal of the Audio Engineering Society. Audio Engineering Society, 49*(6), 472–479.

Algazi, V. R., Duda, R. O., & Avendano, C. (2001). The Cipic HRTF database. In *Proceedings of the IEEE Workshop on Applications of Signal Processing to Audio and Acoustics.*

AuSIM, Inc. (2000). *HeadZap: AuSIM3D HRTF measurement system manual.* Los Altos, CA: Author.

Batteau, D. W. (1967). The role of the pinna in human localization. *Proceedings of the Royal Society of London. Series B. Biological Sciences, 168,* 158–180. doi:10.1098/rspb.1967.0058

Begault, D. (1994). *3-D sound for virtual reality and multimedia.* New York, NY: Academic Press.

Begault, D. R., Wenzel, E. M., & Anderson, M. R. (2001). Direct comparison of the impact of head tracking, reverberation, and individualized head-related transfer functions on the spatial perception of a virtual speech source. *Journal of the Audio Engineering Society. Audio Engineering Society, 49*(10), 904–916.

Brown, C. P., & Duda, R. O. (1997, October). An efficient HRTF model for 3-D sound. In *Proceedings of the IEEE Workshop on Applications of Signal Processing to Audio and Acoustics,* Mohonk, NY.

Brown, C. P., & Duda, R. O. (1998). A structural model for binaural sound synthesis. *IEEE Transactions on Speech and Audio Processing, 6*(5), 476–488. doi:10.1109/89.709673

Carlile, S. (1996). The physical basis and psychophysical basis of sound localization. In Carlile, S. (Ed.), *Virtual auditory space: Generation and applications* (pp. 27–28). Austin, TX: R. G. Landes.

Duda, R. O. (1993). Modeling head related transfer functions. In *Proceedings of the Asilomar Conference on Signals, Systems & Computers* (pp. 996-1000).

Duda, R. O., & Martens, W. L. (1998). Range dependence of the response of a spherical head model. *The Journal of the Acoustical Society of America, 104,* 3048–3058. doi:10.1121/1.423886

Field, A. (2000). *Discovering statistics using SPSS for Windows.* Thousand Oaks, CA: Sage.

Gupta, N., Ordonez, C., & Barreto, A. (2001). The effect of pinna protrusion angle in the localization of virtual sound in the horizontal plane. *The Journal of the Acoustical Society of America, 110*(5), 2679.

Han, H. L. (1994). Measuring a dummy head in search of pinna cues. *Journal of the Audio Engineering Society. Audio Engineering Society, 42*(1-2), 15–37.

Kahn, M., Mackisack, M. S., Osborne, M. R., & Smyth, G. K. (1992). On the consistency of Prony's method and related algorithms. *Journal of Computational and Graphical Statistics, 1,* 329–349. doi:10.2307/1390787

Kuhn, G. F. (1977). Model for the interaural time differences in the azimuthal plane. *The Journal of the Acoustical Society of America, 62*, 157–167. doi:10.1121/1.381498

Lopez-Poveda, E. A., & Meddis, R. (1996). A physical model of sound diffraction and reflections in the human concha. *The Journal of the Acoustical Society of America, 100*, 3248–3259. doi:10.1121/1.417208

Middlebrooks, J. C. (1999). Individual differences in external-ear transfer functions reduced by scaling in frequency. *The Journal of the Acoustical Society of America, 106*(3), 1480–1492. doi:10.1121/1.427176

Middlebrooks, J. C. (1999). Virtual localization improved by scaling nonindividualized external-ear transfer functions in frequency. *The Journal of the Acoustical Society of America, 106*(3), 1493–1510. doi:10.1121/1.427147

Mills, A. W. (1972). Auditory localization. In Tobias, J. V. (Ed.), *Foundations of modern auditory theory* (Vol. 2, pp. 303–348). New York, NY: Academic Press.

Osborne, M. R., & Smyth, G. K. (1995). A modified Prony algorithm for fitting sums of exponential functions. *SIAM Journal on Scientific and Statistical Computing, 16*, 119–138. doi:10.1137/0916008

Parks, T. W., & Burrus, C. S. (1987). *Digital filter design*. New York, NY: John Wiley & Sons.

Shaw, E. A. G., & Teranishi, R. (•••). Sound pressure generated in an external-ear replica and real human ears by a nearby point source. *The Journal of the Acoustical Society of America, 44*(1), 240–249. doi:10.1121/1.1911059

Strutt, J. W. (1904). (Lord Rayleigh). (1904). On the acoustic shadow of a sphere. *Philosophical Transactions of the Royal Society of London. Series A: Mathematical and Physical Sciences, 203*, 87–97.

Strutt, J. W. (Lord Rayleigh). (1945). *The theory of sound* (2nd ed.). New York, NY: Dover.

Tan, C. J., & Gan, W. S. (1998). User-defined spectral manipulation of the HRTF for improved localization in 3D sound systems. *Electronics Letters, 34*(25), 2387–2389. doi:10.1049/el:19981629

Watkins, A. J. (1978). Psychoacoustical aspects of synthesized vertical locale cues. *The Journal of the Acoustical Society of America, 63*(4), 1152–1165. doi:10.1121/1.381823

Wenzel, E. M., Arruda, M., Kistler, D. J., & Wightman, F. L. (1993). Localization using non-individualized head-related transfer functions. *The Journal of the Acoustical Society of America, 94*, 111–123. doi:10.1121/1.407089

Woodworth, R. S., & Schlosberg, H. (1962). *Experimental psychology*. New York, NY: Holt, Rinehard and Winston.

KEY TERMS AND DEFINITIONS

Binaural: Technique of recording and playing sounds that involves two channels.

Concha: Part of the pinna where sound undergoes reflections and reverberations.

HRIR: Head Related Impulse Response.

HRTF: Head Related Transfer Function.

IID: Interaural Intensity Difference.

ITD: Interaural Time Difference.

Monoaural: Sound recorded and played using a single channel (as opposed to stereo).

Pinna: Outer Ear.

Prony's Technique: A method of modeling a signal using a linear combination of exponential and sinusoidal signals.

Spatialization: Projection and localization of sound in physical or virtual space.

Chapter 6
Recent Trends in Speech Recognition Systems

R. K. Aggarwal
National Institute of Technology Kurukshetra, India

M. Dave
National Institute of Technology Kurukshetra, India

ABSTRACT

Ways of improving the accuracy and efficiency of automatic speech recognition (ASR) systems have been a long term goal of researchers to develop the natural language man machine communication interface. In widely used statistical framework of ASR, feature extraction technique is used at the front-end for speech signal parameterization, and hidden Markov model (HMM) is used at the back-end for pattern classification. This chapter reviews classical and recent approaches of Markov modeling, and also presents an empirical study of few well known methods in the context of Hindi speech recognition system. Various performance issues such as number of Gaussian mixtures, tied states, and feature reduction procedures are also analyzed for medium size vocabulary. The experimental results show that using advanced techniques of acoustic models, more than 90% accuracy can be achieved. The recent advanced models outperform the conventional methods and fit for HCI applications.

1. INTRODUCTION

Human computer interaction through natural language conversational interface plays an important role in improving the usage of computers for the common man. The success of such speech enabled man machine communication interface depends mainly upon the performance of automatic speech recognition system. State-of-the-art ASR systems use statistical pattern classification approach, having the two well known phases: feature extraction and pattern classification.

In the architecture of ASR, feature extraction phase comes under front-end, that converts the recorded waveform to some form of acoustic representation known as feature vectors. Back-end covers the different statistical models such as acoustic models and language models, along with searching methods and adaptation techniques for classification. The features are based on time-frequency representation of acoustic signals, which are computed at regular intervals (e.g., every 10ms). The feature vectors are decoded into linguistic units like word, syllable, and phones

DOI: 10.4018/978-1-4666-0954-9.ch006

with the help of hidden Markov models (HMMs) at back-end. For classification, HMMs use either multivariate Gaussian mixtures or artificial neural networks, to emit a state dependent likelihood or posterior probability on a frame by frame basis.

This chapter reviews and compares the existing statistical techniques (i.e., various types of HMMs) which have been used for acoustic-phonetic modeling of ASR in the context of Hindi language. The stochastic models are covered within three categories: conventional techniques, refinements and recently proposed methods. Various experiments are performed in normal field conditions as well as in noisy environments by using well known tools HTK 3.4.1 (Cambridge, University, 2011) and MATLAB. The deficiency in resources like speech and text corpora is the major hurdle in speech research for Hindi or any other Indian language. Unfortunately no standard database for Hindi language is available for public use till yet. Since databases from non-Indian languages cannot be used for Hindi (owing to the language specific effects), we have used self developed corpus which includes documents from popular Hindi news papers. The system includes PLP and PLP-RASTA techniques for feature extraction at front-end.

Rest of the chapter is organized as follows: Section 2 presents the role of speech recognition in HCI with ASR architecture and working. Classical approach of acoustic phonetic modeling is discussed in Section 3. In acoustic modeling, structure of HMM, discrete and continuous type of HMM, modeling unit of HMM, and pronunciation adaptation are covered. Section 4 presents the refinements (variable duration HMM and discriminative techniques) and advancements of HMM such as large margin and soft margin (based on support vector machines), dual stream approach and HMM with wavelet networks proposed by various researchers to overcome the limitations of standard HMM. Feature extraction and reduction techniques are covered in Section 5. In Section 6

ASR challenges and optimization are explained. Experimental results are analyzed in Section 7. Finally conclusions are drawn in Section 8.

2. EFFECTIVE HCI WITH RELIABLE ASR

2.1. Impact of Speech Recognition Performance on HCI

As one of the most natural and comfortable modes of human interaction, speech could be considered an ideal medium for human computer interaction. A simple solution of this problem would be possible if machine could mimic the human production and understanding of speech. To realize that, speech technology, a spectacular evolution of new technical domain, has come into existence over the last four decades. One of the most promising applications of speech technology is spoken dialogue system, which offers the interface for simple, direct and hand free access to information. The system can be loosely divided into three categories: command and control, directed dialogues and natural language interactive systems. Command and control system restricts the users to use only specialized command and is easier to implement. Natural language systems in principle require no previous knowledge or training on the part of the user, and put a burden on system developers by incorporating large vocabulary and complex grammar which is necessary for such systems. Directed dialog systems guide users through a specific dialog path but these steps can be tedious for experienced users who want to achieve their goals more quickly.

ASR is the key component for conversational interface and also a primary source of errors in these systems. The limitations or poor performance of ASR exert a significant negative impact on the overall quality and success of the interactions (Walker et al., 2001). Various mechanisms are required for error recovery introduced by ASR. The impact of recognition errors on overall dialog performance is so prominent that the systems are generally not well prepared to handle the resulting uncertainties. Two important deficiencies are:

- Shortcomings in the ability to accurately detect and diagnose problems.
- A lack of sufficient and effective error recovery strategies.

The reason is that spoken dialog systems typically rely on recognition confidence scores to guard against misunderstandings. It can be a good achievement for human computer interface if the performance of ASR would be more than 90%. If speech recognizers produce perfect results, most of the problems would disappear.

2.2. Statistical Formulation of ASR

In statistical based ASR systems, an utterance is represented by some sequence of acoustic feature observation O, derived from the underlying sequence of words W, and the recognition system needs to find the most likely word sequence, given the observed acoustic signal as formulated by:

$$\widehat{W} = \operatorname{argmax}_w P(W \mid O) \tag{1}$$

In Equation (1) the function $\operatorname{argmax}_w f(x)$ means "the x such that $f(x)$ is maximized". Using Bayes' rules it can be written as:

$$\widehat{W} = \operatorname{argmax}_W \frac{P(O \mid W)P(W)}{P(O)} \tag{2}$$

In Equation (2), $P(O)$ is ignored as it is constant with respect to W. Hence,

$$\widehat{W} = \operatorname{argmax}_w P(O \mid W)P(W) \tag{3}$$

In Equation (3), the observation likelihood $P(O \mid W)$ is evaluated based on an acoustic model and the prior probability $P(W)$ is determined by a language model. The acoustic model $P(O \mid W)$ typically consists of two parts. The first is to describe how a word sequence can be represented by sub-word units, often known as pronunciation modeling. The second is the mapping from each sub word units to acoustic observations (Rabiner & Juang, 2006). The most commonly used language model is the N-gram, which uses the previous (N-1) words to predict the Nth word. The probability of occurrence of a word sequence W is calculated as:

$$\begin{aligned} P(W) &= P(w_1, w_2, \ldots\ldots, w_{m-1}, w_m) \\ &= P(w_1)P(w_2 \mid w_1)P(w_3 \mid w_1 w_2) \\ &\ldots\ldots P(w_m \mid w_{m-n+1} w_{m-n+2} \ldots w_{m-2} w_{m-1}) \end{aligned} \tag{4}$$

Most commonly used N-grams are bigram (N = 2) and trigram (N = 3) language models.

2.3. Architecture of ASR

State-of-the-art ASR systems consist of five basic modules: the signal processing components (i.e., pre-processing and feature extraction), the set of acoustic models (i.e., HMM), the language model (i.e., N-gram estimation), the pronunciation dictionary with a word lexicon and search engine for final decoding as shown in Figure 1. First signal processing module generates features from given speech signal and then pattern classifier module evaluates these features to produce the most likely word sequence as output, with the help of available statistical models and lexicon.

The architecture of ASR is divided into training and decoding (i.e., testing) parts. The training task consists of taking a collection of utterances with associated word labels, and learning an association between the specified word models and observed acoustics. For this, it requires various information sources (i.e., databases and corpus)

Figure 1. Block diagram of automatic speech recognition system

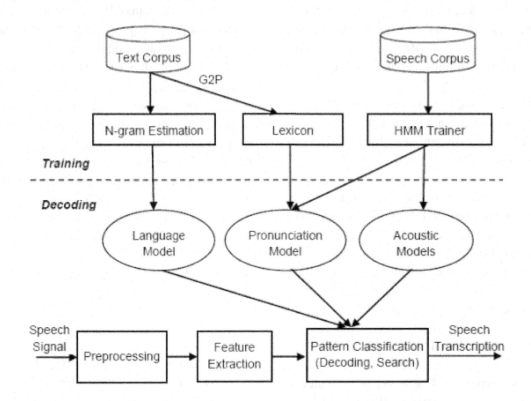

that include waveforms of isolated words or of phonetically labeled phrases. During recognition, the sequence of symbols generated by the acoustic components is compared with the set of words present in the lexicon to produce optimal sequence of words that compose the system's final output. In order to cover the words that are not seen in the acoustic training data, it is necessary to have a grapheme-to-phoneme (G2P) system that uses the word orthography to guess the pronunciation of the word (Goel et al., 2010).

The acoustic and language models resulting from the training procedure are used as knowledge sources during decoding. The decoding process with trained acoustic and language models is often referred to as a search problem. The efficient implementation of the optimal search involves dynamic programming and is typically referred to as Viterbi algorithm (Forney, 1973), which is

borrowed from communication theory. In large vocabulary speech recognition systems, the conventional Viterbi decoder typically generates a word lattice which contains a large number of competing word hypothesis and their associated likelihood scores. Then the recognizer is used to rank these competing hypotheses as the final output (Young, 1996). A lot of methods have been proposed for fast decoding, such as beam search, lexical tree, factored language model probabilities, language model look-ahead, fast likelihood computation, and multi pass search (Ney & Ortmanns, 2000). The task to be carried out by LVCSR decoder (Aubert, 2002) can be divided into the following sections:

• To generate hypothetical word sequences.
• To score the active hypothesis using the knowledge sources.

- To discard the most unpromising paths (pruning).
- To create back-pointers to retrieve the best sentence.

3. CONVENTIONAL APPROACH OF ACOUSTIC PHONETIC MODELING

Most state-of-the-art speech recognition systems typically use continuous density hidden Markov models (CDHMM) underlying technology to obtain a high level of accuracy (Huang et al., 2001). For the estimation of acoustic model parameters, a phonetically rich database is required. Selection of appropriate linguistic unit (i.e., word, syllable, and triphone) for the phonetic representation of speech signals is one of the important issues for acoustic phonetic modeling.

3.1. Structure and Working of HMM

Among the various acoustic models, HMM is so far the most widely used approach due to its efficient algorithm for training and recognition. It is a statistical model for an ordered sequence of symbols, acting as a stochastic finite state machine which is assumed to be built up from a finite set of possible states, each of those states being associated with a specific probability distribution $b_j(o_t)$ for the observation sequence

$O = (o_1, o_2, ..., o_T)$ as shown in Figure 2. These states are interconnected by links describing the conditional probabilities of a transition between the states defined by a state transition matrix, $A = [a_{ij}]$ (Rabiner, 1989). The underlying assumption of the HMM is that the data samples can be well characterized as a parametric random process, and the parameters of the stochastic process can be estimated in a precise and well defined framework. The basic HMM theory was published in a series of classic papers by Baum and his colleagues (Baum & Eagon, 1967).

To model the complex speech signal features, mixtures of Gaussians have been used as emission pdfs in the hidden Markov models. In such systems, the output likelihood of a HMM state S for a given observation vector x_n, can be represented as a weighted sum of probabilities:

$$p(X_n \mid S) = \sum_{k=1}^{K} w_k p_k(X_n) \tag{5}$$

where, the parameters of the pdf are the number of mixture components K; their weighing factor w_k, which satisfies $w_k > 0$ and $\sum_{k=1}^{K} w_k = 1$; the mean vector μ_k and the covariance variance matrix $\sum_k$ of each Gaussian function. The probability terms of Equation (5) are defined by the D-dimensional multivariate Gaussian density function:

Figure 2. HMM for a word RAM

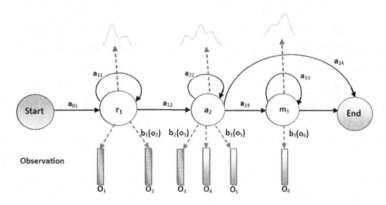

$$p_k(X_n) = \frac{1}{(2\pi)^{D/2} |\Sigma_k|^{1/2}} \exp\left[-\frac{1}{2}(X_n - \mu_k)^T \Sigma_k^{-1}(X_n - \mu_k)\right].$$
$$(6)$$

In practice the full covariance matrices are reduced to diagonal covariance due to computational and data sparseness reasons. The reason is that state likelihoods estimation is computationally intensive and takes about 30–70% of the total recognition time (Gales et al., 1999) and is so time-consuming that it is one of the most important reasons why the recognition is slow. Some LVCSR systems might even decode speech several times slower than real time; that is to say, these systems are not practical for most spontaneous applications, such as man-machine dialogue. Therefore, it is necessary to develop efficient techniques in order to reduce the time consumption of likelihood computation without a significant degradation of recognition accuracy (Cai et al., 2009).

3.2. Types of HMM

In general, HMM are of two types namely, discrete and continuous, depending upon the nature of output probability functions. Discrete HMM first encodes an observed acoustic feature vector into a code (symbol) and then models the sequence of the codes. A codebook is designed to implement it by using vector quantization based minimum distortion methods and multinomial distribution is used to determine the output probabilities of the states. For small vocabulary isolated word recognition, discrete HMM performs well with low computational costs. But these are not capable to model the intrinsic variabilities of the large vocabulary continuous speech recognition (LVCSR) system. Continuous density HMM came into picture to overcome the limitations of discrete HMMs. In CDHMM, to improve the system performance, the database used to train the acoustic model should be large enough covering all possible inter-speaker and intra-speaker variability (Krstulovic et al.,

2006). Several repetitions of each word spoken by several speakers are required for speaker independent systems. Large numbers of parameters are generated for each state depending upon the size of speech corpora to be used. For example a typical system might have approximately 2400 states with 4 mixture components per state giving about 800k parameters in total or approximately 4800 states with 8 mixture components per state giving about 3000k parameters in total. To address this problem in context dependent model, many similar states of the model are tied and the data corresponding to all these states are used to train one global state. HMMs with this type of sharing were proposed in literature under the names semi-continuous and tied-mixture HMMs. The choice of which states to tie is commonly made using decision trees. These tied numbers of states are known are as Senones or Genones with different naming conventions and with slight modification in implementations (Hwang & Huang, 1992). The tied states do not include context independent states, in other words phoneme states are not tied only triphone states are tied.

3.3. Phonetic Representation of Speech Signals

A mapping between acoustic measurements and linguistic units is required which is learned via a finite labeled training set of speech utterances. The main issues in choosing the appropriate modeling units are given below (Huang et al., 2001):

- The unit should be accurate, to represent the acoustic realization that appears in different contexts.
- The unit should be trainable. Sufficient data should be available to estimate the parameters of the unit.
- The units should be generalizable, so that any new word can be derived from a predefined unit inventory for task-independent speech recognition.

For domain specific application, where only small vocabulary are needed, to represent the whole word as basic unit of HMM based acoustic models is the natural choice and exhibit good results (Lee et al., 1993). But this method is unpractical for open systems where new words can be tested as accuracy may be reduced drastically due to out of vocabulary (OOV) words (Fetter et al., 1996). It is also totally infeasible for large vocabulary, speaker independent continuous speech recognition system to use whole word model where several dozens of realizations for every word are required. As the vocabulary size increases, it is no longer possible to train each word explicitly, because neither the training nor the storage is available. Another approach is to construct subword models such as for single phonemes which would solve the flexibility and feasibility problems. Perhaps the simplest set of subword units when trained from real speech material is context independent phone like unit (CI-PLU). Phonemes are a standard and well understood unit, and are easily trainable but they are highly dependent on left, right, and word dependent contexts. Multi-phoneme units such as triphones (crossword and word internal), diphones, demisyllables and syllables have been proposed to capture co-articulatory (contextual) effects (Lee et al., 1993). Triphone modeling is popular because it is more sensitive for co-articulatory effect than other phone modeling. For example two words *how* and *son,* have different sounds of "*o*". In both words, the sound of "*o*" is highly affected with their left and right context. Another advantage is that it is relatively task independent and can be used if the new vocabulary is not the subset of the old one.

3.4. Pronunciation Adaptation

A pronunciation lexicon (or dictionary) is required to map the orthography of each word to its pronunciation. It contains information about which words are known to the system and also how these words are pronounced, i.e., what their phonetic representations look like. Usually a standard pronunciation (also called canonical pronunciation or base form) is used which can be found in ordinary dictionaries. In isolated speech this canonical pronunciation has usually been closer to what speakers actually say, but for some words there might be a mismatch between this standard pronunciation and its phonetic realization. However, in continuous and spontaneous speech, the problem gets more severe, especially at higher speaking rate. It was found by Jost et al. (1997) that in spontaneous speech, 40% of all words are not pronounced as in the standard pronunciation dictionary. The pronounced words tend to deviate more and more from the canonical pronunciation due to co-articulation effects. If different pronunciations of each word are added in lexicon, the error rates could drastically be reduced for a spontaneous speech task (McAllaster et al., 1998). Greenberg (1999) has revealed 80 variants of the word 'the' in a transcription of spontaneous American English speech (Switchboard), which is certainly not possible to cover by any standard English pronunciation dictionary. Frequently used words (like pronouns, articles or function word) deviate quite regularly from the canonical pronunciation in comparison to others.

3.5. Hybrid Approach

ANN is a competent technique for pattern classification but remained unsuccessful in dealing with long time sequences of speech signals. Therefore researchers explored a new paradigm by combining HMM and ANN within single hybrid architecture to take the advantage of both, improving the flexibility and performance of ASR (Trentin & Gori 2001). In this approach, to model the subword units such as phonemes, it is usual to restrict the size of the ANN by using just one ANN output per phoneme. In HMM/GMM systems the state transition probabilities are estimated as part of the expectation maximization training procedure, while this is not the case in HMM/

ANN systems and it is common practice to use the same fixed value (e.g., 0.5) for all transitions (Hagen & Morris 2005).

In HMM/ANN framework, multilayer perceptrons (MLPs) have been used successfully to compute the emission probabilities of the states. If each output unit of an MLP is associated with a particular state of the set of states on which the Markov models are defined, it is possible to train the MLP to generate probabilities for each particular acoustic vector provided to its input (Bourlard & Wellakens 1990). Typically, MLPs have a layered feed forward architecture with an input layer (consisting of the input variables), zero or more hidden (intermediate) layers, and an output layer. Each node in the layer has one corresponding node (i.e., connected) in the next layer and these connections are not all equal. Each connection may have a different strength or weight which encode the knowledge of a network. Data enters at the inputs and passes through the network, layer by layer, until it arrives at the outputs. During normal operation, that is when it acts as a classifier, there is no feedback between layers. This is why they are called feed forward neural networks.

Each layer computes a set of linear discriminant functions (via a weight matrix) followed by a non-linear function, which is often a sigmoid function

$$f(x) = \frac{1}{1 + \exp(-x)}. \tag{7}$$

The actual input x is fed forward to the first hidden layer, where the linear weighted sum of the input values is computed and passed to a sigmoid type function, as given in Equation (7), for every node of that hidden layer. The same computation is performed for all other layers, where the previous hidden layer will provide the input values, until the final output layer is reached. The hidden units serve to generate high order moments of the input; this can be done effectively by many

nonlinear functions, not only by sigmoids. For the output unit a function called the softmax is normally used which approximates a statistical sigmoid function. For an output layer of K units, this function would be defined as

$$f(x_i) = \frac{\exp(x_i)}{\sum_{n=1}^{K} \exp(x_n)}. \tag{8}$$

4. FRAMEWORK FOR ADVANCED MODELING TECHNIQUES

4.1. Refinements of HMM

The easiest way to implement HMM is to compute the parameters for every fixed size frame using the maximum likelihood estimation (MLE) technique. Although this approach has been widely used and is very successful to date, it has three limitations: weak duration modeling, the assumption of conditional independence of observations, and the restrictions on feature extraction imposed by frame based observations. To overcome these deficiencies, researchers have proposed several refinements to the classical HMM including variable duration HMM (segmental), trended HMM, discriminative HMM, connectionist HMM (ANN+HMM) and adaptive models.

4.1.1. Segmental HMM

This technique introduced by Ferguson (1980), is found in literature with various variants including explicit duration HMM, variable duration HMM, generalized HMM, segmental HMM, and more recently hidden semi-Markov model, depending on their assumptions and applications (Yu, 2010). Segmental HMM is an extension of standard HMM, which allows the underline process to be a semi-Markov chain with a variable duration for each state. In this technique each state is trained to model the acoustic variation of a speech segment such as a phoneme. The main difference between the two techniques is that one observation per state is considered in standard HMM while each state can emit a sequence of observations in segmental HMM. The number of observations produced while in a state is determined by the length of time spent in that state. The segment duration distribution can be either parametric or non parametric. Parametric models have used the Poisson distribution (Russel & Moore, 1985), the Gamma distribution (Levinson, 1986) and later extensions conditioning on context. The non parametric models simply use smoothed relative frequencies. For phone-sized units, any reasonable assumption works well empirically, since the contribution of the duration model is small relative to the higher dimensional segment observation probability (Ostendorf et al., 1996). Since we have expanded the state space, interface in a variable duration HMM is slower than in a regular HMM.

4.1.2. Self Adaptive HMM

The number of states in a standard HMM is normally predefined and fixed during training. To search the optimal state, various model selection techniques have been applied such as cross validation principle, Bayesian Information Criterion (BIC) and Akaike's Criterion (AIC). The common drawback of these three methods is that they often have high computational overheads and are almost impractical for complex signals. Fixed state number cannot be an appropriate way to model the speech signal as different number of states may be more meaningful to explain them. In Li et al. (2004), a self adaptive design methodology is proposed to overcome this limitation, which adapts the real state number of the signal source being modeled. The experiments prove that the new HMM has better performance than classical HMMs in modeling signals, and its shrink training algorithm can converge to an accurate and compact model that is the most approximate to the true model.

4.1.3. Discriminative HMM

For acoustic model training there exists two distinct categories of algorithms, namely generative learning and discriminative learning. Although the ML-based generative algorithm (a.k.a. Baum–Welch algorithm) has been highly efficient and practical, it limits the performance of speech recognition. For the last decade, discriminative learning techniques have been proposed as the major driving force to bring down word error rate (WER) in all types of ASR applications. These methods either directly model the class posterior probability, or learn the parameters of the joint-probability model discriminatively so as to minimize classification (recognition) errors. On the basis of optimization criteria, three types of discriminative parameter learning, namely maximum mutual information estimation (MMIE), minimum classification error (MCE), and minimum phone (word) error (MPE/MWE) have been found in literature (Jiang, 2010).

In MLE based HMM we find those HMM model parameters, λ, which maximize the likelihood of the HMMs having generated with training data. Thus, given training data $Y^{(1)}, ..., Y^{(r)}$ the maximum likelihood (ML) training criterion may be expressed as:

$$F_{MLE}(\lambda) = \frac{1}{R} \sum_{r=1}^{R} \log(p(Y^{(r)} \mid w_{ref}^{(r)}; \lambda)) \qquad (9)$$

where $Y^{(r)}$ is the rth training utterance with transcription $w_{ref}^{(r)}$. This optimization is normally performed using expectation maximization. However, for ML to be the best training criterion, the data and models would need to satisfy a number of requirements, in particular, training data sufficiency and model-correctness (Gales & Young, 2007).

The aim of MMI criterion is to maximize the mutual information between the word sequence, and the information extracted by a recognizer with parameters λ from the associated observation sequence, Y (He & Deng, 2008). The conventional

MCE has been based on the generalized probabilistic descent (or gradient descent) method, in which we define the objective function for optimization that is closely related to the empirical classified errors. The objective function which is to be maximized in MCE can be expressed as:

$$F_{MCE}(\lambda) = \sum_{r=1}^{R} \frac{p^k(S_r).p^k(X_r \mid S_r)}{\sum_s p^k(S).p^k(X_r \mid S)} \qquad (10)$$

where X_r is the speech data for r^{th} training sentence, k is the scaling factor typically less than one, $p^k(X_r \mid S_r)$ denotes probability of X_r given its correct transcription S_r, calculated with model λ. Summation in denominator is conducted over all possible labels S, for each X_r.

The MPE criterion is a smoothed approximation to the phone transcription accuracy measured on the output of a word recognition system given the training data. The objective function in MPE, which is to be maximized, is:

$$F_{MPE}(\lambda) = \sum_{r=1}^{R} \frac{\sum_S p^k(S).p^k(X_r \mid S_r).A(S_r,S)}{\sum_s p^k(S).p^k(X_r \mid S)} \qquad (11)$$

where S denotes a variable which may take all possible labels in a hypothesis space. $A(S_r, S)$ is the raw phone transcription accuracy of the sentence S given the reference S_r, which equals the number of reference phones minus the number of errors. $p^k(X_r \mid S)$ denotes the probability of observation for the given sequence.

In discriminative techniques, the choice of competing word sequences and the accumulation of statistics for the selected model are the main issues to be handled carefully for good performance. The major drawback of these techniques is the computational overhead. An iteration of DT requires about 3-4 times the time needed for one ML iteration.

4.2. Recently Proposed Methods

In classical HMM, to estimate the parameters, expectation maximization (EM) algorithm provides an iterative framework for ML estimation with good convergence properties, though it does guarantee finding the global maximum. To create robust and more accurate models, the researchers introduced recently other promising techniques such as support vector machines, wavelets and templates in hybrid framework of statistical models.

4.2.1. Margin Based HMM

Inspired by support vector machines (SVMs), a new algorithm based on large margin estimation (LME) criterion was proposed in literature for multiway classification (Sha & Saul, 2007). A large margin classifier shows more robustness and better generalization capability by yielding lower error rates in new test sets. It estimates HMM parameters using the principle of maximizing minimum margin of the training data as follows:

$$\tilde{\lambda}_{LME} = argmax_\lambda min_{X_r \in D} \ d(X_r \mid \lambda) \qquad (12)$$

where $D = \{X_1, X_2, ..., X_R\}$ denotes the training data set.

In LME, we first define a separation margin for each training data X_r, as follows:

$$d(X_r \mid \lambda) = log[P(S_r).P(X_r \mid S_r)] - max_{S, S \neq S_r} log[P(S).P(X_r \mid S)] \qquad (13)$$

$$d(X_r \mid \lambda) = log[P^k(S_r).P^k(X_r \mid S_r)] - log[\sum_{S \neq S_r} P^k(S).P^k(X_r \mid S)] \qquad (14)$$

Using the margin definition in Equation (12), the LME criterion can be represented as follows:

$$\tilde{\lambda}_{LME} = argmax_\lambda min_{r=1...R} \ ln \frac{P^k(S_r).P^k(X_r \mid S_r)}{\sum_{S, S \neq S_r} P^k(S).P^k(X_r \mid S)} \qquad (15)$$

SVM provides state-of-the-art performance for many applications in pattern recognition but it is challenging to apply the same in large applications like ASR, which does not require binary classification. Another limitation of SVM is the high computation and memory requirements at the time of training and testing (Bishop, 2006). The parameters of large margin GMMs are trained as in SVMs, by a convex optimization that focuses on examples near the decision boundaries. For complex applications like ASR, large margin GMM has certain advantages over SVM. The reason is that large margin GMMs use ellipsoids to model classes, which induce non-linear decision boundaries in the input space, in place of half-spaces and hyperplanes used by SVMs. One potential weakness of LME is that it updates models only with accurately classified samples. However, it is well known that misclassified samples are also critical for classifier learning. Consequently, LME often needs a very good preliminary estimate from the training set to make the influence of ignoring misclassified samples small (Jiang & Li, 2007).

Another approach, soft margin estimation (SME) (Li et al., 2006), was proposed to make a direct use of the successful ideas of soft margin in support vector machines to improve the generalization capability and decision feedback learning in the classifier design. SME outperforms MLE and a discriminative training technique like MCE significantly, and is consistently better than LME. The excellent SME performance is attributed to the well-defined model separation measure and good objective function for generalization. The difference between LME and SME is that LME neglects the misclassified samples; it generally requires a very good preliminary estimate from the training set whereas SME works on all the training data, both the correctly classified as well as misclassified samples.

4.2.2. HMM with Wavelet Networks

To overcome the limitations of Gaussians mixture models, a new approach based on wavelet network was proposed in Ejbali et al. (2010), showing better results compared to typical HMM based systems. This framework combines the two important techniques artificial neural network (ANN) and wavelet, having been used widely, for signal analysis and pattern classification. ANN, also called connectionist network have interesting properties in recognition such as adaptability, resistance to noise and ease of calculation of nonlinear functions. Although, ANN has yielded interesting results on speech recognition to model the subword units such as phonemes and single words but remained unsuccessful in dealing with long time sequences of speech signals by certain types of networks such as multilayer prceptrons. To resolve this problem a new solution, in which wavelets are used as activation functions of neural networks, was searched. It could be very popular and beneficial in future as the wavelets are also excellent approximators and signal analyzers.

In this approach, the wavelet estimates the characteristics of each acoustic unit or different scales. Euclidean distance was used to calculate the similarity between training and testing phases of wavelet network. Experiments were performed on 31 Arabic words using MFCC and PLP both at front end. To compare the results with Gaussian mixtures, a range 32-256 of Gaussian mixtures was used. Wavelet network supersedes the whole Gaussian range used in experiments. The reason is that this framework is capable for the detailed analysis of signals through multiresolution study and access to all frequencies of a signal.

4.2.3. Dual Stream Approach

During the last decade a new theory was suggested by neurolinguistics known as dual stream model of speech processing, which involves two different streams that works in parallel one involved in phonological processing and one in articulatory processing (Hickok et al., 2007). Based on this approach, Puurula et al. (2010) proposed the idea of dual stream speech recognition by utilizing the complementary features of two methods, dynamic time warping (DTW) and HMM (De Wachter et al., 2007). This approach uses the syllables as a modeling unit and log linear interpolation is used to integrate the DTW model scores into the decoding. The interpolation is fundamentally the same as used in (Livescu et al., 2003) where articulatory models were integrated to an ASR.

To solve the data sparsity problem and lack of efficiency in using individual templates for DTW mean templates were introduced with model-based data imputation. To improve accuracy of modeling over simple mean templates constrained covariance matrices were attached to each of the templates. Then clustering of resulting models was performed according to any available context information and mixtures of multivariate Gaussians were estimated for these models. Efficiency in the models is improved by constraining DTW paths according to local and global constraints and integrating the models into a standard token passing decoder at the word level, using the decoder to minimize the number of required DTW computations and caching the results for further identical searches.

5. FEATURE EXTRACTION AND REDUCTION

The purpose of this module is to find a set of properties of an utterance that have acoustic correlations in the speech signal, that is parameters that can somehow be computed or estimated through processing of the signal waveform. Such parameters are termed as features. The two most popular sets of features are cepstrum coefficients obtained with a Mel-frequency cepstrum coefficient (MFCC) (Davis & Mermelstein, 1980) analysis or with a perceptual linear predictive (PLP) (Hermansky, 1990) analysis. In both cases, 39 dimensional feature vectors are formed with the help of the filter-banks designed using the knowledge of the human auditory system. The human auditory system processes the signal in various frequency bands with linear distribution in the initial part of the frequency range and becomes non linear towards the higher frequency range. The other popular techniques of feature extraction are MF-PLP (Woodland et al., 1997), temporal patterns (TRAPs) (Hermansky & Sharma, 1999), wavelets (Sharma et al., 2008) and gravity centroids (Paliwal, 1998). Besides that, a variety of multi stream, multi band and other combinations of features have been proposed in literature to optimize the signal parameterization methods in general field condition as well as in noisy environment (Hagen & Morris, 2005; Aggarwal & Dave, 2011). The steps covered in this phase are preprocessing, feature vector generation, noise compensation, and feature reduction.

5.1. Preprocessing

The analog speech signal is digitized with the sampling rate of the order of 8-16 kHz. In speech production high frequency formants have smaller amplitude with respect to lower frequency formants. A pre-emphasis of high frequencies is therefore required to obtain similar amplitude of all formants. During pre-emphasis, spectrum of the speech is flatten by using a first order FIR filter whose transfer function in the z domain is

$$H(z) = 1 - a.z^{-1} \quad 0 \leq a \leq 1 \qquad (16)$$

where a is the pre-emphasis coefficient, the most common value of which is around 0.95, that gives rise to a more than 20 dB amplification of the high frequency spectrum (Becchetti & Ricotti, 2004).

To extract the short time features, speech signal is blocked into short segments called frames. The duration of each frame varies from 20-35 milliseconds. The speech belonging to each frame is assumed to be stationary as the articulatory configuration stays relatively constant during this short time interval. To reduce the edge effect we need to apply a smoothing window (e.g., Hamming window) to each frame. Successive frames are overlapped to each other so that a more smoothed feature set over time could be generated.

5.2. Mel Frequency Cepstrum Coefficient (MFCC)

Mel cepstral feature extraction is used in some form or another in virtually every state of the art speech and speaker recognition system. In this process Fourier spectrum is computed for the windowed frame signal and then a Mel spaced bank of filters is applied to obtain a vector of log energies. The output of the filter-bank is then converted to cepstral coefficients by using discrete cosine transform (DCT), where only the first 12 coefficients are retained for computing the feature vector. Finally the feature vector consists of 39 values including the 12 cepstral coefficients with one energy, 13 delta cepstral coefficients and 13 delta delta coefficients.

Let $x[n]$ be the input speech signal and 39 dimensional MFCC feature vector is derived as given below:

Fourier transform is applied as:

$$X[k] = \sum_{n=0}^{N-1} x[n] e^{-j2\pi nk/N} \quad 0 \leq k \leq N-1 \tag{17}$$

Mel Spectrum filter bank coefficients are calculated using a window function H_m

$$F[m] = \log(\sum_{k=0}^{N-1} |X[k]|^2 H_m[k]), 0 \leq m \leq M \tag{18}$$

Compute the discrete cosine transform (DCT) of the log filter bank energies to get the MFCCs (c_j):

$$c_j = \sum_{m=1}^{M} F[m] . \cos\left[\frac{\pi j(m-1)}{2M}\right], j = 1, 2, ..., L \tag{19}$$

Generally only the first 12 to 15 values of c_j are retained.

Compute the first and second order time derivatives of the 13 coefficients using the following regression formulae:

$$\frac{\partial c_j}{\partial_\tau} = \frac{\sum_t \tau(c_j^{(t)} - c_j^{(-t)})}{2\sum_t t^2} \tag{20}$$

$$\frac{\partial^2 c_j}{\partial_{\tau^2}} = \frac{\sum_t \tau\left(\frac{\partial c_j^{(t)}}{\partial_\tau} - \frac{c_j^{(-t)}}{\partial_\tau}\right)}{2\sum_t t^2} \tag{21}$$

where t is time, and $c_j^{(t)}$ and $c_j^{(-t)}$ represents the tth following and previous cepstral coefficients in time frame, respectively. The derivatives are appended to the original MFCCs, producing a 39-dimensioanl feature vector for every frame.

5.3. Perceptual Linear Prediction (PLP)

In PLP, the spectrum is multiplied by a mathematical curve modeling the ear's behavior in judging loudness as a function of frequency. The output is then raised to the power 0.33 to simulate the power law of hearing. To obtain the auditory spectrum, 17 band pass filter outputs are used. Their center frequency are equally spaced in Bark domain z (i.e., critical bands), defined by

$$z = 6\log\left(\frac{f}{600} + \sqrt{\left(\frac{f}{600}\right)^2 + 1}\right) \qquad (22)$$

where f is the frequency in Hz and z covers the range 0-5 kHz, into the range 0-17 Bark (i.e., $0 \le z \le 17$ Bark).The center frequency of the kth critical band filter is $z_k = 0.9994k$. Each band is simulated by a spectral weighting,

$$c_k(z) = \begin{cases} 10^{z-x_k} & \text{for } z \le x_k \\ 1 & \text{for } y_k < z < x_k + 1 \\ 10^{-2.5(z-x_k-1)} & \text{for } z \ge x_k + 1 \end{cases}$$

$$(23)$$

where z_k are the center frequencies and $x_k = z_k - 0.5$.

To model the variations in perceived loudness in the human auditory response an equal loudness function $E(\omega)$ is applied to the critical band filter-bank values. The equal-loudness curve is approximated by

$$E(\omega) = 1.151\sqrt{\frac{(\omega^2 + 144 + 10^4)\omega^2}{(\omega^2 + 16 \times 10^4)(\omega^2 + 961 \times 10^4)}}$$

$$(24)$$

where ω is the angular frequency.

If F_k is the equal-loudness weighted output of the kth critical-band filter, it is given by

$$F_k = E(\omega_k)\int_0^\pi C_k(\omega)P(\omega)d\omega. \qquad (25)$$

Finally, the intensity-loudness conversion transforms F_k in the third root:

$$Q(\omega_k) = [F_k]^{\frac{1}{3}} \qquad (26)$$

The output of all these processes is a discrete representation of the auditory spectrum (18 values) which is given to the all pole modeling function (Hermansky, 1990).

Briefly PLP technique employs the following steps:

- Spectral analysis
- Critical-band spectral resolution
- Equal loudness pre-emphasis and intensity loudness conversion
- Inverse discrete Fourier transform
- Solution for autoregressive coefficients

5.4. PLP derived from Mel Filter Bank (MF-PLP)

In this feature extraction technique the best properties of MFCC and PLP are utilized by merging then into one algorithm.

- The first steps are derived from MFCC algorithm up to the application of Mel scale triangular filter bark. The only difference here is that the filter bark is applied to the power spectrum instead of magnitude spectrum.
- The last steps which generate the coefficients are taken from the PLP algorithm. The 20 filter bark outputs are modified by the intensity loudness law.
- 12 to 16 coefficients are calculated from the output of the intensity loudness law via the all-poles approximation.
- In all-pole approximation, autocorrelation coefficients are calculated by applying the inverse discrete Fourier transform (IDFT) to the output of the intensity loudness law. Finally cepstral coefficients are derived from autocorrelation coefficients as followed in LPCC technique (Markel & Gray, 1976).

5.5. RASTA Processing

To improve the accuracy in noisy field conditions we use RASTA which is equally effective on both, background noise and channel distortion. The linguistic components of the speech are governed by the rate of change of the vocal tract shape. The rate of change of nonlinguistic components (i.e., the noise) in speech often lies outside the typical rate of change of the vocal tract shape. The relative spectral (RASTA) technique takes the advantage of this fact and suppresses the spectral components that change more slowly or quickly than the typical rate of change of speech (Hermansky & Morgan, 1994).

RASTA has often been combined with the PLP method and applies a band-pass filter to the energy in each frequency subband in order to smooth over short-term noise variations and to remove any constant offset resulting from static spectral coloration in the speech channel. It is implemented as an IIR filter and the same filter is used for all frequency bands. The band pass range is approximately from 1 Hz to 16 Hz, with a sharp zero at 0 Hz and a time constant of about 160 ms. Events changing more slowly than once a second (e.g., most channel effects, except in severe fading conditions) are thus eliminated by the high pass filtering. The low pass cutoff is more gradual, which smooth parameters over about 40 ms, thus preserving most phonetic events, while suppressing noise. The filtering effects of RASTA try to do normalization, to improve the results of analysis for noisy speech.

5.6. Dimensionality Reduction

An important task for any pattern recognition problem is to find a good feature space, which should be both compact and contain the richest possible discriminant information. Feature dimensions which contain less discriminant information should be discarded because their existence not only slows down the classification process but also degrades the performance in many situations. This step is aimed at incorporating the techniques which project the features into low dimensional subspace, while preserving discriminative information.

These transformations may be supervised or unsupervised. Unsupervised methods are variable directed techniques which make no assumption about the existence of classes or groupings within the data. The simplest form of this criterion is PCA (Duda et al., 2001), which selects the orthogonal projections of the data that maximizes the total variance in the projected subspace. Simply selected subspaces that yield large variances does not necessarily yield subspaces that discriminant between the classes. To address this problem supervised approaches such as LDA (Haeb-Umbach & Ney, 1992) criterion can be used. In LDA the objective is to increase the ratio of the between class variance to the average within class variance for each dimension. This yields an orthonormal transforms such that the average within class covariance matrix is diagonalized, which should improve the diagonal covariance matrix assumption. An alternative extension to LDA is HLDA (Kumar & Andreou, 1998) which outperform approaches like LDA, but are more computationally intensive and require more memory.

6. ASR CHALLENGES AND MODEL OPTIMIZATION

The performance of ASR often degrades under the realistic environment condition or in adverse environment due to the various sources of speech signal variability such as speaker variability, contextual variability, channel distortion and room acoustic (i.e., background noise and reverberation). Sources of degradation of the speech signals may vary in different applications. To optimize the model parameters, we also analyze some of the major factors that led to improvements in performance of ASR such as speaker adaptation and normalization, noise compensation (speech enhancement), handling out of vocabulary words and modeling distant speech signals.

6.1. Speaker Variability

The speaker variability can be categorized into two parts which are intra-speaker variability and inter-speaker variability. A speaker normally changes the quality of his voice, speaking rate and articulation pattern according to his physical and emotional situations, background noise (increase the vocal efforts), and other environmental factors. Due to these reasons, there are a lot of variations in the speech signals even if a unique speaker produces the same linguistic message many times. Physiological differences are an important source of variation between speakers. For example it's well known that vocal tract sizes and shapes are different among speakers. To compensate the effect of inter-speaker variations on ASR performance many solutions have been proposed in literature known as speaker adaptation and normalization.

The goal of speaker adaptation is to modify the acoustic models in light of the data obtained from a specific speaker, so that the models are more closely tuned to the individual. In this area, there are three main techniques:

- Maximum A Posteriori (MAP) adaptation, which is the simplest form of acoustic adaptation (Neumeyer et al., 1995).
- Vocal Tract Length Normalization (VTLN), which warps the frequency scale to compensate for vocal tract differences (Kim et al., 2004).
- Maximum Likelihood Linear Regression, which adjusts the Gaussians and/or feature vectors so as to increase the data likelihood according to an initial transcription (Leggetter & Woodland, 1995).

VTLN tries to adjust input speech to have an average vocal tract length. Variations in vocal tract length cause formant frequencies to shift in frequency in an approximately linear fashion. Thus, one simple form of normalization is to linearly scale the filter bank centre frequencies within the front-end feature extractor to approximate a canonical formant frequency scaling. Since only one parameter needs to be estimated, small amount of adaptation data is sufficient for this purpose. In speaker adaptation techniques the parameters of the model set are adjusted to improve the modeling of the new speaker. To compensate the effect of inter-speaker variations on ASR performance, maximum likelihood linear regression (MLLR) is a successful acoustic model adaptation technique. It takes some adaptation data from a new speaker and updates the model parameters to maximize the likelihood of the adaptation data. It estimates a set of linear transformations for the mean and variance parameters of a Gaussian mixture HMM system. The effect of these transformations is to shift the component means and alter the variances in the initial system so that each state in the HMM system is more likely to generate the adaptation data.

6.2. Variability from Environments

The performance of ASR often degrades in adverse environments due to additive background noise sources, room reverberation and transmission channel distortions. In normal field condition SNR remains between 20-35 dB. Above 35 dB clean speech is assumed. In noisy environment, when SNR is less than 20 dB, speech recognition is a difficult problem. The additive noise n and the convolutional noise h transform the clean speech, x, resulting in noise-corrupted speech y represented as:

$$y(t) = x(t) * h(t) + n(t) \qquad (27)$$

The background noise is generally additive (uncorrelated) in the power spectrum of the acoustic signal. Room reverberation also leads to another kind of additive noise. Depending upon the characteristics in time and frequency domain, various kinds of noises are associated with the speech signals. White noise is characterized by a flat frequency spectrum in linear space. It is loosely analogous to white light which has flat power spectral density with respect to wavelength. Realized as sound, white noise sounds like the hiss of an untuned FM radio or the background noise of a cassette tape player or waterfall. Gaussian noise is a type of statistical noise in which the amplitude of the noise follows that of a Gaussian distribution. It is often incorrectly assume that Gaussian noise in necessarily white noise, yet neither property of one implies the other. A linear combination of Gaussian and white noise is known as white Gaussian noise which is normally additive in nature. Other type of noises those are not pure white noise, are referred to as colored noise. Additive background noise is widely present in various environment scenarios like offices, fans, city streets, factories and helicopters etc. To cope with this the main assumptions are

- Speech and noise signal are uncorrelated at least for a short time interval.
- Noise is either stationary or slowly varying (i.e., quasi stationary)
- Noise can be represented as zero mean random process.

The speech signal can be affected by the quality of microphone (or telephone) used, the number of microphones, the distance between microphone and speaker. High quality speech input is required to improve the performance of speech recognition system. Therefore, close talking super quality microphones should be used to check the multi-path distortion and electrical noise. The characteristics of the environment such as the size of room and the ability of materials used on the walls to absorb frequencies or modify the signal's properties (i.e., room reverberation) (Couvreur & Couvreur, 2004), background noise, also affect the signal quality. Traditionally, fast front-end noise compensation techniques, such as spectral subtraction (Boll, 1979) and more recently SPLICE (stereo-based piecewise linear compensation for

environments) (Deng et al., 2000) have been used to remove noise from the observed noisy and corrupted speech. Spectral-subtraction algorithms estimate the power spectrum of additive noise in the absence of speech, and then subtract that spectral estimate from the power spectrum of the overall input (which normally includes the sum of speech and noise). SPLICE, a frame-based, bias removal algorithm is a brute-force solution for cepstrum enhancement to the acoustic mismatch problem. Instead of blindly transforming the data, it learns the joint probability distribution for noisy speech and clean speech, and uses it to map each received cepstral into a clean estimate. Besides these two techniques the other noise compensation or feature enhancement techniques, proposed in literature to improve the tolerance of ASR system, are Weiner filtering, Kalman filtering, Relative spectra (RASTA) processing, parallel model compensation (PMC), and vector Taylor series approximation (Benesty et al., 2008).

6.3. Out of Vocabulary Words

The usage of words beyond a known vocabulary is major problem in many ASR systems. To locate them, confidence measures are associated with the likelihood of each word. ASR may simply reject the out of vocabulary (OOV) words as irrelevant, or it can choose an appropriate action to handle these words. If no allowance is made for these words, ASR will incorrectly output a word from its dictionary for each OOV occurrence, which reduces the accuracy rates of ASR. Further, if ASR is interactive, users could then be asked to augment the dictionary by defining each new word. This is especially useful in the case of proper names, since training database don't include these names (O'Shaughnessy, 2001).

Confidence scoring has been used to find unreliable regions and label them as out of vocabulary words (OOV). It is performed at various levels such as phone level, word level and utterance level (Kamppari & Hazen, 2000). The confidence measure for a phone is generally computed as the geometric mean of the confidence measures of speech frames in that phone (Pinto & Sitaram, 2005). If a phone p has T frames, its acoustic CM (C_p^A) is given by:

$$C_p^A = (c_1)^{\frac{1}{T}} \times (c_2)^{\frac{1}{T}} \times (c_3)^{\frac{1}{T}} \times ... \times (c_T)^{\frac{1}{T}} \quad (28)$$

where, c_t is the CM of the tth speech frame and geometric mean of n values is the nth root of their product. Equation (28) can be written as

$$C_p^A = exp[log_e\{(c_1)^{\frac{1}{T}} \times (c_2)^{\frac{1}{T}} \times (c_3)^{\frac{1}{T}} \times ... \times (c_T)^{\frac{1}{T}}\}]$$

$$= exp[\frac{1}{T}\{log_e c_1 + log_e c_2 + log_e c_3 + ... + log_e c_T\}]$$

$$= exp[\frac{1}{T}\Sigma_{t=1}^T log_e c_t].$$

$$(29)$$

Another feature that is often used is the difference in scores between first and second best hypothesis in an N-best list or word graph. The recognizer is assumed to be 'sure' about its own recognition results, if the score of the first-best hypothesis is much bigger than the score of the second-best hypothesis. If the scores are very close, the probability that the words are rather similar and that thus one or more words were confused with others is usually higher.

6.4. Distant Speech Signals

In ASR, to avoid the additive background noise and room reverberation close talking microphones are required kept at a distance of about 10cm from the lips of the speaker. For mobile environment and for reason of practical usage, hands free speech input is especially of interest in modern scenario. To use distant speech signals, Hirsch and Finster (2008) proposed an approach for adaptation of HMM to reverberation and background noise. The adaptation is based on an estimation of the noise

characteristics before the beginning of speech is detected. They used the combined adaptation scheme of HMM to cover the effects of both room reverberation as well as background noise based on parallel model combination approach. The Mel spectra of the clean HMM are adapted having the estimates for the noise spectrum, the frequency weighting function and the reverberation time.

7. EXPERIMENTAL RESULTS

7.1. Setup

Among the tools available for the research work in the field of ASR we have used HTK-3.4.1 in conjunction with MATLAB for our experimental work. HTK allows HMMs to be built with any desired topology. HMM definitions can be stored externally as simple text files and hence it is possible to edit them with any convenient text editor. HTK training tools, HINIT, HCOMPV, HEREST, and HHED were used to estimate the parameters of a set of HMMs using training utterances and their associated transcriptions. Among them HEREST is the core HTK training tool which performs embedded training using the entire training set. It is designed to process large databases with the facility of pruning to reduce computation (Young et al., 2009).

The input speech was sampled at 12 kHz sampling rate with 16 bit quantization, and then processed at 10 ms frame rate (i.e., 120 samples/frame) with a Hamming window of 25 milliseconds to obtain the 39 PLP acoustic features. The next step is to decide the unit of acoustic-phonetic transcription for which HMM is to be implemented. Whole word unit based acoustic models are the simplest but successful only in small vocabulary isolated word recognition system. Therefore, crossword triphone model of HMM with linear left-right topology is used to compute the score against a sequence of features for their phonetic transcription. To compute likelihood (probabilistic) of a given word, the word is broken into its constituent phones, and likelihood of the phones is computed from the HMMs. The combined likelihood of all of the phones represents likelihood of the word in the acoustic model.

The experiments were performed on a set of speech data consisting of six hundred words of Hindi language recorded by 10 male and 10 female speakers. The selection of words is made on the basis of that they are phonetically balanced and frequently occurring words of Hindi (Khari Boli). For training, data was recorded in a sound treated room (in clean environment) using a uni-directional close talking standard microphone with 10 cm distance between lips of speaker and transducer. Each time model was trained using 5 repetitions of each word by every speaker. Testing of randomly chosen hundred words, spoken by different speakers is made and recognition rate (i.e., accuracy) is calculated as:

$$Recognition\ rate = \frac{Successfully\ detected\ words}{Number\ of\ words\ in\ test\ set}.$$

7.2. Results

Using the frame synchronous CDHMM statistical model for training and testing the following results were analyzed:

a. Variation in accuracy with number of Gaussian mixtures for phoneme model, syllable model and triphone model.

b. Variation in accuracy with different type of HMM models such as standard HMM, segmental HMM, discriminative HMM and margin based HMM.

c. Variation in accuracy with different projection schemes.

d. Variation in the recognition rate with different SNR.

e. Variation in accuracy with different number of tied states.

The results of the experiments are given below.

7.2.1. Experiment for Various Phonetic Units

Experiments were performed by using standard modeling units viz. phoneme model, syllable model and triphone models. All the models were processed and evaluated with each category of Gaussian mixtures as shown in Table 1. Maximum accuracy was found for cross word triphone model with 16 Gaussian mixtures. At front-end PLP-RASTA was used and at back-end classical HMM was used.

7.2.2. Experiment with Types of HMM

Experiments were performed for different type of Markov models with 16 Gaussian mixtures to achieve best recognition rate and results are given in Table 2. Accuracy is calculated in three different ASR modes- speaker dependent (SD), speaker independent (SI) and speaker adaptation

Table 1. Accuracy by varying mixtures for various phonetic units

Modeling Unit	% Accuracy with varying number of mixture Gaussians				
	2-mix	4-mix	8-mix	16-mix	32-mix
CI Phoneme Model	78.55	80.07	82.11	83.45	82.9
Syllable Model	79.65	81.98	84.25	85.8	84.56
Within word triphone model	80.25	82.23	84.5	85.77	84.91
Cross Word Triphone Model	81.62	83.27	85.88	86.23	85.97

(SA). Two to six percent more accuracy was achieved by the advanced models proposed in literature in comparison to the standard HMM. In our implementation, each discriminative training was initialized with 10 iterations following the initialization with ML training. To reduce the complexity it was assumed that the training data was segmented according to the spoken word sequence, and a uni-gram language model was used for training.

7.2.3. Experiment with Projection Schemes

In this experiment at front-end, the feature vectors were appended upto triple deltas (13 static + $13\Delta + 13\Delta\Delta + 13\Delta\Delta\Delta$) and these 52 dimensional feature vectors were reduced to the standard 39 values, using the projection schemes. At back-end, classical HMM was used with two modeling units, whole word and triphone. Results were compared in case of three projection schemes HLDA, LDA and PCA as shown in Figure 3.

HLDA based reduction shows maximum accuracy in this scenario. The difference between the performance of HLDA and LDA is less. We can also use LDA if less computation is required to make the application fit in real time environment or in embedded system.

Table 2. Accuracy for different types of HMM

Type of HMM	% Accuracy		
	SD	SI	SA
Standard (MLE)	90.4	86.23	88.15
Segmental	91.2	87.05	88.97
MCE	92.15	88.11	90.12
MPE	93.82	89.9	91.34
Large Margin	94.35	90.42	92.37
Soft Margin	95.08	91.36	93.21

7.2.4. Experiments with Different SNR

Experiments were performed by mixing the white Gaussian noise source with the help of NOISEX92 database and accuracy was calculated by varying SNR as shown in Figure 4. At back-end, classical HMM was used and at front-end PLP and PLP RASTA both were used. According to results, RASTA is very useful at low SNR (i.e., less than 25) to check the drop in recognition accuracy.

7.2.5. Experiment with Number of Tied States

Experiments were performed with different number of Senones (tied states) as shown in Table 3. The number of Gaussian mixtures used for each case of tied states is sixteen. With the help of a decision tree, the mixtures of each state were tied for each base phone and the training data triphones are mapped into a smaller set of tied state triphones. Each state position of each phone has a binary tree associated with it. Maximum accuracy was observed around one thousand tied states. While in case of European languages the total number of tied states in a large vocabulary speaker independent system typically ranges from 5,000 to 10,000 states.

8. CONCLUSION

Despite the intensive research in the field of speech technology, many problems still persist for the development of natural language conversational interface between man and machine.

Table 3. Accuracy versus tied states

No. of Senones	50	350	740	1250	1700	2400
Accuracy (%)	82	8	91	90.5	88	84

Figure 3. Accuracy versus projection schemes

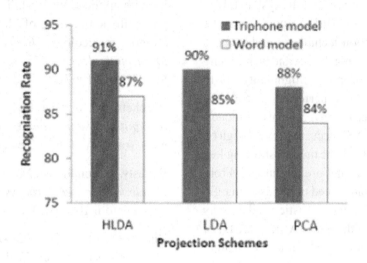

For example, spoken dialogue systems require unbounded variability, yet ASR performs best when the speaker uses a limited vocabulary and syntax. To deal with the large variability problem of acoustic signals, this paper reviewed several promising methods that were proposed in the last two decades. These methods were divided into three categories: conventional techniques, refinement of standard techniques and recently proposed methods. We provided a summary of each method with its merits and demerits.

Experimental results showed the comparison of various statistical acoustic models. Results also illustrate that only 16 Gaussian mixtures and around one thousand tied states yield optimal performance in the context of small training data available for Indian languages. Large number of Gaussian mixtures (i.e., more than 16) and Senones

Figure 4. Accuracy versus SNR

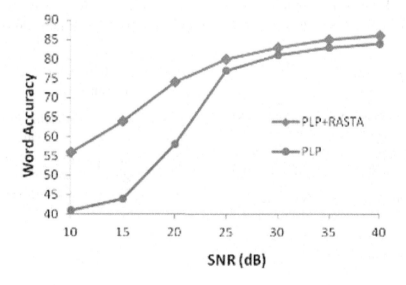

not only increase the computational load but can also reduce the performance of the system due to over fitting of the data. HLDA outperforms the other feature reduction techniques and is more successful in ASR. Using the advanced modeling techniques with appropriate alignment, 2% to 6% improvement in ASR performance could be achieved as compared to conventional techniques.

As the impact of ASR accuracy is very high on the performance of HCI, the models showing less than 10% word error rates are in demand. From this perspective the advanced methods as margin based and discriminative acoustic models may be recommended for the use of ASR in HCI. For future research, various combinations of feature extraction techniques, speech enhancement methods, and acoustic modeling techniques should be used as there is no single technique available which could be labeled as best fit for all environment. Short term features can be added with long term features. Noise compensation techniques effective for additive noise should be used parallely with the noise removal techniques of babble noise. Gaussian mixture models and neural networks should be combined under a single framework to utilize the best features of both. Thus in future, these hybrid models can meet the challenges of the ASR systems. Different types of filterbanks or feature vectors at front-end or different model combinations can be further optimized using genetic algorithms or swarm intelligence.

REFERENCES

Aggarwal, R. K., & Dave, M. (2011). *Performance evaluation of sequentially combined heterogeneous feature streams for Hindi speech recognition system*. Telecommunication Systems Journal.

Aubert, X. L. (2002). An overview of decoding techniques for large vocabulary continuous speech recognition. *Computer Speech & Language, 16*(1), 89–114. doi:10.1006/csla.2001.0185

Baum, L. E., & Eagon, J. A. (1967). An inequality with applications to statistical estimation for probabilistic functions of Markov processes and a model for ecology. *Bulletin of the American Mathematical Society, 73*, 360–363. doi:10.1090/S0002-9904-1967-11751-8

Becchetti, C., & Ricotti, K. P. (2004). *Speech recognition theory and C++ implementation*. New York, NY: John Wiley & Sons.

Benesty, J., Sondhi, M. M., & Huang, Y. (2008). *Handbook of speech processing*. New York, NY: Springer. doi:10.1007/978-3-540-49127-9

Bishop, C. M. (2006). *Pattern recognition and machine learning*. New York, NY: Springer.

Boll, S. F. (1979). Suppression of acoustic noise in speech using spectral subtraction. *IEEE Transactions on Acoustics, Speech, and Signal Processing, 27*, 113–120. doi:10.1109/TASSP.1979.1163209

Bourlard, H., & Wellakens, C. (1990). Links between Markov models and multilayer perceptrons. *IEEE Transactions on Pattern Analysis and Machine Intelligence, 12*(12), 1167–1178. doi:10.1109/34.62605

Cai, J., Bouselmi, G., Laprie, Y., & Haton, J.-P. (2009). Efficient likelihood evaluation and dynamic Gaussian selection for hmm-based speech recognition. *Computer Speech & Language, 23*, 147–164. doi:10.1016/j.csl.2008.05.002

Cambridge University. (2011). *Hidden Markov Model Toolkit*. Retrieved January 15, 2011, from http://htk.eng.cam.ac.uk

Couvreur, L., & Couvreur, C. (2004). Blind model selection for automatic speech recognition in reverberant environments. *The Journal of VLSI Signal Processing, 36*(2-3), 189–203. doi:10.1023/B:VLSI.0000015096.78139.82

Davis, S., & Mermelstein, P. (1980). Comparison of parametric representations for monosyllabic word recognition in continuously spoken sentences. *IEEE Transactions on Acoustics, Speech, and Signal Processing, 28,* 357–366. doi:10.1109/TASSP.1980.1163420

De Wachter, M., Matton, M., Demuynck, K., Wambacq, P., Cools, R., & Van Compernolle, D. (2007). Template based continuous speech recognition. *IEEE Transactions on Audio. Speech and Language Processing, 15*(4), 1377–1390. doi:10.1109/TASL.2007.894524

Deng, L., Acero, A., Plumpe, M., & Huang, X. (2000). Large vocabulary speech recognition under adverse acoustic environments. *Proceedings of Interspeech, 13,* 806–809.

Duda, R. O., Hart, P. E., & Stork, D. G. (2001). *Pattern classification.* New York, NY: John Wiley & Sons.

Ejbali, R., Zaied, M., & Amar, C. B. (2010). Wavelet network for recognition system of Arabic word. *International Journal of Speech Technology, 13,* 163–174. doi:10.1007/s10772-010-9076-y

Ferguson, J. D. (1980). Variable duration models for speech. In *Proceedings of the Symposium on Application of Markov Models to Text and Speech,* Princeton, NJ (pp. 143-179).

Fetter, P., Kaltenmeier, A., Peter, T. K., & Brietzmann, R. (1996). Improved modeling of OOV words in spontaneous speech. In *Proceedings of the IEEE International Conference on Acoustics, Speech, and Signal Processing* (pp. 534-537).

Forney, G. D. (1973). The Viterbi algorithm. *Proceedings of the IEEE, 61,* 268–278. doi:10.1109/PROC.1973.9030

Gales, M., & Young, S. (2007). The application of hidden Markov models in speech recognition. *Foundations and Trends in Signal Processing, 1*(3), 195–304. doi:10.1561/2000000004

Gales, M. J. F., Knill, K. M., & Young, S. J. (1999). State-based Gaussian selection in large vocabulary continuous speech recognition using HMM's. *IEEE Transactions on Speech and Audio Processing, 7*(2), 152–161. doi:10.1109/89.748120

Goel, N., Thomas, S., Agarwal, M., Akyazi, P., Burget, L., & Feng, K..... Schwarz, P. (2010). Approaches to automatic lexicon learning with limited training examples. In *Proceedings of the IEEE Conference on Acoustics, Speech, and Signal Processing* (pp. 5094-5097).

Greenberg, S. (1999). Speaking in shorthand-A syllable-centric perspective for understanding pronunciation variation. *Speech Communication, 29,* 159–176. doi:10.1016/S0167-6393(99)00050-3

Haeb-Umbach, R., & Ney, H. (1992). Linear discriminant analysis for improved large vocabulary continuous speech recognition. In *Proceedings of the International Conference on Acoustics, Speech and Signal Processing* (pp. 13-16).

Hagen, A., & Morris, A. (2005). Recent advances in the multi-stream HMM/ANN hybrid approach to noise robust ASR. *Computer Speech & Language, 19,* 3–30. doi:10.1016/j.csl.2003.12.002

He, X., & Deng, L. (2008). *Discriminative learning for speech recognition: Theory and practice.* Santa Clara, CA: Morgan & Claypool.

Hermansky, H. (1990). Perceptually predictive (PLP) analysis of speech. *The Journal of the Acoustical Society of America, 87*(4), 1738–1752. doi:10.1121/1.399423

Hermansky, H., & Morgan, N. (1994). RASTA processing of speech. *IEEE Transactions on Speech and Audio Processing, 2*(4), 578–589. doi:10.1109/89.326616

Hermansky, H., & Sharma, S. (1999). Temporal patterns (TRAPs) in ASR of noisy speech. In *Proceedings of the IEEE Conference on Acoustic, Speech, and Signal Processing* (pp. 289-292).

Hickok, G., & Poippil, D. (2007). The critical organization of speech processing. *Nature Reviews. Neuroscience, 8*(5), 393–402. doi:10.1038/nrn2113

Hirsch, H.-G., & Finster, H. (2008). A new approach for the adaptation of HMMs to reverberation and background noise. *Speech Communication, 50*, 244–263. doi:10.1016/j.specom.2007.09.004

Huang, X., Acero, A., & Hon, H. W. (2001). *Spoken language processing: A guide to theory algorithm and system development*. Upper Saddle River, NJ: Prentice Hall.

Hwang, M., & Huang, X. (1992). Subphonetic modeling with Markov states—Senone. In *Proceedings of the IEEE International Conference on Acoustics, Speech and Signal Processing*, San Francisco, CA (pp. 33-36).

Jiang, H. (2010). Discriminative training of HMM for automatic speech recognition: A survey. *Computer Speech & Language, 24*, 589–608. doi:10.1016/j.csl.2009.08.002

Jiang, H., & Li, X. (2007). Incorporating training errors for large margin HMMs under semi definite programming framework. In *Proceedings of the IEEE International Conference on Acoustics, Speech, and Signal Processing* (pp. 629-632).

Jost, U., Heine, H., & Evermann, G. (1997). What is wrong with the lexicon- an attempt to model pronunciations probabilistically. In *Proceedings of the 5th European Conference on Speech Communication and Technology*, Rhodes, Greece (pp. 2475-2479).

Kamppari, S. O., & Hazen, T. J. (2000). Word and phone level acoustic confidence scoring. In *Proceedings of the International Conference on Acoustics, Speech and Signal Processing* (Vol. 3, pp. 1799-1802).

Kim, D. Y., Umesh, S., Gales, M. J. F., Hain, T., & Woodland, P. (2004). Using VTLN for broadcast news transcription. In *Proceedings of the International Conference on Spoken Language Processing*, Jeju, Korea.

Krstulovic, S., Bimbot, F., Boëffard, O., Charlet, D., Fohr, D., & Mella, O. (2006). Optimizing the coverage of a speech database through a selection of representative speaker recordings. *Speech Communication, 48*(10), 1319–1348. doi:10.1016/j.specom.2006.07.002

Kumar, N., & Andreou, A. G. (1998). Heteroscedastic discriminant analysis and reduced rank HMMs for improved speech recognition. *Speech Communication, 26*, 283–297. doi:10.1016/S0167-6393(98)00061-2

Lee, C. H., Gauvain, J. L., Pieraccini, R., & Rabiner, L. R. (1993). Large vocabulary speech recognition using subword units. *Speech Communication, 13*, 263–279. doi:10.1016/0167-6393(93)90025-G

Leggetter, C. J., & Woodland, P. (1995). Speaker adaptation using maximum likelihood linear regression. *Computer Speech & Language, 9*(2), 171–185. doi:10.1006/csla.1995.0010

Levinson, S. (1986). Continuously variable duration hidden Markov models for automatic speech recognition. *Computer Speech & Language, 1*(1), 29–45. doi:10.1016/S0885-2308(86)80009-2

Li, J., Wang, J., Zhao, Y., & Yang, Z. (2004). Self-adaptive design of hidden Markov models. *Pattern Recognition Letters, 25*, 197–210. doi:10.1016/j.patrec.2003.10.001

Li, J., Yuan, M., & Lee, C. H. (2006). Soft margin estimation of hidden Markov model parameters. In *Proceedings of the International Conference Interspeech* (pp. 2422-2425).

Livescu, K., Glass, J., & Bilmes, J. (2003). Hidden feature models for speech recognition using dynamic Bayesian networks. In *Proceedings of the International Conference Eurospeech* (pp. 2529-2532).

Markel, J. D., & Gray, A. H. (1976). *Linear prediction of speech*. Berlin, Germany: Springer-Verlag.

McAllaster, D., Gillick, L., Scattone, F., & Newman, M. (1998). Studies with fabricated switchboard data: Exploring sources of model-data mismatch. In *Proceedings of the DARPA Workshop on Conversational Speech Recognition* (Vol. 1).

Neumeyer, L., Sankar, A., & Digalakis, V. (1995). A comparative study of speaker adaptation techniques. In *Proceedings of the International Conference Eurospeech*, Madrid, Spain, (pp. 1127-1130).

Ney, H., & Ortmanns, S. (2000). Progress in dynamic programming search for large vocabulary continuous speech recognition. *Proceedings of the IEEE*, *88*(8), 1224–1240. doi:10.1109/5.880081

O'Shaughnessy, D. (2001). *Speech communications: Human and machines*. Piscataway, NJ: IEEE Press.

Ostendorf, M., Digalakis, V. V., & Kimball, O. A. (1996). From HMM's to segment models: A unified view of stochastic modeling for speech recognition. *IEEE Transactions on Speech and Audio Processing*, *4*(5), 360–378. doi:10.1109/89.536930

Paliwal, K. K. (1998). Spectral subband centroid features for speech recognition. In *Proceedings of the IEEE International Conference on Acoustics, Speech and Signal Processing* (Vol. 2, pp. 617-620).

Pinto, J., & Sitaram, R. N. V. (2005). Confidence measures in speech recognition based on probability distribution of likelihoods. In *Proceedings of the International Conference Interspeech* (pp. 4-8).

Puurula, A., & Van Compernolla, D. (2010). Dual stream speech recognition using articulatory syllable models. *International Journal of Speech Technology*, *13*, 219–230. doi:10.1007/s10772-010-9080-2

Rabiner, L. R. (1989). A tutorial on hidden Markov models and selected applications in speech recognition. *Proceedings of the IEEE*, *77*(2), 257–286. doi:10.1109/5.18626

Rabiner, L. R., & Juang, B. H. (2006). Speech recognition: Statistical methods. In *Encyclopedia of linguistics* (pp. 1–18). Amsterdam, The Netherlands: Elsevier.

Russel, M., & Moore, R. (1985). Explicit modeling of state occupancy in hidden Markov models for automatic speech recognition. In *Proceedings of the International Conference on Acoustic, Speech, and Signal Processing* (pp. 2376-2379).

Sha, F., & Saul, L. K. (2007). Large margin hidden Markov models for automatic speech recognition. In Scholkopf, B., Platt, J., & Hoffman, T. (Eds.), *Advances in neural information processing systems* (pp. 1249–1256). Cambridge, MA: MIT Press.

Sharma, A., Shrotriya, M. C., Farooq, O., & Abbasi, Z. A. (2008). Hybrid wavelet based LPC features for Hindi speech recognition. *International Journal of Information and Communication Technology*, *1*, 373–381. doi:10.1504/IJICT.2008.024008

Trentin, E., & Gori, M. (2001). A survey of hybrid ANN/HMM models for automatic speech recognition. *Neurocomputing*, *37*, 91–126. doi:10.1016/S0925-2312(00)00308-8

Walker, M., Passonneau, R., & Boland, J. (2001). Quantitative and qualitative evaluation of the DARPA communicator spoken dialogue systems. In *Proceedings of the 39th Annual Meeting on Association for Computational Linguistics* (pp. 515-522).

Woodland, P., Gales, M., Pye, D., & Young, S. (1997). Broadcast news transcription using HTK. In *Proceedings of the IEEE International Conference on Acoustics, Speech, and Signal Processing*, Munich, Germany (Vol. 2, 719-722).

Young, S. (1996). A review of large vocabulary continuous speech recognition. *IEEE Signal Processing Magazine*, *13*, 45–57. doi:10.1109/79.536824

Young, S., Evermann, G., Gales, M., Hain, T., Kershaw, D., & Liu, X. …Woodland, P. (2009). *The HTK book*. Cambridge, MA: Microsoft Corporation and Cambridge University Engineering Department.

Yu, S.-Z. (2010). Hidden semi-Markov models. *Artificial Intelligence*, *174*, 215–243. doi:10.1016/j.artint.2009.11.011

KEY TERMS AND DEFINITIONS

Acoustic Model: Used to generate mapping between the basic speech units (phones, syllables) and the observed features of speech signals.

ASR: A task to accurately and efficiently convert the speech signal into a text message independent of the device, speaker or the environment.

Discriminative Techniques: For acoustic model training there exists two distinct categories of algorithms, namely generative learning and discriminative learning. Standard technique of HMM tend toward poor discrimination due to the training algorithm which maximizes likelihoods (MLE criterion) instead of a posteriori probabilities (MAP criterion). Discriminative learning techniques have been proposed as the major driving force to bring down word error rate (WER) in all types of ASR applications. These methods either directly model the class posterior probability, or learn the parameters of the joint-probability model discriminatively so as to minimize classification (recognition) errors.

Feature Extraction: Method of extracting the limited amount of useful information from high dimensional data. One of the goals in such a process is to extract purely the information that distinguishes a given sub unit of a word from another sub-unit. The speech signal contains the characteristics information of the speaker and environment in addition to signal message. A feature extractor for speech recognition needs to maximally discard the speaker and environment information and retaining the signal message information.

Gaussian Mixtures: To model the complex speech signal, mixtures of Gaussian have been used as emission pdf's in the hidden Markov models. Since the evaluation of Gaussian likelihoods dominate the total computational load, the appropriate selection of Gaussian mixtures is very important. A range of 8 to 128 mixture components per state have been found useful depending upon the size of speech corpora to be used to train the HMM.

Hidden Markov Model (HMM): A statistical model for an ordered sequence of symbols, acting as a stochastic finite state machine which is assumed to be built up from a finite set of possible states, each of those states being associated with a specific probability distribution or probability density function (pdf).

Margin Based Approach: Inspired by the great success of margin-based classification techniques (a machine learning approach), researchers incorporated this concept into hidden Markov modeling for speech recognition. They use SVM (support vector machine) framework with a small difference that classes are modeled by collection of ellipsoids in place of half spaces or hyper-planes as used in SVM. For this reason, they are more naturally suited to multi way classification (required in ASR) as opposed to binary classification.

Perceptual Linear Prediction (PLP): Two most popular sets of features are cepstrum coefficients obtained with a Mel-frequency cepstrum coefficient (MFCC) analysis or with a perceptual linear predictive (PLP) analysis. In both cases, 39 dimensional feature vectors are formed with the help of the filter banks designed using the knowledge of the human auditory system. The human auditory system processes the signal in various frequency bands with linear distribution in the initial part of the frequency range and becomes non linear towards the higher frequency range.

State Duration Modeling: The easiest way to implement HMM is to compute the parameters for every fixed size frame. Although the widely used frame based approach is very successful to date, it has some drawbacks. An inherent limitation of HMM technology is that the probability of duration of a state decreases exponentially with time. Therefore, it does not provide adequate representation of temporal structure. To overcome these deficiencies, researchers have proposed segment based alternatives to hidden Markov models which allow the underlying process to be a semi-Markov chain with a variable duration for each state. The main difference between the two techniques is that one observation per state is considered in standard HMM while each state can emit a sequence of observations in segmental HMM.

Chapter 7
Issues in Spoken Dialogue Systems for Human–Computer Interaction

Tanveer J. Siddiqui
University of Allahabad, India

Uma Shanker Tiwary
Indian Institute of Information Technology Allahabad, India

ABSTRACT

Spoken dialogue systems are a step forward towards the realization of human-like interaction with computer-based systems. This chapter focuses on issues related to spoken dialog systems. It presents a general architecture for spoken dialogue systems for human-computer interaction, describes its components, and highlights key research challenges in them. One important variation in the architecture is modeling knowledge as a separate component. This is unlike existing dialogue systems in which knowledge is usually embedded within other components. This separation makes the architecture more general. The chapter also discusses some of the existing evaluation methods for spoken dialogue systems.

1. INTRODUCTION

Ideal communication model for Human-Computer Interaction (HCI) can be derived from human–human interaction which includes both verbal and non-verbal components. Non-verbal communication includes sign languages, facial expressions, gestures, emotions, lip movement, etc., while the main component of verbal communication is a natural language utterances. Understanding

human-human interaction process and deriving a computational model of it is an enigmatic problem and achieving an interaction with computers that can be called close to human–like, if not similar, is still too far to achieve. However, achieving human-like interaction has been a desired goal of human computer interaction and the fascinating idea of using natural languages for interacting with computers has long been a research topic of Artificial Intelligence (AI) and HCI researchers.

DOI: 10.4018/978-1-4666-0954-9.ch007

Systems, like ELIZA, which uses natural language interface, have been developed as early as in 60s. Science fictions are full of wonderful pieces of fantasies about spontaneous human-like conversations with computers. The idea of developing "talking computers" (Samuel et al., 2010) has been haunting researchers in AI and speech technology for past few decades. However, spoken language as a means of communication with computers has become a reality only in recent past owing to the rapid advancements in computing, speech and language technology. Several research prototypes as well as commercial applications are now available that use spoken language communication. Interfaces that use voice as input for controlling appliances, creating documents, searching in an existing database, are already in place. However, systems equipped with such voice-based interfaces have limited capability in that they do not engage the user in a natural conversation. They accept speech inputs, process them and perform some actions or report an error. Research efforts are continuing to develop spoken dialogue systems which "provide an interface between a user and computer-based application in many cycles in a relatively natural manner" (McTear, 2002). Figure 1 shows a wide range of tasks of varying complexity suitable for dialogue-based interfaces. However, supporting such interactions brings additional complexities, such as interpreting the user input to get involved in a conversation, handling uncertainty, knowing its state, confirming, asking to repeat, etc.

In order to have more effective interaction dialogue systems must integrate speech with other natural modalities such as facial expressions, gestures, eye movements, etc. This has lead to the idea of Embodied Conversational Agents (ECA) (Traum & Rickel, 2002) either in the form of animated humanoid avatars or, as talking heads. These agents communicate with the user to plan a task that an agent is able to carry out independently, e.g., book travel tickets, prepare diet chart to improve poor dietary habits, assist in planning investment, etc. Rich models have been developed along this line. However, the core of ECA work is not the use of human language technology but the use of facial expressions and gestures in order to bring emotions and politeness in conversation. Research efforts are being made focusing on in-

Figure 1. Example dialogue applications with increasing order of complexity

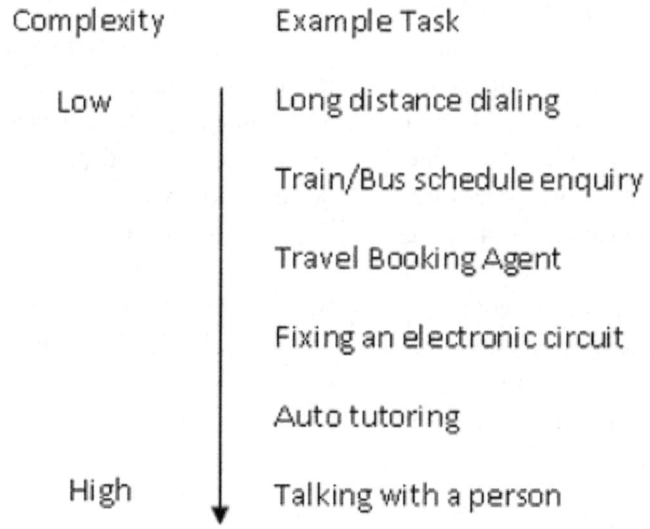

Complexity	Example Task
Low	Long distance dialing
	Train/Bus schedule enquiry
	Travel Booking Agent
	Fixing an electronic circuit
	Auto tutoring
High	Talking with a person

dividual modality as well as to integrate various modalities and to bring emotions in conversation to achieve truly human-like interaction. More recently, particularly the techniques used in the COMPANIONS project (http://www.companions-project.org) has led a group of researchers to believe that emotion and politeness is more dependent on the language than its originator realized, and the best place to locate them may be speech and language phenomenon instead of facial expressions and gestures (Wilks et al., 2011). This has made speech and language processing issues the core concern of dialogue systems. Important challenges in the development of multimodal interface have been discussed in Griol et al. (2011).

In this chapter we restrict the discussion mainly to spoken dialogue systems. Multi-modal interfaces involving other modalities are not within the scope of this chapter. The objective is to provide an overview of issues related to spoken dialogue systems, discuss major components and identify key research challenges in them. Although examples have been cited extensively from the existing dialogue systems, but offering an extensive review of a wide range of existing spoken dialogue system is not our concern. Rest of the chapter is organized as follows:

Section 2 highlights specific characteristics of dialogue. These properties offer new challenges to the development of dialogue systems. Dialogue systems can be categorized in a number of ways. Section 3 discusses some of these categorizations. Dialogue systems use information from a variety of knowledge sources in order to generate dialogue response. These knowledge sources and their roles have been discussed in Section 4, along with a general architecture and major components of a spoken dialogue system for human computer interaction. Some of the existing methods for evaluating a dialogue system are discussed in Section 5. Finally, summary and future research directions appear in Section 6.

2. ISSUES IN DIALOGUE

A spoken dialogue system has to mimic human-human dialogue. In human-human dialogue the two persons engaged in communication wait for their turn to speak. A person, S1, speaks something, then S2, then S1, and so on. This behavior is termed as turn-taking behavior. In general, there can be overlap in utterances. However, the amount of overlap in human-human dialogue is usually very small. This means that the two persons involved in a dialogue are able to figure out whose turn is next and when to take turn to speak. Sacks et al. (1974) argued that the turn-taking behavior is governed by a set of rules that apply at transition relevance places (TRPs) (see Jurafsky & Martin, 2009 for details). A dialogue system has to detect these boundaries in order to have effective communication. Identifying utterance boundary is quite difficult as a single utterance may continue over several turns or a single turn may include several utterances. As in the following example, the system utterance extends to three turns:

S: *Let me check the schedule of your talk.*
U: *hmm*
S: *It is on Monday 26th April at 11:30 am.*
U: *At 11:30 pm?*
S: *And the duration of the talk is 1:30 hours.*

Spoken dialogue systems also require a method to interpret silence. The silence usually occurs when the next speaker has a negative or dispreferred response and plays a significant role in deciding who will speak next and what to speak. Consider the following dialogue.

S: *You ordered for a medium size pizza, a coke and a Mexican wrap. Is it ok?*
U: *Yes*
S: *The bill amount is Rs. 710. Should I confirm the order?*

U: *... [silence]*
S: *Would you like to revise your order?*
U: *Yes*

Here, the silence is being interpreted as a negative response and hence the system takes turn and asks for possibility of revision in the order.

Turn-taking behavior of a dialogue gives rise to several implementational issues in a dialogue system, such as detecting the end of a turn, anticipating the next speaker, handling silence, etc. Cues in this task come from all levels of dialogue: acoustics, prosody, syntax, semantics, lexicon, discourse structure and pragmatics.

Another issue in a dialogue is the constant need of establishing a common ground. Grounding refers to the set of things that are believed by both the speakers. It consists of building a representation of the other's prior knowledge, purpose, and beliefs. The dialogue requires that hearer must acknowledge or ground the speaker's utterance. In human-human communication the hearer uses some continuer words, like mm, hmm, well, ok, etc., to acknowledge the previous utterance. These words indicate that the utterance is reaching to the hearer and hence the current speaker can continue talking. There is a number of other ways in which the hearer can acknowledge, including visual indicators such as nodding, facial expressions or gestures indicating continued attention. However, discussions of visual cues are beyond the scope of this chapter. Inability to apply usual grounding procedures is one of the problems faced by users during human–system interaction. Bubb-Lewis and Scerbo (2002) pointed out that processes like grounding which make human communication so efficient are absent from human-computer communication in its current form.

In human- human dialogue scenario, quite often, utterances are interpreted to mean something different from its literal meaning as in the utterance sequences given:

U: *I have to go to Prague in July.*
S: *What day you want to travel?*
U: *I have to attend a conference from July 28 to August 2.*

Instead of directly communicating the date of travel the user is mentioning the conference dates. What she intends to communicate is that the travel dates should be such that she is able to reach the conference venue to attend the conference on 28th July. U1 is actually communicating more information than is present in the utterance. The dialogue system has to infer the intended meaning.

These properties of conversation play an important role in the spoken dialogue system (SDS) and developing a dialogue system requires addressing issues related to human-human dialogue. The spoken dialogue systems make use of a variety of knowledge sources to handle these issues which will be discussed in Section 4. Table 1 shows example of dialogue systems.

3. TYPES OF DIALOGUE SYSTEMS

Early dialogue systems were used in restricted domains such as telephone-based railway transportation system (Bennacef et al., 1996), weather information system (JUPITER) (Zue et al., 2000) and travel planning (DARAPA communicator) (Walker et al., 2000). More recently dialogue systems have been developed for domains like tutoring, entertainment, and communication (Minker et al., 2004; Lemon et al., 2006; Weng et al., 2006). The EU project TALK (http://www.talk-project.org) focused on the development of new technologies for adaptive dialogue systems using speech, graphics, or a combination of the two in the car (Lee et al., 2010). Chatbots, e.g., ALICE (http://www.alicebot.org), have been developed for domains like entertainment and education.

Table 1. Example dialogue systems

	RAILTEL (Bennacef et al., 1996)	SUNDIAL	TRAINS (Allen et al., 1991)	Circuit-Fix-It Shop	HWYD COMPANION (Pulman et al., 2010)
Objective	Spoken dialogue for train time-table inquiries	To provide information about Flight reservation and enquiries and train enquiries over telephone line	Co-operate to plan railroad transportations.	To fix an electric circuit.	to have conversations about the daily life events mainly related to work and to provide emotional support to users
Task-based or Service-based	Informational	Informational	Task-oriented	Task-oriented	Conversational system
Initiative	System Initiative	System initiative	Mixed-initiative	Mixed-initiative	Mixed-initiative
Dialogue Management	Frame-based	Dialogue grammar and speech act (FSA-based)	Plan-based	Agent-based	Agent-based

Spoken dialogue system development has undergone several generations. We can classify them along a number of dimensions. Based on the functionality provided by dialogue applications, SDSs have been categorized into informational (or simple service-oriented), transactional and problem solving (also known as task oriented) dialogue systems (Wang et al., 2008; Acomb et al., 2007). This categorization corresponds to the three generations through which SDSs evolved. We extend this classification by adding a fourth generation corresponding to non-task oriented dialogue which are conversational entertainment systems with no specific target task. Based on the degree to which the system takes an active role in the conversation the dialogue systems can be categorized as system-initiative or directed-dialogue transactions, mixed-initiative and hybrid (Glass, 1999). On the basis of dialogue management approach used, SDSs can be categorized as Finite State Acceptor (FSA) based system, frame-based system and plan-based system.

3.1. Categorization based on Functionality

Informational Spoken Dialogue Systems

Early-first generation- SDSs were informational in nature. These systems simply retrieve and provide users with the information they require, such as train schedule, flight status, weather information. These are the simplest type of dialogue systems and are characterized by strict directed dialogue interaction. RAILTEL (Bennacef et al., 1996) dialogue system is a service oriented dialogue system which gives information over telephone about railway transportation. This functional categorization refers to chronological developments of SDSs and not to increasing technological difficulties (Wang et al., 2008). Some of the problem in informational SDSs still remains the most challenging topics in spoken dialogue research.

Transactional Spoken Dialogue Systems

Transactional SDSs carry out transactions automatically on behalf of users; e.g., transfer funds between bank accounts, book air flight tickets. Unlike first generation informational SDSs which use strict directed dialogue interaction, these systems allow natural language modality and a longer interaction sequence ranging up to 10 turns. In informational and transactional dialogue systems interaction follows a pre-determined simple script and can be specified using a form filling paradigm (Acomb et al., 2007).

Problem Solving Dialogue Systems (or Task Oriented Dialogue Systems)

The objective of problem solving dialogue systems is to interact with its users to create a plan to carry out a task or solve a problem, e.g., to design a kitchen or fix an electronic circuit. These systems have been deployed to facilitate interaction with callers in speech-based service support systems. TRAINS (Allen et al., 1991) and Circuit-Fix-It Shop (Smith et al., 1995) are examples of dialogue systems that guide its users in accomplishing certain task. The TRAINS system interacts with users to plan routes for transportation whereas Circuit-fix-It Shop assists users in fixing radio circuits in toys over telephone lines. The callers can interact with these systems in order to diagnose problems they are experiencing with a device or to use a service.

Non-Task Oriented Dialogue Systems

Non-task oriented dialogue systems are general conversational systems, also known as chatterbots, designed to chat with the users. These systems assume that its users do not have a specific task to perform. The dialogue systems developed under COMPANION project, e.g., HWYD (Pullman et al., 2010), fall under this category.

3.2. Categorization based on Degree of Initiative

System Initiative Dialogue

In a system initiative dialogue, the computer takes complete control of the interaction and asks well directed questions to get information required for the intended task. Usually, the response to be given by user is too restrictive, may be limited to a few words, e.g., name of city, time, date of travel. Due to restricted amount of linguistic processing these types of systems usually experience error free operation. However, the disadvantage is that it leads to unnatural user's input and longer interaction sequence to get the required information to complete a complex task.

Mixed Initiative Dialogue

In a mixed initiative dialogue approach, system jointly negotiates with the user to extract information needed for the particular tasks. Both the user and the system are capable of controlling the dialogue sequence. Example of mixed initiative dialogue systems include the intelligent tutoring system Auto tutor (Graesser et al., 2005), TRAINS system (Allen et al., 1991) and JUPITER (Zue et al., 2000). These systems offer more flexibility to users, handle complex linguistic inputs but suffer from higher error rate.

Hybrid Dialogue

An alternative approach is hybrid which combines the benefits of both. In hybrid dialogue both the user and the system can control interaction sequence. Whenever, the system experiences difficulty in understanding the user it backs off to a more restrictive system initiative dialogue mode (Rudnicky et al., 1999).

3.3. Categorization based on Dialogue Management Approach

FSA-Based Systems

Finite state machine defines a finite state automaton that contains all possible dialogue states. It requires explicit enumeration of all possible dialogue states and transitions between them. The individual nodes correspond to the specification of certain information or the setting of constraints (corresponding to questions that the DM asks the user) and transitions correspond to action to be taken based on user's response. The control resides with the system. The system produces prompts at each dialogue state, recognizes or rejects specific words or phrases in response to the prompt and produces actions based on the recognized response. The response may consist of the data extracted from a database or it may be concerned with the dialogue management, such as prompting the user to confirm or rephrase the recognized sentence. This approach usually limits user response to single piece of semantic information and verifies the input at each state of the dialogue before proceeding ahead. This approach was used in most of the early dialogue systems. Examples include systems developed under SUNDIAL (Speech UNderstanding and DIALogue) project (Peckham 1991), RAILTEL (Bennacef et al., 1996), ARISE(Automatic Railway Information Systems in Europe) (Minker et al., 1999), spoken dialogue system for monitoring the health status of chronic patients (Giorgino et al., 2005). Here is an example of a dialogue in which the system verifies the user's input at each state of the dialogue:

S: *Hello, How I can help you?*
U: *I want to book an air ticket.*
S: *Do you want to book an air ticket?*
U: *Yes*
S: *What is your destination?*
U: *Toronto*

S: *Was it Toronto?*
U: *Yes*
S: *What day you want to travel?*
U: *Thursday*
S: *Was it Tuesday?*
U: *No*
S: *What day you want to travel?*
U: *Thursday*

Except for the simple tasks, in which it is possible to get relevant information by prompting the user, this approach has a number of limitations. Users often find it convenient to provide more than a single piece of information at a time in a single utterance, as in the following example:

S: *Which date you want to travel?*
U: *I want to leave on 22nd April and return on 26th April.*

FSA-based systems cannot handle this additional information.

Frame-Based Systems

The frame-based systems provide an alternate and less rigid approach. Here the problem is represented as form filling. Instead of representing all possible dialogue states, the information that a dialogue system must obtain from the user is represented as a set of frames composed of slots. For example, a simple railway reservation system might have frames corresponding to train schedule, route information, fare practices, ticket cancellation, etc. Each frame consists of slots for various kinds of information the user might need to specify. Figure 2 shows a template with slots for source and destination stations, departure time, arrival time, fare, class, and whether one way or not. Some of the slots have pre-specified questions that the system asks the user to get the value of the slot, etc. In order to avoid user over-flooding with questions not all the slots have associated questions. The system is able to fill the slots whenever ever user provides a value for any of them.

The frame-based approach eliminates the need to specify information in a particular order and permits the user to supply more information than being asked. A particular system action is associated to a form that specifies all relevant items of information for it. The dialogue manager monitors the form for completion, sets elements as these are specified by the user, identifies empty slots and uses them as trigger for questions to the user (Rudnicky et al., 1999). When all the required items in a form have been specified it takes the associated action. The flow of dialogue is decided by the context of the user's input and the information that the system has to get as in the following example:

S: *Where do you want to go?*
U: *I want to go to Dubai on Saturday.*
S: *Do you need a round trip ticket?*
U: *No*
S: *OK, Let me check for flights for Dubai on Saturday.*

As shown in the example, the system is able to accept the day information which was not requested. The system then checks if any additional information is required before searching in the database.

Another advantage of the frame-based dialogue systems is that they permit for topic switch. The frames in the application domain can be arranged in hierarchal fashion and the user can switch from one topic to another. The system is able to identify the appropriate slot and template to be filled by the input given by the user and then switch control to that template.

The frame-based system is essentially a production rule system. A rule fires when a set of conditions are met. The production rule can switch control based on the user's input and some dialogue history, such as, the last question that was asked (Jurafsky & Martin, 2001). This approach is suitable for informational and transactional SDSs only, where it is easy to get the attribute values of an entity that users are interested in (e.g., the date, and originating and destination cities of a flight). Both FSA and frame-based approach require that the task usually has a fixed goal which can be achieved by having the user specify information on successive turns in response to system's prompt. Using a filled out form the system can perform an action, such as information retrieval. While this capability may suffice for a number of useful applications, it fails to handle more complex communication, such as, communication between the system, the user and the application, in order to create a complex data object representing a plan for solving a problem.

Figure 2. Sample frame for railway enquiry system

Slot	Optional question
From_station	"From what city are you leaving?"
To_station	"Where are you going?"
Preferred_Dep_Time	"When would you like to leave?"
Preferred_Arr_time	"When do you want to arrive?"
Round trip	
Fare class	

Plan-Based Systems

Plan-based approaches take the view that humans plan their actions to achieve goals. The utterances are not just strings but they are actions performing speech acts. The listener has to infer speaker's underlying plan and respond accordingly. A dialogue system, operating under this assumption, needs to infer goals and to construct and activate plans. Elements in plan-based dialogue are plans, actions, mental states and mechanisms for recognizing a specific plan and for reasoning about the speaker's beliefs, intentions, and actions (Flycht-Eriksson, 1999). Plan-based approaches make use of logical inference. The domain knowledge and system behavior are programmed as a set of logical rules and axioms. The system interacts with the user to gather facts, and generates more facts as interaction continues. The relationships among goals and actions that comprise a plan can be represented as a directed graph. Nodes in the graph represent goals, productions, actions and effects and arcs represent relationship between nodes. TRAINS (Allen et al., 1991) takes a plan-based approach. It plans responses to user utterances. Plan-based approaches offer more flexible interaction than FSA-based and frame-based approaches. However, they have been criticized for high computational complexity and lack of sound theoretical background. The process of plan recognition and planning is computationally intensive. Plans are abstract notion and it is difficult to characterize concepts like plans, goals, etc.

4. DIALOGUE SYSTEM ARCHITECTURE

The architecture of existing dialogue systems vary significantly, ranging from interactive voice response system, augmented with isolated word recognition (e.g., "Answer Yes or No") to full-fledged natural language based dialogue systems, supporting unconstrained input from the user, e.g., "How was your day?" as in COMPANION (Pulman et al., 2010). Two commonly used architectures are pipeline and hub. In pipeline architecture various components are connected in tandem, whereas in the hub architecture a central controller module is used through which the communication among various modules takes place. As an HCI system has to deal with unconstrained input, simple pipeline architecture, in which components are connected in tandem, will not work. Instead, it will contain a number of feedback paths particularly due to context sensitiveness or ambiguities arising out of inaccurate speech recognizer or other subsystems. Regardless of the specific architecture, there are some basic components that remain common in all sorts of dialogue systems. These are speech recognition, natural language understanding, dialogue management, natural language generation and speech synthesis. All of them may not be present in each dialogue system and some systems may have additional components. The simplest kind of dialogue system may have only three components: an Automatic Speech Recognizer (ASR) to convert speech into text, some form of dialogue manager to control interaction and a text and/or speech generator for conveying information to the user in textual and/or voice form. More complex systems may have additionally a discourse processing component. Another variation among dialogue systems is in terms of use of knowledge sources. It is not possible to cover all architectures, so we here discuss a general architecture in which knowledge sources are represented as a separate component. Dialogue systems may use a specific implementation involving all, some or none of these knowledge sources, as in case of informational dialogue systems where knowledge is integrated with the control component. The decoupling of knowledge from control has additional benefit of achieving generalization across applications.

4.1. Generalized Architecture

Figure 3 shows a generalized architecture of a spoken dialogue system for human computer interaction. It consists of five functional components, namely Automatic Speech Recognition (ASR), Natural Language Understanding (NLU), Dialogue Management (DM), Natural Language Generation (NLG) and Text to Speech Synthesis (TTS) together with a knowledge component. One important variation in this architecture is modeling knowledge as a separate component instead of integrating it with the control. We feel

decoupling knowledge from control is important from the point of view of achieving generality.

As shown in Figure 3, the ASR takes user utterances (speech signals) and converts it into textual representation. The NLU component interprets the text and creates a semantic representation of it. This analysis may involve complete or partial parsing of the sentence. The dialogue management is the central component. Its job is critical to success of interaction. It takes the semantic representation created by the NLU and decides what action to take? It makes use of long term (user model, domain model, task model) and

Figure 3. Spoken dialogue system architecture for human computer interaction

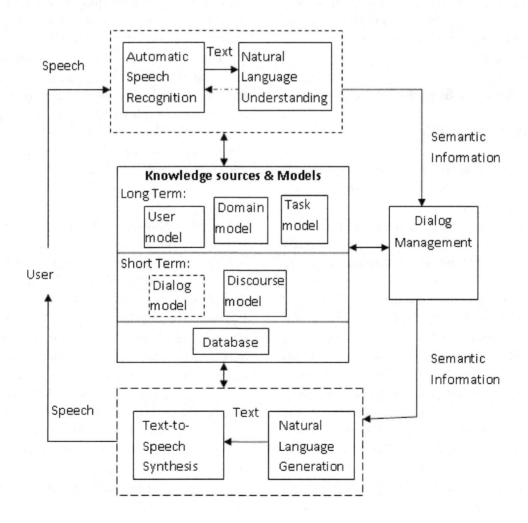

short term knowledge (discourse history) to decide the response of the system. Short term knowledge lasts only during a session, e.g., history of previous utterances, topic of current conversation, system task, etc. Long term knowledge remains valid across sessions, e.g., domain knowledge, user information like age, gender, preferences, and knowledge about the task dialogue system aims at. The dialogue management component decides if all the information related to a task has been gathered or not and accordingly it creates a representation of response of the system to be generated. The NLG component takes this representation and generates natural language sentences corresponding to it which are fed to TTS. The TTS generates spoken form of the text. The implementation of these components varies significantly from system to system. We now discuss these components and the research issues involved in them in a bit detail.

4.2. Dialogue System Components

Speech Recognition

Speech recognizer receives acoustic signal (utterances) and transforms it into recognized sentence. It uses an acoustic model trained from a speech database, a language model that determines the possible sequences of words and a dictionary containing all the possible words that can be recognized. Several approaches have been developed for ASR including expert systems, artificial neural networks (ANNs) and stochastic approaches. State of the art speech recognition systems, e.g., the SPHINX system, uses statistical methods (Hidden Markov Model and bi gram, tri-gram language models) to estimate the most probable sequence of words for a given audio stream and gives encouraging results. A review of statistical approaches can be found in Aggarwal and Dave (2011). Open source toolkits are now available, which can be used to build a speech recognizer easily and quickly. A discussion on some of

these tools can be found in Griol et al. (2011). However, high error rate is still common in a dialogue system where user is allowed to speak freely. For example, 'Let's Go!' bus information system (Raux et al., 2005) has a word error rate of 64%, while the ITSPOKE tutorial system has a word error rate of 34.3% (Litman et al., 2006). The present research challenge is to develop robust speech recognizers that degrade gracefully despite some changes in the input conditions and mispronunciation. Robust speech recognition requires the development of algorithms that are insensitive to irrelevant sources of variabilities and sensitive to variabilities of interest.

Major research issues involved in speech recognition include modeling speech rate, modeling speaker differences, handling microphone phenomenon such as echos, noise, non-linearity and spectral differences due to change in microphone or microphone position. The use of human speech perception model helps in overcoming some of the non-linguistic sources of variability. Various context-based methods have been investigated to reduce speech recognition error (Co´zar et al., 2006; Lieberman et al., 2005; Sarma & Palmer, 2004). These works demonstrate that contextual cues can be exploited to enhance speech recognition using context from the domain information (Huang et al., 2009). In a multi-modal environment visual cues can be used in speech recognition. A discussion on how visual information may help in ASR applications can be found in (Farooq & Datta, 2011; Potamianos et al., 2004). Yet another problem in speech recognition is mistaking background noise for speech sound or recognizing words that have entirely different prosodic structures from the correct words. In order to improve performance of spoken language system an understanding of how people use prosodic information and how it can be used in speech recognition and generation is required. Solving these problems also require research effort to develop robust confidence measures to avoid unreasonable response. Dialogue systems need to support turn-taking behavior. For this, one needs to detect pauses. The detection is complicated by the fact that sometimes pauses within a turn may be longer than between turns. The auditory features like falling pitch at the end of a sentence and lengthening of a final syllable has been used to solve this problem. A natural response must reflect the emotional state of the user. The ASR component is also required to detect emotional states which the dialogue manager can use in response generation. Previous works on emotional classification using speech signal (Vogt at al., 2008) demonstrate that this can be done with good accuracy.

Natural Language Understanding

The language understanding component is responsible for preparing a meaning representation of the recognized strings to be used by dialogue management component. Early dialogue systems lack NLU component. Today's dialogue systems aim to engage the user in a human like conversation for a longer duration. In order to make it possible, NLU, mixed initiative handling, and dynamic response generation are required (Suendermann, 2009). The NLU on a large scale was first introduced in dialogue systems 14 years back (Gorin et al., 1997). It involves syntactic and semantic analysis. The syntactic analysis identifies syntactic structure of the recognized string, whereas the semantic analysis determines the meaning of the constituents. These two phases may exist independently in order to achieve generalization across domains or may be combined for efficiency reasons. The principle of compositional semantics is used to build the semantic representation of sentences by combining semantics of individual syntactic constituents. An alternative approach is to build a semantic representation directly from the recognized string.

The spontaneous speech is accompanied with a number of well-known problems, e.g., unknown or mispronounced words, filled pauses (hmm, oh, ah, etc.), repetition of words or phrases, redundant words or phrases, ellipsis, ungrammatical construction, etc. These problems make it difficult to analyze naturally occurring utterances. A speech recognizer can only handle unknown words problem. Consequently, the output from speech recognizer system often doesn't have the form of a grammatically well-formed string. It consists of sentence fragments, after thought, self- correction, slip of tongue and ungrammatical combinations (McTear, 2002) which make it difficult to parse using traditional CFG formalism. Even in written form, sentences (e.g., in news papers) often lead to a large number of possible parses due to various types of ambiguities. Hence, a full linguistic analysis of sentences is not generally used in dialogue systems. A more flexible approach is to use keyword and phrase spotting which do not attempt to fully analyze an utterance but tries to identify important keywords and phrases. It is relatively easy to design domain specific patterns to extract these keywords. For example, given the utterance "Suggest me a flight from Delhi to Prague." The pattern matching techniques could extract values for the following parameters: the event (suggest), the flight (?), source (Delhi), destination (Prague). This approach has been successfully deployed in commercial applications. However, this approach can be used only in simple domains where it is easy to spot keywords and phrases. In systems with complex interaction this may not be effective. An alternative approach is to take a hybrid approach which first attempts to perform a complete syntax analysis of an utterance; if it fails to find a complete parse then it backs off to robust parsing.

A feature-based grammar can also be used to describe the syntactic properties of words, like gender, number, person, etc. In order to describe the syntactic structure of sentences, usually a set of hand-crafted phrase structure rules are used. These rules determine how the words can be combined. The features of words are used in the combination process. For example, the word 'train' can be combined with 'departs' but not with 'depart' because the agreement features of 'train' and 'depart' are not compatible. The feature-based grammar is often subsumed under the term unification grammar. One major advantage of using the unification grammar is that they permit a declarative encoding of grammatical knowledge, which is independent of any specific processing algorithm. Another advantage is that a similar formalism can be used for semantic representation, with the effect that the simultaneous use of syntactic and semantic constraints improves efficiency of linguistic processing. Each syntactic rule has a corresponding semantic rule and the analysis will simultaneously create a semantic representation of the sentence.

Dialogue Management

The dialogue manager serves as the conversational control mechanism, whose primary operation is to come up with a coherent response given a user utterance. The dialogue management component also deals with the conversational intelligence aspect, e.g., turn-taking management, construction of structured dialogue history, use of discourse markers, requesting for confirmation, etc. It controls the flow of the dialogue by deciding what questions to ask and when to ask. Finite state machines (FSMs), form-filling, plan-based, and agent-based approaches (Section 2) have been used for dialogue management. Several new methods for dialogue management have been proposed, mainly inspired from the success of data-driven approaches in ASR and NLP. Examples include Markovian-based (Levin et al., 2000) and example-based approaches (Lee et al., 2009). Particularly, the use of Partially Observable Markov Decision Process (POMDP) for dialogue modeling (Williams & Young 2007) is gaining interest due to its ability to handle uncertainty. The example-based approach automatically generates response using a corpus containing annotated utterances. As there may be multiple candidate utterances in the corpus, the best utterance is obtained using the utterance

similarity. Recently, combinations of multiple strategies have been used to take advantages of positive points of each strategy (Chu et al., 2007).

Natural Language Generation

Natural language generation has been extensively investigated for generating system response, e.g., in systems that generate reports or summaries (Rambow et al., 2001). The high-level communicative goals in these systems are of the type "make the hearer/reader believe a given set of facts". The dialogue system has similar communicative goals in the final phase when it has obtained information that matches the user's requirements. In the initial phase, dialogue systems have to achieve entirely different high level communicative goals, such as, getting specific information from the user and confirming it either explicitly or implicitly. Confirmation is required because ASR systems are not perfect. These communicative goals can be represented as an unordered list, all of which need to be achieved in the next turn of the system.

While a good NLG component is important for dialogue systems, it is less investigated in this context. Most of the common dialogue applications fall in restricted domain where it is possible to list all desired output strings. Generating utterances in these systems does not require most of the complexities of a full-fledge natural language generation system and can be carried out using only string manipulation. That's why many practical dialogue systems do not use a separate NLG component. In these systems dialogue manager component is responsible for generating the text to be sent to text to speech system. However, the output generated by these systems lacks flexibility and context sensitivity (Theune, 2003) and may not be acceptable in domains requiring complex interaction sequence, e.g., tutoring. If a separate NLG component is used, then DM only decides high level communicative goals to be achieved and sends it to the NLG component. Several general purpose rule-based generation systems have been developed (Elhadad & Robin, 1996) which can be used for generating response. The disadvantage of these systems is the need of hand crafted rules which requires specialized knowledge of the linguistic representations. A much simpler approach to generation is to use the templates. For example, a template might transform *inform ("arrival = 14")* into "The arrival time is 2 pm." However, the time and effort is needed to create templates as the quality of output depends on the set of templates. Even in relatively simple domains the number of templates can become quite large. Rambow et al. (2001) proposed a machine learning approach to avoid the need of hand crafting. The major hindrance in using machine learning approaches is the lack of good corpus of naturally occurring dialogue between human and machine. Samples from human and human communication cannot be used for this purpose because of the obvious differences in communicative goals, e.g., need of explicit or implicit confirmation, using a corpus created by interaction sequences between an existing dialogue system and human users will also mimic its performance and will not help in improving it.

Speech Synthesis

The speech synthesis involves generating waveform for spoken output using the text generated by NLG component. In the simplest form, the output may consist of only prerecorded speech or some templates consisting of prerecorded speech and retrieved data in speech form, e.g., your account balance is <Rs. seventy thousand four hundred> in which the important of the message is prerecorded and the amount in angle bracket has to be either synthesized or played from recorded samples. These techniques for speech synthesis can be used only in cases where the interaction with a system is static in nature and the vocabulary is limited. Such an approach cannot be used in systems involving free form interaction, where the text is not fixed and cannot be predetermined. Hence, the

parametric synthesis is required. It generates the speech signals by mapping the text to phonemes, and then the phonemes to acoustics. As shown in Figure 4, the text is first converted into phonemes for the utterance using either the letter to sound rules or a punctuation dictionary or a combination of both. The traditional approach is to use manually created context sensitive rewrite rules of the form $xY/z \rightarrow w$, which rewrites the letter Y appearing in the context of the letter x and z as phoneme w. However, hand crafting these rules is time consuming, requires an expert depth of knowledge, and is language specific. The use of machine learning techniques is gaining increased attention to learn these rules automatically from a corpus (van den Bosch & Daelemans, 1993). The symbol for "prosody" of the message is also determined using rules and dictionary. This includes the way the voice pitch, intensity, and duration vary for the phoneme sequence. These variations depend on the context. The resulting sequence of discrete symbols is then transformed into continuously varying acoustic parameters.

The main aspects of text to speech synthesis which are relevant to spoken dialogue system include text normalization, morphological analysis, syntactic tagging and parsing, modeling of continuous speech effect such as co-articulation effect, and prosody generation. The text normalization is concerned with the interpretation of abbreviations and other standard forms, such as date, time, currencies and their conversion into a form that can be spoken. Morphological analysis is required to derive pronunciations of morphological variants of words using pronunciation of root forms. This alleviates the need for storing pronunciations of all the morphological variants of a word resulting in significant reduction in the size of pronunciation dictionary. The dictionary will store only the root form of a word, e.g., play, and the pronunciation of its variants, e.g., playing, played, etc. can be derived using the morphological rules. Tagging helps in cases where pronunciation of word varies with its parts of speech.

Figure 4. Parametric synthesis

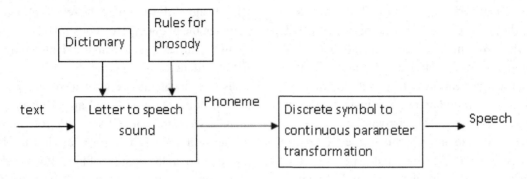

For example, the word record as a verb is pronounced stressing the second part whereas as the noun it gets stress on 're'. In a natural speech certain words get reduced articulation and the sound gets deleted or reduced across word boundaries. These effects need to be modeled in order to generate natural sounding speech. Prosody generation deals with 'pitch', loudness, tempo and rhythm (McTear, 2002). For good quality output adequate prosodic rendering is required to capture the mood and the attitude.

4.3. Knowledge Sources and Models

Dialogue systems require linguistic, task specific, domain specific, contextual and common sense knowledge to resolve linguistic and non-linguistic issues. A variety of knowledge sources and models, both long term and short term, have been developed and used in dialogue systems to provide this knowledge. Different dialogue systems require different knowledge sources. For example, a system that is supposed to suggest a plan to solve a task requires knowledge about task whereas a simple service-based dialogue system do not. Similarly, a system for time-table information for local transport system requires much sophisticated spatial/geographic knowledge than a system that provides information about flight schedule. The system designer has to make a choice regarding how to model them and must be aware of the trade-offs involved. Commonly used knowledge sources and models that have found extensive applications in dialogue systems include dialogue model, discourse model, task model, domain model and user model. Not all dialogue systems make use of all the models, and those that use them differ in their number, nomenclature and scope. Sometimes dialogue history, also known as dialogue memory, and discourse model is treated as synonyms. Some systems view dialogue model as part of the user model. Simple systems usually rely on implicit representation of knowledge, in which knowledge is integrated within the processing modules, whereas complex, problem solving systems make use of multiple interacting knowledge sources and models.

Dialogue Model

Dialogue model consists of a description of general information about dialogue construction, e.g., who will take initiative (system or user), whether to use explicit or implicit confirmation, etc. This knowledge is used to control the dialogue. Representation of this knowledge varies from system to system, plan-based and grammar-based modeling being the most commonly used approaches. SUNDIAL uses a dialogue grammar and speech act to model dialogue whereas the TRAINS system follows a plan-based approach.

Dialogue History

Dialogue history contains a description of results of past utterances which is essentially discourse information. This model is used for dialogue control and resolving linguistic issues like contextual interpretation of utterances, dialogue repair, anaphora resolution, handling of ellipses, etc. As pointed out earlier in this section, dialogue systems use a variety of ways to model this information leading to many different names, e.g., dialogue memory, discourse model, discourse history, history table, context model, etc. The representation may vary from simple, sequential or a complex, hierarchical representation as in SUNDIAL (Peckham, 1991). SUNDIAL uses a tree to describe structure of the dialogue. It uses a contextual model to represent the sequence of beliefs inferred from user's utterances and makes use of status flags to reflect changes in the contextual model. For example, the value 'repeat' means no new contribution has been made.

Task Model

Task model has been used in dialogue systems for two different types of tasks: user task and system task. User task corresponds to nonlinguistic real-world task, whereas system task corresponds to system's communicative and other tasks, e.g., database access. Both kinds of models have been used in dialogue models, though not very common. System model is usually integrated within the dialogue model. Some dialogue systems opt for explicit system model for efficiency and flexibility reasons. It is relatively easy to carry out changes or add a new task in an explicit system model. This model is used by the dialogue manager in deciding its response. For example, in a dialogue system for information retrieval, this model helps in determining if all the required parameters have been specified or not, and to decide what question to ask the user to get missing parameters.

In order to decide what to do next in a given context, dialogue systems require some information about status of the user's task or subtask. One way to provide this knowledge is to make use of an explicit model of the user task. The knowledge about the task is often integrated in the dialogue model and used to interpret utterances and to decide how to proceed ahead. However, few systems (e.g., SUNDIAL and TRAINS system) use an explicit user task model.

Domain Model

The domain model contains a description of domain specific and real-world knowledge. This knowledge is required to reason about the domain, to interpret and understand user utterances and to relate it with domain specific concepts. For example, mapping domain or real world concepts to a specific value for database retrieval such as 3 O'clock afternoon to "3 pm". Domain model helps in understanding user utterances and thereby making the interaction more natural and meaningful.

User Model

User model represents user's goals, intentions, preferences, expertise and beliefs. This information helps in making the dialogue more cooperative. The use of a user model is not common in existing dialogue systems. TRAINS dialogue system uses an elaborate user model.

5. EVALUATION OF DIALOGUE SYSTEM

The dialogue systems have been developed for a wide variety of domains, for many tasks and with varying and sometimes contradictory objectives. This makes it difficult to develop a metrics that generalizes across systems. Nevertheless, we need evaluation methods to assess performance of dialogue systems and to compare the performance of competing systems. The performance can be measured in terms of the extent to which the system achieves its task, the cost or time of achieving the goal, the quality of interaction, user satisfaction, the ability to recover from speech recognition or language understanding errors, etc. There is no agreed upon standard for evaluation of dialogue systems among research communities and a number of metrics have been proposed, both subjective (Larsen, 2003) and objective, to measure these aspects of SDSs. The subjective evaluation consists of judging some parameters by reference to users' opinions. The objective evaluation does not require human subjects and hence reduces personal biases. Ideally, we would like to have quantitative, objective evaluation. However, it is not easy to quantify various human factors and objective evaluation may not exist for all of them.

PARADISE (PARAdigm for DIalogue System Evaluation) is one of the most widely proposed methodologies for evaluating dialogue systems (Walker et al., 97). The performance measure used in PARADISE was a function of weighted combination of task–based success measures and behavior-based cost measures. The framework also provides a methodology to determine weights. It considers the user satisfaction as most important parameter for evaluation and calculates it by combining objective aspects like task success, efficiency, quality, and dialogue cost measures. Usability issues have been discussed in (Dybkjær & Bernsen, 2000). Users are asked to rate on various aspects of their interaction with the system and on a five-point multiple choice scale. The response values are summed to get the user satisfaction measure for each dialogue. The PARADISE framework achieves generalization by making it possible to compare dialogue systems in different domain tasks. Though, this generalization is limited. One problem with PARADISE is that it correlates many factors that are important for interface design but have little to do with dialogue strategy (James et al., 2000).

Eckert et al. (1998) proposed an automatic evaluation framework for spoken dialogue system. Their framework uses a simulated user and performs evaluation based on its interaction with the system. They argued that an automatic evaluation is unbiased, accurate and inexpensive. However, the approach requires a good simulation model which is the major source of difficulty in this approach. Other reported works that attempt to evaluate SDSs using the user simulation techniques include (Schatzmann et al., 2005; Ai & Weng, 2008). Griol et al. (2008) proposed a corpus-based approach to develop and evaluate a spoken dialogue system.

A three tier evaluation methodology for dialogue systems is proposed in Stibler and Denny (2009). Each layer in this method focuses on different aspects. The top layer measures user satisfaction, middle layer focuses on successful task completion in a timely manner, while the lower layer measures the effectiveness of individual system components.

Dybala et al. (2010) proposed a subjective method for evaluating non-task oriented conversational system. They focused on aspects such as human-likeness, humour, likeability or users' emotions towards computers. However, their evaluation was limited to the text-based systems only.

6. SUMMARY AND FUTURE DIRECTIONS

This chapter gives an overview of spoken dialogue systems. We present a generalized architecture for HCI and discuss its components. We outlined key research areas and briefly reviewed existing evaluation methods for spoken dialogue systems. The architecture presented in this chapter considers knowledge an inherent part of the dialogue systems and models it as a separate component. This separation leads to generalization. A spoken dialogue system requires robust speech recognition methods, efficient and robust parsing methods, efficient turn-taking management, emotion handling in speech for good quality dialogues, etc. Regardless of how much efficient an individual component is, a dialogue system cannot work properly unless it is accompanied with a good dialogue control component. Integrating component technologies to produce a robust and acceptable system is one of the major challenges for developers of future spoken dialogue system.

A number of evaluation measures have been proposed and utilized for spoken dialogue system. However, they are far from standard and useful only for task-oriented dialogues. Research efforts are required in the future to develop standard evaluation measures. The non-task-oriented dialogue system poses entirely different challenges in evaluation. Some of the issues, such as sufficiency of task coverage, informativeness, etc., become irrelevant for them. The research community has to respond to these challenges by proposing evaluation methods for non-task-oriented dialogues. Lack of domain independent framework is another area that requires attention of research community. Producing human like natural response requires integration of various modalities, like gestures, gaze, emotional state of the user, etc. Multi-modal human computer interaction is the future technology. A lot of research efforts are continued in this direction. Research prototypes are already in place. However, a lot need still to be done in this direction and this is likely to remain an important research area in future.

REFERENCES

Acomb, K., Bloom, J., Dayanidhi, K., Hunter, P., Krogh, P., Levin, E., & Pieraccini, R. (2007, April 26). Technical support dialog systems: Issues, problems, and solutions. In *Proceedings of the HLT Workshop on Bridging the Gap: Academic and Industrial Research in Dialog Technology*, Rochester, NY.

Aggarwal, R. K., & Dave, M. (2011). *Towards the recent trends of acoustic models for speech recognition system*. Hershey, PA: IGI Global.

Allen, J., Schubert, L., Ferguson, G., Heeman, P., Hwang, C. H., & Kato, T. (1991). The TRAINS project a case study in building a conversational planning agent. *Journal of Experimental & Theoretical Artificial Intelligence*, *7*, 7–48. doi:10.1080/09528139508953799

Bennacef, S., Devillers, L., Rosset, S., & Lamel, L. (1996). Dialog in the RAILTEL telephone-based system. In *Proceedings of the International Conference on Spoken Language Processing*.

Bubb-Lewis, C., & Scerbo, M. W. (2002). The effects of communication modes on performance and discourse organization with an adaptive interface. *Applied Ergonomics*, *33*, 15–26. doi:10.1016/S0003-6870(01)00046-1

Chu, S.-W., O'Neill, I., & Hanna, P. (2007). Using multiple strategies to manage spoken dialogue. In *Proceedings of the International Conference Interspeech* (pp. 158-161).

Co'zar, R. L., & Callejas, Z. (2006). Two-level speech recognition to enhance the performance of spoken dialogue systems. *Knowledge-Based Systems*, *19*, 153–163. doi:10.1016/j.knosys.2005.11.004

Dybala, P., Ptaszynski, M., Rzepka, R., & Araki, K. (2010). Evaluating subjective aspects of HCI on an example of a non-task oriented conversational system. *International Journal of Artificial Intelligence Tools*, *20*(10), 1–39.

Dybkjær, L., & Bernsen, N. O. (2000). Usability issues in spoken language dialogue systems. *Natural Language Engineering*, *6*, 243–272. doi:10.1017/S1351324900002461

Eckert, W., Levin, E., & Pieraccini, R. (1998). *Automatic evaluation of spoken dialogue systems* (Tech. Rep. No. TR98.9.1). Florham Park, NJ: ATT Labs Research.

Elhadadm, M., & Robin, J. (1996). *An overview of SURGE: A reusable comprehensive syntactic realization component* (Tech. Rep. No. 96–03). Beer Sheva, Israel: Ben Gurion University.

Farooq, O., & Datta, S. (2011). *Enhancing robustness in speech recognition using visual information*. Hershey, PA: IGI Global.

Flycht-Eriksson, A. (1999). A survey of knowledge sources in dialogue systems. In *Proceedings of the IJCAI Workshop on Knowledge and Reasoning in Practical Dialogue Systems* (p. 48).

Giorgino, T., Azzini, I., Rognoni, C. S. Q., Stefanelli, M., Falavigna, D., & Gretter, R. (2005). Automated spoken dialog system for hypertensive patient home management. *International Journal of Medical Informatics, 74*(2-4). doi:10.1016/j.ijmedinf.2004.04.026

Glass, J. R. (1999). Challenges for spoken dialogue system. In *Proceedings of the IEEE Workshop on Automatic Speech Recognition and Understanding*.

Gorin, A., Giuseppe, L., Jeremy, R., & Wright, H. (1997). How may I help you? *Speech Communication, 23*(1-2), 113–127. doi:10.1016/S0167-6393(97)00040-X

Graesser, A. C., Chipman, P., Hayens, B. C., & Olney, A. (2005). Auto Tutor: An intelligent tutoring system with mixed-initiative dialog. *IEEE Transactions on Education, 48*(4), 612–619. doi:10.1109/TE.2005.856149

Griol, D., Callejas, Z., López-Cózar, R., Espejo, G., Ábalos, N., & Molina, J. M. (2011). On the development of adaptive and user-centred interactive multimodal. In Tiwary, U. S., & Siddiqui, T. J. (Eds.), *Speech, image and language processing for human computer interaction*. Hershey, PA: IGI Global.

Griol, D., Hurtado, L. F., Segarra, E., & Sanchis, E. (2008). A statistical approach to spoken dialog systems design and evaluation. *Speech Communication, 50*, 666–682. doi:10.1016/j.specom.2008.04.001

Hua, A., & Weng, F. (2008). User simulation as testing for spoken dialog systems. In *Proceedings of the 9th SIGdial Workshop on Discourse and Dialogue*.

Hung, V., Gonzalez, A., & DeMara, R. (2009). Towards a context-based dialog management layer for expert systems. In *Proceedings of the International Conference on Information, Process, and Knowledge Management* (pp. 60-65).

James, F., Rayner, M., & Hockey, B. A. (2000). Accuracy, coverage, and speed: What do they mean to users? In *Proceedings of the CHI Workshop on Natural-Language Interaction*.

Jurafsky, D., & Martin, J. H. (2001). *Speech and language processing: An introduction to natural language processing, computational linguistics and speech recognition*. Upper Saddle River, NJ: Prentice Hall.

Larsen, L. B. (2003). Assessment of spoken dialogue system usability – what are we really measuring. In *Proceedings of the Eurospeech Conference*, Geneva, Switzerland.

Lee, C., Jung, S., Kim, K., Lee, D., & Lee, G. G. (2010). Recent approaches to dialog management for spoken dialog systems. *Journal of Computing Science and Engineering, 4*(1), 1–22.

Lee, C., Jung, S., Seokhwan, K., & Lee, G. G. (2009). Example-based dialog modeling for practical multi-domain dialog system. *Speech Communication, 51*, 466–484. doi:10.1016/j.specom.2009.01.008

Lemon, O., Liu, X., Shapiro, D., & Tollander, C. (2006). Hierarchical reinforcement learning of dialogue policies in a development environment for dialogue systems: REALLDUDE. In *Proceedings of the 10th SemDial Workshop on the Semantics and Pragmatics of Dialogue: Demonstration Systems*.

Levin, E., Pieraccini, R., & Eckert, E. (2000). A stochastic model of human-machine interaction for learning dialog strategies. *IEEE Transactions on Speech and Audio Processing, 8*(1), 11–23. doi:10.1109/89.817450

Lieberman, H., Faaborg, A., Daher, W., & Espinosa, J. (2005, January 9-12). How to wreck a nice beach you sing calm incense. In *Proceedings of the International Conference on Intelligent User Interfaces*, San Diego, CA.

Litman, D. J., Ros, C. P., Forbes-Riley, K., Van-Lehn, K., Bhembe, D., & Silliman, S. (2006). Spoken versus typed human and computer dialogue tutoring. *International Journal of Artificial Intelligence in Education, 16*, 145–170.

McTear, M. F. (2002). Spoken dialog technology: Enabling the conversational user interface. *ACM Computing Surveys, 34*(1), 90–169. doi:10.1145/505282.505285

Minker, W. (1999). Stochastically-based semantic analysis for ARISE - Automatic railway information systems for Europe. *Grammars, 2*(2), 127–147. doi:10.1023/A:1009943728288

Minker, W., Haiber, U., Heisterkaml, P., & Scheible, S. (2004). SENECA spoken language dialogue system. *Speech Communication, 43*, 89–102. doi:10.1016/j.specom.2004.01.005

Peckham, J. (1991, February 14-27). Speech understanding and dialogue over the telephone: an overview of the ESPRIT SUNDIAL project. In *Proceedings of the DARPA Workshop on Speech and Language*, Pacific Gove, CA.

Potamianos, G., Neti, C., Luettin, J., & Matthews, I. (2004). Audio–visual automatic speech recognition: an overview. In Vatikiotis-Bateson, E., & Perrier, P. (Eds.), *Issues in visual and audio–visual speech processing*. Cambridge, MA: MIT Press.

Pulman, S. G., Boye, J., Cavazza, M., Smith, C., & Santos de la Camara, R. (2010). How was your day? In *Proceedings of the Workshop on Companionable Dialogue Systems* (pp. 37-42).

Rambow, O., Bangalore, S., & Walker, M. (2001). Natural language generation in dialog systems. In *Proceedings of the First International Conference on Human Language Technology Research*, San Diego, CA.

Raux, A., Langner, B., Bohus, D., Black, A., & Eskenazi, M. (2005). Let's go public! Taking a spoken dialog system to the real world. In *Proceedings of the Interspeech/Eurospeech Conference*, Lisbon, Portugal.

Rudnicky, A., Thayer, E., Constantinides, P., Tchou, C., Shern, R., & Lenzo, K. ….Oh, A. (1999). Creating natural dialogs in the Carnegie Mellon communicator system. In *Proceedings of the Conference Eurospeech* (Vol. 4, pp. 1531-1534).

Sacks, H., Schegloff, E. A., & Jefferson, G. (1974). A simplest systematics for the organization of turn-taking for conversation. *Language, 50*(4), 697–735. doi:10.2307/412243

Samuel, M., Gómez-García-Bermejo, J., & Zalama, E. (2010). A realistic, virtual head for human–computer interaction. *Interacting with Computers, 22*, 176–192. doi:10.1016/j.intcom.2009.12.002

Sarma, A., & Palmer, D. (2004). Context-based speech recognition error detection and correction. In *Proceedings of the Human Language Technology Conference North American Chapter of the Association for Computational Linguistics Annual Meeting: Short Papers* (pp. 85-88).

Schatzmann, J., Georgila, K., & Young, S. (2005). Quantitative evaluation of user simulation techniques for spoken dialogue systems. In *Proceedings of the 6th SIGdial Workshop on Discourse and Dialogue*.

Smith, R. W., Hipp, D. R., & Biermann, A. W. (1995). An architecture for voice dialog systems based on Prolog-style theorem-proving. *Computational Linguistics*, *21*, 281–320.

Stibler, K., & Denny, J. (2001). A three-tiered evaluation approach for interactive spoken dialogue systems. In *Proceedings of the First International Conference on Human Language Technology Research* (pp. 1-5).

Suendermann, D., Evanini, K., Liscombe, J., Hunter, P., Dayanidhi, K., & Pieraccini, R. (2009). From rule-based to statistical grammar: Continuous improvement of large scale spoken dialog system. In *Proceedings of the IEEE International Conference on Acoustics, Speech and Signal Processing* (pp. 4713-4716).

Theune, M. (2003). *Natural language generation for dialog: system survey*. Twente, The Netherlands: University of Twente.

Traum, D., & Rickel, J. (2002, July 15-19). Embodied agents for multi-party dialogue in immersive virtual worlds. In *Proceedings of the First international Joint Conference on Autonomous Agents and Multiagent Systems: Part 2*, Bologna, Italy (pp. 766-773).

van den Bosch, A., & Daelemans, W. (1993). Data-oriented methods for grapheme-to-phoneme conversion. In *Proceedings of the Sixth Conference on European Chapter of the Association for Computational Linguistics* (pp. 45-53).

Vogt, T., André, E., & Johannes, W. (2008). Automatic recognition of emotions from speech: A review of the literature and recommendations for practical realisation. In Peter, C., & Beale, R. (Eds.), *Affect and emotion in human-computer interaction* (pp. 75–91). Berlin, Germany: Springer-Verlag. doi:10.1007/978-3-540-85099-1_7

Walker, M., Langkilde, I., Wright, J., Gorin, A., & Litman, D. (2000). Learning to predict problematic situations in a spoken dialogue system: experiments with How May I Help You? In *Proceedings of the North American Chapter of the Association for Computational Linguistics* (pp. 210-217).

Walker, M., Litman, D., Kamm, C., & Abella, A. (1997). PARADISE: a general framework for evaluating spoken dialog agents. In *Proceedings of the 35th Annual Meeting of the Association of Computational Linguistics* (pp. 271-280).

Wang, Y.-Y., Yu, D., Ju, Y.-C., & Acero, A. (2008). An introduction to voice search. *IEEE Signal Processing Magazine*, *25*(3), 29–38.

Weng, F., Varges, S., Raghunathan, B., Ratiu, F., Pon-Barry, H., & Lathrop, B. …Prieto, R. (2006). CHAT: A conversational helper for automotive tasks. In *Proceedings of the International Conference on Spoken Language Processing* (pp. 1061-1064).

Wilks, Y., Catizone, R., Worgan, S., & Turunen, M. (2011). Some background on dialogue management and conversational speech for dialogue systems. *Computer Speech & Language*, *25*(2), 128–139. doi:10.1016/j.csl.2010.03.001

Williams, J. D., & Young, S. (2007). Partially observable Markov decision processes for spoken dialog systems. *Computer Speech & Language*, *21*, 393–422. doi:10.1016/j.csl.2006.06.008

Zue, V., Seneff, S., Glass, J., Polifroni, J., Pao, C., Hazen, T., & Hetherington, L. (2000). Jupiter: a telephone-based conversatioinal interface for weather information. *IEEE Transactions on Speech and Audio Processing*, *8*, 85–96. doi:10.1109/89.817460

Chapter 8
Enhancing Robustness in Speech Recognition using Visual Information

Omar Farooq
Aligarh Muslim University, India

Sekharjit Datta
Loughborough University, UK

ABSTRACT

The area of speech recognition has been thoroughly researched during the past fifty years; however, robustness is still an important challenge to overcome. It has been established that there exists a correlation between speech produced and lip motion which is helpful in the adverse background conditions to improve the recognition performance. This chapter presents main components used in audio-visual speech recognition systems. Results of a prototype experiment conducted on audio-visual corpora for Hindi speech have been reported of simple phoneme recognition task. The chapter also addresses some of the issues related to visual feature extraction and the integration of audio-visual and finally present future research directions.

1. INTRODUCTION

Speech is a complex signal which has variability not only from one speaker to another, but also a lot of variations within the same speaker. The variations of speech signal within a speaker may be attributed to factors like age, stress, emotional state or biological reasons (such as sore throat, flu, etc.) and is also called intra-speaker variability. Pronunciation of same word differs among people from different geographical backgrounds due to variations in accents. The recent advances in the

signal processing algorithms and availability of fast computational machines have enabled practical implementation of speaker independent automatic speech recognition (ASR) systems feasible.

In an ASR system, attempts are made to imitate human speech recognition which has tremendous recognition capabilities; however, the knowledge of exact mechanism of human speech recognition is still limited. Due to this reason, the current ASR can perform equally well as humans in the case of quite background conditions, but their performance degrade severely when there is a

DOI: 10.4018/978-1-4666-0954-9.ch008

mismatch between training and test conditions. In practical scenario, these mismatch conditions are frequently encountered because of the difference in background conditions in which the speech is to be recognized. Due to this reason realizing an ASR system which matches human speech recognition capabilities under adverse conditions has been a big challenging task.

To achieve robustness in ASR various techniques have been proposed, which could be grouped into the following four categories:

- Robust feature extraction
- Compensation techniques
- Noise filtering during pre-processing
- Audio visual speech recognition

The first approach is based on the extraction of the features that are inherently resistant to noise. The techniques used under this category are RASTA (RelAtiveSpecTrA) processing (Hermansky & Morgan, 1994), one-sided auto-correlation LPC (You & Wang, 1999) and auditory model processing of speech (Kim, Lee, & Kil, 1999). The assumption made here is that the noise is additive and white with Gaussian distribution. The second approach is based on the compensation model, which tries to recover the original speech from the corrupted speech in the feature parameter domain or at the pattern-matching stage. Methods using the second approach are cepstral normalization (Acero & Stern, 1990), probabilistic optimum filtering (Kim & Un, 1996; Neumeyer & Weintraub, 1994) and parallel model combination (Gales & Young, 1996).

Spectral enhancement techniques like spectral subtraction and Wiener filtering have been used resulting in improved recognition performance. To reduce the effect of noise present the speech signal, robust amplitude modulation, frequency modulation (AM-FM) features in combination with MFCCs have shown considerable error rate reduction for mismatched noisy conditions (Dimitriadis, Maragos, & Potamianos, 2005). Specialized order statistics filters which work on the sub-band log-energies also have been implemented for noise reduction (Ramírez, Segura, Benítez, Torre, & Rubio, 2005). Denoising process based on soft and hard thresholding of wavelet coefficients has also been proposed (Donoho & Johnston, 1995; Mallat, 1998).

Although the above techniques improves the recognition performance, but the improvement is limited to low background noise levels only. It is well documented that humans use visual information from speaker's lip region for speech recognitions particularly in presence of noise or by people with hearing impairment (Chibelushi, Deravi, & Mason, 2002). A strong correlation has also been reported between face and speech acoustics (Grant & Braida, 1991; Williams & Katsaggelos, 2002).

The idea of using visual information along with the audio for ASR applications started only recently due to the fact that higher computational and storage was required for video processing. Lips are one of the most important regions of interest which is of particular interest. The movement of lips conveys dynamic information complimentary to the information obtained from the acoustic speech. Since this visual information from the lips is not affected by the poor acoustic conditions; hence, its use is logical along with the audio information. Many experimental results have shown that modelling visual dynamics along with the speech, can improve speech and speaker recognition performance not only in noisy environment (in the SNR range of 15dB to -10dB) but also in noise-free environments (Chaudhari, Ramaswamy, Potamianos, & Neti, 2003; Potamianos, Neti, Gravier, Garg, & Senior, 2003).

An audio visual speech recognition system (AVASR) uses both audio as well as visual information and integrates them to achieve recognition. The choice and reliable extraction of visual features strongly affect the performance of AVASR systems. In 1984, Petajan was first to propose shape-based features such as height and width of the mouth for visual speech recognition. Later on different feature extraction techniques combined with different classifiers such as Neural Network (Yuhas, Goldstein, & Sejnowski, 1989), time-delayed Neural Network (TDNN) (Stork, Wolff, & Levine, 1992; Bregler & Omohundro, 1995), fuzzy logics (Silsbee & Bovik, 1996) Boltzmann zippers and Hidden Markov Model. Exploiting bimodal information form a speaker is also useful in speaker recognition applications. The dynamic visual information reduces the chances of misclassification (impostor attacks) as compared to audio-only or static-image-based (face recognition) speaker recognition systems.

Although, Hindi is spoken by about 366 million people as their first language and is the world and is the second most spoken language, but there have been little research in the area of speech recognition systems for Hindi (Shrotriya, Verma, Gupta, & Agrawal, 1996; Samudravijaya, 2001; Gupta, 2006). Most of the reported work use the standard techniques used for English speech recognition (Samudravijaya, 2001; Gupta, 2006) and report word accuracy in the range of 90%-95%. In Hindi, there are 16 stop consonants, while English has only six which increase the level of difficulty in recognition.

Due to lack of English knowledge for a large population of Indians, it is highly imperative to develop a spoken native language interface for easier information access. The chapter presents some results of an ongoing research in the area of audio visual Hindi speech recognition. Few of the preliminary results obtained from the new database developed are reported here in this chapter. Section 2 gives an introduction to ASR system with an overview of different blocks use in it. The issues of pre-processing, feature extraction and its integration for AVASR is discussed in Section 3. Different feature extraction techniques for audio as well as video signal have been elaborated in this section. Section 4 presents the details of Hindi audio visual database and the results obtained. Finally the summary of the chapter is given in Section 5.

2. AUDIO SPEECH RECOGNITION SYSTEM

Speech recognition is a class of pattern recognition problems where different sound patterns are to be identified. These sound patterns may correspond to phonemes, syllables or word durations, but most commonly phonemes are used for continuous speech recognition task. The phoneme are the basic acoustically distinguishably unit or the basic sound of speech that conveys linguistic information. The number of phonemes depends on the languages e.g., in American English, there are approximately 42 phonemes (Deller, Hansen, & Proakis, 1993), while in the case of Hindi the phonemes as about 60. Features derived from these phonemes are used to develop and train models that are used for recognition. Once a phoneme is recognized, they are concatenated to form a valid word which is then verified by the dictionary. A simplified block diagram of a speech recognition system is shown in Figures 1 and 2. Similar to phonemes, for visual speech, the basic visually distinguishably unit are called viseme. For the case of Hindi speech the visemes can be broadly classified into 14 categories. Table 1 shows the mapping of frequently used Hindi phonemes to visemes. The subsequent section gives a brief description of the various blocks in an ASR system.

2.1. Signal Processing Front-End

There is a lot of variation in the front-end processing for a speech recognition system. The analog speech is first sampled and quantized to convert it into a digital form to enable subsequent processing by a computer. The sampling frequency influences the decision about the design of the filter bank, if the frequency domain features are to be used for recognition. The output of the ADC is pre-emphasized using a pre-emphasis filter, which is motivated by the human speech production model.

For the voiced speech, there is an overall of -6 dB/octave decay (-12 dB/octave due to excitation source and +6 dB/octave due to the radiation compensation) in speech radiated from lips, as frequency increases (Picone, 1993). The spectrum of speech is flattened by a pre-emphasis filter of the form $1-az^{-1}$. Commonly the value of 'a' chosen is 0.97 for pre-emphasis application. Since it is impossible to correctly locate the phoneme start and end point due to the co-articulation effects in continuous speech, therefore, a constant duration of the speech signal is used. To extract the short-time features of a speech signal, it is broken up into short segments called frames. The duration of each frame varies from 5ms to 20ms. To reduce the boundary effect at the edge of each frame, a smoothing window is applied to each frame. The

window duration can be in the range of 10ms to 30ms. The most commonly used window function is the Hamming function given by:

$$w[n] = 0.54 - 0.46 \cos\left(\frac{2\pi n}{L}\right) \qquad (1)$$

where L is the length of the window function.

2.2. Feature Extraction

Feature extraction in general is a process by which some important distinct information of a pattern is extracted which can differentiate it from other patterns. Good features have small spread within a given pattern class, while between different pattern classes the spread is large. Here a spread can be simply calculated by evaluating the distance between the feature vectors. Since much of the speech information is usually conveyed in the spectrum, it becomes a logical choice for feature selection. Thus, the compact representation of the speech spectrum during a frame duration can be used as feature vector. The most popular speech feature currently in use for speech and speaker recognition is the cepstrum and its derivatives. The details of the feature extraction process are discussed in Feature Extraction Section 3.4.

Figure 1. Block diagram of Speech recognition system

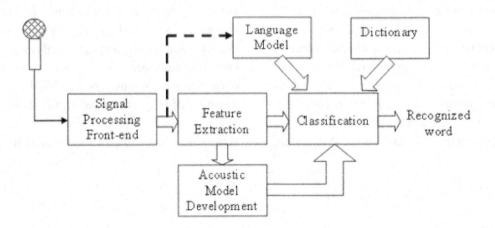

2.3. Acoustic and Language Model

For a small vocabulary speech recognition system the acoustic and the language model can be avoided and the feature vector can be directly given to a classifier. However, when the dictionary size increases, confusion between the classes increases due to the co-articulation effect, which causes an overall reduction in the recognition performance.

For developing the acoustic model Hidden Markov's Models (HMMs) are commonly used. These models are trained for individual phoneme feature vector derived from training speech data (Young, Kershaw, Odell, Ollason, Valtchev, & Woodland, 2011). A Markov Chain (MC) of N unique states is given as: $S_1, S_2, ...,S_N$. At regular discrete time intervals, the system can change from one state to another with a certain probability. At any given time, the current state of the system is denoted by q_n, for $n = 1, 2, ...,T$. For a first-order system, the state transition only depends on the current state, while for a second-order system it depends on the current and previous states (Rabiner, 1989). For a first-order system, the probability of going from the current state i to the next state j, called the transition probability, is:

$$a_{ij} = P\left(q_n = S_j \mid q_{n-1} = S_i\right), \quad \text{for} \quad 1 \le i \text{ and } j \le N. \tag{2}$$

The state transition probabilities are always positive $a_{ij} \ge 0$ and the sum of probabilities of the path leaving a state is unity, i.e.

Table 1. Groups of phonemes that are mapped to the same viseme category

Viseme Class	Phonemes
1	ɖ
2	eː, ɛː
3	ɪ, iː, ə, aː, j
4	uː, ʊ
5	ɔː
6	g, gʱ, ɦ, k̪, kʰ, ʈ
7	r
8	l, d̪, ɳ, n, t̪, ɭ, t̪ʰ
9	s, z
10	tʃ, tʃʰ, ʃ, dʒ, ʒ
11	t̪ʰ, ɖ, ɖʱ
12	f, ʋ
13	m, b, p, pʰ, bʱ
14	oː

$$\sum_{j=1}^{N} a_{ij} = 1. \tag{3}$$

A complete description of an HMM requires the specification of N (the number of states) and M (the number of models), and the specification of the probability measures A, B and π. A common compact notation for an HMM is:

$$\lambda = \left(A, B, \pi\right) \tag{4}$$

where A is a matrix of transition probabilities, B is matrix of observable probabilities π and is an initial state vector consisting of initial probabilities.

Figure 2. Block diagram of an ASR front-end

To perform recognition using HMM first these parameters are to be optimized. To achieve this training is carried out on the training speech dataset. The dataset should contain the transcription of the speech and a dictionary to convert the words into phonetic transcription. The training is done to adjust the model parameters to maximize the likelihood *P(y/M)* by taking a model (Baum, Petrei, Soules & Weiss, 1970; Liporace, 1982; Moon, 1996) $M = \{S, \pi, A, B, y\}$ and training observation $y = y_1^T$, to compute a new model M'. If the likelihood has increased such that

$$P\left(y/M'\right) - P\left(y/M\right) \geq \varepsilon \qquad (5)$$

where ε is a given tolerance, then re-estimate the model with $M = M'$.

Based on the training data a language model evaluates the occurrence probability of a word or sequence of N words for a given utterance. This probabilistic language model is used to predict the N word sequence is known as an N-gram model. Since the statistics of the model are developed during the training phase it is therefore known as static model. In the case of dynamic or adaptive language model the word probability depends on the input text observed until that time. This helps in improving the performance of the system in places where a large language source has sub-language structures within itself (Picone, Ebel, & Deshmukh, 1995; Young, 1996).

2.4. Classification

Once the features are extracted, they are given to the HMM to estimate the value of the model parameters explained in previous section. These model parameters are optimized using the training data from individual phonemes and is called as an acoustic model. There should be a sufficient number of examples for each phoneme in order to have proper training (parameter estimation) of the HMM. For testing the recognizer, the observation vector is passed through these models and the one which gives the maximum probability is considered to be recognized. The acoustic model may be based on the single phoneme (monophone) or on the combination of three phonemes (triphone) model. The triphone model has an advantage that it gives higher recognition performance since it takes into consideration the effect of co-articulation. However, it requires a very large dataset to build and train all the possible triphone combinations, which may not be practically possible.

The recognized word units are used to construct the whole sentence with the help of language models.

The brief description of the speech recognition systems shows that there are many steps involved in speech recognition process. An improvement in any one of these will result in an increase in recognition performance. Integration of visual information has been tried by different researchers at different level. They are tested on different databases, with different number of speakers and with different complexity level like, isolated words and digit recognition (Nefian, Liang, Pi, Xiaoxiang, Mao, & Murphy, 2002), and large vocabulary continuous speech (Neti et al., 2000). The following section gives an overview of audio-visual ASRs system design.

3 AVASR DESIGN

The block diagram of an audio visual speech recognition system is shown in Figure 3. Due to the bimodal nature of the AVASR system, a video camera is used to collect information from a speaker. The classification stage of an AVASR is usually based on the HMM model which is the same as of ASR shown in Figure 1. Apart from this, the pre-processing and the feature extraction/integration are carried out separately for both speech and video signals. The video camera samples the speech considering the audio bandwidth, which is at a much higher rate than required for speech recognition application. Hence the speech signal is usually down sampled to 16 kHz. The details of the front end processing of the speech signal have already been discussed in the previous section.

The design of video front-end is challenging task as video data contains information about speaker and background which has no relevance to the speech. The rate at which data is generated in video stream is higher than that of speech signal; this requires special processing of video stream to make it compatible to audio rate.

3.1. Visual Front End

The function of a video front end is to pre-process the video and make it suitable for feature extraction. Captured video is first of all converted into frames, which are usually at the rate of 25 or 30 frames per second. Since the features are usually extracted from the individual frames, therefore, the feature vector generated will be at the rate of 25 or 30 per second. This rate is not compatible with the audio feature vector rate which is about 100 per second. In order to synchronize the two feature vectors, the video frames are interpolated to 100 frames per second which will result into same feature vector rate as the audio. The front end also tries to reduce the effect of variations due to lighting conditions, distance from the camera and orientation prior to feature extraction. Audio and visual front-end processing is performed in parallel on the two streams and feature vectors are extracted. The integration information extracted from the audio and video stream results into different fusion schemes discussed in the later section.

3.2. Face Detection and Mouth Tracking

For audio-visual speech recognition facial information plays an important part. The first step in extracting visual information is the detection of face. In AVASR, the prime concern is the extraction of robust features; face detection is generally

taken as a trivial task. Most of the corpora used for AVASR are usually face centered and variations in orientation and lighting conditions are limited. For face detection, a template matching method with sequential application of the support vectors (Romdhani, Torr, Scholkopf, & Blake, 2001) can be used to determine the face boundary in the gray level image was used.

The algorithm can detect multiple faces, but sometimes it detects non-face objects as well which can be seen in Figure 4. This algorithm has been altered to serve the purpose of single face detection by selecting the largest dimension detected object as the desired face. The results obtained improves the face detection possibility except for some frames where either some part

Figure 3. Block diagram of an AVASR

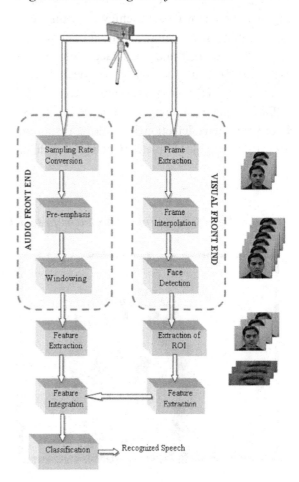

of the face is been clipped. Various other face detection algorithms (Nilsson, Nordberg, & Claesson, 2007; Yang & Waibel, 1996) have also been reported in literature.

3.3. Lip Localization

In AVASR systems, Region Of Interest (ROI) used for features extraction may include the entire face, lower half of face containing speakers' mouth or only the mouth region, the last one being most commonly used. Manual extraction of ROI from a single frame have been used, this ROI can be extended to other frames with the assumption that face has minimum movement during the speech. Another simple approach is based on developing corpora having the lips colored (Kaynak, Zhi, Cheok, Sengupta, Jian, & Chung, 2004) so that the lip region can be detected easily by using color segmentation. However, to achieve real-time and general purpose speech recognition system, it is essential to extract and track face without any pre-defined marking. Various techniques based on edge detection techniques (Zhang & Mersereau, 2000), template matching (Cristinacce & Cootes, 2006), symmetry detection (Reisfeld, & Yeshurun, 1992), deformable templates (Chandramohan, &

Silsbee, 1996) etc. have been used for ROI extraction. In Jian, Kaynak, Vheok, and Chung (2001) a lip detection algorithms based on normalized RGB pixel value is reported. The lip detection is further refined by using neighborhood based processing.

Lip Color and Intensity Mapping is a method proposed by Ooi, Jeon, Kim, Ko, and Han (2009), is based on a color mapping of the lips by integrating color and intensity information. A linear transformation of RGB components and Principal Component Analysis (PCA) is employed to estimate the optimum coefficients of transformation. From a set of training images, N pixels of lip and non-lip are sampled and its distribution is evaluated. Each pixel is regarded as a 3 dimensional vector $X_i=(R_i, G_i, B_i)$. The covariance matrix is obtained from the three dimensional vector and the associated eigenvectors and eigenvalues are determined from the covariance matrix. If $V=(V_1, V_2, V_3)$ is an eigenvector corresponding to the smallest eigenvalues where lip and non-lip pixels have the least overlapping then the color space, C is defined as:

$$C=0.2\times R-0.6\times G+0.3\times B \qquad 6a$$

Figure 4. Detected face (in red box) One false detection is also seen

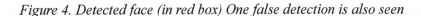

The new color space C is normalized as:

$$C_{norm} = \frac{\left(C - C_{min}\right)}{\left(C_{max} - C_{min}\right)} \qquad \text{6b}$$

After normalization, the lip region shows higher value than the non-lip region which is further enhanced by squaring. After the color transformation, this image may still show low contrast in the upper lip region, which can be resolved by using the intensity information (*I*). The upper lip region typically consists of lower intensity values, therefore, by combining the image (which is separable in the lower lip region) and intensity image (which has a stronger boundary in the upper lip region), an enhanced version of the lip color can be obtained as follows:

$$C_{map} = \alpha C_{squared} + \frac{\gamma}{I} \ \ where \ \alpha + \gamma = 1. \qquad 7$$

The result of lip color intensity mapping on an extracted frame from the database is shown in Figure 5a. The binarization is performed using a global threshold that is selected based on Otsu (Otsu, 1979) method. Empirically, $\alpha = 0.75$, $\gamma = 0.25$ are derived. Higher weight is given to the C squared image since it captures most of the lip shape except the upper part and corners of lips.

Pseudo-Hue Approach: Although it has been well established that skin hue is fairly consistent across different people, colors of lip and skin region usually overlap. This approach takes into account the Pseudo Hue ($\hat{H}$) value, of the lips defined as:

$$\hat{H} = \frac{R}{\left(R + G\right)}. \qquad 8$$

The concept of Pseudo Hue is useful because the difference between R and G for the lip pixels is greater than that for the skin pixels (Eveno, Caplier, & Coulon, 2001; Rohani, Alizadeh, Sobhanmanesh, & Boostani, 2008). It uses the pseudo hue plane to separate the lips from the skin. Indeed, $\hat{H}$ has higher values for the lips than for the skin and is robust for lips and skin pixels discrimination even when dealing with different subjects. However, the $\hat{H}$ of beard and shadow can be very similar as that of the lip. The reason lies in that the pseudo hue value may be very high when all components of RGB are low.

After the application of one of the transform, the image is binarized by using Otsu threshold method. Figures 5b and 5c shows the image obtained using lip detection using Pseudo-Hue Method and subsequent Otsu thresholding respectively. The result of lip color intensity mapping on an extracted frame from the database is shown in Figure 5a. By evaluating the black pixel intensity histogram both row-wise and column-wise the position ROI around the lips can be extracted. This operation is confined to the lower one-third of the face, since the lip is assumed to be located in the lower half of the face extracted.

3.4. Feature Extraction

Feature extraction is essentially a dimensionality reduction process in which information relevant for differentiating different patterns is retained. This also helps to reduce the computational time and resources at the classification stage. This compact set of feature is referred as feature vector and the performance of speech recognition system is greatly dependent on the extraction of features which are robust, stable, and ideally retain all the speech information contained in the original source (Picone, 1993). A good feature must satisfy the following properties:

- Maximize variance between different classes and at the same time minimize variance between members of same class.

Figure 5. (a) Lip detection using lip colour and intensity method. (b) Lip detection using pseudo-hue method. (c) Otsu thresholding on the image obtained in (b).

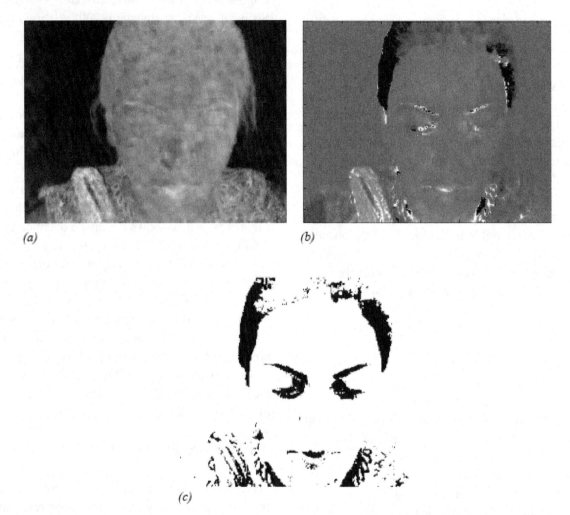

(a)

(b)

(c)

- Capture the characteristic properties from speech and video.
- Robust to change in environment, lighting conditions and background.
- Speaker independent.

In case of an AVASR, the feature extraction phase for audio and visual signals are carried out in parallel. Although many feature extraction techniques have been proposed for speech recognition, some of the commonly used are Mel Frequency Cepstral Coefficients (MFCCs), linear prediction coefficient derived cepstral coefficients (LPCCs), and wavelet based features (Farooq & Datta, 2004; Sarikaya & Hansen, 2000). Wavelet based features when compared to MFCC features have shown better recognition performance for phoneme recognition (Farooq et al., 2004), isolated digit recognition task and monophone recognition under stressed speech (Sarikaya et al., 2000). The use of MFCC features for Hindi speech may not be a good choice because of the presence of large number of stops, with some of them having duration as short as 5ms and cannot be considered stationary for 10ms frame duration.

3.4.1. Audio Feature Extraction

The common techniques used for speech feature extraction are LPC based approach, MFCC and wavelet based techniques.

Linear Predictive Analysis

Linear prediction technique is used to derive the filter coefficients (corresponding to the vocal tract) by minimizing the mean square error between the input and the estimated sample. It assumes an all pole model for speech production of order P as shown in Equation (9).

$$X(z) = G(z)\frac{1}{A(z)} = G(z)\left(\frac{1}{1 + a_1 z^{-1} + a_2 z^{-2} + \dots + a_p z^{-P}}\right)$$

(9)

where $G(z)$ is the glottal excitation and $\frac{1}{A(z)}$ transfer function of the synthesis filter. Normally 12 coefficients are sufficient to predict the speech. These coefficients are extracted using the auto-correlation method or the covariance method.

After linear predictive analysis cepstral coefficients can be extracted or further filtering can be applied to calculate the power in each band to be used as features. Perceptual weighting has also been applied after the linear predictive analysis to shape the spectrum similar to that of the human ear response.

The cepstral coefficients reduce the word error rate in speech recognition systems because it compresses the magnitude spectrum, and reduces correlation between coefficients. Compressing the magnitude spectrum reduces the dynamic range making it easier to represent with fewer coefficients. Linear predictive cepstral coefficients (LPCC) and Mel-frequency cepstral coefficients (MFCC) are two important variant of cepstral coefficients.

Mel Frequency Cepstral Coefficient

An ASR tries to emulate the human auditory system which follows the Mel scale. In order to extract features from the speech signal a bank of filters is used to decompose the signal. For a signal of bandwidth 8 kHz a bank of 24-filters with Mel spacing is used. Mel filters used are triangular and they are equally spaced along the Mel-scale (almost linear below 1000 Hz and logarithmically increases thereafter) as shown in Figure 6. The Mel scale is defined by Equation 10. The energy in all these bands is calculated and a logarithmic compression is applied. The Discrete Cosine Transform (DCT) of these compressed energies is then taken and the first 13 coefficients are used as features.

$$f_{mel} = 2595 \log_{10}\left(1 + \frac{f_{lin}}{700}\right).$$

(10)

The MFCC features derived are not very robust to additive noise and give the spectral information of the signal. In order to include the temporal information of the speech signal in the extracted features, delta and delta-delta coefficients are used. This is calculated by taking the time derivative of the features, which is insensitive to a constant bias. This has the disadvantage of having only the transition information and hence it has to be used along with the MFCC features for recognition.

Wavelet Based Features

In recent years a number of features extraction approaches based on Wavelet Transform and Wavelet Packets have been proposed (Sarikaya & Hansen, 2000; Long & Datta, 1998; Farooq & Datta, 2004). The wavelet based features used were similar to that of MFCC features except for

Figure 6. Mel filter bank used for filtering

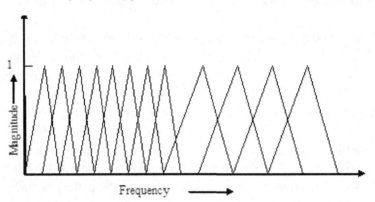

the filter banks used. However, the advantage of having better temporal resolution provided by the wavelet transform was not exploited in those features.

The Discrete Wavelet Transform (DWT) has been suggested (Long et al., 1998; Fonseca, Guido, Scalassara, Maciel, & Pereira, 2007) for feature extraction applications in speech processing. In their techniques high energy wavelet coefficients were used as features. These features are not very reliable because the DWT is shift variant and would require additional processing for shift adjustment. To overcome this problem, total energy of the wavelet coefficients in each frequency band was proposed as feature vector (Chang, Kwon, & Yang, 1998; Farooq & Datta, S. 2001). Another problem with the DWT is that it recursively decomposes the lower frequency band only which does not always have useful information for classification. The Wavelet Packet (WP) decomposition, which is a generalization of the DWT, can decompose the lower as well as higher frequency bands. This results into an over-complete set of basis which is not desirable for speech compression application, but does not create problem for speech recognition application. Admissible Wavelet Packet (AWP) is a flexible form of the WP, which can decompose either lower or higher frequency band.

Admissible wavelet packet based features were proposed in Farooq et al. (2001) which decom-

posed the signal into 24-bands that followed the Mel scale. These filters were implemented using the 'Daubechies 6' mother wavelet. The features were calculated by taking the first 13 coefficients of DCT which were applied on the logarithm of the energies obtained at the output of the filter bank. Although this scheme showed some limited improvement in phoneme recognition task, however, the ability of the wavelet transform was not exploited fully. The advantage of having better time resolution gained by using the AWP was lost by calculating the total energy in each band.

In Farooq, Datta, and Shrotriya (2010) AWP was used for Hindi phoneme recognition problem. In this AWP was applied to divide the signal into seven sub-bands and output of each sub-band is divided into three segments. Features were selected by applying DCT on the logarithm of sample energies in each segment. The results were found to be superior to MFCC based features under clean as well as noisy conditions.

3.4.2. Visual Features Extraction

Feature extraction from the visual domain is relatively new area of research for speech recognition application and extracting appropriate features still remains a challenge. Although speech production is a dynamic activity, but mostly visual features are extracted from the static frames (extracted during the pre-processing) of video to provide important information about the speech. These static features along with first and second derivative of the features extracted from the frames are used to include dynamic visual information. Different techniques of visual features used in AVASR can be classified into three main categories (Potamianos, Neti, Luettin, & Matthews, 2004). Low level or appearance based features, High level or shape based features and Hybrid features which is the combination of both the appearance and shape based features.

Low Level, Appearance or Pixel Based Features

Appearance based features consider mouth pixel values as the source of information. The ROI may be chosen as the mouth region, lower part (i.e., half of face containing lower jaw and chin) or the entire face. The shape of the ROI may be rectangular, square or a disc around mouth region.

Due to the high dimensionality of this ROI various transformations are performed to reduce this bulk of data to relatively low dimensions, suitable for use with the recognition system. Amongst the commonly used techniques are principal component analysis (Aleksic & Katsaggelos, 2004; Gurban & Thiran, 2009; Bregler & Konig, 1994), discrete cosine transform (DCT) (Nefian, Liang, Pi, Liu, & Murphy, 2002), Linear Discriminant Analysis (LDA) and Maximum Likelihood Linear Transformation (MLLT). The main idea in these transformations is to transform the ROI data in such a way as to retain the maximum speech information in a sufficiently low number of dimensions.

High Level or Shape Based Features

In this approach, the shape of speaker lips and other parts of face are assumed to contain speech related information. Under this category, lips or face contour based features are used for speech recognitions. One of such approach use the ge-

ometry of mouth or lips i.e., length, width, area, perimeter of inner and outer lips or a combination of these (Heckmann, Berthommier, & Kroschel 2001). In another approach, a model for lip or face contour has been used (Cootes, Taylor, & Edward, 1998). These are statistical models whose parameters model the shape of lips or face. Active shape models (Cootes et al., 1998) use deformable templates that iteratively adjust itself on to an object in an image.

Snakes (Jang, 2007), which track edges in image sequence is another such approaches. In Cristinacce et al. (2006) a shape constrained search for face detection and then using the nearest neighbour approach for adjusting the templates using training data have been used. These features are inherently of low dimensionality and are unaffected by the lighting condition and orientation. However they are difficult to be extracted robustly and are computationally expensive.

Hybrid Features

To take the advantage of both appearance and shape based features a hybrid approach is also been proposed. Appearance based features can be extracted with more accuracy as they do not need sophisticated algorithms for extraction, but are sensitive to lighting conditions (such as shadows) and pose. Shape based features on the other hand are robust to lighting and orientation but are difficult to extract accurately. These techniques include the simple concatenation of the two types of features (Chan, 2001). The PCA projection of mouth pixels is combined with lip geometric features. Other examples of shape and appearance based features (Mok, Lau, Leung, Wang, & Yan, 2004) combine the ASM based features with PCA.

3.5. Audio Visual Integration

Integration of audio and video features for optimum recognition performance is an open area of research in audio-visual ASR system design.

There are different possibilities to integrate audio and visual information modalities. It could be integrated at features level, state level, word level or even combining the scores on a sentence level. AVASR design attempts to integrate the information from audio and visual modalities as near to human speech recognition system as possible.

The fusion of audio and visual features is a complex task and it has various unanswered questions. Although for audio, 13 MFCC based features are typically used, but for visual based features there are no standard features as yet. Further, the number of visual features may be dynamic in nature due to the variation in the background conditions and different weighting factors may be assigned while fusion. The fusion of audio and video streams of information can be categorized into three main approaches. This classification is based on when the integration of information takes place early, late or at intermediate level.

3.5.1. Early Integration or Data Fusion

This is simple fusion approach, where the information from both audio and visual modality is map onto a common space of lower dimension. Another variant in this category is concatenation of features extracted from the two modalities. Although concatenation is simple in use, it suffers from a number of limitations. One of the major problems in implementing this technique is that the dynamic range of audio and visual features is different. Further, the mapping from phoneme to viseme set is not one to one as shown in Table 1. The concatenated features in higher dimension may be mapped onto a lower dimension using transforms like PCA and ICA. Apart from being simple to implement data fusion, this technique uses a single classifier which reduces the overall computational complexity of the system.

3.5.2. Late Integration or Decision Fusion

In late integration, also known as the decision fusion, the decision of the two classifiers (based on audio and video) are fused (Stork & Hennecke; 1996, Verma, Faruquie, Neti, Basu, & Senior, 1999). This fusion of the two output decisions is an important step in this approach as it has to account for the orthogonality between the two channels and the channel reliability. It is possible that the reliability of the channels change with time e.g., under varying background conditions. Since the classifiers for audio and video channels are separate more weight may be assigned to video classifier output than audio before the fusion at the output level. Usually n-best hypothesis from audio and visual classifier outputs are selected to evaluate likelihoods based on the reliability weights to give likelihood score for final recognition. Although this technique requires two classifiers, but they are simpler as they operate at a lower dimension.

3.5.3. Intermediate Level Integration or Hybrid Fusion

The integration of visual information can also be carried out at the intermediate level. Here audio and visual modalities are integrated at level in between the two extremes. This integration gives a better control over the previous two techniques (Farooq & Datta, 2001) and exploits the individual advantages of both data and decision fusion. There are different possibilities at which integration could take place but the most common is the state level integration where the audio and visual likelihood at state level are combined. In general the integration strategies used are not as sharp and a number of variations of these categories have been used.

4. CASE STUDY: HINDI VISEME CLASSIFICATION

Classification of the stops is one of the most challenging tasks in speech classification due to its dynamic, variable context and speaker-dependent nature. The stop phonemes are produced by complex movements in the vocal tract. With the nasal cavity closed, a rapid closure or opening is affected at some points in the oral cavity. Behind the point of closure pressure is built which is suddenly released with release of closure in vocal tract.

In Hindi, there are 16 stops, while English has only six. The study of Hindi stop is important in order to understand its time and frequency domain characteristics and the improvement that can be achieved by using the visual features. This will enables us to identify distinguishing features to uniquely classify the Hindi stop. Two things required to uniquely identify the stop are the voicing during their closure intervals and the place of articulation. The place of articulation classification is an important task that must be solved in order to develop a module responsible for identifying stop. The task is difficult since the acoustic properties of these stop consonants change abruptly during the course of their production. Due to the abrupt nature of stop, traditional statistical methods do not classify them distinctly without the assistance of semantic information. More studies of the acoustic cues for the classification of stop are also needed for the knowledge based approach. But most of these studies are for English and other languages (i.e., two or three category languages). Hindi, an Indo-Aryan language, has four manner categories of stops; voiceless unaspirated, voiced unaspirated, voiceless aspirated and voiced aspirated at four places of articulation- bilabial, dental, post alveolar (retroflex stops), and velar (Ahmed & Agrawal, 1969). Phonemes with identical manner of articulation are difficult to distinguish based on acoustic information alone, can have different place of articulation, and hence, are easier to distinguish visually than acoustically. Various mappings between phonemes and visemes have been described in the literature. They are usually derived by human speech reading studies, but they can also be generated using statistical clustering techniques (Goldschen, Garcia, & Petajan, 1996). There is no general agreement about the exact grouping of phonemes into visemes; however, some clusters are well-defined.

4.1. Hindi Audio Visual Speech Database

There has been very little research work carried out on Hindi audio (Shrotriya et al., 1996; Samudravijaya, 2001; Gupta, 2006) or audio visual speech recognition system (Khanam, Mumtaz, Farooq, Datta, & Vyas, 2009). Primarily it was due to the non-availability of standard database in native Hindi language. Phonetically balanced Hindi sentences were constructed and an audio-visual recognition was carried out by choosing 17 subjects (9 male and 8 female in the age group of 20-30 years. During the recording the background conditions of all the speakers were kept almost the same and the recording room had no sound proofing. The speakers had considerably different speaking-speeds. The recording was performed using a digital camera, with a resolution of 640 x 480 pixels, frame rate of 30 fps and stereo-audio sampling frequency of 48 kHz.

4.2. Experimental Results

Pre-processing of audio and video signals was performed to extract the area of interest. The task of endpoint detection of stops in the audio signal was done manually by listening to the sentences. In the speech representation, these stops were characterized by a low-energy gap preceding a high-energy burst. The detection of the stops was done with the help of vowels properties that followed or preceded the stops. The events of interest (instances of /b/, /g/, /p/ and /k/) were then extracted from continuous speech.

Frames from the video were extracted using the detected endpoints obtained from the audio signal. The features were obtained by choosing a suitable region of interest (ROI) around the lips for viseme recognition. To obtain the ROI first the face detection and then the lip localization is carried out.

A new method to extract ROI by using the black pixel intensity histogram both row-wise and column-wise (Raihan, Khan, Farooq, Datta, & Vyas, 2010) was used. This operation was confined to the lower one-third of the face, an approximation that turns out to be satisfactory. Further, in order to determine the left and right limits of the lips coordinates, the minima of the two histograms were used. Figure 7 shows the lips end point detection using row-wise histogram.

A new features extraction technique for video features is used which is based on the two-dimensional Discrete Cosine Transform (DCT) on blocks of 8x8 pixels (Khanam et al., 2009). The DCT coefficients represent frequencies from starting from the lowest frequency to the highest in a zig-zag form shown in Figure 8. Since the information is mainly present in the lower frequencies, only the first fifteen coefficients selected in a zigzag fashion were taken as feature.

A 13-dimensional MFCC based features were extracted for the Hindi stops recognition task. The DCT uses the spatial correlation to obtain a set of uncorrelated coefficients. The spatial and tem-poral correlations between the different frames of the video instance were exploited by subtracting consecutive frames, before applying DCT. Since all the stop instances did not have the same number of frames, the first frame was subtracted from the second and the penultimate frame from the ultimate. DCT was applied separately on the two difference frames and the first 15 coefficients taken in a zigzag manner. The two 15-dimensional vectors obtained there from were alternated and the first fifteen coefficients chosen to create the final feature vector.

The audio and video features were combined using Early Integration as well as Late Integration techniques. 13 MFCC based features and 15 visual features were simply concatenated, to obtain a 28-features vector, before performing classification for the Early Integration.

The database was doubly-randomized and split into two parts; 75% of it was used in the training of the classifier and the remaining 25% was used as an unknown test input. Around 1000 runs were performed to make the results statistically pure. Table 2 shows the recognition accuracy achieved by an LDA classifier for the four-class (stop consonants /b/, /g/, /p/ and /k/) classification.

Further, the 4-class recognition accuracy is as shown in Table 3. It is evident that the addition of visual information in the ASR leads to a relative improvement in recognition accuracy of the stops both for Early as well as Late Integration. The

Figure 7. Shows the lips end point detection using row-wise histogram

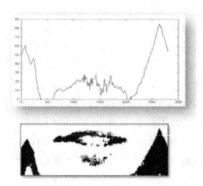

Figure 8. Zig-zag selection of DCT coefficients

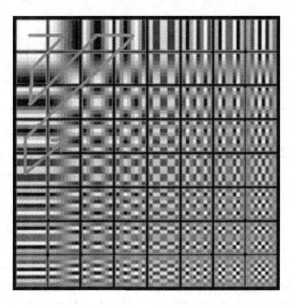

recognition accuracy appears to be on the lower side, because the recognition was performed at phoneme level without the use of any language model or dictionary used.

Additive white Gaussian noise was injected into the speech signal to achieve different signal to noise ratio (SNR). The classification results for audio only, video only and audio-visual (with late integration) is shown in Table 4. It is apparent from the figure that the AVASR gives the best performance among the three and shows better robustness.

The fricatives are considered to be amongst the set of phonemes which are difficult to recognize due to their noise like spectral characteristics. In the next experiment three fricatives (/s/, /f/, /ʋ/)

were chosen for the task of recognition and the results obtained is shown in Table 5 (Khanam et al., 2009). As seen from Table 1, the last two fricatives fall in the same viseme category due to which the recognition with video only features is very low. However, when the audio and visual features are combined, the result shows considerable improvement in the recognition performance. This is due to the fact that the voicing information present in the acoustic signal along with the visual information derived from the lip region helps to increase the between class feature separation, thereby improving the classification result using linear discriminant function.

Table 2. Phoneme confusion-matrix linear discriminant function

Stops	b	g	p	k
b	35.82	36.91	12.12	15.15
g	22.43	44.25	14.28	19.04
p	11.90	9.5	46.37	24.97
k	9.25	22.22	26.92	36.06

Table 3. Recognition accuracy using audio only, video only and audio-visual features for four-class stop recognition

Features	Recognition Accuracy (%)
Audio only	40.63
Video only	25.25
Audio + Video(Early integration)	43.62
Audio + Video(Late integration)	44.29

Table 4. Recognition accuracy using audio only, video only and audio-visual features for four-class stop recognition

Features	30dB	20dB	10dB	5dB	0dB	-5dB
Audio	36.45	34.83	32.74	30.21	25.00	20.10
Video	25.25	25.25	25.25	25.25	25.25	25.25
Audio + Video(Late integration)	39.93	38.05	37.79	37.52	36.34	28.64

5. SUMMARY AND CONCLUSION

Audio-visual speech recognition is a relatively new area of research, which requires optimal feature selection and extraction in audio as well as visual domain. Although many features have been proposed for the audio signal, MFCC are most commonly used audio feature. Features in the visual domain are still widely open research field and there are no commercial systems available for AVASR.

Due to the non-availability of the Hindi audio-visual database, there has been no research in this area. The paper proposes a new visual feature extraction technique based on 2D-DCT for AVASR application. It is observed that early as well as late integration of the audio and visual features improve the stops as well as fricative recognition performance over the audio only and video only recognizer. As seen in the previous section, addition of video features improve the robustness of the stop phoneme recognition system in the presence of background noise, therefore, it is

expected that in case of full AVASR for Hindi speech the robustness will improve. Further, the enhancement in the recognition performance can be improved by the use of HMM along with the language model and dictionary.

Since Hindi has different phonemes and visemes as compared to English a detailed study of this language is needed. This will result into identification of new viseme classes which are not present in English speech. This type of study will enable developing an AVASR which accounts for the differences in Hindi phoneme-viseme set thereby improving the recognition performance under adverse conditions.

The current state of research focuses on effective extraction and tracking of lips to extract features and better understand of how human brain fuses the audio and visual information. Success in this direction will help to develop effective fusion techniques of audio and visual information to further improve the robustness and recognition accuracy. Studies on weighted fusion of information from audio and visual domain can be carried out, where the weighting factor could be decided by the amount of background noise present. Secondly, different hidden Markov model (HMM) based recognizer architectures can be explored, which attempts to implicitly include reliability information into the models.

Table 5. Recognition accuracy using audio only, video only and audio-visual features for fricative recognition

Features	Recognition Accuracy (%)
	Linear
Audio only	37.74
Video only	21.37
Audio + Video(Early integration)	47.91
Audio + Video(Late integration)	61.52

ACKNOWLEDGMENT

The authors would like to thank the British Council and Council of Science and Technology, UP India for partially funding this on-going research project.

REFERENCES

Acero, A., & Stern, R. M. (1990). Environmental robustness in automatic speech recognition. In *Proceedings of the International Conference on Acoustic, Speech and Signal Processing* (pp. 849-852).

Ahmed, R., & Agrawal, S. S. (1969). Significant features in the perception of Hindi consonants. *The Journal of the Acoustical Society of America, 45*, 758–763. doi:10.1121/1.1911459

Aleksic, P. S., & Katsaggelos, A. K. (2004). Comparison of low and high-level visual features for audio-visual continuous automatic speech recognition. In *Proceedings of the IEEE International Conference on Acoustics, Speech, and Signal Processing* (Vol. 5, pp. 917-920).

Baum, L. E., Petrei, S. T. G., & Weiss, N. (1970). A maximisation technique occurring in the statistical analysis of probabilistic functions of Markov chains. *Annals of Mathematical Statistics, 41*, 164–171. doi:10.1214/aoms/1177697196

Bregler, C., & Konig, Y. (1994). Eigenlips for robust speech recognition. In *Proceedings of the International Conference on Acoustics, Speech and Signal Processing*, Adelaide, Australia (pp. 669-672).

Bregler, C., & Omohundro, S. (1995). Nonlinear manifold learning for visual speech recognition. In *Proceedings of the IEEE International Conference on Computer Vision* (pp. 494-499).

Chan, M. T. (2001). HMM-based audio-visual speech recognition, integrating geometric and appearance-based visual features. In *Proceedings of the Fourth Workshop on Multimedia Signal Processing* (pp. 9-14).

Chandramohan, D., & Silsbee, P. L. (1996). Multiple deformable template approach for visual speech recognition. In *Proceedings of the Fourth International Conference on Spoken Language*, Philadelphia, PA (Vol. 1, pp. 50-53).

Chang, S., Kwon, Y., & Yang, S. (1998). Speech feature extracted from adaptive wavelet for speech recognition. *Electronics Letters, 34*(23), 2211–2213. doi:10.1049/el:19981486

Chaudhari, U. V., Ramaswamy, G. N., Potamianos, G., & Neti, C. (2003, April 6-10). Audio-visual speaker recognition using time-varying stream reliability prediction. In *Proceedings of the International Conference on Acoustics, Speech Signal Processing*, Hong Kong, China (Vol. 5, pp. 712-715).

Chibelushi, C. C., Deravi, F., & Mason, J. S. D. (2002). A review of speech-based bimodal recognition. *IEEE Transactions on Multimedia, 4*(1), 23–37. doi:10.1109/6046.985551

Cootes, T. F., Taylor, C. J., & Edward, G. J. (1998). Active appearance models. In *Proceedings of the European Conference on Computer Vision*, Freiburg, Germany (pp. 484-498).

Cristinacce, D., & Cootes, T. F. (2006). Facial feature detection and tracking with automatic template selection. In *Proceedings of the 7th International Conference on Automatic Face and Gesture Recognition* (pp. 429-434).

Deller, J. R., Hansen, J. H. L., & Proakis, J. G. (1993). *Discrete-time processing of speech signals*. New York, NY: Macmillan.

Dimitriadis, D., Maragos, P., & Potamianos, A. (2005). Robust AM-FM features for speech recognition. *IEEE Signal Processing Letters, 12*(9), 621–624. doi:10.1109/LSP.2005.853050

Donoho, D. L., & Johnston, I. M. (1995). Denoising by soft-thresholding. *IEEE Transactions on Information Theory*, *41*(3), 613–627. doi:10.1109/18.382009

Eveno, N., Caplier, A., & Coulon, P. Y. (2001). A new color transformation for lips segmentation. In *Proceedings of the Fourth Workshop on Multimedia Signal Processing* (pp. 3-8).

Farooq, O., & Datta, S. (2001). Mel filter-like admissible wavelet packet structure for speech recognition. *IEEE Signal Processing Letters*, *8*(7), 196–198. doi:10.1109/97.928676

Farooq, O., & Datta, S. (2004). Wavelet based robust sub-band features for phoneme recognition. *IEEE Proceedings on Vision Image Signal Processing*, *151*(3), 187–193. doi:10.1049/ip-vis:20040324

Farooq, O., Datta, S., & Shrotriya, M. C. (2010). Wavelet sub-band based temporal features for robust Hindi phoneme recognition. *International Journal of Wavelets, Multresolution, and Information Processing*, *8*(6), 847–859. doi:10.1142/S0219691310003845

Fonseca, E. S., Guido, R. C., Scalassara, P. R., Maciel, C. D., & Pereira, J. C. (2007). Wavelet time-frequency analysis and least squares support vector machines for the identification of voice disorders. *Computers in Biology and Medicine*, *37*(4), 571–578. doi:10.1016/j.compbiomed.2006.08.008

Gales, M. J. F., & Young, S. J. (1996). Robust continuous speech recognition using parallel model combination. *IEEE Transactions on Speech and Audio Processing*, *4*(5), 352–359. doi:10.1109/89.536929

Goldschen, A. J., Garcia, O. N., & Petajan, E. D. (1996). Rationale for phoneme-viseme mapping and feature selection in visual speech recognition. In Stork, D. G., & Hennecke, M. E. (Eds.), *Speech reading by humans and machines* (pp. 505–515). Berlin, Germany: Springer-Verlag.

Grant, K. W., & Braida, L. D. (1991). Evaluating the articulation index for auditory-visual input. *The Journal of the Acoustical Society of America*, *89*, 2950–2960. doi:10.1121/1.400733

Gupta, R. (2006). *Speech recognition for Hindi (M. Tech. Project Report)*. Bombay, Mumbai, India: Indian Institute of Technology.

Gurban, M., & Thiran, J.-P. (2009). Information theoretic feature extraction for audio-visual speech recognition. *IEEE Transactions on Signal Processing*, *57*(12), 4765–4776. doi:10.1109/TSP.2009.2026513

Heckmann, M., Berthommier, F., & Kroschel, K. (2001). A hybrid ANN/HMM audio-visual speech recognition system. In *Proceedings of the International Conference on Auditory-Visual Speech Processing*, Aalborg, Denmark (pp. 190-195).

Hermansky, H., & Morgan, N. (1994). RASTA processing of speech. *IEEE Transactions on Speech and Audio Processing*, *2*(4), 578–589. doi:10.1109/89.326616

Jang, K. S. (2007). Lip contour extraction based on active shape model and snakes. *International Journal of Computer Science and Network Security*, *7*(10), 148–153.

Jian, Z., Kaynak, M. N., Vheok, A. D., & Chung, K. C. (2001). Real-time lip tracking for virtual lip implementation in virtual environments and computer games. In *Proceedings of the 10th IEEE International Conference on Fuzzy Systems*, Melbourne, VIC, Australia (vol. 3, pp. 1359-1362).

Kaynak, M. N., Zhi, Q., Cheok, A. D., Sengupta, K., Jian, Z., & Chung, K. C. (2004). Analysis of lip geometric features for audio-visual speech recognition. *IEEE Transactions on Systems, Man, and Cybernetics. Part A, Systems and Humans, 34*(4), 564–570. doi:10.1109/TSMCA.2004.826274

Khanam, R., Mumtaz, S. M., Farooq, O., Datta, S., & Vyas, A. L. (2009). Audio-visual features for stop recognition from continuous Hindi speech. In *Proceedings of the National Symposium on Acoustics* (pp. 91-96).

Kim, D. S., Lee, S. Y., & Kil, R. M. (1999). Auditory processing of speech signals for robust speech recognition in real world noisy environment. *IEEE Transactions on Speech and Audio Processing, 7*(1), 55–69. doi:10.1109/89.736331

Kim, D. Y., & Un, C. K. (1996). Probabilistic vector mapping with trajectory information for noise-robust speech recognition. *Electronics Letters, 32*(17), 1550–1551. doi:10.1049/el:19961081

Liporace, L. A. (1982). Maximum likelihood estimation for multivariate observations of Markov source. *IEEE Transactions on Information Theory, 28*, 729–734. doi:10.1109/TIT.1982.1056544

Long, C. J., & Datta, S. (1998). Discriminant wavelet basis construction for speech recognition. In *Proceedings of the 5th International Conference on Spoken Language Processing*, Sydney, Australia (Vol. 3, pp. 1047-1049).

Mallat, S. (1998). *A wavelet tour of signal processing*. New York, NY: Academic Press.

Mok, L. L., Lau, W. H., Leung, S. H., Wang, S. L., & Yan, H. (2004). Person authentication using ASM based lip shape and intensity information. In *Proceedings of the International Conference on Image Processing* (Vol. 1, pp. 561-564).

Moon, T. K. (1996). The expectation-maximization algorithm. *IEEE Signal Processing Magazine, 13*(6), 47–60. doi:10.1109/79.543975

Nefian, A. V., Liang, L., Pi, X., Liu, X., & Murphy, K. (2002). Dynamic Bayesian networks for audio-visual speech recognition. *EURASIP Journal on Applied Signal Processing*, (1): 1274–1288. doi:10.1155/S1110865702206083

Nefian, A. V., Liang, L., Pi, X., Xiaoxiang, L., Mao, C., & Murphy, K. (2002). A coupled HMM for audio-visual speech recognition. In *Proceedings of the IEEE International Conference on Acoustics, Speech, and Signal Processing*, Orlando, FL (Vol. 2, pp. 2013-2016).

Neti, C., Potamianos, G., Luettin, J., Matthews, I., Glotin, H., & Vergyri, D. …Zhou, J. (2000). *Audio-visual speech recognition: Workshop 2000 final report*. Baltimore, MD: Centre for Language and Speech Processing.

Neumeyer, L., & Weintraub, M. (1994). Probabilistic optimum filtering for robust speech recognition. In *Proceedings of the International Conference on Acoustic, Speech and Signal Processing* (Vol. 1, pp. 417-420).

Nilsson, M., Nordberg, J., & Claesson, I. (2007). Face detection using local SMQT features and split up snow classifier. In *Proceedings of the International Conference on Acoustics, Speech and Signal Processing* (pp. 589-592).

Ooi, W. C., Jeon, C., Kim, K., Ko, H., & Han, D. K. (2009). Effective lip localization and tracking for achieving multimodal speech recognition. *Multisensor Fusion and Integration for Intelligent Systems, 35*(1), 33–43. doi:10.1007/978-3-540-89859-7_3

Otsu, N. (1979). A threshold selection method from gray-level histograms. *IEEE Transactions on Systems, Man, and Cybernetics, 9*(1), 62–66. doi:10.1109/TSMC.1979.4310076

Picone, J. W. (1993). Signal modelling techniques in speech recognition. *Proceedings of the IEEE, 81*(9), 1215–1247. doi:10.1109/5.237532

Picone, J. W., Ebel, W. J., & Deshmukh, N. (1995). Automatic speech understanding: The next generation. *Digital Signal Processing Technology, 57*, 101–114.

Potamianos, G., Neti, C., Gravier, G., Garg, A., & Senior, A. W. (2003). Recent advances in the automatic recognition of audio-visual speech. *Proceedings of the IEEE, 91*, 1306–1326. doi:10.1109/JPROC.2003.817150

Potamianos, G., Neti, C., Luettin, J., & Matthews, I. (2004). Audiovisual automatic speech recognition: An overview. In Bailly, G., Bateson, V. V., & Perrier, P. (Eds.), *Issues in visual and audio-visual speech processing*. Cambridge, MA: MIT Press.

Rabiner, L. R. (1989). A tutorial on hidden Markov models and selected applications in speech recognition. *Proceedings of the IEEE, 77*(2), 257–285. doi:10.1109/5.18626

Raihan, H., Khan, N., Farooq, O., Datta, S., & Vyas, A. L. (2010). Comparative performance of audio and audio-visual features for Hindi fricative recognition. *Proceedings of the National Symposium on Acoustics, 37*(1), 7-12.

Ramírez, J., Segura, J. C., Benítez, C., Torre, A., & Rubio, A. (2005). An effective subband OSF-based VAD with noise reduction for robust speech recognition. *IEEE Transactions on Speech and Audio Processing, 13*(6), 1119–1129. doi:10.1109/TSA.2005.853212

Reisfeld, D., & Yeshurun, Y. (1992). Robust detection of facial features by generalised symmetry. In *Proceedings of the 11ᵗʰ International Conference on Pattern Recognition* (Vol. 1, pp. 117-120).

Rohani, R., Alizadeh, S., Sobhanmanesh, F., & Boostani, R. (2008). Lip segmentation in color images. In *Proceedings of the International Conference on Innovations in Information Technology* (p. 747).

Romdhani, S., Torr, P., Scholkopf, B., & Blake, A. (2001). Computationally efficient face detection. In *Proceedings of the International Conference on Computer Vision* (pp. 695-700).

Samudravijaya, K. (2001). Hindi speech recognition. *Journal of Acoustical Society of India, 29*(1), 385–393.

Sarikaya, R., & Hansen, J. H. L. (2000). High resolution speech feature parametrization for monophone-based stressed speech recognition. *IEEE Signal Processing Letters, 7*(7), 182–185. doi:10.1109/97.847363

Shrotriya, N., Verma, R., Gupta, S. K., & Agrawal, S. S. (1996). Durational characteristics of Hindi consonant clusters. In *Proceedings of the International Conference on Spoken Language Processing* (pp. 2427-2430).

Silsbee, P., & Bovik, A. (1996). Computer lip reading for improved accuracy in automatic speech recognition. *IEEE Transactions on Speech and Audio Processing, 4*(5), 337–351. doi:10.1109/89.536928

Stork, D. G., & Hennecke, M. E. (1996). Speech reading: An overview of image processing, feature extraction, sensory integration and pattern recognition techniques. In *Proceedings of the 2nd International Conference on Automatic Face and Gesture Recognition* (pp. 16-26).

Stork, D. G., Wolff, G., & Levine, E. (1992). Neural network lipreading system for improved speech recognition. In *Proceedings of the International Joint Conference on Neural Networks* (pp. 285-295).

Verma, A., Faruquie, T., Neti, C., Basu, S., & Senior, A. (1999). Late integration in audio-visual continuous speech recognition. In *Proceedings of the Automatic Speech Recognition and Understanding Workshop* (pp. 71-77).

Williams, J. J., & Katsaggelos, A. K. (2002). An HMM-based speech-to-video synthesizer. *IEEE Transactions on Neural Networks. Special Issue on Intelligent Multimedia, 13*(4), 900–915.

Yang, J., & Waibel, A. (1996). A real-time face tracker. In *Proceedings of the 3rd IEEE Workshop on Applications of Computer Vision* (pp. 142-147).

You, K. H., & Wang, H. C. (1999). Robust features for noisy speech recognition based on temporal trajectory filtering of short-time autocorrelation sequences. *Speech Communication, 28*, 13–24. doi:10.1016/S0167-6393(99)00004-7

Young, S. (1996). A review of large vocabulary continuous speech recognition. *IEEE Signal Processing Magazine*, 45–57. doi:10.1109/79.536824

Young, S., Kershaw, D., Odell, J., Ollason, D., Valtchev, V., & Woodland, P. (2011). *The HTK book*. Retrieved from http://htk.eng.cam.ac.uk

Yuhas, B. P., Goldstein, M. H., & Sejnowski, T. J. (1989). Integration of acoustic and visual speech signals using neural networks. *IEEE Communications Magazine*, 65–71. doi:10.1109/35.41402

Zhang, X., & Mersereau, R. M. (2000). Lip feature extraction towards an automatic speech reading system. In *Proceedings of the International Conference on Image Processing* (Vol. 3, pp. 226-229).

Chapter 9
On Applying the Farey Sequence for Shape Representation in Z^2

Sanjoy Pratihar
Indian Institute of Technology Kharagpur, India

Partha Bhowmick
Indian Institute of Technology Kharagpur, India

ABSTRACT

Describing the shape of an object is a well-studied, yet ever-engrossing problem, because an appropriate description can improve the efficiency of a shape matching algorithm, thereby enriching subsequent applications. The authors propose a novel boundary-based shape description using the Farey sequence to capture an object shape represented as a sequence of discrete straight line segments. The straight edges are extracted directly from a gray-scale image without resorting to any edge map detection, and without using any thinning procedure. Then we merge the straight pieces, which are almost collinear but usually small in length, by employing the novel idea of an Augmented Farey Table (AFT). An AFT is a preprocessed data structure that provides us the Farey indices based on which the amount of linearity of three consecutive vertices of a polygon in the digital plane, is decided. Using the final straight pieces after AFT-based merging, the authors build a shape description using the Farey indices of the merged/ larger pieces. In particular, the method would be computationally attractive for polygonal approximation and shape description of a large database of gray-scale images. Experimental results demonstrate its usefulness, efficiency, and elegance.

INTRODUCTION

Shape is an attributive embodiment of human perception. Various shape description and matching techniques, therefore, are found to play important roles in the automated machine recognition of digital objects and patterns. Understanding the shape of a graphic object as a polygon described as a numeric sequence — of its vertex coordinates or some other attributes — can be of great interest, as a numeric representation can be analyzed easily and efficiently by an algorithm working on the integer input. Description of the shape of an object in a digital image can be also given as

DOI: 10.4018/978-1-4666-0954-9.ch009

a sequence of internal angles of the underlying polygon, and the resultant representation of the object leads towards compactness and reduced memory requirement. Further, it also becomes almost invariant to rotation and also to isotropic scaling. However, the internal angle at a vertex of the polygon being a real value lying in the open interval $(0, 2\pi)$, floating-point computations and allied procedural complexities do play significant roles in determining the runtime of an algorithm that deals with shapes. This paper shows how a Farey sequence can be used to represent the edge slopes, and the vertex angles thereof, to describe a polygon for its readiness to subsequent applications.

Once we get a proper descriptor of digital images, we can apply some shape matching algorithm for shape-based retrieval. There are a number of methods that build classifiers without finding correspondences. These approaches have been used for handwritten digit recognition (LeCun, Bottou, Bengio, & Haffner, 1998), face recognition (Moghaddam, Jebara, & Pentland, 2000), hand recognition (Shamaie, Hai, & Sutherland, 2011), etc. Methods are also there to perform recognition based on shape information. For example, silhouettes have been described using Fourier descriptors in Zahn and Roskies (1972). Skeleton extraction and feature descriptions based on medial-axis transform are discussed in Sharvit, Chan, Tek, and Kimia (1998). Other approaches that treat the shape as a set of points, extracted using an edge detector, are available in Borgefors (1988), Gavrila and Philomin (1999), and Huttenlocher, Lilien, and Olson (1999).

Polygonal approximation/polygonization itself is also used as intermediate steps in various applications such as volume rendering and multi resolution modeling (De-Haemer, Jr. & Zyda, 1991; Shirley & Tuchman, 1990), image and video retrieval (Mokhtarian & Mohanna, 2002), shape coding (O'Connell, 1997), etc. There exists a rich literature of different techniques for polygonal (or poly-chain) approximation of a digital curve (Bhowmick & Bhattacharya, 2007; Chen & Chung, 2001; Climer & Bhatia, 2003; Dunham, 1986; Imai & Iri, 1986; Perez & Vidal, 1994; Rosin, 1997; Teh & Chin, 1989; Wall & Danielsson, 1984; Yin, 2003, 2004). However, none of these algorithms can be used for approximating a gray-level curve or an object in a gray-scale image. Hence, for polygonal approximation of (objects in) a gray-scale image, at first the edge map needs to be extracted, and then the edge map has to be thinned for obtaining strictly one-pixel-thick curves. We can use edge detection operators (e.g., Prewitt operator, Sobel operator, etc.) or an well-known edge extraction algorithm, e.g., Canny's edge detection algorithm (Canny, 1986), to get the edge map first. Thus, with the existing practice, polygonal approximation of a gray-scale image is realizable only after the extraction of the thinned edges of objects present in the image. And then only we can apply one of the above-mentioned algorithms on the thinned edge/curve to get polygonal (or poly-chain) approximation of the objects. The entire procedure is, therefore, not only susceptible to pitfalls of the adopted edge extraction algorithm and subsequent thinning, but also affected by inter-stage dependence and high runtime.

In this paper, we first deal with polygonization of objects present in a gray-scale image to obtain the boundary representation, and then we describe the boundary as a numeric sequence, which serves as a high-level geometric figure that captures the underlying shape. The work proposed here is divided into the following two stages:

Stage 1: We find the digitally straight edges defining the boundary of an object, and then merge the almost collinear edges to derive a tighter description of the object, which has been explained in the section of Detection of Straight Edges. By this algorithm, an edge is detected as a sequence of piecewise linear components. We extract the straight edges by inspecting the corresponding edge points one by one until there is a break in the chain because of the digital-straightness properties

(Klette & Rosenfeld, 2004b). The ordered set of endpoints of the straight edges provides the polygonal shape of the object. The notion of Farey sequence (Graham, Knuth, & Potashnik, 1994) and the resultant Farey indices, which are in correspondence with slopes of line segments, have been used in tandem with the digital-geometric properties of straightness to get the final result of polygonal approximation. Merging of extracted straight edges has been implemented using differences of indices of slope fractions in the *Augmented Farey Table* (*T*), newly introduced in this work, where each index is available by a single probe in *T*, and the decision on collinearity of two or more straight edges is taken using addition/subtraction operations in the integer domain only.

Stage 2: After the polygonization, we use the Farey index corresponding to (the slope of) each line-segment/edge that defines the polygonal form of an object. We obtain a shape description of the boundary using the difference of Farey indices of each pair of consecutive straight edges in the sequence. It has been also shown in brief how the resultant numeric sequence can be used for an effective shape matching algorithm. Figure 3 demonstrates the basic steps of a shape decomposition algorithm using Farey sequence (Pratihar & Bhowmick, 2010). As shown in this figure, we first obtain the digitally straight edges defining the object boundary, and then merge the almost collinear edges to derive a tighter description of the object (Figures 1b and 1c). The notion of Farey sequence (Graham et al., 1994) and the resultant Farey indices, which are in correspondence with the edge slopes, have been used to get the final polygonal cover (Figure 1c). For an efficient implementation, the Farey indices are stored in the augmented Farey table (T) of order 200. Each Farey index corresponds to the slope of a line segment connecting two points with integer coordinates, and is available by a single probe in T. The Farey indices, corresponding to the (slopes of) edges of the polygonal cover, form a numeric sequence that serves as a high-level geometric

abstraction of the underlying shape. We use this numeric sequence to obtain a turn sequence, which is a 2-element string consisting of L (left turn) and R (right turn) only. From this turn sequence, a sequence of saddle points and the corresponding L-containing substrings are obtained to form a visibility graph, which is finally used for component detection (Figure 1d).

DETECTION OF STRAIGHT EDGES

To detect the straight edges of locally maximum lengths, we have used an algorithm based on chain-code properties and exponential averaging of edge strengths (Prewitt responses) (Gonzalez & Woods, 1993), which has been reported recently (Pratihar & Bhowmick, 2009). To decide the maximal straightness of an edge, certain regularity properties of digital straightness have been used, which can be derived from the chord property (Klette & Rosenfeld, 2004a; Rosenfeld, 1974). A curve C is digitally straight if and only if its chain codes have at most two values in {0, 1, 2,..., 7}, differing by ±1 (mod 8) and for one of these, the run-length must be unity (Property R1). Also, if s and n be the respective singular code and non-singular code in a digital curve C, then the runs of n can have only two lengths, which are consecutive integers (Property R2).

To obtain the start point of a straight edge, each point p of the image is visited (in row-major order). If the Prewitt response at p exceeds the threshold value, $T(=100$ in our experiments), and the response is a local maximum in the 8-neighborhood (8N) of p, then p is the start point, p_s. The next point on the edge commencing from p_s is obtained from the responses in 8N of p_s. The direction d_s from p_s is the chain code from p_s to its neighbor having the maximum response. In case of multiple maxima (which indicates multiple edges incident at p_s), we consider each of them, one by one, for finding the straight edges from p_s.

Figure 1. Basic steps of a Farey-based shape-decomposition algorithm

(a) Input shape.

(b) Extracted straight edges, using exponential averaging and digital straightness.

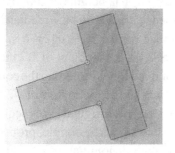

(c) Polygonal cover, using AFT (N = 200; T_f = 5000).

(d) Final decomposition, using saddle points and visibility graph.

To get the (straight-)edge point next to any current point p, we need not apply the convolution at each neighbor (in 8N) of p with the Prewitt operator (in order to get their responses, and the maximum/maxima, thereof). Instead, in our algorithm, checking the Prewitt responses at three neighbors corresponding to three directions suffices: d, $(d+1)(\mod 8)$, and $(d+7)(\mod 8)$, where d is the chain code of p. For, from Property R1, no other neighbor can be the next point on the current edge. We have used an effective method of exponential averaging to estimate the strength of an edge point using its own response and the weighted contribution of responses at the previous edge points. In other words, to compute the exponential average of the responses in and around a point p, we consider the responses — which have been already computed and stored — at the points preceding p up the straight edge. A detailed explanation of the algorithm is given in (Pratihar & Bhowmick, 2009).

Using the Farey Sequence for Integer Computation

Farey sequences are named after the British geologist, John Farey, Sr. [Philosophical Magazine, 1816]. He guessed that each new term in a Farey sequence is the mediant of its neighbors, but, so far as is known, he did not prove this property (Beiler, 1964). Later, Cauchy gave a proof in *Exercises de mathmatique* and attributed this result to Farey.

Interestingly, C. Haros had also published similar results in 1802, which were possibly not known either to Farey or to Cauchy.

The Farey sequence F_i of order i is the sequence of completely reduced (i.e., simple/irreducible), proper, and positive fractions that have denominators less than or equal to i, and are arranged in increasing order of their values. There are several studies and related works related with Farey sequences and their indices, some of which may be seen in Graham et al. (1994), Hardy and Wright (1968), Neville (1950), and Schroeder (2006). As shown in this work, a Farey sequence can be of interesting and practical use to decide whether three points, sorted lexicographically by their x and y (integer) coordinates, are collinear. It involves only addition, comparison, and memory access, but no multiplication, to check the linearity. Thus, it helps in reducing the running time for the linearity-checking function compared to the existing procedures.

For example, for three given points $p_1(i_1, j_1)$, $p_2(i_2, j_2)$, and $p_3(i_3, j_3)$ in succession, one of the common practices is to use the metric $D(p_1, p_2, p_3)/\max(|i_1 - i_3|, |j_1 - j_3|)$ for computing the deviation of p_2 from $p_1 p_3$ (Berg, Kreveld, Overmars, & Schwarzkopf, 2000). However, computation of the triangle area given by $D(p_1, p_2, p_3)$ involves multiplication, and is therefore computationally expensive. Such multiplications are avoided by us using Farey sequences. When we have a huge database of images to be processed one after another, we can compute a Farey table of an appropriate size and use it for computational optimization. As a result, the total time of polygonal approximation for all images in the database would be significantly reduced.

Augmented Farey Table

A Farey sequence starts with the fraction 0/1 and ends with the fraction 1/1. For example, the Farey sequence of orders 1 to 5 are as follows:

$$F_1 = \frac{0}{1}, \frac{1}{1}$$

$$F_2 = \frac{0}{1}, \frac{1}{2}, \frac{1}{1}$$

$$F_3 = \frac{0}{1}, \frac{1}{3}, \frac{1}{2}, \frac{2}{3}, \frac{1}{1}$$

$$F_4 = \frac{0}{1}, \frac{1}{4}, \frac{1}{3}, \frac{1}{2}, \frac{2}{3}, \frac{3}{4}, \frac{1}{1}$$

$$F_5 = \frac{0}{1}, \frac{1}{5}, \frac{1}{4}, \frac{1}{3}, \frac{2}{5}, \frac{1}{2}, \frac{3}{5}, \frac{2}{3}, \frac{3}{4}, \frac{4}{5}, \frac{1}{1}$$

Interestingly, each F_i can be computed from F_{i-1}. If p/q has neighbors a/b and c/d in a Farey sequence, then p/q is the mediant of a/b and c/d. In other words, $p/q=(a+c)/(b+d)$. For example, since 3/5 is the mediant of 1/2 and 2/3 in F_5, 3/5 is obtained for F_5 by adding the corresponding numerators and denominators of 1/2 and 2/3 from F_4.

Clearly, the original Farey sequence F_i of order i consists of all the simple, proper, positive fractions with denominators less than or equal to i. Compound fractions (that can be reduced to simple fractions of F_i), improper fractions (with numerators less than or equal to i), and negative fractions do not find any place in F_i. With simple operations, we obtain an augmented Farey sequence F'_i from the Farey sequence F_i in order to include the above fractions as well. The augmented sequence F_i aids the linearity checking procedure while merging the end points of straight edges, which are almost collinear. For each member a/b of F_i, we prepare a sub-list containing the equivalent compound fractions with denominators less than or equal to i. Corresponding to each a/b, a new fraction $(a+a')/(b+b')$ is computed, where a'/b' is already a member of the sub-list corresponding to a/b, and b' is the highest denominator in the sub-list corresponding to a/b, such that $(b+b') \le i$. This new fraction is kept in the sub-list of F'_i linked to a/b. The first member $a'/b' = (a+a)/(b+b)$ of such a sub-list is obtained by adding the numerator a of a/b with itself and the denominator b of it with itself, provided $2b' \le i$. Since F_i is derived as stated above, it contains all positive fractions (simple and compound) with denominators less than or equal to i. Now we take mirror reflection of this list about 1/1, such that in the reflected part each member is the reciprocal of its counterpart. The compound fraction in the sub-lists linked to the simple fractions are also treated in the same way, i.e., numerators become denominators, and vice versa. This reflected part is appended to the original list. Next, we again take a reflection of this enlarged list, with the signs of all denominators in the reflected part changed to negative. Thus, finally we get all the fractions with positive numerator and positive/negative denominator. Taking their positions in the list we build the *augmented Farey table*, namely T_i, corresponding to F_i, as shown in Figure 2.

For example, when compound fractions are included in F4, it gets augmented to

$$F_4' = \frac{0}{1}\left(\frac{0}{2},\frac{0}{3},\frac{0}{4}\right),\frac{1}{4},\frac{1}{3},\frac{1}{2}\left(\frac{2}{4}\right),\frac{2}{3},\frac{3}{4},\frac{1}{1}\left(\frac{2}{2},\frac{3}{3},\frac{4}{4}\right).$$

On including the improper fractions, it is further augmented to

$$F_4' = \frac{0}{1}\left(\frac{0}{2},\frac{0}{3},\frac{0}{4}\right),\frac{1}{4},\frac{1}{3},\frac{1}{2}\left(\frac{2}{4}\right),\frac{2}{3},\frac{3}{4},\frac{1}{1}\left(\frac{2}{2},\frac{3}{3},\frac{4}{4}\right),$$
$$\frac{4}{3},\frac{3}{2},\frac{2}{1}\left(\frac{4}{2}\right),\frac{3}{1},\frac{4}{1},\frac{1}{0}\left(\frac{2}{0},\frac{3}{0},\frac{4}{0}\right).$$

When negative fractions (positive numerator and negative denominator) are included, we get

$$F_4' = \frac{4}{-1},\frac{3}{-1},\frac{2}{-1}\left(\frac{4}{-2}\right),\frac{3}{-2},\frac{4}{-3},\frac{1}{-1}\left(\frac{2}{-2},\frac{3}{-3},\frac{4}{-4}\right),$$
$$\frac{3}{-4},\frac{2}{-3},\frac{1}{-2}\left(\frac{2}{-4}\right),\frac{1}{-3},\frac{1}{-4},\frac{0}{-1}\left(\frac{0}{-2},\frac{0}{-3},\frac{0}{4}\right),$$
$$\frac{0}{1}\left(\frac{0}{2},\frac{0}{3},\frac{0}{4}\right),\frac{1}{4},\frac{1}{3},\frac{1}{2}\left(\frac{2}{4}\right),\frac{2}{3},\frac{3}{4},\frac{1}{1}\left(\frac{2}{2},\frac{3}{3},\frac{4}{4}\right),$$
$$\frac{4}{3},\frac{3}{2},\frac{2}{1}\left(\frac{4}{2}\right),\frac{3}{1},\frac{4}{1},\frac{1}{0}\left(\frac{2}{0},\frac{3}{0},\frac{4}{0}\right).$$

For other two types of fractions, i.e., fractions with negative numerator and positive denominator, and fractions with negative numerator and negative denominator, we have to take reflection of the above list F_4' and then change the signs of numerators and denominators accordingly. Thus, F_4' becomes a complete list of all possible fractions.

Clearly, all fractions $\{a/b\}$, where $|a| \le 4$ and $|b| \le 4$, can be kept in a list divided into four sub-lists, which keep fractions of types a/b, $a/(-b)$, $(-a)/(-b)$, and $(-a)/b$ respectively; and for each sub-list, the fractions are in increasing order. For each fraction in each sub-list, we can easily access its position in the sub-list by accessing the table T, as shown in Figure 2.

Merging of Straight Edges using T

Extraction of straight edges from a gray-scale image generates an ordered set E (endpoints of straight edges), as explained earlier. Now, in order to reduce the number of straight edges defining the boundary of the object, vertices are taken out from E, and if they are "almost collinear", then they are combined together to form a longer straight edge. If $\langle e_i, e_{i+1},..., e_j \rangle$ be a maximal (ordered) subset of straight edges that are almost collinear, then these $j - i + 1$ edges are combined to a single edge. The process is repeated for all such maximal subsets in succession to obtain a reduced set of (almost) straight edges corresponding to the object boundary. There are several techniques available in the literature to replace the almost-collinear pieces by a single piece (Bhowmick & Bhattacharya, 2007; Rosin & West, 1995).

We have used a novel technique using differences of indices corresponding to line slopes — which are equivalent to fractions — in the augmented Farey table, T. Each T-index is obtained by a single probe in T and the decision on linearity of three points is taken in the integer domain using addition/subtraction operation only. For a straight edge with end points $p(x_p, y_p)$ and $q(x_q, y_q)$, we do access the index of the fraction $(y_p - y_q)/(x_p - x_q)$,

Figure 2. AFT T$_4$ of order 4 containing indices of all fractions in {a/b: 4 ≤a, b ≤4}.

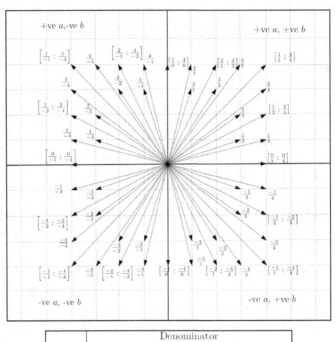

		\multicolumn{9}{c}{Denominator}								
		-4	-3	-2	-1	0	1	2	3	4
N	4	19	18	16	14	13	12	10	8	7
u	3	20	19	17	15	13	11	9	7	6
m	2	22	21	19	16	13	10	7	5	4
e	1	24	23	22	19	13	7	4	3	2
r	0	25	25	25	25	–	1	1	1	1
a	-1	26	27	28	31	37	43	46	47	48
t	-2	28	29	31	34	37	40	43	45	46
o	-3	30	31	33	35	37	39	41	43	44
r	-4	31	32	34	36	37	38	40	42	43

which is the slope of the line segment *pq*, in *T*. If two line segments L_1 and L_2 are having their respective *T*-indices as f_1 and f_2, then L_1 and L_2 are merged if the difference of f_1 and f_2 is less than a threshold T_f, which is a differential Farey index and a parameter of our algorithm. Results for T_f = 2000 and 5000 (order of Farey table being 200) are shown in Figure 3.

SHAPE DESCRIPTION METHOD

Method Overview

As the boundary of an object gives an idea about its shape, we have described the boundary as a sequence of straight line segments. If all the internal angles (in degree) are written in order for a polygon, we get an idea about the shape of the polygon. For example, for a rectangular shape, the angular description will be ⟨90°, 90°, 90°, 90°⟩ irrespective of its orientation; for an equilateral triangle it will be ⟨60°, 60°, 60°⟩. In general, for a polygon having *n* vertices, there will be *n* entries in the description. The process involves computation of the angles magnitude, which is ultimately based on multiplication and division. For every line segment/edge we have to compute its slope and then the angle between each pair of consecutive edges. Instead of writing these angles in succession, we use the Farey indices to provide a description in the integer domain. Every straight edge of the boundary contributes an index (Farey index). Every two consecutive indices (as discussed) do generate a difference, and the sequence of these differences is used as a (circular chain) description for a (closed) polygon.

Shape Description

In our method a sequence of differences between the slopes of adjacent segments/edges has been used as a reliable descriptor of the boundary. The difference between the slopes of an edge e_k and of its next edge e_{k+1} is estimated as the difference of their Farey indices. If the respective Farey indices of e_k and e_k+1 be f_k and f_{k+1}, then the deviation of e_{k+1} from e_k is realized using an appropriate difference of f_k+1 from f_k (Figure 5). The method has been demonstrated in Figure 4. We consider the traversal of a polygon P such that the interior of P always lies right during the traversal. For three consecutive vertices of P, namely $v_k := (x_k, y_k)$, $v_{k+1} := (x_k+1, y_{k+1})$, and $v_{k+2} := (x_{k+2}, y_{k+2})$, which define two consecutive edges e_k and e_{k+1} of P ($0 \leq k < n$), we decide whether there is a left turn or a right turn at the vertex v_{k+1}, using the respective Farey indices f_k and f_{k+1} of e_k and e_{k+1} incident at v_{k+1}. Depending on a few combinatorial cases and their sub-cases, the differential Farey index, namely f'_{k+1}, corresponding to v_{k+1}, is hence obtained from f_k and f_{k+1}, as explained next.

The procedure of computing f'_{k+1} is given in Figure 5, where N_f denotes the number of positive and simple (proper and improper) fractions in the Farey table corresponding to $[0, \pi/2)$. Total number of simple fractions in T_i is, therefore, $4N_f$, which increases with the order i of AFT; for example, $N_f(T_4) = 12$ (Figure 2), $N_f(T_{200}) = 24464$.

As shown in Figure 4a, we start at the vertex v_0 and traverse the edges/line segments clockwise, as explained above. The Farey indices of the edges $e_0, e_1, ..., e_{15}$ are obtained from the coordinates of

Figure 3. Results of straight edge extraction from a sample image for two different values of the Farey threshold, T_f. Preliminary edges (without thinning) detected by exponential averaging are shown in green; final edges using AFT are shown in blue with endpoints highlighted in red. Note that, as T_f increases from 2000 to 5000, number of edges decrease, implying coarser approximation.

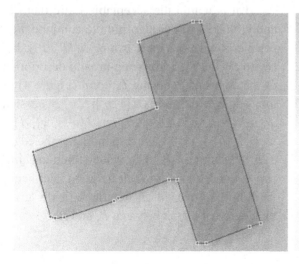

the vertices corresponding to them. For example, for edge e_0, the vertices are v_0 (24, 53) and v_1 (28, 213), wherefore we get its Farey index as $f_0 = 73098$ from the AFT, T_{200}. As v_1 and v_2 (220, 211) correspond to the edge e_1, we get its index as $f_1 = 48820$. Using the procedure shown in Figure 5, we get $f'_1 = f_0 - f_1 = 24278$ corresponding to v_1. The complete description of differential Farey indices are computed this way, which is shown in the table of Figure 4a. The feature sequence of the polygon P in Figure 4a based on differential Farey indices is, therefore, given by

$P_T = \langle 24547, 24650, 24453, 24511, 24436,$
$24339, 24400, 25055, 26427, 74380, 73014,$
$73257, 73905, 73392, 72937, 24387 \rangle.$

Similarly, for the polygon Q in Figure 4b, we get

$Q_T = \langle 23644, 24739, 24407, 24344, 24432,$
$24432, 24644, 23855, 24241, 71686, 72551,$
$73287, 73500, 73466, 73497, 23591 \rangle.$

It can be noticed from Figure 4a and Figure 4b that, effectively, the differential Farey indices of the corresponding edges of P and Q are almost similar instead of an arbitrary orientation of Q relative to P. It may be mentioned here that for T_{200} (Table 2), a deviation of differential index by 1000 on the average actually represents an angular deviation of $1000 \times 0.0036° = 3.6°$; clearly, for higher values of order i of the augmented Farey table, T_i, this deviation will be reduced (see Results Section).

Shape Matching

After generating a numeric sequence as the descriptor of the boundary of each polygonal object, we use an algorithm to compute the distance between two such descriptors, namely A_1 and A_2, having n_1 and n_2 elements, corresponding to two polygons, P_1 and P_2, respectively. The distance is computed in two phases. In Phase 1, we consider a modified form of the *Levenshtein distance* as the metric in *Wagner-Fischer algorithm* for *edit distance* between A_1 and n_2 successive elements of A_2A_2 (Damerau, 1964; Gusfield, 1997; Navarro, 2001; Wagner & Fischer, 1974). Note that, A_2A_2 is prepared by concatenating A_2 with itself for its wrap-around consideration. Each element of A_1 and A_2 lies in the interval $[0, 4N_f]$, where $4N_f$ is the total number of all simple fractions stored in T_i. Let d_v be the matrix having n_1 rows and n_2 columns, where the first column corresponds to (t)th element of A_2A_2 and the last one to its $(n_2 - \square t + 1)$th element. In the *dynamic-programming* portion (Cormen, Leiserson, & Rivest, 2000; Wagner & Fischer, 1974) of the algorithm, we assign

$d_v[u,v] \leftarrow d[u-1, j-1]$ if $|A_1[u] - A_2[v]| < T_f$;

where, T_f = *Farey threshold*; otherwise, we make

$d_v[u,v] \leftarrow 1 + \min\{d_v[u-1,v], d_v[u,v-1],$
$d_v[u-1,v-1]\},$

corresponding to the three edit operations of deletion, insertion, and substitution respectively.

We run Phase 1 for $t = 1, 2, ..., n_2$ — each time after initializing d_v — thus obtaining the minimum $d_v[n_1][n_2]$ over n_2 iterations, which signifies the effective Levenshtein distance between A_1 and A_2. If it is within the acceptable limit, then we apply Phase 2 of our algorithm to compute their perimeter-wise distance, namely $d_e(P_1, P_2)$, between P_1 and P_2P_2 (for wrap-around description of the edges of P_2) using L_2 norm (Figure 4) of their edges. In the matrix $d_e[1..n_1][1..n_2]$, we assign $de[u, v] = |L_2(e_u) - L_2(e_v)| + \min\{d_v[u-1, v], d_v[u, v-1], d_v[u-1, v-1]\}$, corresponding to the edges e_u in P_1 and e_v in P_2. The value stored at $d_e[n_1][n_2]$ is the distance for (t)th iteration, and hence its minimum over all n_2 iterations finally gives the degree of match between P_1 and P_2.

Figure 4. Description using differential Farey indices $f'_0, f'_1, ..., f'_{n-1}$, based on actual experiments. $L_1(e_k) = |x_{k+1}-x_k| + |y_{k+1}-y_k|$, $L_2(e_k) = round(\sqrt{((x_{k+1}-x_k)^2 + (y_{k+1}-y_k)^2)})$. See the section on Shape Description for explanation

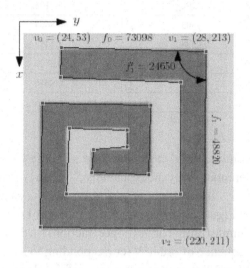
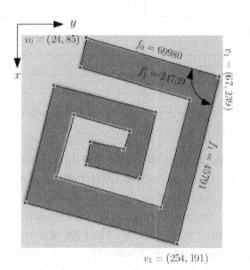

k	$e_k := \langle v_k, v_k+1 \rangle$	f_k	f'_k	L_1	L_2		k	$e_k := \langle v_k, v_k+1 \rangle$	f_k	f'_k	L_1	L_2
0	$\langle(24,53),(28,213)\rangle$	73098	24547	164	160		0	$\langle(24,85),(67,239)\rangle$	69980	23644	197	159
1	$\langle(28,213),(220,211)\rangle$	48820	24650	194	192		1	$\langle(67,239),(254,191)\rangle$	45791	24739	235	193
2	$\langle(220,211),(218,30)\rangle$	24345	24453	183	181		2	$\langle(254,191),(208,15)\rangle$	21270	24407	222	181
3	$\langle(218,30),(84,32)\rangle$	97690	24511	136	134		3	$\langle(208,15),(77,48)\rangle$	94782	24344	164	135
4	$\langle(84,32),(86,152)\rangle$	73198	24436	122	120		4	$\langle(77,48),(107,166)\rangle$	70286	24432	148	121
5	$\langle(86,152),(161,150)\rangle$	48609	24339	77	75		5	$\langle(107,166),(181,147)\rangle$	45790	24432	93	76
6	$\langle(161,150),(159,87)\rangle$	24081	24400	65	63		6	$\langle(181,147),(166,85)\rangle$	21506	24644	77	63
7	$\langle(159,87),(134,89)\rangle$	96882	25055	27	25		7	$\langle(166,85),(140,90)\rangle$	95507	23855	31	26
8	$\langle(134,89),(131,126)\rangle$	74381	26427	40	37		8	$\langle(140,90),(148,128)\rangle$	70820	24241	46	38
9	$\langle(131,126),(113,126)\rangle$	1	74380	18	18		9	$\langle(148,128),(128,135)\rangle$	93578	71686	27	21
10	$\langle(113,126),(111,62)\rangle$	24087	73014	66	64		10	$\langle(128,135),(110,71)\rangle$	21027	72551	82	66
11	$\langle(111,62),(182,59)\rangle$	48416	73257	74	71		11	$\langle(110,71),(179,51)\rangle$	45386	73287	89	71
12	$\langle(182,59),(182,185)\rangle$	73393	73905	126	126		12	$\langle(179,51),(213,172)\rangle$	69958	73500	155	125
13	$\langle(182,185),(61,185)\rangle$	1	73392	121	121		13	$\langle(213,172),(93,205)\rangle$	94496	73466	153	124
14	$\langle(61,185),(56,52)\rangle$	24010	72937	138	133		14	$\langle(93,205),(57,78)\rangle$	20999	73497	163	132
15	$\langle(56,52),(24,53)\rangle$	97479	24387	33	32		15	$\langle(57,78),(24,85)\rangle$	95264	23591	40	33

(a)   (b)

SHAPE DECOMPOSITION

For every edge of P, we need to compute its slope, and then the angle between each pair of consecutive edges. Instead of writing these angles in succession, we use the Farey indices to provide a description in the integer domain. Every straight edge of P corresponds to an index, namely the Farey index, which, for a "positive slope" of the edge, is the rank[1] of the fraction (equaling the slope of the edge) in F_N. For example, the rank of 3/4 in F_4 is 6, since there are five smaller fractions (0/1,

1/4, 1/2, 2/3, 3/4) in F_4. For other fractions, the indices are computed in a convenient way (Figure 2) and used for subsequent analysis, as explained in the following sections. Every two consecutive indices generate a difference, and the sequence of these differences is used as a (circular chain) description for the (closed) polygon, P.

Turn Checking Using T-Indices

The difference between the slopes of an edge e_k and of its next edge e_{k+1} is estimated as the difference

Table 2. Average, minimum, and maximum angular differences of two consecutive slopes in degree

Order	Avg.	Min.	Max
10	1.4062	0.6296	5.7105
20	0.3515	0.1503	2.8624
50	0.0581	0.0234	1.1457
100	0.0147	0.0058	0.5729
200	0.0036	0.0015	0.2856
300	0.0016	0.0007	0.1909

of their Farey indices. We call it the differential Farey index. If the respective Farey indices of e_k and e_{k+1} be f_k and f_{k+1}, then the differential Farey index of e_{k+1} from e_k is realized using an appropriate difference of f_{k+1} from f_k. The procedure of computing these Farey differences has been given in Figure 5. It is based on the analysis of various possible cases apropos the signs of the numerators and the denominators of fk and f_{k+1}.

We consider the traversal of a polygon P such that the interior of P, and the corresponding object thereof, always lies right during the traversal. For three consecutive vertices of P, namely $v_{k-1} := (x_{k-1}, y_{k-1})$, $v_k := (x_k, y_k)$, $v_k+1 := (x_k+1, y_k+1)$, which define two consecutive edges e_k and e_{k+1} of P, we decide whether there is a left turn or a right turn at the vertex v_k, using the respective Farey indices f_k and f_{k+1} of e_k and e_{k+1} incident at v_k. Depending on a few

combinatorial cases and their sub-cases, the differential Farey index, namely f'_{k+1}, corresponding to v_k, is hence obtained from f_k and f_{k+1}, as given in Figure 5. If N_f denotes the number of positive, simple (proper or improper fractions) in the Farey sequence of order N (corresponding to slopes in $[0, \pi/2]$), then the total number of simple fractions in T_N is $4(N_f-1)$, which increases with the order N of T_N; for example, $N_f(T_4) = 13$, whereby the total number of fractions in T_N is 48 (Figure 2).

The turn checking at a vertex is done using its differential Farey index. There is a right turn at the vertex v_{k+1} if $f'_{k+1} \leq 2N_f$, and a left turn if $f'_{k+1} \geq 2N_f$, since $2N_f$ corresponds to the angular measure π. An illustration is given in Figure 6 for a right and a left turn. For example, f'_{k+1} is computed as $f'_{k+1} = 2N_f - {}_\square (f_k - f_{k+1})$ because $f_k > f_{k+1}$ (Figure 5). So, $f'_{k+1} = 13$, which is less than $2N_f = 22$ (as N_f

Figure 5. Procedure for computing the differential Farey index, f'_{k+1}, for two consecutive edges, e_k and e_{k+1}

$$
\begin{aligned}
&\textbf{if } (y_k \geq y_{k+1} \geq y_{k+2} \textbf{ or } y_k \leq y_{k+1} \leq y_{k+2}) \\
&\qquad \textbf{if } (f_k > f_{k+1}) \textbf{ then } f'_{k+1} \leftarrow 2 \cdot N_f - (f_k - f_{k+1}) \\
&\qquad \textbf{else } f'_{k+1} \leftarrow 2 \cdot N_f + (f_{k+1} - f_k) \\
&\textbf{else} \\
&\qquad \textbf{if } |f_k - f_{k+1}| < 2 \cdot N_f \\
&\qquad\qquad \textbf{if } (f_k > f_{k+1}) \textbf{ then } f'_{k+1} \leftarrow 2 \cdot N_f - (f_k - f_{k+1}) \\
&\qquad\qquad \textbf{else } f'_{k+1} \leftarrow 2 \cdot N_f + (f_{k+1} - f_k) \\
&\qquad \textbf{else} \\
&\qquad\qquad \textbf{if } (f_k > f_{k+1}) \textbf{ then } f'_{k+1} \leftarrow f_k - f_{k+1} \\
&\qquad\qquad \textbf{else } f'_{k+1} \leftarrow 4 \cdot N_f - (f_{k+1} - f_k)
\end{aligned}
$$

Figure 6. Examples of turn checking with N = 5: F'$_5$ = ⟨0/1, 1/5, 1/4, 1/3, 2/5, 1/2, 3/5, 2/3, 3/4, 4/5, 1/1, 5/4, 4/3, 3/2, ...⟩; N$_f$ = 11. (a) Right turn, as f'$_{k+1}$ = 2N$_f$ − (f$_k$ − f$_{k+1}$) = 13 ≤ 2N$_f$ = 22. (b) Left turn, as f'$_{k+1}$ = 2N$_f$ + (f$_{k+1}$ − f$_k$) = 27 > 2N$_f$ = 22.

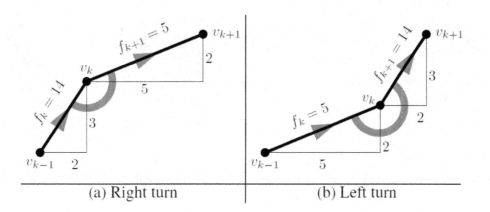

(a) Right turn　　　　　　　(b) Left turn

= 11 for order N = 5), which implies a right turn (Figure 6a). On the contrary, in Figure 6b, as f'_{k+1} exceeds $2N_f$ = 22, we have a left turn.

A demonstration of preparing the turn sequence for a polygon P by our algorithm on a test image is shown in Figure 7. Starting at v_1, as we traverse the polygon in clockwise manner, the Farey indices of its edges e_1, e_2,..., e_{27} are computed from the vertex coordinates. For example, for edge e_1, the vertices are $v_1(33, 166)$ and $v_2(37, 252)$, wherefore we get its Farey index as f_1 = 72827 from the AFT, T_{200}, with N = 200. As v_2 and v_3 (90, 225) correspond to the edge e_2, we get its index as f_2 = 42701. Using the procedure given in Figure 5, we get $f'_1 = f_1 - f_2$ = 30126, which indicates a right turn at v_2, because $f'_1 ≤ 2N_f$ = 48928 (as N_f (T_{200}) = 24464).

The feature sequence of the polygon P in Figure 7 based on differential Farey indices is, therefore, given by

PT = ⟨30126, 90019, 55100, 4039, 27982, 16817, 55908, 62684, 55554, 54164, 52740, 15277, 17948, 94673, 88106, 16817, 20359, 59928, 22382, 26464, 67016, 55729, 6005, 9998, 51744, 56564, 17165⟩.

We enumerate the above sequence of differential Farey indices as a turn sequence, using the turn types at their vertices, namely L (left turn) and R. Such a turn sequence for the boundary of the shape of Figure 7a has been shown in Figure 7b.

Finding Saddle Points

It can be noticed from the turn sequence that a sub-sequence (i.e., a contiguous segment) of L represents a local concavity and that of R, a local convexity. In particular, the L-segments represent the concave parts, and the R-segments represent the convex parts. Further, the end of an L-segment (concave part) marks the beginning of an R-segment (convex part), and vice versa. We define a saddle point[2] as the first or the last point of an L-segment, before or after which an R-segment ends or starts. Evidently, in every L-segment there will be at least one and at most two saddle points. For, if an L-segment consists of a single L, then it marks the end of its preceding R-segment and also the beginning of the next R-segment. And if it is made up of two or more L's, then its first L marks the end of the preceding R-segment and its last L marks the beginning of the next R-segment. For example, in Figure 7, ⟨v_3,v_4⟩ is an L-segment;

Figure 7. Critical points (vertices), turn sequence, saddle points (encircled), and visibility graph resulting to the final set of saddle points, obtained by our algorithm

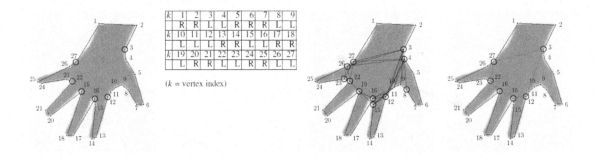

k	1	2	3	4	5	6	7	8	9
	R	R	L	L	R	R	R	L	L
k	10	11	12	13	14	15	16	17	18
	L	L	L	R	R	L	L	R	R
k	19	20	21	22	23	24	25	26	27
	L	R	R	L	L	R	R	L	L

(k = vertex index)

(a) Initial saddle points.	(b) Turn sequence at the vertices (*7, *4, ..., *4A) of P.	(c) Visibility graph.	(d) Final saddle points.

its first vertex v_3 signifies the end of the preceding R-segment $\langle v_1, v_2 \rangle$ and its last vertex v_4 signifies the start of the next R-segment $\langle v_5, v_6, v_7 \rangle$. Vertex v_{19} is the degenerate case of an L-segment with a single L, which marks the end of the R-segment $\langle v_{17}, v_{18} \rangle$ and the start of the R-segment $\langle v_{20}, v_{21} \rangle$.

Component Detection

After obtaining the sequence of saddle points, namely $S_p := \langle s_1, s_2, ... \rangle$, we construct the visibility graph, namely $G_p(V_p, E_p)$, defined on P. The graph G_p is constructed based on S_p for component detection as explained (Figure 7c), which is subsequently used for object decomposition. Observe that, each point s_i in S_p occurs before each other point s_j in S_p if and only if s_i is traversed before s_j while obtaining the vertex set of P.

To construct the node set V_p, for each s_i in S_p, we consider the corresponding L-segment, S_i, from the turn sequence, and add a vertex v_i in V_p for each saddle point or critical point/vertex (of type L, if any) of S_i. For example, in Figure 7c, the L-segments are denoted as $S_1, S_2, ..., S_6$, and for the L-segment $S_1 := \langle v_3, v_4 \rangle$, we have two

saddle points considered as nodes in V_p; for $S_2 := \langle v_8, ..., v_{12} \rangle$, we have two saddle points (v_8 and v_{12}) and three other critical points (v_9, v_{10}, v_{11}) in V_p; and so forth. For the (j)th vertex (saddle point or critical point) v_{ij} in S_i, which is added as a node u_{ij} in V_p, we also store the id i of the segment S_i as an auxiliary information of u_{ij} for construction of the edge set as follows.

For construction of the edge set E_p, we consider each pair of nodes ($u_{ij}, u_{i'j'}$) from V_p such that the following conditions are satisfied:

(e1) $i - i' = 1 \pmod{m}$, m being the total number of L-segments.

(e2) The line segment $l(v_{ij}, v_{i'j'})$ joining v_{ij} and $v_{i'j'}$ lies entirely inside P.

Condition e1 ensures that there is no edge between two saddle points or critical points belonging to the same L-segment (by this, we do not have any line segment lying outside P). Condition e2 is to guarantee that, after the decomposition, no part of any component lies outside the polygonal cover P of the concerned object. To decide whether $l(v_{ij}, v_{i'j'})$ lies entirely inside P, we consider each side/

Table 1. Summary of results for some images

Image	Straight Edges	n	Components	CPU Time (seconds)
t001	77	39	6	0.0289
t002	87	72	8	0.0419
t003	76	48	7	0.0372
bird	64	32	7	0.0256
camel-1	111	69	11	0.0418
camel-2	84	53	10	0.0389
hammer	20	13	4	0.0277
jar	45	29	5	0.0249
palm-1	55	25	7	0.0324
stem	37	28	7	0.0283

edge of P and find its intersection, if any, with l $(v_{ij}, v_{i'j'})$. The line segment l $(v_{ij}, v_{i'j'})$ is considered to be lying inside P if it has no point of intersection with any of the edges of P.

The components are extracted based on the visibility graph, G_p, as illustrated in Figure 7c. The basic steps are as follows. We consider the first two L-segments, and check from G_p whether there exists an edge between the nodes corresponding to the first vertex of S_1 and the last vertex of S_2. If so, then the line segment joining these two vertices—one from S_1 and the other from S_2—is considered to be the first partition line of the decomposition (for example, the line segment connecting v_3 and v_{12} in Figure 7d; and the part of the object contained in the sub-polygon starting from the first vertex of S_1, ending at the last vertex of S_2, and bounded by the concerned partition line is reported as the first component. Otherwise, we consider the second vertex of S_1 and the last (or its previous, in the next iteration) vertex of S_2, and so on, until there is a success. If there is a failure, then it implies that there exists no edge in G_p between any vertex of S_1 and any vertex of S_2; hence, no partition line is formed between S_1 and S_2, and the process is repeated between S_2 and S_3, starting from the first vertex of S_2 and the last one of S_3. In general, if a partition line is formed between jth vertex of S_i and j'th vertex of S_{i+1}, then in the next iteration, we consider j'th vertex of S_{i+1} as its resultant first vertex and check whether edges exist between it and the last vertex of S_{i+2}. If yes, then the corresponding partition line is formed. Otherwise, we consider the $(j'+1)$th vertex of S_{i+1} and do a similar checking until we get a success or all the vertices of S_{i+1} and S_{i+2} get exhausted. If it is a success, then the vertex of S_{i+2} incident on the partition line is set as the resultant first vertex in the next iteration; otherwise, the actual first vertex of S_{i+2} remains the first vertex in the next iteration. The procedure is repeated until all the L-segments are considered for forming the partition lines in succession. The red-colored lines in Figure 7d illustrate the final partition lines, as reported by our algorithm.

IMPLEMENTATION AND RESULTS

We have implemented the algorithm in C in Linux Fedora Release 7, Kernel version 2.6.21.1.3194. fc7, Dual Intel Xeon Processor 2.8 GHz, 800 MHz FSB. To reduce the number of edges by merging the "almost collinear" edges, we have considered T_f as the Farey threshold and have tested on several datasets for various T_f. If two consecutive edges e and e' are having AFT indices f and f', then they will be almost collinear if $|f-f'|$ is appreciably

Figure 8. Results of decomposition by our algorithm (N = 200, T_f = 5000)

(a) Input   (b) Extracted edge   (c) Polygonal cover   (d) Components

small, or, $|f-f'|$ is less than the threshold, T_f. Thus, the threshold T_f realizes the tolerance of merging two or more edges in succession, where the value of T_f, in turn, depends on the order N of T_N.

As T_f increases for a fixed AFT, the number of straight edges in P gets reduced. For example, when the order $N = 100$, total number of fractions is 24352. These 24352 slopes/fractions divide the interval of [0, 360o) into 24352 divisions. Similarly, for $N = 200$, there exist 24464×4 = 97856 slope vectors, wherefore each division amounts to 0.0037°. Hence $T_f = 1000, 2000,$ and 4000, for $N = 200$, provides tolerances of 3.679°, 7.356°, and 14.716° respectively. Although theoretically all the divisions will not be equal, the impact on practical applications is relatively negligible when

Figure 9. Some final decomposition by our algorithm (N = 200, T_f = 5000)

the number of divisions is significantly large. Hence, in our implementation, we have taken N = 200. Table 1 shows test results for some typical real-world shapes whose decompositions are shown in Figure 8 and Figure 9.

Table 2 gives an idea of the average, the minimum, and the maximum angular differences (in degrees) between two consecutive slopes for various orders of the AFT. As the order increases, the precision increases and so the difference between two consecutive slopes decreases.

CONCLUSION

Shape analysis is a pertinent problem in content-based image retrieval and computer vision. The simple-yet-efficient shape description method presented here is based on Farey sequences, which, if employed appropriately, can expedite an algorithm by its strength of integer computation. As evidenced by experimental results, our descriptor is found to be almost invariant to rotation and in compliance with shape matching using dynamic programming on the integer input. A suitable metric defined on differential Farey indices and L_2 norm of polygon edges may be designed in future to estimate the shape similarity more efficiently. We are presently working on this, which will be reported in future.

ACKNOWLEDGMENT

This chapter is mostly based on two preliminary works reported in Pratihar and Bhowmick (2009, 2010).

REFERENCES

Beiler, A. H. (1964). *Recreations in the theory of numbers: The queen of mathematics entertains.* New York, NY: Dover.

Berg, M. D., Kreveld, M. V., Overmars, M., & Schwarzkopf, O. (2000). *Computational geometry algorithms and applications.* Berlin, Germany: Springer-Verlag.

Bhowmick, P., & Bhattacharya, B. B. (2007). Fast polygonal approximation of digital curves using relaxed straightness properties. *IEEE Transactions on Pattern Analysis and Machine Intelligence, 29*(9), 1590–1602. doi:10.1109/TPAMI.2007.1082

Borgefors, G. (1988). Hierarchical chamfer matching: A parametric edge matching algorithm. *IEEE Transactions on Pattern Analysis and Machine Intelligence, 10*(6), 849–865. doi:10.1109/34.9107

Canny, J. (1986). A computational approach to edge detection. *IEEE Transactions on Pattern Analysis and Machine Intelligence, 8*, 679–714. doi:10.1109/TPAMI.1986.4767851

Chen, T. C., & Chung, K. L. (2001). A new randomized algorithm for detecting lines. *Real Time Imaging, 7*, 473–481. doi:10.1006/rtim.2001.0233

Climer, S., & Bhatia, S. K. (2003). Local lines: A linear time line detector. *Pattern Recognition Letters, 24*, 2291–2300. doi:10.1016/S0167-8655(03)00055-2

Cormen, T. H., Leiserson, C. E., & Rivest, R. L. (2000). *Introduction to algorithms.* New Delhi, India: Prentice Hall of India.

Damerau, F. J. (1964). A technique for computer detection and correction of spelling errors. *Communications of the ACM, 7*(3), 171–176. doi:10.1145/363958.363994

DeHaemer, M. Jr, & Zyda, M. (1991). Simplification of objects rendered by polygonal approximations. *Computers & Graphics, 15*(2), 175–184. doi:10.1016/0097-8493(91)90071-O

Dunham, J. G. (1986). Optimum uniform piecewise linear approximation of planar curves. *IEEE Transactions on Pattern Analysis and Machine Intelligence, 8*, 67–75. doi:10.1109/TPAMI.1986.4767753

Flanigan, F. J., & Kazdan, J. L. (1990). *Calculus two: Linear and nonlinear functions.* Berlin, Germany: Springer-Verlag.

Gavrila, D., & Philomin, V. (1999). Real-time object detection for smart vehicles. In *Proceedings of the 7th International Conference on Computer Vision* (pp. 87-93).

Gonzalez, R. C., & Woods, R. E. (1993). *Digital image processing.* Reading, MA: Addison-Wesley.

Graham, R., Knuth, D., & Potashnik, O. (1994). *Concrete mathematics.* Reading, MA: Addison-Wesley.

Gusfield, D. (1997). *Algorithms on strings, trees, and sequences: Computer science and computational biology.* Cambridge, UK: Cambridge University Press. doi:10.1017/CBO9780511574931

Hardy, G. H., & Wright, E. M. (1968). *An introduction to the theory of numbers*. New York, NY: Oxford University Press.

Huttenlocher, D., Lilien, R., & Olson, C. (1999). View-based recognition using an eigen-space approximation to the Hausdorff measure. *IEEE Transactions on Pattern Analysis and Machine Intelligence, 21*(9), 951–955. doi:10.1109/34.790437

Imai, H., & Iri, M. (1986). Computational geometric methods for polygonal approximations of a curve. *Computer Vision Graphics and Image Processing, 36*, 31–41. doi:10.1016/S0734-189X(86)80027-5

Klette, R., & Rosenfeld, A. (2004a). *Digital geometry: Geometric methods for digital picture analysis*. San Francisco, CA: Morgan Kaufmann.

Klette, R., & Rosenfeld, A. (2004b). Digital straightness: A review. *Discrete Applied Mathematics, 139*(1-3), 197–230. doi:10.1016/j.dam.2002.12.001

LeCun, Y., Bottou, L., Bengio, Y., & Haffner, P. (1998). Gradient based learning applied to document recognition. *Proceedings of the IEEE, 86*(11), 2278–2324. doi:10.1109/5.726791

Moghaddam, B., Jebara, T., & Pentland, A. (2000). Bayesian face recognition. *Pattern Recognition, 33*(11), 1771–1782. doi:10.1016/S0031-3203(99)00179-X

Mokhtarian, F., & Mohanna, F. (2002). Content-based video database retrieval through robust corner tracking. In *Proceedings of the IEEE Workshop on Multimedia Signal Processing* (pp. 224-228).

Navarro, G. (2001). A guided tour to approximate string matching. *ACM Computing Surveys, 33*(1), 31–88. doi:10.1145/375360.375365

Neville, E. H. (1950). *The Farey series of order 1025*. Cambridge, UK: Cambridge University Press.

O'Connell, K. (1997). Object-adaptive vertex based shape coding method. *IEEE Transactions on Circuits and Systems for Video Technology, 7*, 251–255. doi:10.1109/76.554440

Perez, J. C., & Vidal, E. (1994). Optimum polygonal approximation of digitized curves. *Pattern Recognition Letters, 15*, 743–750. doi:10.1016/0167-8655(94)90002-7

Pratihar, S., & Bhowmick, P. (2009). A thinning-free algorithm for straight edge detection in a gray-scale image. In *Proceedings of the 7th International Conference on Advances in Pattern Recognition* (pp. 341-344).

Pratihar, S., & Bhowmick, P. (2010). Shape decomposition using Farey sequence and saddle points. In *Proceedings of the Seventh Indian Conference on Computer Vision, Graphics and Image Processing* (pp. 77-84).

Rosenfeld, A. (1974). Digital straight line segments. *IEEE Transactions on Computers, 23*(12), 1264–1268. doi:10.1109/T-C.1974.223845

Rosin, P. L. (1997). Techniques for assessing polygonal approximation of curves. *IEEE Transactions on Pattern Analysis and Machine Intelligence, 19*(6), 659–666. doi:10.1109/34.601253

Rosin, P. L., & West, G. A. W. (1995). Non-parametric segmentation of curves into various representations. *IEEE Transactions on Pattern Analysis and Machine Intelligence, 17*, 1140–1153. doi:10.1109/34.476507

Schroeder, M. (2006). Fractions: Continued, Egyptian and Farey. In Schroeder, M. (Ed.), *Number theory in science and communication: With applications in cryptography, physics, digital information, computing, and self-similarity (Springer Series in Information Sciences)* (*Vol. 7*). New York, NY: Springer.

Shamaie, A., Hai, W., & Sutherland, A. (2011). *Hand gesture recognition for HCI.* Retrieved from http://www.ercim.eu/publication/Ercim News/enw46/shamaie.html

Sharvit, D., Chan, J., Tek, H., & Kimia, B. (1998). Symmetry based indexing of image databases. *Journal of Visual Communication and Image Representation, 9*(4), 366–380. doi:10.1006/jvci.1998.0396

Shirley, P., & Tuchman, A. A. (1990). Polygonal approximation to direct scalar volume rendering. *SIGGRAPH Computer Graphics, 24*(5), 63–70. doi:10.1145/99308.99322

Teh, C.-H., & Chin, R. T. (1989). On the detection of dominant points on digital curves. *IEEE Transactions on Pattern Analysis and Machine Intelligence, 2*(8), 859–872. doi:10.1109/34.31447

Wagner, R. A., & Fischer, M. J. (1974). The string-to-string correction problem. *Journal of the ACM, 21*(1), 168–173. doi:10.1145/321796.321811

Wall, K., & Danielsson, P.-E. (1984). A fast sequential method for polygonal approximation of digitized curves. *Computer Vision Graphics and Image Processing, 28,* 220–227. doi:10.1016/S0734-189X(84)80023-7

Yin, P. Y. (2003). Ant colony search algorithms for optimal polygonal approximation of plane curves. *Pattern Recognition, 36,* 1783–1797. doi:10.1016/S0031-3203(02)00321-7

Yin, P. Y. (2004). A discrete particle swarm algorithm for optimal polygonal approximation of digital curves. *Journal of Visual Communication and Image Representation, 15*(2), 241–260. doi:10.1016/j.jvcir.2003.12.001

Zahn, C., & Roskies, R. (1972). Fourier descriptors for plane closed curves. *IEEE Transactions on Computers, 21*(3), 269–281. doi:10.1109/TC.1972.5008949

ENDNOTES

[1]   A simple, proper fraction p/q in F_N has a rank (i.e., index) f in F_N if and only if there exists $f-1$ simple fractions in F_N whose values are less than p/q.

[2]   Mathematically, a *saddle point* for a curve is a stationary point such that the curve in the neighborhood of that point is not entirely on any side of the tangent space at that point (Flanigan & Kazdan, 1990).

Chapter 10
Multi Finger Gesture Recognition and Classification in Dynamic Environment under Varying Illumination upon Arbitrary Background

Armin Mustafa
Samsung India Software Operations, India

K.S. Venkatesh
Indian Institute of Technology Kanpur, India

ABSTRACT

This chapter aims to develop an 'accessory-free' or 'minimum accessory' interface used for communication and computation without the requirement of any specified gadgets such as finger markers, colored gloves, wrist bands, or touch screens. The authors detect various types of gestures, by finding fingertip point locations in a dynamic changing foreground projection with varying illumination on an arbitrary background using visual segmentation by reflectance modeling as opposite to recent approaches which use IR (invisible) channel to do so. The overall performance of the system was found to be adequately fast, accurate, and reliable. The objective is to facilitate in the future, a direct graphical interaction with mobile computing devices equipped with mini projectors instead of conventional displays. The authors term this a dynamic illumination environment as the projected light is liable to change continuously both in time and space and also varies with the content displayed on colored or white surface.

1. INTRODUCTION

With an ever increasing role of computerized machines in society, the need for more ergonomic and faster Human Computer Interaction (HCI) systems has become an imperative. Here, we aim to develop an 'accessory-free' or 'minimum accessory' interface suitable for communication and computation without the requirement of often used gadgets such as finger markers, colored gloves, wrist bands, or touch screens. We describe here a robust method to detect various types of gestures.

DOI: 10.4018/978-1-4666-0954-9.ch010

Our approach works by locating different salient parts, specifically fingertips, in a spatio-temporally dynamic foreground projection. This projection itself constitutes the varying illumination which the gestures have to be detected: moreover, we allow this projection to fall upon a nearly arbitrary background surface. The overall performance of the system was found to be adequate for real-time use, in terms of speed, and accurate and reliable enough in a practical setting. The long term objective is to eventually facilitate a direct graphical interaction with mobile computing devices equipped with mini projectors instead of conventional displays. It must be noted that unlike the conventional setting in which intrusions are detected as regions of major change in a 'learned' static background, our 'background' is in fact the instantaneous displayed output of the computing device, and is therefore generally liable to vary in space and time with the content displayed. Furthermore, keeping in mind the exigencies of anywhere-anytime computing, the system we propose does not require a plain white surface to be available to display upon: instead, it only requires that the surface should have at all points, a certain minimum non-specular reflectance and also be planar, even if not strictly normal to the projector-camera axis. According to most currently reported approaches, such an unconstrained problem specification would necessitate the use of an IR (invisible) channel for the finger intrusion detection. Our approach operates exclusively with visual detection and applies the principle of reflectance modeling on the scene where intrusion needs to be detected and also on intrusion which in our case is hand to achieve this. Briefly, it consists of the following two steps:

1. A process we call Dynamic Background Subtraction, under varying illumination upon an arbitrary background using a reflectance modeling technique that carries out visual detection of the shape of intrusion on the front side projected background. This par-

ticular process in patented by us in India (Application No: 974/DEL/2010)

2. Detecting the gestures and quantifying them: this is achieved by specially tuned light algorithms for the detection of the contour trajectory of the intruding hand through time, and tracking multiple salient points of this intrusion contour. Gestures can then be classified and subsequently quantified in terms of the extracted multi trajectory parameters such as position, velocity, acceleration, curvature, direction, etc.

A special, simplified, case of the above general approach is the demonstrated Paper Touchpad which functions as a virtual mouse for a computer, operating under conditions of stable (non-dynamic) illumination on arbitrary backgrounds, with the requirement of a single webcam and a piece of paper upon which the 'touchpad' is printed. This is an interactive device easy to use anywhere, anytime and employs a homographic mapping between screen and piece of paper. The paper touchpad, however, does not obviate the display.

In the end, we aim to design a robust real time system which can be embedded into a mini-projector and camera equipped mobile device that can be used without accessories anywhere a flat surface and some shade (from excessively bright light such as direct sunlight) is available. The single unit would substitute for the computer or communicator, the display, keyboard, mouse, a piano, a calculator etc.

2. RELATED WORK

Most reported techniques have usually been using some gadgets/accessories or other sort of assistive tools. For example visual ways to interact with the computer using hand gestures involved the use of a rather unique and quite ingenious Omni-directional sensor (Hofer, Naeff, & Kunz, 2009), which adds to the system cost and assumes the availability of the Omni-directional sensor. Many other researchers have studied and used glove-based or wrist band based devices (Oka, Sato, & Koike, 2002) to measure hand postures, shape and location with high accuracy and speed, especially for virtual reality. But they aren't suitable for several applications because the cables connected to the gloves restrict unfettered hand motion. Besides, the apparatus is difficult to carry and use anywhere and anytime. Some have also proposed hand gesture recognition in which the camera was placed a few meters away (Lockton, 2009), but this can't be used for direct interaction with a computer system in the most common modes of computer use. The method in Kim, Kim, and Lee (2007) detects hand and finger gestures in projected light but they require a color camera, an infrared camera, front and rear projection and are used specifically for an augmented desk interface as opposed to our system, which just requires one color camera and one projector and can be used nearly anywhere.

At the same time, single- and multitouch technologies, essentially touch (contact detection) based, were used for human computer interaction, employing devices like a touch screen (e.g., computer display, table and wall) or touchpad, as well as software that recognizes multiple simultaneous touch points. But this requires the use of specifically multi touch hardware surfaces and specific systems interfaced with it as observed in Grossman, Balakrishnan, Kurtenbach, Fitzmaurice, Khan, and Buxton (2001) and Fukumoto, Suenaga, and Mase (1994). The techniques used were mostly amongst the following: Frustrated Total Internal Reflection (FTIR), Rear Diffused Illumination (Rear DI) such as Microsoft's Surface Table, Laser Light Plan (LLP), LED-Light Plane (LED-LP) and finally Diffused Surface Illumination (DSI) to be found in Segan and Kumar (1999). Such specialized surfaces hardly qualify for anywhere-anytime application.

Certain optical or light sensing (camera) based solutions were attempted sometime later. The scalability, low cost and ease of setup are suggestive reasoning for the popularity of optical solutions. Each of these techniques consists of an optical sensor (typically a camera), infrared light source, and visual feedback in the form of projection or LCD as seen in Wu, Shah, and Lobo (2000) and Eldridge and Rudolph (2008). Monocular camera views were also used for 3D pose estimation of hand gestures like in Shimada, Shirai, Kuno, and Miura (1998) which was very computationally expensive

Infrared imagings for building an interface as in Lin and Chang (2007) and augmented desktops as in Han (2005) and Oka, Sato, and Koike (2002) also appear in the literature. Such techniques employ infrared cameras, infrared light source, IR LED's with few inches of acrylic sheets, baffles, compliant surfaces etc. for proper operation. Similarly, Westerman, Elias, and Hedge (2001) requires capacitive sensor array, keyboard and pointing device. All these types of Multi touch devices used for HCI require complicated setups and sophisticated devices which make the system much more costly and difficult to manage. Similarly, Kim, Kim, and Lee (2007) used infrared cameras to segment skin regions from background pixels in order to track two hands for interaction on a 2D tabletop display. Their method then used a template matching approach in order to recognize a small set of gestures that could be interpreted as interface commands. However, no precise fingertip position information was obtained using their technique.

After some time, techniques using Stereo Vision came into existence but didn't gain much popularity because of certain drawbacks like the need for some complex calibration and the subject having to adjust according to the needs of the camera, which makes it difficult to use for real-life situations (Mitra & Acharya, 2007) as well as diminishing user friendliness. Some have used simple CRT/LCD displays but the capture was done with two cameras placed at two different accurately maintained angles (Thomas, 1994) which were again unsuitable for day to day applications.

Many approaches use markers attached to a user's hands or fingertips to facilitate their detection in the video stream captured by the camera as seen in Mistry, Maes, and Chang (2007). While markers help in more reliably detecting hands and fingers, they present obstacles to natural interaction similar to glove-based devices, though perhaps less cumbersome than the former. Besides, the user has to remember to carry the markers around without fail. A few works provide a comprehensive survey of hand tracking methods and gesture analysis algorithms (Jones & Rehg, 1999). But these are meant for whole-body gestures which are unsuitable for acting as a direct interface with the computer or any system for a seated subject 'before a desk'.

Depth information obtained using 2 cameras were used for classification into background and foreground in Gordon, Darrell, Harville, and Woodfill (1999). Another approach is to extract image regions corresponding to human skin by either color segmentation or background image subtraction or both. Because human skin isn't uniformly colored and changes significantly under different lighting conditions, such methods often produce unreliable segmentation of human skin regions and are user (skin color) dependent. Methods based on background image modeling followed by subtraction also prove unreliable when applied to images with a complex background and time varying illumination conditions as in Thomas (1994). For an effective and practical solution, we need that the system, even with a dynamic background must give good results. Only this will allow our proposed approach to operate directly under fore-projected illumination to come to fruition.

After a system identifies image regions in input images, it can analyze the regions to estimate hand posture. Researchers in Pavlovic, Sharma, and Huang (2001) and Vladimir, Rajeev, and Thomas (1993) have developed several techniques to estimate pointing directions of one or multiple fingertips based on 2D hand or fingertip geometrical features. Wu, Lin, and Huang (2001) uses a 3D human hand model for hand gesture analysis. To determine the model's posture, this approach matches the model to a hand image obtained by one or more cameras as seen in Yuan and Zhang (2010) and Wren, Azarbayejani, Darrell, and Pentland (1997). Using a 3D human hand model solves the problem of self-occlusion, but these methods don't work well for natural or intuitive interactions because they're too computationally expensive for real-time processing and require controlled environments with a relatively simple background.

Moreover, all these approaches either assume the background to be static or use infrared light as a fourth invisible channel for visual segmentation. In Hofer, Naeff, and Kunz (2009) detection of hand gestures for the replacement of mouse is shown but this works only for a static background, and we also need a separate monitor for operation. Our formulation is generic and aims to replace monitor, keyboard, piano, mouse etc. Motonorihi, Ueda, and Akiyama (2003) and Helman, Juan, Leone, and Aderito (2007) detect hand gestures but not in dynamic background and highly changing lighting conditions and does not eliminate the use of monitor, keyboard etc. Also in Utsumi and Ohya (1999), hand gestures are detected to interact with sound/music system which is a rather specific application, whereas our system is much more general. Similarly, in Jenab and Reiterer (2008) finger movement is used to interact with the mobile screen but only a few gestures are supported, suitable for a static background only. Apart from all this, Xing, Wang, Zhao, and Huang (2009) gives a survey of almost all existing algorithms in gesture recognition for various applications and most of them used Hidden Markov Models, Finite State Machines, Artificial Neural Networks, wavelets etc. but none of the existing algorithm satisfies all the criteria and conditions of our problem.

In an era where people dislike carrying large gadgets, or complex setups and assistive tools or accessories with them, we need to rework our paradigm. It isn't enough to simply make the devices smaller and better. We need a 'minimum accessory interface' which uses visual segmentation techniques for foreground segmentation on dynamic backgrounds, in fact, even operates under projector front-illumination conditions, and forgoes an infrared channel. With reducing prices of cameras and projectors, our proposed system should eventually become cost-competitive and replace hardware like items mouse, keyboard, monitor etc.

3. OUR APPROACH: PRINCIPLES, ASSUMPTIONS AND CALIBRATION

3.1. The Projector Camera System

Projection systems are used for various esoteric purposes such as to implement augmented reality, as well as to simply create both displays and interfaces on ordinary surfaces. Ordinary surfaces have varying reflectance, color (texture), and geometry. These variations can be accounted for by integrating a camera into the projection system and applying methods from computer vision. Projector-camera systems became popular in these years, and one of the popular purposes of them is 3D measurement. The only difference between camera and projector is the direction of flow of optical information. 3D scene is projected onto the 2D image plane in camera; and 2D pattern in projector is projected onto 3D scene. Hence, a straightforward solution for projector calibration is using camera calibration methods, which generally require 3D-2D projection maps (homographies).

In most such applications, the projector serves, that is to say, interacts with, only the camera. Our system uses a projector-camera pair in a subtly different and more powerful role: both to provide device output to the user and to simultaneously provide user input to the system. Both the camera and the user utilize the projector's output, and both the user and the projector provide necessary inputs to the camera. In short, the projection surface serves as the medium of communication between user and machine. The set-up is shown in the Figure 1.

3.2. Surface Types and Reflectance

For our purpose in the following discussion, we can afford to use the terms *reflectivity* and *reflectance* interchangeably, as our concern is with thick surfaces whose reflection properties are not contributed to by thin reflection (multi layered surface) phenomena. Reflectivity is a directional property, and on the basis of this directionality, most surfaces can be grossly divided into those that are specular reflectors and those that are diffuse reflectors, though we keep in mind that the terms specular and diffuse are relative. For specular surfaces, such as glass or polished metal, reflectivity will be nearly zero at all angles except at the appropriate reflected angle. For diffuse surfaces,

Figure 1. Projector camera system

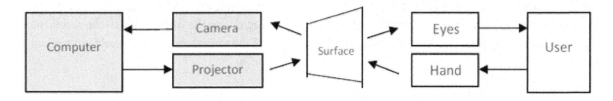

such as matte white paint, reflectivity is uniform; radiation is reflected in all angles equally or near-equally. Such surfaces are said to be Lambertian. Most real objects have some mixture of diffuse and specular reflective properties.

Besides, the output of a light-sensitive device depends on the color of the light incident upon it. Radiant sensitivity is considered as a function of wavelength i.e., the response of a device or material to monochromatic light is a function of wavelength, also known as spectral response. It is a means of relating the physical nature of change in light to the changes in image and color spaces. Recent computational models of color vision demonstrate that it is possible to achieve exact color constancy over a limited range of lights and surfaces described by linear models. The success of these computational models hinges on whether any sizable range of surface spectral reflectances can be described by a linear model with about three parameters. A visual system exhibits perfect or exact color constancy if its estimates of object color are unaffected by changes in ambient lighting. Human color vision is approximately color constant across certain ranges of illumination, although the degree of color constancy exhibits changes with the range of lighting examined.

As long as the lighting and surface spectral reflectances in the scene approximately lie within limited ranges, the color estimates are approximately correct. Spectral response on the plane upon which projection takes place will differ with the spectral response of the intruding object, thus giving evidence of intrusion. We have used the concept of reflectance modeling in our work. The reflectances of various objects like hand, arbitrary background etc to create different models which are in turn used for intrusion detection under varying illumination. Since it is not the appearance of the surface that is being modeled, but its reflectance, intrusion detection becomes possible over

a wide range of spatially and temporally varying illumination conditions. Using these concepts we develop an algorithm which first models, and then uses, reflectance properties of the projection surface to detect intrusion.

3.3. Assumptions

We expect the surface, the user and the system (consisting of the computing device, its projector and its camera) to meet some general criteria.

1. The surface must be near-flat, with a Lambertian (non-specular) reflectivity uniform over the projection surface.

2. The reflectance coefficient is not too low either at any wavelength in the visible band, or at any point or region upon the surface. This is the first part of a *singularity-avoidance* requirement.

3. We allow the surface to possess some space-varying texture, subject to meeting the criteria set down above at each point individually.

4. Surface reflectance spectrum should differ sufficiently from that of human skin at all points.

5. We allow ambient illumination to be present, and to have any spectral bias, so long as its intensity allows the projector output to sufficiently dominate and so long as the ambient illumination is constant over time during the entirety of a user session.

6. Ambient illumination must preferably be non-specular (diffuse) to avoid shadow casting.

7. There should not be instances of regions or times where both ambient and projector illumination are zero, resulting in very dark regions on the surface. This is the second part of the *singularity-avoidance* requirement

8. The camera-projector combination is assumed to be fixed in space relative to each other (by sharing a common chassis, for example) as well as fixed in space relative to the projection surface during an interaction session.

9. Bounded depth: While capturing the videos, the light intensity reflected by the fingers should be nearly constant to avoid abrupt intensity changes due to intrusions occurring too close to the camera/projector. This is ensured by keeping the hand and fingers close to the projection surface at all times. In other words, the depth variation across the projection surface during the gesturing action should be a reasonably small fraction of the camera/projector distance.

10. Each finger gesture video should be brief and last for no more than about 3-4 seconds. Longer gesture times will delay the identification of the gesture as identification and appropriate consequent action is only possible after each gesture performed is completed.

11. The optics of projector and camera are kept as nearly co-axial and coincident as possible to reduce the shadow and parallax effects.

12. We confine ourselves to an image size of 640 x 480 pixels because larger sizes, while improving spatial resolution of the gestures, would increase the computational burden, and adversely affect real time performance.

13. At a maximum, 2 fingers were used to make a proper sign. This choice varies from signer to signer and programmer to programmer. More the skin region, more is the complexity of the coding for tracking the motion of the fingers.

14. Good computing power.

15. Camera, preferably without AGC and white balance adaptation

3.4. Experimental Setup and Calibration

Under the abovementioned set of assumptions, the system's operation during a session is initiated with a session calibration phase which process consists of the following steps in sequence.

1. Calibration to ambient illumination.
2. Calibration to skin color under ambient illumination.
3. Surface texture calibration under projector illumination.
4. Skin color calibration under projector illumination.
5. Camera-projector co-calibration for white balance.

Apart from all these session-specific parameter settings, the system has to be one-time factory-calibrated to map camera and projector spatial and temporal resolutions to one other.

Gestures are captured through the use of a single web camera facing towards the hand of the user and the projection surface. The details of calibration will be discussed in Section 4.

The experimental setup of our system is shown in the Figure 2. Dynamic data is projected on a surface and gesture is performed on respective surface which is captured by camera and the video stream obtained is processed to define the gestures.

4. RELIABLE INTRUSION DETECTION UNDER PROJECTOR ILLUMINATION

4.1. The Statistical Gaussian Model Based Approach

What we present in the following is, to the best of our knowledge, original. There are hardly any reports we could find in the literature we could find dealing with intrusion detection in a

Figure 2. Experimental setup of the invention: 1-Projector, 2-Screen on which random scenes are being projected and hand is inserted as an intrusion and 3-Camera recording the screen

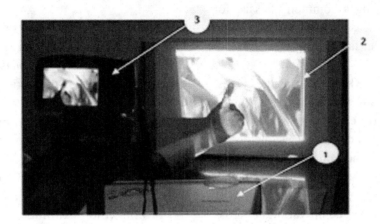

dynamically illuminated environment. In Nadia and Cooperstock (2004) the authors deal with intrusion detection in camera projector system handles geometry and color compensation, but does not gives any compensation for factors like Luminance, Camera parameters etc. The methods outlined in this subsection were actually developed and implemented at our lab chronologically prior to the reflectance modeling approach we present next. This approach is more pedagogically intuitive, and while original, represents less radical innovation than reflectance modeling.

In the process of arriving at a method that effectively achieves our goals, we first describe an approach to change/intrusion detection that is more preliminary and is in common use: it makes more assumptions about the environment such as that no ambient illumination is present (an unrealistic assumption). Further it reality does not constitute what may properly be termed reflectance modeling in the rigorous sense, as surface and skin reflectance models are not estimated. Thus the performance of the preliminary approach we present in this section is markedly inferior under even compliant conditions, and places more restrictions upon the environment. On the other hand, we do choose to present it in some detail because this

method was actually first implemented before our more refined final approach was conceived. It also has some pedagogic value, as it directly addresses many of the most important challenges of the problem of intrusion detection. Extracting intrusion based on color image segmentation or background subtraction often fails when the scene has a complicated background and dynamic lighting. In the case of intrusion monitoring, simple motion detection, or an approach based on color modeling, may be sufficient. But variations in lighting conditions, constantly changing background, as well as camera hardware settings and behavior complicate the intrusion detection problem. It is often necessary to cope with the phenomenon of illumination variations as it can falsely trigger the change detection module. Further, motion detection as a means of intrusion detection may also fail in the scenario we plan to work in, where the background can be dynamic, with moving entities flying across the screen at times giving rise to what may be termed spurious flow artifacts. The information in each band of the RGB color space of the video sequences activates our pixel wise change detection algorithm in the observed input frame in spite of a continuously changing background. This is achieved by recursively updating the background on the basis of the known projected information and seeking conformance in each camera captured frame to the current reference frame. Ordinary surfaces can have space varying reflectance, color, and geometry. These variations can be accounted for by integrating a camera into the projection system and applying methods from computer vision. The methods currently in use are fundamentally limited since they assume the camera, illumination, and scene as static. Steps involved in the method are as follows:

Step 1: Before we start our learning phase we need to assume that the projector screen surface has complete uniformity.

Step 2: Matching frames of the projected and captured videos

In the experiment conducted we fixed the no of frames in both captured and projected video and hence calibrated and matched the captured and projected videos.

- Projected video has 100 frames between two black frames
- Captured video has 500 frames between two nearest black frames
- Result: 1 frame of projector was temporally equal to 5 frames of captured video

Step 3: Calibration of colors for projector camera system:

Pure red, green and blue colors are sent via the projector and captured by the camera for a set of 'n' frames. The camera output is not pure red, green or blue. Here, every pure input has all its corresponding response RGB components non zero. This is on account of an imperfect color balance match between projector and camera.

Since the color values which are projected and the ones which are captured from the camera

don't match we carry out color calibration over 'n' frames.

Considering the red input only:

a. Find the mean red, mean green and mean blue of the output for the 'n' frames

b. Find the maximum and minimum for each red, green and blue output from the 'n' frames.

c. Find the difference between maximum and the mean value for every RGB output component for the red input which gives the deviation.

d. Follow the same procedure for green as well as blue input for 'n' frames.

The projected RGB values are represented by R_P, G_P and B_P and the corresponding camera captured colour values are represented by R_C, G_C and B_C. With the projector output held constant, we in fact capture 'n' frames with the camera for the purpose of statistical averaging over camera noise, and denote these time indexed camera capture components as $R_C(t)$, $G_C(t)$ and $B_C(t)$.

An imperfect match between the white balances of projector and camera results in a certain amount of crosstalk between different colour channels, so that $R_P = [255\ 0\ 0]^T$; $G_P = [0\ 255\ 0]^T$; $B_P = [0\ 0\ 255]^T$, whereas $R_C = [R^r_C\ R^g_C\ R^b_C]^T$; $G_C = [G^r_C\ G^g_C\ G^b_C]^T$; $B_C = [B^r_C\ B^g_C\ B^b_C]^T$. Each component X^y_C; $X = R, G, B$ and $y = r, g, b$ in each output vector of these equations is the time and space average of the n resp. captures:

$$X_C^{\ y} = \frac{\sum\limits_{k,l=1,1}^{M,N} \sum\limits_{t=1}^{n} X_C^{\ y}(t)}{n \times M \times N} \tag{1}$$

where M, N are the numbers of pixel rows and columns in the captured image, and k,l are the row and column indices.

Step 4: Now for detecting the intrusion blob we need to calculate the mean and maximum deviation for each input RGB component. Ideally, the mean as well as the deviation for each RGB output component for every individual pure input is determined. For simplicity we take the mean and maximum values only. x_r, x_g, x_b are respective maximum deviations from mean value for red, green and blue components

$$x_r = R^r_{max} - R^r_C, x_g = R^g_{max} - R^g_C, x_b = R^b_{max} - R^b_C \qquad (2)$$

where $R^r_{max}, R^g_{max}, R^b_{max}$ are the extreme red green and blue components under the red input. Similarly, we define and compute:

$$y_r = G^r_{max} - G^r_C, y_g = G^g_{max} - G^g_C, y_b = G^b_{max} - G^b_C \qquad (3)$$

$$z_r = B^r_{max} - B^r_C, z_g = B^g_{max} - B^g_C, z_b = B^b_{max} - B^b_C \qquad (4)$$

Step 5: Formation of color bias matrix: This matrix is formed by the mean values and maximum deviations in each of the red, green and blue inputs and outputs. The color bias matrix is as shown in Equation (5). This matrix is used to calculate the expected values by performing matrix multiplication with known input

$$\begin{pmatrix} R^r_C & G^r_C & B^r_C \\ R^g_C & G^g_C & B^g_C \\ R^b_C & G^b_C & B^b_C \end{pmatrix} \qquad (5)$$

Step 6: Calculating the total maximum deviations in RGB

The total deviation for each component is the sum of deviation or variance at each input. To find these values we need to follow the equation given below:

Dev(R) =deviation due to red input + deviation due to green input+ deviation due to blue input

$$(6)$$

$$dev(R) = \sigma(R) = x_r + y_r + z_r \qquad (7)$$

Similarly,

$$dev(G) = \sigma(G) = x_g + y_g + z_g \qquad (8)$$

$$dev(B) = \sigma(B) = x_b + y_b + z_b \qquad (9)$$

Step 7: Finding expected values
- Project the video
- Convert it into number of frames
- Every pixel of every single frame is now decomposed into its RGB components
- These RGB values are then normalized by dividing each by 255
- Now we multiply this normalized RGB with the color bias matrix to get the expected values

For any single pixel $p(i,j)$ of the projected video, let the value of RGB components be given by $[R,G,B]^T$. To calculate the expected value in the absence of intrusion, we need to do matrix multiplication of the pixels RGB values and the color bias matrix. Let the final expected (normalized) values for the red, green and blue be R_e, G_e and B_e, calculated as shown in Equation (10).

$$\begin{pmatrix} R^r_C & G^r_C & B^r_C \\ R^g_C & G^g_C & B^g_C \\ R^b_C & G^b_C & B^b_C \end{pmatrix} * \begin{pmatrix} R \div 255 \\ G \div 255 \\ B \div 255 \end{pmatrix} = \begin{pmatrix} R_e \\ G_e \\ B_e \end{pmatrix} \qquad (10)$$

Step 8: Steps for finding the observed values

- ◦ Interpolate and resize the captured video to projected video for pixel matching.
- ◦ Convert the captured videos to frames
- ◦ Every pixel of every single frame is now decomposed into its RGB components
- ◦ Intrusion detection is done according to the equations below
- ◦ Equations are derived which relate the image coordinates in the camera to the external coordinate system.

Step 9: Each red green and blue will have their individual Gaussian models. According to the Statistical Gaussian models obtained above we can do background subtraction by defining a range of around '$2\sigma_x$' around the mean which constitutes the background and the values obtained outside that range is considered to be intrusion. Here subscript 'x' represents the colors Red(r), Green(g) or Blue(b)

Now we take each red (R_v), green (G_v) and blue (B_v) component of the observed value V of each pixel, which can generically be represented as X_v, where X represents R, G or B and apply following equations on it to detect the intrusion. 'σ_x' is the variance and expected values are R_e, G_e and B_e of the respective RGB components which can be represented as X_e, where X represents R, G or B.

The RGB values of every pixel of the captured frames are now taken and compared with the expected values as given before. Here, k is chosen to be 0.73 based upon the empirical tests and is used for thresholding. After the detection of intrusions a binary image is created with 1s at pixels where intrusion has occurred and 0s elsewhere. The decision equations are written below:

$$X_e - (k\,{}^*\sigma_x) < X_v < X_e + (k\,{}^*\sigma_x)\ ;\ \text{Then it is}$$
Background $\hspace{3cm}$ (11)

Else it is intrusion

The flowchart of the statistical approach to find intrusion is shown in Figure 3

4.2. Compensations

4.2.1. Correction for Camera Auto Gain and Auto Colour Balance

The approach assumes that the camera does not implement automatic gain control and automatic white balance. If this is not the case additional measures are required for proper detection. This subsection deals with those additional measures. When a camera implements automatic gain control, and the feature is not optional (cannot be turned off), changes in the content of the projected scene $D[n]$ will result in global luminance adjustments in the camera output, affecting, essentially, every pixel. By our decision rule, this will affect the results of the detector, which it should not. We now outline briefly a method to undo this effect, by remapping the luminance function suitably to defeat the auto gain effect. The equations that follow invariably contain some empirical constants that could change with the camera in use.

The method estimates the illumination conditions of the observed image and normalizes the brightness before carrying out background subtraction. The first step towards this is a color space transformation to transform the image into YC_bC_r colour space. Our subsequent interest is confined to the Y component.

The RGB color space does not provide sufficient information about the illumination conditions and effect of such conditions on any surface. So we transform to YC_bC_r space and then apply threshold to Y component to enhance the segmentation by using the intensity properties of the image. Threshold segmentation was implemented as the first step to decrease the details in the image set greatly for efficient processing. Hence we calculate luminance at each pixel and then calculate

Figure 3. The statistical approach to detect intrusion

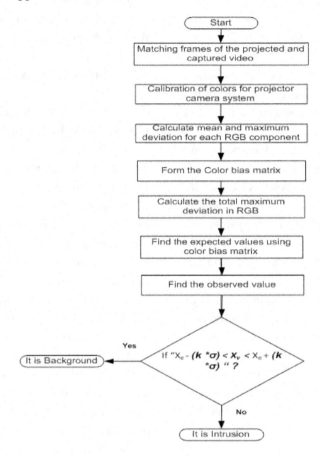

the new value for 'k' the deflection coefficient at each pixel according to the value of luminance.

This is done by developing a linear relationship between luminance and *'k'*

$$k^y - .82 = (slope*(Y - Y_{min})) \qquad (12)$$

$$k^y = (slope*Y) + (.82) - (slope*Y_{min}) \qquad (13)$$

where, k^y - The factor by which the old value of *'k'* must be multiplied

$$slope = (0.06/(Y_{max} - Y_{min})); \qquad (14)$$

L_{min}, L_{max} -Minimum and Maximum Luminance for pixels in the frame respectively.

4.2.2. Dominant Color Compensation

This compensates for possible inbuilt white balance adaptation by the camera. Automatic white balance adaptation in the camera tends to suppress the dominate color. We therefore artificially increase sensitivity to the dominant color to compensate for the adaptation. The value of *'k'* is set as follows:

$$k^c = [(R+G+B) \div (3 * Dom\_color)] + 0.9 \qquad (15)$$

where, *Dom_color* is the dominant color for that particular pixel (either R or G or B) and *'k^c'* is a new constant for modulating *'k'*. Hence, the final value of constant *'k'* is given by:

$$k_{final} = k^* \, k^y/k^c \qquad (16)$$

After this dominant color and luminance compensation, we replace k with k_{final} in the detection Equation.(11).

4.3. Intrusion Detection using Reflectance Model

The methods outlined in this subsection were actually developed and implemented at our lab. It is more general and all encompassing formulation of the problem; it introduces and uses the method of reflectance modeling. It gives additional advantages to the user by allowing use of non white and textured surfaces for projection which was not permissible in the Gaussian model approach. What follows in this subsection constitutes the main and most significant innovative part of our work.

Reflectance modeling represents the more refined approach to the problem of intrusion detection in highly varying and dynamic illumination in the presence of near-constant non-dominant ambient illumination. We now launch into a discussion of this method in a systematic manner. The main aim of the problem was detection of events that differ from what is considered normal. The normal in this case, is, arguably, the possibly highly dynamic scene projected on the user specified surface by the computer through the mini projector. We aim to detect the intrusion through a novel process of reflectance modeling. The session begins with a few seconds of calibration which itself includes generating models of the hand, the surface, and the ambient illumination. Subsequently, we proceed to detect the hand in constantly changing background caused by the mixture of unchanging ambient illumination and the highly varying projector illumination under front projection. This kind of detection requires carefully recording the camera output with certain constraints followed by the learning phase and projector-camera co-calibration to match the no of frames per second and number of pixels per frame. This is executed with the steps explained below:

4.3.1. Calculation of Expected RGB Values and Detecting Intrusion at Initial Stages under Controlled Projector Illumination

1. Recording and modeling surface under ambient lighting (ambient lighting is on and projector is off). This defines a model say S_A, which is surface under ambient lighting and is true for any sort of arbitrary texture plane surface.

2. Now, the hand is introduced on the surface illuminated by the ambient lighting and a model for hand is obtained, say H_A, which is hand/skin under ambient light. This is done through the following steps: first the region occupied by the hand is segmented by subtraction and a common Gaussian model for all the sample pixels of the hand available over the space of the foreground and over all the frames of the exposure.

3. Hand is removed from the visibility of camera and the projector is switched on with three lights one by one, Red, Green and Blue. This is followed by observing and modeling of the surface in ambient light in addition to the colored light of projector, which can be represented by $S_{AP}{}^R$, $S_{AP}{}^G$ and $S_{AP}{}^B$ respectively. It is assumed that we cannot switch off the ambient light as we wish. Each $S_{AP}{}^Y$ = $[\, R_S{}^Y, \, G_S{}^Y, \, B_S{}^Y \,]$, where Y represents the projection of lighting and may take values as R, G or B

4. Now the surface in colored(R, G, B) projector light $(S_P{}^Y)$ is determined by differencing $S_{AP}{}^Y$ and S_A at each pixel. The relationship of the session parameters is as shown in Equation (18). This specifies the green, red and blue component of the surface under projection. The subtraction should be done component wise i.e., for each red, green and blue color

$$S_p^Y = [R_p^Y, G_p^Y, B_p^Y]^T \qquad (17)$$

$$S_p^Y = S_{AP}^Y - S_A; \qquad (18)$$

5.   The hand is introduced under a scenario when the ambient light is on, and the projector is displaying three lights one by one, Red, Green and Blue. We get new models of hand which are H_{AP}^R, H_{AP}^G and H_{AP}^B for red, green and blue light respectively captured under combination of ambient light and projector white light. Each $H_{AP}^Y = [R_H^Y, G_H^Y, B_H^Y]$, where Y represents the projection of lighting and may take values as R, G or B

6.   Hence, the model of the hand in projected white light is obtained, H_p^Y which is obtained in the same way as S_p^Y.

$$H_p^Y = [R_{PH}^Y, G_{PH}^Y, B_{PH}^Y]^T \qquad (19)$$

$$H_p^Y = H_{AP}^Y - H_A; \qquad (20)$$

7.   Color bias matrix is constructed for both models of hand(M_H) and surface(M_S) like we construct in the Gaussian model

8.   Now project the known changing data on the surface under observation by camera. Let us assume the data is $D[n]$ where 'n' is the frame number. But the camera receives a sum of the reflections of the ambient lighting from the surface.

9.   Normalization of the models H_p^Y and S_p^Y is done to obtain values which are less than or equal to one by dividing each component by 255, which is the maximum value that each component can reach.

10.   Now the expected values of the dynamic background when projected on the surface(S_e) is obtained which is ought to be seen through the camera by performing a matrix multiplication of the $D[n]$ and the M_S followed by addition of S_A

$$S_e = (M_S \times D[n]) + S_A; \; S_e = [S_e^R, S_e^G, S_e^B]^T \qquad (21)$$

11.   Next we calculate the expected values of the hand pixels when dynamic background is projected on the hand (H_e) which is ought to be seen through the camera by performing matrix multiplication of the $D[n]$ and the M_H followed by addition of the H_A image

$$H_e = (M_H \times D[n]) + H_A; \; H_e = [H_e^R, H_e^G, H_e^B]^T \qquad (22)$$

The average result of the net outcome of the above calculation and the Gaussian model method is the values expected in the region of the hand skin pixels during intrusion in the combination of ambient lighting and foreground projection on the hand. Now these values can be used to detect the blobs for the fingers of the hand entering the frames by detecting skin regions manipulated by the models obtained earlier.

12.   Now consider the 'n^{th}' of the time and space normalized camera output. The value of the observation at any given pixel be 'V' while H_e and S_e are the expected values for the same pixel in that frame. Evaluate the ratio:

$$\eta = \frac{\|V - H_e\|}{\|V - S_e\|} \qquad (23)$$

Decision rule is as follows: If $\eta > 1$ then it is intrusion, else it is background. The majority decision of all the three RGB components is taken as final decision.

The flowchart of the use of reflectance modeling method to detect intrusion is shown in Figure 4.

4.3.2. Shadow Removal and other Post Processing

Shadows are often a problem in background subtraction because they can show up as a foreground object under segmentation by change detection. A shadow may be viewed as a geometrically distorted version of the pattern that together with

Figure 4. Flowchart representation of reflectance modelling method

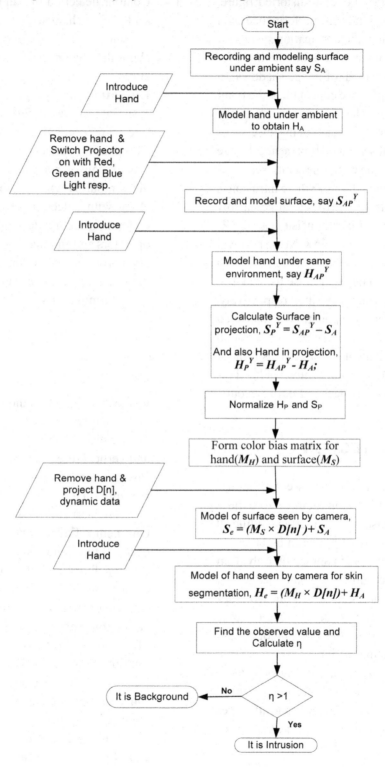

the pattern produces an overall distorted figure. Shadows can greatly hinder the performance level of pattern detection and classification systems.

There are a number of possible methods for the detection and removal of image shadows. In our method we employ the concept that the point where shadows are cast has the same ratio between the RGB components expected in the absence of intrusion to those observed in its presence. Hence the red, green and blue component ratios are calculated at each point in the area where intrusion is detected and this ratio is used to determine shadow regions where these ratios is consistent across R, G, B. After removing the shadow, Noise removal algorithm is applied on the image to remove both salt and pepper and Gaussian noise using a 4×4 median filter and Gaussian filter respectively. This is then followed by application of connected component analysis by performing foreground cleanup in a raw segmented image. This form of analysis returns the required contour of hand removing the other disturbances and extra contours.

5. GESTURE DETECTION

In this section, we present the essential gesture detection and quantification methods to build a complete gesture based visual interface. While all the techniques outlined below were most certainly independently developed in our lab literally from first principles, we ourselves acknowledge that despite being original, this part of our work applies relatively straightforward and well known elementary image operations and cannot be said to constitute major innovation.

After detection of the binary images by techniques outlined in the previous sections, we need to detect the finger tips and the type and attributes of the gestures. The aim of this project is to propose a video based approach to recognize gestures (one or more fingers). The algorithm includes the following steps and is shown in Figure 5.

1. Contour detection of hand which is represented by a chain sequence in which every entry in the sequence encodes information about the location of the next point on the curve

2. **Curvature mapping:** The curvature of a smooth curve is defined as the curvature of its osculating circle at each point. Curvature may either be negative or positive. Calculation of curvature at each point in the contour by applying the usual formula, along with detection of corner points by computing second derivatives using Sobel operators and finding eigenvalues from the autocorrelation function obtained. Using the first method of curvature, we apply the usual formula for signed curvature k:

$$k = \frac{x'y'' - y'x''}{(x'^2 + y'^2)^{3/2}} \tag{24}$$

where x' and y' gives the first derivative in horizontal and vertical direction. y'' and x'' are the second derivatives in the horizontal and vertical direction

3. **Positive curvature extrema extraction on contour** (determining the highest positive corner points) **This is done by two methods:** One method finds out the maximum positive peaks of the signed curvature calculated in the step above and other method finds the corner points by computing second derivatives. In case of more than one positive curvature points of almost equivalent magnitude of curvature, we classify the gesture to be multiple fingers. The two methods are applied jointly upon each frame, because it was found that corner detection alone produced many false positives.

4. **Segregating the gesture into single or multiple finger:** Single finger gestures: Click, Rotate (Clockwise and Anticlockwise), Move arbitrary and Pan Multiple finger

Figure 5. Flowchart representation of gesture detection from intrusion

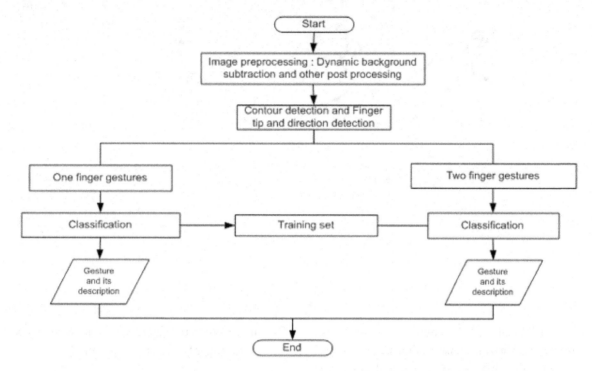

gestures: Zoom (Zoom-In and Zoom-Out), Drag.

5. **Frame to frame fingertip tracking by using motion model estimation:** The trajectory, direction evolution, starts and end points of each finger in the gesture performed is traced through the frames. This is done by applying motion model upon the high curvature point in every frame on the retrieved contour and verifying if the detected point lies in the vicinity of the prediction made using the preceding frames. Tracking motion feedback is used to handle momentary errors or occlusions.

6. **Gesture classification and quantification:** The final classification and subsequent gesture quantification is performed using the information represented diagrammatically in Figure 6.

The gestures shown in Figure 6 are described as follows:

Single finger gestures:

Click: When there is no significant movement in the finger tip except for a vibration.

Pan: When the comparative thickness of the contour is above some threshold.

Move: When there is significant movement in the finger tip in any direction.

Rotate: For this slope is calculated at each point along the trajectory and the and following equations are implemented: Let at time '*t*' the coordinates of finger tip are *(x, y)* and at some time '*t + k*' the fingertip coordinates are *(x',y')*

$$a = \frac{y' - y}{x' - x} , \; b = \frac{x' - x}{y' - y} \tag{29}$$

where 'a' and 'b' represents the slope and inverse slope respectively

When the gesture ends, we find out how many times both '*a*' and '*b*' becomes zero and what is

Figure 6. Gesture classification criteria

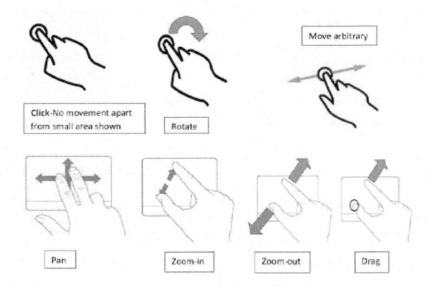

their sum. The times *'a'* becomes zero represents that the line is horizontal and the times *'b'* becomes zero represents that the line is vertical line. The presence of line represents absence of curve and thereby helps us to find out whether our gesture is rotate or not.

Two finger gestures:

Drag: When one of the finger tip stays constant and other finger tip moves.

Zoom out: When the Euclidean distance between the two finger tips decrease gradually.

Zoom-in: When the Euclidean distance between two finger tips increase gradually

Tables 1 and 2 describe each gesture that is how it is performed and what it represents.

6. RESULTS AND CONCLUSION

First a clean binary image of the hand is obtained using the method of reflectance modeling, and then gesture detection can be achieved by applying the algorithms explained above. Specifically, the

Table 1. For single finger gestures

No	Gesture	Meaning	Signing Mode
1	Click	It is derived from normal clicking action as we do on mouse of PC's or laptop so as to open something	Tapping index finger on the surface. The position specifies the action location
2	Move Arbitrary	Move in random directions from current position	Move index finger in arbitrary direction on the surface
3	Rotate		Complete or incomplete circle is drawn with index finger in Clockwise and Anti clockwise direction
	(a)Anti-Clockwise	Rotating object in Anti-clockwise direction like taking turn	
	(b)Clockwise	Rotating an object in clockwise direction	
4	Pan	Movement of object or window from one place to another	Index and middle finger stay and move together moving in arbitrary direction

Table 2. For multi-finger gestures

No.	Gesture		Meaning	Signing mode
1	Drag		It signifies movement of window or object in one direction	Enacted by fixed thumb and arbitrary movement of index finger
2	Zoom			
		(a)Zoom-in	Increase in size of window or object	Move index finger and thumb away from each other
		(b)Zoom-out	Decrease in size of window or object	Move index finger and thumb away from each other

system can track the tip positions and motions of the fingers to classify the gestures and find out their attributes. The figure shows the detection of contour of hand and tip of finger(s) in dynamic projection on arbitrary background, followed by tracking the trajectories, velocities and direction of the movement thereby classifying the gestures. These positions depict the commonly held positions of hand, common to all gestures (Figure 7).

By application of our algorithms for both plain and arbitrary backgrounds, we detect the intrusion successfully. This method is accurate and robust and works over a wide range of ambient lighting and varying illumination conditions.

The performance analysis of the reflectance modeling method is as follows:

1. The algorithm was run on:
    a. Three kinds of skin samples- Fair, Dusky and Black.
    b. Three kinds of background surfaces on which projection was made
2. Scale limitation: This represents the area occupied by the hand in the surface area which is being captured by the camera. The minimum value came out be 10% of the screen area approximately and maximum value came out to be 80% of screen area. Outside this range performance is negatively affected
3. Gesture should not contain more than two fingers.

4. 1% error in fingertip detection in the gesture performed i.e., 1 frame missed out of 80 frames approximately in a video
5. Pixel level accuracy of tip is in 10 pixel diameter circle

7. APPLICATIONS

This work finds many applications for new era systems which can act such as both mobile and computers. The best application is in the making of a human computer interface (HCI) where the interfacing devices like keyboard, mouse, calculator, piano etc would become obsolete. It will help in creating a new era system consisting of a projector-camera combined with a processor which can be used as a computing device much smaller than any of the existing systems.

There are several factors that make creating applications in HCI difficult. They can be listed as:

*   The information is very complex and variable
*   Intrusion detection techniques should be highly robust
*   Developers must understand exactly what it is that the end user of their computer system will be doing.

Certain conditions may be relaxed to get attractive applications:

Figure 7. Shows detection of contour and finger tip for single and multiple finger gesture on arbitrary background

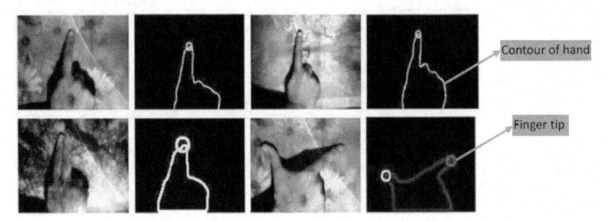

- When the front projection is absent i.e., when no dynamic or white light is being projected on to the screen, we can design systems like paper touchpad, virtual keyboard, virtual piano etc. These applications just have a static arbitrary background. Equations given for the dynamic reflectance model simplify accordingly

- Considering a case of back lit projection where dynamic data is being projected at the back allows us to design a system where we can directly interact with the monitor or screen. Here again, the general equations we have given will simplify appropriately. We omit the details here.

Figure 8. Paper touch pad setup on left and the printed touchpad on shhet of paper on right. 1.Paper touchpad, 2. Webcamera just above the paper touchpad and 3. Monitor which is mapped to the touchpad

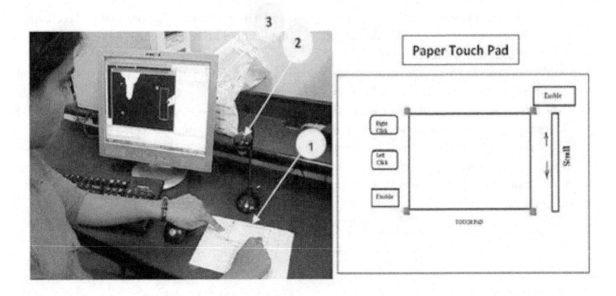

Figure 9. Paper touch pad showing operation of left click

One of the key applications is Paper Touch-pad. The paper touchpad is a kind of a virtual mouse used for providing mouse cursor and its functions in any computer system using an ordinary sheet of paper with a few fixed markings on it for calibration. The setup and the layout of paper touch pad is shown in Figure 8. The red dots on the corner of the printout of the touchpad are used for homographic mapping. The figures show the movement of the cursor and left click operation of the mouse. In Figure 9, the first picture shows left click operation on 'My Pictures' icon in start menu and the picture besides it shows the window of My Pictures opened on the display screen as a result. Along similar lines, we can design application specific keyboards/keypads, and use our techniques to enable 'paper keyboards.'

9. FUTURE POSSIBILITIES

1. This may be further extended for whole body gestures which may be used for sign language recognition or for robotic and other applications

2. We may also use an infra-red laser or flood illumination as an invisible 4th channel for detecting more details of gestures performed and to further eliminate the effects of the visible band varying illumination.

3. Extract more information like speed and acceleration from the gesture performed and allowing the user to communicate through these parameters as well.

4. As the end result, we aim to design a robust real time system which can be embedded into a mobile device that can be used without accessories anywhere a flat surface and some shade is available. The single unit would substitute for the computer/communicator, the display, keyboard and pointing device which may require a projector, camera, processor and memory.

5. We can move on to develop vision techniques to recognize gesture sequences, instead of just individual gestures as well as more complicated finger gestures, which can be a great help in faster communication.

REFERENCES

Eldridge, R., & Rudolph, H. (2008). *Stereo vision for unrestricted human computer interaction*. Rijeka, Croatia: InTech.

Fukumoto, M., Suenaga, Y., & Mase, K. (1994). Finger-pointer: Pointing interface by image processing. *Computers & Graphics*, *18*(5), 633–642. doi:10.1016/0097-8493(94)90157-0

Gordon, G., Darrell, T., Harville, M., & Woodfill, J. (1999). Background estimation and removal based on range and color. In *Proceedings of the International IEEE Conference on Computer Vision and Pattern Recognition*.

Grossman, T., Balakrishnan, R., Kurtenbach, G., Fitzmaurice, G., Khan, A., & Buxton, B. (2001). Interaction techniques for 3D modeling on large displays. In *Proceedings of the Symposium on Interactive 3D Graphics* (p. 1723).

Han, J. Y. (2005). Low-cost multi-touch sensing through frustrated total internal reflection. In *Proceedings of the 18th Annual ACM Symposium on User Interface Software and Technology*.

Helman, S., Juan, W., Leonel, V., & Aderito, M. (Eds.). (2007, May 23-25). *Proceedings of the GW 7th International Workshop on Gesture in Human-Computer Interaction and Simulation*, Lisbon, Portugal.

Hofer, R., Naeff, D., & Kunz, A. (2009). FLATIR: FTIR multi touch detection on a discrete distributed sensor array. In *Proceedings of the International Conference on Tangible and Embedded Interaction* (pp. 317-322).

Jenabi, M., & Reiterer, H. (2008, October). *Fint-teraction: Finger interaction with mobile phones*. Paper presented at the Future Mobile Experiences Workshop, Lund, Sweden.

Jones, M., & Rehg, J. (1999). Statistical color models with application to skin detection. In *Proceedings of the IEEE Conference on Computer Vision and Pattern Recognition* (Vol. 1).

Kim, S. G., Kim, J. W., & Lee, C. W. (2007). Implementation of multi-touch tabletop display for HCI (human computer interaction). In *Proceedings of the 12th International Conference on Human-Computer Interaction: Interaction Platforms and Techniques* (pp. 854-863).

Lin, H. H., & Chang, T. W. (2007). A camera based multitouch interface builder for designers. In J. A. Jacko (Ed.), *Proceedings of the 12th International Conference on Human-Computer Interaction: Applications and Services* (LNCS 4553, pp. 1102-1109).

Lockton, R. (2009). *Hand gesture recognition using special glove and wrist*. Oxford, UK: Oxford University.

Mistry, P., Maes, P., & Chang, L. (2007). WUW - Wear Ur World - A wearable gestural interface. In *Proceedings of the 27th International Conference Extended Abstracts on Human Factors in Computing Systems* (pp. 4111-4116).

Mitra, S., & Acharya, T. (2007). Gesture recognition: A survey. *IEEE Transactions on Systems, Man and Cybernetics. Part C, Applications and Reviews*, *37*(3), 311–324. doi:10.1109/TSMCC.2007.893280

Motonorihi, S., Ueda, S., & Akiyama, K. (2003). Human interface based on finger gesture recognition using omni-directional image sensor. In *Proceedings of the IEEE International Symposium on Virtual Environments, Human-Computer Interfaces and Measurement Systems* (pp. 68-72).

Nadia, M., & Cooperstock, J. (2004). Occlusion detection for front projected interactive displays. In *Proceedings of Pervasive Computing and Advances in Pervasive Computing*.

Oka, K., Sato, Y., & Koike, H. (2002). Real-time fingertip tracking and gesture recognition tracking. *IEEE Computer Graphics and Applications*, *22*(6), 64–71. doi:10.1109/MCG.2002.1046630

Pavlovic, V., Sharma, R., & Huang, T. (2001). Visual interpretation of hand gestures for HCI. *IEEE Transactions on Pattern Analysis and Machine Intelligence*, *19*(7), 677–695. doi:10.1109/34.598226

Segan, J., & Kumar, S. (1999). Shadow gestures: 3D hand pose estimation using a single camera. In *Proceedings of the IEEE Conference on Computer Vision and Pattern Recognition* (pp. 479-485).

Shimada, N., Shirai, Y., Kuno, Y., & Miura, J. (1998) Hand gesture estimation and model refinement using monocular camera-ambiguity limitation by inequality constraints. In *Proceedings of the 3rd IEEE International Conference on Automatic Face and Gesture Recognition* (pp. 268-273).

Thomas, M. (1994). *Finger Mouse: A freehand computer pointing interface* (Unpublished doctoral dissertation). The University of Illinois, Chicago, IL.

Utsumi, A., & Ohya, J. (1999). Multiple-hand-gesture tracking using multiple cameras. In *Proceedings of the IEEE Conference on Computer Vision and Pattern Recognition* (pp. 473-478).

Vladimir, I., Rajeev, S., & Thomas, S. (1993). *Visual interpretation of hand gestures for HCI: A review*. Chicago, IL: The University of Illinois.

Westerman, W., Elias, J. G., & Hedge, A. (2001). A multi touch: A new tactile 2-D gesture interface for HCI. In *Proceedings of the Human Factors and Ergonomics Society Annual Meeting* (Vol. 45, pp. 632-636).

Wren, C., Azarbayejani, A., Darrell, T., & Pentland, A. P. (1997). Pfinder: Real-time tracking of the human body. *IEEE Transactions on Pattern Analysis and Machine Intelligence*, *19*(7), 780–785. doi:10.1109/34.598236

Wu, A., Shah, M., & Lobo, N. (2000). A virtual 3D blackboard: 3D finger tracking using single camera. In *Proceedings of the Fourth International IEEE Conference on Automatic Face and Gesture Recognition*, Grenoble, France (pp. 536-543).

Wu, Y., Lin, J. Y., & Huang, T. S. (2001). Capturing natural hand articulation. In *Proceedings of the IEEE International Conference on Computer Vision* (Vol. 2, pp. 426-432).

Xing, J., Wang, W., Zhao, W., & Huang, J. (2009). A novel multi-touch human-computer-interface based on binocular stereo vision. In *Proceedings of the International Symposium on Intelligent Ubiquitous Computing and Education* (pp. 319-323).

Yuan, W., & Zhang, W. (2010). A novel hand-gesture recognition method based on finger state projection for control of robotic hands. In H. Liu, H. Ding, Z. Xiong, & X. Zhu (Eds.), *Proceedings of the Third International Conference on Intelligent Robotics and Applications* (LNCS 6425, pp. 671-682).

Chapter 11
Human Computer Interaction for Effective Metasearching

Rashid Ali
Aligarh Muslim University, India

M. M. Sufyan Beg
Jamia Millia Islamia, India

ABSTRACT

Metasearching is the process of combining search results of different search systems into a single set of ranked results which, in turn, is expected to provide us the collective benefit of using each of the participating search systems. Since, user is the direct beneficiary of the search results; this motivates the researchers in the field of Human Computer Interaction (HCI) to measure user satisfaction. A user is satisfied if he receives good quality search results in response to his query. To measure user satisfaction, we need to obtain feed back from user. This feedback might also be used to improve the quality of metasearching. The authors discuss the design of a metasearch system that is based on human computer interaction. We compare our method with two other methods Borda's method and modified Shimura technique. The authors use Spearman's footrule distance as the measure of comparison. Experimentally, the method performs better than the Borda's method. The authors argue that the method is significant as it models the user feedback based metasearching and has spam-fighting capabilities.

1. INTRODUCTION

Metasearching is the process of combining the search results obtained from a number of search engines in order to get better overall results. The need of metasearching arises from the fact that no search engine is comprehensive in its coverage of the Web. Also, no ranking algorithm can be thought of being universally acceptable. So, it is a good idea to combine results of different search engines into a better overall ranking that gives the combined advantage of different ranking techniques, which are employed by the participating search engines. The goal is to get a system that gives results better than the best of the participating search engines. In today's world, where every

DOI: 10.4018/978-1-4666-0954-9.ch011

organization is putting its information on world wide web, the issue becomes more interesting as more and more metasearching will be needed to suit specific information search applications. We sometimes divide the metasearch engines into two categories namely external metasearch engines and internal metasearch engines. External metasearch engines take lists of results from popular public search systems and return an overall ranked list of results by combining them. In this case, the different ranked lists returned by the different search systems might contain different sets of documents. While in the case of internal metasearch engines, different rankings of the same set of documents, which are returned by the participating sub-engines, are combined into a single overall ranking. Sometimes, it is also called rank aggregation. On the other hand, in the case of external metasearch engines, the ranked lists from participating search engines are not permutations of the same set of documents. Therefore, the process of combining these ranked lists into a single ranked list may be called as rank aggregation of partial lists. If we take the participating search engines as voters and the ranked documents as candidates, then metasearching may be considered simply as developing a system that returns a group preference on these documents.

But, whatever the type of metasearching, the goal remains the same. That is to get a system, which gives results better than that of the best of the participating search engines. The results are better if they satisfy a user with his information need. For this, the user feedback should be taken. We can obtain user feedback by asking the user to fill in a feedback form after he has finished searching. But, it is too demanding for the user. Human Computer Interaction models the interaction between human and Web search engines to obtain user feedback implicitly. In this implicit feedback, we infer the feedback from the user by watching the actions of the user on search results presented before him in response to his query. On the basis of which, a weight is assigned to each

result instead of the search engines. Then, the overall ordering of the results may be obtained by sorting the results in descending order of their weights. This overall ordering is in fact overall ordering by the user. But, the problem with the user feedback based method is that it is a time costly affair. Therefore, it is also not scalable. That means it can be performed with a small number of queries but not with a very large number of queries. For larger data sets, automatic method is the only answer. So, it motivated us to look for some automated mean to approximate user's behavior.

In this Chapter, we discuss a method for effective metasearching based on human computer interaction. Our system learns ranking rules using rough set theory to estimate an aggregated ranking for the rankings obtained from the participating search systems. Our system learns the ranking rules on the basis of user's ranking, which is available for a given set of rankings in the training set.

This chapter is organized as follows. In Section 2, we briefly look at the background and related work. In Section 3, we discuss the method of obtaining user feedback implicitly. Then, we briefly review the theoretical details of rough set theory and related terminologies. After that, we discuss the rough set based method for metasearching that models the user feedback based metasearching and present the metasearching algorithms. We show our results in Section 4. Finally, we conclude in Section 5.

2. BACKGROUND AND RELATED WORK

Here, we first discuss related work and then list some important definitions.

2.1. Related Work

In past, HCI researchers have shown interest in Web search. With the growth of World Wide Web, the importance of HCI aspects of search engines has been increasing consistently. Many HCI Web studies discussed the Web search using interactive variables like Web search queries, search duration, ease of user interface and may other human interaction variables. Su and Chen (1999) proposed a methodology for evaluating search engines from a user perspective. Spink, in her user centric approach (2002), asked twenty-two volunteers to search their own information tasks and then, rate the top 20 Web documents on relevance, using a four-point scale. In another study, Jansen and Spink (2006) compared interactions occurring between users and Web search engines from the perspectives of session length, query length, query complexity, and content viewed among the Web search engines. Recently, Capra (2010) proposed a HCI browser to support studies on Web search The HCI browser helps the researcher investigating user's activities on search results to collect data for their study.

Metasearching, too, has been widely discussed in literature. Aslam and Montogue used the classical Borda's method (Borda 1781) for metasearching (2001). They also discussed a weighted Borda's method, where a linear combination of weighted Borda's score was used to compute the total score for a document in place of the sum of the normal Borda's score.

Fox and Shaw experimented over a set of retrieval systems in TREC competitions (1994). They experimented with a group of rank aggregation methods (CombMNZ, CombSUM etc.), which are based on unweighted min, max, or sum of each document's relevance score over the constituent systems. For combining the result from different systems, Vogt and Cottrell used the linear combination (LC) model (1999). In the LC model, the final score of a document d is computed by simply linearly (each weighted differently) combining the normalized relevance scores and is given by

$$S_{LC}(d) = \sum_i w_i s_i(d) \qquad (1)$$

where, w_i is the weight given to the ith retrieval systems and $s_i(d)$ is the relevance score given to the document by the ith retrieval system. Renda and Straccia (2003) compared rank based methods (Borda, Markov chain based methods) with score based methods(CombMNZ, CombSUM, LC methods) for the metasearching.

In all of these studies on metasearching, the measure used for comparing different rank aggregation technique is precision, which may be defined as the ability to retrieve documents that are mostly relevant. But, they do not consider the relative rankings of documents in search results. By relative ranking, we mean that the relevant search results should presented in decreasing order of relevance. They also do not discuss any distance criterion for the purpose of comparison of different metasearch techniques. A good work in the context of metasearching that makes use of popular distance measures is reported by Dwork et al. (2001). Beg and Ahmad (2003) investigated the use of soft computing techniques for rank aggregation on the Web in the context of metasearching.

Minimizing the distance measure in order to get a consensus ranking for the given set of different rankings is appreciable and truly applicable in many fields like sports, election etc. But, this is not very useful in the context of metasearching. In metasearching, we collate search results of different search engines and we cannot consider all search engines to be of equal importance. Indexing algorithms of search engines are prone to spamming. Dwork et al. (2001) method also discussed the spam fighting A page p is said to spam a search engine S, if there is another page q, which S ranks lower than p, but most human evaluators would rank it higher. So, if a search engine is spammed and we consider all the search engine of equal importance, this will affect the results of metasearcing. Therefore, we feel that human intelligence should be used in determining the true overall ordering of the documents. It is universally accepted that human experts are the best judges. Use of human intelligence is helpful in spam fighting and also promises to give better results in the context of metasearching. But, for this, user feedback is needed. But, the problem with the user feedback based method is that it is very costly with respect to the time required. So, it cannot be performed with a very large number of queries. For larger size of data, we can not bear the time required by the user feedback based method. This motivated us to look for some automated mean to approximate user's behavior. In the way, we moved towards the rough set theory, which is as an efficient approach to deal with uncertainty and vagueness in artificial intelligence. In the present work, we discuss the design of a user feedback based metasearching system that first learns the ranking rules using rough set theory considering the user feedback based ranking as aggregated ranking in the training data sets and then, uses the learned ranking rules to estimate the aggregated ranking for the other data sets, for which user feedback is not available. Our method for getting ranking rules is similar to that proposed by Yao and Sai (2001) for mining ordering rules. But, there is difference with respect to input data. In Yao and Sai (2001), ordering of objects is available in form of attribute values for the objects but in our case there are no attributes values available at all. We are only provided with the rankings of documents from different search engines. Therefore, we need to change these rankings in some scores so that the documents can be compared.

2.2. Useful Definitions

Now, we list some of the important definitions.

Definition 1. Rank Aggregation: Given a set of n candidates say $C=\{1,2,3, \ldots, n\}$ and a set of m voters say $V=\{1,2,3, \ldots, m\}$. A ranked list l_i on C for each voter i, where, $l_i(j) < l_i(k)$ indicates that voter i prefers the candidate j to k. Rank aggregation is the process of combining the ranked lists $l_1, l_2, l_3, \ldots, l_m$ into a single list of candidates say l that represents the *collective choice* of the voters. The function used to get l from the ranked lists $l_1, l_2, l_3, \ldots, l_m$ (i.e., $f(l_1, l_2, l_3, \ldots, l_m) = l$) is known as the rank aggregation function.

Definition 2. Given a universe U and $S \subseteq U$, an ordered list (or simply, a list) l with respect to U is given as $l = [e_1, e_2, \ldots, e_{|s|}]$, with each $e_i \in S$, and $e_1 \succ e_2 \succ \ldots \succ e_{|s|}$, where "$\succ$" is some ordering relation on S. Also, for $j \in U$ and $j \in l$, let $l(j)$ denote the position or rank of j, with a higher rank having a lower numbered position in the list. We may assign a unique identifier to each element in U and thus, without loss of generality, we may get $U = \{1, 2, \ldots, |U|\}$.

Definition 3. Full List: If a list contains all the elements in U, then it is said to be a full list.

Example 1. A full list l_f given as $[e, a, d, c, b]$ has the ordering relation $e \succ a \succ d \succ c \succ b$. The Universe U may be taken as $\{1, 2, 3, 4, 5\}$ with say $a \equiv 1, b \equiv 2, c \equiv 3, d \equiv 4, e \equiv 5$. With such an assumption, we have $l_f = [5, 1, 4, 3, 2]$. Here $l_f(5) \equiv l_f(e) = 1, l_f(1) \equiv l_f(a) = 2, l_f(4) \equiv l_f(d) = 3, l_f(3) \equiv l_f(c) = 4, l_f(2) \equiv l_f(b) = 5$.

Definition 4. Partial List: A list l_p containing elements, which are a strict subset of universe U, is called a partial list. We have a strict inequality $|l_p| < |U|$.

There are different non-parametric techniques for statistical inference like Spearman Correlation, kendall's tau and Spearman's footrule distance. If different rankings are assumed as some points in a metric space and d as some distance measure on this space, then a better rank aggregation is one which presents a ranking l such that its distance to all the m rankings $l_1, l_2, l_3, \ldots, l_m$ is minimum. The two most popular distance measures (Diaconis, 1988) for rankings are kendall's tau and Spearman's footrule distance.

Definition 5. Kendall Tau distance counts the number of pairwise disagreement between two lists. It is also known as bubble sort distance since it is equal to number of pairwise adjacent transpositions needed to transform from one list to other. The normalized version of *Kendall Tau distance* between two full lists l_1 and l_2, each of cardinality $|l|$, is given as follows.

$$K\left(l_1,l_2\right) = \frac{\left|\left\{(i,j)|\forall l_1(i) < l_1(j), l_2(i) > l_2(j)\right\}\right|}{(1/2)|l|(|l|-1)}$$

(2)

Definition 6. Spearman footrule distance is the summation of absolute difference between rank of all the elements in the two list. The normalized version of *Spearman footrule distance* (SFD) between two full lists l_1 and l_2, each of cardinality $|l|$, is given as follows.

$$F\left(l_1,l_2\right) = \frac{\sum_{\forall i}\left|l_1(i) - l_2(i)\right|}{\left|\left(\frac{1}{2}\right)|l|^2\right|}$$

(3)

Definition 7. Given a set of k full lists as $L=\{l_1, l_2,..., l_k\}$, the normalized aggregated footrule distance of a full list l to the set of full lists L is given as

$$F\left(l,L\right) = \frac{\sum_{i=1}^{k} F\left(l,l_i\right)}{k}$$

(4)

In external metasearching, when the results from participating search engines are collated, the ranked lists are almost invariably always the partial ones. The aggregation of partial lists that minimizes Spearman footrule distance is stated by Dwork et al. (2001) to be a NP-hard problem. Beg and Ahmad (2002) presented an improved version

of Shimura technique of fuzzy ordering (Shimura, 1973), which makes use of OWA operator (Yager, 1988) for the problem of aggregation of partial lists that minimizes Spearman footrule distance.

In this work, we compare the performance of the rough set based external metasearching with the improved Shimura technique and Borda's method based external metasearching using normalized aggregated footrule distance. We discuss these two methods namely Borda's method and improved Shimura technique in subsequent subsections.

2.3. Borda's Method

Given k lists $l_1, l_2, ..., l_k$, a score $S_i(c_j) = |cp: l_i(cp) > l_i(c_j)|$ is assigned to each candidate c_j in list l_i. The candidates are then sorted in a decreasing order of their total Borda score

Example 2. Given lists $l_1 = \{c,d,b,a,e\}$ and $l_2 = \{b,d,e,c,a\}$.

- $S_1(a)=|e|=1$, as $l_1(e)=5 > l_1(a)=4$.
- Similarly,
- $S_1(b)=|a,e|=2$, as $l_1(e)=5 > l_1(b)=3$ and $l_1(a)=4 > l_1(b)=3$.
- Proceeding this way, we get
- $S_1(c) = |a,b,d,e| = 4$,
- $S_1(d) = |a,b,e| = 3$,
- $S_1(e) = | | = 0$,
- $S_2(a) = | | = 0$,
- $S_2(b) = |a,c,d,e| = 4$,
- $S_2(c) = |a| = 1$,
- $S_2(d) = |a,c,e| = 3$,
- $S_2(e) = |a,c| = 2$,
- $S(a) = S_1(a)+S_2(a) = 1+0 = 1$,
- $S(b) = S_1(b)+S_2(b) = 2+4 = 6$,
- $S(c) = S_1(c)+S_2(c) = 4+1 = 5$,
- $S(d) = S_1(d)+S_2(d) = 3+3 = 6$,
- $S(e) = S_1(e)+S_2(e) = 0+2 = 2$

Now, sorting the elements based on their total scores, we get the aggregated ranking as $b = d > c > e > a$. The symbol '=' indicates a tie.

2.4. Improved Shimura Technique

In this section, we briefly discuss the improved Shimura technique (Beg & Ahmad, 2002). We begin with the Shimura technique of fuzzy ordering (Shimura, 1973).

Shimura Technique

For variables x_i and x_j defined on a universe X, a relativity function $f(x_i|x_j)$ is taken to be the membership of preferring x_i over x_j. This function is given as

$$f\left(x_i \middle| x_j\right) = \frac{f_{x_j}\left(x_i\right)}{\max\left(f_{x_j}\left(x_i\right), f_{x_i}\left(x_j\right)\right)} \qquad (5)$$

where, $f_{x_j}\left(x_i\right)$ is the membership function of x_i with respect to x_j, and $f_{x_i}\left(x_j\right)$ is the membership function of x_j with respect to x_i. For $X = \left[x_1, x_2, \ldots, x_n\right]$, $f_{x_i}\left(x_i\right) = 1$. $C_i = \min_{j=1}^n f\left(x_i \middle| x_j\right)$ is the membership ranking value for the ith variable. Now, if a descending sort on C_i ($i=1$ to n) is carried out, the sequence of i's thus obtained would constitute the aggregated rank. For the m lists $l_1, l_2, \ldots, l_m$ from the m voters, we can have

$$f_{x_j}\left(x_i\right) = \frac{\left|k \in \left[1, m\right] \wedge l_k\left(x_i\right) < l_k\left(x_j\right)\right|}{m} \qquad (6)$$

Example 3. Given $l_1 = [3, 4, 2, 1]$, $l_2 = [2, 4, 3, 1]$ and $l_3 = [4, 2, 1, 3]$

$j \rightarrow$

$$fx_i\left(x_j\right) = \;\; i \downarrow \begin{bmatrix} 1 & 0 & 0.33 & 0 \\ 1 & 1 & 0.67 & 0.33 \\ 0.67 & 0.33 & 1 & 0.33 \\ 1 & 0.67 & 0.67 & 1 \end{bmatrix}$$

$j \rightarrow$

$$f\left(x_i \middle| x_j\right) = \;\; i \downarrow \begin{bmatrix} 1 & 0 & 0.5 & 0 \\ 1 & 1 & 1 & 0.5 \\ 1 & 0.5 & 1 & 0.5 \\ 1 & 1 & 1 & 1 \end{bmatrix} \rightarrow C_i = \begin{matrix} 1 \\ 2 \\ 3 \\ 4 \end{matrix} \begin{bmatrix} 0 \\ 0.5 \\ 0.5 \\ 1 \end{bmatrix}$$

A descending sort on C_i gives the aggregated rank as either $l = [4, 3, 2, 1]$ or $l = [4, 2, 3, 1]$.

Improved Version of Shimura Technique

To improve the performance of that classical Shimura technique, the use of OWA operator (Yager, 1988) is suggested in Beg and Ahmad (2003). It is observed that the performance of Shimura technique is poor primarily due to the employment of *min* function in finding $C_i = \min_{j=1}^n f\left(x_i \middle| x_j\right)$. The *min* function results in many ties, when a descending order sort is applied on C_i and thus, deteriorates the performance of Shimura technique. Therefore, in modified Shimura technique, the *min* function is replaced by an *OWA* operator. The OWA operators, in fact, provide a parameterised family of aggregation operators, which include many of the well-known operators such as the maximum, the minimum, the k-order statistics, the median and the arithmetic mean. The vector C_i is computed using relative fuzzy quantifier as follows.

$$C_i = \sum_j w_j . z_j \qquad (7)$$

here, z_j is the jth largest element in the ith row of the matrix $f(x_i|x_j)$. w_j is the weight of *OWA* based aggregation and is computed from the membership function Q describing the quantifier. In the case of a relative quantifier, with N criteria we have, $w_j = Q(j/N) - Q((j-1)/N)$, $j=0,1,2,\ldots,N$ with $Q(0)=0$. The membership function Q of relative quantifier can be represented as

$$Q(r) = \begin{cases} 0 & if \quad r < a \\ \dfrac{r-a}{b-a} & if \quad b \le r \le a \\ 1 & if \quad r > b \end{cases} \qquad (8)$$

In this work, we will be using the relative fuzzy linguistic quantifier "at least half" with the pair (a = 0.0, b = 0.5) for the purpose of finding the vector C_i as above. Now, as with the Shimura technique, if a descending sort on C_i (i=1 to n) is carried out, the sequence of i's thus obtained would constitute the aggregated rank.

3. USER FEEDBACK BASED METASEARCHING

For metasearching, in the learning phase, we present a union say U_SET of all the lists from the different search engines before the user and get user feedback implicitly by watching actions of user on the list U_SET.

3.1. Human Computer Interaction based User Feedback

We characterize the feedback of the user by a vector (*V, T, P, S, B, E, C*), , which consists of the following (Beg, 2002).

a. The sequence V in which the user visits the documents, $V = (v_1, v_2, …, v_N)$. If document i is the kth document visited by the user, then we set $v_i = k$.
b. The time t_i that a user spends examining the document i. We denote the vector $(t_1, t_2, …, t_N)$ by T. For a document that is not visited, the corresponding entry in the array T is 0.
c. Whether or not the user prints the document i. This is denoted by the Boolean p_i. We denote the vector $(p_1, p_2, …, p_N)$ by P.

d. Whether or not the user saves the document i. This is denoted by the Boolean s_i. We denote the vector $(s_1, s_2, …, s_N)$ by S.
e. Whether or not the user book-marked the document i. This is denoted by the Boolean b_i. We denote the vector $(b_1, b_2, …, b_N)$ by B.
f. Whether or not the user e-mailed the document i to someone. This is denoted by the Boolean e_i. We denote the vector $(e_1, e_2, …, e_N)$ by E.
g. The number of words that the user copied and pasted elsewhere. We denote the vector $(c_1, c_2, …, c_N)$ by C.

After that, weighted sum σ_j for each document j selected by the user is computed as follows

$$\sigma_j = \left(w_V \frac{1}{2^{(v_j-1)}} + w_T \frac{t_j}{t_j^{max}} + w_P p_j + w_S s_j + w_B b_j + w_E e_j + w_C \frac{c_j}{c_j^{total}} \right) \qquad (9)$$

where, t_j^{max} represents the maximum time a user is expected to spend in examining the document j, and c_j^{total} is the total number of words in the document j. Here, w_V, w_T, w_P, w_S, w_B, w_E and w_C, all lying between 0 and 1, give the respective weights that we want to give to each of the seven components of the feedback vector. The sum σ_j represents the importance of document j.

The sum σ_j represents the importance of document j in the eyes of the user. The intuition behind this formulation as pointed out in Beg (2002) is as follows. The importance of the document should decrease monotonically with the postponement being afforded by the user in picking it up. More the time spent by the user in glancing through the document, more important that must be for him. If the user is printing the document, or saving it, or book-marking it, or e-mailing it to someone else, or copying and pasting a portion of the document, it must be having some importance in the eyes of the user. A combination of the above seven factors by simply taking their weighted sum gives the overall importance the document holds in the eyes of the user. As regards the maximum time a user is expected to spend in examining the document j, it is clarified that this is taken to be directly proportional to the size of the document. We assume that an average user reads at a speed of about 10 bytes per second. This includes the pages containing text as well as images. So a document of size 1 kB is expected to take a minute and 40 seconds to go through. The above mentioned default reading speed of 10 bytes per second may be set differently by the user, if he wishes so.

It may be noted that depending on his preferences and practice, the user would set the importance of the different components of the feedback vector. For instance, if a user does not have a printer at his disposal, then there is no sense in setting up the importance weight (w_p) corresponding to the printing feedback component (P). Similarly, if a user has a dial-up network connection, and so he is in a habit of saving the relevant documents rather than spending time on it while online, it would be better to give a higher value to w_S, and a lower value to w_T. In such a case, lower values may also be given to w_p, w_E and w_C, as he would not usually be printing or e-mailing or copying and pasting a document at a stretch while online. So, after explaining the modalities to him, the user is to be requested to modify the otherwise default values of 1 for all these weights. It may, however, be noted that the component of the feedback vector corresponding to the sequence of clicking, always remains to be the prime one and so w_V must always be 1.

Now, sorting the documents on the descending values of their weighted sum σ_j will yield a sequence say R_{UF}, which is the ranking of documents on the basis of the user's feedback. Our metasearching system learns the ranking rules on the basis of this ranking. In other words, this user feedback based ranking is considered as the overall ranking to mine the ranking rules.

3.2. Rough Set Theory

Rough set theory, proposed by Pawlak in 1982, is a novel mathematical approach to vagueness (Pawlak, 1982). Rough set philosophy is based on the assumption that, in contrast to the classical set theory, we have some additional information (knowledge, data) about elements of a set. Objects characterized by the same information are indiscernible (similar) in view of the available information about them and form groups. These groups are called elementary sets or concepts. Elementary concepts can be combined into compound concepts. Any union of some elementary sets is called a crisp set. A set, which is not crisp, is referred to as rough (vague, imprecise). Consequently, each rough set has boundary-line cases, i.e., objects that cannot be with certainty classified, by employing the available knowledge, as members of the set or its complement. In rough set approach, it is assumed that a pair of precise concepts – called the lower and the upper approximation of the vague concept, replaces any vague concept. Therefore, for each rough set, two crisp sets, called the lower and the upper approximation of the rough set, are associated. The lower approximation consists of all objects, which surely belong to the set, and the upper approximation contains all objects, which possibly belong to the set. The difference between the upper and the lower approximation constitute the boundary region of the rough set. Hence, rough set theory expresses vagueness by employing a boundary region of a set and not by a partial membership, like in fuzzy set theory.

The rough set theory has been shown to be of great importance in artificial intelligence especially in knowledge discovery and data analysis. The main advantage of rough set theory in data analysis is that it does not need any preliminary or additional information about data like a grade of membership or the value of possibility in fuzzy set theory, probability distributions in statistics etc. Use of rough set is particularly advantageous when we have missing data or incomplete data or inconsistent data. Rough set can very easily deal with the inconsistencies in contrast to other techniques.

For data analysis, objects are generally represented in terms of their values on a set of attributes. Specifically, to present specific information about objects notion of an information table is used. An information table is a two-dimensional structure where rows correspond to objects of the universe, the columns correspond to a set of attributes, and each cell is the value of an object with respect to an attribute. Formally, an information table is a quadruple $T = (U, A_t, \{V_a \mid a \in A_t\}, \{I_a \mid a \in A_t\})$, where U is a finite nonempty set of objects, A_t is a finite nonempty set of attributes, V_a is a nonempty set of values for $a \in A_t$, $I_a: U \rightarrow V_a$ is an information function. When, we are dealing with a special attribute d called decision attribute, then the information table is specifically called decision table and all attributes other than d are called conditional attributes.

In our case, the user feedback based ranking R_{UF} forms the decision attribute and the rankings from participating search engines form the conditional attributes. To reduce the size of decision table, two tasks are performed on the table. The first is to identify equivalence classes i.e., the objects that are indiscernible using the available attributes. So that, only one element is needed to represent entire class. An equivalence relation E_A for a subset of attributes $A \subseteq A_t$ can be defined. The attribute corresponding to user feedback based ranking, R_{UF} partitions all pairs of documents into disjoint classes. The lower and upper approximation of each of these classes can simultaneously be obtained based on attributes in A.

The second task is to search for attributes that preserve indiscernibility relation and consequently set approximation. The rest of the attributes are redundant. There are too many such subsets of attributes and those that are minimal are called reducts. The intersection of all reducts is called core. Finding minimal reduct i.e., reduct having minimum cardinality among all reducts is NP hard

but there are genetic algorithm based heuristics, which find many reducts in reasonable time for systems with a small number of attributes. In our case two, the Reducts and core of attributes in A can also be computed to eliminate the redundant ones. Then, for each equivalence class present in lower approximation class, a certain rule can be drawn. A possible rule can also be drawn from equivalence class present in upper approximation. These possible rules are useful in case of larger data sets where inconsistencies may reduce lower approximation and hence the finding of strong rules. For example, in our case, it is quite possible that for the same set of attributes we are getting different values of decision attribute based on user feedback for different queries. In such cases, rough set is especially useful as it can deal with this inconsistency by drawing a possible rule from the upper approximation.

Example 4. In a table containing information about items in a store (strictly speaking their ID's), attributes can be, for example, *cost, durable, portable* etc., *Information table* is a *attribute-value* table, where the value corresponding to an item *AirConditioner* and the attribute *cost* can be *High*. Suppose we are given data about 6 items, as shown in Table 1.

Columns of the table are labeled by attributes and rows by objects (items), whereas entries of the table are attribute-values. Thus each row of the table can be seen as information about specific item. For example, item *I5* is characterized in the table by the following attribute-value set

(*Portable, yes*), (*Durable, no*), (*Cost, high*), (*Buy, No*),

which form the information about the item.

In the given table, items *I2, I3* and *I5* are indiscernible with respect to the attribute *Portable*, items *I3* and *I6* are indiscernible with respect to attributes *Durable* and *Buy*, and items *I2* and *I5* are indiscernible with respect to attributes *Portable, Durable* and *Cost*. Hence, for example, the attribute *Portable* generates two elementary sets {*I2*, *I3*, *I5*} and {*I1*, *I4*, *I6*}, whereas the attributes *Portable* and *Durable* form the following elementary sets: {*I1*, *I4*, I6}, {*I2*, *I5*} and {*I3*}. Similarly one can define elementary sets generated by any subset of attributes.

For Item *I2*, decision is to buy, whereas for item *I5* decision is not to buy, and they are indiscernible with respect to the attributes *Portable*, *Durable* and *Cost*, hence the decision attribute *Buy* cannot be characterized in terms of attributes *Portable*, *Durable* and *Cost*. Hence, *I2* and *I5* are the boundary-line cases, which cannot be properly classified in view of the available knowledge. The remaining items *I1*, *I3* and *I6* have values, which enable us to classify them as the items surely to be bought, items *I2* and *I5* cannot be decided to be bought or not, and item *I4* surely can not be bought, in view of the available information. Thus the lower approximation of the set of items to be bought is the set {*I1*, *I3*, *I6*} and the upper approximation of this set is the set {*I1*, *I2*, *I3*, *I5*, I6}, whereas the boundary-line cases are items *I2* and *I5*. Similarly, *I4* surely should not be bought and *I2*, *I5* cannot be excluded as to be bought, thus the lower approximation of this concept is the set {*I4*} whereas - the upper approximation – is the set {*I2*, *I4*, *I5*} and the boundary region of the concept "not buy" is the set {*I2*, *I5*}, the same as in the previous case. In Table 1, if we drop either the attribute Portable or Durable we get the data set which is equivalent to the original one, in regard to approximations and dependencies. Therefore,

attribute-pairs, {*Portable*, *Cost*} and {*Durable*, *Cost*} are reducts for the data in above Table and the attribute {*Cost*}, which is intersection of both the reducts is the core.

A good description of rough set theory and its application can be found in Komorowski et al. (1999).

3.3. Effective Meta Searching using Rough Set Theory

For metasearching, our system first learns the ranking rules using rough set theory from training data. For this, we first issue a query to the participating search engines and get the results. The search results from the participating search engines are combined and presented before the user. Let us assume the cardinality of the union, U_SET of all the lists from the different search engines is $|n|$. The user feedback on the U_SET is obtained implicitly as discussed in Section 3.1. Then, we build an information table say ranked information table by using the ranked lists from the participating search engines and the user feedback based ranking R_{UF}. Now, if the number of participating search engines is m, we have a total of $m+1$ rankings. In the ranked information table, we have $m+1$ columns corresponding to these $m+1$ rankings. We place a value $-k$ in the cell (i, j), if a document $i \in$ U_SET is present at k^{th} position in the jth ranking. We are setting the values to $-k$ in order to convert the ranked list R_j into a scored list, where the score for each

Table 1. Example of information on 6 items

Item	Portable	Durable	Cost	Buy
I1	*no*	*yes*	*high*	*yes*
I2	*yes*	*no*	*high*	*yes*
I3	*yes*	*yes*	*very high*	*yes*
I4	*no*	*yes*	*normal*	*no*
I5	*yes*	*no*	*high*	*no*
I6	*no*	*yes*	*very high*	*yes*

document is given on the basis of its position in the ranked list (higher the position, higher is the score). As in Yao and Sai (2001), we also convert our information table called ranked information table to binary information table. In the binary information table, an equivalence relation E_A for a subset of attributes $A \subseteq A_t$ can be defined. The attribute corresponding to user feedback based ranking, R_{UF} partitions all pairs of documents into two disjoint classes. The lower and upper approximation of each class can simultaneously be obtained based on attributes in A. Reducts and core of attributes in A can also be found to eliminate the redundant ones. Then, for each equivalence class present in lower approximation class, a certain rule can be drawn. A possible rule can also be drawn from equivalence class present in upper approximation. These possible rules are useful in case of larger data sets where inconsistencies

may reduce lower approximation and hence the finding of strong rules. Rosetta-a rough set toolkit for analyzing data (Rosetta), may be used to get a minimal set of ranking rules from the binary information table. The whole process is illustrated in Figure 1. We repeat the whole process for a good number of queries in the training set. Then, we select the best set of ranking rules by performing cross-validation test.

The best set of ranking rules from the learning phase is used to estimate the aggregated ranking of the documents for a new query in the running phase. In the running phase, we issue the new query to the m participating search engines and get the m ranked lists. We use these m rankings to construct a ranked information table and convert the ranked information table into binary information table, by following the same procedure as in the learning phase. In this case, since we do

Figure 1. Learning ranking rules

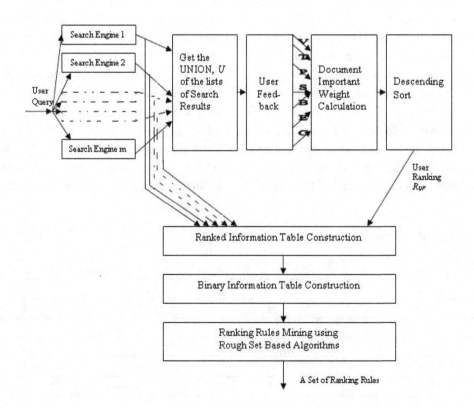

not have user feedback based ranking, the values of the attribute corresponding to the user feedback based ranking in the ranked information table may be initialized as all zeroes. We estimate the values of the attribute corresponding to the user feedback in the binary information table by using the selected ranking rules. Then, we convert the binary information table back into the ranked information table. The attribute corresponding to the user feedback based ranking in the ranked information table gives the predicted overall ranking of the documents R_{ag}. Thus, the documents in the U_SET ranked on the basis of this aggregating ranking R_{ag} can then be returned as the result of the metasearching for the new query. The overall procedure of metasearching is illustrated in Figure 2.

3.4. Metasearching Algorithms

Here, we present two algorithms. The first algorithm learns the ranking rules using rough set theory from training data and the second algorithm uses the ranking rules to estimate the aggregated rank.

Algorithm for Learning Phase

This algorithm learns the ranking rules for metasearching.

- Get the query and pass it to all the participating search engines. Obtain the ranked results from all participating m search engines, i.e., m rankings and combine the elements in these ranked lists to get the

Figure 2. Metasearching using the best set of ranking rules

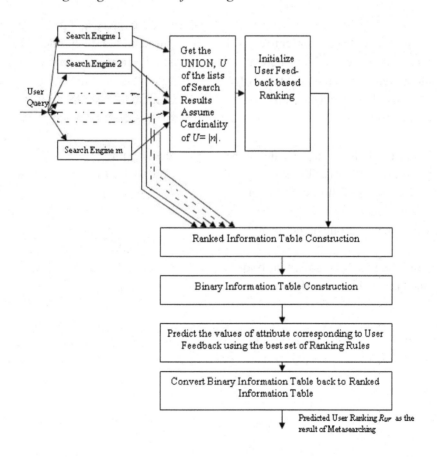

union of the documents in these set of results, called U_SET. Let n be the cardinality of the U_SET. Display these results in U_SET to the user.

- Observe the implicit feedback from the user on these results, compute document importance weight for each of the result in U_SET, and compute R_{UF}, the user feedback based ranking of documents in U_SET by sorting the documents in descending order of their document importance weight.

- Construct an information table, called Ranked Information Table (RIT), $T_{n*(m+1)}$ with n documents and the (m+1) rankings, $R_{j, j=1 \text{ to } m+1}$ (m ranking by m search engines and one R_{UF} by the user) as follows:

```
For i=1 to n
    For j=1 to (m+1)
        If the document D_i is at k_th
position in R_j, then set T_i,j= -k.
```

We are setting the values to –k in order to convert the ranked list R_j into a scored list, where the score for each document is given on the basis of its position in the ranked list(higher the position, higher is the score).

- Convert the RIT built in step 3 into the Binary information table (BIT) as $B_{s*(m+1)}$, where s=(n*(n-1)), as follows: Each pair (p,q) of the n documents in U_SET such that p≠q corresponds to one object in BIT.

For each document pair (p,q) such that p≠q, which corresponds to an object i in BIT

```
For j=1 to (m+1)
        If T_p,j>T_q,j then set B_i,j=1 else
set B_i,j=0.
```

- If a considerable number of queries have been searched, then go to step 6, else repeat steps 1 to 4 for a number of instances in the training data.

- Get all the latest BITs, perform cross validation and find the ranking rules using rough set theory i.e., apply the rough set based algorithms on the BITs to find the association between the ranking by user and rankings by the m search engines. Thus, obtain the ranking rule set, called the best ranking rule set that gives maximum accuracy. Save these ranking rules in the database and go to the running phase.

Algorithm for Running Phase

This algorithm uses the ranking rules learnt in learning phase to obtain the results of metasearching

- Get the query and pass it to all the participating m search engines. Obtain the ranked results from all participating m search engines, i.e., m rankings and combine the elements in these ranked lists to get the union of the documents in these set of results, called U_SET. Let n be the cardinality of the U_SET.

- consists of following sub steps.
  a. Convert U_SET into RIT, $T_{n*(m+1)}$ with n documents and the m rankings by m search engines (leaving the user feedback field, R_{UF}) as follows:

```
For i=1 to n
    For j=1 to (m+1)
        If the document D_i is at k_th
position in R_j, then set T_i,j= -k.
```

We are setting the values to –k in order to convert the ranked list R_j into a scored list, where the score for each document is given on the basis of its position in the ranked list(higher the position, higher is the score).

b. Convert the RIT built in step (a) into the Binary information table (BIT) as $B_{s*m,}$ where $s = (n*(n-1))$ and m is the ranking by m search engines (leaving the user feedback field, UF), as follows: Each pair (p,q) of the n documents in U_SET such that p≠q corresponds to one object in BIT.

For each document pair (p,q) such that p≠q, which corresponds to an object i in BIT

```
    For j=1 to (m)
        If T_{p,j}>T_{q,j} then set B_{i,j}=1
else set B_{i,j}=0.
```

c. Using the best set of ranking rules with their respective confidence values as saved in learning phase, estimate the $(m+1)_{th}$ column in the Binary information table (BIT) corresponding to (UF), so that the table becomes $B_{s*(m+1)}$.

d. Set l=1, and repeat the following for l=1 to n

` For each document $D_o \in$ U_SET, compute a score S_o as

```
1+n-2
      S_o= Σ B_{i,m+1}
i=1
Then, set l=l+(n-1)
```

e. Sort the n documents in U_SET on descending values of their score $S_{o \ o=1 \ to \ n}$ and get a ranking of the documents, which is the desired aggregated ranking R_{ag}. Display the results in U_SET to the user according to this aggregated ranking. This is the output of user feedback based metasearching. Again, obtain the user's feedback implicitly and build the corresponding RIT and BIT and save in database.

o   Learn the ranking rules internally. Get all the latest 15 BITs, perform validation and find ranking rules using rough set theory. Thus, obtain the rule set, called the best ranking rule set that gives maximum accuracy. Save these ranking rules in the database as the new best rule set.

Our algorithms in original form may be used for internal metasearching. But, for external metasearching, some slight modifications is required because ranked lists from participating search engines are not the permutation of same set of documents. Let us assume the cardinality of set U_SET, the union of partial lists obtained by participating search engines, is $|n|$. Then, in the construction of Ranked Information table, we place a value $-(|n+1|)$ in the cell (i,j) for a document $i \in$ U-SET but not present in the partial ranked list R_j of the results returned by the jth search engine to ensure that the document i gets minimum possible score in the jth column.

With these modifications, our algorithms work for external meta-searching too and we get an aggregated ranked list of cardinality $|n|$, which is given as the output of the metasearching. This is illustrated in example 5.

Example 5. Given the 7 ranked lists consisting the top ten search results from seven search engines (SEs) as follows-

```
R_1={1,2,3,4,5,6,7,8,9,10}
R_2={11,12,1,2,13,6,7,8,4,3}
R_3={1,3,12,2,13,14,7,8,15,9}
R_4={2,11,16,9,17,18,1,8,6,3}
R_5={1,2,7,19,20,21,3,8,22,6}
R_6={11,12,17,9,5,1,23,3,2,8}
R_7={1,2,9,5,24,22,25,3,4,7}
```

So, UNION of these seven ranked lists constitute 25 documents and therefore RIT will also have 25 rows, (1,2,......25). Let user selects only 12 of these documents say (documents numbered 1, 2, 3, 4, 7, 8, 11, 12, 16, 17, 19, 20) with document weights being (2.6, 2, 1.2, 0.5, 0.4, 1.1, 2.8, 2.2, 0.6, 0.5, 0.6, 0.5), then RIT would be as shown in Table 2. We give the document 0 to the document not selected by the user assuming that the document is of not any importance in the eyes of the user.

5. EXPERIMENTS AND RESULTS

For the training of our metassearch system, we experimented with 15 queries on seven popular search engines, namely, *AltaVista*, *Ask*, *Excite*, *Google*, *HotBot*, *Lycos* and *Yahoo*. These queries are listed in Table 3. Using the search results returned from the seven search engines in response to each of the 15 queries and implicit user's feedback, we constructed a ranked information table and converted that into binary information table. Then, using Rosetta, we mined the ranking rules. Then, we performed cross-validation with

Table 2. RIT

Document	SE1	SE2	SE3	SE4	SE5	SE6	SE7	User's Weight
1	-1	-3	-1	-7	-1	-6	-1	2.6
2	-2	-4	-4	-1	-2	-9	-2	2
3	-3	-10	-2	-10	-7	-8	-8	1.2
4	-4	-9	-26	-26	-26	-26	-9	0.5
5	-5	-26	-26	-26	-26	-5	-4	0
6	-6	-6	-26	-9	-10	-26	-26	0
7	-7	-7	-7	-26	-3	-26	-10	0.4
8	-8	-8	-8	-8	-8	-10	-26	1.1
9	-9	-26	-10	-4	-26	-4	-3	0
10	-10	-26	-26	-26	-26	-26	-26	0
11	-26	-1	-26	-2	-26	-1	-26	2.8
12	-26	-2	-3	-26	-26	-2	-26	2.2
13	-26	-5	-5	-26	-26	-26	-26	0
14	-26	-26	-6	-26	-26	-26	-26	0
15	-26	-26	-9	-26	-26	-26	-26	0
16	-26	-26	-26	-3	-26	-26	-26	0.6
17	-26	-26	-26	-5	-26	-3	-26	0.5
18	-26	-26	-26	-6	-26	-26	-26	0
19	-26	-26	-26	-26	-4	-26	-26	0.6
20	-26	-26	-26	-26	-5	-26	-26	0.5
21	-26	-26	-26	-26	-6	-26	-26	0
22	-26	-26	-26	-26	-9	-26	-6	0
23	-26	-26	-26	-26	-26	-7	-26	0
24	-26	-26	-26	-26	-26	-26	-5	0
25	-26	-26	-26	-26	-26	-26	-7	0

these rules. Result of cross-validation is shown in Table 4.

From Table 4, it is clear that rule set corresponding to query 7 is most applicable since it has highest average correctness of prediction when applied to other queries. So, we select the rule set corresponding to query 7 as ranking rules and use it for getting aggregated rank for the data set for which we do not have user feedback. The rule set consists of the following rules:

- SE2(1) AND SE3(1) AND SE4(1) AND SE6(0)=> SE8(1)
- SE2(0) AND SE3(1) AND SE4(1) AND SE6(0)=> SE8(1)
- SE2(1) AND SE3(1) AND SE4(1) AND SE6(1)=> SE8(1)
- SE2(1) AND SE3(1) AND SE4(0) AND SE6(0)=> SE8(1)
- SE2(1) AND SE3(1) AND SE4(0) AND SE6(1)=> SE8(1)

Here, SE2, SE3, SE4, SE6 correspond to the search engines Ask, Excite, Google and Lycos respectively. The SE8 corresponds to the implicit

Table 3. List of queries used in learning phase

1	*measuring search quality*
2	*mining access patterns from web logs*
3	*pattern discovery from web transactions*
4	*distributed associations rule mining*
5	*document categorization query generation*
6	*term vector database*
7	*client -directory-server-model*
8	*Similarity measure for resource discovery*
9	*hypertextual web search*
10	*IP routing in satellite networks*
11	*focussed web crawling*
12	*concept based relevance feedback for information retrieval*
13	*parallel sorting neural network*
14	*spearman rank order correlation coefficient*
15	*web search query benchmark*

user feedback. That means, using partial lists from only these four search engines and above rule set, we could approximate the aggregated ranking by the user with 77% accuracy for all the 15 queries. Here, we conclude that only results of the four search engines are sufficient to provide us with the approximate result of user feedback based metasearching of seven search engines. Using these rules we can predict the aggregated rank Rag for other queries. Top few results for the query parallel architecture obtained using our method are listed in Table 5. Table 5 shows that not only these results are relevant but also presented in proper order of relevance.

Using the best set of ranking rules from the learning phase, we predict the overall ranking for the results returned from the seven search engines in response to the following 37 queries.

affirmative action, alcoholism, amusement parks, citrus groves, classical guitar, architecture, bicycling, blues, cheese, computer vision, cruises, Death Valley, field hockey, gardening, graphic design, Gulf war, HIV, java, Lipari, lyme disease, mutual funds, National parks, parallel architecture, Penelope Fitzgerald, recycling cans, rock climbing, San Francisco, Shakespeare, stamp collecting, sushi, table tennis, telecommuting, Thailand tourism, vintage cars, volcano, zen buddhism, and Zener.

The same queries were also used in Beg and Ahmad (2003). We also implemented Borda's method and Modified Shimura Technique and obtained the results of metasearching using these two techniques for the above 37 queries. We compare the rough set based metasearching with Borda's method and Modified Shimura Technique by computing the normalized footrule distance F (l, L) (Dwork et al., 2001) for the results of above 37 queries. The results of comparison of performance of Rough Set based method with these two techniques are listed in Table 4. As shown in Table 4, we find that our rough based technique

Table 4. Results of cross validation for the 15 queries

Query	1	2	3	4	5	6	7	8	9	10	11	12	13	14	15
1	.705	.623	.588	.587	.614	.561	.662	.617	.519	.637	.631	.619	.705	.579	.588
2	.612	.7	.563	.635	.632	.602	.671	.619	.6	.638	.652	.621	.651	.589	.628
3	.809	.667	.743	.649	.675	.685	.791	.698	.671	.742	.697	.667	.704	.661	.641
4	.644	.805	.707	.796	.745	.715	.784	.768	.675	.789	.768	.764	.779	.741	.757
5	.603	.743	.578	.719	.837	.64	.718	.687	.566	.703	.705	.694	.649	.695	.667
6	.68	.801	.668	.706	.76	.84	.828	.716	.72	.76	.738	.767	.772	.734	.745
7	.697	.73	.765	.664	.767	.633	.796	.796	.632	.732	.796	.776	.736	.739	.688
8	.636	.735	.664	.715	.74	.66	.831	.901	.613	.768	.778	.788	.678	.701	.661
9	.591	.672	.592	.566	.64	.668	.654	.595	.767	.663	.617	.616	.63	.617	.606
10	.631	.813	.618	.803	.823	.703	.843	.782	.623	.869	.779	.742	.724	.743	.78
11	.688	.686	.596	.609	.681	.718	.715	.71	.625	.725	.814	.667	.667	.592	.607
12	.705	.73	.716	.682	.748	.682	.783	.761	.641	.713	.761	.764	.711	.73	.68
13	.666	.866	.741	.778	.781	.809	.815	.795	.785	.85	.778	.754	.882	.74	.795
14	.687	.691	.551	.661	.575	.55	.782	.546	.427	.627	.54	.654	.628	.822	.558
15	.672	.889	.717	.778	.848	.859	.848	.848	.777	.882	.838	.817	.788	.801	.899
Avg.	**.668**	**.743**	**.654**	**.690**	**.724**	**.688**	**.768**	**.723**	**.643**	**.740**	**.726**	**.714**	**.714**	**.699**	**.687**

performs better than the Borda's method as the average of normalized footrule distance $F(l, L)$ over the 37 queries for rough set based method is less than that for Borda's method. From Table 6, we also observe that our technique does not perform better than the modified Shimura technique in the minimization of the distance measure. But, as pointed out in Section 2, the minimization of the distance measure is not the real objective in metasearching. In metasearching, the aim is to get relevant results in proper order of relevance. Therefore, our technique is highly useful since it returns the highly relevant results in proper order of relevance. Our algorithm performs well in this consideration because it models the user feedback based metasearching. Due to the same reason, the method also has spam-fighting capabilities.

Table 5. Top few results for the query parallel architecture

1	http://www.cs.berkeley.edu/~culler/cs258-s99/
2	http://www.parl.clemson.edu/
3	http://www.cs.berkeley.edu/~culler/book.alpha/index.html
4	http://www.amazon.com/Parallel-Computer-Architecture-HardwareSoftware/dp/1558603433,
5	http://en.wikipedia.org/wiki/Parallel_computing
6	http://www.npac.syr.edu/
7	http://www.cc.gatech.edu/computing/Architecture/arch.html
8	http://www.acm.org/crossroads/xrds5-3/pisma.html
9	http://www.ecs.umass.edu/ece/andras/courses/ECE669/
10	http://www.cs.unc.edu/Research/aipdesign/

Table 6. Comparison of performance of rough set based method with Borda's method and improved Shimura technique

Query	Cardinality of Universe |U|	Borda's method	Improved Shimura	Rough set based method
1	521	0.529668	0.528342	0.526371
2	518	0.522198	0.519018	0.528178
3	538	0.522651	0.504351	0.505723
4	453	0.530741	0.524387	0.537214
5	494	0.52562	0.524123	0.536604
6	440	0.5269	0.503925	0.514953
7	497	0.5231	0.509758	0.528778
8	398	0.534704	0.515644	0.52362
9	445	0.529207	0.517985	0.537314
10	543	0.515572	0.483936	0.48948
11	423	0.518057	0.492168	0.490749
12	516	0.531133	0.518960	0.533232
13	541	0.528662	0.522996	0.5219
14	456	0.53217	0.52533	0.534838
15	533	0.528188	0.529523	0.532856
16	525	0.515764	0.508453	0.520074
17	536	0.51757	0.507098	0.509275
18	434	0.52448	0.516996	0.528837
19	557	0.530019	0.529626	0.529509
20	519	0.524267	0.505575	0.503671
21	466	0.517326	0.512944	0.507112
22	503	0.525281	0.514127	0.537811
23	591	0.525325	0.523778	0.531497
24	532	0.517106	0.489026	0.493441
25	529	0.521945	0.51154	0.529573
26	511	0.530577	0.518527	0.531795
27	416	0.51862	0.490827	0.500691
28	499	0.526542	0.521856	0.533863
29	544	0.529831	0.515517	0.518008
30	532	0.533748	0.523962	0.538228
31	491	0.511521	0.494784	0.502908
32	499	0.504895	0.489950	0.488755
33	604	0.522599	0.509598	0.527837
34	556	0.514339	0.499206	0.502936
35	489	0.52742	0.52025	0.538332
36	534	0.52091	0.508204	0.508409
37	540	0.51939	0.512694	0.529829
Average	**506**	**0.523731**	**0.512027**	**0.520384**

7. CONCLUSION

In this chapter, we presented a system for effective metasearching using human computer interaction and rough set theory. We infer user's feedback by watching user's actions on the search results returned in response to his query. We design a metasearch system based on the feedback obtained through human computer interaction. Our approach is very much useful since it models the user's preference for metasearching without actual user's involvement. Our system merges the results of different search engines using the ranking rules that are based on the user's feedback. Our approach removes the cost incurred in getting user's feedback by automating the whole process, once the system is trained. Since, our system models user's based metasearching, it promises to have spam-fighting capabilities.

REFERENCES

Aslam, J. A., & Montague, M. (2001). Models for metasearch. In *Proceedings of the Twenty Fourth Annual International ACM SIGIR Conference on Research and Development in Information Retrieval* (pp. 276-284). New York, NY: ACM.

Beg, M. M. S. (2002). *On measurement and enhancement of Web search quality* (Unpublished doctoral dissertation). International Institute of Technology, Delhi, India.

Beg, M. M. S., & Ahmad, N. (2002). Improved Shimura technique for rank aggregation on the World Wide Web. In *Proceedings of the 5th International Conference on Information Technology*, Bhubaneswar, India.

Beg, M. M. S., & Ahmad, N. (2003). Soft computing techniques for rank aggregation on the World Wide Web. *World Wide Web -. International Journal (Toronto, Ont.)*, *6*(1), 5–22.

Borda, J. C. (1781). *Memoire Sur les Election au Scrutiny*. Paris, France: Histoire de l'Academie Royale des Sciences.

Capra, R. (2010, October 22-27). HCI Browser: A tool for studying Web search behavior. In *Proceedings of the American Society for Information Science and Technology Annual Meeting*, Pittsburgh, PA.

Condorcet, M. J. (1785). E'ssai Sur l'Application de l'Analyse. In *Probabilite' des De'cisions Rendues a` la Pluralite.'*. Paris, France: Des Voix.

Diaconis, P. (1988). Group representations in probability and statistics: *Vol. 11. Lecture Notes — Monograph series*. Hayward, CA: Institute of Mathematical Statistics.

Dwork, C., Kumar, R., Naor, M., & Sivakumar, D. (2001). Rank aggregation methods for the Web. In *Proceedings of the Tenth International World Wide Web Conference* (pp. 613-622). New York, NY: ACM.

Fox, E. A., & Shaw, J. A. (1994). Combination of multiple searches. In *Proceedings of the Second Text REtreival Conference* (pp. 243-249). Gaithersburg, MD: NIST.

Jansen, B. J., & Spink, A. (2006). How are we searching the World Wide Web? A comparison of nine search engine transaction logs. *Information Processing & Management*, *42*(2), 248–263. doi:10.1016/j.ipm.2004.10.007

Kierczak, M. (2009). *Rosetta- A rough set toolkit for analyzing data*. Retrieved August 12, 2011, from http://www.lcb.uu.se/tools/rosetta/

Komorowski, J., Pawlak, Z., Polkowski, L., & Skowron, A. (1999). Rough sets: A tutorial. In Pal, S. K., & Skowron, A. (Eds.), *Rough fuzzy hybridization: A new trend in decision-making* (pp. 3–98). Berlin, Germany: Springer-Verlag.

Pawlak, Z. (1982). Rough sets. *International Journal of Computer and Information Sciences, 11*, 341–356. doi:10.1007/BF01001956

Renda, M. E., & Straccia, U. (2003). Web Metasearch: Rank vs. score based rank aggregation methods. In *Proceedings of the Eighteenth Annual ACM Symposium on Applied Computing* (pp. 841-846). New York, NY: ACM.

Shimura, M. (1973). Fuzzy sets concept in rank ordering objects. *Journal of Mathematical Analysis and Applications, 43*, 717–733. doi:10.1016/0022-247X(73)90287-4

Spink, A. (2002). A user centered approach to evaluating human interaction with Web search engines: an exploratory study. *Information Processing & Management, 38*(3), 410–426. doi:10.1016/S0306-4573(01)00036-X

Su, L. T., & Chen, H. (1999). Evaluation of Web search engines by undergraduate students. In *Proceedings of the 62nd American Society for Information Science*, Washington, DC (Vol. 36, pp. 98-114).

Truchon, M. (1998). *An extension of the condorcet criterion and Kemeny Orders*. Montreal, QC, Canada: Centre de Recherche en Economie et Finance Appliquees.

Vogt, C. C., & Cottrell, G. W. (1999). Fusion via a linear combination of scores. *Information Retrieval, 1*(3), 151–173. doi:10.1023/A:1009980820262

Yager, R. R. (1988). On ordered weighted averaging aggregation operators in multicriteria decision making. *IEEE Transactions on Systems, Man, and Cybernetics, 18*(1), 183–190. doi:10.1109/21.87068

Yao, Y. Y., & Sai, Y. (2001). Mining ordering rules using rough set theory. *Bulletin of International Rough Set Society, 5*, 99–106.

KEY TERMS AND DEFINITIONS

Human Computer Interaction: Study of interaction between users and computers.

Learning Ranking Rules: Learning the rules which are used for obtaining overall ranking of a set of items in a rank aggregation process.

Metasearching: Process of presenting the user with the search results from different search systems in response to the user query as a single ranked list.

Rank Aggregation: Combining ranking from different sources to a single aggregated ranking.

Rough Set Theory: Approach to deal vagueness in data, which expresses vagueness by employing a boundary region of a set. A non-empty boundary region means that the set is rough. Otherwise, the set is crisp.

Spam-Fighting Capability: Ability of a search system to handle manipulation of its indexing algorithm by the spam pages.

User Feedback: Feedback taken from the user.

Chapter 12
Science of Emoticons:
Research Framework and State of the Art in Analysis of Kaomoji–Type Emoticons

Michal Ptaszynski
Hokkai-Gakuen University, Japan

Rafal Rzepka
Hokkaido University, Japan

Jacek Maciejewski
Independent Researcher, Poland

Kenji Araki
Hokkaido University, Japan

Pawel Dybala
Kotoken Language Laboratory, Poland

Yoshio Momouchi
Hokkai-Gakuen University, Japan

ABSTRACT

Emoticons are string of symbols representing body language in text-based communication. For a long time they have been considered as unnatural language entities. This chapter argues that, in over 40-year-long history of text-based communication, emoticons have gained a status of an indispensable means of support for text-based messages. This makes them fully a part of Natural Language Processing. The fact the emoticons have been considered as unnatural language expressions has two causes. Firstly, emoticons represent body language, which by definition is nonverbal. Secondly, there has been a lack of sufficient methods for the analysis of emoticons. Emoticons represent a multimodal (bimodal in particular) type of information. Although they are embedded in lexical form, they convey non-linguistic information. To prove this argument the authors propose that the analysis of emoticons was based on a theory designed for the analysis of body language. In particular, the authors apply the theory of kinesics to develop a state of the art system for extraction and analysis of kaomoji, Japanese emoticons. The system performance is verified in comparison with other emoticon analysis systems. Experiments showed that the presented approach provides nearly ideal results in different aspects of emoticon analysis, thus proving that emoticons possess features of multimodal expressions.

DOI: 10.4018/978-1-4666-0954-9.ch012

INTRODUCTION

One of the primary functions of the Internet is to connect people online. The first developed online communication media, such as e-mail or BBS forums, were based on text messages. Although later improvement and popularization of Internet connections allowed for phone calls or video conferences, the text-based message did not lose its popularity. However, its sensory limitations in communication modalities (no view or sound of the interlocutors) prompted users to develop communication strategies compensating for these limitations. One such strategy is the use of emoticons, strings of symbols imitating body language (faces or gestures). Today, the use of emoticons in online conversation contributes to the facilitation of the online communication process in e-mails, BBS, instant messaging applications, or blogs (Suzuki & Tsuda, 2006b; Derks et al., 2007; Chiu, 2007). Therefore obtaining a sufficient level of computation for this kind of communication is likely to improve machine understanding of language used online, and contribute to the creation of more natural human-machine interfaces. Thus analysis of emoticons is of great importance in such fields as Human-Computer Interaction (HCI), Computational Linguistics (CL), or Artificial Intelligence (AI). However, for a long time emoticons have been considered as unnatural language entities and included in a subfield of NLP called Unnatural Language Processing (UNLP). The term "Unnatural Language Processing" (UNLP), as roughly defined for the needs of Baidu UNLP Contest (http://www.baidu.jp/unlp/) in 2010, refers to a subfield of NLP dealing with language phenomena which cannot be captured by conventional language processing methods (Hagiwara, 2011). UNLP defined this way[1] includes such problems as informal expressions, typos, emoticons, onomatopoeia, or unknown words. This chapter focuses on emoticons, and in particular on their Japanese type called *kaomoji*. We claim that emoticons are far from being unnatural entities in

language and mention some empirical proofs for this claim. We notice further that there are two reasons for the emoticons to have been included in UNLP. Firstly, since emoticons are said to be representing body language, the information they convey is by definition nonverbal. Secondly, there is a lack of sufficient methodology for emoticon analysis. We propose such methodology in a form of a framework for the research on emoticons. Moreover, we present our research in developing a system for analysis of emoticons, based on the idea taking advantage of the fact that emoticons incorporate both linguistic and nonlinguistic information.

The outline of this chapter is as follows. After providing definitions and explanations of the nomenclature used in this chapter, we present our approach to the analysis of emoticons and explain the general idea the research is based upon. Next, we present a review of other research dealing with emoticons. We describe two general fields that take emoticons as research objects, namely, social sciences and NLP. Next, we propose a general framework for the research on emoticons. Following, we explain the particular procedures applied during automatic generation of the emoticon database applied in our research. We also describe the structure and statistics of the database. Then we describe CAO, a system for emotiCon Analysis and decOding of affective information, built on the database. We describe the evaluation settings for the system and present the results of the evaluation. Finally, the chapter is finalized with concluding remarks, future directions, and planned applications for the system.

BACKGROUND

Classification of Emotion Types

We focused on emoticons used in online communication in Japanese. Therefore, for the classification of emotions, we needed to choose the one proven to be the most appropriate for the Japanese language. We applied the general definition of emotions as every temporary state of mind, feeling, or affective state evoked by experiencing different sensations (Lewis et al., 2008). As for the classification of emotions, we applied that of Nakamura (1993), who, after over 30 years of thorough study in the lexicography of the Japanese language and emotive expressions, distinguishes 10 emotion types as the most appropriate for the Japanese language and culture. These are: *ki/yorokobi* (joy, delight), *do/ikari* (anger), *ai/aware* (sadness, gloom), *fu/kowagari* (fear), *chi/haji* (shame, shyness), *ko/suki* (liking, fondness), *en/iya* (dislike), *ko/takaburi* (excitement), *an/yasuragi* (relief), and *kyo/odoroki* (surprise, amazement). Emoticons in our research are then annotated according to this classification.

Definition of Emoticons

Emoticons are representations of body language in text-based messages, where the communication channel is limited to transmission of letters and punctuation marks. It is not certain when the first emoticon in the history was used, however, different sources point to many interesting discoveries. The oldest known reference (Lee, 2009) is to Abraham Lincoln's speech from 1862, where he used a mark looking like a smiley face ";)". Although there is some doubt on whether it is a deliberately used emoticon, or a typo, the mark is used in a humorous context (after a short annotation "applause and laughter"), which supports the emoticon thesis. The first known typographical

emoticons annotated with emotion classes, such as "joy", or "melancholy", appeared probably in the U.S. satirical magazine *Puck*[2] in 1881 (Figure 1). In the digital era some of the first widely used emoticons were the ones emerged on PLATO, a system for assisted university coursework (Dear, 2008). As for the emoticons known today, it is assumed that the first ones were introduced in 1982 by Scott Fahlman of Carnegie Mellon University on a Computer Science BBS (Fahlman, 1982), from where they spread to Usenet and later to the Internet.

Emoticons have been used in online communication for many years and their numbers have developed depending on the language of use, letter input system, the kind of community they are used in, etc. However, they can be roughly divided into three types: 1) Western one-line type, 2) Eastern one-line type, and 3) multiline ASCII art type. Western emoticons exhibit characteristics as being rotated by 90 degrees, such as ":-)" (smiling face), or ":-D" (laughing face). They are the simplest of the three as they are usually made of two to four characters and are of a relatively small number. We excluded them from our research as not being challenging enough. Moreover, our research focuses on the use of emoticons by Japanese users, and this type of emoticon is rarely used in Japanese online communities. However, as the Western-type emoticons can be gathered in a list of about 50, such a list could be simply added to our system at the end in a subprocedure. Multiline ASCII art-type emoticons, on the other hand, consist of a number of charac-

Figure 1. Emoticons presented in the Puck magazine

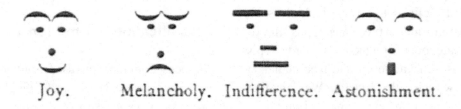

Joy. Melancholy. Indifference. Astonishment.

ters written in several, or even up to several dozens of lines. When looked at from a distance, this makes up a picture, often representing a face or several faces. Their multiline structure leads their analysis to be considered more as a task for image processing than language processing, as this would be the only way for the computer to obtain an impression of the emoticon from a point of view similar to a user looking at the computer screen. Because of the above, we do not include multiline ASCII art emoticons in our research. Finally, Eastern emoticons, in contrast to the Western ones are usually not rotated and present faces, gestures, or postures from a point of view easily comprehensible to the reader. Some examples are: "(^o^)" (laughing face), "(^_^)" (smiling face), and "(ToT)" (crying face). They arose in Japan, where they were called *kaomoji*, in the 1980s and since then have been developed in a number of online communities. They are made up of three to over twenty characters written in one line and consist of a representation of at least one face or posture, up to a number of different face-marks. In the research described in this chapter, we focused mainly on this type of emoticon for the following reason. The *kaomoji* emoticons have a large variation of forms and are sophisticated enough to express different mean-

ings. See Figure 2 for some examples of this type of emoticon. Emoticons defined as above can be considered as representations of body language in text-based conversation, where the communication channel is limited to the transmission of letters and punctuation marks. Therefore, we based our approach on the analysis of emoticons on assumptions similar to those from research on body language. In particular, we apply the theory of kinesics to define semantic areas as separate kinemes, and then automatically assign to them emotional affiliation.

Theory of Kinesics

The word kinesics, as defined by Vargas (1986), refers to all nonverbal behavior related to movement, such as postures, gestures, and facial expressions, and functions as a term for body language in current anthropology. It is studied as an important component of nonverbal communication, together with paralanguage (e.g., voice modulation) and proxemics (e.g., social distance). The term was first used by Birdwhistell (1952, 1970), who founded the theory of kinesics. The theory assumes that nonverbal behavior is used in everyday communication systematically and can be studied in a similar way to language. A minimal

Figure 2. Examples of emoticon division into sets of semantic areas: [M] – mouth, [E_L], [E_R] – eyes, [B_1], [B_2] - emoticon borders, [S_1] - [S_4] - additional areas

No. of sets	Emoticon	S₁	B₁	S₂	E_L	M	E_R	S₃	B₂	S₄	...
1	٧(｡·ω·)٧	٧	(	｡	·	ω	·	N/A	)	٧	
1	(――;)	N/A	(	N/A	—	N/A	—	;	)	N/A	
					SET 01					SET 02	
2	(＾＾)人(＾＾)	N/A	(	N/A	＾	N/A	＾	N/A	)	人	(＾＾)
2	☆-(•≧▽)人(▽≦•)-☆	☆-	(	•	≧	▽	N/A	N/A	)	人	(▽≦•)-☆
				SET 01		SET 02		SET 03		SET 04	
4	(▽´o)Ⅲ´★)ω´☆)∀´•)			(▽´o)		Ⅲ´★)		ω´☆)		∀´•)	

part distinguished in kinesics is a *kineme*—the smallest meaningful set of body movement, e.g., raising eyebrows or moving the eyes upward. Birdwhistell developed a complex system of *kinegraphs* to annotate kinemes for the research on body language. Some examples of kinemes are given in Figure 3.

Emoticons from the Viewpoint of Kinesics

Emoticons represent a multimodal (or specifically bimodal) type of information. On the one hand, they are embedded in lexical form. On the other hand, they convey non-linguistic information. This claim is supported by research both in social sciences (Rezabek & Cochenour, 1998) as well as

in recent fMRI studies of brain responses to emoticons (Yuasa et al., 2006). In general, emoticons are abstract representations of body language in online text-based communication. Therefore the same (or similar) method of analysis performed in studies on body language, such as kinesics, should be also valid in the analysis of emoticons. One of the current applications of kinesics is in annotation of affect display in psychology to determine which emotion is represented by which body movement or facial expression. This reasoning applied in kinesics should be applicable to emoticons as well. For the purposes of this research we specified the definition of "emoticon" (in the meaning of *kaomoji* emoticon) to: "a one-line string of symbols containing at least one set of semantic areas", where the semantic areas are classified

Figure 3. Some examples of kinegraphs used by Birdwhistell to annotate body language

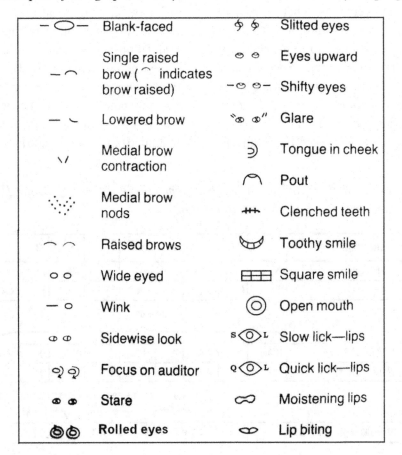

as: "mouth" [M], "eyes" [E_L], [E_R], "emoticon borders" [B_1], [B_2], and "additional areas" [S_1] - [S_4] placed between the above. Each area can include any number of characters. We also allowed part of the set to be of empty value, which means that the system can analyze an emoticon precisely even if some of the areas are absent. The minimal emoticon set considered in this research contains of two eyes (a set represented as "E_L,E_R", e.g., "^^" (a happy face)), mouth and an eye ("E_L,M" or "M,E_R", e.g., "(^o)" (a laughing face) and "(_^)" (a smiling face) respectively), or mouth/eye with one element of the additional areas ("M/E_R,S_3/S_4" or "S_1/S_2,E_L/M", e.g., "(^)/~" (a happy face) and "\(`)" (a sad face) respectively). However, many emoticons contain all or most of the areas, as in the following example showing a crying face "･ﾟ･(/Д`;)･ﾟ･". See Figure 2 for some examples of emoticons and their semantic areas. The analysis of emotive information conveyed in emoticons can therefore be based on annotations of the particular semantic areas grouped in a database. Such a database used in this research is described later in the chapter along with a method for its automatic construction.

Research on Emoticons - Review of the Field

In this section we shortly describe most relevant previous research on emoticons. Research on emoticons has developed in two general streams. Firstly, social sciences and communication studies have investigated the effects of emoticons on social interaction. Secondly, in NLP much effort has been put into generating and analyzing emoticons in order to improve computer-related text-based communication and contribute to fields like Computer-Mediated Communication or Human-Computer Interaction.

Emoticons in Social Sciences

As for social sciences, there are several examples worth mentioning. Ip (2002) investigated the impact of emoticons on affect interpretation in Instant Messaging. She concluded that the use of emoticons helps the interlocutors in conveying their emotions during online conversation. Wolf (2004) showed further, in her study on newsgroups, that there are significant differences in the use of emoticons by men and women. Derks et al. (2007) investigated the influence of social context on the use of emoticons in Internet communication. Finally, linguistic analysis of student chat conversations done by Maness (2008) proved emoticons as an important means of online communication.

A thorough research showing the importance of emoticons in communication was presented by Ptaszynski in 2006. He performed a study on emotive expressions used online and included emoticons as one of such expressions. Firstly, he performed a linguistic analysis of a part of a robust online forum *2channel* (http://www.2ch.net/) to find out which types of emotive expressions appear most often. Secondly, Ptaszynski performed a survey on 110 people (48 women, 62 men of different age groups). In the survey he asked about the types of expressions the participants use to express their feelings when communicating online. Both, the survey and the linguistic analysis showed that emoticons are the second, after direct lexical expressions, most often used type of expressions of emotions (Figure 4). Moreover, on the lists of ten most popular particular expressions, emoticons appeared most often, four times for positive emotions and five times for negative emotions (for details see Ptaszynski, 2006, p. 90).

All of the research are important and prove that emoticons appear frequently in online conversation, and often are necessary for the communication to take place.

Figure 4. Results presented by Ptaszynski (2006, p. 92) Left: Percentage of each type of emotive expression used on 2channel; Right: Popularity of each emotive expression type among survey participants (graphs simplified)

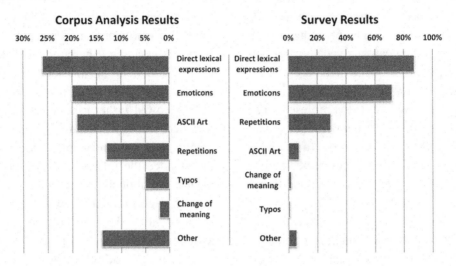

Emoticons in NLP

Two practical applications of research on emoticons in the field of Natural Language Processing are to generate and analyze emoticons. One of the first significant attempts to emoticon generation was done by Nakamura et al. (2003). They used a Neural Networks-based algorithm to learn a set of emoticon areas (mouths, faces, etc.) and used them later in a dialog agent. Unfortunately, the lack of a firm formalization of the semantic areas made the choice of emoticons eventually random, and the final performance far from ideal. This was one of the reasons for abandoning the idea of emoticon areas as base elements for emoticon-related systems. From that time most of the research on emoticon generation focused on preprogrammed emoticons (Suzuki & Tsuda 2006a, 2006b; Takami et al., 2009). In our research (Ptaszynski, Dybala, Komuda, Rzepka, & Araki, 2010; Ptaszynski, Dybala, Rzepka, & Araki, 2010) Ptaszynski, Maciejewski, Dybala, Rzepka, & Araki, 2010a, 2010b) we revived the idea of exploiting the emoticon areas, however, not in the research on emoticon generation, but

in emoticon extraction and analysis. There have been several attempts to analyze emoticons or use them to detect user emotions in sentences. For example, Reed (2005) showed that the use of emoticons can be useful in sentiment classification. Yang et al. (2007) made an attempt to use emoticons as seeds to automatically build a lexicon of emotional expressions. Both research focus on preprogrammed Western-type emoticons. As for attempts to analyze Eastern-type emoticons there have been three significant ones, namely, Tanaka et al. (2005), Yamada et al. (2007) and Kawakami (2008). To provide a wider view of our system's capabilities we reconstructed and compared CAO to those systems where it was possible. In particular, the emoticon extraction was compared to the system developed by Tanaka et al. (2005). Emotion estimation of emoticons was compared to the system developed by Yamada et al. (2007), as their approach is similar to ours in the method of exploiting the statistical occurrence of parts of emoticons. The method by Kawakami (2008) was fully manual and therefore was not a subject for comparison with automatic analysis methods. The three methods are described in detail.

Kernel Method for Emoticon Extraction

The system for extraction and analysis of emoticons with kernel methods was proposed by Tanaka et al. (2005). In their method, they used popular tools for processing sentences in Japanese, a POS tagger, *ChaSen* (Matsumoto et al., 2000), and a Support Vector Machine-based chunker, *yamcha* (Kudo & Matsumoto, 2001), to chunk sentences and separate parts of speech from "other areas in the sentence." which they defined as potential emoticons. However, their method was significant as it was the first evaluated attempt to extract emoticons from input. Unfortunately, the method was unable to perform many important tasks. First, as the method is based on a POS tagger, it could not extract emoticons from input other than a chunkable sentence. Therefore, if their system got a non-chunkable input (e.g., a sentence written in a hurry, with spelling mistakes, etc.), the method would not be able to proceed or would give an erroneous output. Moreover, if a spelling mistake appeared inside a parenthesis, a non-emoticon content could be recognized as a potential emoticon. All this made their method highly vulnerable to user creativity, although in a closed test on a set of prepared sentences their best result was somewhat high with 85.5% of Precision and 86.7% of Recall (balanced F-score = 86%). Their classification of emoticons into emotion types however, was not ideal. The set of six emotion types was determined manually and the classification process was based on a small sample set. Therefore as the system for comparison of emotion-type classification we used the one developed by Yamada et al. (2007).

N-Gram Method for Emoticon Affect Estimation

Yamada et al. (2007) used statistics of n-grams to determine emotion types conveyed by emoticons. Although their method was not able to detect or extract emoticons from input, their set of emotion types was not set by the researchers, but borrowed from a classification appearing on BBS Web sites with emoticon dictionaries. Although not ideal, such classification was less subjective than their predecessors. To classify emoticons, they used simple statistics of all characters occurring in emoticons without differentiating them into semantic areas. Eventually, this caused errors, as some characters were calculated as "eyes" although they represented "mouths," etc. However, the accuracy of their method still achieved somewhat high scores of about 76-83%. For comparison with CAO, we built a second system similar to theirs, but improved in several ways. Firstly, we applied our emotion-type classification, without which in the evaluation their system would always score 0% for the lacking emotion types. We also added the ability for emoticon extraction from input not present in the original system of Yamada et al. Moreover, we also used our database of raw emoticon samples, which improved the coverage of their system's database to 10,137 from 693 (6.8% of the improved database). Improved this way, we used this system in evaluation of CAO to verify the performance of our system in comparison with other methods in the fairest way possible. We also used three versions of Yamada's system, based on unigrams, bigrams, and trigrams.

Manual Analysis of Small Emoticon Database

Kawakami (2008) gathered and thoroughly analyzed a database of 31 emoticons. Unfortunately, his analysis was done manually. Moreover, the small number of samples made his research inapplicable in affect analysis of the large numbers of original emoticons appearing on the Internet. As mentioned, this method was fully manual, and was not a subject for comparison with automatic analysis methods. However, we made CAO provide all sufficient information Kawakami was dealing with as well.

Figure 5. Previous research on emoticon analysis in comparison to our system

Research (approach) / Capability	Tanaka et al (2005) (kernel methods)	Yamada et al (2007) (n-grams)	Kawakami (2008) (database)	CAO (theory of kinesics)
1. Detection whether input equals emoticon	×	×	×	○
2. Detection of emoticon in sentence input	○ (included in **3.**)	×	×	○
3. Extraction of emoticon from any other string of characters	○	×	×	○
4. Division into semantic areas	×	×	×	○
5. Database coverage	1,075	693	31	10,137 expanded automatically to over 3 mln.
6. Classification of emotion types	6 types (Subjective)	7 types (BBS-based; Subjective)	6 types (Subjective)	10 types (Language/ Culture Based)
7. Emotion estimation of separate emoticons	○ (included in **8.**)	○	○	○
8. Affect Analysis of sentences with emoticons	○	×	×	○

All of the methods strictly depend on their primary emoticon databases and therefore are highly vulnerable to user creativity in generating new emoticons. In our research, we aimed to deal with this problem. Our system is capable of extraction of emoticons from input and fully automatic affect analysis based on a coherent emotion classification. It also takes into consideration semantic areas (representations of mouth, eyes, etc.). The system is based on a large emoticon database collected from the Internet and enlarged automatically, providing coverage of over 3 million possibilities. The system is thoroughly evaluated with a training set (the database) and a test set (a corpus of over 350 million sentences in Japanese). We summarize the above previous research in comparison to our system in Figure 5.

FRAMEWORK FOR NLP RESEARCH ON EMOTICONS

Hagiwara includes emoticons in Unnatural Language Processing task (endnote 2). This puts emoticons in a position of an unnatural entity in language. In our research on emoticons we got to the contrary conclusions. Emoticons function as generic representations of body language in text-based communication, and are not only natural, but frequent and often necessary entities in natural language used online. This is also proved by a long history of development and use of emoticons, which emerged along with the first computer-mediated communication environments. Moreover, authors were not able to identify any online communication environment NOT using emoticons as a support for text-based messages. Despite the firm position in communication, the phenomenon of emoticons has not yet had enough attention (e.g., search engines, including Yahoo or Google, are still incapable of detecting and parsing even the simplest emoticons, which influences search results on informal media, like blogs, etc.). To fill this gap, we propose including research on emoticons as a challenge in NLP. To help researchers investigate this topic in the future we present a framework for the research on emoticons consisting of tasks necessary to fulfill within the research on emoticons.

Figure 6 presents our proposal of a framework for research on emoticons. It consists of 12 tasks (11 plus one additional) divided into 6 groups. The first two groups indicate emoticon detection and extraction. Although these two tasks could be performed with the same procedure, for some tasks it is enough only to confirm the presence

Figure 6. Framework for NLP research on emoticons

Task to perform with Emoticon	Type of Emoticon (1-line)	
	A (Western)	**B (Eastern)**
1. Emoticon Detection		
1.1. Input = emoticon?	--	CAO
1.2. In sentence input	Changhua et al. 2007	Tanaka et al. 2005; Ptaszynski et al. 2010a,b,c,d
1.3. In any input	--	Ptaszynski et al. 2010 a,b,c,d
2. Emoticon Extraction		
2.1. From sentence input	--	Tanaka et al. 2005; Ptaszynski et al. 2010 a,b,c,d
2.2. From any input	--	Ptaszynski et al. 2010 a,b,c,d
3. Parsing / Division into semantic areas		Nakamura, et al. 2003; Ptaszynski et al. 2010 a,b,c,d
4. Semantic Analysis		
4.1. Affect / Sentiment	Read, 2005; Changhua et al. 2007	Tanaka et al. 2005; Yamada et al. 2007; Ptaszynski et al. 2010 a,b,c,d
4.2. Actions	Changhua et al. 2007	Tanaka et al. 2005
4.3. Other	Politeness: Suzuki and Tsuda (2006b)	--
5. Emoticon Generation	--	Nakamura, et al. 2003; Suzuki and Tsuda, 2006
6. Evaluation on		
6.1. emoticons alone	Changhua et al. 2007	Tanaka et al. 2005; Yamada et al. 2007; Ptaszynski et al. 2010 a,b,c,d
6.2. sentences with emoticons	Read, 2005	Nakamura, et al. 2003; Suzuki and Tsuda, 2006; Ptaszynski et al. 2010 a,b,c,d

of an emoticon (e.g., classifying sentences into emotive and non-emotive). Detection is usually simpler and therefore consumes less time and resources. In extraction, the detected emoticon is further stored in memory, which can be used in further analysis. The next task is emoticon parsing, or dividing into particular semantic areas. It is useful, when one aspires to deal with human creativity in emoticon generation (Nakamura et al., 2003). We also proved that it can help in emoticon analysis (Ptaszynski, Maciejewski, et al., 2010a, 2010b). Task 4 includes analysis of the meaning emoticons convey. The most popular task is to analyze affect, although it is also possible to analyze actions the emoticons depict. Other areas, still unchallenged or challenged only briefly, could include the analysis of influence the emoticons have on politeness strategies. However, it has to be remembered that all these represent different

dimensions and should be dealt as separate tasks. Emoticon generation is one of the most challenging tasks, as it aims to generate original emoticons to match other contents (e.g., sentence, like in Nakamura et al., 2003). Recently this task has been simplified to preprogrammed emoticons. Final task to perform within this framework is thorough evaluation of the system. It can be performed on separate emoticons, or sentences the emoticons appear in.

To create a system capable to thoroughly analyze emoticons and use them in a way close to human creativity, all of the above tasks need to be included in the research. However, it is difficult to deal with all emoticon types and tasks at once. Therefore in the table we indicated the research that already dealt with each task to some extent. We did not however compare the results, as all research used different datasets and evaluation criteria.

DATABASE OF EMOTICONS

To create a system for emoticon analysis, we first needed a coherent database of emoticons classified according to the emotions they represent. The database development was performed in several steps. First, raw emoticon samples were collected from the Internet. Then, the naming of emotion classes expressed by the emoticons was unified according to Nakamura's (1993) classification of emotions. Next, the idea of kinemes was applied in order to divide the extracted emoticons into semantic areas. Finally, the emotive affiliations of the semantic areas were determined by calculating their occurrences in the database.

Resource Collection

The raw emoticons were extracted from seven online emoticon dictionaries available on seven popular Web pages dedicated to emoticons: *Facemark Party, Kaomojiya, Kao-moji-toshokan, Kaomoji-café, Kaomoji Paradise, Kaomojisyo* and *Kaomoji Station*[3]. The dictionaries are easily accessible from the Internet.

Database Naming Unification

The data in each dictionary is divided into numerous categories, such as "greetings," "affirmations," "actions," "hobbies," "expressing emotions," etc.

However, the number of categories and their nomenclature is not unified. To unify them, we used Ptaszynski, Dybala, Rzepka, and Araki (2009) affect analysis system. One of the procedures in this system is to classify words according to the emotion type they express, based on Nakamura's emotion classification. Categories with names suggesting emotional content were selected and emoticons from those categories were extracted, giving a total of 11,416 emoticons. However, as some of them could appear in more than one collection, we performed filtering to extract only the unique ones. The number of unique emoticons after the filtering was 10,137 (89%). Most of the emoticons appearing in all seven collections were unique. Only for the emoticons annotated as expressions of "joy" was a large amount, over one-third, repeated. This means that all of the dictionaries from which the emoticons were extracted provided emoticons that did not appear in other collections. On the other hand, the high repeating frequency of emoticons annotated as expressions of "joy" suggests that this emotion type is expressed by Internet users with a certain number of popular emoticons. The emotion types for which the number of extracted emoticons was the highest were, in order, joy, fondness, anger, surprise, gloom, and excitement. This suggests that Internet users express these emotion types more often than the rest, which were, in order, dislike, shame/bashfulness, fear, and relief. The ratio of unique emoticons to all extracted ones and their distribution across the emotion types are shown in Figure 7.

Figure 7. Ratio of unique emoticons to all extracted emoticons and their distribution in the database according to emotion types

joy, delight	liking, fondness	anger	surprise, amazement	sadness, gloom	excitement	dislike	shame, shyness	fear	relief	Overall	Emoticons
3128	1988	1238	1227	1203	1124	704	526	179	99	**11416**	All extracted
1972	1972	1221	1196	1169	1120	698	511	179	99	**10137**	Unique
63%	99%	99%	97%	97%	99%	99%	97%	100%	100%	**89%**	Ratio

Extraction of Semantic Areas

After gathering the database of raw emoticons and classifying them according to emotion types, we performed an extraction of all semantic areas appearing in unique emoticons. The extraction was done in agreement with the definition of emoticons and according to the following procedure. Firstly, possible emoticon borders are defined and all unique eye-mouth-eye triplets are extracted together ($E_L ME_R$). From those triplets we extracted mouths (M) and pairs of eyes (E_L, E_R). The rule for extracting eye-patterns from triplets goes as follows. If the eyes consist of multiple characters, each eye has the same pattern. If the eyes consist only of one character, they can be the same or different (this was always true among the 10,137 emoticons in our database). Finally, having extracted the $E_L ME_R$ triplets and defined the emoticon borders we extracted all existing additional areas (S1,...,S4). The flow chart of the whole procedure is represented on Figure 8. The details of the process with an example are represented in Figure 10.

Emotion Annotation of Semantic Areas

Having divided the emoticons into semantic areas, occurrence frequency of the areas in the emotion-type database was calculated for every triplet, eyes, mouth, and each of the additional areas. All unique areas were summarized in the order of occurrence within the database for each emotion type. Each area's occurrence rate is considered as the probability of which emotion they tend to express.

Database Statistics

The number of unique combined areas of $E_L ME_R$ triplets was 6,185. The number of unique eyes (E_L, E_R) was 1,920. The number of unique mouth areas (M) was 1,654. The number of unique additional areas was respectively $S_1 = 5,169$, $S_2 = 2,986$, $S_3 = 3,192$, $S_4 = 8,837$ (Overall 20,184). The distribution of all area types for which the statistics were calculated is shown in Figure 9.

Database Coverage

In previous research on emoticon classification one of the most popular approaches was the as-

Figure 8. Flow chart of the database construction

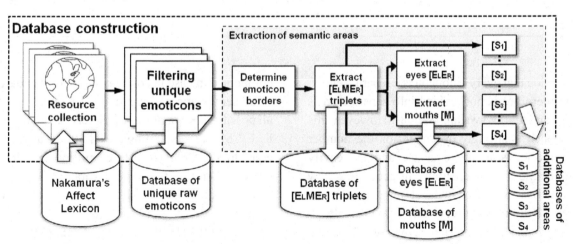

Figure 9. Distribution of all types of unique areas for which occurrence statistics were calculated across all emotion types in the database

Area type	$E_L M E_R$	S_1	B_1	S_2	E_L E_R	M	S_3	B_2	S_4
joy, delight	1298	1469	--	653	349	336	671	--	2449
anger	741	525	--	321	188	239	330	--	1014
sorrow, sadness, gloom	702	350	--	303	291	170	358	--	730
fear	124	72	--	67	52	62	74	--	133
shame, shyness	315	169	--	121	110	85	123	--	343
liking, fondness	1079	1092	--	802	305	239	805	--	1633
dislike	527	337	--	209	161	179	201	--	562
excitement	670	700	--	268	243	164	324	--	1049
relief	81	50	--	11	38	26	27	--	64
surprise, amazement	648	405	--	231	183	154	279	--	860
Overall	6185	5169	--	2986	1920	1654	3192	--	8837

Figure 10. The flow of the procedure for semantic area extraction

```
1.Input: (.*) - STRING OF CHARACTERS
2.Determine emoticon borders:
  B₁{NULL,(, (,<,<,... }, B₂{NULL,>,>) ,),...}:B₁(.*)B₁
3.Localize E_LME_R triplet in the potential emoticon: B₁(.*)E_LME_R(.*)B₂;
4.Separate eyes E_L,E_R and mouth M areas:
5. from E_LME_R take n characters from the left n_L and
   right n_R;
6. if n_L=n_R, n_L is E_L and n_R=E_R; if no match take n-1
   characters;
7. if the above fails, take one character form left as E_L and from right as
   E_R.
8. mouth area M is what is left between E_L and E_R
9.Determine additional areas S₁,...,S₄ according to the regular expression:
  S₁B₁S₂E_LME_RS₃B₂S₄
10.Calculate occurrence frequencies separately for triplet E_LME_R, pair E_L,E_R,
   mouth M, additional areas S₁,...,S₄, for all emotion types;
```

sumption that every emoticon is a separate entity, and therefore is not divided into separate areas or characters (Kawakami, 2008). However, this approach is strongly dependent on the number of emoticons in the database and is heavily vulnerable to user creativity in generating new emoticons. We aimed in developing an approach as much immune to user creativity as possible. To verify that, we estimated the coverage of the raw emoticon database in comparison to the database of all semantic areas separately. The number of all possible combinations of triplets calculated as $E_L,E_R \times M$, even excluding the additional areas, is equal to 3,175,680 (over three million combinations[4]). Therefore the basic coverage of the raw emoticon database, which contains a somewhat large number of 10,137 unique samples, does not exceed 0.32% of the whole coverage of this method. This means that a method based only on a raw emoticon database would lose 99.68% of possible coverage, which is retained in our approach.

CAO: EMOTICON ANALYSIS SYSTEM

The databases of emoticons and their semantic areas described were applied in CAO - *a system for emotiCon Analysis and decOding of affective information*. The system performs three main procedures. First, it detects whether input contains any emoticons. Second, if emoticons were detected, the system extracts all emoticons from the input. Third, the system estimates the expressed emotions by matching the extracted emoticon in stages until it finds a match in the databases of:

1. raw emoticons,
2. $E_L M E_R$ triplets and additional areas $S_1;...; S_4$,
3. separately for the eyes $E_L; E_R$, mouth M, and the additional areas.

Emoticon Detection in Input

The first procedure after obtaining input is responsible for detecting the presence of emoticons. The presence of an emoticon is determined when at least three symbols usually used in emoticons appear in a row. A set of 455 symbols was statistically selected as symbols appearing most frequently in emoticons.

Emoticon Extraction from Input

In the emoticon extraction procedure the system extracts all emoticons from input. This is done in stages, looking for a match with: 1) the raw emoticon database; in case of no match, 2) any $E_L M E_R$ triplet from the triplet database. If a triplet is found the system matches the rest of the elements of the regular expression: $m/[S_1?][B_1?][S_2?][E_L M E_R][S_3?][B_2?][S_4?]/$, with the use of all databases of additional areas and emoticon borders; 3) in case the triplet match was not found, the system searches for: 3a) any triplet match from all 3 million $E_L M E_R$ combinations with one of the four possible $E_L M E_R$ patterns matched gradually ($[E_L][M][E_R]$, $[E_L][E_R]$, $[M][E_R]$, $[E_L][M]$); or as a last resort 3b) a match for any of all the areas separately. The flow of this procedure is represented in Figure 11.

Although the extraction procedure could function also as a detection procedure, it is more time consuming. The differences in processing time are not noticeable when the number of consecutive inputs is small. However, we plan to use CAO to annotate large corpora including over several

Figure 11. The flow of the procedure for emoticon extraction

```
1.Input: "SOME CHARACTERS ·°·(/Д`;)·°·SOME CHARACTERS"
2.Find match in raw emoticon database: ·°·(/Д`;)·°·
3. If no match, localize E_LME_R triplet in the E_LME_R triplet database: /Д`
4. If no triplet found, look for any E_LME_R combination;
5. If no combination matched, find any E_LE_R or M from separate semantic area
   database: /`, Д
6.Localize emoticon borders B_1,B_2 : (,)
7.Localize additional areas S_1,S_2,S_3,S_4 : ·°·,;,·°·
8.Determine the emoticon structure: S_1: ·°·, B_1:(, S_2:N/A, E_LE_R: /`, M: Д,
  S_3:;, B_2:), S_4: ·°·
9.Look for next emoticon;
```

million entries. With this code improvement the system skips sentences with no potential emoticons, which shortens the processing time.

Affect Analysis Procedure

In the affect analysis procedure, the system estimates which emotion types are the most probable for an emoticon to express. This is done by matching the recognized emoticon to the emotions annotated on the database elements and checking their occurrence statistics. This procedure is performed as an extension to the extraction procedure. The system first checks which emotion types were annotated on raw emoticons. If no emotion was found, it looks for a match with emotion annotations with E_LME_R triplet. If no match was found, the semantic area databases for eyes E_LE_R and mouth M are considered separately and the matching emotion types are extracted. Finally, emotion type annotations for additional areas are determined. The flow of this procedure is shown with an example in Figure 12. Flow chart of the system as a whole is represented on Figure 13.

Output Calculation

After extracting the emotion annotations of emoticons and/ or semantic areas, the final emotion ranking output was calculated. In the process of evaluation, we calculated the score in five different ways to specify the most effective method of result calculation.

Occurrence

The processing of one emoticon provides a set of lists—one for each emoticon part (mouth, eyes, additional areas, etc.). Any part of emoticon may appear in databases belonging to different emotion types (e.g., in the crying emoticon,, element representing "mouth"—appears 53 times in the sorrow database, 52 times in excitement, 28 times in joy, etc. (see Figure 8 for details). Each of those lists contains emotion types with assigned numbers of occurrences of the element in the database of each emotion type. Having these lists, it is possible to perform different calculations to summarize/generalize them. First, all results can be added and then the emotion type appearing most often will be the most probable for the emoticon to express. In other words, occurrence is the straightforward

Figure 12. The flow of the procedure for affect analysis of emoticon

```
1. Input; (e.g.: ˚•(/Д`;)•˚•)
2. Determine emotion types according to raw emoticon database; (•˚•(/Д`;)•˚• :
   sorrow/sadness(3), excitement(2))
3. If no match, determine emotion types for E_LME_R triplet;
   ( /Д`:excitement(14),anger(2),sorrow(1),fear(1),joy(1),fondness(1) )
4. If no emotion types for triplet found, find emotion types for separate
   semantic areas E_LE_R and M;
   (/`:sorrow(3),shame(3),joy(2),fondness(2),fear(1),excitement(1),anger(1))
   ( Д:sorrow(53),excitement(52),anger(42),surprise(37), joy(28),
   fondness(25),dislike(22),fear(12),shame(9))
5. Determine emotion types for additional areas;
   (•˚•:..., ;:..., •˚•:...)
6. Proceed to next emoticon in the character string;
7. If no more emoticons, summarize scores;
```

Figure 13. Flow chart of the CAO system

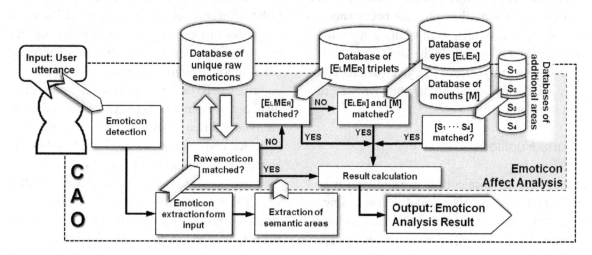

number of occurrences of an element (emoticon/triplet/semantic area). The higher the occurrence of an element in the emotion-type database, the higher it scored. For more elements, the final score for an emotion type was calculated as the sum of all occurrence scores for all emotion types. The final emotion scores were placed in descending order of the final sums of their occurrences.

Frequency

However, it might be said that to simply add the numbers is not a fair way of score summarization since there are a different number of elements in each database and a database with a small number of elements will have a tendency to lose. To avoid such biases, we divided the emotion score by the number of all elements in the database. Therefore, frequency is calculated as the occurrence number of a matched element (emoticon or semantic area) divided by the number of all elements in the particular emotion-type database. The higher the frequency rate for a matched element in the emotion-type database, the higher it scored. For more elements, the final score for an emotion type was calculated as the sum of all frequency scores of the matched elements for an

emotion type. The final scores for each emotion type were placed in descending order of the final sums of their frequencies.

Unique Frequency

It could be further said that just dividing by all elements is also not ideally fair since there are elements appearing more often which are therefore stronger, which will also cause a bias in the results. To avoid this, we also divided the occurrences by the number of all unique elements. Unique frequency is thus calculated similarly to the usual frequency. The difference is that the denominator (division basis) is not the number of all elements in the particular emotion-type database, but the number of all unique ones.

Position

Position is calculated in the following way. The strings of characters in all databases (raw emoticons, triplets, and semantic areas) are sorted by their occurrence in descending order. By position, we mean the place of the matched string in the database. Position is determined by the number of strings, occurrence of which was greater than the occurrence of a given string. For example, in a set of strings with the following occurrences: $n_1=5, n_2=5, n_3=5, n_4=3, n_5=3, n_6=2, n_7=2, n_8=1$, the strings n6 and n7 will be in the sixth position. If the string was not matched in a given database, it is assigned a position of the last plus one element from this database.

Unique Position

Unique Position is calculated in a similar way to the normal Position, with one difference. Since some strings in the databases have the same number of occurrences, they could be considered as appearing in the same position. Therefore, here we considered the strings with the same occurrences as the ones with the same position. For example, in a set of strings with the following occurrences: $n_1=5, n_2=5, n_3=5, n_4=3, n_5=3, n_6=2, n_7=2, n_8=1$, the strings n_6 and n_7 will be in the third position. If the string was not matched in a given database, it is assigned a position of the last plus one element from this database.

Two-Dimensional Model of Affect

According to Solomon (1993), people sometimes misinterpret specific emotion types, but rarely their valence. One might, for example, confuse such emotions as anger and irritation, but it is unlikely they would confuse admiration with detestation. Therefore, we checked whether the general features of the extracted emotion types were in agreement. By "general features," we mean those proposed by Russell (1980) in his theory of a 2D model of affect, where he argues that all emotions can be described in a space of two dimensions: valence and activation. An example of positive-activated emotion would be elation, positive-deactivated would be relief; negative-activated and negative-deactivated emotions would be indignation and depression, respectively. Nakamura's emotion types were mapped onto Russell's model and their affiliation to the spaces was determined as

in Ptaszynski, Dybala, Shi, Rzepka, and Araki (2009). For some emotion types, the affiliation is somewhat obvious, e.g., gloom is never positive or activated. However, for other emotion types, the emotion affiliation is not that obvious, e.g., surprise can be both positive as well as negative, dislike can be either activated or deactivated, etc. The emotion types with uncertain affiliation were mapped on all groups they could belong to. However, no emotion type was mapped on more than two adjacent fields. These groups are then used for estimating whether the emotion types extracted by CAO belong to the same quarter. For the details of the mapping of the emotion types, see Figure 14.

EVALUATION OF CAO

To fully verify the system's performance, we carried out an exhaustive evaluation. The system was evaluated using a training set and a test set. The evaluated areas were: emoticon detection in a sentence, emoticon extraction from input, division of emoticons into semantic areas, and emotion classification of emoticons.

Training Set Evaluation

The training set for the evaluation included all 10,137 unique emoticons from the raw emoticon database. However, to avoid perfect matching with the database (and therefore scoring 100% accuracy), we made the system skip the first step - matching to the raw emoticon database - and continue with further procedures (matching triplets and separate semantic areas).

The system's score was calculated as follows: If the system annotated an emoticon taken from a specific emotion-type database with the name of the database as the highest one on the list of all annotated emotions, it counted as 1 point. Therefore, if the system annotated five emotion types on an emoticon taken from the "joy" da-

Figure 14. Grouping Nakamura's classification of emotions on Russell's 2D space

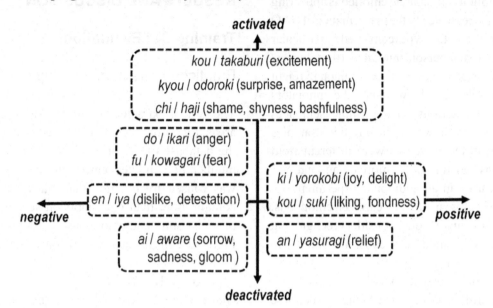

tabase and the "joy" annotation appeared as the first one on the list of 5, the system's score was 5/5 (1 point). If the name of the emotion database from which the emoticon was taken did not appear in the first place, the score was calculated as the rank number the emotion achieved divided by the number of all emotions annotated. Therefore, if the system annotated five emotion types on an emoticon taken from the "joy" database and the "joy" annotation appeared as the second one on the list of five, the system's score was 4/5 (0.8 point), and so on. These calculations were further performed for all five ways of score calculation.

Test Set Evaluation

In the test set evaluation, we used Yacis Blog Corpus (Maciejewski et al., 2010).

Yacis Blog Corpus

Yacis Blog Corpus is an unannotated corpus consisting of 354,288,529 Japanese sentences. Average sentence length is 28.17 Japanese characters, which fits in the definition of a short sentence in

the Japanese language (Kubota et al., 2002). Yacis Corpus was assembled using data obtained automatically from the pages of Ameba Blog (www.ameblo.co.jp), one of the largest Japanese blogging services. It consists of 12,938,606 downloaded and parsed Web pages written by 60,658 unique bloggers. There were 6,421,577 pages containing 50,560,024 comments (7.873 comments per page that contains at least one comment). All pages were obtained between 3rd and 24th of December 2009. We used this corpus as it has been shown before that communication on blogs is rich in emoticons.

Experiment Settings

From Yacis Blog Corpus, we randomly extracted 1,000 middle-sized sentences as the test set; 418 of those sentences included emoticons. Using Cohen's kappa agreement coefficient and balanced F-score, we calculated CAO's performance in detecting emoticons in sentences (with Cohen's agreement coefficient and kappa), and emoticon extraction (including division of emoticons into semantic areas). In the evaluation of the emotion estimation procedure, we asked 42 people to annotate emotions on separate emoticons appearing in the sentences to verify the performance of CAO in specifying emotion types conveyed by particular emoticons (each person annotated 10 sentences/emoticons, except one person, who annotated eight samples). Additionally, we asked the annotators to annotate emotions on the whole sentences with emoticons (however, the emoticon samples appearing in the sentences were different from the ones assigned in only emoticon annotation). This was used in an additional experiment not performed before in other research on emoticons. The usual evaluation only considers recognizing emotions of separate emoticons. We wanted to check how much of the emotive information encapsulated in a sentence could be conveyed with the addition of emoticons and whether it is possible to recognize the emotion expressed by the whole sentence looking only at the emoticons used in the sentence. Emoticons are something like an addition to this meaning. The question was how much does the emoticon match the meaning expressed by the sentence? We checked this appearance of the emotion types and the general emotive features (valence and activation). However, the meaning of written/typed sentences is mostly understood on the basis of lexical information, and we expected these results to be lower than those from only emoticon evaluation. The system's results were calculated in a similar way to the training set, considering human annotations as a gold standard. Moreover, we checked the results of annotations for specific emotion types and groups of emotions belonging to the same quarters from Russell's 2D affect space. The calculations were performed for the best three of the five ways of score calculation selected in training set evaluation.

RESULTS AND DISCUSSION

Training Set Evaluation

Emoticon Extraction from Input

The system extracted and divided into semantic areas a total number of 14,570 emoticons from the database of the original 10,137. The larger number of extracted emoticons on the output was caused by the fact that many emoticons contain more than one emoticon set (examples of such compound emoticons are represented in Figure 2). In primary evaluation of the system (Ptaszynski, Dybala, Rzepka, & Araki, 2010), approximately 82% of all extracted emoticons were extracted correctly. The problem appeared in erroneously extracting additional areas as separate emoticons. We solved this problem by detecting the erroneously extracted additional areas in a post-procedure, using the additional area database and reattaching the erroneously extracted areas with the actual emoticons they belonged to. This optimized the extraction procedure. There were still 73 cases (from 14,570) of erroneously extracting additional areas as emoticons. The analysis of errors showed that these erroneously extracted additional areas contained elements appearing in databases of semantic areas of eyes or mouths and emoticon borders. To solve this problem, the error cases would have to be added as exceptions; however, this would prevent the extraction of such emoticons in the future if they actually appeared as emoticons. Therefore, we agreed to this minimal error rate (0.5%), with which the extraction accuracy of CAO is still near ideal (99.5%). Finally, the results for the emoticon extraction and division into semantic areas, when represented by the notions of Precision and Recall, were as follows: CAO was able to extract and divide all of the emoticons; therefore, the Recall rate was 100%. As for the Precision, 14,497 out of 14,570 were extracted and divided correctly, which gives the rate of 99.5%. The balanced F-score for these results equals 99.75%, which clearly outperforms the system of Tanaka et al. (2005).

Affect Analysis of Emoticons

First, we calculated how many of the extracted emoticons the system was able to annotate any emotions for. This was done with a near-ideal accuracy of 99.5%. The only emoticons for which the system could not find any emotions were the 73 errors that appeared in the extraction evaluation. This means that the emotion annotation procedure was activated for all of the correctly extracted emoticons (100%).

Second, we calculated the accuracy in annotation of the particular emotion types on the extracted emoticons. From the five ways of result calculation, two (Position and Unique Position) achieved much lower results than the other three, about 50%, and were discarded from further evaluation. All of the other three (Occurrence, Frequency, and Unique Frequency) scored high, from over 80% to over 85%. The highest overall score in the training set evaluation was achieved by, in order: Occurrence (85.2%), Unique Frequency (81.8%), and Frequency (80.4%). Comparison with the other

emoticon analysis system showed that even after the improvements that we made, the best score it achieved (80.2%) still did not exceed our worst score (80.4%). For details see Figure 15.

Test Set Evaluation

Emoticon Detection in Input

The system correctly detected the presence or absence of emoticons in 976 out of 1,000 sentences (97.6%). In 24 cases (2.4% of all sentences), the system failed to detect that an emoticon appeared in the sentence. However, the system achieved an ideal score in detecting the absence of emoticons. This means that there are no errors in the detecting procedure itself, but that the database does not cover all possibilities of human creativity. However, it can be reasonably assumed that if our system, with the database coverage of over 3 million possibilities, still has 2.4% of error in emoticon detection, the methods based on smaller databases would fail even more often in similar tasks. The strength of the Cohen's coefficient of agreement with human annotators was considered

Figure 15. Training set evaluation results for emotion estimation of emoticons for each emotion type with all five score calculations in comparison to another system

| Emotion type | Yamada et al (2007) improved | | | CAO: | | Unique | | Unique |
	1-gram	2-gram	3-gram	Occurrence	Frequency	Frequency	Position	Position
anger	0.702	0.815	**0.877**	**0.811**	0.771	0.767	0.476	0.476
dislike	0.661	0.809	**0.919**	0.631	**0.800**	0.719	0.556	0.591
excitement	0.700	0.789	**0.846**	0.786	0.769	**0.797**	0.560	0.516
fear	**0.564**	0.409	0.397	0.451	**0.936**	0.858	0.652	0.671
fondness	**0.452**	0.436	0.448	**0.915**	0.778	0.783	0.460	0.389
joy	0.623	0.792	**0.873**	**0.944**	0.802	0.860	0.522	0.421
relief	**1.000**	0.999	**1.000**	0.600	**0.990**	0.985	0.599	0.621
shame	0.921	0.949	**0.976**	0.706	**0.922**	0.910	0.538	0.566
sorrow	0.720	0.861	**0.920**	**0.814**	0.809	0.791	0.553	0.520
surprise	0.805	0.904	**0.940**	0.862	0.866	**0.874**	0.520	0.523
All approx.	0.675	0.751	**0.802**	**0.852**	0.804	0.818	0.517	0.469

Figure 16. Results of the CAO system in emoticon detection, extraction from input and estimation of emotions

		Detection		Extraction		
		System		R	P	F-score
		Emoticon	No emoticon	94.3%	100%	97.1%
Users	Emoticon	394	24			
	No emoticon	0	582	$\left[\frac{394}{418}\right]$	$\left[\frac{394}{394}\right]$	$\frac{2*P*R}{(P+R)}$
No. of agreements=976 (97.6%), Kappa= 0.95						

to be very good (kappa = 0.95). The results are summarized in Figure 16.

Emoticon Extraction from Input

From 418 sentences containing emoticons, CAO extracted 394 (Recall = 94.3%). All of them were correctly extracted and divided into semantic areas (Precision = 100%), which gave an overall extraction score of over 97.1% of balanced F-score. With such results, the system clearly outperformed Tanaka et al.'s (2005) system in emoticon extraction and presented ideal performance in emoticon division into semantic areas, a capability not present in the compared system. As an interesting remark, it should be noticed that in the evaluation on the training set, the Recall scored perfectly, but the Precision did not, and in the evaluation on the test set it was the opposite. This suggests that sophisticated emoticons, which

CAO had problems detecting, do not appear very often in the corpora of natural language such as blog contents, and the database applied in CAO is sufficient for the tasks of emoticon extraction from input and emoticon division into semantic areas. However, as human creativity is never perfectly predictable, sporadically (in at least 2.4% of cases), new emoticons still appear which the system is not able to extract correctly. This problem could be solved by frequent updates of the database. The race against human creativity is always an uphill task, although, with close to ideal extraction (over 97%), CAO is already a large step forward. The results are summarized in Figure 17.

Affect Analysis of Separate Emoticons

The highest score was achieved by, in order: Unique Frequency (93.5% for specific emotion types and 97.4% for estimating groups of emo-

Figure 17. Results of the CAO system in Affect Analysis of emoticons. The results summarize three ways of score calculation, specific emotions types and 2-dimensional affect space. The CAO system showed in comparison to another system.

Emotion Estimation on Separate Emoticons								
Yamada et al. (2007)			CAO					
1-gram	2-gram	3-gram	Occurrence		Frequency		Unique Frequency	
			Types	2D space	Types	2D space	Types	2D space
0.721347	0.865117	**0.877049**	0.891472	0.966778	0.934319	0.971044	**0.935364**	**0.973925**
Emotion Estimation on Sentences								
Yamada et al. (2007)			CAO					
1-gram	2-gram	3-gram	Occurrence		Frequency		Unique Frequency	
			Types	2D space	Types	2D space	Types	2D space
0.685714	**0.797659**	0.714819	0.755171	0.908911	0.800896	0.940582	**0.802012**	**0.946291**

tions mapped on Russell's affect space model), Frequency (93.4% and 97.1%), and Occurrence (89.1% and 96.7%). The compared system by Yamada et al. (2007), despite the numerous improvements we made to this system, did not score well, achieving its best score (for trigrams) far below our worst score (Occurrence/Types). The scores are shown in the top part of Figure 17. The best score was achieved by Unique Frequency, which, in training set evaluation, achieved the second highest score. This method of score calculation will therefore be used as default score calculation in the system. However, to confirm this, we also checked the results of evaluation of affect analysis of sentences with CAO.

Affect Analysis of Emoticons in Sentences

The highest score was achieved by, in order: Unique Frequency (80.2% for specific emotion types and 94.6% for estimating groups of emotions mapped on Russell's affect space model), Frequency (80% and 94%), and Occurrence (75.5% and 90.8%). It is the same score order, although the evaluation was not of estimating emotions of separate emoticons, but of whole sentences with the use of CAO. This proves that Unique Frequency is the most efficient method of output calculation for our system. The compared system scored poorly here as well, achieving only one score (for bigrams) higher than our worst score (Occurrence/Types). The scores are shown in the bottom part of Figure 17. The score for specific emotion-type determination was, as we expected, not ideal (from 75.5% to 80.2%). This confirms that, using only emoticons, affect analysis of sentences can be performed at a reasonable level (80.2%). However, as the emotive information conveyed in sentences also consists of other lexical and contextual information, it is difficult to achieve a result close to ideal. Although the results for 2D affect space were close to ideal (up to nearly 95%), which means that the emotion types for

which human annotators and the system did not agree still had the same general features (valence polarity and activation), this also confirms the statement from Section 5.5 that people sometimes misinterpret (or use interchangeably) the specific emotion types of which general features remain the same (in the test data people annotated, e.g., "fondness" on sentences with emoticons expressing "joy," or "surprise" on "excitement," etc., but never, e.g., "joy" on "fear"). The above can also be interpreted as further proof for the statement from the Section "Definition of Emoticons", where emoticons are defined as expressions used in online communication as representations of body language. In direct communication, body language is also often used to convey a supportive meaning for the contents conveyed through language. Moreover, some sets of behavior (or kinemes) can be used to express different specific meanings for which the general emotive feature remains the same. For example, wide opened eyes and mouth might suggest emotions like fear, surprise, or excitement; although the specificity of the emotion is determined by the context of a situation, the main feature (activation) remains the same. In our evaluation, the differences in the results for specific emotions types and 2D affect model prove this phenomenon. Some examples illustrating this have been presented in Figure 18.

CONCLUSION

In this chapter we presented an interdisciplinary review of research on emoticons, string of symbols representing body language in text-based communication. We showed that although emoticons have been a part of text-based communication for a long time, relatively little have been done in NLP to understand this important phenomenon. We suggested to include emoticon processing as frequent NLP challenge and proposed a framework, containing tasks to be included in the future research on emoticons.

Figure 18. Examples of analysis performed by CAO. Presented abilities include: emoticon extraction, division into semantic areas, and emotion estimation in comparison with human annotations of separate emoticons and whole sentences. Emotion estimation (only the highest scores) given for unique frequency.

Example 1: *Chakku-shime wasure-san ga ooidesu ne, watashi mo tama ni yarakashite hitori sekimen* (;^_^A
Translation: Many people forget to close their fly. I sometimes do that too and when I notice, I get all red (;^_^A

S_1	B_1	S_2	E_LME_R	S_3	B_2	S_4
N/A	(	;	^_^	A	N/A	N/A

CAO	Human Annotation	
fear / anxiety (0.06450746)	emoticon	sentence
...	fear / anxiety	fear / anxiety, shame

Example 2: *Itsumo, "Mac, ne-----"tte shibui kao sareru n desu. Windows to kurabete meccha katami ga semai desu* (丿 Д`):・° +:・。
Translation: People would pull a wry face on me saying "Oh, you're using a Mac...?" . It makes me feel so down when compared to Windows (丿 Д`):・° +:・。

S_1	B_1	S_2	E_LME_R	S_3	B_2	S_4
N/A	(	N/A	丿 Д`	N/A	)	:・° +:・。

CAO	Human Annotation	
sadness / sorrow (0.00698324)	emoticon	sentence
excitement (0.004484305)	sadness /	sadness / sorrow, dislike
dislike (0.001897533)	sorrow	
...		

Example 3: >*Aki-san, eee,* (丿° o °)丿 *ipod wa nai to iya dakara sugu ni juden da yo!!*
Translation: >>Aki-san, What!? (丿° o °)丿 I couldn't imagine a day without my ipod! Recharge your battery at once!

S_1	B_1	S_2	E_LME_R	S_3	B_2	S_4
N/A	(	丿	° o °	N/A	)	丿

CAO	Human Annotation	
surprise (0.02686763)	emoticon	sentence
joy (0.02679939)	surprise	surprise
excitement (0.02238806)		
...		

Example 4: *2000 bon anda wo tassei shita ato ni iroiro to sainan tsuzuita node nandaka o-ki no doku*・・・(°. °)
Translation: All these sudden troubles, after scoring 2000 of safe hits. Unbelievable pity・・・(°. °)

S_1	B_1	S_2	E_L	M	E_R	S_3	B_2	S_4
・・・	(	N/A	°	.	°	N/A	)	N/A

CAO	Human Annotation	
surprise (0.4215457)	emoticon	sentence
...	surprise	surprise , dislike

We also presented a prototype system for automatic affect analysis of Eastern-style emoticons, CAO. The system was created using a database of emoticons containing over 10,000 of unique emoticons collected from the Internet. These emoticons were automatically distributed into emotion-type databases with the use of an affect analysis system developed by Ptaszynski, Dybala, Rzepka, and Araki (2009). Finally, the emoticons were automatically divided into semantic areas, such as mouths or eyes and their emotion affiliations were calculated based on occurrence statistics. The division of emoticons into semantic areas was based on Birdwhistell's (1970) idea of kinemes as minimal meaningful elements in body language. The database applied in CAO contains over 10,000 raw emoticons and several thousands of elements for each unique semantic area (mouths, eyes, etc.). This gave the system coverage of over 3 million combinations. With such a coverage, the system is capable of automatically annotating potential emotion types of any emoticon. There are a finite number of semantic areas used by users in emoticons generated during online communication. The number CAO can match over 3 million emoticon face (eye-mouth-eye) triplets and is sufficient to cover most possibilities. The evaluation on both the training set and the test set showed that the system outperforms previous methods, achieving results close to ideal, and has other capabilities not present in its predecessors: detecting emoticons in input with very strong agreement coefficient (kappa = 0.95) and extracting emoticons from input and dividing them into semantic areas, which, calculated using balanced F-score, reached over 97%. Among the five methods of calculating emotion rank score we compared in evaluation of emotion estimation of emoticons, the highest and the most balanced score was based on Unique Frequency and this method of score calculation will be used as a default setting in CAO. Using Unique Frequency, the system estimated emotions of separate emoticons with an accuracy of 93.5% for the specific emotion types and 97.3% for groups of emotions belonging to the same 2D affect space (Russell, 1980). There were some minor errors, however not exceeding the standard error level, which can be solved by optimization of CAO's procedures during future usage. Also, in affect analysis of whole sentences, CAO annotated the expressed emotions with a high accuracy of over 80% for specific emotion types and nearly 95% for 2D affect space.

FUTURE WORK

At present, CAO is the most accurate and reliable system for emoticon analysis known to the authors. In the near future, we plan to apply it to numerous tasks. Beginning with a contribution to computer-mediated communication, we plan to make CAO a support tool for e-mail reader software. Although emoticons are used widely in online communication, there is still a wide spectrum of users (often elderly) who do not understand the emoticon expressions. Such users, when reading a message including emoticons, often get confused, which causes future misunderstandings with other people. CAO could help such users interpret the emoticons appearing in e-mails. As processing time in CAO is very short (processing of both training and test sets took no more than a few seconds), this application could also be extended to instant messaging services to help interlocutors understand each other in the text-based communication. As a support system for Affect and Sentiment Analysis systems, such as the one by Ptaszynski et al. (2009), CAO could also contribute to preserving online security (Abbasi & Chen, 2007), which has been an urgent problem for several years. To standardize emoticon interpretation, we plan to contribute to the Smiley Ontology Project (Radulovic & Milikic, 2009). Finally, we plan to annotate large corpora of online communication, like Yacis Corpus, to contribute to linguistic research on emotions in language.

ACKNOWLEDGMENT

This research was supported by (JSPS) KAKENHI Grant-in-Aid for JSPS Fellows (22-00358).

REFERENCES

Abbasi, A., & Chen, H. (2007). Affect intensity analysis of dark Web forums. In *Proceedings of the IEEE Conference on Intelligence and Security Informatics* (pp. 282-288).

Birdwhistell, R. L. (1952). *Introduction to kinesics: an annotation system for analysis of body motion and gesture*. Lexington, KY: University of Kentucky Press.

Birdwhistell, R. L. (1970). *Kinesics and context*. Philadelphia, PA: University of Pennsylvania Press.

Chiu, K. C. (2007). *Explorations in the effect of emoticon on negotiation process from the aspect of communication* (Unpublished master's thesis). National Sun Yatsen University, Kaohsiung, Taiwan.

Dear, B. L. (2008). *Emoticons and smileys emerged on the PLATO system in the 1970s in a unique and different way*. Retrieved December 17, 2009, from http://www.platopeople.com/emoticons.html

Derks, D., Bos, A. E. R., & von Grumbkow, J. (2007). Emoticons and social interaction on the Internet: the importance of social context. *Computers in Human Behavior, 23*, 842–849. doi:10.1016/j.chb.2004.11.013

Fahlman, S. (1982). *Original Bboard Thread in which:-) was proposed*. Retrieved from http://www.cs.cmu.edu/~sef/Orig-Smiley.htm

Hagiwara. (2011). *UnNatural language processing blog*. Retrieved from http://blog.lilyx.net/

Ip, A. (2002). *The impact of emoticons on affect interpretation in instant messaging*. Retrieved January 20, 2011 from http://amysmile.com/doc/emoticon_paper.pdf

Kawakami, M. (2008). The database of 31 Japanese emoticon with their emotions and emphases. *The Human Science Research Bulletin of Osaka Shoin Women's University, 7*, 67–82.

Kubota, H., Yamashita, K., Fukuhara, T., & Nihsida, T. (2002). POC caster: Broadcasting agent using conversational representation for internet community. *Transactions of the Japanese Society for Artificial Intelligence, 17*, 313–321. doi:10.1527/tjsai.17.313

Kudo, T., & Matsumoto, Y. (2001). Chunking with support vector machines. In *Proceedings of the Second Meeting of the North American Chapter of the Association for Computational Linguistics* (pp. 192-199).

Lee, J. (2009, January 19). Is that an emoticon in 1862? *The New York Times*. Retrieved from http://cityroom.blogs.nytimes.com/2009/01/19/hfo-emoticon/

Lewis, M., Haviland-Jones, J. M., & Feldman, B. L. (Eds.). (2008). *Handbook of emotions*. New York, NY: Guilford.

Maciejewski, J., Ptaszynski, M., & Dybala, P. (2010). Developing a large-scale corpus for natural language processing and emotion processing research in Japanese. In *Proceedings of the International Workshop on Modern Science and Technology* (pp. 192-195).

Maness, J. M. (2008). A linguistic analysis of chat reference conversations with 18-24 year-old college students. *Journal of Academic Librarianship, 34*(1), 31–38. doi:10.1016/j.acalib.2007.11.008

Matsumoto, Y., Kitauchi, A., Yamashita, T., Hirano, Y., Matsuda, H., Takaoka, K., & Asahara, M. (2000). *Japanese Morphological Analysis System ChaSen version 2.2.1*. Retrieved January 20, 2011, from http://chasen.aist-nara.ac.jp/hiki/ChaSen/

Nakamura, A. (1993). *Kanjo hyogen jiten* (Dictionary of emotive expressions). Tokyo, Japan: Tokyodo.

Nakamura, J., Ikeda, T., Inui, N., & Kotani, Y. (2003). Learning face mark for natural language dialogue system. In *Proceedings of the IEEE International Conference on Natural Language Processing and Knowledge Engineering* (pp. 180-185).

Ptaszynski, M. (2006). *Boisterous language: Analysis of structures and semiotic functions of emotive expressions in conversation on Japanese Internet bulletin board forum '2channel'* (Unpublished master's thesis). UAM, Poznan, Poland.

Ptaszynski, M., Dybala, P., Komuda, R., Rzepka, R., & Araki, K. (2010). Development of emoticon database for affect analysis in Japanese. In *Proceedings of the 4th International Symposium on Global COE Program of the Knowledge Federation* (pp. 203-204).

Ptaszynski, M., Dybala, P., Rzepka, R., & Araki, K. (2009). Affecting corpora: Experiments with automatic affect annotation system - a case study of the 2channel forum. In *Proceedings of the Conference of the Pacific Association for Computational Linguistics* (pp. 223-228).

Ptaszynski, M., Dybala, P., Rzepka, R., & Araki, K. (2010). Towards fully automatic emoticon analysis system (^o^). In *Proceedings of the Sixteenth Annual Meeting of the Association for Natural Language Processing* (pp. 583-586).

Ptaszynski, M., Dybala, P., Shi, W., Rzepka, R., & Araki, K. (2009). Towards context aware emotional intelligence in machines: Computing contextual appropriateness of affective states. In *Proceedings of the 21st International Joint Conference on Artificial Intelligence* (pp. 1469-1474).

Ptaszynski, M., Maciejewski, J., Dybala, P., Rzepka, R., & Araki, K. (2010a). CAO: A fully automatic emoticon analysis system. In *Proceedings of the Twenty-Fourth AAAI Conference on Artificial Intelligence* (pp. 1026-1032).

Ptaszynski, M., Maciejewski, J., Dybala, P., Rzepka, R., & Araki, K. (2010b). CAO: A fully automatic emoticon analysis system based on theory of kinesics. *IEEE Transactions on Affective Computing, 1*(1), 46–59. doi:10.1109/T-AFFC.2010.3

Radulovic, F., & Milikic, N. (2009). Smiley ontology. In *Proceedings of the Social Network Interoperability Workshop, held in conjunction with the Asian Semantic Web Conference.*

Read, J. (2005). Using emoticons to reduce dependency in machine learning techniques for sentiment classification. In *Proceedings of the ACL Student Research Workshop* (pp. 43-48).

Rezabek, L. L., & Cochenour, J. J. (1998). Visual cues in computer-mediated communication: Supplementing text with emoticons. *Journal of Visual Literacy, 18*, 201–215.

Russell, J. A. (1980). A circumplex model of affect. *Journal of Personality and Social Psychology, 39*(6), 1161–1178. doi:10.1037/h0077714

Solomon, R. C. (1993). *The passions: Emotions and the meaning of life.* Cambridge, MA: Hackett.

Suzuki, N., & Tsuda, K. (2006a). Automatic emoticon generation method for web community. In *Proceedings of the IADIS International Conference on Web Based Communities* (pp. 331-334).

Suzuki, N., & Tsuda, K. (2006b). Express emoticons choice method for smooth communication of e-business. In B. Gabrys, R. J. Howlett, & L. C. Jain (Eds.), *Proceedings of the 10th International Conference on Knowledge-Based Intelligent Information and Engineering Systems* (LNCS 4252, pp. 296-302).

Takami, K., Yamashita, R., Tani, K., Honma, Y., & Goto, S. (2009). Deducing a user's state of mind from analysis of the pictographic characters and emoticons used in mobile phone emails for personal content delivery services. *International Journal on Advances in Telecommunications, 2*(1), 37–46.

Tanaka, Y., Takamura, H., & Okumura, M. (2005, January 9-12). Extraction and classification of facemarks with kernel methods. In *Proceedings of the 10th International Conference on Intelligent User Interfaces*, San Diego, CA.

Vargas, M. F. (1986). *Louder than words: An introduction to nonverbal communication.* Ames, IO: Iowa State University Press.

Wolf, A. (2004). Emotional expression online: Gender differences in emoticon use. *Cyberpsychology & Behavior*, *3*(5), 827–833. doi:10.1089/10949310050191809

Yamada, T., Tsuchiya, S., Kuroiwa, S., & Ren, F. (2007). Classification of facemarks using n-gram. In *Proceedings of the International Conference on NLP and Knowledge Engineering* (pp. 322-327).

Yang, C., Hsin-Yih Lin, K., & Chen, H.-H. (2007). Building emotion lexicon from weblog corpora. In *Proceedings of the ACL Demo and Poster Sessions* (pp. 133-136).

Yuasa, M., Saito, K., & Mukawa, N. (2006). Emoticons convey emotions without cognition of faces: an fMRI study. In *Proceedings of the CHI Extended Abstracts on Human factors in Computing Systems* (pp. 1565-1570).

KEY TERMS AND DEFINITIONS

Affect Analysis: A subfield of AI and Information Extraction. It focuses on classifying user expressions of emotions. It takes as an object the human user and aims to estimate his/her emotional states, such as anger, excitement, joy, etc., with the use of different modalities (language, facial expressions, voice, etc.).

Emoticons: Strings of symbols representing other than lexical layers of human communication in online media. In particular, emoticons most often represent facial expressions, poses, or other elements of body language. They are often used to express emotions to support text-based online communication.

Natural Language Processing (NLP): A field of Computer Science and Linguistics focused on processing different aspects of natural (human) language. Research within NLP includes such topics as machine translation, ontology generation, natural language generation, or sentiment analysis.

ENDNOTES

[1]   The term is also defined differently much earlier as an insufficiency for explaining natural language phenomena by computer-based logic or programming languages in general (for details see Oberlander et al., 1999; Aho, 2009)

[2]   *Puck*, No. 212, p. 65, 30 March 1881.

[3]   Respectively: http://www.facemark.jp/facemark.htm, http://kaomojiya.com/, http://www.kaomoji.com/kao/text/, http://kaomoji-cafe.jp/, http://rsmz.net/kaopara/, http://matsucon.net/material/dic/, http://kaosute.net/jisyo/kanjou.shtml

[4]   However, including the additional areas in the calculation gives an overall number of possibilities equal to at least $1.382613544823877 \times 10^{21}$

Section 3
Multimodal Developments

Chapter 13

On the Development of Adaptive and User-Centred Interactive Multimodal Interfaces

David Griol
Carlos III University of Madrid, Spain

Ramón López-Cózar
University of Granada, CITIC-UGR, Spain

Zoraida Callejas
University of Granada, CITIC-UGR, Spain

Gonzalo Espejo
University of Granada, CITIC-UGR, Spain

Nieves Ábalos
University of Granada, CITIC-UGR, Spain

ABSTRACT

Multimodal systems have attained increased attention in recent years, which has made possible important improvements in the technologies for recognition, processing, and generation of multimodal information. However, there are still many issues related to multimodality which are not clear, for example, the principles that make it possible to resemble human-human multimodal communication. This chapter focuses on some of the most important challenges that researchers have recently envisioned for future multimodal interfaces. It also describes current efforts to develop intelligent, adaptive, proactive, portable and affective multimodal interfaces.

1. INTRODUCTION TO MULTIMODAL INTERFACES

With the advances of speech, image and video technology, human-computer interaction (HCI) has reached a new phase, in which multimodal information is a key point to enhance the communication between humans and machines. Unlike traditional keyboard- and mouse-based interfaces, multimodal interfaces enable greater flexibility in the input and output, as they permit users to employ different input modalities as well as to obtain responses through different means, for example, speech, gestures and facial expressions.

DOI: 10.4018/978-1-4666-0954-9.ch013

This is especially important for users with special needs, for whom the traditional interfaces might not be suitable (McTear, 2004; López-Cózar & Araki, 2005; Wahlster, 2006).

In addition, the widespread use of mobile technology implementing wireless communications such as personal digital assistants (PDAs) and smart phones enables a new type of advanced applications to access information. As the number of ubiquitous, connected devices continues to grow, the heterogeneity of client capabilities and the number of methods for accessing information services also increases. As a result, users can effectively access huge amounts of information and services from almost everywhere and through different communication modalities.

Multimodality has been traditionally addressed from two perspectives. On the one hand, human-human multimodal communication. Within this area we can find in the literature studies concerned with speech-gesture systems (Catizone et al., 2003), semiotics of gestures (Radford, 2003; Flecha-García, 2010), structure and functions of face-to-face communication (Bailly et al., 2010), emotional relations (Cowie & Cornelius, 2003; Schuller et al., 2011), and intercultural variations (Endrass et al., 2011; Edlung et al., 2008). On the other hand, human-machine communication and interfaces. Topics of interest in this area include, among others, talking faces, embodied conversational agents (Cassell et al., 2000), integration of multimodal input, fission of multimodal output (Wahlster, 2003), and understanding of signals from speech, text, and visual images (Benesti et al., 2008).

This chapter focuses on some of the most important challenges that researchers have recently envisioned for future multimodal interfaces. It describes current efforts to develop intelligent, adaptive, proactive, portable and affective multimodal interfaces. All these concepts are not mutually exclusive, for example, the system's intelligence can be concerned with the system's adaptation enabling better portability to different environments.

There are different levels in which the system can adapt to the user (Jokinen, 2003). The simplest one is through personal profiles in which the users have static choices to customize the interaction (e.g., whether they prefer a male or female system's voice), which can be further improved by classifying users into preference groups. Systems can also adapt to the users' environment, for example, Ambient Intelligence (AmI) applications such as ubiquitous proactive systems. The main research topics are the adaptation of systems to different expertise levels (Haseel & Hagen, 2005), knowledge (Forbes-Riley & Litman, 2004), and special needs of users. The latter topic is receiving a lot of attention nowadays in terms of how to make systems usable by handicapped and elderly people (Heim et al., 2007; Batliner et al., 2004; Langner & Black, 2005), and how to adapt them to user features such as age, proficiency in the interaction language (Raux et al., 2003) or expertise in using the system (Haseel & Hagen, 2005).

Despite their complexity, these characteristics for the design of user centred multimodal interfaces are to some extent rather static, i.e., they are usually gathered a priori and not during the dialog, and thus they are not used to dynamically adapt the multimodal interface at some stage in the interaction. There is another degree of adaptation in which the system not only adapts to the messages conveyed during the interaction, but also to the user's intentions and emotional states (Martinovski & Traum, 2003; Prendinger et al., 2003). It has been demonstrated that many breakdowns in man-machine communication could be avoided if the machine was able to recognize the emotional state of the user and responded to it more sensitively, for instance, by providing more explicit feedback if the user is frustrated. Emotional intelligence not only includes the ability to recognize the user's emotional state, but also the ability to act on it appropriately (Salovey & Mayer, 1990).

To deal with all these important topics required for the design of adaptive and user-centred interactive multimodal interfaces, this chapter is organized as follows. Section 2 provides an overview on the main architectures and toolkits available for the development of such systems. Section 3 describes the main principles involved in the development of multimodal interfaces which are adaptive to the user's location and activities without requiring explicit user inputs. The section also provides examples of multimodal systems implemented to incorporate such contextual information, and discusses various aspects concerned with emotion recognition and affective responsivity of multimodal systems. Section 4 describes our work related to the development of interactive multimodal interfaces. Finally, Section 5 presents the conclusions and outlines possibilities for future research directions.

2. DEVELOPMENT OF MULTIMODAL INTERFACES: ARCHITECTURES AND TOOLKITS

Multimodal interfaces involve several user senses simultaneously during the communication with the computer. We are particularly interested in systems which employ voice as a relevant communication modality for the input and output (Griol et al., 2008; Callejas & López-Cózar, 2008a). In this section we provide an overview on the main architectures and development toolkits available for the development of such systems.

Multimodal dialogue systems can be defined as computer programs designed to interact with users *similarly* as human beings would do, using more or less interaction modalities depending on their complexity (McTear, 2004; López-Cózar & Araki, 2005). These programs are employed for a number of applications, including tutoring (Forbes-Riley & Litman, 2011), entertainment (Ibrahim & Johansson, 2002), command and control (Stent et al., 1999), healthcare (Beveridge & Fox, 2006),

call routing (Paek & Horvitz, 2004) and retrieval of information about a variety of services, for example, weather forecasts (Maragoudakis, 2007), apartment rental (Cassell et al., 1999) and travels (Huang et al., 1999). A detailed classification of these systems using different criteria (languages, domains, functionalities, interaction degrees, input and output modalities, etc.) can be found in López-Cózar and Araki (2005) and McTear (2004).

2.1. Approaches to Incremental Development

In order to develop usable multimodal interfaces, it is necessary to take the user perspective into account from the early stages in the development cycle. The system-in-the-loop technique is based on the fact that software systems improve cyclically by means of user interactions. For example, the performance of a speech-based multimodal interface can be improved by means of analyses of sentences previously uttered by users. If modifications are needed in the design of the system, the technique is employed again to obtain new experimental results. These steps (collection of data and test of system) are repeated until the system designers are satisfied with the performance. Among others, Van de Burgt et al. (1996) used this technique to implement the SCHISMA system. In particular, the technique was used to collect user utterances and analyse them in order to improve the performance of the system.

It is possible to collect user utterances from an early design of the system using the Wizard of Oz (WOz) technique, in which a human *Wizard* plays the role of the computer in a human-computer interaction (Fraser & Gibert, 1991). The users are made to believe that they interact with a computer but actually they interact with the Wizard, who decides the system's responses considering the current design planned for the interface. Salber and Coutaz (1993) discussed some requirements of WOz for multimodal systems. They indicated that a multimodal system is more complex to simulate than a system based on speech only, which increases the task complexity and the bandwidth necessary for the simulation. For multimodal interaction, the authors suggested to employ a multi-wizard configuration, which requires properly organising the work of several wizards. A platform for multimodal WOz experiments must have a high performance and flexibility, and should include a tool to retrieve and manipulate data collected during the experiments.

2.2. From Speech to Multimodality

The implementation of multimodal systems is a complex task in which a number of technologies are involved, including signal processing, phonetics, linguistics, natural language processing, affective computing, graphics and interface design, animation techniques, telecommunications, sociology and psychology. The complexity is usually addressed by dividing the implementation into simpler problems, each associated with a system's module that carries out specific functions. Usually, this division is based on the traditional architecture of spoken dialogue systems: automatic speech recognition (ASR), spoken language understanding (SLU), dialogue management (DM), natural language generation (NLG) and text-to-speech synthesis (TTS).

ASR is the process of obtaining a sentence (text string) from a voice signal (Rabiner & Huang, 1993). It is a very complex task given the diversity of factors that can affect the input, basically concerned with the speaker, the interaction context and the transmission channel. Different applications demand different complexity on the speech recognizer. Cole et al. (1997) identified eight parameters that allow an optimal tailoring of the recognizer: speech mode, speech style, dependency, vocabulary, language model, perplexity, signal-to-noise ratio (SNR) and transduction. Nowadays, general-purpose ASR systems are usually based on Hidden Markov Models (HMMs) (Rabiner & Juang, 1993).

SLU is the process of extracting the semantics from a text string (Minker, 1998). It generally involves employing morphological, lexical, syntactical, semantic, discourse and pragmatic knowledge. In a first stage, lexical and morphological knowledge allow dividing the words in their constituents distinguishing lexemes and morphemes. Syntactic analysis yields a hierarchical structure of the sentences, whereas the semantic analysis extracts the meaning of a complex syntactic structure from the meaning of its constituents. There are currently two major approaches to carry out SLU: rule-based (Mairesse et al., 2009) and statistical (Meza-Ruiz et al., 2008), including some hybrid methods (Liu et al., 2006).

DM is concerned with deciding the next action to be carried out by the dialogue system. The simplest dialogue model is implemented as a finite-state machine, in which machine states represent dialogue states and the transitions between states are determined by the user's actions. Frame-based approaches have been developed to overcome the lack of flexibility of the state-based dialogue models, and are used in most current commercial systems. For complex application domains, plan-based dialogue models can be used. They rely on the fact that humans communicate to achieve goals, and during the interaction, the humans' mental state might change (Chu et al., 2005). Currently, the application of machine-learning approaches to model dialogue strategies is a very active research area (Griol et al., 2008; Williams & Young, 2007; Cuayáhuitl et al., 2006; Lemon et al., 2006).

NLG is the process of obtaining texts in natural language from a non-linguistic representation of information. It is usually carried out in five steps: content organization, content distribution in sentences, lexicalization, generation of referential expressions and linguistic realization. The simplest approach uses predefined text messages (e.g., error messages and warnings). Although intuitive, this approach is very inflexible (Reiter, 1995). The next level of sophistication is template-based generation, in which the same message structure can be produced with slight differences. This approach is used mainly for multi-sentence generation, particularly in applications where texts are fairly regular in structure, such as business reports (Reiter, 1995). Phrase-based systems employ what can be considered generalized templates at the sentence level (in which case the phrases resemble phrase structure grammar rules), or at the discourse level (in which case they are often called text plans) (Elhadad & Robin, 1996). Finally, in feature-based systems, each possible minimal alternative of expression is represented by a single feature to obtain the maximum level of generalization and flexibility (Oh & Rudnicky, 2000).

TTS synthesizers transform text strings into acoustic signals. A TTS system is composed of two parts: front-end and back-end. The front-end carries out two major tasks. Firstly, it converts text strings containing symbols such as numbers and abbreviations into their equivalent words. This process is often called text normalization, pre-processing or tokenization. Secondly, it assigns a phonetic transcription to each word, which requires dividing and marking the text into prosodic units, i.e., phrases, clauses, and sentences. The back-end (often referred to as the synthesizer) converts the words in text format into sound. Concatenative synthesis employs pre-recorded units of human voice that are put together to obtain words. It generally produces the most natural synthesized speech; however, differences between variations in speech and in the nature of the automated techniques for segmenting the waveforms sometimes result in audible glitches.

Once the speech-based response of the system has been designed, it is possible to gradually incorporate other modalities. In order to do so, it is important to design a *fusion* module to combine information chunks provided by different input modalities of a multimodal interface. The result is a data structure that enables the multimodal system in handling different information types

simultaneously. Using this data structure, the system's dialogue manager can decide what to do next. A number of methods have been proposed to represent the combined data. For example, Faure and Julia (1993) employed *Triplets*, which are a syntactic formalism to represent multimodal events in the form: (verb, object, location). The authors found this method very useful to represent speech information combined with deictic information generated by means of gestures. Allen (1995) proposed to use semantic structures called frames. The information from each modality was interpreted separately and transformed into frames, the slots which determined the parameters of the action to be made. Frames contain partial information if some slots are empty. During the fusion the frames are combined, fulfilling the empty slots. For example, Lemon et al. (2006a) used frames to combine multimodal information in a multimodal interface that provided information about hotels, restaurants and bars in a town. XML-based languages are other method to represent multimodal information. For example, Wahlster et al. (2001) used an XML-based language called M3L to represent all the information flows between the processing components of the SmartKom system.

2.3. Architectures for the Design of Multimodal Interfaces

It is important to properly select the architecture to be used for implementing a multimodal interface, since it should allow further enhancement or porting it from one application domain to another. We can find in the literature a number of architectures to implement multimodal interfaces.

Galaxy Communicator is a distributed, message-based, hub-centred architecture (Seneff et al., 1998), in which the main components are interconnected by means of client-server connections. This architecture has been used to set up, among others, the MIT's Voyager and Jupiter systems (Glass et al., 1995; Zue et al., 2000).

The Open Agent Architecture (OAA) architecture was designed to ease the implementation of agent-based applications, enabling intelligent, cooperative, distributed, and multimodal agent-based user interfaces (Moran et al., 1997). The agents can be developed in several high-level languages (e.g., C or Java) and platforms (e.g., Windows and Solaris). The communication with other agents is possible using the Interagent Communication Language (ICL). The cooperation and communication between the agents is carried out by means of an agent called Facilitator. Several authors have used this architecture to implement multimodal interfaces for a variety of application domains, including map-based tourist information (Moran et al., 1997), interaction with robots (Bos et al., 2003), and control of user movements in a 2D game (Corradini & Samuelsson, 2008).

The blackboard architecture was released considering principles of Artificial Intelligence. Its name denotes the metaphor of a group of expert people who work together and collaboratively around a blackboard to solve a complex problem. All the resources available are shared by the agents. Each agent can collaborate, generate new resources and use resources from other agents. A Facilitator agent controls the resources and acts as intermediary among the agents which compete to write on the blackboard, taking into account the relevance of the contribution of each agent. This architecture has been used to implement a number of multimodal interfaces (Raux & Eskenazi, 2007; Huang et al., 2007).

R-Flow is an extensible XML-based architecture for multimodal interfaces (Li et al., 2007). It is based on a recursive application of the Model-View-Controller (MVC) design. The structure is based on three layers: modality independent dialogue control, synchronization of logical modalities and physical presentation. Each one is codified in different XML-based languages. For example, State-Chart XML (SCXML) is used for dialogue control, whereas SMIL (Synchronized Multimedia Integration Language) and EMMA (Extensible Multimodal Interface Language) (Li et al., 2006) are used for modality synchronization and interpretation.

In addition to the architectures discussed above, which are amongst the most employed, it is possible to find other architectures in the literature. For example, Leßmann and Wachsmuth (2003) used the classical architecture Perceive-Reason-Act for the design of a multimodal interface. The *Perceive* module handles the input information, which is collected by auditory, tactile and visual sensors. The *Act* module generates the output information. Actions can be carried out by means of either *deliberative* or *reactive* behaviour. The component for deliberative behaviour uses knowledge about the domain, which is updated by perceptions, and generates intentions employing a plan library, which represents what the agent wants to do next. The second way of generating an action is by means of the reactive behaviour, which is reserved for actions that do not need deliberation, for example, making the agent appear more lifelike.

Following a different approach, Wei and Rudnicky (2000) proposed an architecture based on a task decomposition and an expectation agenda. The agenda is a list of topics represented by handlers. A handler encapsulates the knowledge necessary for interacting with the user about a specific information slot. The agenda defines a "plan" for carrying out a specific task, which is represented as a specific order of handlers.

2.4. Tools for the Development of Multimodal Systems

This section describes a number of tools and standards for developing multimodal systems that we consider relevant for this chapter. The discussion includes tools such as HTK, CSMU Sphinx, CMU SLM, NLTK, and standards such as VoiceXML, among others.

The Hidden Markov Model Toolkit (HTK) is free software for building and using Hidden

Markov Models (HMMs), which was developed by Cambridge University (Young et al., 2000). In the community of multimodal interfaces this software is primarily used for ASR, but it also has been used for a number of applications including speech synthesis, character recognition and DNA sequencing. It consists of a set of libraries and tools that provide facilities for speech analysis, HMM training, testing, and results analysis. The software supports HMMs using both continuous density mixture Gaussians and discrete distributions and can be used to build complex HMM systems.

CMU Sphinx (Lee et al., 1990) is an ASR system developed at the Carnegie Mellon University. There are several versions of it (Sphinx 2 - 4), each including an acoustic model trainer (SphinxTrain). The recogniser can deal with continuous, speaker-independent speech using HMMs and n-gram language models. Sphinx 2 focuses on real-time recognition suitable for speech-based applications and uses a semi-continuous representation for acoustic modelling. Sphinx 3 adopted the prevalent continuous HMM representation and has been used primarily for high-accuracy, non-real-time recognition. Sphinx 4 is written entirely in Java with the goal of providing a more flexible framework for research. PocketSphinx has been designed to run in real time on handhelds and be integrated with live applications. There is also a number of proprietary software for ASR, including AT&T WATSON, Windows speech recognition system, IBM ViaVoice, Microsoft Speech API, Nuance Dragon NaturallySpeaking, MacSpeech, Loquendo ASR and Verbio ASR.

The Carnegie Mellon Statistical Language Modeling Toolkit (CMU SLM) is a set of Unix tools designed to facilitate language modelling (Rosenfeld, 1995). The toolkit allows processing corpora of data (text strings) in order to obtain word frequency lists and vocabularies, word bigram and trigram counts, bigram and trigram-related statistics and a number of back-off bigram

and trigram language models. Using these tools it is also possible to compute statistics such as perplexity, out-of-vocabulary words (OOV) and distribution of back-off cases.

The Natural Language Toolkit (NLTK) (Bird et al., 2008) is a suite of libraries and programs for symbolic and statistical natural language processing for the Python programming language. Other tools include Phoenix, designed by the Carnegie Mellon University in combination with the Helios confidence annotation module (Ward & Issar, 1994), and Tina, developed by the MIT and based on context free grammars, augmented transition networks, and lexical functional grammars (Seneff, 1989).

The Center for Spoken Language Understanding (CSLU) at the Oregon Health and Science University developed a graphical tool called CSLU Toolkit for the design of dialogue managers based on finite-state dialogue models (McTear, 1998). The toolkit includes tools for working with audio, display, speech recognition, speech generation, and animated faces.

The AT&T FSM library is a set of Unix tools for building, combining and optimizing weighted finite-state systems (Mohri, 1997). Some systems based on finite states were created under the SUNDIAL (Müller & Runge, 1993) and SUNSTAR projects (Nielsen & Baekgaard, 1992).

VoiceXML is the W3C's standard XML format for specifying interactive voice dialogues between humans and computers (McGlashan et al., 2004). The language is the result of the joint efforts of several companies and institutions (AT&T, IBM, Lucent, Motorola, etc) which make up the so-called VoiceXML Forum. The language has been designed to ease the creation of multimodal dialogue systems employing audio, ASR, speech synthesis and recording, and mixed-initiative dialogues.

The W3C's Speech Interface Framework defines other standards related to VoiceXML, including:

- SRGS (Speech Recognition Grammar Specification),
- SISR (Semantic Interpretation for Speech Recognition),
- PLS (Pronunciation Lexicon Specification), and
- CCXML (Call Control eXtensible Markup Language).

SALT (Speech Application Language Tags) is also an XML based markup language that is used in HTML and XHTML pages to add ASR to web based applications. Multimodality using this language is possible in different ways: keyboard, speech, keypad, mouse and/or stylus. XHTML+Voice (X+V) is a new technology that combines XHTML and voice-based interfaces on small devices, such as PDAs and tablets. This technology uses web standards such as ECMAScript and JavaScript.

TRINDIKIT is a toolkit for building and experimenting with information states (TRINDIConsortium, 2001). The term information state means, roughly, the information stored internally by a system, in this case a dialogue system. A dialogue move engine (DME) updates the information state on the basis of observed dialogue moves and selects appropriate moves to be performed. Apart from proposing a general system architecture, TRINDIKIT also specifies formats for defining information states, update rules, dialogue moves, and associated algorithms. It further provides a set of tools for experimenting with different formalizations of information-state implementations, rules, and algorithms.

The Galatea Toolkit (Shin-ichi et al., 2003) is an open-source software for the development of anthropomorphic animated multimodal agents. The toolkit comprises four fundamental modules for ASR, speech synthesis, face animation, and dialogue control, which can be used to set up multimodal dialogue systems.

HephaisTK is a toolkit for rapid prototyping of multimodal interfaces that uses SMUIML, a simple mark-up language for describing human-machine multimodal interaction and integration mechanisms (Dumas et al., 2010). This toolkit includes the exploration and assessment of different fusion mechanisms applied to data coming from different human-computer interaction means, such as speech, gesture or ink-based applications.

WebSphere Everyplace Multimodal Environment and WebSphere Multimodal Toolkit, from IBM, enable to integrate graphical and voice interaction in a single application.

The WAMI toolkit (Gruenstein et al., 2008) provides a framework for developing, deploying, and evaluating Web-Accessible Multimodal Interfaces in which users interact using speech, mouse, pen, and/or touch. The toolkit uses modern web-programming techniques, enabling the development of browser-based applications available on a wide array of Internet-connected devices. Several sophisticated multimodal applications have been developed using the toolkit, which can be used by means of desktop, laptop, tablet PCs and mobile devices.

The Multi-Modal Interface Designer (MMID) provides a combination of visual and speech-based interaction. The main way of interaction with the toolkit is vocal: speech-recognition and TTS. However, it includes an additional visual modality.

Festival (Clark et al., 2004) is a C++ general multi-lingual speech synthesis system developed at Centre for Speech Technology Research (CSTR) at the University of Edinburgh. It is distributed under a free software license and offers a number of APIs as well as an environment for development and research on speech synthesis. Supported languages include English, Spanish, Czech, Finnish, Italian, Polish and Russian. An alternative is FreeTTS (Walker et al., 2002), another open source speech synthesis system written entirely in Java. It allows employing markers to specify when speech generation should not be interrupted, to concatenate speech, and to generate speech using different voices. There are also many commercial systems for TTS like Cepstral, Loquendo TTS and Kalliope.

Xface (Balci, 2005) is an open source toolkit for generating and animating 3D talking heads. The toolkit relies on MPEG-4 Facial Animation Parameters (FAPs) and a keyframe-based rendering which uses the SMIL-Agent scripting language. The toolkit is multi-platform as it can be compiled with any ANSI C++ standard compliant compiler.

The CSLR's Conversational Agent Toolkit (CAT) (Cole et al., 2003) provides a set of modules and tools for research and development of advanced embodied conversational agents. These modules include an audio server, the Sonic speech recognition system, and the Phoenix natural language parser. The CU Animate toolkit (designed for research, development, control and real time rendering of 3D animated characters) is used for the design of the facial animation system.

The Microsoft Agent toolkit (Walsh & Meade, 2003) includes animated characters, TTS engines, and speech recognition software. It is preinstalled in several versions of MS Windows and can be easily embedded in web pages and Office applications with VBScript. Microsoft also provides tools to create new agents, such as the Agent Character Editor.

Maxine (Seron et al., 2006) is an open source engine for embodied conversational agents developed by the University of Zaragoza (Spain). The agents created with this tool can interact with the user by means of text, voice, mouse and keyboard. The agents can gather information from the user and the environment (noise level in the room, position of the user to establish visual contact, image-based estimate of the user's emotional state, etc.), and are able to render emotional states that vary with the relationship that they establish with the user.

3. ADAPTIVE MULTIMODAL INTERFACES

Nowadays, we are surrounded by technology: mobile devices, wearable computing, smart environments and ambient intelligence applications provide new ubiquitous computing capabilities for which multimodal interfaces are in most cases essential (Nihei, 2004; Truong & Dustdar, 2009; Strauss & Minker, 2010). In this section we describe the main principles involved in the development of multimodal interfaces for this pervasive paradigm, highlighting the importance of the adaptivity of the interface.

Adaptivity refers to several aspects in dialogue systems. Novice users and experienced users may want the interface to behave completely differently, for example to have system-initiative instead of mixed-initiative. An example of the benefits of adaptivity in the interaction level can be found in Seneff et al. (2007). The processing of context is essential to achieve this adapted behaviour and also cope with the ambiguities derived from the use of natural language. For instance, context information can be used to resolve anaphoric references, to take into account the current user position as a data to be used by the system, or to decide the strategy to be used by the dialogue management module by taking into account specific user preferences.

3.1. The Role of Context in the Interaction

Although there is not a complete agreement on the definition of *context information*, the most widely accepted is the one proposed by Dey and Abowd (2000): "*Any information that can be used to characterize the situation of an entity (...) relevant to the interaction between a user and an application, including the user and the application themselves*". As can be observed from this definition, any information source can be considered context as long as it provides knowledge relevant to handle the communication between the user and the system.

Kang et al. (2008) differentiate two types of context: *internal* and *external*. The former describes the user state (e.g., communication context and emotional state), whereas the latter refers to the environment state (e.g., location and temporal context). Most of studies in the literature focus only on external context. However, it is very important to combine both types of context information to provide a personalized and meaningful interaction which takes into account both the users' current location and their preferences (Strauss & Minker, 2010).

In the literature, there are several approaches developing mobile and context aware systems such as platforms, frameworks and multimodal applications for offering context-aware services. These applications include location-based services, e.g., suggesting points or events of interest taking place near the user's current location (Poslad et al., 2001). Other types of context information are device profiles, user preferences, user's activities and interactions, devices, and the network status. These types of context play an important role when context is used to support adaptation in service/ task selection (Prezerakos et al., 2007; Truong et al., 2008).

Context information is usually gathered from a wide variety of sources, which produces heterogeneity in terms of quality and persistence. This is why some authors distinguish between static context, which deals with invariant features, and dynamic context, that is able to cope with information that changes (Henricksen et al., 2002). The frequency of such changes is very variable and can deeply influence the way dynamic context is obtained and shared. It is reasonable to obtain largely static context directly from users, and frequently changing context from indirect means such as sensors. To share context some authors have develop tools that make the transfer of contextual information transparent to the interface, which can be placed at a higher level of abstraction. This has

been addressed for example by using web services (Keidl & Kemper, 2004).

An important issue to be considered is which language and model is best suited to describe context. A number of methods have been proposed to create these models, from the simple key-value method (in which a variable contains the actual context), to tagged encoding approaches (which uses context profiles to enable modelling and processing context recursively, and to employ efficient context retrieval algorithms), and object oriented models (which have the benefits of encapsulation and reusability). UML, XML, RDF, and OWL-based representations are also widely used because they are considered open and interoperable. In existing context-aware systems, XML is already used widely for modelling and implementing context information.

Regarding context storage techniques, relational databases are frequently employed to store context information in context aware systems out of the web services domain (Naguib et al., 2001; Henricksen et al., 2002). A number of formalisms have been defined to represent the information of the user interaction captured by the sensors in the environment. Many multimodal dialogue systems typically employ the semantic representation based on the concept of dialogue acts (DA) (Stolcke et al., 2000). A DA represents the meaning of the user and system utterances (e.g., question, answer, response, etc.). User's DAs are usually represented by frames (Minsky, 1975). A frame is a structure for representing a concept or situation. Each concept in a domain has usually associated a group of attributes (slots) and values. Recently, machine-learning approaches have been applied to create simple statistical user models trainable on existing human-computer dialogue data, which provide more dynamism to compute internal context (Eckert et al., 1998; Georgila et al., 2005; Schatzmann et al., 2007).

The performance of a dialogue system highly depends on context information. In fact, the result of the interaction can be completely different depending on the environment conditions (e.g., people speaking near the system, noise generated by other devices) and user skills. In the literature we can find different methodologies to take into account contextual information for adapting the different modules of a dialogue system. In Pargellis et al. (2004) a profile manager is integrated in a spoken dialogue system to code the user preferences about services and modify the dialogue structure by taking them into account. In different dialogue systems, users' skills and preferences are also used to personalize the interaction, set the system initiative, and select specific prompts and modalities (Minker et al., 2004; Seneff et al., 2007).

3.2. The Role of Affect

One of the main research objectives of multimodal systems is to achieve human-like communication between people and machines. This eliminates the need for keyboard and mouse in favour of more intuitive ways of interaction, such as natural language, thus leading to a new paradigm in which technologies can be accessed by non-expert users or handicapped people.

However, multimodal human-computer interaction is still not comparable to human dialogue. One of the reasons for this is that human interaction involves exchanging not only explicit content, but also implicit information about the affective state of the interlocutor. Systems that make use of such information are described as incorporating affective computing as they emulate human emotional intelligence as they are able to recognize, interpret, manage and/or generate emotions. The concept of emotional intelligence was introduced in Salovey and Mayer (1990) to denote "the subset of social intelligence that involves the ability to monitor one's own and others' feelings and emotions, to discriminate among them and to use this information to guide one's thinking and actions". Salovey and Mayer proposed a model that identified four different factors of emotional intelligence: the

perception of emotion, the ability reason using emotions, the ability to understand emotion and the ability to manage emotions. According to Salovey and Mayer, the four branches of their model are "arranged from more basic psychological processes to higher, more psychologically integrated processes." For example, the lowest level branch concerns abilities of perceiving and expressing emotion.

To endow multimodal interfaces with affective computing capabilities makes it possible to recognize the user's emotions and adapt the interface functionalities to better accomplish his requirements, thus partly simulating the four branches of human emotional intelligence mentioned. Stern (2003) also provides empirical evidence that if a user encounters a virtual character that seems to be truly emotional, there is also a potential to form emotional relationships with each other. Emotion recognition has been used in Human Computer Interaction (HCI) systems for several purposes. In some application domains it is necessary to recognize the affective state of the user to adapt the systems to it or even change it. For example, in emergency services (Bickmore & Giorgino, 2004) or intelligent tutors (Ai et al., 2006), it is necessary to know the users' emotional state to calm them down, or to encourage them in learning activities. However, there are also some applications in which emotion management is not a central aspect, but contributes to the better functioning of the system as a whole. In these systems emotion management can be used to resolve stages of the dialogue that cause negative emotional states, as well as to avoid them and foster positive ones in future interactions (Burkhardt et al., 2005). Furthermore, emotions are of interest not just for their own sake, but also because they affect the explicit message conveyed during the interaction: they change peoples' voices, facial expressions, gestures, speed of speech, etc. This is usually addressed as "emotional colouring" and can be of great importance for the interpretation of the user input. For example, Wahlster (2006) use emotional colouring in the context of the SmartKom system to detect sarcasm and thus tackle false positive sentences.

Additionally, the similarity-attraction principle states that users have a better attitude toward agents which exhibit a personality similar to their own. Thus, personality plays a very important role on how users assess multimodal interfaces and their willingness to interact with them. In the same way as humans understand other humans' behaviour and react accordingly to it in terms of the observation of everyday behaviour (Lepri et al., 2009), the personality of the system can be considered as a relatively stable pattern that affects its emotion expression and behaviour and differentiates it from other multimodal interfaces (Xiao et al., 2005).

Emotion recognition for multimodal interfaces is usually treated as a classification problem in which the input is the user last response (voice, facial expressions, body gestures…) and the output is the most probable emotional state. Many different machine learning classifiers have been employed for emotion recognition and frequently the final emotion is decided considering the results of several of these classification algorithms (López-Cózar et al., 2008). Some of the classifiers most widely used are K-nearest neighbours (Lee & Narayanan, 2005), Hidden Markov Models (Pitterman & Pitterman, 2006; Ververidis & Kotropoulos, 2006), Support Vector Machines (Morrison, Wang, & Silva, 2007), Neural Networks (Morrison, Wang, & Silva, 2007; Callejas & López-Cózar, 2008) and Boosting Algorithms (Sebe et al., 2004; Zhu & He, 2008).

Emotion recognition can be carried out with invasive and non invasive methods. Invasive methods are based on physiological measures like breathing rate or conductivity of skin (Picard, 1997). One of the most widespread methods consists in measuring the galvanic skin response (GSR) as there is a relationship between the arousal of emotions and changes in GSR (Lee et al., 2005). Some other methods are EMG, which measures facial muscles (Mahlke, 2006), heart rate or more recently the usage of brain images (Critchley et al., 2005). Non invasive methods are usually based on audio and video. On the one hand, audio emotion recognition can be carried out from the acoustic information or from linguistic information. Speech is deeply affected by emotions: acoustic, contour, tone, voice quality and articulation change with different emotions, a comprehensive study of those changes is presented in Cowie et al. (2001). Language information deals with linguistic changes depending on the emotional state of the user. For this purpose the technique of word emotional salience has gained remarkable attention. This measure represents the frequency of apparition of a word in a given emotional state or category and it is calculated from a corpus of user-system interactions (Lee et al., 2005). On the other hand, video recognition usually pays attention to facial expression, body posture and movements of the hands; a summary of all these features can be found in Picard and Daily (2005). Other authors emphasize that emotions are influenced by cultural and social settings and defend an "interactional approach" (Boehner et al., 2007) to be considered along with physiological, audio or video measures.

Due to its benefits and huge variety of applications, affective computing has become an outstanding research topic in the field of HCI, and numerous important international and interdisciplinary related projects have appeared. Some of the latest are, to mention just a few:

- **MEGA** (Camurri et al., 2004): Its purpose was the modelling and real-time analysis, synthesis, and networked communication of expressive and emotional content in non-verbal interaction (e.g., music or dance) by multi-sensory interfaces, from a multimodal perspective.
- **NECA** (Gebhard et al., 2004): Its purpose was the creation of multi-user and multi-agent virtual spaces populated by affec-

tive conversational agents able to express themselves through synchronised emotional speech and non-verbal expression.

- **VICTEC** (Hall et al., 2005): Its purpose was the development of a toolkit that supports the creation of believable synthetic characters in a virtual environment who establish credible and empathic relations with children.
- **NICE** (Corradini et al., 2005): Its purpose was to foster universal natural interactive access, in particular for children and adolescents, by developing natural, fun and experientially rich communication between humans and embodied historical and literary characters.
- **HUMAINE** (Cowie & Schröder, 2005): Its purpose is to lay the foundations for European development of systems that can register, model and influence human emotional and emotion-related states coordinating efforts to come to a shared understanding of the issues involved.
- **COMPANIONS** (Wilks, 2006): Its purpose is the creation of companions: personalized, conversational interface to the Internet that knows its owner, on a range of platforms, indoor and nomadic, based on integrated high-quality research in multi-modal human-computer interfaces, intelligent agents, and human language technology.

4. EXAMPLES OF MULTIMODAL DIALOGUE SYSTEMS

In this section we describe the interactive multimodal interfaces which we have developed covering some of the issues described in the previous sections.

4.1. The Mayordomo Multimodal Dialogue System

Mayordomo (Ábalos et al., 2010) is a multimodal dialogue system developed in our laboratory which aims to centralize the control of appliances in a home. Specifically, users can employ either spontaneous speech or a traditional GUI interfaces based on keyboard and mouse. The system has been designed to operate in an AmI environment in order to ease the interaction. For example, Mayordomo can find out the room in which the user is at any time through RFID devices. This information is then used to optimize the dialogue with the user, thus ridding him off about providing unnecessary information. Mayordomo also allows parental control of some appliances in order to restrict the interaction with them. For instance, parents can forbid that children watch TV after 10 p.m. The system administrator has privileges to perform special actions, for example, installing and uninstalling appliances and handling the parental control. The system creates a log of all actions carried out within the environment by any user.

To provide spoken interaction, we used Windows Vista Speech Recognition (WVSR). This package includes both the engine for ASR and the engine for TTS. Windows Vista includes two development tools for programmers: SAPI 5.3 (Speech API) and System.Speech (.NET Framework 3.0 namespace). To implement the system we employed System.Speech as it is oriented mainly to programming languages for Microsoft .NET. Each appliance has an associated configuration file that allows the user to control it orally.

Speech understanding is based on what we have noted as an "action". In our application domain, an action consists of four fields of data: room, appliance, attribute, and value. Using these four elements, the system can execute a particular order on an appliance, or provide the information requested by the user. To implement the speech understanding process, we employed a method that searches in the recognized sentence for the four fields of data in the action concept.

Once the semantic analysis of the sentence is finished, the dialogue manager must decide what will be the answer to be generated by the system. In particular it must determine whether to provide the information requested by the user or perform a specific action on an appliance. To do this it checks if there is information missing in the recognized sentence. If there is no data missing and the user is requesting information, the dialogue manager invokes the module *Provide Information*, which organizes the information to be provided to the user in well-formed sentences. The system uses speech synthesis (TTS) to communicate verbally with the user, employing as input the sentences in text format created by the module for sentence generation.

The GUI interface designed for Mayordomo (Figure 1) includes a status bar, and a text field which displays each system's response. The status bar can be very useful in case users want to interact with the system in noisy environments where understanding the messages generated by TTS might be difficult. The interface also provides a command prompt that allows users to communicate with the system in text format.

A set of tools have been developed to carry out the evaluation of the system (Ábalos et al., 2011). These tools include a corpus of spoken sentences, two transcribers, an orthographic and a semantic one, and a user simulator. The corpus is a set of audio files, spoken sentences recorded by users, which our system uses in order to perform the actions in the domain to which it is defined. Our current corpus design contains two scenarios: the scenario to switch on any appliances, called scenario 1, and a scenario designed to provide only names of rooms, appliances, attributes, values and actions, called scenario 2. Each of these scenarios contains 75 sentences divided into three sets of 25 sentences. Currently, our corpus contains 1500 sentences recorded: half of them, 750 sentences, are from scenario 1 and the other half are from scenario 2, that is, there have been recorded 10 whole set of sentences for each scenario. The collaboration of fifteen volunteers has been indispensable for recording and obtaining this corpus.

The orthographic automatic transcriber is a module that receives an audio file (.wav) of our corpus and creates a text file (.txt) with the same name, whose content is the orthographic transcription of the audio spoken sentence. The text file created is extremely important in the evaluation of the dialogue system because it contains the sentence designed of the scenario, without any recognition errors, i.e., the correct sentence. The semantic automatic transcriber module, which works as a semantic analyser, receives as input the text file containing a sentence created with the corpus automatic transcriber, and creates a text file with the same name as the input text file.

The user simulator is basically an additional dialogue system which automatically interacts with the dialogue system to assess, representing in this way the behaviour of a real user. The simulator uses the files which contains the corpus in order to create dialogues and interacting with the dialogue system as if it were a user, with goals and answering to questions which are made by the dialogue system. Through this simulation, the dialogue system receives as input spoken sentences previously recorded by users, with the advantage of considering real phenomenon which appear in speech recognition. Several steps are followed to implement the interaction between the user simulator and the dialog system: i) Determine the purpose of the interaction with the dialogue system; ii) Choose the file to be used as a user's turn in the dialogue; iii) Speech recognition; iv) Dialogue management and sentence generation; v) Next dialogue turn or end of interaction.

These tools have been applied to the specific case of Mayordomo dialogue system. In particular, the contributions allow us to assess the dialogue system using two approaches. To perform an overall evaluation of the system, the user simulator tool

Figure 1. GUI interface of the Mayordomo system

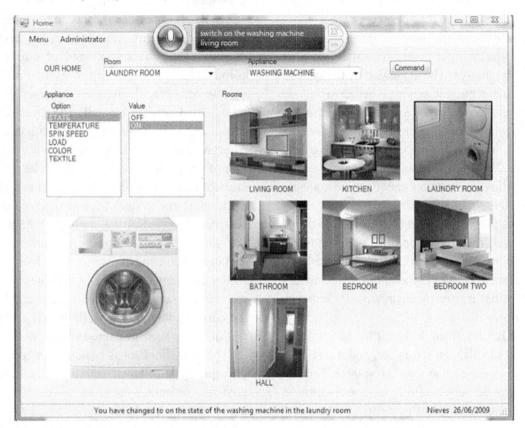

has been developed. Meanwhile, to accomplish an evaluation of the individual components of the dialogue system (in our case, speech recognizer, natural language understanding and dialogue manager), the automatic transcribers and a number of secondary tools to calculate statistical measures have been elaborated. With these tools, measures obtained are Word Accuracy, Keyword Accuracy, Sentence Understanding, Sentence Recognition, Task Completion and Implicit Recovery. These measures allow us to obtain experimental results from which to draw conclusions, for instance, which components of the dialogue system must be improved.

In order to perform an overall evaluation of Mayordomo, the user simulator has been applied to our corpus. The simulation result is shown in Table 1. In this case, Microsoft Speech Recog-

nizer 8.0 for Windows (American English) is the recognizer used in the simulation. 1000 dialogues have been generated with sentences recorded of our corpus of which 4751 sentences recorded have been correctly analyzed whereas there have been 263 sentences with recognition errors.

The number of completed dialogues is 274 so task completion is 27.4% which means that in three of every four cases the dialogue does not end satisfactorily. The reason is that sentence recognition rate (SR) and sentence understanding rate (SU) are not quite good because of the recognition errors. In fact, sentences from scenario 2 are names of appliances, rooms, attributes and values. Therefore, these spoken sentences are quite short (only a word or two) and in case there is any recognition error, the speech recognizer finds them difficult to understand. If we want to

Table 1. Simulation results obtained for the May-ordomo system

Analyzed Sentences	4751
Recognition Errors	263
Sentence Recognition Rate (SR)	
Sentence Recognition	28,23%
Correctly Recognized	1341
Sentence Understanding Rate (SU)	
Sentence Understanding Rate	17,7%
Correctly Understood	841
Implicit Recovery (IR)	
Implicit Recovery Rate	0,91%
Not recognized sentences but understood	43
Task Completion (TC)	
Total of dialogues	1000
Finished dialogues	274
Task completion	27,4%
Word Accuracy (WA)	24,86%
Keyword Accuracy (KWA)	24,86%

improve our dialogue system we must take into account these shortages. For example, we could change the speech recognizer engine and evaluate the dialogue system again to compare results and to find the speech recognizer which one is appropriate for our system.

4.2. An Academic Assistant in the SecondLife Virtual World

The stunning increase in the amount of time people are spending socializing online is creating new ways of communication and cooperation. With the advances in the so-called Web 2.0, virtual worlds have grown dramatically over the last decade. These worlds or "metaverses" are computer-simulated multimodal environments in which humans, through their avatars cohabit with other users. Traditionally, virtual worlds have had a predefined structure and fixed tasks that the user could carry out. However, social virtual worlds have emerged to emphasize the role of social

interaction in these environments, allowing the users to determine their own experiences.

We decided to use Second Life (SL) as a testbed for our research for several reasons. Firstly, because it is one of the most popular social virtual worlds available: its population is nowadays of millions of enthusiastic residents from around the world. Secondly, because it uses a sophisticated physics engine which generates very realistic simulations including collision detection, vehicle dynamics and animation look & feel, thus making the avatars and the environment more credible and similar to the real world. Thirdly, because SL's capacity for customization is extensive and encourages user innovation and participation, which increases the naturalness of the interactions that take place in the virtual world.

We have developed a conversational metabot (Griol et al., 2010) that facilitates academic information (courses, professors, doctoral studies and enrolment) in SL based on the functionalities provided by a previously developed dialogue system (Callejas & López-Cózar, 2008a). Figure 2 shows the architecture developed for the integration of conversational metabot both in the Second Life and OsGrid virtual worlds. The conversational agent that governs the metabot is outside the virtual world, using external servers that provide both data access and speech recognition and synthesis functionalities.

The speech signal provided by the text to speech synthesizer is captured and transmitted to the voice server module in Second Life (SLVoice) using code developed in Visual C#. NET and the SpeechLib library. This module is external to the client program used to display the virtual world and is based on the Vivox technology, which uses the RTP, SIP, OpenAL, TinyXPath, OpenSSL and libcurl protocols to transmit voice data. We also use the utility provided by Second Life lipsynch to synchronize the voice signal with the lip movements of the avatar. In addition, we have integrated a keyboard emulator that allows the transmission of the text transcription generated

Figure 2. Architecture designed for the development of the conversational metabot

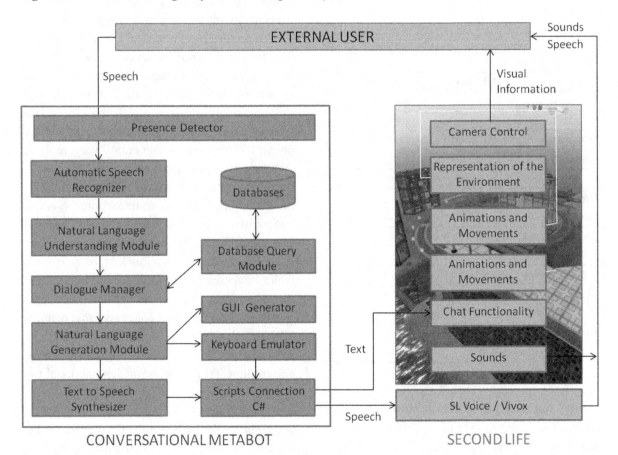

by the conversational avatar directly to the chat in Second Life. The system connection with the virtual world is carried out by using the libOpen-Metaverse library. This .Net library, based on the Client /Server paradigm, allows accessing and creating three-dimensional virtual worlds, and it is used to communicate with servers that control the virtual world of Second Life.

Speech recognition and synthesis are performed using the Microsoft Speech Application Programming Interface (SAPI), integrated into the Windows Vista operating system. To enable the interaction with the conversational bot in Spanish using the chat in Second Life, we have integrated synthetic voices developed by Loquendo. Using this architecture user's utterances can be easily recognized, the transcription of these utterances can be transcribed in the chat in Second Life, and the result of the user's query can be communicated using both text and speech modalities. To do this, we have integrated modules for the semantic understanding and dialogue management implemented for the original dialogue system, which are based on grammars and VoiceXML files. Figure 3 shows the developed metabot providing information about tutoring hours of a specific professor.

A set of 150 dialogs was acquired with the conversational metabot by means of its interaction with students and professors of our university. Figure 4 shows an example of a dialog extracted from this corpus and translated from Spanish to English. Turns with S refer to system turns, and turns with U refer to user turns.

Figure 3. Conversational metabot developed to interact in virtual worlds (dialogue in the Spanish original version)

We considered the following measures for the evaluation:

1. Dialog success rate (%success). This is the percentage of successfully completed dialogs in which the metabot provides the correct information to each one of the required questions.
2. Average number of turns per dialog (nT).
3. Confirmation rate (%confirm). It was computed as the ratio between the number of explicit confirmations turns (nCT) and the number of turns in the dialog (nCT/nT).
4. Average number of corrected errors per dialog (nCE). This is the average of errors detected and corrected by the dialog manager of the conversational metabot. We have considered only those errors that modify the values of the attributes and that could cause the failure of the dialog.
5. Average number of uncorrected errors per dialog (nNCE). This is the average of errors not corrected by the dialog manager. Again, only errors that modify the values of the attributes are considered.
6. Error correction rate (%ECR). The percentage of corrected errors, computed as nCE/(nCE + nNCE).

The results presented in Table 2 show that the developed conversational can interact correctly with the users in most cases, achieving a success rate of 94%. The dialog success depends on whether the system provides the correct data for every objective defined in the scenario. The analysis of the main problems detected in the acquired dialogs shows that, in some cases, the system did not detect that the user wanted to finish the dialog. A second problem was related to the introduction of data with a high confidence value

Figure 4. Example of a dialog acquired with the interaction of the system with real users

---

S1: Hi! You can ask me for information about subjects, lecturers, doctoral studies and registrations.
U1: I want to know information about subjects in Computer Science.
S2: Which subject do you want to consult?
U2: Language Processors I.
S3: Here you can consult the information of the subject. Anything else?
U3: Can you inform me about the schedules of Group D?
S4: I give the information for the Group D of Language Processors I: Monday 9:00-11:00, Wednesday 11:00-13:00. Anything else?
U4: Can you tell me the name of the lecturer?
S5: I give the information for the Group D of Language Processors I. The name of the lecturer is David Griol. Anything else?
U5: No, thank you.
S6: Bye!

---

due to errors generated by the automatic speech recognizer that were not detected by the dialog manager. However, the evaluation confirms a good operation of the approach since the information is correctly provided by the metabot in the majority of cases, as it is also shown in the value of the error correction rate.

In addition, we have already completed a preliminary evaluation of this functionality of the conversational metabot based on questionnaire to assess the students' subjective opinion about the metabot performance. The questionnaire had 10 questions: i) Q1: State on a scale from 1 to 5 your previous knowledge about new technologies for information access.; ii) Q2: How many times

have you accessed virtual worlds like Second Life?; iii) Q3: How well did the metabot understand you?; iv) Q4: How well did you understand the messages generated by the metabot?; v) Q5: Was it easy for you to get the requested information?; vi) Q6: Was the interaction rate adequate?; vii) Q7: Was it easy for you to correct the metabot errors?; viii) Q8: Were you sure about what to say to the system at every moment?; ix) Q9: Do you believe the system behaved similarly as a human would do?; x) Q10: In general terms, are you satisfied with the metabot performance?

The possible answers for each one of the questions were the same: Never, Seldom, Sometimes, Usually, and Always. All the answers were

Table 2. Results of the objective evaluation of the conversational metabot

	%success	nT	%confirm	%ECR	nCE	nNCE
Conversational Metabot	94%	11.6	28%	93%	0.89	0.06

Table 3. Results of the subjective evaluation of the conversational metabot (1=worst, 5=best evaluation)

	Q1	Q2	Q3	Q4	Q5	Q6	Q7	Q8	Q9	Q10
Average Value	4.6	2.8	3.6	3.8	3.2	3.1	2.7	2.3	2.4	3.3
Maximum Value	5	3	4	5	5	4	3	3	4	4
Minimal Value	4	1	2	3	2	3	2	2	1	3

assigned a numeric value between one and five (in the same order as they appear in the questionnaire). Table 3 shows the average, minimal and maximum values for the subjective evaluation carried out by a total of 15 students from one of the groups in the subject.

From the results of the evaluation, it can be observed that students positively evaluates the facility of obtaining the data required to fulfill the complete set of objectives of the proposed in the exercises defined for the subject, the suitability of the interaction rate during the dialog. The sets of points that they mention to be improved include the correction of system errors and a better clarification of the set of actions expected by the platform at each time.

5. CONCLUSION AND FUTURE RESEARCH DIRECTIONS

The development of multimodal systems is a very active research topic. The design and performance of these systems is very complex, not only because of the complexity of the different technologies involved, but also because of the required interconnection of very heterogeneous components. In this chapter we have provided an overview of the most representative architectures, techniques and toolkits available for the development of such systems. We have paid special attention to context adaptation as a key aspect of these systems, and provided examples of the multimodal dialogue systems developed in our lab that cover the issues discussed.

For future research additional work is needed in several directions to make these systems more usable by a wider range of potential users. For example, the development of emotional conversational agents represents a promising field of research, as emotions play a very important role in the rational decision-making, perception and

human-to-human interaction. Also a very interesting trend are multimodal social systems which rely on the fact that in real settings people do not only speak about topics concerned with the task at hand, but also about other topics, especially at the beginning of the conversation, for example, weather conditions, family or current news. Hence, additional efforts must be made by the research community in order to make conversational agents more human-like employing dialogue strategies based on this kind of very genuine human behaviour.

REFERENCES

Ábalos, N., Espejo, G., López-Cózar, R., Callejas, Z., & Griol, D. (2010). A multimodal dialogue system for an ambient intelligent application in home environments. *In Proceedings of the 13th International Conference on Text, Speech and Dialogue* (pp. 491-498).

Ábalos, N., Espejo, G., López-Cózar, R., Callejas, Z., & Griol, D. (2011). A toolkit for the evaluation of spoken dialogue systems in ambient intelligence domains. In *Proceedings of the Second International Workshop on Human-Centric Interfaces for Ambient Intelligence*, Nottingham, UK.

Ai, H., Litman, D., Forbes-Riley, K., Rotaru, M., Tetreault, J., & Purandare, A. (2006). Using systems and user performance features to improve emotion detection in spoken tutoring dialogs. In *Proceedings of the International Conference on Spoken Language Processing*, Pittsburgh, PA (pp. 797-800).

Bailly, G., Raidt, S., & Elisei, F. (2010). Gaze, conversational agents and face-to-face communication. *Speech Communication, 52*(6), 598–612. doi:10.1016/j.specom.2010.02.015

Balci, K. (2005). XfaceEd: Authoring tool for embodied conversational agents. In *Proceedings of the International Conference on Multimodal Interfaces* (pp. 208-213).

Batliner, A., Hacker, C., Steidl, S., Nöth, E., D'Arcy, S., Russel, M., & Wong, M. (2004). Towards multilingual speech recognition using data driven source/target acoustical units association. In *Proceedings of the International Conference on Acoustics, Speech, and Signal Processing*, Montreal, QC, Canada (pp. 521-524).

Benesty, J., Sondhi, M. M., & Huang, Y. (2008). *Springer handbook of speech processing*. New York, NY: Springer. doi:10.1007/978-3-540-49127-9

Beveridge, M., & Fox, J. (2006). Automatic generation of spoken dialogue from medical plans and ontologies. *Biomedical Informatics*, *39*(5), 482–499. doi:10.1016/j.jbi.2005.12.008

Bickmore, T., & Giorgino, T. (2004). Some novel aspects of health communication from a dialogue systems perspective. In *Proceedings of the AAAI Fall Symposium on Dialogue Systems for Health Communication*, Washington, DC (pp. 275-291).

Bird, S., Klein, E., Loper, E., & Baldridge, J. (2008). Multidisciplinary instruction with the Natural Language Toolkit. In *Proceedings of the Third ACL Workshop on Issues in Teaching Computational Linguistics* (pp. 62-70).

Boehner, K., DePaula, R., Dourish, P., & Sengers, P. (2007). How emotion is made and measured. *International Journal of Human-Computer Studies*, *65*(4), 275–291. doi:10.1016/j.ijhcs.2006.11.016

Bos, J., Klein, E., & Oka, T. (2003). Meaningful conversation with a mobile robot. In *Proceedings of the Tenth Conference on European Chapter of the Association for Computational Linguistics* (pp. 71-74).

Burkhardt, F., van Ballegooy, M., Englert, R., & Huber, R. (2005). An emotion-aware voice portal. In *Proceedings of the Electronic Speech Signal Processing Conference*, Prague, Czech Republic (pp. 123-131).

Callejas, Z., & López-Cózar, R. (2008a). Relations between de-facto criteria in the evaluation of a spoken dialogue system. *Speech Communication*, *50*(8-9), 646–665. doi:10.1016/j.specom.2008.04.004

Callejas, Z., & López-Cózar, R. (2008b). Influence of contextual information in emotion annotation for spoken dialogue systems. *Speech Communication*, *50*(5), 416–433. doi:10.1016/j.specom.2008.01.001

Camurri, A., Mazzarino, B., & Volpe, G. (2004). Expressive interfaces. *Cognition Technology and Work*, *6*(1), 15–22. doi:10.1007/s10111-003-0138-7

Cassell, J., Bickmore, T., Billinghurst, M., Campbell, L., Chang, K., Vilhálmsson, H., & Yan, H. (1999). Embodiment in conversational interfaces: Rea. In *Proceedings of the Conference on Computer-Human Interaction* (pp. 520-527).

Cassell, J., Sullivan, J., Prevost, S., & Churchill, E. F. (2000). *Embodied conversational agents*. Cambridge, MA: MIT Press.

Catizone, R., Setzer, A., & Wilks, Y. (2003). Multimodal dialogue management in the COMIC Project. *Proceedings of the European Chapter of the Association for Computational Linguistics Workshop on Dialogue Systems: Interaction, Adaptation, and Styles of Management*, Budapest, Hungary (pp. 25-34).

Chu, S.-W., O'Neill, I., Hanna, P., & McTear, M. (2005). An approach to multistrategy dialogue management. In *Proceedings of the Interspeech/Eurospeech Conference*, Lisbon, Portugal (pp. 865-868).

Clark, R., Richmond, K., & King, S. (2004). Festival 2 - build your own general purpose unit selection speech synthesizer. In *Proceedings of the 5th ISCA Workshop on Speech Synthesis* (pp. 173-178).

Cole, R., Mariani, J., Uszkoreit, H., Varile, G. B., Zaenen, A., Zampolli, A., & Zue, V. (Eds.). (1997). *Survey of the state of the art in human language technology.* Cambridge, UK: Cambridge University Press.

Cole, R., Van Vuuren, S., Pellom, B., Hacioglu, K., Ma, J., & Movellan, J. …Wade-stein, D. (2003). Perceptive animated interfaces: first steps toward a new paradigm for human-computer interaction. *Proceedings of the IEEE, 91*(9), 1391-1405.

Corradini, A., Mehta, M., Bernsen, N. O., & Charfuelán, M. (2005). Animating an interactive conversational character for an educational game system. In *Proceedings of the International Conference on Intelligent User Interfaces*, San Diego, CA (pp. 183-190).

Corradini, A., & Samuelsson, C. (2008). A generic spoken dialogue manager applied to an interactive 2D game. In E. André, L. Dybkjær, W. Minker, H. Neumann, R. Pieraccini, & M. Weber (Eds.), *Proceedings of the 4th IEEE Tutorial and Research Workshop on Perception and Interactive Technologies for Speech-Based Systems: Perception in Multimodal Dialogue Systems* (LNCS 5078, pp. 2-13).

Cowie, R., & Cornelius, R. (2003). Describing the emotional states that are expressed in speech. *Speech Communication, 40*(1-2), 5–32. doi:10.1016/S0167-6393(02)00071-7

Cowie, R., Douglas-Cowie, E., Tsapatsoulis, N., Votsis, G., Kollias, S., Fellenz, W., & Taylor, J. (2001). Emotion recognition in human-computer interaction. *IEEE Signal Processing Magazine, 18*(1), 32–80. doi:10.1109/79.911197

Cowie, R., & Schröder, M. (2005). Piecing together the emotion jigsaw. In S. Bengio & H. Bourlard (Eds.), *Proceedings of the First International Conference on Machine Learning for Multimodal Interaction* (LNCS 3361, pp. 305-317).

Critchley, H. D., Rotshtein, P., Nagai, Y., O'Doherty, J., Mathias, C. J., & Dolana, R. J. (2005). Activity in the human brain predicting differential heart rate responses to emotional facial expressions. *NeuroImage, 24*, 751–762. doi:10.1016/j.neuroimage.2004.10.013

Cuayáhuitl, H., Renals, S., Lemon, O., & Shimodaira, H. (2006). Reinforcement learning of dialogue strategies with hierarchical abstract machines. In *Proceedings of the IEEE/ACL Spoken Language Technology Workshop*, Palm Beach, Aruba (pp. 182-186).

Dey, A., & Abowd, G. (2000). Towards a better understanding of context and context-awareness. In *Proceedings of the 1st international symposium on Handheld and Ubiquitous Computing* (pp. 304-307).

Dumas, B., Lalanne, D., & Ingold, R. (2009). Description languages for multimodal interaction: a set of guidelines and its illustration with SMUIML. *Journal on Multimodal User Interfaces, 3*, 237–247. doi:10.1007/s12193-010-0043-3

Eckert, W., Levin, E., & Pieraccini, R. (1998). *Automatic evaluation of spoken dialogue systems* (Tech. Rep. No. TR98.9.1). Florham Park, NJ: ATT Labs Research.

Edlund, J., Gustafson, J., Heldner, M., & Hjalmarsson, A. (2008). Towards human-like spoken dialogue systems. *Speech Communication, 50*(8-9), 630–645. doi:10.1016/j.specom.2008.04.002

Elhadad, M., & Robin, J. (1996). An overview of SURGE: A reusable comprehensive syntactic realization component. In *Proceedings of the Eighth International Natural Language Generation Workshop* (pp. 1-4).

Endrass, B., Rehm, M., & André, E. (2011). Planning small talk behavior with cultural influences for multiagent systems. *Computer Speech & Language*, *25*(2), 158–174. doi:10.1016/j.csl.2010.04.001

Faure, C., & Julia, L. (1993). Interaction homme-machine par la parole et le geste pour l'édition de documents. In *Proceedings of the International Conference on Real and Virtual Worlds* (pp. 171-180).

Flecha-García, M. L. (2010). Eyebrow raises in dialogue and their relation to discourse structure, utterance function and pitch accents in English. *Speech Communication*, *52*(6), 542–554. doi:10.1016/j.specom.2009.12.003

Forbes-Riley, K., & Litman, D. (2011). Designing and evaluating a wizarded uncertainty-adaptive spoken dialogue tutoring system. *Computer Speech & Language*, *25*(1), 105–126. doi:10.1016/j.csl.2009.12.002

Forbes-Riley, K. M., & Litman, D. (2004). Modelling user satisfaction and student learning in a spoken dialogue tutoring system with generic, tutoring, and user affect parameters. In *Proceedings of the North American Chapter of the Association for Computational Linguistics on Human Language Technologies*, New York, NY (pp. 264-271).

Fraser, N., & Gilbert, G. (1991). Simulating speech systems. *Computer Speech & Language*, *5*, 81–99. doi:10.1016/0885-2308(91)90019-M

Gebhard, P., Klesen, M., & Rist, T. (2004). Coloring multi-character conversations through the expression of emotions. In *Proceedings of the Tutorial and Research Workshop on Affective Dialogue Systems*, Kloster Irsee, Germany (pp. 128-141).

Georgila, K., Henderson, J., & Lemon, O. (2005). Learning user simulations for information state update dialogue systems. In *Proceedings of the Eurospeech Conference* (pp. 893-896).

Glass, J., Flammia, G., Goodine, D., Phillips, M., Polifroni, J., & Sakai, S. (1995). Multilingual spoken-language understanding in the MIT Voyager system. *Speech Communication*, *17*(1-2), 1–18. doi:10.1016/0167-6393(95)00008-C

Griol, D., Hurtado, L. F., Segarra, E., & Sanchis, E. (2008). A statistical approach to spoken dialog systems design and evaluation. *Speech Communication*, *50*(8-9), 666–682. doi:10.1016/j.specom.2008.04.001

Griol, D., Rojo, E., Arroyo, Á., Patricio, M. A., & Molina, J. M. (2010). A conversational academic assistant for the interaction in virtual worlds. *Advances in Soft Computing*, *79*, 283–290. doi:10.1007/978-3-642-14883-5_37

Gruenstein, A., McGraw, I., & Badr, I. (2008). The WAMI toolkit for developing, deploying, and evaluating web-accessible multimodal interfaces. In *Proceedings of the International Conference on Multimodal Interfaces*.

Hall, L., Woods, S., Aylett, R., Paiva, A., & Newall, L. (2005). Achieving empathic engagement through affective interaction with synthetic characters. In J. Tao, T. Tan, & R. W. Picard (Eds.), *Proceedings of the International Conference on Affective Computing and Intelligent Interaction*, Beijing, China (LNCS 3784, pp. 731-738).

Haseel, L., & Hagen, E. (2005). Adaptation of an automotive dialogue system to users' expertise. In *Proceedings of the Interspeech/Eurospeech Conference*, Lisbon, Portugal (pp. 222-226).

Heim, J., Nilsson, E. G., & Skjetne, J. H. (2007). User profiles for adapting speech support in the opera Web browser to disabled users. In C. Stephanidis & M. Pieper (Eds.), *Proceedings of the 9th ECRIM Workshop on Universal Access in Ambient Intelligence Environments* (LNCS, 4397, pp. 154-172).

Henricksen, K., Indulska, J., & Rakotonirainy, A. (2002). Modeling context information in pervasive computing systems. In *Proceedings of the 1ˢᵗ International Conference on Pervasive Computing* (pp. 167-180).

Huang, C., Xu, P., Zhang, X., Zhao, S., Huang, T., & Xu, B. (1999). LODESTAR: A Mandarin spoken dialogue system for travel information retrieval. In *Proceedings of the Conference Eurospeech* (pp. 1159-1162).

Huang, H., Cerekovic, A., Pandzic, I., Nakano, Y., & Nishida, T. (2007). A script driven multimodal embodied conversational agent based on a generic framework. In *Proceedings of the 7th International Conference on Intelligent Virtual Agents* (pp. 381-382).

Ibrahim, A., & Johansson, P. (2002). Multimodal dialogue systems for interactive TV applications. In *Proceedings of the 4ᵗʰ IEEE International Conference on Multimodal Interfaces* (pp. 117-122).

Jokinen, K. (2003). Natural interaction in spoken dialogue systems. In *Proceedings of the Workshop on Ontologies and Multilinguality in User Interfaces*, Crete, Greece (pp. 730-734).

Kang, H., Suh, E., & Yoo, K. (2008). Packet-based context aware system to determine information system user's context. *Expert Systems with Applications, 35*, 286–300. doi:10.1016/j.eswa.2007.06.033

Keidl, M., & Kemper, A. (2004). A framework for context-aware adaptable Web services. In E. Bertino, S. Christodoulakis, D. Plexousakis, V. Christophides, M. Koubarakis, K. Böhm, & E. Ferrari (Eds.), *Proceedings of the 9th International Conference on Advances in Database Technology* (LNCS 2992, pp. 826-829).

Langner, B., & Black, A. (2005). Using speech in noise to improve understandability for elderly listeners. In *Proceedings of the Conference on Automatic Speech Recognition and Understanding*, San Juan, Puerto Rico (pp. 392-396).

Lee, C., Yoo, S. K., Park, Y. J., Kim, N. H., Jeong, K. S., & Lee, B. C. (2005). Using neural network to recognize human emotions from heart rate variability and skin resistance. In *Proceedings of the Annual International Conference on Engineering in Medicine and Biology Society*, Shanghai, China (pp. 5523-5525).

Lee, C. M., & Narayanan, S. S. (2005). Toward detecting emotions in spoken dialogs. *IEEE Transactions on Speech and Audio Processing, 13*(2), 293–303. doi:10.1109/TSA.2004.838534

Lee, K., Hon, H., & Reddy, R. (1990). An overview of the SPHINX speech recognition system. In Waibel, A., & Lee, K.-F. (Eds.), *Readings in speech recognition* (pp. 600–610). San Francisco, CA: Morgan Kaufmann. doi:10.1109/29.45616

Lemon, O., Georgila, K., & Henderson, J. (2006). Evaluating effectiveness and portability of reinforcement learned dialogue strategies with real users: the TALK TownInfo evaluation. In *Proceedings of the IEEE-ACL Spoken Language Technologies Conference*, Palm Beach, Aruba (pp. 178-181).

Lepri, B., Mana, N., Cappelletti, A., Pianesi, F., & Zancanaro, M. (2009). Modeling the personality of participants during group interactions. In G.-J. Houben, G. McCalla, F. Pianesi, & M. Zancanaro (Eds.), *Proceedings of the 17th International Conference on User Modeling, Adaptation, and Personalization* (LNCS 5535, pp. 114-125).

Leßmann, N., & Wachsmuth, I. (2003). A cognitively motivated architecture for an anthropomorphic artificial communicator. In *Proceedings of the International Conference on Computing and Mission* (pp. 277-278).

Li, L., Cao, F., Chou, W., & Liu, F. (2006). XMflow: An extensible micro-flow for multimodal interaction. In *Proceedings of the 8th Workshop on Multimedia Signal Processing* (pp. 497-500).

Li, L., Li, L., Chou, W., & Liu, F. (2007). R-Flow: An extensible XML based multimodal dialogue system architecture. In *Proceedings of the 9th Workshop on Multimedia Signal Processing* (pp. 86-89).

Litman, D. J., & Pan, S. (2002). Designing and evaluating an adaptive spoken dialogue system. *User Modeling and User-Adapted Interaction, 12*, 111–137. doi:10.1023/A:1015036910358

López-Cózar, R., & Araki, M. (2005). *Spoken, multilingual and multimodal dialogue systems. development and assessment*. New York, NY: John Wiley & Sons.

López-Cózar, R., Callejas, Z., Kroul, M., Nouza, J., & Silovský, J. (2008). Two-level fusion to improve emotion classification in spoken dialogue systems. In P. Sojka, A. Horák, I. Kopecek, & K. Pala (Eds.), *Proceedings of the 11th International Conference on Text, Speech and Dialogue* (LNCS 5246, pp. 617-624).

Mahlke, S. (2006). Emotions and EMG measures of facial muscles in interactive contexts. In *Proceedings of the Conference on Human Factors in Computing Systems*, Montreal, QC, Canada.

Maragoudakis, M. (2007). MeteoBayes: Effective plan recognition in a weather dialogue system. *IEEE Intelligent Systems, 22*(1), 66–77. doi:10.1109/MIS.2007.14

Martinovski, B., & Traum, D. (2003). Breakdown in human-machine interaction: the error is the clue. In *Proceedings of the ISCA Tutorial and Research Workshop on Error Handling in Dialogue Systems*, Chateau d'Oex, Vaud, Switzerland (pp. 11-16).

McGlashan, S., Burnett, D. C., Carter, J., Danielsen, P., Ferrans, J., & Hunt, A. …Tryphonas, S. (2004). *Voice Extensible Markup Language (VoiceXML)*. Retrieved from http://www.w3.org/TR/voicexml21/

McTear, M. F. (1998). Modelling spoken dialogues with state transition diagrams: experiences with the CSLU toolkit. In *Proceedings of the International Conference on Spoken Language Processing* (pp. 1223-1226).

McTear, M. F. (2004). *Spoken dialogue technology*. New York, NY: Springer. doi:10.1007/978-0-85729-414-2

Minker, W. (1998). Stochastic versus rule-based speech understanding for information retrieval. *Speech Communication, 25*(4), 223–247. doi:10.1016/S0167-6393(98)00038-7

Minker, W., Haiber, U., Heisterkamp, P., & Scheible, S. (2004). The Seneca spoken language dialogue system. *Speech Communication, 43*(1-2), 89–102. doi:10.1016/j.specom.2004.01.005

Minsky, M. (1975). A framework for representing knowledge. In Winston, P. H. (Ed.), *The psychology of computer vision* (pp. 211–277). New York, NY: McGraw-Hill.

Mohri, M. (1997). Finite-state transducers in language and speech processing. *Computational Linguistics, 23*(2), 269–311.

Moran, D. B., Cheyer, A. J., Julia, L. E., Martin, D. L., & Park, S. (1997). Multimodal user interface in the open agent architecture. In *Proceedings of the 2nd International Conference on Intelligent User Interfaces* (pp. 61-68).

Morrison, D., Wang, R., & Silva, L. C. D. (2007). Ensemble methods for spoken emotion recognition in call-centers. *Speech Communication, 49*(2), 98–112. doi:10.1016/j.specom.2006.11.004

Müller, C., & Runge, F. (1993). Dialogue design principles - key for usability of voice processing. In *Proceedings of the Eurospeech Conference* (pp. 943-946).

Naguib, H., Coulouris, G., & Mitchell, S. (2001). Middleware support for context-aware multimedia applications. In *Proceedings of the 3rd International Working Conference on New Developments in Distributed Applications and Interoperable Systems* (pp. 9-22).

Nielsen, P. B., & Baekgaard, A. (1992). Experience with a dialogue description formalism for realistic applications. In *Proceedings of the International Conference on Spoken Language Processing* (pp. 719-722).

Nihei, K. (2004). Context sharing platform. *NEC Journal of Advanced Technology, 1*(3), 200–204.

Oh, A., & Rudnicky, A. (2000). Stochastic language generation for spoken dialog systems. In *Proceedings of the ANLP North American Chapter of the Association for Computational Linguistics Workshop on Conversational Systems* (pp. 27-32).

Paek, T., & Horvitz, E. (2004). Optimizing automated call routing by integrating spoken dialogue models with queuing models. In *Proceedings of the North American Chapter of the Association for Computational Linguistics on Human Language Technologies* (pp. 41-48).

Pargellis, A., Kuo, H., & Lee, C. (2004). An automatic dialogue generation platform for personalized dialogue applications. *Speech Communication, 42*, 329–351. doi:10.1016/j.specom.2003.10.003

Picard, R. W. (1997). *Affective computing*. Cambridge, MA: MIT Press.

Picard, R. W., & Daily, S. B. (2005). Evaluating affective interactions: Alternatives to asking what users feel. In *Proceedings of the CHI Workshop on Evaluating Affective Interfaces-Innovative Approaches*, Portland, OR.

Pitterman, J., & Pitterman, A. (2006). Integrating emotion recognition into an adaptive spoken language dialogue system. In *Proceedings of the 2nd IEEE International Conference on Intelligent Environments* (pp. 213-219).

Poslad, S., Laamanen, H., Malaka, R., Nick, A., Buckle, P., & Zipf, A. (2001). Crumpet: Creation of user-friendly mobile services personalized for tourism. In *Proceedings of the 2nd International Conference on 3G Mobile* (pp. 28-32).

Prendinger, H., Mayer, S., Mori, J., & Ishizuka, M. (2003). Persona effect revisited. using bio-signals to measure and reflect the impact of character-based interfaces. In *Proceedings of the Intelligent Virtual Agents*, Kloster Irsee, Germany (pp. 283-291).

Rabiner, L. R., & Juang, B. H. (1993). *Fundamentals of speech recognition*. Upper Saddle River, NJ: Prentice Hall.

Radford, L. (2003). Gestures, speech, and the sprouting of signs: A semiotic-cultural approach to students' types of generalization. *Mathematical Thinking and Learning, 5*(1), 37–70. doi:10.1207/S15327833MTL0501_02

Raux, A., & Eskenazi, M. (2007). A multi-layer architecture for semi-synchronous event-driven dialogue management. In *Proceedings of the International Conference on Automatic Speech Recognition and Understanding* (pp. 514-519).

Raux, A., Langner, B., Black, A. W., & Eskenazi, M. (2003). LET'S GO: Improving spoken dialog systems for the elderly and non-natives. In *Proceedings of the Eurospeech Conference*, Geneva, Switzerland (pp. 753-756).

Reiter, E. (1995). NLG vs. templates. In *Proceedings of the Fifth European Workshop in Natural Language Generation* (pp. 95-105).

Rosenfeld, R. (1995). The CMU statistical language modeling toolkit and its use in the 1994 ARPA CSR evaluation. In *Proceedings of the ARPA Spoken Language Systems Technology Workshop*.

Salber, D., & Coutaz, J. (1993). Applying the wizard of oz technique to the study of multimodal systems. In *Proceedings of the Selected papers from the Third International Conference on Human-Computer Interaction* (pp. 219-230).

Salovey, P., & Mayer, J. D. (1990). Emotional intelligence. *Imagination, Cognition and Personality, 9*, 185–211.

Schatzmann, J., Thomson, B., Weilhammer, K., Ye, H., & Young, S. (2007). Agenda-based user simulation for bootstrapping a POMDP dialogue system. In *Proceedings of the North American Chapter of the Association for Computational Linguistics on Human Language Technologies* (pp. 149-152).

Schuller, B., Batliner, A., Steidl, S., & Seppi, D. (2011). Recognising realistic emotions and affect in speech: State of the art and lessons learnt from the first challenge. *Speech Communication, 53*, 1062–1087. doi:10.1016/j.specom.2011.01.011

Schultz, T., & Kirchhoff, K. (2006). *Multilingual speech processing*. Amsterdam, The Netherlands: Elsevier.

Sebe, N., Sun, Y., Bakker, E., Lew, M. S., Cohen, I., & Huang, T. S. (2004). Towards authentic emotion recognition. In *Proceedings of the IEEE Conference on Systems, Man and Cybernetics* (pp. 623-628).

Seneff, S. (1989). TINA: A probabilistic syntactic parser for speech understanding systems. In *Proceedings of ACL Workshop on Speech and Natural Language* (pp. 168-178).

Seneff, S., Adler, M., Glass, J., Sherry, B., Hazen, T., Wang, C., & Wu, T. (2007). Exploiting context information in spoken dialogue interaction with mobile devices. In *Proceedings of the International Workshop on Improved Mobile User Experience* (pp. 1-11).

Seneff, S., Hurley, E., Lau, R., Pao, C., Schmid, P., & Zue, V. (1998). Galaxy-II: A reference architecture for conversational system development. In *Proceedings of the International Conference on Spoken Language Processing* (pp. 931-934).

Seron, F., Baldassarri, S., & Cerezo, E. (2006). MaxinePPT: Using 3D virtual characters for natural interaction. In *Proceedings of the 2nd International Workshop on Ubiquitous Computing and Ambient Intelligence* (pp. 241-250).

Shin-ichi, K., Shimodaira, H., Nitta, T., Nishimoto, T., Nakamura, S., & Itou, K. …Sagayama, S. (2003). Galatea: Open-source software for developing anthropomorphic spoken dialog agents. In H. Prendinger & M. Ishizuka (Eds.), *Life-like characters: Tools, affective functions, and applications* (pp. 187-212). Berlin, Germany: Springer-Verlag.

Stent, A., Dowding, J., Gawron, J. M., Bratt, E., & Moore, R. (1999). The CommandTalk spoken dialogue system. In *Proceedings of the Association for Computational Linguistics* (pp. 183-190).

Stern, A. (2003). Creating emotional relationships with virtual characters. In Trappl, R., Petta, P., & Payr, S. (Eds.), *Emotions in humans and artifacts* (pp. 333–362). Cambridge, MA: MIT Press.

Stolcke, A., Coccaro, N., Bates, R., Taylor, P., Ess-Dykema, C. V., & Ries, K. (2000). Dialogue act modelling for automatic tagging and recognition of conversational speech. *Computational Linguistics, 26*(3), 339–373. doi:10.1162/089120100561737

Strauss, P., & Minker, W. (2010). *Proactive spoken dialogue interaction in multi-party environments*. New York, NY: Springer. doi:10.1007/978-1-4419-5992-8

TRINDIConsortium. (2001). *Task Oriented Instructional Dialogue Book Draft*. Retrieved from http://www.ling.gu.se/projekt/trindi/book.ps

Truong, H. L., & Dustdar, S. (2009). A survey on context-aware web service systems. *International Journal of Web Information Systems, 5*(1), 5–31. doi:10.1108/17440080910947295

Truong, H. L., Dustdar, S., Baggio, D., Corlosquet, S., Dorn, C., Giuliani, G., & Gombotz, R. (2008). inContext: A pervasive and collaborative working environment for emerging team forms. In *Proceedings of the International Symposium on Applications and the Internet* (pp. 118-125).

Van de Burgt, S. P., Andernach, T., Kloosterman, H., Bos, R., & Nijholt, A. (1996). Building dialogue systems that sell. In *Proceedings of the NLP and Industrial Applications Conference* (pp. 41-46).

Ververidis, D., & Kotropoulos, C. (2006). Emotional speech recognition: resources, features and methods. *Speech Communication, 48*, 1162–1181. doi:10.1016/j.specom.2006.04.003

Wahlster, W. (2001). SmartKom: Multimodal dialogues with mobile Web users. In *Proceedings of the International Cyber Assist Symposium* (pp. 33-40).

Wahlster, W. (2003) Towards symmetric multimodality: Fusion and fission of speech, gesture, and facial expression. In *Proceedings of the 26th German Conference on Artificial Intelligence* (pp. 1-18).

Wahlster, W. (Ed.). (2006). *SmartKom: Foundations of multimodal dialogue systems*. New York, NY: Springer. doi:10.1007/3-540-36678-4

Walker, W., Lamere, P., & Kwok, P. (2002). *FreeTTS: A performance case study*. Santa Clara, CA: Sun Microsystems.

Walsh, P., & Meade, J. (2003). Speech enabled e-learning for adult literacy tutoring. In *Proceedings of the International Conference on Advanced Learning Technologies* (pp. 17-21).

Ward, W., & Issar, S. (1994). Recent improvements in the CMU spoken language understanding system. In *Proceedings of the ACL Workshop on Human Language Technology* (pp. 213-216).

Wei, X., & Rudnicky, A. (2000). Task-based dialogue management using an agenda. In *Proceedings of the ANLP/NAACL Workshop on Conversational Systems* (pp. 42-47).

Wilks, Y. (2006). *Artificial companions as a new kind of interface to the future internet* (Tech. Rep. No. 13). Oxford, UK: Oxford Internet Institute.

Williams, J., & Young, S. (2007). Partially observable Markov decision processes for spoken dialog systems. *Computer Speech & Language, 21*(2), 393–422. doi:10.1016/j.csl.2006.06.008

Xiao, H., Reid, D., Marriott, A., & Gulland, E. K. (2005). An adaptive personality model for ECAs. In J. Tao, T. Tan, & R. W. Picard (Eds.), *Proceedings of the First International Conference on Affective Computing and Intelligent Interaction* (LNCS 3784, pp. 637-645).

Young, S., Kershaw, D., Odell, J., Ollason, D., Valtchev, V., & Woodland, P. (2000). *The HTK book*. Redmond, WA: Microsoft Corporation.

Zhu, Z., & He, K. (2008). A novel approach of emotion recognition based on selective ensemble. In *Proceedings of the 3rd International Conference on Intelligent Systems and Knowledge Engineering* (pp. 695-698).

Zue, V., Seneff, S., Glass, J., Polifroni, J., Pao, C., Hazen, T., & Hetherington, L. (2000). JUPITER: A telephone-based conversational interface for weather information. *IEEE Transactions on Speech and Audio Processing, 8*(1), 85–96. doi:10.1109/89.817460

ADDITIONAL READING

Bernsen, N. O., & Dybkjaer, L. (2010). *Multimodal usability*. New York, NY: Springer.

Bezold, M., & Minker, W. (2011). *Adaptive multimodal interactive systems*. New York, NY: Springer. doi:10.1007/978-1-4419-9710-4

Grifoni, P. (Ed.). (2009). *Multimodal human-computer interaction and pervasive services*. Hershey, PA: IGI Global. doi:10.4018/978-1-60566-386-9

Jokinen, K. (2009). *Constructive dialogue modelling: speech interaction and rational agents*. New York, NY: John Wiley & Sons.

Kurkovsky, S. (Ed.). (2009). *Multimodality in mobile computing and mobile devices: methods for adaptable usability*. Hershey, PA: IGI Global. doi:10.4018/978-1-60566-978-6

Macías, J. A., Granollers, A., & Latorre, P. M. (Eds.). (2009). *New trends on human-computer interaction*. New York, NY: Springer. doi:10.1007/978-1-84882-352-5

Maragos, P., Potamianos, A., & Graos, P. (Eds.). (2010). *Multimodal processing and interaction: Audio, video, text*. New York, NY: Springer.

Tzovaras, D. (Ed.). (2010). *Multimodal user interfaces: from signals to interaction*. New York, NY: Springer.

KEY TERMS AND DEFINITIONS

Affective Computing: Interdisciplinary field of study concerned with developing computational systems which are able to understand, recognize, interpret, synthesize, predict and/or respond to human emotions.

Automatic Speech Recognition (ASR): Technique to determine the word sequence in a speech signal. To do this, this technology first detects basic units in the signal, e.g., phonemes, which are then combined to determine words.

Context Information: Any information that can be used to characterize the situation of an entity relevant to the interaction between a user and an application, including the user and the application themselves (Dey & Abowd, 2000).

Dialogue Management (DM): Iimplementation of the "intelligent" behaviour of the conversational system. It receives some sort of internal representation obtained from the user input and decides the next action the system must carry out.

Fission of Multimodal Information: Opposite to the *fusion* operation, chooses the output to be produced through each output modality and coordinates the output across the modalities in order to generate a system response appropriately for the user.

Fusion of Multimodal Information: Operation that combines the information chunks provided by the diverse input modules of the conversational agent in order to obtain a better understanding of the intention of the user.

Natural Language Generation (NLG): Creation of messages in text mode, grammatical and semantically correct, which will be either displayed on screen or converted into speech by means of text-to-speech synthesis.

Second Life: A three dimensional virtual world developed by Linden Lab in 2003 and accessible via the Internet.

Speech Synthesis: Artificial generation of human-like speech. A particular kind of speech synthesis technique is called Text-To-Speech synthesis (TTS), the goal of which is to transform into speech of any input sentence in text format.

Spoken Language Understanding (SLU): Technique to obtain the semantic content of the sequence of words provided by the ASR module. It must face a variety of phenomena, for example, ellipsis, anaphora and ungrammatical structures typical of spontaneous speech.

Virtual World/Environment: Synthetic environment which resembles real world or can be perceived as a real world by their users.

VoiceXML: Standard XML-based language to access web applications by means of speech.

Wizard of Oz (WOz): Technique that uses a human called *Wizard* to play the role of the computer in a human-computer interaction. The users are made to believe that they interact with a computer but actually they interact with the Wizard.

XHTML+Voice (X+V): XML-based language that combines traditional web access using XHTML and speech-based access to web pages using VoiceXML.

Chapter 14
A Survey of Mobile Vision Recognition Applications

Andrew Molineux
Lancaster University, UK

Keith Cheverst
Lancaster University, UK

ABSTRACT

In recent years, vision recognition applications have made the transition from desktop computers to mobile phones. This has allowed a new range of mobile interactions and applications to be realised. However, this shift has unearthed new issues in mobile hardware, interactions and usability. As such the authors present a survey into mobile vision recognition, outlining a number of academic and commercial applications, analysing what tasks they are able to perform and how they achieve them. The authors conclude with a discussion on the issues and trends found in the survey.

INTRODUCTION

Mobile phones are becoming an ever more ubiquitous resource in modern society. This, paired with the increasing range of mobile resources (e.g., GPS, digital cameras, etc.) has allowed for different application domains to evolve, one of which is mobile vision recognition. In this chapter we survey a number of academic and commercial applications that use mobile vision recognition, analysing what tasks they perform, how they achieve them, and compare them according to five criteria which are: *system architecture, target range, restricted domain, interaction style*

and *modification required to the environment*. We focus largely on mobile phone-based vision recognition applications although an early PDA and tablet PC based system are also described as they represent key work in this field.

Vision recognition uses statistical methods to disentangle image data, using models constructed with the aid of geometry, physics and learning theory (Forsyth & Ponce, 2002).It also has the ability to extend beyond the visible spectrum of humans, and may include other forms of vision such as infrared (Cao & Balakrishnan, 2006), heat, x-ray and radar. Some examples of vision recognition applications include object recognition,

DOI: 10.4018/978-1-4666-0954-9.ch014

motion detection, optical character recognition (OCR) and barcode scanning. Vision recognition is also often used within augmented reality applications. One example of an augmented reality interaction style that we will be exploring in our survey is the magic lens metaphor. First envisaged in 1993 (Bier, Stone, Pier, Buxton, & DeRose, 1993) the magic lens metaphor was designed to work using small lenses placed over objects. The concept used these lenses to reveal hidden information, enhance data of interest or suppress distracting information. This metaphor was later realised on camera phones (Schöning, Krüger, & Müller, 2006), where the screen and camera acted as a magic lens by augmenting content beneath the phone that was visible to the phone's camera.

Historically, vision recognition applications were most commonly found on desktop computers due to their high processing overhead. This limited the domain in which applications of this nature could be used to a desktop environment, with some impractical exceptions (Höllerer & Feiner, 2004). However, more recently vision recognition applications have made the transition onto mobile phones, which is the focus of this chapter. This change can mostly be attributed to increased processor speeds, and improved mobile resources. One significant development is the introduction of cameras to mobile phones. It is estimated that there are currently 4.6 billion mobile phones in use worldwide, and of those more than one billion are equipped with cameras ("Camera-phones dotty but dashing," 2010). The first commercial camera phone, the Sharp J-SH04, was released in 2000 (Sharp, 2010) and contained a 110,000-pixel CMOS sensor. Since then, major strides have been made in the field of camera phones including: xenon/LED flashes, front facing cameras and a vast improvement in image quality such as the Nokia N8 (Nokia, 2010) which has a 12 megapixel camera with HD video recording. However, mobile phone hardware is far from ideally setup for vision recognition. At the time of writing (2011) there is still a lack of mobile devices with hardware support for floating point mathematics, which greatly hinders the performance of vision recognition algorithms. Recent trends in handset hardware have shown improvement in this area (Yoskowitz, 2010).

Vision recognition allows applications to build a picture of the visual setting surrounding them. When an application/device can read information about the surrounding environment and act upon this information, it is often said that it is context-aware. In a standard usecase, a mobile phone could be set up to be contextually aware of a number of environmental variables including location, light levels, sound levels and even the phones poise/momentum. Through placing a normal camera phone within a room, an application has the potential to acquire a range of visual contextual elements such as who is in the room (face recognition), what items are in the room (object recognition) or even the position of the device within the room (using stereo vision techniques). For example the Nexus S (Google, 2011a) has an ambient light sensor that allows the screen's backlight to automatically adapt to varying lighting conditions.

In the remainder of this chapter we present a number of key mobile vision recognition applications. These are analysed and compared according to a number of criteria (described in the analysis section). The chapter concludes with a discussion on the current issues and trends prevalent in the field of mobile vision recognition.

REPRESENTATIVE SURVEY OF MOBILE VISION RECOGNITION APPLICATIONS

The aim of this survey is to present a subset of academic and commercial case studies which represent a wide range of application domains, ranging from augmented reality (Wagner & Schmalstieg, 2003) to data organisation for the homeless (Gebrekristos, Aljadaan, & Bihani,

2008). In the following section we outline our15 selectedcase studies, spanning the last decade, in chronological order.

C1: First Steps towards Handheld Augmented Reality (Signpost)

Wagner and Schmalstieg (2003) performed early work in augmented reality with mobile devices. They defined fiveprocesses involved in their augmented reality task: capturing video, tracking markers, application processing, rendering and display. The main focus was to investigate the effects of offloading the tasks to a server, and the impact this has on the running system. They claim to be the first to have developed a working, stand-alone mobile 3D augmented reality application with off-the-shelf hardware. The test application (*Signpost*) consisted of a PDA which read visual markers within an office environment. When the user held the phone up and peered through the display,they were presented with either a map of the area or visual directions (e.g., a 3D arrow) augmented over the camera output.

C2: PhoneGuide: Museum Guidance Supported by On-Device Object Recognition on Mobile Phones (PhoneGuide)

Föckler, Zeidler, Brombach, Bruns, and Bimber (2005)developed a camera phone-based museum guide called *PhoneGuide*. On taking a picture of an exhibit, the *PhoneGuide*applicationperformed image recognition to determine the exhibit in the scene, and once detected itprovided information on said item. A custom object recognition algorithm was developed for this purpose, such that feature detection was completed using image structure, and colour histograms and recognition were performed using an artificial neural network. The average recognition time was around one second for a database of ~50 objects (using multiple images from different perspectives) and they found an average success rate of 90%. However, with varying lighting conditions, the recognition rate dropped. This also was true if the data set was trained on one phone and used on another style of phone due to the varying colour levels in the cameras.

C3: Sweep and Point and Shoot: Phonecam-Based Interactions for Large Public Displays (Sweep Point-Shoot)

Rohs, Sheridan, and Ballagas (2004) and Ballagas, Rohs, and Sheridan (2005) developed two interaction techniques that weredesigned to enable users to interact with large public displays usinga camera phone. The first of these, termed *Sweep*allowed the camera phone to act as an optical mouse by using optical flow image processing to detect movement. The second, *Point and shoot*allowed usersto select content by aligning it within the camera's viewfinder window. Once the item was within the viewfinder, it could be selected by clicking a button on the phone, which triggered the large display to briefly flash a grid of visual codes. These codeswere used to enable the phone to calculate the location of the viewfinder on the large screen and thus the object they have selected.

C4: Conceptual Framework Camera Phone-Based Interaction Techniques (Camera Phone Interactions)

Rohs and Zweifel (2005) devised a number of camera phone interactions that used 2D markers. Rather than allowing the marker to serveonly as a visual code, they exploited the fact that the phone's orientation could also be derived from monitoring the 2D barcode. For example, if a user were to arrive at a bus station and align their camera phone's viewfinder at the 2D marker next to the sign for the bus they are interested in, they could view timetable information augmented over the camera's video feed. Further, rotating the phone clockwise/anticlockwise enabled the user to scroll through the bus times. The gestures they proposed included rotation, tilting, changing the distance and entering values on the keypad.

C5: Interactive Museum Guide: Fast and Robust Recognition of Museum Objects (Interactive Museum)

Bay, Fasel, and Van Gool (2006) developed an application with functionality akin to that described in *PhoneGuide*. Their main focus was to evaluate SURF (Speeded Up Robust Features) (Bay, Ess, Tuytelaars, & Van Gool, 2006) and SIFT (Scale Invariant Feature Transformation)(Lowe, 1999) when implemented on mobile devices. Similar to *PhoneGuide,* their test involved recognising museum exhibits from different perspectives angles and lighting conditions. They found that SURF outperformed SIFT in both detection time and success rate in the detection of 20 museum artefacts.

C6: Electronic Clipping System with Invisible Barcodes (Invisible Barcodes)

Kamijo, Kamijo, and Sakamoto (2006) explored how visual markers (QR codes) could be embedded into printed medium with no visual impact on the reader. By using ultraviolet ink and specially adapted camera phones, they were able to hide fully functional QR codes within printed text. Their motivation was to enable users to query physical items with a low processing overhead, high recognition rate and little visual impact on the user. Recognising that lighting is a factor when using ultraviolet, they performed a number of tests in various lighting conditions and found that between 300 lx and 1000 lx (the recommended ISO standard for office lighting) their application worked sufficiently.

C7: Camera Phone-Based Motion Sensing: Interaction Techniques, Applications and Performance Study (TinyMotion)

Wang and Canny (2006) explored markerless device motion detection using computer vision techniques on camera phone video feeds. They investigated a number of motion-based interactions including text entry via handwriting capture, gaming controls and target acquisition (Wang, Zhai, & Canny, 2006). As *TinyMotion* didn't use markers, the interactions could be performed in many different environments and against a range of backdrops. Their testing showed it was over 95% effective in a range of lighting conditions (outdoor direct sunlight, outdoor shade, indoor ambient light, indoor fluorescent lamp).

C8: Wayfinding for Individuals with Cognitive Impairments (Wayfinding: Cognitive Impairments)

This application exploited the visual presence of QR codes by using them as visual cues in a wayfinding task with cognitively impaired users (Chang, Tsai, Chang, & Wang, 2007; Chang, Tsai, & Wang, 2008). Certain mental disorders such as Alzheimer's cause a number of unique challenges that affect a user's ability to perform wayfinding tasks. Their system investigated how QR codes positioned at key waypoints could provide turn-by-turn directions to the users via their camera phone. When the user encountered a QR code, they could take a picture of it for navigational information. The phone would then upload the decoded information to a central server, after which pictures and text instructions of the user's next steps would be downloaded onto the phone, providing the user with detailed directions to their next waypoint or end destination.

C9: Creating and Sharing Multi-media Packages Using Large Situated Public Displays and Mobile Phones (Snap 'n Grab)

Maunder, Marsden, and Harper (2007, 2008) investigated ways in which camera phones can access content on situated displays using vision recognition and wireless communication (Bluetooth). They focused heavily on a usercentric design, adopting a user evaluation-based design cycle, beginning with paper prototypes (Maunder, 2010). The proposed interaction coined *"Snap 'n Grab"* envisaged users taking pictures of content on public displays with camera phones. This was then sent to a server that performed object recognition. Finally, the server returned relevant content back to the user's phone based on the object recognition results. This allowed image recognition interactions to be performed on Bluetooth enabled mobile phones without having to install any additional software on the user's phone.

C10: Map Navigation With Mobile Devices (Mobile Map Navigation)

Rohs, Schöning, Raubal, Essl, and Krüger (2007) investigated different methods in which users could explore and navigate digital maps. Their approach investigated three styles: joystick, dynamic peephole without visual context, and magic lens with visual context. The joystick style allowed the user to pan up, down, left and right on the digital map using the phone's built in joystick. Dynamic peephole worked in a similar manner to the joystick style, but instead of the user pressing buttons to traverse the map, they physically moved the phone over a digital marker grid. Motion estimation was then calculated by monitoring the markers captured by the phone's camera and the direction they moved in. Lastly, the magic lens approach was similar to dynamic peephole,

but instead of the motion being performed over a non-contextual surface (grid of markers), a map was used. Small markers were embedded into the image to aid the positioning phase.

C11: QR Codes for the Chronically Homeless (QR for Homeless)

Gebrekristos et al. (2008) performed a number of observations on homeless shelters in Detroit, America. They found that many homeless people, despite lacking many basic necessities, were still able to afford and maintain mobile phones. They also observed the lack of structure in the day to day living of the average homeless person. Based on their observations they created an application that involved encoding information about the homeless person onto QR codes, enabling the homeless community to use QR codes to manage their own information. Many homeless shelters required some registration information, which could be stored on the QR code providing a cost effective system for fast data transfers. Printed QR codes were seen as a preferable solution to storing the information on the user's phone, as the frequency in which the phones were charged implied that a mobile only solution couldn't provide a sufficiently reliable solution.

C12: Map Torchlight: A Mobile Augmented Reality Camera Projector Unit (Map Torchlight)

Schöning, Rohs, Kratz, Löchtefeld, and Kruger (2009) investigated ways in which physical maps could be augmented using vision recognition and projector phones. When the projected area was overlaid onto part of the map, the projector augmented the map by adding additional content. In the case of *Map Torchlight*, the projector highlighted places of interest. Vision recognition techniques were used to calculate the position of the projected area using small markers encoded into the map similar to the markers used in *Mobile Map Navigation*.

C13: Supporting Hand Gesture Manipulation of Projected Content with Mobile Phones (Gesture Manipulation)

Baldauf and Fröhlich (2009) focused on camera equipped wearable devices with projection capabilities. This work investigated how hand gestures could used to control projected content from a small wearable device. Coloured markers were attached to the wearer's fingers to facilitate the gesture detection stage. They implemented three gestures: panning, zooming and rotating, all of which track two markers (although the application could track more). One key benefit of such an interaction style was that it lowered potential context switches between the physical device and the projected content (Greaves & Rukzio, 2008).

C14: Server-Side Object Recognition and Client-Side Object Tracking for Mobile Augmented Reality (Server-Side Object Recognition)

Gammeter et al. (2010)developed an application that combined object recognition and augmented reality, by allowing visual feedback from the object recognition results to be overlaid onto the video feed. This is often referred to as the looking glass metaphor. This augmented reality interaction was similar to the commercial application Layar (http://www.layar.com). However, Layar used the phone's compass gyroscope and GPS, rather than vision recognition, to calculate the augmented reality overlay.

C15: Image Recognition Techniques for use in a Mobile Public Interactive Display (Snap 'n Grab Lite)

Smith and Marsden (2010) modified the *Snap 'n Grab* system by incorporating barcodes that resembled picture frames to aid the object recognition task. The addition of barcodes lowered the complexity of the object recognition task on the server, thereby allowing the code to be ported to a mobile phone. This hardware change from the initial server hardware (Mac Mini) to a mobile device (HTC touch pro mobile phone) lowered the cost of the *Snap 'n Grab* system hardware. Their user study involved a number of participants taking pictures of the media content with their own camera phones, which were then sent to the server for processing. The study concluded that *Snap 'n Grab Lite* achieved an 87% success rate of detecting the images and they attributed a large proportion of the failures to poorly photographed images i.e., where some of the barcode was occluded.

COMPARISON/ANALYSIS

Having outlined the 15 selected applications, we can now compare and analyse them according to our five comparison criteria, which are system architecture, target range, restricted domain, interaction style and modification of environment. System architecture refers to the distributed nature of the application, for example, whether or not the application uses client-server architecture. Target range refers to the set of objects/environments that the application is designed to work in. For example, in the case of *PhoneGuide* the application is designed to recognise 50 exhibits within a single museum. Restricted Domain outlines whether or not the application has restrictions imposed upon it, which therefore restricts the domain in which it can function. Interaction style compares the different user interaction styles that are supported by the applications. Finally, Modification of environment refers to the extent to which the physical environment needs to be modified in order for the application to work. For example, an application that uses QR codes would be considered to have a high level of modification due to the fact that a significant visual modification to the environment is required. These terms are discussed in greater detail in the remainder of this section. Table 1 gives a comparison for all surveyed mobile vision recognition applications.

System Architecture

The functionality and scalability of mobile vision recognition applications are linked to the system architecture. All of the applications surveyed adopt one of two styles namely *standalone,* where the entire application is contained within the mobile

device and *client-server*, where some aspect of the application relies on a server. The latter approach can be used to offload processing from the mobile device, or to exploit resources on the server such as object databases for object recognition. However, rather than this being a dichotomy, we consider this concept as a scale of varying levels of dependence on the server. For example, *Wayfinding: Cognitive Impairments* performs the entire image processing locally and only interacts with the server to gain media content, whereas *Server-Side Object Recognition* uploads the entire image to the server to perform the entire object recognition task.

Applications that adopt a standalone architecture tend to have a narrow target range, such as barcode readers or object recognition applications with a limited object data set. *PhoneGuide, Interactive Museum, QR for Homeless, TinyMotion, Invisible Barcode, Map Torchlight* and *Mobile Map Navigation* all adopt a standalone approach. For image recognition applications such as *Phone Guide* and *Interactive Museum,* all application

Table 1. Comparison table for all surveyed mobile vision recognition applications (AR-Augmented Reality)

	Application	System Architecture	Target Range	Restricted Domain	Interaction Style	Modification Of Environment
C1	Signpost	Client-Server	Narrow	No	AR	Perceptible
C2	Phone Guide	Standalone	Narrow	No	Point-Shoot	No Modification
C3	Sweep Point-Shoot	Client-Server	Narrow	Yes	Point-Shoot, Motion	Perceptible
C4	Camera Phone Interactions	Standalone	Narrow	Yes	Motion, AR	Perceptible
C5	Interactive Museum	Standalone	Narrow	No	Point-Shoot	No Modification
C6	Invisible barcodes	Standalone	Wide	Yes	Point-Shoot	Imperceptible
C7	TinyMotion	Standalone	Wide	No	Motion	No Modification
C8	Wayfinding: Cognitive impairments	Client-Server	Narrow	Yes	Point-Shoot	Perceptible
C9	Snap 'n Grab	Client-Server	Narrow	Yes	Point-Shoot	Imperceptible
C10	Mobile Map Navigation	Standalone	Narrow	Yes	AR	Imperceptible
C11	QR for Homeless	Standalone	Narrow	Yes	Point-Shoot	Perceptible
C12	Map Torchlight	Standalone	Narrow	Yes	AR	Imperceptible
C13	Gesture Manipulation	Standalone	Wide	Yes	Hand Gestures	Perceptible
C14	Server-Side Object Recognition	Client-Server	Wide	No	AR	No Modification
C15	Snap 'n Grab Lite	Client-Server	Narrow	Yes	Point-Shoot	Perceptible

data is stored on the mobile device. This allows such an application to operate in domains where data connectivity may be intermittent (such as a museum where certain exhibits areas may not have wireless data connectivity), allowing for a much more reliable application. This has an impact on the possible number of objects the system can recognise and the time in which it can perform the recognition task, as with limited storage and processing capabilities some compromises have to be made, and often with standalone architectures, compromises are made in the target range.

Of the applications that fit into the client-server category, the type of data that is passed between client and server differs quite significantly. For example, *Server-Side Object Recognition, Snap 'n Grab* and *Snap 'n Grab Lite* all upload the entire image (or video frame) to the server for object recognition, thus allowing the complex tasks of feature detection and feature matching to be offloaded from the mobile device. In the case of *Server-Side Object Recognition*, this is done for two main reasons. Firstly, the client side object tracking is performed on the device, therefore by offloading the task of object recognition, the processing overhead on the device is lowered. Secondly, the application's object database contains over 300,000 objects and will therefore take up considerable storage space. The second style of client-server interaction can be seen in *Wayfinding: Cognitive Impairments*. This application performs the object detection on the mobile device, and queries the server for additional information. *Signpost* presents an informative insight into client-server architectures with early augmented reality applications. They experiment with offloading tracking, application code and rendering. One consideration was that they were unable to offload the entire task to the server due to network constraints, as there was not sufficient bandwidth to upload the video stream and download the edited video stream with any real time interactivity.

Target Range

The target range can be considered as the set of objects/targets or the constraints that the application is designed to work with. For example, *PhoneGuide* is designed to work within the domain of a single museum recognising ~50 exhibits, hence its target range would be the 50 objects. In our surveyed applications we have found two types of target range: narrow and wide. An application with a narrow target range may only be able to recognise a limited number of objects. For example *PhoneGuide* is sat to have a narrow target range due to the fact it can only perform object recognition tasks on a small set of objects. A wide target ranged application has a much broader scope in which it can successfully function. For example, *Server-Side Object Recognition* has a wide target range as it has the ability to recognize over 300,000 objects such as landmarks, product logos and DVD covers.

PhoneGuide and *Interactive Museum* have a narrow target range as both are designed to recognise a small set of objects/exhibits within a museum. These applications will not be able to fully function (return correct image recognition results) on any object not included in the exhibit. *Server-Side Object Recognition, Invisible Barcodes* and *TinyMotion* have wide target ranges. *TinyMotion* uses markerless feature tracking to calculate motion, meaning that the interaction can be performed over a multitude of surfaces. Given the nature of the vision recognition problem, clearly there is no perfect object recognition application that has an unlimited target range. Google Goggles for example has a very large image database and works well in a number of object categories such as landmarks, product logos, OCR and barcodes, but will not perform well on objects such as animals, furniture and faces (Google, 2011b).

Restricted Domain

An application is said to have a restricted domain if the developers have enforced restrictions in which the application can function. For example, with respect to *Invisible Barcodes*, the interactions will only be possible on print that has a marker upon it, which must have been placed within the environment prior to the interaction occurring. *Invisible Barcodes* would be classed as having a restricted domain as it can only function on print with the adapted markers on.

Applications that use physical markers such as QR codes fall under the category of restricted domain. This is because the vision recognition task can only be performed in the presence of a visual marker, thus limiting the applications scope to a restricted domain. *Signpost, Sweep Point-Shoot, Camera Phone Interactions, Invisible Barcodes, Wayfinding: Cognitive Impairments, Snap 'n Grab Lite, Mobile Map Navigation, QR for Homeless, Map Torchlight and Gesture Manipulation* all have predefined target ranges and use some form of marker.

Interaction

Mobile applications that use vision recognition differ a great deal from standard mobile applications in terms of interface and interaction, as vision recognition applications often involve users utilizing a viewfinder metaphor on the phone. The user is thus required to align content in the viewfinder window.

Applications in the category of augmented reality base their interaction on an augmented reality style such as the magic lens metaphor and the looking glass metaphor. In our survey, *Map Torchlight* and *Mobile Map Navigation* all adopt the magic lens metaphor. One key requirement of this metaphor is to have knowledge of the content below the magic lens device, which is realised through vision recognition. *Server-Side Object Recognition* and *Signpost* adopt the look-ing glass metaphor. This differs from the magic lens metaphor in that the device is peered into and used to survey bigger areas, whereas magic lens interactions tend to involve the device being placed directly over real world artefacts e.g., maps.

Arguably, the most established interaction for camera phone users is the point and shoot interaction. Similar to that of a normal camera interaction, the user aligns the object in the viewfinder and presses a button; a vision recognition process is then performed on this image and once complete, results are returned to the user. *PhoneGuide, Interactive Museum, Wayfinding: Cognitive Impairments, Snap 'n Grab, Snap 'n Grab Lite, Sweep Point-Shoot Camera Phone Interactions* and *QR for Homeless* all adopt this interaction style.

Sweep, Point-Shoot, Mobile Map Navigation, Gesture Manipulation, TinyMotion and *Camera Phone Interactions* all have interactions that are based on calculating the phone's movement. *Sweep, Point-Shoot and TinyMotion* use markerless tracking. This allows the interaction to be performed on most surfaces. Markerless motion sensing in mobile computing has gained commercial appeal in recent years. One of the first examples of such was Mozzies (Siemans, 2004), and more recently, Nintendo's 3DS console was shipped with an Augmented Reality game based on markerless tracking called Face Raiders (Nintendo, 2011). *Camera Phone Interaction* uses physical markers (Visual Codes) to calculate the movement of the phone, although with this system multiple interactions are possible. Each marker allows different styles of interaction and aids the camera phone in the detection of what interaction should be performed.

Augmented reality applications generally have to provide a high level of interactivity when compared to a point and shoot interaction style. This is due to the real-time nature of augmented reality applications. For example, with the magic lens metaphor, if the visual output was delayed when compared to the user's movement, the user may become confused as the resulting output would not fit their mental model of the interaction. Early augmented reality applications tended to have a relatively low refresh rate. *Signpost* for example was able to achieve approximately 5 frames per second (fps). More recent examples such as *Server-Side Object Recognition* (2010) were able to achieve 12 fps using client side object tracking and server side object recognition. Frame rates are likely to improve over time as the processing capabilities of mobile phones increases. Point and shoot style interactions tend not to have such a strict time constraint due to the interaction being less interactive, i.e., a query is submitted and the user waits for the results. However it is still important to deliver relevant content within a reasonable time scale. Client approaches such as *PhoneGuide and Interactive Museum* were able to achieve recognition speeds as low as 0.8 and 0.75 seconds respectively.

Modification of Environment

Vision recognition applications rely on recognising physical objects based on visual information, and using this information within the application. For example, if you were to take a picture of a closed and open umbrella, from a visual perspective they look very different even though they are clearly the same object. Vision recognition applications use a range of techniques to gain information from the environment. These techniques can be considered to lie along a spectrum, such that at one end, applications will capture and recognise real world objects and features with no modification of the environment whereas at the other end, the environment is modified with visual markers and icons that are perceptible to the user. In between these two extremities lie imperceptible changes, which for example may take the form of specially adapted text so that OCR applications can read them with ease (such as in car registration plates) or small markers hidden within a map

image (*Map Torchlight*). Within the scope of this chapter to "modify the environment" is defined as changing the physical environment in some form i.e., place markers, change objects poise/shape or inject objects into the scene, in order to aid the recognition.

Phone guide, Interactive Museum, Server-Side Object Recognition, Snap 'n Grab and *Tiny Motion* are all examples of applications that require no modification of the environment. In all these cases, the application relies solely on real world objects for its tasks. *Phone guide, Interactive Museum, Server-Side Object Recognition* use object recognition in some form to visually query objects. *Server-Side Object Recognition, TinyMotion and Sweep Point-Shoot* use markerless tracking to detect motion using vision recognition.

Applications that require the physical environment to be modified can be split into two categories: imperceptible and perceptible. Imperceptible modifications are subtle changes that are either unnoticeable or invisible to the human eye. *Map Torchlight* and *Mobile Map Navigation* embed small dots within the map to allow the phone to easily calculate the area it is viewing, and accurately overlay information by using the dots as anchor points. Rohs, Schöning, Raubal, Essl, and Krüger (2007)commented, *"Participants didn't notice them. They can be replaced by gridlines commonly found on many city maps"*. This research showed how the addition of small markers could ease the processing overhead on the mobile device, while having little visual effect on the user. This was further supported by their user evaluation. *Invisible barcode*s hides the visual markers by using UV ink, which is out of the spectrum of human vision, thus allowing quite complex and high fidelity markers to be hidden within normal print with no visual modifications.

Applications that fit into the category of perceptible modifications use visual markers such as QR codes to aid vision recognition tasks. *QR for Homeless and Camera Phone Interactions* exploit the visual presence of the markers by using them as visual cues, informing the user that a potential interaction can take place at this spot. *Sweep Point-Shoot, Signpost* and *Snap 'n Grab Lite* don't exploit the visual presence from the user's perspective; rather they use the markers solely for their technical benefits. For example, *Sweep Point-Shoot* uses a grid of visual codes, which are flashed on public displays to determine a camera's viewfinder position. This grid has no aesthetic benefit, but is used to lower the complexity of the task. Table 2 gives a technical summary of the surveyed applications.

DISCUSSION

Trends in exploiting contextual information on mobile devices are likely to develop over coming years as mobile phones become ever more ubiquitous in modern society. This doesn't necessarily mean vision recognition on mobile devices will mature equally, due to the fact the number of sensors built into mobile devices is also growing, thereby lowering the need to perform vision recognition in a number of scenarios. One example of the range of sensors available in a mobile device at the time of writing is the Nexus S by Google (2011a), which has a camera, accelerometers,

Table 2. A technical summary of the surveyed applications (additional information regarding toolkits is available in our toolkit section)

	Application	Year	Hardware	Operating system	Software	Implementation Details
C1	Signpost	2003	iPAQ 5450	Pocket PC 2002	C++	Studierstube ARToolKit
C2	PhoneGuide	2005	Nokia 6600	S60	C++	Custom object recognition algorithm
C3	Sweep Point-Shoot	2005	Nokia 6600	S60	C++	Visual Codes
C4	Camera Phone Interactions	2005	Nokia 7650	S60	C++	Magic lens toolkit
C5	Interactive Museum	2006	Tablet PC (1.7 GHz)	Linux	-	SIFT, SURF
C6	Invisible barcodes	2006	W21 CAII	REX OS	BREW	QR codes
C7	TinyMotion	2006	Motorola V710	Proprietary	BREW (C++)	Custom Motion detection algorithm
C8	Wayfinding: Cognitive impairments	2007	Asus P525	Windows Mobile 5	-	QR codes, web browser based
C9	Snap 'n Grab	2007	(Server) Mac Mini	-	-	Bluetooth, SIFT
C10	Mobile Map Navigation	2007	Nokia N80	S60	C++	Magic lens toolkit
C11	QR for Homeless	2008	-	-	-	QR codes
C12	Map Torchlight	2009	Nokia N95 +Pico Projector	S60	C++	Magic lens toolkit
C13	Gesture Manipulation	2009	Nokia N95 +Pico Projector	S60	Java, C	Nokia CV, Java ME
C14	Client-Server Object Recognition	2010	Nexus One	Android	Android, C	Kooaba API, FAST edge detection
C15	Snap 'n Grab Lite	2010	(Server) HTC Touch Pro	Windows Mobile 6	C#	UPC, binary barcode with guide lines

GPS, digital compass, proximity sensor, light sensor and NFC reader.

The acceptance of vision recognition applications by the general public depends on a number of key factors, one of which is the management of their expectations. For example, from a user's perspective, narrow scoped vision recognition applications that use QR codes differ from applications that rely on traditional image recognition. Museum guides that only support a limited range of exhibits such as *PhoneGuide* may appear inaccurate or unreliable if a user was to unknowingly attempt to use the application out of its target range. Whereas with applications that exploit visual markers, the user would be aware of locations that they were able to use them as the marker would be present.

We believe that without ecologically valid user testing, true recognition rates can't be discovered in vision recognition applications, as the task of getting the user to accurately take a picture of the object in question is as important as the choice of object recognition algorithm. *PhoneGuide* and *Interactive Museum, Invisible Barcodes, Signpost* and *Server-Side Object Recognition* do not perform user testing, but provide statistics on recognition rate based on lab testing/field surveys. Consider *PhoneGuide,* in which the interaction involves the user framing the exhibit within the cameras viewfinder window. Even within this task there is a degree of ambiguity. Is the user meant to capture the exhibit's description plaque? Are they to capture the entire object? Or is capturing a portion of the object sufficient? We believe the user's understanding and subsequent performance of the object recognition task will significantly affect recognition rates. This is supported by the findings of a user study performed by *Snap 'n Grab Lite*, which observed that one of their biggest sources of error in their recognition task was due to users poorly framing images.

Large-scale adoption of certain technologies hinders vision recognition applications becoming more prevalent in the domestic market. Denso Wave first created QR codes in 1994, yet there are still many mobile operating systems which do not natively support these valuable vision tools e.g., core Android (after market applications are available). There are multitudes of 2D barcodes available, many of which have different niches that allow for different functionality. However, if 2D barcodes were to adopt a similar standardisation as 1D barcodes, such that one standard were to be adopted world-wide, and other variants were used for more niche activities (such as internal tracking on parcels), this would allow high perceptibility vision recognition applications to be used much more easily within the domestic market.

Although mobile phone hardware has seen vast technological improvements over the last decade, it still remains one of the key problem domains for mobile vision recognition applications. One hardware constraint mentioned by many of our surveyed applications (*Signpost, Server-Side Object Recognition, Camera Phone Interactions)* is the lack of floating point units (FPU) within mobile phone hardware platforms. Floating point arithmetic is often used within graphics and computer vision tasks. When no FPU is present, it can be either emulated at the cost of a high processing overhead, or algorithms have to be adapted to not include floating point arithmetic (Henrysson, Billinghurst, & Ollila, 2005; Rohs, Schöning, Krüger, & Hecht, 2007). However, floating support on mobile devices is improving. For example, a floating-point benchmark test was undertaken (Yoskowitz, 2010) to compare the HTC Hero (released June 2009) and the Google Nexus One (released January 2010). It showed that the Nexus One had a 450% increase in performance when compared to the Hero, achieving 37.5 MFLOPS (Millions of FLoating-point Operations Per Second) compared to 2MFLOPS. However, processing isn't the only hardware constraint affecting mobile vision recognition. For example, camera phone hardware often contains a range of tools that enable vision recognition applications to function e.g., camera, display and processor.

With small hardware changes, the range of possible mobile vision recognition applications can be increased. For example, if a phone containing two rear-facing cameras were to be developed, applications could then be developed that use stereovision to measure distances. This could aid future technologies such as projector phones in tasks such as calibration.

When considering applications that use augmented reality, they must perform a range of tasks which include: displaying the camera feed, performing vision processing to extract the appropriate information and rendering some form of graphical display that augments the input appropriately. Consider the magic lens metaphor. One issue that arises when developing such an interaction is when we consider how users would expect to interact with a similar real world object such as a magic lens or magnifying glass. If the content was not properly displayed or rendered this could cause frustration and confusion to the user, as the augmentation would not reflect the real world data correctly and not conform to their mental model of how the interaction should take place. Further, when developing for mobile devices one must also consider that the battery is a limited resource. Computationally expensive applications have an adverse effect on the battery life of the mobile device. This was noted by Wang et al. (2006), who recorded a considerable decrease in battery life when using vision recognition to monitor motion while playing an interactive game on a mobile device. The average battery life when playing was ~3hours 20min.

SUMMARY

In this chapter we have presented a survey of mobile vision recognition applications from a HCI perspective. Although the field of mobile vision recognition in its infancy, commercial applications that use vision recognition are beginning to emerge. Many unique interactions can be realised from vision recognition and such interactions can serve to enrich user experience on mobile devices. However, much research into interaction styles is still needed, as traditional mobile interaction methods may not be able to be applied to this new interaction paradigm. Visual markers such as QR codes can be used to lower the complexity of object recognition tasks, allowing complex and computationally intensive applications to be simplified and thus more conceivable on mobile phones.

ACKNOWLEDGMENT

This work is funded by the EPSRC funded EX-TRAMS project (grant ref: EP/H004289/1).

REFERENCES

Baldauf, M., & Fröhlich, P. (2009). Supporting hand gesture manipulation of projected content with mobile phones. In *Proceedings of the Workshop on Mobile Interaction with the Real World* (pp. 1-4).

Ballagas, R., Rohs, M., & Sheridan, J. (2005). Sweep and point and shoot: phonecam-based interactions for large public displays. In *Proceedings of the Extended Abstracts on Human Factors in Computing Systems* (pp. 1200-1203). New York, NY: ACM.

Bay, H., Ess, A., Tuytelaars, T., & Van Gool, L. (2006). Speeded up robust features (SURF). *Computer Vision and Vision Understanding, 110*(3), 404–417.

Bay, H., Fasel, B., & Van Gool, L. (2006). Interactive museum guide: Fast and robust recognition of museum objects. In *Proceedings of the First International Workshop on Mobile Vision*.

Bier, E., Stone, M., Pier, K., Buxton, W., & DeRose, T. (1993).Toolglass and magic lenses: the see-through interface. In *Proceedings of the 20th Annual Conference on Computer Graphics and Interactive Techniques* (pp. 73-80). New York, NY: ACM.

Camera-phones dotty but dashing. (2010). *The Economist.* Retrieved January 10, 2011, from http://www.economist.com/node/15865270

Cao, X., & Balakrishnan, R. (2006). Interacting with dynamically defined information spaces using a handheld projector and a pen. In *Proceedings of the 19th Annual ACM Symposium on User Interface Software and Technology* (p. 225). New York, NY: ACM.

Chang, Y.-J., Tsai, S.-K., Chang, Y., & Wang, T.-Y. (2007). A novel wayfinding system based on geo-coded QR codes for individuals with cognitive impairments. In *Proceedings of the 9th International ACM SIGACCESS Conference on Computers and Accessibility* (p. 231). New York, NY: ACM.

Chang, Y.-J., Tsai, S.-K., & Wang, T.-Y. (2008). A context aware handheld wayfinding system for individuals with cognitive impairments.Proceedings of the 10th international ACM SIGACCESS conference on Computers and accessibility - Assets '08, 27. New York, NY: ACM.

Föckler, P., Zeidler, T., Brombach, B., Bruns, E., & Bimber, O. (2005). PhoneGuide: museum guidance supported by on-device object recognition on mobile phones. In *Proceedings of the 4th International Conference on Mobile and Ubiquitous Multimedia* (pp. 3-10). New York, NY: ACM.

Forsyth, D. A., & Ponce, J. (2002). *Computer vision: A modern approach.* Upper Saddle River, NJ: Prentice Hall.

Gammeter, S., Gassmann, A., Bossard, L., Quack, T., & Van Gool, L. (2010). Server-side object recognition and client-side object tracking for mobile augmented reality. In *Proceedings of the IEEE Conference on Computer Vision and Pattern Recognition Workshops* (pp. 1-8). Washington, DC: IEEE Computer Society.

Gebrekristos, M., Aljadaan, A., & Bihani, K. (2008). QR-Codes for the chronically homeless. In *Proceedings of the Twenty-Sixth Annual CHI Conference Extended Abstracts on Human Factors in Computing Systems* (p. 3879). New York, NY: ACM.

Google. (2011a). *Nexus S.* Retrieved January 10, 2011, from http://www.google.com/nexus/

Google. (2011b). *Google goggles.* Retrieved January 10, 2011, from http://www.google.com/mobile/goggles/#text

Greaves, A., & Rukzio, E. (2008). Evaluation of picture browsing using a projector phone. In *Proceedings of the 10th International Conference on Human Computer Interaction with Mobile Devices and Services* (Vol. 5, p. 351). New York, NY: ACM.

Henrysson, A., Billinghurst, M., & Ollila, M. (2005). Face to face collaborative AR on mobile phones. In *Proceedings of the 4th IEEE/ACM International Symposium on Mixed and Augmented Reality* (pp. 80-89). Washington, DC: IEEE Computer Society.

Höllerer, T. H., & Feiner, S. K. (2004). Mobile augmented reality. In Karimi, H., & Hammad, A. (Eds.), *Telegeoinformatics: Location-based computing and services.* London, UK: Taylor and Francis Books.

Kamijo, K., Kamijo, N., & Sakamoto, M. (2006). Electronic clipping system with invisible barcodes. In *Proceedings of the 14th Annual ACM International Conference on Multimedia* (p. 753). New York, NY: ACM.

Lowe, D. (1999). Object recognition from local scale-invariant features. In *Proceedings of the International Conference on Computer Vision* (Vol. 2, pp. 1150-1157). Washington, DC: IEEE Computer Society.

Maunder, A. (2010). *Designing appropriate interactive systems for the developing world*. Cape Town, South Africa: University of Cape Town.

Maunder, A., Marsden, G., & Harper, R. (2007). Creating and sharing multi-media packages using large situated public displays and mobile phones. In *Proceedings of the 9th International Conference on Human Computer Interaction with Mobile Devices and Services* (pp. 222-225). New York, NY: ACM.

Maunder, A., Marsden, G., & Harper, R. (2008). SnapAndGrab: accessing and sharing contextual multi-media content using Bluetooth enabled camera phones and large situated displays. In *Proceedings of the CHI Extended Abstracts on Human Factors in Computing Systems* (pp. 2319-2324). New York, NY: ACM.

Nintendo. (2011). *Face Raiders*. Retrieved June 1, 2011, from http://www.nintendo.com/3ds/built-in-software#/5

Nokia. (2010). *Nokia N8*. Retrieved January 10, 2011, from http://events.nokia.com/nokian8/home.html

Rohs, M., Schöning, J., Krüger, A., & Hecht, B. (2007). Towards real-time markerless tracking of magic lenses on paper maps. In *Adjunct Proceedings of the 5th International Conference on Pervasive Computing, Late Breaking Results* (pp. 69-72).

Rohs, M., Schöning, J., Raubal, M., Essl, G., & Krüger, A. (2007). Map navigation with mobile devices: virtual versus physical movement with and without visual context. In *Proceedings of the 9th International Conference on Multimodal Interfaces* (pp. 146-153). New York, NY: ACM.

Rohs, M., Sheridan, J., & Ballagas, R. (2004). Direct manipulation techniques for large displays using camera phones. In *Proceedings of the 2nd International Symposium on Ubiquitous Computing Systems* (pp. 1-2).

Rohs, M., & Zweifel, P. (2005). A conceptual framework for camera phone-based interaction techniques. In H.-W. Gellersen, R. Want, & A. Schmidt (Eds.), *Proceedings of the Third International Conference on Pervasive Computing* (LNCS 3468, pp. 171-189).

Schöning, J., Krüger, A., & Müller, H. J. (2006). Interaction of mobile camera devices with physical maps. In *Adjunct Proceedings of the Fourth International Conference on Pervasive Computing* (pp. 121-124).

Schöning, J., Rohs, M., Kratz, S., Löchtefeld, M., & Kruger, A. (2009). Map torchlight: a mobile augmented reality camera projector unit. In *Proceedings of the 27th International Conference on Extended Abstracts on Human Factors in Computing Systems* (pp. 3841-3846). New York, NY: ACM.

Sharp. (2010). *Sharp chronology*. Retrieved January 10, 2011, from http://www.sharp-world.com/corporate/info/his/chronology/p14.html

Siemans. (2004). *Pictures of the future*. Retrieved January 10, 2011, from http://www.siemens.com/innovation/en/publikationen/publications_pof/pof_fall_2004/research_cooperation.htm

Smith, G., & Marsden, G. (2010). Image recognition techniques for use in a mobile public interactive display. In *Proceedings of the Annual Southern Africa Telecommunication Networks and Applications Conference* (pp. 345-355).

Wagner, D., & Schmalstieg, D. (2003). First steps towards handheld augmented reality. In *Proceedings of the Seventh IEEE International Symposium on Wearable Computers* (pp. 127-135). Washington, DC: IEEE Computer Society.

Wang, J., & Canny, J. (2006). TinyMotion: camera phone based interaction methods. In *Proceedings of the CHI Extended Abstracts on Human Factors in Computing Systems* (pp. 339-344). New York, NY: ACM.

Wang, J., Zhai, S., & Canny, J. (2006). Camera phone based motion sensing: interaction techniques, applications and performance study. In *Proceedings of the 19th Annual ACM Symposium on User Interface Software and Technology* (pp. 101-110). New York, NY: ACM.

Yoskowitz, A. (2010). *Nexus One with Android 2.2 had strong performance gains*. Retrieved June 1, 2011, from http://www.afterdawn.com/news/article.cfm/2010/05/12/nexus_one_with_android_2_2_has_strong_performance_gains

ADDITIONAL READING

Ballard, D. H., & Brown, C. M. (1982). *Computer vision*. Upper Saddle River, NJ: Prentice Hall.

Borntrager, C., Cheverst, K., Davies, N., Dix, A., Friday, A., & Seitz, J. (2003). Experiments with multi-modal interfaces in a context-aware city guide. In *Proceedings of the International Conference on Human-Computer Interaction with Mobile Devices and Services* (pp. 116-130).

Dix, A., Finlay, J., Abowd, G. D., & Beale, R. (2004). *Human-computer interaction* (3rd ed.). Upper Saddle River, NJ: Prentice Hall.

Kato, H., & Tan, K. T. (2007). Pervasive 2D barcodes for camera phone applications. *IEEE Pervasive Computing / IEEE Computer Society IEEE Communications Society, 6*(4), 76–85. doi:10.1109/MPRV.2007.80

Kato, H., & Tan, K. T. (2009). 2D barcodes for mobile phones. In *Proceedings of the 2nd International Conference on Mobile Technology, Applications and Systems* (p. 8).

Löchtefeld, M., Schöning, J., Rohs, M., & Kruger, A. (2009). LittleProjectedPlanet: An augmented reality game for camera projector phones. In *Proceedings of the Workshop on Mobile Interaction with the Real World, Bonn, Germany*.

Rekimoto, J., & Ayatsuka, Y. (2000). CyberCode: designing augmented reality environments with visual tags. In *Proceedings of the DARE Conference on Designing Augmented Reality Environments* (pp. 1-10).

Rodden, T., Cheverst, K., Davies, K., & Dix, A. (1998). Exploiting context in HCI design for mobile systems. In *Proceedings of the Workshop on Human Computer Interaction with Mobile Devices* (pp. 21-22).

Rohs, M. (2005). Real-world interaction with camera phones. In H. Murakami, H. Nakashima, H. Tokuda, & M. Yasumura (Eds.), *Proceedings of the Second International Symposium on Ubiquitous Computing Systems* (LNCS 3598, pp. 74-89).

Rohs, M., & Gfeller, B. (2004). Using camera-equipped mobile phones for interacting with real-world objects. *Advances in Pervasive Computing, 21*(3), 265–271.

Zhang, Z., & Pollefeys, M. (Eds.). (2010). *Proceedings of the IEEE International Workshop on Mobile Vision*. Washington, DC: IEEE Computer Society.

KEY TERMS AND DEFINITIONS

Augmented Reality: Monitors contextual data, and visually adapts the environment by adding additional content using a visual metaphor (e.g., the looking glass metaphor).

Feature Detection: The process of applying mathematical processes to images/ video frames to extract and define areas of interest. The features change depending on the vision recognition task and can be edges, corners, blobs or colour histograms.

Feature Tracking: Monitors the movement of these features over different frames enabling motion information to be calculated from the video data.

Magic Lens Metaphor: The initial concept was to use the lenses to reveal hidden information, enhance data of interest or suppress distracting information. This metaphor was later realised on camera phones.

Mobile Computing: Interacting with small computational devices while moving and in the field.

Object Recognition: The process of finding an object within an image or video. This process commonly involves two steps, feature detection and feature matching.

Spectrum of Vision Recognition: The scale of how much the environment must be adapted to facilitate their vision recognition application. The spectrum ranges from the use of predefined markers in the environment, to applications that can interpret real world objects and features.

Torchlight Metaphor: Sometimes called searchlight; is similar to the magic lens metaphor as its main purpose is to augment real world content. Instead of the user peering through the 'lens', the torchlight metaphor uses a projector to superimpose the content onto the object.

Vision Recognition: Using computational methods to extract and define elements in the visual context.

Wizard of Oz: An application architecture where some process is controlled by an experimenter without necessarily informing the user of this process. The analogy of the "man behind the curtain" controlling the system.

APPENDIX

Toolkits/Resources

ARToolKit

ARToolKit is a C and C++ library that has functionality for 2D markers to be tracked, thereby allowing virtual reality components to be anchored to real-world components through the viewfinder. ARToolKit is released under the GNU general public licence allowing free use for non-commercial use.
   Link- http://www.hitl.washington.edu/artoolkit/

OpenCV

OpenCV is an open source Computer Vision library written in C (with support for C++, C# and Java) with functionally for functions such as image processing, tracking, transformation, and object recognition.
   Link- http://opencv.willowgarage.com/wiki/

NyARToolkit

NyARToolkit is an augmented reality toolkit allowing prototyping of augmented reality applications for Android, Java and C# and is based on ARToolKit.
   Link- http://nyatla.jp/nyartoolkit/wiki/index.php?FrontPage.en

Studierstube

A computer vision library for detection and pose estimation of 2D marker. Similar to that of ARToolKit and is written from scratch with high performance pcs and mobile devices in mind.
   Link-http://studierstube.icg.tugraz.at/handheld_ar/stbtracker.php

VisualCodes

This project creates a toolkit that allows you to read VisualCodes, a 2D barcode similar to QR codes. The toolkit also allows you to investigate different actions such as rotations and selecting a single Vi-sualCode from multiple ones.
   Link- http://www.vs.inf.ethz.ch/res/proj/visualcodes/

ZXing (Barcode Reader)

ZXing (Zebra crossing) is an open-source multi-format 1D/2D barcode processing library. ZXing is written in Java and allows local decoding of barcoding without any server communication. The library currently supports UPC, EAN, QR Code, Code 39 and many more barcode styles. They have also also sup-port for iPhone, C++ and Java ME.
   Link- http://code.google.com/p/zxing/

Chapter 15
Speech Disorders Recognition using Speech Analysis

Khaled Necibi
University of Annaba, Algeria

Halima Bahi
University of Annaba, Algeria

Toufik Sari
University of Annaba, Algeria

ABSTRACT

Speech disorders are human disabilities widely present in young population but also adults may suffer from such disorders after some physical problems. In this context, the detection and further the correction of such disabilities may be handled by Automatic Speech Recognition (ASR) technology. The first works on the speech disorders detection began early in the 70s and seem to follow the same evolution as those on the ASR. Indeed, these early works were more based on the signal processing techniques. Progressively, systems dealing with speech disorders incorporate more ideas from ASR technology. Particularly, Hidden Markov Models, the state-of-the-art approaches in ASR systems, are used. This chapter reviews systems that use ASR techniques to evaluate pronunciation of people who suffer from speech or voice impairments. The authors investigate the existing systems and present the main innovation and some of the available resources.

INTRODUCTION

When a person is unable to produce speech sounds correctly or fluently, or has problems with his or her voice, then he/she has a speech disorder. Difficulties pronouncing sounds, or articulation disorders, and stuttering are examples of speech disorders.

When a person has trouble understanding others (receptive language), or sharing thoughts, ideas, and feelings completely (expressive language), then he/she has a language disorder. A stroke can result in aphasia, or a language disorder. Both children and adults can have speech and language disorders. They can occur as a result of a medical problem or have no known cause.

DOI: 10.4018/978-1-4666-0954-9.ch015

Recent advances in ASR promoted developments of ASR-based applications dedicated to people with disabilities like blindness or physical handicaps. However, in this chapter, we are particularly, interested with researches which address the problem of speech disorders.

The first works on the speech disorders detection began very early by the beginning of the 70s and seem to follow the same evolution as those on the ASR. Indeed, these early works were more based on the signal processing techniques (Childers, 1990). Later, systems dedicated to speech disorders incorporate more ideas from ASR technology, particularly, Hidden Markov Models, which are the state-of-the-art approaches in ASR systems.

This chapter is particularly dedicated to the presentation of available works in speech disorders detection based on speech recognition technology. In the following section we introduce the principles of the use of ASR technology in the speech impairments evaluation. This is done throughout the presentation of an illustrative example: Vocaliza which is a system devoted to speech disorder assessment.

We make an overview of the available researches in the field. The works are mainly grouped by the kind of disorder. Thus, disorders like: apraxia, dysarthria, or stuttering are presented.

We present the available resources in the field in terms of dataset for speech impairments and available software. We give the new trends in the fields and we suggest some possible directions to investigate.

ASR IN SPEECH IMPAIRMENT DETECTION

Speech disorders are human disabilities widely present in young population but also adults may suffer from such disorders after some physical problems. So, the detection and further the correction of such disabilities may be handled by ASR technology. At the beginning, works were essentially based on signal processing techniques. In particular, these works were mainly based on the fundamental computation and the harmonics of the signal, and then the principal of the detection consists on looking for dissimilarities between the normal speech and the abnormal one.

Recently, the need of the computer-aided speech therapy systems has increased. Such systems are getting more attention for researchers since the number of persons suffering from speech impairment is great. The main purpose of these systems is to provide methods for improving the communication skills of person who suffer from disorder in speech or voice.

Among the available systems devoted to speech disorder, we would like first to present Vocaliza, a system which is developed in the context of the National Project TIN in Spain.

Vocaliza (Vaquero et al., 2008a), is a Speech-Technology-based application for computer-aided speech therapy in Spanish language. This software provides a user interface especially designed to be attractive even to the youngest users. It works on three level of language: phonological, semantic and syntactic. Each level was trained by a different method which was shown as a game, in order to attract young users. In fact, all games were based on ASR techniques. The goal here was to decide if the user has completed the game successfully. The system includes speech synthesis to show how a word must be pronounced, speaker adaptation to estimate the acoustic models adapted to the user and utterance verification to evaluate user pronunciation.

Most of Vocaliza functionalities are provided by different Human Languages Technologies (HLTs) like ASR which is the core module of Vocaliza application. Each game needs an ASR decoder to decode the user utterances, and to decide which word sequence has been pronounced, so that the application will be able to let the user know if the game has been completed successfully.

The ASR integrated in Vocaliza uses an utterance verification procedure in order to decide if the user has pronounced the requested word or if there is a phoneme sequence with more probability.

In Rodríguez et al. (2008), an informatics application for speech therapy in Spanish language has been introduced. The objective was to improve communication skills of children having speech impairment. Speech technology, in fact, provides methods which can help children to improve pre-language (crying, speech activity detection, intensity and intonation control, generation of vocal sounds and others) and language. Vocaliza was used in Rodríguez et al. (2008) only for improving the children's language. It was very useful tool for the training of children with different speech disorder at several levels of language.

LTTERATURE REVIEW

As already said, several works address the use of ASR technology in speech disorders context. In the following, we present some of these works mainly grouped by the disorder they address.

Apraxia vs. Dysarthria of Speech

Dysarthria and Apraxia are two distinct types of motor speech disorders. Dysarthria is a disorder of motor execution, while Apraxia is a disorder of motor programming.

Apraxia of Speech is a motor speech disorder. It is caused by damage to the parts of the brain related to speaking. It may result from stroke or be developmental, and involves inconsistent production of speech sounds and rearranging of sounds in a word ("potato" may become "topato" and next "totapo"). Production of words becomes more difficult with effort, but common phrases may sometimes be spoken spontaneously without effort.

On the other side, dysarthria is a weakness or paralysis of speech muscles caused by damage to

the nerves and/or brain. Dysarthria is often caused by strokes, parkinsons disease, Amyotrophic Lateral Sclerosis (ALS), head or neck injuries, surgical accident, or cerebral palsy.

Many researchers have investigated both types of disorders. In Hosom et al. (2004), Hosom, Shribreg and Green have reported finding from two feasibility studies using automatic speech recognition methods in childhood speech sound disorders. The studies have evaluated and implemented the automation of two proposed diagnostic markers for suspected apraxia of speech called the Lexical Stress Ratio (LSR) and the Coefficient of Variation Ratio (CVR). The Lexical Stress Ratio is a weighted composite of amplitude area, frequency area and duration in the stressed compared to the unstressed vowel as obtained from the productions of a speaker. The Coefficient of Variation Ratio represents the average normalized variability of durations of pause and speech events obtained from a conversational speech sample. As results, the Lexical Stress Ratio values obtained with ASR were within 1.6% to 6.7% of the Lexical Stress Ratio values obtained manually using Computerized Speech Lab (CSL). The Coefficient of Variation Ratio values obtained using ASR were within 0.7% to 2.7% of the Coefficient of Variation Ratio obtained manually using Matlab. Finally, the authors have affirmed that these results indicate the potential of ASR-based techniques to process these and other diagnostic markers of childhood speech sound disorders.

Vijayalakshmi, Nagarajan, and Reddy (2009) have developed a continuous speech, an isolated-style monophone-based, and a triphone-based speech recognition systems. As in Vijayalakshmi et al. (2009) a triphone is a contex-dependant phoneme which takes both the left and right phonetic contexts into consideration, thus avoiding the variability. The authors in Vijayalakshmi et al. (2009) have shown that triphone modeling with more numbers of examples is more powerful than monophone models, as it models the co-articulatory effect also. For each of the phonemes, the number of contexts (left and right) was depended on the number of phonemes under consideration. The contexts were derived from the Nemours database of dysarthric speech. Word-internal triphones alone were considered. There were 231 word-internal triphones derived from dysarthric speech data. Out of the 231 triphones only 128 had more than 10 examples in the TIMIT speech corpus. As in Vijayalakshmi et al. (2009), the triphone training procedure involves the following steps:

- Generation of monophone models with a nominal number of states and a single mixture/state, and re-estimation of these models.
- Creation of triphone transcriptions from monophone transcriptions.
- Initial triphone training by cloning the single-mixture monophone models. Re-estimation of the cloned triphone models.
- Triphone clustering. Triphones were clustered and acoustically similar states were tied using a tree-based clustering procedure.
- Splitting the single mixture gaussian distributions by a divide-by-two algorithm. Re-estimation of these triphone models.

As explained above, these speech recognition systems were trained with the TIMIT speech corpus and tested with the Nemours database of dysarthric speech. The correlation coefficient between the performance of the speech recognition systems and the Frenchay Dysarthria Assessment (FDA) scores was computed for the assessment of articulatory sub-systems. It was observed that triphone-based system after necessary phoneme grouping based on place of articulation correlates well with the FDA scores. The authors have also observed that apart from the articulatory problems, some of the speakers were affected with velopharyngeal incompetence. It was analyzed with group delay function-based acoustic measure for the detection of hypernasality on dysarthric speech and found that 4 out of 10 dysarthric speakers in the Nemours database were hypernasal.

Cleft Lip and Palate Works

Cleft Lip and Palate is the most common malformation of the head. In fact, speech of children with Cleft Lip and Palate is still disordered even after surgery and it might show some special characteristics such as hypernasality, backing and weakening of consonants. The most known feature of disordered speech in Cleft Lip and Palate is the hypernasality in vowels (also called nasality) and nasalizes consonants. This may reduce the speech intelligibility. Both features, hypernasality and nasality consonants, can be summarizes as nasal air emission.

The term nasality was often used in the literature for two different kinds of nasality: hypernasality and hyponasality. While hypernasality is caused enhanced nasal emissions, as in children with Cleft Lip and palate, hyponasality is caused by a blockage of the nasal airway, e.g., when a patient has a cold. There are several studies on both nasality types.

The disordered speech in Cleft Lip and Palate might also contain secondary cleft cleft-type characteristics. These may be caused by compensatory articulation, which is still present even after adequate closure of the clefting. For example, pharyngeal backing is caused by a shift in the localization of the tongue toward the palate during the articulation. Glottal articulation, also called laryngeal replacement, is an extreme backing of articulation. Another typical characteristic of secondary phonetic disorders is the absence or weakening of consonants, also called weakened plosives.

In clinical practice, articulation disorders are evaluated perceptually, and the evaluation procedures are performed by a speech therapist. Previous studies have shown that experience is an important factor that influences the judgment of speech disorders and the perceptual evaluation of persons with limited experience tends to vary considerably. For scientific purposes, usually the mean score judged by a panel of experienced speech therapists serves as a reliable evaluation of speech and is sometimes called objective. This is consuming in term of time and human-power.

Maier, Hönig, Bocklet, and Nöth (2009b) have presented a new technical procedure for the objective measurement and evaluation of phonetic disorders in connected speech. They have compared the obtained results with perceptual ratings of an experienced speech therapist. The experiments performed were:

1. An ASR system was applied to evaluate the detection of these features of Cleft Lip and palate: hypernasality, nasality consonants, pharyngeal backing, laryngeal replacement and weakened plosives. The experiment was based on the transcription of the tests that was created manually.
2. A second experiment was conducted to examine whether it is possible to perform the fully automatic assessment without manual transcription.

The system proposed by Maier et al. (2009b) detects speech disorders at the speaker level as well as an expert. The correlations between the automatic system and the human expert for the different articulation disorders and features of Cleft Lip and Palate were in the same range.

Authors in Scipioni et al. (2009) have shown that the diagnosis of speech disorders, such as the speech produced by persons with Cleft Lip and Palate, is of crucial importance for the speech quality which would be a great help for speech therapists. The goal of the study presented in Scipioni et al. (2009) was to provide support to clinical procedures by means of an automatic assessment.

On German Cleft Lip and Palate data high and significant correlations between human ratings and the recognition accuracy of a speech recog-

nition system were mentioned in Scipioni et al. (2009). The authors have investigated whether the approach was also suitable for other languages. They have compared the correlations obtained on German data with the correlations on Italian data. A high and significant correlation (r=0.76; p < 0.01) was identified on the Italian data. These results were not significantly different from the results on German data (p > 0.05).

Works on Stuttering

Stuttering affects approximately 1% of the adult population. Stuttering affects the fluency of speech. It begins during childhood and, in some cases, lasts throughout life. The disorder is characterized by disruptions in the production of speech sounds, also called "disfluencies." Most people produce brief disfluencies from time to time. For instance, some words are repeated and others are preceded by "um" or "uh". Since stuttering is relatively widespread in the population, a lot of researches tried to assist the rehabilitation process. As for many other troubles, one of the main problems still unsolved in the domain of speech fluency disorders is an objective and an automatic way of judgment of patient performance before and after speech therapy sessions and an assessment of gains made after intervention. A lot of researches were based on vocal pitch and higher formants

As stuttering is often associated to "repetitions", one of the important parameter in assessing the stuttered speech objectively is the automatic detection of syllable repetition. Indeed, Ravikumar et al. (2008) propose an automatic detection method for syllable repetition in read speech for objective assessment of stuttered disfluencies which uses a novel approach. The method has four stages comprising of segmentation, feature extraction, score matching and decision logic (Figure 1). Feature extraction is implemented using well know Mel Frequency Cepstra Coefficient (MFCC). Score matching is done using Dynamic

Figure 1. Block diagram of automatic detection method

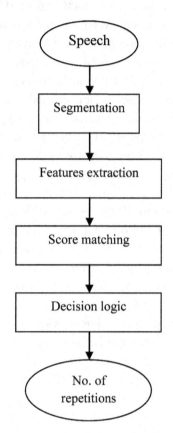

Time Warping (DTW) between the syllables. The Decision logic is implemented by Perceptron based on the score given by score matching.

In Czyzewski et al. (2003), the authors propose a methodology of analysis of formants in stuttered speech. This study focuses on vowels pronunciation and provides an analysis of "vowels prolongation" and "vowels repetition" cases.

A more recent work (as in Wisniewski et al., 2010) proposes an improved approach based on hidden Markov models. The study aims to detect and classify prolonged fricative phonemes in the Polish language.

From practical side, Awad, Curless, and Merson (1999) have developed a software tool to help stuttering children and Parkinson disease clients improve their speech fluency. This tool is used by speech therapists in hospitals and by the patients themselves in their own homes.

The following steps describe the integrated speech fluency treatment system (Figure 2):

1. The client visits the clinician for an initial evaluation of the speech fluency disorder.

Figure 2. Integration of computerized home treatment

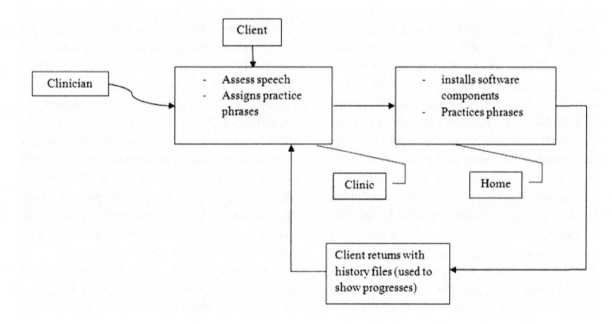

2. Subsequently, the clinician assesses the disorder and assigns a set of homework phrases for the client to practice using the treatment tool.

3. The client installs the software components at home (guided by the manual supplied).

4. The client practices the homework phrases. The software provides video and audio feedback to let the client see and hear how closely the attempted speech pattern matched the clinician's goal pattern. The software compares the similarity of the client and clinician's speech patterns and displays scores to client. The client creates a history disk containing a record of the client's past attempts. The client returns to the clinic where the clinician uses the history disk to evaluate the client's progress and assigns new homework goal phrases for the client to practice.

5. The client takes home the new phases to practice and the treatment process continues with step 4.

Works of Lieida et al.

Saz, Miguel, Lleida, Ortega, and Buera (2005) have studied the variations in the time and frequency domains inside a Spanish language corpus of speakers who have non-pathological and pathological speech. They have shown how pathological speech had a greater variability in the duration of words than non-pathological speech. In the frequency domain, the authors have shown that the vowels confusability increases by 18%. The experimentation performed using ASR with this corpus have demonstrated that this variability was the main cause of the loss in the performance of the ASR systems. To reduce the impact of the time and the variability of the frequency the authors have used a recent Vocal Tract Length Normalization (VTLN) system: MATE (augMented stAte space acoustic modE) to improve the ASR systems when dealing with speakers who suffer from any kind

of speech pathology. The experimentation with MATE have shown a 17.04% and 11.19% Word Error Recognition (WRE) reduction by using frequency and time MATE respectively.

Vaquero et al. (2008b) have addressed the problem that disabled people face when accessing new systems and technologies available nowadays. As a way to include speech impaired people in the technological society of today, two lines of work were carried out by Vaquero et al., the first one was a computer-aided speech therapy software; VOCALIZA, developed for the speech training of children with different disabilities. This tool makes use of different state of the art speech technologies to train different levels of the language. On the other hand, research on the use of ASR Systems for the speech impaired was carried out. This works has focused on current techniques of speaker adaptation to know how this technique can deal with this kind of speech.

Yin et al. (2008) have addressed the problem of neuromuscular disorders affecting in speech. They have proposed a phone level pronunciation verification scenario to detect the influence of mispronunciations induced by neuromuscular disorders in dysarthric speech. The maximum a posteriori (MAP) based task domain adaptation and the maximum likelihood linear regression (MLLR) based speaker adaptation were applied to reduce the influence of extraneous sources of variability on verification performance. When both task-dependent MAP adaptation and speaker-dependent MLLR adaptation were applied, an improvement in the error rate of approximately 25% relative the performance obtained using a baseline ASR system was obtained, resulting in an error rate of 18.6%. So, the performance of the measures used in this system achieve a performance that is close to that necessary to provide useful feedback to impaired speakers in language learning and speech therapy applications.

Saz et al. (2009a) have presented an approach for lexical adaptation in automatic speech recognition of the disordered speech from a group of young impaired speakers. The outcome of an Acoustic Phonetic Decoder (APD) was used to learn new lexical variants of the 57-word vocabulary and add them to a lexicon personalized to each user. The possibilities of combination of this lexical adaptation with acoustic adaptation achieved through traditional Maximum A Posteriori (MAP) approaches were furtherer explored. The results have shown the importance of matching the lexicon in the ASR decoding phase to the lexicon used for the acoustic adaptation.

Saz et al. (2009b) studied the problem of Computer-Aided Speech and Language Therapy (CASLT). The goal of this study was to develop and evaluate a semi-automated ASR-based system in order to provide an interactive speech therapy to the increasing population of impaired individuals and help professional speech therapists. In this work, some interactive tools were designed to facilitate the acquisition of language skills in the areas of basic phonatory skills, phonetic articulation and language understanding for children with neuromuscular disorders like dysarthria. The performance of the ASR systems and subword-based pronunciation verification used for this domain have provided adequate performance similar to the experts agreement rate, for supporting the presented CASLT applications.

The Detection of Parkinson's Disease

The aim of the study presented by Little, McSharry, Hunter, Spielman, and Ramig (2008) was to discriminate healthy people from people with Parkinson's Disease by detecting dysphonia. Dysphonia is an impairment in the normal production of vocal sounds. Dysphonic symptoms typically include reduced loudness, breathiness, roughness, decreased energy in the higher parts of the harmonic spectrum, and exaggerated vocal tremor. The authors have introduced a new measure of dysphonia, Pitch Period Entropy (PPE), which is robust to many uncontrollable confounding effects

including noisy acoustic environments and normal healthy variations in voice frequency.

At a first stage, the authors have performed many experiments to select a features set to be considered in the features extraction stage. In the classification stage, authors have chosen the support vector machine (SVM) as classifier to discriminate between healthy and dysphonic subject.

Their main finding was that non-standard measures significantly outperform the traditional measures in separating healthy controls from people with Parkinson, in terms of overall correct classification performance. They have also found that traditional noise-to-harmonics methods contain some useful information that increases the performance.

The Detection and Evaluation of Edentulous Speakers

Dental rehabilitation by complete dentures is a state of the art approach to improve functional aspects of the oral cavity of edentulous patients and it is important to assure that these dentures have a sufficient fit (Bocklet et al., 2010). Patients that make part of the work presented in Bocklet et al. (2010) have been rated according to their sufficient/insufficient fit of their dentures. The authors, in this work, have shown that sufficient dentures increase the performance of an ASR system by 27%.

A dataset of 13 edentulous speakers that have been recorded with and without complete dentures was used. These dentures have been rated not to have a perfect fit i.e., an insufficient. The authors have used three recordings types for each of these 13 patients: one without complete dentures, one with insufficient dentures and one with sufficient dentures.

In fact, the main goal of this work was to create a system that is able to detect on a spoken text whether the complete dentures have a sufficient fit or not. So, three different systems were used to achieve this goal: The first system takes the word accuracy results of a speech recognizer and uses this single value as feature. The second system calculates the distance between the spoken text of an edentulous patient and a reference speaker by Dynamic Time Warping (DTW). These distances were used as features for a classifier. The third system models each speaker by Gaussian Mixture Models (GMM) and uses the concatenated mean vectors of these GMMs as input vector for a classifier.

The authors have performed an ASR-based experiments on the dataset previously mentioned. The experiments on these dataset have shown word accuracy improvement of 10% between recordings without any dentures and recordings with insufficient dentures. Sufficient dentures have improved these results by another 18%.

The authors have also achieved another goal: the automatic detection of incomplete dentures. So the authors have compared the recognition results of the three different systems previously presented (that use word accuracy, DTW and GMM). The results obtained have shown a recognition rate of 80%.

The Detection of Vocal Fold Paralysis and Edema

Ziogas and Kotropoulos (2006) have studied two class pattern recognition problem, namely the automatic detection of speech disorders such as vocal fold paralysis and edema by processing the speech signal recorded from patients affected by this kind of disorder as well as speakers unaffected by this disorder. The data used were extracted from the Massachusetts Eye and Ear Infirmary database of disorders speech (MEEI). The Linear Prediction Coefficients (LPC) were used as input to the pattern recognition module. Two techniques were developed. The first one was an optimal linear classifier design, while the second one was based on the dual-space linear discriminant analysis. The authors have performed two experiments in order to assess the performance of the techniques

developed namely the detection of vocal fold paralysis for male speakers and the detection of vocal fold edema for female speakers. Long-term mean feature vectors have proved very efficient in detecting the voice disorders yielding a probability of detection that may approach 100% for a probability of false alarm equal to 9.52%.

Kotropoulos and Arce (2009) have studied the same subject, but they have employed utterances of the sustained vowel "ah" from the Massachusetts Eye and Ear Infirmary database (MEEI) of disordered speech. The receiver operating characteristic curve of the linear classifier, that stems from the Bayes classifier when Gaussian class conditional probability density functions with equal covariance matrices were assumed, was derived. The optimal operating point of the linear classifier was specified with and without reject option. The reject option has shown to improve the accuracy of a linear classifier in detecting vocal fold paralysis for male patients as well as detecting vocal fold edema for female ones than that obtained without reject option. Moreover, the reported improvements were been shown to be statistically significant at 95% confidence level. In addition, the linear classifier with reject option outperforms the previously employed classifiers in Ziogas et al. (2006).

The Detection of Articulation Disorders: Approaches and Solutions

Georgoulas, Georgopoulos, and Stylios (2006) have proposed a new integrated methodology to extract features and classify speech sounds to detect any speech articulation disorder in a speaker. For the feature extraction phase, the authors have used the discrete wavelet transform method. They have also used Support Vectors Machines (SVMs) for the classification of speech sounds and detection of articulation disorders. The proposed method was implemented on a data set where different sets of features and different schemes of SVMs were tested leading to satisfactory performance.

Su, Wu, and Tsai (2008) have presented an approach to automatic assessment on articulation disorders using unsupervised acoustic model adaptation. They have shown that there are two problems for modeling the articulation disorders speech: 1) insufficient training database and unpredictable variations from speakers with articulation disorders generally degrades the recognition performance and 2) traditional speaker adaptation adapts the acoustic models to overfit the incorrect pronunciation while miss the purpose for articulation disorder assessment. In the assessment of the articulation disorders, the purpose was to identify the mispronounced phones from the speech pronounced by the speaker with speech disorders. Instead of adapting the acoustic models to fit the articulation disordered speech, the study in Su et al. (2008) tries to adapt the acoustic models using the correctly pronounced speech from the speaker with speech disorder, while keeps the incorrectly pronounced units unchanged. Finally, the speaker-dependent acoustic models can be applied for articulation disorder assessment of the speaker with articulation disorder.

Strategies of speaker adaptation can be divided into supervised or unsupervised and incremental or batch. The authors in Su et al. (2008) have proposed an unsupervised, incremental adaptation to adapt the acoustic models for the speakers with articulation disorders from the acoustic models of normal speakers.

The manual articulation disorders assessments of 453 children who suffer from articulation disorder were conducted by the authors to obtain the mispronounced phenomenon between phones. This information was adopted to re-estimate the confusion matrix of the phones for the speaker with articulation disorder. The re-estimation process keeps the confident/consistent recognition results of the speech pronounced by the speaker with articulation disorders for adaptation. Incrementally, the adapted acoustic models recognize the speech of the speaker with articulation disorders

and obtain more confident recognition results. The process is ended until no more new phones are confirmed for adaptation. The final re-estimated confusion matrix provides the mispronunciations of the phones for the speakers with articulation disorders and the results can be analyzed based on the pre-defined articulation and phonological error types to obtain the assessment results.

To achieve this aim, phonological information was considered as the prior knowledge to choose the correctly pronounced and recognized phones for adaptation.

Georgoulas et al. (2009) have proposed a novel integrated method for the detection of a common substitution articulation error in Greek language. They have introduced a novel approach based on signal processing methods to extract features from speech signals and based on them to detect a specific type of articulation disorders. The Empirical Mode Decomposition algorithm and the Hilbert Huang Transform were applied to the speech signal in order to calculate the marginal spectrum of the signal. The marginal spectrum is subsequently subject to a mel-cepstrum like processing to extract features which are fed to a neural network classifier which is responsible for the identification of the articulation disorder. The preliminary result of this work suggests that this approach was very promising for the detection of the disorder under study.

Miyamoto, Komai, Takiguchi, Ariki, and Li (2010) have investigated the speech recognition of a person with articulation disorders resulting from athetoid cerebral palsy. The authors have performed the extraction of the acoustic feature using MAF (for Multiple Acoustic Frames) instead of MFFC-delta, and a pose-robust audio-visual speech recognition method using AAM (for Active Appearance Model) to increase noise robustness in a real environment. The main goal was to recognize the speech of one person with articulation disorders problems. The proposed method has yielded an improvement of 7.3% (from 51.6% to 58.9%) in the recognition rate compared to the audio-only method.

AVAILABLE TOOLS

PEAKS: A System for the Automatic Evaluation of Voice and Speech Disorders

Maier, Haderlein, Eysholdt, Rosanowski, Batliner, Schuster, and Noth (2009a) have introduced a Program for the Evaluation and the Analyze of all Kinds of Speech disorders: PEAKS, a recording and analyze environment for the automatic or manual evaluation of voice and speech disorders. This system can be assessed via Internet platform independently. The system works on this way. The patient reads a text or names pictures. His or her speech is then analyzed by ASR module and prosodic analysis. For patients who had their larynx removed due to cancer and for children with cleft lip and palate, the system can achieve significant correlations between the automatic analysis and the judgment of human experts. A correlation of 0.90 for the evaluation of the laryngectomees and 0.87 for the evaluation of the children's data was obtained which was comparable to human inter-rater correlations (Maier et al., 2009a).

Features Extraction et MFCCs Coefficients

Signal processing which use suitable features extraction is the first step to successful trained models of speech recognizer and any other ASR-based application. This operation is very important in term of obtaining parameters describing the speech signal as closely as possible, and in the same time, reducing its high redundancy. This initial operation is important in implementing recognizer because on the used feature extraction of speech signal depends their success.

The most commonly feature extraction method used in current ASR systems is MFCC (Mel-Frequency Cepstral Coefficients). Such a speech parameterization is designed to maintain the characteristic of human sound perception.

The compensation for non-linear perception of frequency is implemented by the bank of triangular band filters with the linear distribution of frequencies along so called mel-frequency range. The linear deployment of filters to mel-frequency axis results in a non-linear distribution for the standard frequency axis in hertz. The definition of the mel-frequency range is described by the following equation (Equation 1):

$$\text{fm} = 2595\log 10\left(1 + \frac{f}{700}\right) \qquad (1)$$

where is frequency in linear range and is the corresponding frequency in nonlinear mel-frequency range.

The procedure applied for the gaining of the MFCCs coefficients consists of several steps. The input of the system is supplied with signal samples and the signal pre-emphasis is done. It is a filtration to emphasis the higher frequencies of speech signals which show a greater attenuation. The main frequency components of the speech spectrum are amplified too. Pre-emphasis of the speech signal is realized with this simple FIR filter (Equation 2):

$$\text{H}\left(z\right) = 1 - az^{-1} \qquad (2)$$

where is from interval [0.9,1].

In the next step, signal segmentation and hamming window are applying and the window length is set to 10 - 30 ms. The exact time length of window (number of samples in the frequency of sampling) is chosen equal to the power of 2 due to the subsequent processing of fast fourier transformation.

In the next step the Fast Fourier Transform (FFT) is used to calculate components of magnitude spectrum $|S(f)|$ of the analyzed signal.

The most important step in this signal processing is mel-freqency transformation. The algorithm is carried out by the bank of triangular band filters with a uniform distribution of center frequencies of each triangular filter along the frequency axis in mel-frequency range.

The next step is to calculate the logarithm of the outputs of individual filters, which affects the dynamics of the signal.

The final step in calculation of the MFCC coefficients which is, instead of inverse Fourier transform, the application of the Discrete Cosine Transform (DCT) which is defined by the following equation (Equation 3):

$$Cmf(n) = \sqrt{(\frac{2}{K})} \sum_{j=1}^{K} \log mj \cos\left[n(j-0.5)\frac{\pi}{K}\right]$$

(3)

where is the number of MFCC coefficients and is the number of mel-frequency band filters in the bank of filters. The Discrete Cosine Transformation (DCT) tend to produce non-correlated coefficients for wide range of signals Cmf(n).

Coefficients of MFCC can be considered as static because all the vector items are obtained from the current weighted microsegment of the signal defined by window functions (Hamming). But there exists the so called dynamic parameters (also called temporal cepstral derivative) known as delta (ΔCm) (first derivative) and delta delta $(\Delta^2 Cm)$ (second derivative). For delta-MFCC,

we can compute it by Equation (4) where and are an appropriate normalization constant.

$$\Delta Cm(t) = \frac{\partial Cm(t)}{\partial t} \approx \mu \sum_{k=-K}^{K} kCm(t+k).$$

(4)

The following equation (Equation 5) shows the approximation of the second derivative, where is the estimated weight m[th] delta cepstral coefficient evaluated at frame.

$$\Delta^2 Cm(t) = \Delta Cm(t+1) - \Delta Cm(t-1).$$

(5)

The Available Corpus

In fact, there is a lot of databases and corpus used in the field of the speech disorder detection. The most used among them is The Massachusetts Eye et Ear Infirmary (MEEI) Voice Disorders Database. Generally, not all data have been standardized or were available in such web site. Some researchers have chosen to create their own corpus that seems to be well suited to subject in question because not all available data can be employed in such case. In the following, we will present the corpus of data available and not those created manually or that were created when subject have taken place.

Table 1. Available datasets

Works	corpus
(Su et al., 2008)	The TCC300 speech corpus
(Miyamoto et al., 2010)	the ATR Japanese speech database
(Maier et al., 2009)	VERBMOBIL data
(Nayak et al., 2003)	The "Baby Chilanto" database Baby Chillanto" database from "Instituto Nacional de Astrofisica Optica y Electronica – CONACYT, Mexico".
(Saz et al., 2005)	The corpus recorded by the Department of Signals and Communications from the University of Las Palmas de Gran Canaria (Spain)
(Kotropoulos et al., 2009; Vijayalakshmi et al., 2009; Ziogos et al., 2006)	The Massachusetts Eye & Ear Infirmary (MEEI) Voice Disorders Database
(Scipioni et al., 2009)	The ChildIt speech corpus

Table 1 illustrates the different corpus used in the field of speech disorder detection.

INNOVATIVE APPROACHES

Danubianu, Pentiuc, and Socaciu (2009) have performed a short analysis of the use opportunity of the data mining techniques in order to improve the personalized therapy of speech disorders framework. The authors have also presented the Logo-DM system. It is a data mining system designed to be associated with TERAPERS system in order to use the data from TERAPERS for analysis and to provide new information based on which one could improve the process of therapy. The novelty of the study presented in Danubianu et al. (2009) consist in using data mining to make predictions regarding the outcome of personalized therapy of speech disorders and to enrich the knowledge base of an expert system designed to assist therapy.

As another direction of research, we suggest the use of Computer Assisted Pronunciation Teaching (CAPT) approaches during the assessment of the pathological pronunciation. Such approaches may provide an interesting feedback in a rehabilitation process for patients.

REFERENCES

Awad, S. S., Curless, M. W., & Merson, R. (1999). Computer assisted treated for motor speech disorders. In *Proceedings of the 16th IEEE International Conference on Instrumentation and Measurement Technology* (pp. 595-600).

Bocklet, T., Hönig, F., Haderlein, T., Stelzle, F., Knipfer, C., & Nöth, E. (2010). Automatic detection and evaluation of edentulous speakers with insufficient dentures. In *Proceedings of the 13th International Conference on Text, Speech and Dialogue* (pp. 237-244).

Childers, D. G. (1990). Speech processing and synthesis for assessing vocal disorders. *IEEE Engineering in Medicine and Biology Magazine, 9*(1), 69–71. doi:10.1109/51.62911

Czyzewski, A., Kaczmarek, A., & Kostek, B. (2003). Intelligent processing of stuttered speech. *Journal of Intelligent Information Systems, 21*(2), 143–171. doi:10.1023/A:1024710532716

Danubianu, M., Pentiuc, S. G., & Socaciu, T. (2009). Towards the optimized personalized therapy of speech disorders by data mining techniques. In *Proceedings of the IEEE Fourth International Multi-Conference on Computing in the Global Information Technology* (pp. 20-25).

Georgoulas, G., Georgopoulos, V. C., & Stylios, C. D. (2006). Speech sound classification and detection of articulation disorders with support vector machines and wavelets. In *Proceedings of the 28th IEEE Annual International Conference on Engineering in Medicine and Biology Society* (pp. 2199-2202)

Georgoulas, G., Georgopoulos, V. C., Stylios, G. D., & Stylios, C. D. (2009). Detection of articulation disorders using empirical mode decomposition and neural networks. In *Proceedings of the International Joint Conference on Neural Networks*, Atlanta, GA (pp. 959-964).

Hosom, J. P., Shriberg, L., & Green, J. R. (2004). Diagnostic assessment of childhood apraxia of speech using automatic speech recognition (ASR) methods. *Journal of Medical Speech-Language Pathology, 12*(4), 171–176.

Kotropoulos, C., & Arce, G. R. (2009). Linear classifier with reject option for the detection of vocal fold paralysis and vocal fold edema. *EURASIP Journal on Advances in Signal Processing, 2009*, 1–13. doi:10.1155/2009/203790

Little, M. A., McSharry, P. E., Hunter, E. J., Spielman, J., & Ramig, L. O. (2008). Suitability of dysphonia measurements for telemonitoring of Parkinson's disease. *IEEE Transactions on Bio-Medical Engineering, 56*(4), 1015–1022. doi:10.1109/TBME.2008.2005954

Maier, A., Haderlein, T., Eysholdt, U., Rosanowski, F., Batliner, A., Schuster, M., & Noth, E. (2009a). PEAKS – A system for the automatic evaluation of voice and speech disorders. *Speech Communication, 51*, 425–437. doi:10.1016/j.specom.2009.01.004

Maier, A., Hönig, F., Bocklet, T., & Nöth, E. (2009b). Automatic detection of articulation disorders in children with cleft lip and palate. *The Journal of the Acoustical Society of America, 126*(5), 2589–25602. doi:10.1121/1.3216913

Miyamoto, C., Komai, Y., Takiguchi, T., Ariki, Y., & Li, I. (2010). Multimodal speech recognition of a person with articulation disorders using AAM (Active Appearance Model) and MAF (Multiple Acoustic Frames). In *Proceedings of the IEEE International Workshop on Multimedia Signal Processing*, Saint Malo, France (pp. 517-520).

Ravikumar, K. M., Reddy, B., Rajagopal, R., & Nagaraj, H. C. (2008). Automatic detection of syllable repetition in read speech for objective assessment of stuttered disfluencies. In *Proceedings of the World Academy of Science, Engineering and Technology* (pp. 270-273).

Rodríguez, W. R., Vaquero, C., Saz, O., & Lleida, E. (2008). *Speech technology applied to children with speech disorders* (pp. 1–4). Saragossa, Spain: Communication Technology Group.

Saz, O., Lleida, E., & Miguel, A. (2009a). Combination of acoustic and lexical speaker adaptation for disordered speech recognition. In *Proceedings of the Conference InterSpeech* (pp. 554-547).

Saz, O., Miguel, A., Lleida, E., Ortega, A., & Buera, L. (2005). *Study of time and frequency variability in pathological speech and error reduction methods for automatic speech recognition.* Saragossa, Spain: Aragon Institute of Technology (I3A), University of Zaragozas.

Saz, O., Yin, S. C., Lleida, E., Rose, R., Vaquero, C., & Rodríguez, W. R. (2009b). Tools and technologies for computer-aided speech and language therapy. *Speech Communication, 51*(10), 948–967. doi:10.1016/j.specom.2009.04.006

Scipioni, M., Gerosa, M., Giuliani, D., Noth, E., & Maier, A. (2009). Intelligibility assessment in children with cleft lip and palate in Italian and German. In *Proceedings of the International Conference InterSpeech*, Brighton, UK (pp. 967-970).

Su, H., Wu, C. H., & Tsai, P. J. (2008). Automatic assessment of articulation disorders using confident unit-based model adaptation. In *Proceedings of the International Conference on Speech, Acoustics and Signal Processing* (pp. 4513-4526).

Vaquero, C., Saz, O., Lleida, E., & Rodríguez, W. R. (2008b). E-inclusion technologies for the speech handicapped. In *Proceedings of the International Conference on Speech, Acoustics and Signal Processing* (pp. 4509-4512).

Vaquero, C., Saz, O., Rodríguez, W. R., & Lleida, E. (2008a). *Human language technologies for speech therapy in Spanish language* (pp. 129–132). Zaragoza, Spain: University of Zaragoza.

Vijayalakshmi, P., Nagarajan, T., & Reddy, M. R. (2009). Assessment of articulatory and velopharyngeal sub-systems of dysarthric speech. *Biomedical Soft Computing and Human Sciences, 14*(2), 87–94.

Wisniewski, M., Jozkowiak, W. K., SmoŁka, E., & Suszynski, E. (2010). Improved approach to automatic detection of speech disorders based on the HMM approach. *Journal of Medical Informatics and Technologies*, 1-8.

Yin, S. C., Rose, R., Saz, O., & Lleida, E. (2008). *Verifying pronunciation accuracy from speakers with neuromuscular disorders. Zaragoza, Spain: NSERC Program and the national project TIN.*

Ziogas, E., & Kotropoulos, C. (2006). *Detection of vocal fold paralysis and edema using linear discriminant classifiers* (pp. 1–11). Brussels, Belgium: European Union MUSCLE Network.

Compilation of References

Ábalos, N., Espejo, G., López-Cózar, R., Callejas, Z., & Griol, D. (2010). A multimodal dialogue system for an ambient intelligent application in home environments. *In Proceedings of the 13th International Conference on Text, Speech and Dialogue* (pp. 491-498).

Ábalos, N., Espejo, G., López-Cózar, R., Callejas, Z., & Griol, D. (2011). A toolkit for the evaluation of spoken dialogue systems in ambient intelligence domains. In *Proceedings of the Second International Workshop on Human-Centric Interfaces for Ambient Intelligence*, Nottingham, UK.

Abbasi, A., & Chen, H. (2007). Affect intensity analysis of dark Web forums. In *Proceedings of the IEEE Conference on Intelligence and Security Informatics* (pp. 282-288).

Abdellatif, R., & Calderon, C. (2007). SecondLife: A computer-mediated tool for distance-learning in architecture education? In *Proceedings of Em'body'ing Virtual Architecture: The Third International Conference of the Arab Society for Computer Aided Architectural Design* (pp. 17-34).

Acero, A., & Stern, R. M. (1990). Environmental robustness in automatic speech recognition. In *Proceedings of the International Conference on Acoustic, Speech and Signal Processing* (pp. 849-852).

Acomb, K., Bloom, J., Dayanidhi, K., Hunter, P., Krogh, P., Levin, E., & Pieraccini, R. (2007, April 26). Technical support dialog systems: Issues, problems, and solutions. In *Proceedings of the HLT Workshop on Bridging the Gap: Academic and Industrial Research in Dialog Technology*, Rochester, NY.

Aggarwal, R. K., & Dave, M. (2011). *Performance evaluation of sequentially combined heterogeneous feature streams for Hindi speech recognition system*. Telecommunication Systems Journal.

Aggarwal, R. K., & Dave, M. (2011). *Towards the recent trends of acoustic models for speech recognition system*. Hershey, PA: IGI Global.

Ahmed, R., & Agrawal, S. S. (1969). Significant features in the perception of Hindi consonants. *The Journal of the Acoustical Society of America, 45*, 758–763. doi:10.1121/1.1911459

Ai, H., Litman, D., Forbes-Riley, K., Rotaru, M., Tetreault, J., & Purandare, A. (2006). Using systems and user performance features to improve emotion detection in spoken tutoring dialogs. In *Proceedings of the International Conference on Spoken Language Processing*, Pittsburgh, PA (pp. 797-800).

Akin, O. (1986). *Psychology of architectural design*. London, UK: Pion.

Alejandro, J., & Nicu, S. (2007). Multimodal human-computer interaction. *Computer Vision and Image Understanding, 108*(1-2), 116–134. doi:10.1016/j.cviu.2006.10.019

Aleksic, P. S., & Katsaggelos, A. K. (2004). Comparison of low and high-level visual features for audio-visual continuous automatic speech recognition. In *Proceedings of the IEEE International Conference on Acoustics, Speech, and Signal Processing* (Vol. 5, pp. 917-920).

Algazi, V. R., Duda, R. O., & Avendano, C. (2001). The Cipic HRTF database. In *Proceedings of the IEEE Workshop on Applications of Signal Processing to Audio and Acoustics*.

Algazi, V. R., Avendano, C., & Duda, R. O. (2001). Estimation of a spherical-head model from anthropometry. *Journal of the Audio Engineering Society. Audio Engineering Society, 49*(6), 472–479.

Allen, J., Schubert, L., Ferguson, G., Heeman, P., Hwang, C. H., & Kato, T. (1991). The TRAINS project a case study in building a conversational planning agent. *Journal of Experimental & Theoretical Artificial Intelligence, 7*, 7–48. doi:10.1080/09528139508953799

Anderson, J. R. (1996). ACT – A simple theory of complex cognition. *The American Psychologist, 51*, 355–365. doi:10.1037/0003-066X.51.4.355

Anderson, J. R. (2005). Human symbol manipulation within an integrated cognitive architecture. *Cognitive Science, 29*, 313–341. doi:10.1207/s15516709cog0000_22

Anderson, J. R., & Lebiere, C. (1998). *The atomic components of thought*. Mahwah, NJ: Lawrence Erlbaum.

Antonieta, A., Fillwalk, J., & Vásquez, G. V. (2009). Collaborating in a virtual architectural environment: The Las Americas Virtual Design Studio (LAVDS) populates Second Life. In *Proceedings of Anais do XIII Congresso da Sociedade Ibero Americana de Gráfica Digital*.

Aslam, J. A., & Montague, M. (2001). Models for metasearch. In *Proceedings of the Twenty Fourth Annual International ACM SIGIR Conference on Research and Development in Information Retrieval* (pp. 276-284). New York, NY: ACM.

Aubert, X. L. (2002). An overview of decoding techniques for large vocabulary continuous speech recognition. *Computer Speech & Language, 16*(1), 89–114. doi:10.1006/csla.2001.0185

AuSIM, Inc. (2000). *HeadZap: AuSIM3D HRTF measurement system manual*. Los Altos, CA: Author.

Awad, S. S., Curless, M. W., & Merson, R. (1999). Computer assisted treated for motor speech disorders. In *Proceedings of the 16th IEEE International Conference on Instrumentation and Measurement Technology* (pp. 595-600).

Bailly, G., Raidt, S., & Elisei, F. (2010). Gaze, conversational agents and face-to-face communication. *Speech Communication, 52*(6), 598–612. doi:10.1016/j.specom.2010.02.015

Balci, K. (2005). XfaceEd: Authoring tool for embodied conversational agents. In *Proceedings of the International Conference on Multimodal Interfaces* (pp. 208-213).

Baldauf, M., & Fröhlich, P. (2009). Supporting hand gesture manipulation of projected content with mobile phones. In *Proceedings of the Workshop on Mobile Interaction with the Real World* (pp. 1-4).

Ballagas, R., Rohs, M., & Sheridan, J. (2005). Sweep and point and shoot: phonecam-based interactions for large public displays. In *Proceedings of the Extended Abstracts on Human Factors in Computing Systems* (pp. 1200-1203). New York, NY: ACM.

Bannon, L. J., & Schmidt, K. (1991). CSCW: four characters in search of a context. In Bowers, J. M., & Bendford, S. D. (Eds.), *Studies in computer supported cooperative work*. Amsterdam, The Netherlands: North Holland.

Barnard, P. (2007). *The Emotion Research Group Website: MRC Cognition and Brain Sciences Unit*. Retrieved from http://www.mrc-cbu.cam.ac.uk/~philb

Batliner, A., Hacker, C., Steidl, S., Nöth, E., D'Arcy, S., Russel, M., & Wong, M. (2004). Towards multilingual speech recognition using data driven source/target acoustical units association. In *Proceedings of the International Conference on Acoustics, Speech, and Signal Processing*, Montreal, QC, Canada (pp. 521-524).

Batteau, D. W. (1967). The role of the pinna in human localization. *Proceedings of the Royal Society of London. Series B. Biological Sciences, 168*, 158–180. doi:10.1098/rspb.1967.0058

Baum, L. E., & Eagon, J. A. (1967). An inequality with applications to statistical estimation for probabilistic functions of Markov processes and a model for ecology. *Bulletin of the American Mathematical Society, 73*, 360–363. doi:10.1090/S0002-9904-1967-11751-8

Baum, L. E., Petrei, S. T. G., & Weiss, N. (1970). A maximisation technique occurring in the statistical analysis of probabilistic functions of Markov chains. *Annals of Mathematical Statistics, 41*, 164–171. doi:10.1214/aoms/1177697196

Bay, H., Fasel, B., & Van Gool, L. (2006). Interactive museum guide: Fast and robust recognition of museum objects. In *Proceedings of the First International Workshop on Mobile Vision*.

Bay, H., Ess, A., Tuytelaars, T., & Van Gool, L. (2006). Speeded up robust features (SURF). *Computer Vision and Vision Understanding, 110*(3), 404–417.

Becchetti, C., & Ricotti, K. P. (2004). *Speech recognition theory and C++ implementation*. New York, NY: John Wiley & Sons.

Beg, M. M. S. (2002). *On measurement and enhancement of Web search quality* (Unpublished doctoral dissertation). International Institute of Technology, Delhi, India.

Beg, M. M. S., & Ahmad, N. (2002). Improved Shimura technique for rank aggregation on the World Wide Web. In *Proceedings of the 5th International Conference on Information Technology*, Bhubaneswar, India.

Begault, D. (1994). *3-D sound for virtual reality and multimedia*. New York, NY: Academic Press.

Begault, D. R., Wenzel, E. M., & Anderson, M. R. (2001). Direct comparison of the impact of head tracking, reverberation, and individualized head-related transfer functions on the spatial perception of a virtual speech source. *Journal of the Audio Engineering Society. Audio Engineering Society, 49*(10), 904–916.

Beg, M. M. S., & Ahmad, N. (2003). Soft computing techniques for rank aggregation on the World Wide Web. *World Wide Web -. International Journal (Toronto, Ont.), 6*(1), 5–22.

Beiler, A. H. (1964). *Recreations in the theory of numbers: The queen of mathematics entertains*. New York, NY: Dover.

Benesty, J., Sondhi, M. M., & Huang, Y. (2008). *Handbook of speech processing*. New York, NY: Springer. doi:10.1007/978-3-540-49127-9

Benesty, J., Sondhi, M. M., & Huang, Y. (2008). *Springer handbook of speech processing*. New York, NY: Springer. doi:10.1007/978-3-540-49127-9

Bennacef, S., Devillers, L., Rosset, S., & Lamel, L. (1996). Dialog in the RAILTEL telephone-based system. In *Proceedings of the International Conference on Spoken Language Processing*.

Bennett, A. (2006). *Design studies: theory and research in graphic design*. New York, NY: Princeton Architectural Press.

Benyon, D., & Murray, D. (1993). Applying user modeling to human computer interaction design. *Artificial Intelligence Review, 7*(3-4), 199–225. doi:10.1007/BF00849555

Berg, M. D., Kreveld, M. V., Overmars, M., & Schwarzkopf, O. (2000). *Computational geometry algorithms and applications*. Berlin, Germany: Springer-Verlag.

Beveridge, M., & Fox, J. (2006). Automatic generation of spoken dialogue from medical plans and ontologies. *Biomedical Informatics, 39*(5), 482–499. doi:10.1016/j.jbi.2005.12.008

Beyer, H., & Holtzblatt, K. (1998). *Contextual design: Defining customer-centered systems*. San Francisco, CA: Morgan Kaufmann.

Bhowmick, P., & Bhattacharya, B. B. (2007). Fast polygonal approximation of digital curves using relaxed straightness properties. *IEEE Transactions on Pattern Analysis and Machine Intelligence, 29*(9), 1590–1602. doi:10.1109/TPAMI.2007.1082

Bickmore, T., & Giorgino, T. (2004). Some novel aspects of health communication from a dialogue systems perspective. In *Proceedings of the AAAI Fall Symposium on Dialogue Systems for Health Communication*, Washington, DC (pp. 275-291).

Bier, E., Stone, M., Pier, K., Buxton, W., & DeRose, T. (1993).Toolglass and magic lenses: the see-through interface. In *Proceedings of the 20th Annual Conference on Computer Graphics and Interactive Techniques* (pp. 73-80). New York, NY: ACM.

Bird, S., Klein, E., Loper, E., & Baldridge, J. (2008). Multidisciplinary instruction with the Natural Language Toolkit. In *Proceedings of the Third ACL Workshop on Issues in Teaching Computational Linguistics* (pp. 62-70).

Birdwhistell, R. L. (1952). *Introduction to kinesics: an annotation system for analysis of body motion and gesture*. Lexington, KY: University of Kentucky Press.

Birdwhistell, R. L. (1970). *Kinesics and context*. Philadelphia, PA: University of Pennsylvania Press.

Bishop, C. M. (2006). *Pattern recognition and machine learning*. New York, NY: Springer.

Biswas, P., & Robinson, P. (2008b). Automatic evaluation of assistive interfaces. In *Proceedings of the 13th ACM International Conference on Intelligent User Interfaces* (pp. 247-256).

Biswas, P., & Robinson, P. (2009a). Modelling perception using image processing algorithms. In *Proceedings of the 23rd British HCI Group Annual Conference on People and Computers: Celebrating People and Technology* (pp. 494-503).

Biswas, P., & Robinson, P. (2009b). Predicting pointing time from hand strength. In A. Holzinger & K. Miesenberger (Eds.), *Proceedings of the 5th Symposium of the Workgroup Human-Computer Interaction and Usability on HCI and Usability for e-Inclusion* (LNCS 5889, pp. 428-447).

Biswas, P., Bhattacharyya, S., & Samanta, D. (2005). User model to design adaptable interfaces for motor-impaired users. In *Proceedings of the IEEE TENCON Region 10 Conferences* (pp. 1801-1844).

Biswas, P., & Robinson, P. (2008a). A new screen scanning system based on clustering screen objects. *Journal of Assistive Technologies, 2*(3). doi:10.1108/17549450200800023

Blandford, A., Butterworthb, R., & Curzonb, P. (2004). Models of interactive systems: a case study on programmable user modelling. *International Journal of Human-Computer Studies, 60*, 149–200. doi:10.1016/j.ijhcs.2003.08.004

Bocklet, T., Hönig, F., Haderlein, T., Stelzle, F., Knipfer, C., & Nöth, E. (2010). Automatic detection and evaluation of edentulous speakers with insufficient dentures. In *Proceedings of the 13th International Conference on Text, Speech and Dialogue* (pp. 237-244).

Boden, M. A. (1985). *Computer models of mind: Computational approaches in theoretical psychology*. Cambridge, UK: Cambridge University Press.

Boehner, K., DePaula, R., Dourish, P., & Sengers, P. (2007). How emotion is made and measured. *International Journal of Human-Computer Studies, 65*(4), 275–291. doi:10.1016/j.ijhcs.2006.11.016

Boll, S. F. (1979). Suppression of acoustic noise in speech using spectral subtraction. *IEEE Transactions on Acoustics, Speech, and Signal Processing, 27*, 113–120. doi:10.1109/TASSP.1979.1163209

Borda, J. C. (1781). *Memoire Sur les Election au Scrutiny*. Paris, France: Histoire de l'Academie Royale des Sciences.

Borgefors, G. (1988). Hierarchical chamfer matching: A parametric edge matching algorithm. *IEEE Transactions on Pattern Analysis and Machine Intelligence, 10*(6), 849–865. doi:10.1109/34.9107

Bos, J., Klein, E., & Oka, T. (2003). Meaningful conversation with a mobile robot. In *Proceedings of the Tenth Conference on European Chapter of the Association for Computational Linguistics* (pp. 71-74).

Bourlard, H., & Wellakens, C. (1990). Links between Markov models and multilayer perceptrons. *IEEE Transactions on Pattern Analysis and Machine Intelligence, 12*(12), 1167–1178. doi:10.1109/34.62605

Bovair, S., Kieras, D. E., & Poison, P. G. (1988). *The acquisition and performance of text editing skill: A production system analysis* (Tech. Rep. No. 28). Ann Arbor, MI: University of Michigan.

Bovair, S., Kieras, D. E., & Polson, P. G. (1990). The acquisition and performance of text-editing skill: A cognitive complexity analysis. *Human-Computer Interaction, 5*, 1–48. doi:10.1207/s15327051hci0501_1

Branko, K., Schmitt, G., Hirschberg, U., Kurmann, D., & Johnson, B. (2000). An experiment in design collaboration. *Automation in Construction, 9*, 73–81. doi:10.1016/S0926-5805(99)00050-3

Bregler, C., & Konig, Y. (1994). Eigenlips for robust speech recognition. In *Proceedings of the International Conference on Acoustics, Speech and Signal Processing*, Adelaide, Australia (pp. 669-672).

Bregler, C., & Omohundro, S. (1995). Nonlinear manifold learning for visual speech recognition. In *Proceedings of the IEEE International Conference on Computer Vision* (pp. 494-499).

Broadfoot, O., & Bennett, R. (2003). Design studios: Online? Comparing traditional face to face design studio education with modern Internet-based design studios. In *Proceedings of the Apple University Consortium Conference: Digital Voyages*.

Brown, C. P., & Duda, R. O. (1997, October). An efficient HRTF model for 3-D sound. In *Proceedings of the IEEE Workshop on Applications of Signal Processing to Audio and Acoustics*, Mohonk, NY.

Brown, C. P., & Duda, R. O. (1998). A structural model for binaural sound synthesis. *IEEE Transactions on Speech and Audio Processing, 6*(5), 476–488. doi:10.1109/89.709673

Brusilovsky, P. (1996). Methods and techniques of adaptive hypermedia. *User Modeling and User-Adapted Interaction, 6*(2), 87–129. doi:10.1007/BF00143964

Brusilovsky, P. (2001). Adaptive hypermedia. *User Modeling and User-Adapted Interaction, 11*(1-2), 87–110. doi:10.1023/A:1011143116306

Bubb-Lewis, C., & Scerbo, M. W. (2002). The effects of communication modes on performance and discourse organization with an adaptive interface. *Applied Ergonomics, 33*, 15–26. doi:10.1016/S0003-6870(01)00046-1

Burkhardt, F., van Ballegooy, M., Englert, R., & Huber, R. (2005). An emotion-aware voice portal. In *Proceedings of the Electronic Speech Signal Processing Conference*, Prague, Czech Republic (pp. 123-131).

Butterworth, R., & Blandford, A. (1997). *Programmable user models: The story so far*. Retrieved June 30, 2007, from http://www.cs.mdx.ac.uk/puma/wp8.pdf

Buxton, W. (2009). (2010). *Human input to computer systems: Theories, techniques and technology*. Retrieved October 27, 2009, from http://www.billbuxton.com/inputManuscript.html

Byrne, M. D. (2001). ACT-R/PM and menu selection: Applying a cognitive architecture to HCI. *International Journal of Human-Computer Studies, 55*, 41–84. doi:10.1006/ijhc.2001.0469

Cai, J., Bouselmi, G., Laprie, Y., & Haton, J.-P. (2009). Efficient likelihood evaluation and dynamic Gaussian selection for hmm-based speech recognition. *Computer Speech & Language, 23*, 147–164. doi:10.1016/j.csl.2008.05.002

Callejas, Z., & López-Cózar, R. (2008a). Relations between de-facto criteria in the evaluation of a spoken dialogue system. *Speech Communication, 50*(8-9), 646–665. doi:10.1016/j.specom.2008.04.004

Callejas, Z., & López-Cózar, R. (2008b). Influence of contextual information in emotion annotation for spoken dialogue systems. *Speech Communication, 50*(5), 416–433. doi:10.1016/j.specom.2008.01.001

Cambridge University. (2011). *Hidden Markov Model Toolkit*. Retrieved January 15, 2011, from http://htk.eng.cam.ac.uk

Camera-phones dotty but dashing. (2010). *The Economist*. Retrieved January 10, 2011, from http://www.economist.com/node/15865270

Camurri, A., Mazzarino, B., & Volpe, G. (2004). Expressive interfaces. *Cognition Technology and Work, 6*(1), 15–22. doi:10.1007/s10111-003-0138-7

Canny, J. (1986). A computational approach to edge detection. *IEEE Transactions on Pattern Analysis and Machine Intelligence, 8*, 679–714. doi:10.1109/TPAMI.1986.4767851

Cao, X., & Balakrishnan, R. (2006). Interacting with dynamically defined information spaces using a handheld projector and a pen. In *Proceedings of the 19th Annual ACM Symposium on User Interface Software and Technology* (p. 225). New York, NY: ACM.

Capra, R. (2010, October 22-27). HCI Browser: A tool for studying Web search behavior. In *Proceedings of the American Society for Information Science and Technology Annual Meeting*, Pittsburgh, PA.

Card, S. K., Moran, T. P., & Newell, A. (1986). The model human processor: An engineering model of human performance. In K. R. Boff, L. Kaufman, & J. P. Thomas (Eds.), *Handbook of perception and human performance. Vol. 2: Cognitive processes and performance* (pp. 1-35). Wright-Patterson AFB, OH: Harry G. Armstrong Aerospace Medical Research Lab.

Card, S. K., Moran, T. P., & Newell, A. (1983). *The psychology of human computer interaction*. Mahwah, NJ: Lawrence Erlbaum.

Card, S., Moran, T., & Newell, A. (1983). *The psychology of human-computer interaction*. Mahwah, NJ: Lawrence Erlbaum.

Carlile, S. (1996). The physical basis and psychophysical basis of sound localization. In Carlile, S. (Ed.), *Virtual auditory space: Generation and applications* (pp. 27–28). Austin, TX: R. G. Landes.

Carroll, J. M., & Olson, J. M. (1990). Mental models in human-computer interaction. In Helander, M. (Ed.), *Handbook of human-computer interaction* (pp. 135–158). Amsterdam, The Netherlands: Elsevier.

Cassell, J., Bickmore, T., Billinghurst, M., Campbell, L., Chang, K., Vilhálmsson, H., & Yan, H. (1999). Embodiment in conversational interfaces: Rea. In *Proceedings of the Conference on Computer-Human Interaction* (pp. 520-527).

Cassell, J., Sullivan, J., Prevost, S., & Churchill, E. F. (2000). *Embodied conversational agents*. Cambridge, MA: MIT Press.

Castellano, G., Fanelli, A. M., & Torsello, M. A. (2006). Dynamic link suggestion by a neuro-fuzzy web recommendation system. In *Proceedings of the IADIS International Conference on World Wide Web/Internet* (pp. 219-225).

Catizone, R., Setzer, A., & Wilks, Y. (2003). Multimodal dialogue management in the COMIC Project. *Proceedings of the European Chapter of the Association for Computational Linguistics Workshop on Dialogue Systems: Interaction, Adaptation, and Styles of Management*, Budapest, Hungary (pp. 25-34).

Chan, M. T. (2001). HMM-based audio-visual speech recognition, integrating geometric and appearance-based visual features. In *Proceedings of the Fourth Workshop on Multimedia Signal Processing* (pp. 9-14).

Chandramohan, D., & Silsbee, P. L. (1996). Multiple deformable template approach for visual speech recognition. In *Proceedings of the Fourth International Conference on Spoken Language*, Philadelphia, PA (Vol. 1, pp. 50-53).

Chang, Y.-J., Tsai, S.-K., & Wang, T.-Y. (2008). A context aware handheld wayfinding system for individuals with cognitive impairments.Proceedings of the 10th international ACM SIGACCESS conference on Computers and accessibility - Assets '08, 27. New York, NY: ACM.

Chang, Y.-J., Tsai, S.-K., Chang, Y., & Wang, T.-Y. (2007). A novel wayfinding system based on geo-coded QR codes for individuals with cognitive impairments. In *Proceedings of the 9th International ACM SIGACCESS Conference on Computers and Accessibility* (p. 231). New York, NY: ACM.

Chang, S., Kwon, Y., & Yang, S. (1998). Speech feature extracted from adaptive wavelet for speech recognition. *Electronics Letters*, *34*(23), 2211–2213. doi:10.1049/el:19981486

Chaudhari, U. V., Ramaswamy, G. N., Potamianos, G., & Neti, C. (2003, April 6-10). Audio-visual speaker recognition using time-varying stream reliability prediction. In *Proceedings of the International Conference on Acoustics, Speech Signal Processing*, Hong Kong, China (Vol. 5, pp. 712-715).

Chen, S. (2002). A cognitive model for non-linear learning in hypermedia programmes. *British Journal of Educational Technology*, *33*(4). doi:10.1111/1467-8535.00281

Chen, T. C., & Chung, K. L. (2001). A new randomized algorithm for detecting lines. *Real Time Imaging*, *7*, 473–481. doi:10.1006/rtim.2001.0233

Chibelushi, C. C., Deravi, F., & Mason, J. S. D. (2002). A review of speech-based bimodal recognition. *IEEE Transactions on Multimedia*, *4*(1), 23–37. doi:10.1109/6046.985551

Childers, D. G. (1990). Speech processing and synthesis for assessing vocal disorders. *IEEE Engineering in Medicine and Biology Magazine*, *9*(1), 69–71. doi:10.1109/51.62911

Chiu, K. C. (2007). *Explorations in the effect of emoticon on negotiation process from the aspect of communication* (Unpublished master's thesis). National Sun Yatsen University, Kaohsiung, Taiwan.

Chiu, M. L. (1998). The design guidance of CSCW: learning from collaborative design studios' in Sasada. In *Proceedings of the 3rd International Conference of the Association for Computer-Aided Architectural Design Research in Asia* (pp. 261-270).

Chong, H.-Q., Tan, A.-H., & Ng, G.-W. (2007). Integrated cognitive architectures: a survey. *Artificial Intelligence Review*, *28*, 103–130. doi:10.1007/s10462-009-9094-9

Chu, S.-W., O'Neill, I., Hanna, P., & McTear, M. (2005). An approach to multistrategy dialogue management. In *Proceedings of the Interspeech/ Eurospeech Conference*, Lisbon, Portugal (pp. 865-868).

Chu, S.-W., O'Neill, I., & Hanna, P. (2007). Using multiple strategies to manage spoken dialogue. In *Proceedings of the International Conference Interspeech* (pp. 158-161).

Clark, R., Richmond, K., & King, S. (2004). Festival 2 - build your own general purpose unit selection speech synthesizer. In *Proceedings of the 5th ISCA Workshop on Speech Synthesis* (pp. 173-178).

Climer, S., & Bhatia, S. K. (2003). Local lines: A linear time line detector. *Pattern Recognition Letters*, *24*, 2291–2300. doi:10.1016/S0167-8655(03)00055-2

Co'zar, R. L., & Callejas, Z. (2006). Two-level speech recognition to enhance the performance of spoken dialogue systems. *Knowledge-Based Systems*, *19*, 153–163. doi:10.1016/j.knosys.2005.11.004

Coffield, F., Moseley, D., Hall, E., & Ecclestone, K. (2010). *Learning styles and pedagogy in Post-16 Learning: a systematic and critical review*. UK: Learning and Skills Research Centre. Retrieved November 20, 2010, from http://www.lsda.org.uk/files/pdf/1543.pdf

Cole, R., Van Vuuren, S., Pellom, B., Hacioglu, K., Ma, J., & Movellan, J. …Wade-stein, D. (2003). Perceptive animated interfaces: first steps toward a new paradigm for human-computer interaction. *Proceedings of the IEEE*, *91*(9), 1391-1405.

Cole, R., Mariani, J., Uszkoreit, H., Varile, G. B., Zaenen, A., Zampolli, A., & Zue, V. (Eds.). (1997). *Survey of the state of the art in human language technology*. Cambridge, UK: Cambridge University Press.

Condorcet, M. J. (1785). E'ssai Sur l'Application de l'Analyse. In *Probabilite´ des De´cisions Rendues a` la Pluralite.´*. Paris, France: Des Voix.

Cooper, R. P. (2002). *Modeling high - Level cognitive processes*. Mahwah, NJ: Lawrence Erlbaum.

Cootes, T. F., Taylor, C. J., & Edward, G. J. (1998). Active appearance models. In *Proceedings of the European Conference on Computer Vision*, Freiburg, Germany (pp. 484-498).

Cormen, T. H., Leiserson, C. E., & Rivest, R. L. (2000). *Introduction to algorithms*. New Delhi, India: Prentice Hall of India.

Corradini, A., & Samuelsson, C. (2008). A generic spoken dialogue manager applied to an interactive 2D game. In E. André, L. Dybkjær, W. Minker, H. Neumann, R. Pieraccini, & M. Weber (Eds.), *Proceedings of the 4th IEEE Tutorial and Research Workshop on Perception and Interactive Technologies for Speech-Based Systems: Perception in Multimodal Dialogue Systems* (LNCS 5078, pp. 2-13).

Corradini, A., Mehta, M., Bernsen, N. O., & Charfuelán, M. (2005). Animating an interactive conversational character for an educational game system. In *Proceedings of the International Conference on Intelligent User Interfaces*, San Diego, CA (pp. 183-190).

Couvreur, L., & Couvreur, C. (2004). Blind model selection for automatic speech recognition in reverberant environments. *The Journal of VLSI Signal Processing*, *36*(2-3), 189–203. doi:10.1023/B:VLSI.0000015096.78139.82

Cowie, R., & Schröder, M. (2005). Piecing together the emotion jigsaw. In S. Bengio & H. Bourlard (Eds.), *Proceedings of the First International Conference on Machine Learning for Multimodal Interaction* (LNCS 3361, pp. 305-317).

Cowie, R., & Cornelius, R. (2003). Describing the emotional states that are expressed in speech. *Speech Communication*, *40*(1-2), 5–32. doi:10.1016/S0167-6393(02)00071-7

Cowie, R., Douglas-Cowie, E., Tsapatsoulis, N., Votsis, G., Kollias, S., Fellenz, W., & Taylor, J. (2001). Emotion recognition in human-computer interaction. *IEEE Signal Processing Magazine*, *18*(1), 32–80. doi:10.1109/79.911197

Cristinacce, D., & Cootes, T. F. (2006). Facial feature detection and tracking with automatic template selection. In *Proceedings of the 7th International Conference on Automatic Face and Gesture Recognition* (pp. 429-434).

Critchley, H. D., Rotshtein, P., Nagai, Y., O'Doherty, J., Mathias, C. J., & Dolana, R. J. (2005). Activity in the human brain predicting differential heart rate responses to emotional facial expressions. *NeuroImage, 24,* 751–762. doi:10.1016/j.neuroimage.2004.10.013

Cuayáhuitl, H., Renals, S., Lemon, O., & Shimodaira, H. (2006). Reinforcement learning of dialogue strategies with hierarchical abstract machines. In *Proceedings of the IEEE/ACL Spoken Language Technology Workshop,* Palm Beach, Aruba (pp. 182-186).

Czyzewski, A., Kaczmarek, A., & Kostek, B. (2003). Intelligent processing of stuttered speech. *Journal of Intelligent Information Systems, 21*(2), 143–171. doi:10.1023/A:1024710532716

Damerau, F. J. (1964). A technique for computer detection and correction of spelling errors. *Communications of the ACM, 7*(3), 171–176. doi:10.1145/363958.363994

Danubianu, M., Pentiuc, S. G., & Socaciu, T. (2009). Towards the optimized personalized therapy of speech disorders by data mining techniques. In *Proceedings of the IEEE Fourth International Multi-Conference on Computing in the Global Information Technology* (pp. 20-25).

Davis, S., & Mermelstein, P. (1980). Comparison of parametric representations for monosyllabic word recognition in continuously spoken sentences. *IEEE Transactions on Acoustics, Speech, and Signal Processing, 28,* 357–366. doi:10.1109/TASSP.1980.1163420

De Wachter, M., Matton, M., Demuynck, K., Wambacq, P., Cools, R., & Van Compernolle, D. (2007). Template based continuous speech recognition. *IEEE Transactions on Audio. Speech and Language Processing, 15*(4), 1377–1390. doi:10.1109/TASL.2007.894524

Dear, B. L. (2008). *Emoticons and smileys emerged on the PLATO system in the 1970s in a unique and different way.* Retrieved December 17, 2009, from http://www.platopeople.com/emoticons.html

DeHaemer, M. Jr, & Zyda, M. (1991). Simplification of objects rendered by polygonal approximations. *Computers & Graphics, 15*(2), 175–184. doi:10.1016/0097-8493(91)90071-O

Deller, J. R., Hansen, J. H. L., & Proakis, J. G. (1993). *Discrete-time processing of speech signals.* New York, NY: Macmillan.

Deng, L., Acero, A., Plumpe, M., & Huang, X. (2000). Large vocabulary speech recognition under adverse acoustic environments. *Proceedings of Interspeech, 13,* 806–809.

Derks, D., Bos, A. E. R., & von Grumbkow, J. (2007). Emoticons and social interaction on the Internet: the importance of social context. *Computers in Human Behavior, 23,* 842–849. doi:10.1016/j.chb.2004.11.013

Dey, A., & Abowd, G. (2000). Towards a better understanding of context and context-awareness. In *Proceedings of the 1st international symposium on Handheld and Ubiquitous Computing* (pp. 304-307).

Diaconis, P. (1988). Group representations in probability and statistics: *Vol. 11. Lecture Notes — Monograph series.* Hayward, CA: Institute of Mathematical Statistics.

Dimitriadis, D., Maragos, P., & Potamianos, A. (2005). Robust AM-FM features for speech recognition. *IEEE Signal Processing Letters, 12*(9), 621–624. doi:10.1109/LSP.2005.853050

Dix, A., Finlay, J., Abowd, G., & Beale, R. (1998). *Human-computer interaction* (2nd ed.). London, UK: Prentice Hall.

Donoho, D. L., & Johnston, I. M. (1995). Denoising by soft-thresholding. *IEEE Transactions on Information Theory, 41*(3), 613–627. doi:10.1109/18.382009

Doorenbos, R. B. (1994). Combining left and right unlinking for matching a large number of learned rules. In *Proceedings of the Twelfth National Conference on Artificial Intelligence,* Seattle, WA.

Dordevic, N., Rančic, D., & Dimitrijevic, A. (2007, July). Evaluation of user cognitive ability. In *Proceedings of the 11th WSEAS International Conference on Computers,* Agios Nikolaos, Crete Island, Greece (pp. 469-474).

Dorst, K., & Dijkhuis, J. (1995). Comparing paradigms for describing design activity. *Design Studies, 16*(2), 261–274. doi:10.1016/0142-694X(94)00012-3

Duda, R. O. (1993). Modeling head related transfer functions. In *Proceedings of the Asilomar Conference on Signals, Systems & Computers* (pp. 996-1000).

Duda, R. O., Hart, P. E., & Stork, D. G. (2001). *Pattern classification*. New York, NY: John Wiley & Sons.

Duda, R. O., & Martens, W. L. (1998). Range dependence of the response of a spherical head model. *The Journal of the Acoustical Society of America, 104*, 3048–3058. doi:10.1121/1.423886

Duffy, V. G. (2008). *Handbook of digital human modeling: Research for applied ergonomics and human factors engineering*. Boca Raton, FL: CRC Press.

Dumas, B., Lalanne, D., & Ingold, R. (2009). Description languages for multimodal interaction: a set of guidelines and its illustration with SMUIML. *Journal on Multimodal User Interfaces, 3*, 237–247. doi:10.1007/s12193-010-0043-3

Dunham, J. G. (1986). Optimum uniform piecewise linear approximation of planar curves. *IEEE Transactions on Pattern Analysis and Machine Intelligence, 8*, 67–75. doi:10.1109/TPAMI.1986.4767753

Dwork, C., Kumar, R., Naor, M., & Sivakumar, D. (2001). Rank aggregation methods for the Web. In *Proceedings of the Tenth International World Wide Web Conference* (pp. 613-622). New York, NY: ACM.

Dybala, P., Ptaszynski, M., Rzepka, R., & Araki, K. (2010). Evaluating subjective aspects of HCI on an example of a non-task oriented conversational system. *International Journal of Artificial Intelligence Tools, 20*(10), 1–39.

Dybkjær, L., & Bernsen, N. O. (2000). Usability issues in spoken language dialogue systems. *Natural Language Engineering, 6*, 243–272. doi:10.1017/S1351324900002461

Eckert, W., Levin, E., & Pieraccini, R. (1998). *Automatic evaluation of spoken dialogue systems* (Tech. Rep. No. TR98.9.1). Florham Park, NJ: ATT Labs Research.

Eco, U. (1980). Function and sign: the semiotics of architecture. In Broadbent, G., Bunt, R., & Jencks, C. (Eds.), *Signs, symbols and architecture* (pp. 11–69). Chichester, UK: John Wiley & Sons.

Edlund, J., Gustafson, J., Heldner, M., & Hjalmarsson, A. (2008). Towards human-like spoken dialogue systems. *Speech Communication, 50*(8-9), 630–645. doi:10.1016/j.specom.2008.04.002

Ejbali, R., Zaied, M., & Amar, C. B. (2010). Wavelet network for recognition system of Arabic word. *International Journal of Speech Technology, 13*, 163–174. doi:10.1007/s10772-010-9076-y

Eldridge, R., & Rudolph, H. (2008). *Stereo vision for unrestricted human computer interaction*. Rijeka, Croatia: InTech.

Elhadad, M., & Robin, J. (1996). An overview of SURGE: A reusable comprehensive syntactic realization component. In *Proceedings of the Eighth International Natural Language Generation Workshop* (pp. 1-4).

Ellis, C. A., & Keddara, K. (1995). *Dynamic change within workflow systems (Tech. Rep.)* (pp. 1–20). Boulder, CO: University of Colorado.

Endrass, B., Rehm, M., & André, E. (2011). Planning small talk behavior with cultural influences for multiagent systems. *Computer Speech & Language, 25*(2), 158–174. doi:10.1016/j.csl.2010.04.001

Eng, K., Lewis, R. L., Tollinger, I., Chu, A., Howes, A., & Vera, A. (2006). Generating automated predictions of behavior strategically adapted to specific performance objectives. In *Proceedings of the ACM/SIGCHI Conference on Human Factors in Computing Systems* (pp. 621-630).

Eveno, N., Caplier, A., & Coulon, P. Y. (2001). A new color transformation for lips segmentation. In *Proceedings of the Fourth Workshop on Multimedia Signal Processing* (pp. 3-8).

Fahlman, S. (1982). *Original Bboard Thread in which:-) was proposed*. Retrieved from http://www.cs.cmu.edu/~sef/Orig-Smiley.htm

Farooq, O., & Datta, S. (2001). Mel filter-like admissible wavelet packet structure for speech recognition. *IEEE Signal Processing Letters, 8*(7), 196–198. doi:10.1109/97.928676

Farooq, O., & Datta, S. (2004). Wavelet based robust sub-band features for phoneme recognition. *IEEE Proceedings on Vision Image Signal Processing, 151*(3), 187–193. doi:10.1049/ip-vis:20040324

Farooq, O., & Datta, S. (2011). *Enhancing robustness in speech recognition using visual information*. Hershey, PA: IGI Global.

Farooq, O., Datta, S., & Shrotriya, M. C. (2010). Wavelet sub-band based temporal features for robust Hindi phoneme recognition. *International Journal of Wavelets, Multresolution, and Information Processing, 8*(6), 847–859. doi:10.1142/S0219691310003845

Faure, C., & Julia, L. (1993). Interaction hommemachine par la parole et le geste pour l'édition de documents. In *Proceedings of the International Conference on Real and Virtual Worlds* (pp. 171-180).

Felder, R. M., & Silverman, L. K. (1988). Learning and teaching styles in engineering education. *English Education, 78*(7), 674–681.

Ferguson, J. D. (1980). Variable duration models for speech. In *Proceedings of the Symposium on Application of Markov Models to Text and Speech*, Princeton, NJ (pp. 143-179).

Fetter, P., Kaltenmeier, A., Peter, T. K., & Brietzmann, R. (1996). Improved modeling of OOV words in spontaneous speech. In *Proceedings of the IEEE International Conference on Acoustics, Speech, and Signal Processing* (pp. 534-537).

Field, A. (2000). *Discovering statistics using SPSS for Windows*. Thousand Oaks, CA: Sage.

Finholt, T., Sproull, L., & Kiesler, S. (1990). Communication and performance in ad hoc task groups. In Galegher, J., Kraut, R. E., & Egido, C. (Eds.), *Intellectual teamwork: Social and technological foundations of cooperative work* (pp. 291–325). Mahwah, NJ: Lawrence Erlbaum.

Fish, J., & Scrivener, S. (1990). Amplifying the mind's eye: sketching and visual cognition. *Leonardo, 23*, 117–126. doi:10.2307/1578475

Fitts, P. M. (1954). The information capacity of the human motor system in controlling the amplitude of movement. *Journal of Experimental Psychology, 47*, 381–391. doi:10.1037/h0055392

Flanigan, F. J., & Kazdan, J. L. (1990). *Calculus two: Linear and nonlinear functions*. Berlin, Germany: Springer-Verlag.

Flecha-García, M. L. (2010). Eyebrow raises in dialogue and their relation to discourse structure, utterance function and pitch accents in English. *Speech Communication, 52*(6), 542–554. doi:10.1016/j.specom.2009.12.003

Flycht-Eriksson, A. (1999). A survey of knowledge sources in dialogue systems. In *Proceedings of the IJCAI Workshop on Knowledge and Reasoning in Practical Dialogue Systems* (p. 48).

Föckler, P., Zeidler, T., Brombach, B., Bruns, E., & Bimber, O. (2005). PhoneGuide: museum guidance supported by on-device object recognition on mobile phones. In *Proceedings of the 4th International Conference on Mobile and Ubiquitous Multimedia* (pp. 3-10). New York, NY: ACM.

Fonseca, E. S., Guido, R. C., Scalassara, P. R., Maciel, C. D., & Pereira, J. C. (2007). Wavelet time-frequency analysis and least squares support vector machines for the identification of voice disorders. *Computers in Biology and Medicine, 37*(4), 571–578. doi:10.1016/j.compbiomed.2006.08.008

Forbes-Riley, K. M., & Litman, D. (2004). Modelling user satisfaction and student learning in a spoken dialogue tutoring system with generic, tutoring, and user affect parameters. In *Proceedings of the North American Chapter of the Association for Computational Linguistics on Human Language Technologies*, New York, NY (pp. 264-271).

Forbes-Riley, K., & Litman, D. (2011). Designing and evaluating a wizarded uncertainty-adaptive spoken dialogue tutoring system. *Computer Speech & Language, 25*(1), 105–126. doi:10.1016/j.csl.2009.12.002

Forney, G. D. (1973). The Viterbi algorithm. *Proceedings of the IEEE, 61*, 268–278. doi:10.1109/PROC.1973.9030

Forslund, K., Dagman, A., & Söderberg, R. (2006). Visual sensitivity: communicating poor quality. In *Proceedings of the International Design Conference* (pp. 713-720).

Forsyth, D. A., & Ponce, J. (2002). *Computer vision: A modern approach*. Upper Saddle River, NJ: Prentice Hall.

Fox, E. A., & Shaw, J. A. (1994). Combination of multiple searches. In *Proceedings of the Second Text REtreival Conference* (pp. 243-249). Gaithersburg, MD: NIST.

Franck, T., & Halima, H. M. (2005). Modelling elementary cognitive abilities for adaptive hypermedia presentation. *User Modeling and User-Adapted Interaction, 15*, 459–495. doi:10.1007/s11257-005-2529-3

Frankie, J., & Rama, G. (2009). Multimodal and federated interaction. In Chen, S., & Magoulas, G. (Eds.), *Adaptable and adaptive hypermedia systems* (pp. 102–122). Hershey, PA: IRM Press.

Fraser, N., & Gilbert, G. (1991). Simulating speech systems. *Computer Speech & Language, 5*, 81–99. doi:10.1016/0885-2308(91)90019-M

Frias-Martinez, E., Magoulas, G., Chen, S., & Macredie, R. (2005). Modelling human behaviour in user adaptive systems: Recent advances using soft computing techniques. *Expert Systems with Applications, 29*, 320–329. doi:10.1016/j.eswa.2005.04.005

Fukumoto, M., Suenaga, Y., & Mase, K. (1994). Finger-pointer: Pointing interface by image processing. *Computers & Graphics, 18*(5), 633–642. doi:10.1016/0097-8493(94)90157-0

Gabriel, G. C., & Maher, M. L. (2002). Coding and modeling communication in architectural collaborative design. *Automation in Construction, 11*, 199–211. doi:10.1016/S0926-5805(00)00098-4

Gajos, K. Z., Wobbrock, J. O., & Weld, D. S. (2007). Automatically generating user interfaces adapted to users' motor and vision capabilities. In *Proceedings of the ACM Symposium on User Interface Software and Technology* (pp. 231-240).

Gales, M. J. F., Knill, K. M., & Young, S. J. (1999). State-based Gaussian selection in large vocabulary continuous speech recognition using HMM's. *IEEE Transactions on Speech and Audio Processing, 7*(2), 152–161. doi:10.1109/89.748120

Gales, M. J. F., & Young, S. J. (1996). Robust continuous speech recognition using parallel model combination. *IEEE Transactions on Speech and Audio Processing, 4*(5), 352–359. doi:10.1109/89.536929

Gales, M., & Young, S. (2007). The application of hidden Markov models in speech recognition. *Foundations and Trends in Signal Processing, 1*(3), 195–304. doi:10.1561/2000000004

Gammeter, S., Gassmann, A., Bossard, L., Quack, T., & Van Gool, L. (2010). Server-side object recognition and client-side object tracking for mobile augmented reality. In *Proceedings of the IEEE Conference on Computer Vision and Pattern Recognition Workshops* (pp. 1-8). Washington, DC: IEEE Computer Society.

Garcia, E., & Sicilia, M. A. (2010). Information imperfection as inherent characteristics of adaptive hypermedia: imprecise models of users and interactions. In Chen, S., & Magoulas, G. (Eds.), *Adaptable and adaptive hypermedia systems* (pp. 150–167). Hershey, PA: IRM Press.

Garrido, J. L., & Gea, M. (2001). Modelling dynamic group behaviours. In C. Johnson (Ed.), *Proceedings of the 8th International Workshop on Interactive Systems: Design, Specification and Verification* (LNCS 2220, pp. 128-143).

Gavrila, D., & Philomin, V. (1999). Real-time object detection for smart vehicles. In *Proceedings of the 7th International Conference on Computer Vision* (pp. 87-93).

Gebhard, P., Klesen, M., & Rist, T. (2004). Coloring multi-character conversations through the expression of emotions. In *Proceedings of the Tutorial and Research Workshop on Affective Dialogue Systems*, Kloster Irsee, Germany (pp. 128-141).

Gebrekristos, M., Aljadaan, A., & Bihani, K. (2008). QR-Codes for the chronically homeless. In *Proceedings of the Twenty-Sixth Annual CHI Conference Extended Abstracts on Human Factors in Computing Systems* (p. 3879). New York, NY: ACM.

Georgila, K., Henderson, J., & Lemon, O. (2005). Learning user simulations for information state update dialogue systems. In *Proceedings of the Eurospeech Conference* (pp. 893-896).

Georgoulas, G., Georgopoulos, V. C., & Stylios, C. D. (2006). Speech sound classification and detection of articulation disorders with support vector machines and wavelets. In *Proceedings of the 28th IEEE Annual International Conference on Engineering in Medicine and Biology Society* (pp. 2199-2202)

Georgoulas, G., Georgopoulos, V. C., Stylios, G. D., & Stylios, C. D. (2009). Detection of articulation disorders using empirical mode decomposition and neural networks. In *Proceedings of the International Joint Conference on Neural Networks*, Atlanta, GA (pp. 959-964).

Gero, J. S. (1990). Design prototypes: A knowledge representation schema for design. *AI Magazine, 2009*, 27–36.

Giorgino, T., Azzini, I., Rognoni, C. S. Q., Stefanelli, M., Falavigna, D., & Gretter, R. (2005). Automated spoken dialog system for hypertensive patient home management. *International Journal of Medical Informatics, 74*(2-4). doi:10.1016/j.ijmedinf.2004.04.026

Glass, J. R. (1999). Challenges for spoken dialogue system. In *Proceedings of the IEEE Workshop on Automatic Speech Recognition and Understanding.*

Glass, J., Flammia, G., Goodine, D., Phillips, M., Polifroni, J., & Sakai, S. (1995). Multilingual spoken-language understanding in the MIT Voyager system. *Speech Communication, 17*(1-2), 1–18. doi:10.1016/0167-6393(95)00008-C

Gluck, K. A., & Pew, R. W. (Eds.). (2005). *Modeling human behavior with integrated cognitive architectures: Comparison, evaluation, and validation.* London, UK: Psychology Press.

Goel, N., Thomas, S., Agarwal, M., Akyazi, P., Burget, L., & Feng, K..... Schwarz, P. (2010). Approaches to automatic lexicon learning with limited training examples. In *Proceedings of the IEEE Conference on Acoustics, Speech, and Signal Processing* (pp. 5094-5097).

Goel, V. (1995). *Sketches of thought.* Cambridge, MA: MIT Press.

Goldschen, A. J., Garcia, O. N., & Petajan, E. D. (1996). Rationale for phoneme-viseme mapping and feature selection in visual speech recognition. In Stork, D. G., & Hennecke, M. E. (Eds.), *Speech reading by humans and machines* (pp. 505–515). Berlin, Germany: Springer-Verlag.

Goldschmidt, G. (1991). The dialectics of sketching. *Creativity Research Journal, 4*(2), 123–143. doi:10.1080/10400419109534381

Goldschmidt, G. (1992). Serial sketching: visual problem solving in designing. *Cybernetics and Systems: An International Journal, 23*, 191–219. doi:10.1080/01969729208927457

Goldschmidt, G. (1994). On visual design thinking: the via kids of architecture. *Design Studies, 15*(2), 158–174. doi:10.1016/0142-694X(94)90022-1

Gonzalez, R. C., & Woods, R. E. (1993). *Digital image processing.* Reading, MA: Addison-Wesley.

Google. (2011a). *Nexus S.* Retrieved January 10, 2011, from http://www.google.com/nexus/

Google. (2011b). *Google goggles.* Retrieved January 10, 2011, from http://www.google.com/mobile/goggles/#text

Gordon, G., Darrell, T., Harville, M., & Woodfill, J. (1999). Background estimation and removal based on range and color. In *Proceedings of the International IEEE Conference on Computer Vision and Pattern Recognition.*

Gorin, A., Giuseppe, L., Jeremy, R., & Wright, H. (1997). How may I help you? *Speech Communication, 23*(1-2), 113–127. doi:10.1016/S0167-6393(97)00040-X

Graesser, A. C., Chipman, P., Hayens, B. C., & Olney, A. (2005). Auto Tutor: An intelligent tutoring system with mixed-initiative dialog. *IEEE Transactions on Education, 48*(4), 612–619. doi:10.1109/TE.2005.856149

Graham, R., Knuth, D., & Potashnik, O. (1994). *Concrete mathematics.* Reading, MA: Addison-Wesley.

Grant, K. W., & Braida, L. D. (1991). Evaluating the articulation index for auditory-visual input. *The Journal of the Acoustical Society of America, 89*, 2950–2960. doi:10.1121/1.400733

Gray, P., England, D., & McGowan, S. (1994). XUAN: Enhancing the UAN to capture temporal relationships among actions. In *Proceedings of the 9th Conference on People and Computers* (pp. 301-312).

Gray, W. D., & Sabnani, H. (1994). Why you can't program your VCR, or, predicting errors and performance with production system models of display-based action. In *Proceedings of the Conference Companion on Human Factors in Computing Systems in ACM/SIGCHI Conference on Human Factors in Computing Systems* (pp. 79-80).

Gray, W., Young, R. M., & Kirschenbaum, S. (1997). Introduction to this special issue on cognitive architectures and human-computer interaction. *Human-Computer Interaction, 12*, 301–309. doi:10.1207/s15327051hci1204_1

Greaves, A., & Rukzio, E. (2008). Evaluation of picture browsing using a projector phone. In *Proceedings of the 10th International Conference on Human Computer Interaction with Mobile Devices and Services* (Vol. 5, p. 351). New York, NY: ACM.

Greenberg, S. (1999). Speaking in shorthand-A syllable-centric perspective for understanding pronunciation variation. *Speech Communication, 29*, 159–176. doi:10.1016/S0167-6393(99)00050-3

Griffiths, T. L., Kemp, C., & Tenenbaum, J. B. (2008). *Bayesian models of inductive learning.* Tutorial presented at the Annual Meeting of the Cognitive Science Society.

Griol, D., Callejas, Z., López-Cózar, R., Espejo, G., Ábalos, N., & Molina, J. M. (2011). On the development of adaptive and user-centred interactive multimodal. In Tiwary, U. S., & Siddiqui, T. J. (Eds.), *Speech, image and language processing for human computer interaction.* Hershey, PA: IGI Global.

Griol, D., Hurtado, L. F., Segarra, E., & Sanchis, E. (2008). A statistical approach to spoken dialog systems design and evaluation. *Speech Communication, 50*(8-9), 666–682. doi:10.1016/j.specom.2008.04.001

Griol, D., Rojo, E., Arroyo, Á., Patricio, M. A., & Molina, J. M. (2010). A conversational academic assistant for the interaction in virtual worlds. *Advances in Soft Computing, 79*, 283–290. doi:10.1007/978-3-642-14883-5_37

Grossman, T., Balakrishnan, R., Kurtenbach, G., Fitzmaurice, G., Khan, A., & Buxton, B. (2001). Interaction techniques for 3D modeling on large displays. In *Proceedings of the Symposium on Interactive 3D Graphics* (p. 1723).

Gruenstein, A., McGraw, I., & Badr, I. (2008). The WAMI toolkit for developing, deploying, and evaluating web-accessible multimodal interfaces. In *Proceedings of the International Conference on Multimodal Interfaces.*

Gupta, N., Ordonez, C., & Barreto, A. (2001). The effect of pinna protrusion angle in the localization of virtual sound in the horizontal plane. *The Journal of the Acoustical Society of America, 110*(5), 2679.

Gupta, R. (2006). *Speech recognition for Hindi (M. Tech. Project Report).* Bombay, Mumbai, India: Indian Institute of Technology.

Gurban, M., & Thiran, J.-P. (2009). Information theoretic feature extraction for audio-visual speech recognition. *IEEE Transactions on Signal Processing, 57*(12), 4765–4776. doi:10.1109/TSP.2009.2026513

Gusfield, D. (1997). *Algorithms on strings, trees, and sequences: Computer science and computational biology.* Cambridge, UK: Cambridge University Press. doi:10.1017/CBO9780511574931

Haeb-Umbach, R., & Ney, H. (1992). Linear discriminant analysis for improved large vocabulary continuous speech recognition. In *Proceedings of the International Conference on Acoustics, Speech and Signal Processing* (pp. 13-16).

Hagen, A., & Morris, A. (2005). Recent advances in the multi-stream HMM/ANN hybrid approach to noise robust ASR. *Computer Speech & Language, 19*, 3–30. doi:10.1016/j.csl.2003.12.002

Hagiwara. (2011). *UnNatural language processing blog.* Retrieved from http://blog.lilyx.net/

Hall, L., Woods, S., Aylett, R., Paiva, A., & Newall, L. (2005). Achieving empathic engagement through affective interaction with synthetic characters. In J. Tao, T. Tan, & R. W. Picard (Eds.), *Proceedings of the International Conference on Affective Computing and Intelligent Interaction*, Beijing, China (LNCS 3784, pp. 731-738).

Hampson, P. J., & Moris, P. E. (1996). *Understanding cognition.* Oxford, UK: Blackwell.

Han, J. Y. (2005). Low-cost multi-touch sensing through frustrated total internal reflection. In *Proceedings of the 18th Annual ACM Symposium on User Interface Software and Technology.*

Han, H. L. (1994). Measuring a dummy head in search of pinna cues. *Journal of the Audio Engineering Society. Audio Engineering Society, 42*(1-2), 15–37.

Hardy, G. H., & Wright, E. M. (1968). *An introduction to the theory of numbers.* New York, NY: Oxford University Press.

Harrison, M. D., & Duke, D. J. (1995). A review of formalisms for describing interactive behavior. In R. N. Taylor & J. Coutaz (Eds.), *Proceedings of the Workshop on Software Engineering and Human-Computer Interaction* (LNCS 896, pp. 49-75).

Haseel, L., & Hagen, E. (2005). Adaptation of an automotive dialogue system to users' expertise. In *Proceedings of the Interspeech/Eurospeech Conference*, Lisbon, Portugal (pp. 222-226).

Heckmann, M., Berthommier, F., & Kroschel, K. (2001). A hybrid ANN/HMM audio-visual speech recognition system. In *Proceedings of the International Conference on Auditory-Visual Speech Processing*, Aalborg, Denmark (pp. 190-195).

Heim, J., Nilsson, E. G., & Skjetne, J. H. (2007). User profiles for adapting speech support in the opera Web browser to disabled users. In C. Stephanidis & M. Pieper (Eds.), *Proceedings of the 9th ECRIM Workshop on Universal Access in Ambient Intelligence Environments* (LNCS, 4397, pp. 154-172).

Helman, S., Juan, W., Leonel, V., & Aderito, M. (Eds.). (2007, May 23-25). *Proceedings of the GW 7th International Workshop on Gesture in Human-Computer Interaction and Simulation*, Lisbon, Portugal.

Henricksen, K., Indulska, J., & Rakotonirainy, A. (2002). Modeling context information in pervasive computing systems. In *Proceedings of the 1st International Conference on Pervasive Computing* (pp. 167-180).

Henrysson, A., Billinghurst, M., & Ollila, M. (2005). Face to face collaborative AR on mobile phones. In *Proceedings of the 4th IEEE/ACM International Symposium on Mixed and Augmented Reality* (pp. 80-89). Washington, DC: IEEE Computer Society.

Hermansky, H., & Sharma, S. (1999). Temporal patterns (TRAPs) in ASR of noisy speech. In *Proceedings of the IEEE Conference on Acoustic, Speech, and Signal Processing* (pp. 289-292).

Hermansky, H. (1990). Perceptually predictive (PLP) analysis of speech. *The Journal of the Acoustical Society of America, 87*(4), 1738–1752. doi:10.1121/1.399423

Hermansky, H., & Morgan, N. (1994). RASTA processing of speech. *IEEE Transactions on Speech and Audio Processing, 2*(4), 578–589. doi:10.1109/89.326616

He, X., & Deng, L. (2008). *Discriminative learning for speech recognition: Theory and practice*. Santa Clara, CA: Morgan & Claypool.

Hickok, G., & Poippil, D. (2007). The critical organization of speech processing. *Nature Reviews. Neuroscience, 8*(5), 393–402. doi:10.1038/nrn2113

Hick, W. E. (1952). On the rate of gain of information. *Journal of Experimental Psychology, 4*, 11–26.

Hirsch, H.-G., & Finster, H. (2008). A new approach for the adaptation of HMMs to reverberation and background noise. *Speech Communication, 50*, 244–263. doi:10.1016/j.specom.2007.09.004

Hofer, R., Naeff, D., & Kunz, A. (2009). FLATIR: FTIR multi touch detection on a discrete distributed sensor array. In *Proceedings of the International Conference on Tangible and Embedded Interaction* (pp. 317-322).

Hollan, J., Hutchins, E., & Kirsh, D. (2000). Distributed cognition: Toward a new foundation for human computer interaction research. *ACM Transactions on Computer-Human Interaction, 7*(2), 174–196. doi:10.1145/353485.353487

Höllerer, T. H., & Feiner, S. K. (2004). Mobile augmented reality. In Karimi, H., & Hammad, A. (Eds.), *Telegeoinformatics: Location-based computing and services*. London, UK: Taylor and Francis Books.

Hoog, J., Falkner, C., & Seifried, P. (2007). Collaborative spaces as learning environments. In *Proceedings of the Conference of the Arab Society for Computer Aided Architectural Design* (pp. 357-364).

Hoog, J., Falkner, C., & Seifried, P. (2008). Second City: A three-dimensional city model as interdisciplinary platform for research. In *Proceedings of the Conference on Education and Research in Computer Aided Architectural Design in Europe* (pp. 359-366).

Hornof, A. J., & Kieras, D. E. (1997). Cognitive modeling reveals menu search is both random and systematic. In *Proceedings of the ACM/SIGCHI Conference on Human Factors in Computing Systems* (pp. 107-114).

Horvitz, E., Breese, J., Heckerman, D., Hovel, D., & Rommelse, K. (1995). *The Lumiere Project: Bayesian user modeling for inferring the goals and needs of software users*. Redmond, WA: Microsoft Research. Retrieved from http://research.microsoft.com/en-us/um/people/horvitz/lumiere.HTM

Hosom, J. P., Shriberg, L., & Green, J. R. (2004). Diagnostic assessment of childhood apraxia of speech using automatic speech recognition (ASR) methods. *Journal of Medical Speech-Language Pathology, 12*(4), 171–176.

Howes, A., Vera, A., Lewis, R. L., & Mccurdy, M. (2004). Cognitive constraint modeling: A formal approach to reasoning about behavior. In *Proceedings of the 26th Annual Meeting of the Cognitive Science Society*.

Hsu, H. P. (2010). Design behavior in the interactive virtual environment on the network space. In *Proceedings of the Second IEEE International Conference on Intelligent Human Computer Interaction* (pp. 320-327).

Hua, A., & Weng, F. (2008). User simulation as testing for spoken dialog systems. In *Proceedings of the 9th SIGdial Workshop on Discourse and Dialogue*.

Huang, C., Xu, P., Zhang, X., Zhao, S., Huang, T., & Xu, B. (1999). LODESTAR: A Mandarin spoken dialogue system for travel information retrieval. In *Proceedings of the Conference Eurospeech* (pp. 1159-1162).

Huang, H., Cerekovic, A., Pandzic, I., Nakano, Y., & Nishida, T. (2007). A script driven multimodal embodied conversational agent based on a generic framework. In *Proceedings of the 7th International Conference on Intelligent Virtual Agents* (pp. 381-382).

Huang, X., Acero, A., & Hon, H. W. (2001). *Spoken language processing: A guide to theory algorithm and system development*. Upper Saddle River, NJ: Prentice Hall.

Hung, V., Gonzalez, A., & DeMara, R. (2009). Towards a context-based dialog management layer for expert systems. In *Proceedings of the International Conference on Information, Process, and Knowledge Management* (pp. 60-65).

Huseyinov, I. N. (2011, July 9-14). Fuzzy linguistic modelling cognitive styles/learning styles for adaptation through multi-level granulation. In J. A. Jacko (Ed.), *Proceedings of the 14th International Conference on Human Computer Interaction: Users and Applications*, Orlando, FL (LNCS 6764, pp. 39-47).

Huseyinov, I. N., & Akin, C. (2009) Collaborative filtering recommender systems with fuzzy set theory. In *Proceedings of the International Conference on e-Learning, e-Business, EIS, and e-Government*, Las Vegas, NV (pp. 397-400).

Huseyinov, I. N., & Akin, C. (2010). Adaptation based on psychological factors using fuzzy logic. In *Proceedings of the International Conference on e-Learning, e-Business, EIS, and e-Government*, Las Vegas, NV (pp. 297-303).

Hutchins, E. (1995). How a cockpit remembers its speeds. *Cognitive Science, 19*, 265–288. doi:10.1207/s15516709cog1903_1

Huttenlocher, D., Lilien, R., & Olson, C. (1999). View-based recognition using an eigen-space approximation to the Hausdorff measure. *IEEE Transactions on Pattern Analysis and Machine Intelligence, 21*(9), 951–955. doi:10.1109/34.790437

Hwang, M., & Huang, X. (1992). Subphonetic modeling with Markov states—Senone. In *Proceedings of the IEEE International Conference on Acoustics, Speech and Signal Processing*, San Francisco, CA (pp. 33-36).

Ibrahim, A., & Johansson, P. (2002). Multimodal dialogue systems for interactive TV applications. In *Proceedings of the 4th IEEE International Conference on Multimodal Interfaces* (pp. 117-122).

Imai, H., & Iri, M. (1986). Computational geometric methods for polygonal approximations of a curve. *Computer Vision Graphics and Image Processing, 36*, 31–41. doi:10.1016/S0734-189X(86)80027-5

Ip, A. (2002). *The impact of emoticons on affect interpretation in instant messaging*. Retrieved January 20, 2011 from http://amysmile.com/doc/emoticon_paper.pdf

James, F., Rayner, M., & Hockey, B. A. (2000). Accuracy, coverage, and speed: What do they mean to users? In *Proceedings of the CHI Workshop on Natural-Language Interaction*.

Jang, K. S. (2007). Lip contour extraction based on active shape model and snakes. *International Journal of Computer Science and Network Security, 7*(10), 148–153.

Jansen, B. J., & Spink, A. (2006). How are we searching the World Wide Web? A comparison of nine search engine transaction logs. *Information Processing & Management*, *42*(2), 248–263. doi:10.1016/j.ipm.2004.10.007

Jenabi, M., & Reiterer, H. (2008, October). *Fintteraction: Finger interaction with mobile phones*. Paper presented at the Future Mobile Experiences Workshop, Lund, Sweden.

Jian, Z., Kaynak, M. N., Vheok, A. D., & Chung, K. C. (2001). Real-time lip tracking for virtual lip implementation in virtual environments and computer games. In *Proceedings of the 10ᵗʰ IEEE International Conference on Fuzzy Systems*, Melbourne, VIC, Australia (vol. 3, pp. 1359-1362).

Jiang, H., & Li, X. (2007). Incorporating training errors for large margin HMMs under semi definite programming framework. In *Proceedings of the IEEE International Conference on Acoustics, Speech, and Signal Processing* (pp. 629-632).

Jiang, H. (2010). Discriminative training of HMM for automatic speech recognition: A survey. *Computer Speech & Language*, *24*, 589–608. doi:10.1016/j.csl.2009.08.002

John, B. E., & Kieras, D. (1996). The GOMS family of user interface analysis techniques: Comparison and contrast. *ACM Transactions on Computer-Human Interaction*, *3*, 320–351. doi:10.1145/235833.236054

John, B. E., & Kieras, D. E. (1996). The GOMS family of user interface analysis techniques: Comparison and contrast. *ACM Transactions on Computer-Human Interaction*, *3*(4), 320–351. doi:10.1145/235833.236054

Johnson-Laird, P. A. (1988). *The computer and the mind*. Cambridge, MA: Harvard University Press.

Johnson, P. (1992). *Human computer interaction: psychology, task analysis and software engineering*. New York, NY: McGraw-Hill.

Jokinen, K. (2003). Natural interaction in spoken dialogue systems. In *Proceedings of the Workshop on Ontologies and Multilinguality in User Interfaces*, Crete, Greece (pp. 730-734).

Jones, M., & Rehg, J. (1999). Statistical color models with application to skin detection. In *Proceedings of the IEEE Conference on Computer Vision and Pattern Recognition* (Vol. 1).

Jost, U., Heine, H., & Evermann, G. (1997). What is wrong with the lexicon- an attempt to model pronunciations probabilistically. In *Proceedings of the 5ᵗʰ European Conference on Speech Communication and Technology*, Rhodes, Greece (pp. 2475-2479).

Jurafsky, D., & Martin, J. H. (2001). *Speech and language processing: An introduction to natural language processing, computational linguistics and speech recognition*. Upper Saddle River, NJ: Prentice Hall.

Kahn, M., Mackisack, M. S., Osborne, M. R., & Smyth, G. K. (1992). On the consistency of Prony's method and related algorithms. *Journal of Computational and Graphical Statistics*, *1*, 329–349. doi:10.2307/1390787

Kamijo, K., Kamijo, N., & Sakamoto, M. (2006). Electronic clipping system with invisible barcodes. In *Proceedings of the 14th Annual ACM International Conference on Multimedia* (p. 753). New York, NY: ACM.

Kamppari, S. O., & Hazen, T. J. (2000). Word and phone level acoustic confidence scoring. In *Proceedings of the International Conference on Acoustics, Speech and Signal Processing* (Vol. 3, pp. 1799-1802).

Kang, H., Suh, E., & Yoo, K. (2008). Packet-based context aware system to determine information system user's context. *Expert Systems with Applications*, *35*, 286–300. doi:10.1016/j.eswa.2007.06.033

Kaptelinin, V., Nardi, B. A., & Macaulay, C. (1999). The activity checklist: a tool for representing the space of context. *Interactions Magazine*, *6*(4), 27–39.

Kathryn, M., Lou, M. M., & Saunders, R. (2008). Achieving adaptable behavior in intelligent rooms using curious supervised learning agents. In *Proceedings of the 13th International Conference of the Association for Computer-Aided Architectural Design Research in Asia* (pp. 185-192).

Kaur, M., & Tanwar, P. (2010). Developing brain computer interface using fuzzy logic. *International Journal of Information Technology and Knowledge Management*, *2*(2), 429–434.

Kavcic, A. (2004). Fuzzy user modelling for adaptation in educational hypermedia. *IEEE Transactions on Systems, Man and Cybernetics. Part C, Applications and Reviews*, *34*(4), 439–449. doi:10.1109/TSMCC.2004.833294

Kawakami, M. (2008). The database of 31 Japanese emoticon with their emotions and emphases. *The Human Science Research Bulletin of Osaka Shoin Women's University, 7,* 67–82.

Kaynak, M. N., Zhi, Q., Cheok, A. D., Sengupta, K., Jian, Z., & Chung, K. C. (2004). Analysis of lip geometric features for audio-visual speech recognition. *IEEE Transactions on Systems, Man, and Cybernetics. Part A, Systems and Humans, 34*(4), 564–570. doi:10.1109/TSMCA.2004.826274

Keates, S., Clarkson, J., & Robinson, P. (2000). Investigating the applicability of user models for motion impaired users. In *Proceedings of the ACM/SIGACCESS Conference on Computers and Accessibility* (pp. 129-136).

Keidl, M., & Kemper, A. (2004). A framework for context-aware adaptable Web services. In E. Bertino, S. Christodoulakis, D. Plexousakis, V. Christophides, M. Koubarakis, K. Böhm, & E. Ferrari (Eds.), *Proceedings of the 9th International Conference on Advances in Database Technology* (LNCS 2992, pp. 826-829).

Khanam, R., Mumtaz, S. M., Farooq, O., Datta, S., & Vyas, A. L. (2009). Audio-visual features for stop recognition from continuous Hindi speech. In *Proceedings of the National Symposium on Acoustics* (pp. 91-96).

Kieras, D. E. (1994). GOMS modeling of user interfaces using NGOMSL. In *Proceedings of the Conference Companion on Human Factors in Computing Systems,* Boston, MA (pp. 371-372).

Kieras, D. E. (2005). Fidelity issues in cognitive architectures for HCI Modelling: Be careful what you wish for. In *Proceedings of the International Conference on Human Computer Interaction.*

Kieras, D. E., Wood, S. D., Abotel, K., & Hornof, A. (1995). GLEAN: A computer-based tool for rapid GOMS model usability evaluation of user interface designs. In *Proceedings of the ACM Symposium on User Interface and Software Technology* (pp. 91-100).

Kieras, D. E., & Meyer, D. E. (1997). An overview of the EPIC architecture for cognition and performance with application to human-computer interaction. *Human-Computer Interaction, 4*(12), 391–438.

Kieras, D. E., Meyer, D. E., Ballas, J. A., & Lauber, E. J. (2000). Modern computational perspectives on executive mental processes and cognitive control: Where to from here? In Monsell, S., & Driver, J. (Eds.), *Attention and performance, XVIII: Control of cognitive processes* (pp. 681–712). Cambridge, MA: MIT Press.

Kieras, D. E., & Polson, P. G. (1985). An approach to the formal analysis of user complexity. *International Journal of Man-Machine Studies, 22,* 365–394. doi:10.1016/S0020-7373(85)80045-6

Kierczak, M. (2009). *Rosetta- A rough set toolkit for analyzing data.* Retrieved August 12, 2011, from http://www.lcb.uu.se/tools/rosetta/

Kim, D. Y., Umesh, S., Gales, M. J. F., Hain, T., & Woodland, P. (2004). Using VTLN for broadcast news transcription. In *Proceedings of the International Conference on Spoken Language Processing,* Jeju, Korea.

Kim, S. G., Kim, J. W., & Lee, C. W. (2007). Implementation of multi-touch tabletop display for HCI (human computer interaction). In *Proceedings of the 12th International Conference on Human-Computer Interaction: Interaction Platforms and Techniques* (pp. 854-863).

Kim, D. S., Lee, S. Y., & Kil, R. M. (1999). Auditory processing of speech signals for robust speech recognition in real world noisy environment. *IEEE Transactions on Speech and Audio Processing, 7*(1), 55–69. doi:10.1109/89.736331

Kim, D. Y., & Un, C. K. (1996). Probabilistic vector mapping with trajectory information for noise-robust speech recognition. *Electronics Letters, 32*(17), 1550–1551. doi:10.1049/el:19961081

Klette, R., & Rosenfeld, A. (2004a). *Digital geometry: Geometric methods for digital picture analysis.* San Francisco, CA: Morgan Kaufmann.

Klette, R., & Rosenfeld, A. (2004b). Digital straightness: A review. *Discrete Applied Mathematics, 139*(1-3), 197–230. doi:10.1016/j.dam.2002.12.001

Koenig, G. K. (1974). *Architettura e comunicazione Seconda edizione accresciutia da un saggio su Schindler e Neutra.* Florence, Italia: Liberia Editrice Fiorentina.

Komorowski, J., Pawlak, Z., Polkowski, L., & Skowron, A. (1999). Rough sets: A tutorial. In Pal, S. K., & Skowron, A. (Eds.), *Rough fuzzy hybridization: A new trend in decision-making* (pp. 3–98). Berlin, Germany: Springer-Verlag.

Kotropoulos, C., & Arce, G. R. (2009). Linear classifier with reject option for the detection of vocal fold paralysis and vocal fold edema. *EURASIP Journal on Advances in Signal Processing, 2009,* 1–13. doi:10.1155/2009/203790

Krenn, B., & Schollum, C. (2008, April 2-4). The RAS-CALLI platform for a flexible and distributed development of virtual systems augmented with cognition. In *Proceedings of the International Conference on Cognitive Systems,* Karlsruhe, Germany.

Krstulovic, S., Bimbot, F., Boëffard, O., Charlet, D., Fohr, D., & Mella, O. (2006). Optimizing the coverage of a speech database through a selection of representative speaker recordings. *Speech Communication, 48*(10), 1319–1348. doi:10.1016/j.specom.2006.07.002

Kubota, H., Yamashita, K., Fukuhara, T., & Nihsida, T. (2002). POC caster: Broadcasting agent using conversational representation for internet community. *Transactions of the Japanese Society for Artificial Intelligence, 17,* 313–321. doi:10.1527/tjsai.17.313

Kudo, T., & Matsumoto, Y. (2001). Chunking with support vector machines. In *Proceedings of the Second Meeting of the North American Chapter of the Association for Computational Linguistics* (pp. 192-199).

Kuhn, G. F. (1977). Model for the interaural time differences in the azimuthal plane. *The Journal of the Acoustical Society of America, 62,* 157–167. doi:10.1121/1.381498

Kumar, N., & Andreou, A. G. (1998). Heteroscedastic discriminant analysis and reduced rank HMMs for improved speech recognition. *Speech Communication, 26,* 283–297. doi:10.1016/S0167-6393(98)00061-2

Kuniavsky, M. (2003). *Observing the user experience: A practitioner's guide to user research.* San Francisco, CA: Morgan Kaufmann.

Kvan, T. (2000). Collaborative design: what is it? *Automation in Construction, 9,* 409–415. doi:10.1016/S0926-5805(99)00025-4

Kvan, T. (2001). The pedagogy of virtual design studio. *Automation in Construction, 10,* 345–354. doi:10.1016/S0926-5805(00)00051-0

Laird, J. E. (2008). Extending the soar cognitive architecture. In *Proceedings of the First Conference on Artificial General Intelligence* (pp. 224-235).

Laird, J. E., Rosenbloom, P. S., & Newell, A. (1984). Towards chunking as a general learning mechanism. In *Proceedings of the National Conference on Artificial Intelligence,* Austin, TX (pp. 188-192).

Laird, R., Newell, J., & Paul, A. (1987). Soar: An architecture for general intelligence. *Artificial Intelligence, 33,* 1–64. doi:10.1016/0004-3702(87)90050-6

Lallement, Y., & Alexandre, F. (1997). Cognitive aspects of neurosymbolic integration. In Sun, R., & Alexandre, F. (Eds.), *Connectionist-symbolic integration.* London, UK: Lawrence Erlbaum.

Langner, B., & Black, A. (2005). Using speech in noise to improve understandability for elderly listeners. In *Proceedings of the Conference on Automatic Speech Recognition and Understanding,* San Juan, Puerto Rico (pp. 392-396).

Larkin, J. H., & Simon, H. A. (1987). Why a diagram is (sometimes) worth ten thousand words. *Cognitive Science, 11,* 65–99. doi:10.1111/j.1551-6708.1987.tb00863.x

Larsen, L. B. (2003). Assessment of spoken dialogue system usability – what are we really measuring. In *Proceedings of the Eurospeech Conference,* Geneva, Switzerland.

Laseau, P. (1993). *Graphic thinking for architects and designers.* New York, NY: Van Nostrand Reinhold.

Lawson, B., & Loke, S. (1997). Computers, words and pictures. *Design Studies, 18*(7), 171–183. doi:10.1016/S0142-694X(97)85459-2

LeCun, Y., Bottou, L., Bengio, Y., & Haffner, P. (1998). Gradient based learning applied to document recognition. *Proceedings of the IEEE, 86*(11), 2278–2324. doi:10.1109/5.726791

Lee, C., Yoo, S. K., Park, Y. J., Kim, N. H., Jeong, K. S., & Lee, B. C. (2005). Using neural network to recognize human emotions from heart rate variability and skin resistance. In *Proceedings of the Annual International Conference on Engineering in Medicine and Biology Society*, Shanghai, China (pp. 5523-5525).

Lee, J. (2009, January 19). Is that an emoticon in 1862? *The New York Times*. Retrieved from http://cityroom.blogs.nytimes.com/2009/01/19/hfo-emoticon/

Lee, C. H., Gauvain, J. L., Pieraccini, R., & Rabiner, L. R. (1993). Large vocabulary speech recognition using subword units. *Speech Communication, 13*, 263–279. doi:10.1016/0167-6393(93)90025-G

Lee, C. M., & Narayanan, S. S. (2005). Toward detecting emotions in spoken dialogs. *IEEE Transactions on Speech and Audio Processing, 13*(2), 293–303. doi:10.1109/TSA.2004.838534

Lee, C., Jung, S., Kim, K., Lee, D., & Lee, G. G. (2010). Recent approaches to dialog management for spoken dialog systems. *Journal of Computing Science and Engineering, 4*(1), 1–22.

Lee, C., Jung, S., Seokhwan, K., & Lee, G. G. (2009). Example-based dialog modeling for practical multi-domain dialog system. *Speech Communication, 51*, 466–484. doi:10.1016/j.specom.2009.01.008

Lee, K., Hon, H., & Reddy, R. (1990). An overview of the SPHINX speech recognition system. In Waibel, A., & Lee, K.-F. (Eds.), *Readings in speech recognition* (pp. 600–610). San Francisco, CA: Morgan Kaufmann. doi:10.1109/29.45616

Leggetter, C. J., & Woodland, P. (1995). Speaker adaptation using maximum likelihood linear regression. *Computer Speech & Language, 9*(2), 171–185. doi:10.1006/csla.1995.0010

Lemon, O., Georgila, K., & Henderson, J. (2006). Evaluating effectiveness and portability of reinforcement learned dialogue strategies with real users: the TALK TownInfo evaluation. In *Proceedings of the IEEE-ACL Spoken Language Technologies Conference*, Palm Beach, Aruba (pp. 178-181).

Lemon, O., Liu, X., Shapiro, D., & Tollander, C. (2006). Hierarchical reinforcement learning of dialogue policies in a development environment for dialogue systems: REALLDUDE. In *Proceedings of the 10th SemDial Workshop on the Semantics and Pragmatics of Dialogue: Demonstration Systems*.

Lepri, B., Mana, N., Cappelletti, A., Pianesi, F., & Zancanaro, M. (2009). Modeling the personality of participants during group interactions. In G.-J. Houben, G. McCalla, F. Pianesi, & M. Zancanaro (Eds.), *Proceedings of the 17th International Conference on User Modeling, Adaptation, and Personalization* (LNCS 5535, pp. 114-125).

Leßmann, N., & Wachsmuth, I. (2003). A cognitively motivated architecture for an anthropomorphic artificial communicator. In *Proceedings of the International Conference on Computing and Mission* (pp. 277-278).

Levin, E., Pieraccini, R., & Eckert, E. (2000). A stochastic model of human-machine interaction for learning dialog strategies. *IEEE Transactions on Speech and Audio Processing, 8*(1), 11–23. doi:10.1109/89.817450

Levinson, S. (1986). Continuously variable duration hidden Markov models for automatic speech recognition. *Computer Speech & Language, 1*(1), 29–45. doi:10.1016/S0885-2308(86)80009-2

Lewis, M., Haviland-Jones, J. M., & Feldman, B. L. (Eds.). (2008). *Handbook of emotions*. New York, NY: Guilford.

Li, J., Yuan, M., & Lee, C. H. (2006). Soft margin estimation of hidden Markov model parameters. In *Proceedings of the International Conference Interspeech* (pp. 2422-2425).

Li, L., Cao, F., Chou, W., & Liu, F. (2006). XM-flow: An extensible micro-flow for multimodal interaction. In *Proceedings of the 8th Workshop on Multimedia Signal Processing* (pp. 497-500).

Li, L., Li, L., Chou, W., & Liu, F. (2007). R-Flow: An extensible XML based multimodal dialogue system architecture. In *Proceedings of the 9th Workshop on Multimedia Signal Processing* (pp. 86-89).

Lieberman, H., Faaborg, A., Daher, W., & Espinosa, J. (2005, January 9-12). How to wreck a nice beach you sing calm incense. In *Proceedings of the International Conference on Intelligent User Interfaces*, San Diego, CA.

Li, J., Wang, J., Zhao, Y., & Yang, Z. (2004). Self-adaptive design of hidden Markov models. *Pattern Recognition Letters*, *25*, 197–210. doi:10.1016/j.patrec.2003.10.001

Lin, H. H., & Chang, T. W. (2007). A camera based multitouch interface builder for designers. In J. A. Jacko (Ed.), *Proceedings of the 12th International Conference on Human-Computer Interaction: Applications and Services* (LNCS 4553, pp. 1102-1109).

Liporace, L. A. (1982). Maximum likelihood estimation for multivariate observations of Markov source. *IEEE Transactions on Information Theory*, *28*, 729–734. doi:10.1109/TIT.1982.1056544

Litman, D. J., & Pan, S. (2002). Designing and evaluating an adaptive spoken dialogue system. *User Modeling and User-Adapted Interaction*, *12*, 111–137. doi:10.1023/A:1015036910358

Litman, D. J., Ros, C. P., Forbes-Riley, K., VanLehn, K., Bhembe, D., & Silliman, S. (2006). Spoken versus typed human and computer dialogue tutoring. *International Journal of Artificial Intelligence in Education*, *16*, 145–170.

Little, M. A., McSharry, P. E., Hunter, E. J., Spielman, J., & Ramig, L. O. (2008). Suitability of dysphonia measurements for telemonitoring of Parkinson's disease. *IEEE Transactions on Bio-Medical Engineering*, *56*(4), 1015–1022. doi:10.1109/TBME.2008.2005954

Livescu, K., Glass, J., & Bilmes, J. (2003). Hidden feature models for speech recognition using dynamic Bayesian networks. In *Proceedings of the International Conference Eurospeech* (pp. 2529-2532).

Lockton, R. (2009). *Hand gesture recognition using special glove and wrist*. Oxford, UK: Oxford University.

Long, C. J., & Datta, S. (1998). Discriminant wavelet basis construction for speech recognition. In *Proceedings of the 5th International Conference on Spoken Language Processing*, Sydney, Australia (Vol. 3, pp. 1047-1049).

López-Cózar, R., Callejas, Z., Kroul, M., Nouza, J., & Silovský, J. (2008). Two-level fusion to improve emotion classification in spoken dialogue systems. In P. Sojka, A. Horák, I. Kopecek, & K. Pala (Eds.), *Proceedings of the 11th International Conference on Text, Speech and Dialogue* (LNCS 5246, pp. 617-624).

López-Cózar, R., & Araki, M. (2005). *Spoken, multilingual and multimodal dialogue systems. development and assessment*. New York, NY: John Wiley & Sons.

Lopez-Poveda, E. A., & Meddis, R. (1996). A physical model of sound diffraction and reflections in the human concha. *The Journal of the Acoustical Society of America*, *100*, 3248–3259. doi:10.1121/1.417208

Lowe, D. (1999). Object recognition from local scale-invariant features. In *Proceedings of the International Conference on Computer Vision* (Vol. 2, pp. 1150-1157). Washington, DC: IEEE Computer Society.

Maciejewski, J., Ptaszynski, M., & Dybala, P. (2010). Developing a large-scale corpus for natural language processing and emotion processing research in Japanese. In *Proceedings of the International Workshop on Modern Science and Technology* (pp. 192-195).

Maher, M. L., Simoff, S. J., & Cicognani, A. (1997). Observations from an experimental study of computer-mediated collaborative design. In *Proceedings of the Third International IFIP WG 5.2 Workshop on Formal Design Methods for CAD* (pp. 165-186).

Mahlke, S. (2006). Emotions and EMG measures of facial muscles in interactive contexts. In *Proceedings of the Conference on Human Factors in Computing Systems*, Montreal, QC, Canada.

Maier, A., Haderlein, T., Eysholdt, U., Rosanowski, F., Batliner, A., Schuster, M., & Noth, E. (2009a). PEAKS – A system for the automatic evaluation of voice and speech disorders. *Speech Communication*, *51*, 425–437. doi:10.1016/j.specom.2009.01.004

Maier, A., Hönig, F., Bocklet, T., & Nöth, E. (2009b). Automatic detection of articulation disorders in children with cleft lip and palate. *The Journal of the Acoustical Society of America*, *126*(5), 2589–25602. doi:10.1121/1.3216913

Mallat, S. (1998). *A wavelet tour of signal processing*. New York, NY: Academic Press.

Mamdani, E. M. (1974). Applications of fuzzy algorithms for simple dynamic plants. *Proceedings of the IEEE*, *21*(2), 1585–1588.

Maness, J. M. (2008). A linguistic analysis of chat reference conversations with 18-24 year-old college students. *Journal of Academic Librarianship*, *34*(1), 31–38. doi:10.1016/j.acalib.2007.11.008

Mankoff, J., Fait, H., & Juang, R. (2005). Evaluating accessibility through simulating the experiences of users with vision or motor impairments. *IBM Systems Journal*, *44*(3), 505–518. doi:10.1147/sj.443.0505

Maragoudakis, M. (2007). MeteoBayes: Effective plan recognition in a weather dialogue system. *IEEE Intelligent Systems*, *22*(1), 66–77. doi:10.1109/MIS.2007.14

Markel, J. D., & Gray, A. H. (1976). *Linear prediction of speech*. Berlin, Germany: Springer-Verlag.

Martinovski, B., & Traum, D. (2003). Breakdown in human-machine interaction: the error is the clue. In *Proceedings of the ISCA Tutorial and Research Workshop on Error Handling in Dialogue Systems*, Chateau d'Oex, Vaud, Switzerland (pp. 11-16).

Matsumoto, Y., Kitauchi, A., Yamashita, T., Hirano, Y., Matsuda, H., Takaoka, K., & Asahara, M. (2000). *Japanese Morphological Analysis System ChaSen version 2.2.1.* Retrieved January 20, 2011, from http://chasen.aist-nara.ac.jp/hiki/ChaSen/

Maunder, A., Marsden, G., & Harper, R. (2007). Creating and sharing multi-media packages using large situated public displays and mobile phones. In *Proceedings of the 9th International Conference on Human Computer Interaction with Mobile Devices and Services* (pp. 222-225). New York, NY: ACM.

Maunder, A., Marsden, G., & Harper, R. (2008). SnapAndGrab: accessing and sharing contextual multi-media content using Bluetooth enabled camera phones and large situated displays. In *Proceedings of the CHI Extended Abstracts on Human Factors in Computing Systems* (pp. 2319-2324). New York, NY: ACM.

Maunder, A. (2010). *Designing appropriate interactive systems for the developing world*. Cape Town, South Africa: University of Cape Town.

McAllaster, D., Gillick, L., Scattone, F., & Newman, M. (1998). Studies with fabricated switchboard data: Exploring sources of model-data mismatch. In *Proceedings of the DARPA Workshop on Conversational Speech Recognition* (Vol. 1).

McGlashan, S., Burnett, D. C., Carter, J., Danielsen, P., Ferrans, J., & Hunt, A. ...Tryphonas, S. (2004). *Voice Extensible Markup Language (VoiceXML)*. Retrieved from http://www.w3.org/TR/voicexml21/

Mckim, R. H. (1980). *Experiences in visual thinking*. Florence, KY: Brooks/Cole Press.

Mcmillan, W. W. (1992). Computing for users with special needs and models of computer-human interaction. In *Proceedings of the ACM/SIGCHI Conference on Human Factors in Computing Systems* (pp. 143-148).

McTear, M. F. (1998). Modelling spoken dialogues with state transition diagrams: experiences with the CSLU toolkit. In *Proceedings of the International Conference on Spoken Language Processing* (pp. 1223-1226).

McTear, M. F. (2002). Spoken dialog technology: Enabling the conversational user interface. *ACM Computing Surveys*, *34*(1), 90–169. doi:10.1145/505282.505285

McTear, M. F. (2004). *Spoken dialogue technology*. New York, NY: Springer. doi:10.1007/978-0-85729-414-2

Middlebrooks, J. C. (1999). Individual differences in external-ear transfer functions reduced by scaling in frequency. *The Journal of the Acoustical Society of America*, *106*(3), 1480–1492. doi:10.1121/1.427176

Middlebrooks, J. C. (1999). Virtual localization improved by scaling nonindividualized external-ear transfer functions in frequency. *The Journal of the Acoustical Society of America*, *106*(3), 1493–1510. doi:10.1121/1.427147

Mills, A. W. (1972). Auditory localization. In Tobias, J. V. (Ed.), *Foundations of modern auditory theory* (*Vol. 2*, pp. 303–348). New York, NY: Academic Press.

Minker, W. (1998). Stochastic versus rule-based speech understanding for information retrieval. *Speech Communication*, *25*(4), 223–247. doi:10.1016/S0167-6393(98)00038-7

Minker, W. (1999). Stochastically-based semantic analysis for ARISE - Automatic railway information systems for Europe. *Grammars, 2*(2), 127–147. doi:10.1023/A:1009943728288

Minker, W., Haiber, U., Heisterkamp, P., & Scheible, S. (2004). The Seneca spoken language dialogue system. *Speech Communication, 43*(1-2), 89–102. doi:10.1016/j.specom.2004.01.005

Minsky, M. (1975). A framework for representing knowledge. In Winston, P. H. (Ed.), *The psychology of computer vision* (pp. 211–277). New York, NY: McGraw-Hill.

Mistry, P., Maes, P., & Chang, L. (2007). WUW - Wear Ur World - A wearable gestural interface. In *Proceedings of the 27th International Conference Extended Abstracts on Human Factors in Computing Systems* (pp. 4111-4116).

Mitchell, T. J., Chen, S., & Macredie, R. D. (2010). *Cognitive styles and adaptive Web-based learning.* Retrieved October 12, 2010, from http://bura.brunel.ac.uk/handle/2438/388

Mitchell, W. J. (1995). *City of Bits: Space, Place, and the Infobahn.* Cambridge, MA: MIT Press.

Mitra, S., & Acharya, T. (2007). Gesture recognition: A survey. *IEEE Transactions on Systems, Man and Cybernetics. Part C, Applications and Reviews, 37*(3), 311–324. doi:10.1109/TSMCC.2007.893280

Miyamoto, C., Komai, Y., Takiguchi, T., Ariki, Y., & Li, I. (2010). Multimodal speech recognition of a person with articulation disorders using AAM (Active Appearance Model) and MAF (Multiple Acoustic Frames). In *Proceedings of the IEEE International Workshop on Multimedia Signal Processing,* Saint Malo, France (pp. 517-520).

Mobasher, B., & Anand, S. S. (2010). *Intelligent techniques for Web personalization.* Retrieved November 3, 2010, from http://www.inf.unibz.it/~ricci/ATIS/papers/itwp-v5.pdf

Moghaddam, B., Jebara, T., & Pentland, A. (2000). Bayesian face recognition. *Pattern Recognition, 33*(11), 1771–1782. doi:10.1016/S0031-3203(99)00179-X

Mohri, M. (1997). Finite-state transducers in language and speech processing. *Computational Linguistics, 23*(2), 269–311.

Mok, L. L., Lau, W. H., Leung, S. H., Wang, S. L., & Yan, H. (2004). Person authentication using ASM based lip shape and intensity information. In *Proceedings of the International Conference on Image Processing* (Vol. 1, pp. 561-564).

Mokhtarian, F., & Mohanna, F. (2002). Content-based video database retrieval through robust corner tracking. In *Proceedings of the IEEE Workshop on Multimedia Signal Processing* (pp. 224-228).

Moon, T. K. (1996). The expectation-maximization algorithm. *IEEE Signal Processing Magazine, 13*(6), 47–60. doi:10.1109/79.543975

Moran, D. B., Cheyer, A. J., Julia, L. E., Martin, D. L., & Park, S. (1997). Multimodal user interface in the open agent architecture. In *Proceedings of the 2nd International Conference on Intelligent User Interfaces* (pp. 61-68).

Moran, T. P. (1981). Command language grammar: A representation for the user interface of interactive computer systems. *International Journal of Man-Machine Studies, 15*(1), 3–50. doi:10.1016/S0020-7373(81)80022-3

Morrison, D., Wang, R., & Silva, L. C. D. (2007). Ensemble methods for spoken emotion recognition in call-centers. *Speech Communication, 49*(2), 98–112. doi:10.1016/j.specom.2006.11.004

Motomura, Y., Yoshida, K., & Fujimoto, K. (2000). Generative user models for adaptive information retrieval. In *Proceedings of the IEEE International Conference on Systems, Man and Cybernetics* (pp. 665-670).

Motonorihi, S., Ueda, S., & Akiyama, K. (2003). Human interface based on finger gesture recognition using omni-directional image sensor. In *Proceedings of the IEEE International Symposium on Virtual Environments, Human-Computer Interfaces and Measurement Systems* (pp. 68-72).

Müller, C., & Runge, F. (1993). Dialogue design principles - key for usability of voice processing. In *Proceedings of the Eurospeech Conference* (pp. 943-946).

Nadia, M., & Cooperstock, J. (2004). Occlusion detection for front projected interactive displays. In *Proceedings of Pervasive Computing and Advances in Pervasive Computing.*

Naguib, H., Coulouris, G., & Mitchell, S. (2001). Middleware support for context-aware multimedia applications. In *Proceedings of the 3rd International Working Conference on New Developments in Distributed Applications and Interoperable Systems* (pp. 9-22).

Nakamura, J., Ikeda, T., Inui, N., & Kotani, Y. (2003). Learning face mark for natural language dialogue system. In *Proceedings of the IEEE International Conference on Natural Language Processing and Knowledge Engineering* (pp. 180-185).

Nakamura, A. (1993). *Kanjo hyogen jiten* (Dictionary of emotive expressions). Tokyo, Japan: Tokyodo.

Nason, S., & Laird, J. E. (2004, July 30-August 1). Soar-RL: Integrating reinforcement learning with soar. In *Proceedings of the International Conference on Computing and Mission* (pp. 208-211).

Nasraoui, O., & Petenes, C. (2003). Combining web usage mining and fuzzy inference for web personalization. In *Proceedings of the WEBKDD Conference on Web Mining as Premise to Effective Web Applications* (pp. 37-46).

Navarro, G. (2001). A guided tour to approximate string matching. *ACM Computing Surveys*, *33*(1), 31–88. doi:10.1145/375360.375365

Nefian, A. V., Liang, L., Pi, X., Xiaoxiang, L., Mao, C., & Murphy, K. (2002). A coupled HMM for audio-visual speech recognition. In *Proceedings of the IEEE International Conference on Acoustics, Speech, and Signal Processing*, Orlando, FL (Vol. 2, pp. 2013-2016).

Nefian, A. V., Liang, L., Pi, X., Liu, X., & Murphy, K. (2002). Dynamic Bayesian networks for audio-visual speech recognition. *EURASIP Journal on Applied Signal Processing*, (1): 1274–1288. doi:10.1155/S1110865702206083

Nejime, Y., & Moore, B. C. J. (1997). Simulation of the effect of threshold elevation and loudness recruitment combined with reduced frequency selectivity on the intelligibility of speech in noise. *The Journal of the Acoustical Society of America*, *102*, 603–615. doi:10.1121/1.419733

Nelson, G. (1979). *Problems of design*. New York, NY: Whitney Library of Design.

Nesson, R. (2007). *A Harvard Law school lecture in Second Life*. New York, NY: Christine Lagorio.

Neti, C., Potamianos, G., Luettin, J., Matthews, I., Glotin, H., & Vergyri, D. ...Zhou, J. (2000). *Audio-visual speech recognition: Workshop 2000 final report*. Baltimore, MD: Centre for Language and Speech Processing.

Neumeyer, L., & Weintraub, M. (1994). Probabilistic optimum filtering for robust speech recognition. In *Proceedings of the International Conference on Acoustic, Speech and Signal Processing* (Vol. 1, pp. 417-420).

Neumeyer, L., Sankar, A., & Digalakis, V. (1995). A comparative study of speaker adaptation techniques. In *Proceedings of the International Conference Eurospeech*, Madrid, Spain, (pp. 1127-1130).

Neville, E. H. (1950). *The Farey series of order 1025*. Cambridge, UK: Cambridge University Press.

Newell, A. (1973). *You can't play 20 questions with nature and win: Projective comments on the papers of this symposium*. Pittsburgh, PA: Carnegie Mellon University.

Newell, A. (1990). *Unified theories of cognition*. Cambridge, MA: Harvard University Press.

Newell, A., & Simon, H. A. (1995). *GPS: A program that simulates human thought*. Cambridge, MA: MIT Press.

Ney, H., & Ortmanns, S. (2000). Progress in dynamic programming search for large vocabulary continuous speech recognition. *Proceedings of the IEEE*, *88*(8), 1224–1240. doi:10.1109/5.880081

Nielsen, P. B., & Baekgaard, A. (1992). Experience with a dialogue description formalism for realistic applications. In *Proceedings of the International Conference on Spoken Language Processing* (pp. 719-722).

Nihei, K. (2004). Context sharing platform. *NEC Journal of Advanced Technology*, *1*(3), 200–204.

Nikos, T., Panagiotis, G., Zacharias, L., Constantinous, M., & George, S. (2009). An assessment of human factors in adaptive hypermedia environments. In Chen, S., & Magoulas, G. (Eds.), *Adaptable and adaptive hypermedia systems* (pp. 1–34). Hershey, PA: IRM Press.

Nikos, T., Panagiotis, G., Zacharias, L., & Costas, M. (2009). Individual differences in adaptive educational hypermedia: the effect of cognitive style and visual working memory. In Chen, S., & Magoulas, G. (Eds.), *Adaptable and adaptive hypermedia systems* (pp. 147–163). Hershey, PA: IRM Press.

Nilsson, M., Nordberg, J., & Claesson, I. (2007). Face detection using local SMQT features and split up snow classifier. In *Proceedings of the International Conference on Acoustics, Speech and Signal Processing* (pp. 589-592).

Nintendo. (2011). *Face Raiders*. Retrieved June 1, 2011, from http://www.nintendo.com/3ds/built-in-software#/5

Nokia. (2010). *Nokia N8*. Retrieved January 10, 2011, from http://events.nokia.com/nokian8/home.html

Norcio, F., & Chen, Q. (1992). Modeling user's with neural architecture. In *Proceedings of the International Joint Conference on Neural Networks* (pp. 547-552).

Norcio, F. (1989). Adaptive interfaces: Modelling tasks and users. *IEEE Transactions on Systems, Man, and Cybernetics, 19*(2), 399–408. doi:10.1109/21.31042

O'Connell, K. (1997). Object-adaptive vertex based shape coding method. *IEEE Transactions on Circuits and Systems for Video Technology, 7*, 251–255. doi:10.1109/76.554440

O'Shaughnessy, D. (2001). *Speech communications: Human and machines*. Piscataway, NJ: IEEE Press.

Oh, A., & Rudnicky, A. (2000). Stochastic language generation for spoken dialog systems. In *Proceedings of the ANLP North American Chapter of the Association for Computational Linguistics Workshop on Conversational Systems* (pp. 27-32).

Oka, N. (1991). Hybrid cognitive model of conscious level processing and unconscious level processing. In *Proceedings of the IEEE International Joint Conference on Neural Networks* (pp. 485-490).

Oka, K., Sato, Y., & Koike, H. (2002). Real-time fingertip tracking and gesture recognition tracking. *IEEE Computer Graphics and Applications, 22*(6), 64–71. doi:10.1109/MCG.2002.1046630

Ooi, W. C., Jeon, C., Kim, K., Ko, H., & Han, D. K. (2009). Effective lip localization and tracking for achieving multimodal speech recognition. *Multisensor Fusion and Integration for Intelligent Systems, 35*(1), 33–43. doi:10.1007/978-3-540-89859-7_3

Osborne, M. R., & Smyth, G. K. (1995). A modified Prony algorithm for fitting sums of exponential functions. *SIAM Journal on Scientific and Statistical Computing, 16*, 119–138. doi:10.1137/0916008

Ostendorf, M., Digalakis, V. V., & Kimball, O. A. (1996). From HMM's to segment models: A unified view of stochastic modeling for speech recognition. *IEEE Transactions on Speech and Audio Processing, 4*(5), 360–378. doi:10.1109/89.536930

Otsu, N. (1979). A threshold selection method from gray-level histograms. *IEEE Transactions on Systems, Man, and Cybernetics, 9*(1), 62–66. doi:10.1109/TSMC.1979.4310076

Paek, T., & Horvitz, E. (2004). Optimizing automated call routing by integrating spoken dialogue models with queuing models. In *Proceedings of the North American Chapter of the Association for Computational Linguistics on Human Language Technologies* (pp. 41-48).

Paliwal, K. K. (1998). Spectral subband centroid features for speech recognition. In *Proceedings of the IEEE International Conference on Acoustics, Speech and Signal Processing* (Vol. 2, pp. 617-620).

Pargellis, A., Kuo, H., & Lee, C. (2004). An automatic dialogue generation platform for personalized dialogue applications. *Speech Communication, 42*, 329–351. doi:10.1016/j.specom.2003.10.003

Parks, T. W., & Burrus, C. S. (1987). *Digital filter design*. New York, NY: John Wiley & Sons.

Pavlovic, V., Sharma, R., & Huang, T. (2001). Visual interpretation of hand gestures for HCI. *IEEE Transactions on Pattern Analysis and Machine Intelligence, 19*(7), 677–695. doi:10.1109/34.598226

Pawlak, Z. (1982). Rough sets. *International Journal of Computer and Information Sciences, 11*, 341–356. doi:10.1007/BF01001956

Payne, S. J., & Green, T. R. G. (1986). Task-action grammars: A model of mental representation of task languages. *Human-Computer Interaction*, *2*, 93–133. doi:10.1207/s15327051hci0202_1

Peck, V. A., & John, B. E. (1992). Browser-Soar: a computational model of a highly interactive task. In *Proceedings of the ACM/SIGCHI Conference on Human Factors in Computing Systems* (pp. 165-172).

Peckham, J. (1991, February 14-27). Speech understanding and dialogue over the telephone: an overview of the ESPRIT SUNDIAL project. In *Proceedings of the DARPA Workshop on Speech and Language*, Pacific Gove, CA.

Perez, J. C., & Vidal, E. (1994). Optimum polygonal approximation of digitized curves. *Pattern Recognition Letters*, *15*, 743–750. doi:10.1016/0167-8655(94)90002-7

Phillips, N. (2009). *Graphical modification for partially sighted gamer accessibility (Tripos Part II)*. Cambridge, UK: University of Cambridge.

Picard, R. W., & Daily, S. B. (2005). Evaluating affective interactions: Alternatives to asking what users feel. In *Proceedings of the CHI Workshop on Evaluating Affective Interfaces-Innovative Approaches*, Portland, OR.

Picard, R. W. (1997). *Affective computing*. Cambridge, MA: MIT Press.

Picone, J. W. (1993). Signal modelling techniques in speech recognition. *Proceedings of the IEEE*, *81*(9), 1215–1247. doi:10.1109/5.237532

Picone, J. W., Ebel, W. J., & Deshmukh, N. (1995). Automatic speech understanding: The next generation. *Digital Signal Processing Technology*, *57*, 101–114.

Pile, J. F. (1979). *Design: purpose, form and meaning*. Amherst, MA: University of Massachusetts Press.

Pinto, J., & Sitaram, R. N. V. (2005). Confidence measures in speech recognition based on probability distribution of likelihoods. In *Proceedings of the International Conference Interspeech* (pp. 4-8).

Pitterman, J., & Pitterman, A. (2006). Integrating emotion recognition into an adaptive spoken language dialogue system. In *Proceedings of the 2nd IEEE International Conference on Intelligent Environments* (pp. 213-219).

Poslad, S., Laamanen, H., Malaka, R., Nick, A., Buckle, P., & Zipf, A. (2001). Crumpet: Creation of user-friendly mobile services personalized for tourism. In *Proceedings of the 2nd International Conference on 3G Mobile* (pp. 28-32).

Potamianos, G., Neti, C., Gravier, G., Garg, A., & Senior, A. W. (2003). Recent advances in the automatic recognition of audio-visual speech. *Proceedings of the IEEE*, *91*, 1306–1326. doi:10.1109/JPROC.2003.817150

Potamianos, G., Neti, C., Luettin, J., & Matthews, I. (2004). Audiovisual automatic speech recognition: An overview. In Bailly, G., Bateson, V. V., & Perrier, P. (Eds.), *Issues in visual and audio-visual speech processing*. Cambridge, MA: MIT Press.

Pratihar, S., & Bhowmick, P. (2009). A thinning-free algorithm for straight edge detection in a gray-scale image. In *Proceedings of the 7th International Conference on Advances in Pattern Recognition* (pp. 341-344).

Pratihar, S., & Bhowmick, P. (2010). Shape decomposition using Farey sequence and saddle points. In *Proceedings of the Seventh Indian Conference on Computer Vision, Graphics and Image Processing* (pp. 77-84).

Prendinger, H., Mayer, S., Mori, J., & Ishizuka, M. (2003). Persona effect revisited. using bio-signals to measure and reflect the impact of character-based interfaces. In *Proceedings of the Intelligent Virtual Agents*, Kloster Irsee, Germany (pp. 283-291).

Ptaszynski, M. (2006). *Boisterous language: Analysis of structures and semiotic functions of emotive expressions in conversation on Japanese Internet bulletin board forum '2channel'* (Unpublished master's thesis). UAM, Poznan, Poland.

Ptaszynski, M., Dybala, P., Komuda, R., Rzepka, R., & Araki, K. (2010). Development of emoticon database for affect analysis in Japanese. In *Proceedings of the 4th International Symposium on Global COE Program of the Knowledge Federation* (pp. 203-204).

Ptaszynski, M., Dybala, P., Rzepka, R., & Araki, K. (2009). Affecting corpora: Experiments with automatic affect annotation system - a case study of the 2channel forum. In *Proceedings of the Conference of the Pacific Association for Computational Linguistics* (pp. 223-228).

Ptaszynski, M., Dybala, P., Rzepka, R., & Araki, K. (2010). Towards fully automatic emoticon analysis system (^o^). In *Proceedings of the Sixteenth Annual Meeting of the Association for Natural Language Processing* (pp. 583-586).

Ptaszynski, M., Dybala, P., Shi, W., Rzepka, R., & Araki, K. (2009). Towards context aware emotional intelligence in machines: Computing contextual appropriateness of affective states. In *Proceedings of the 21st International Joint Conference on Artificial Intelligence* (pp. 1469-1474).

Ptaszynski, M., Maciejewski, J., Dybala, P., Rzepka, R., & Araki, K. (2010a). CAO: A fully automatic emoticon analysis system. In *Proceedings of the Twenty-Fourth AAAI Conference on Artificial Intelligence* (pp. 1026-1032).

Ptaszynski, M., Maciejewski, J., Dybala, P., Rzepka, R., & Araki, K. (2010b). CAO: A fully automatic emoticon analysis system based on theory of kinesics. *IEEE Transactions on Affective Computing, 1*(1), 46–59. doi:10.1109/T-AFFC.2010.3

Pulman, S. G., Boye, J., Cavazza, M., Smith, C., & Santos de la Camara, R. (2010). How was your day? In *Proceedings of the Workshop on Companionable Dialogue Systems* (pp. 37-42).

Puurula, A., & Van Compernolla, D. (2010). Dual stream speech recognition using articulatory syllable models. *International Journal of Speech Technology, 13*, 219–230. doi:10.1007/s10772-010-9080-2

Rabiner, L. R. (1989). A tutorial on hidden Markov models and selected applications in speech recognition. *Proceedings of the IEEE, 77*(2), 257–285. doi:10.1109/5.18626

Rabiner, L. R., & Juang, B. H. (1993). *Fundamentals of speech recognition*. Upper Saddle River, NJ: Prentice Hall.

Rabiner, L. R., & Juang, B. H. (2006). Speech recognition: Statistical methods. In *Encyclopedia of linguistics* (pp. 1–18). Amsterdam, The Netherlands: Elsevier.

Radford, L. (2003). Gestures, speech, and the sprouting of signs: A semiotic-cultural approach to students' types of generalization. *Mathematical Thinking and Learning, 5*(1), 37–70. doi:10.1207/S15327833MTL0501_02

Radulovic, F., & Milikic, N. (2009). Smiley ontology. In *Proceedings of the Social Network Interoperability Workshop, held in conjunction with the Asian Semantic Web Conference*.

Raihan, H., Khan, N., Farooq, O., Datta, S., & Vyas, A. L. (2010). Comparative performance of audio and audio-visual features for Hindi fricative recognition. *Proceedings of the National Symposium on Acoustics, 37*(1), 7-12.

Rambow, O., Bangalore, S., & Walker, M. (2001). Natural language generation in dialog systems. In *Proceedings of the First International Conference on Human Language Technology Research*, San Diego, CA.

Ramírez, J., Segura, J. C., Benítez, C., Torre, A., & Rubio, A. (2005). An effective subband OSF-based VAD with noise reduction for robust speech recognition. *IEEE Transactions on Speech and Audio Processing, 13*(6), 1119–1129. doi:10.1109/TSA.2005.853212

Raux, A., & Eskenazi, M. (2007). A multi-layer architecture for semi-synchronous event-driven dialogue management. In *Proceedings of the International Conference on Automatic Speech Recognition and Understanding* (pp. 514-519).

Raux, A., Langner, B., Black, A. W., & Eskenazi, M. (2003). LET'S GO: Improving spoken dialog systems for the elderly and non-natives. In *Proceedings of the Eurospeech Conference*, Geneva, Switzerland (pp. 753-756).

Raux, A., Langner, B., Bohus, D., Black, A., & Eskenazi, M. (2005). Let's go public! Taking a spoken dialog system to the real world. In *Proceedings of the Interspeech/Eurospeech Conference*, Lisbon, Portugal.

Ravikumar, K. M., Reddy, B., Rajagopal, R., & Nagaraj, H. C. (2008). Automatic detection of syllable repetition in read speech for objective assessment of stuttered disfluencies. In *Proceedings of the World Academy of Science, Engineering and Technology* (pp. 270-273).

Read, J. (2005). Using emoticons to reduce dependency in machine learning techniques for sentiment classification. In *Proceedings of the ACL Student Research Workshop* (pp. 43-48).

Reisfeld, D., & Yeshurun, Y. (1992). Robust detection of facial features by generalised symmetry. In *Proceedings of the 11ᵗʰ International Conference on Pattern Recognition* (Vol. 1, pp. 117-120).

Reisner, P. (1981). Formal grammar and human factors design of an interactive graphics system. *IEEE Transactions on Software Engineering*, 7, 229–240. doi:10.1109/TSE.1981.234520

Reiter, E. (1995). NLG vs. templates. In *Proceedings of the Fifth European Workshop in Natural Language Generation* (pp. 95-105).

Renda, M. E., & Straccia, U. (2003). Web Metasearch: Rank vs. score based rank aggregation methods. In *Proceedings of the Eighteenth Annual ACM Symposium on Applied Computing* (pp. 841-846). New York, NY: ACM.

Rezabek, L. L., & Cochenour, J. J. (1998). Visual cues in computer-mediated communication: Supplementing text with emoticons. *Journal of Visual Literacy*, 18, 201–215.

Rieman, J., & Young, R. M. (1996). A dual-space model of iteratively deepening exploratory learning. *International Journal of Human-Computer Studies*, 44, 743–775. doi:10.1006/ijhc.1996.0032

Rodríguez, W. R., Vaquero, C., Saz, O., & Lleida, E. (2008). *Speech technology applied to children with speech disorders* (pp. 1–4). Saragossa, Spain: Communication Technology Group.

Rohani, R., Alizadeh, S., Sobhanmanesh, F., & Boostani, R. (2008). Lip segmentation in color images. In *Proceedings of the International Conference on Innovations in Information Technology* (p. 747).

Rohs, M., & Zweifel, P. (2005). A conceptual framework for camera phone-based interaction techniques. In H.-W. Gellersen, R. Want, & A. Schmidt (Eds.), *Proceedings of the Third International Conference on Pervasive Computing* (LNCS 3468, pp. 171-189).

Rohs, M., Schöning, J., Krüger, A., & Hecht, B. (2007). Towards real-time markerless tracking of magic lenses on paper maps. In *Adjunct Proceedings of the 5th International Conference on Pervasive Computing, Late Breaking Results* (pp. 69-72).

Rohs, M., Schöning, J., Raubal, M., Essl, G., & Krüger, A. (2007). Map navigation with mobile devices: virtual versus physical movement with and without visual context. In *Proceedings of the 9th International Conference on Multimodal Interfaces* (pp. 146-153). New York, NY: ACM.

Rohs, M., Sheridan, J., & Ballagas, R. (2004). Direct manipulation techniques for large displays using camera phones. In *Proceedings of the 2nd International Symposium on Ubiquitous Computing Systems* (pp. 1-2).

Romdhani, S., Torr, P., Scholkopf, B., & Blake, A. (2001). Computationally efficient face detection. In *Proceedings of the International Conference on Computer Vision* (pp. 695-700).

Rosenfeld, R. (1995). The CMU statistical language modeling toolkit and its use in the 1994 ARPA CSR evaluation. In *Proceedings of the ARPA Spoken Language Systems Technology Workshop*.

Rosenfeld, A. (1974). Digital straight line segments. *IEEE Transactions on Computers*, 23(12), 1264–1268. doi:10.1109/T-C.1974.223845

Rosin, P. L. (1997). Techniques for assessing polygonal approximation of curves. *IEEE Transactions on Pattern Analysis and Machine Intelligence*, 19(6), 659–666. doi:10.1109/34.601253

Rosin, P. L., & West, G. A. W. (1995). Non-parametric segmentation of curves into various representations. *IEEE Transactions on Pattern Analysis and Machine Intelligence*, 17, 1140–1153. doi:10.1109/34.476507

Rudnicky, A., Thayer, E., Constantinides, P., Tchou, C., Shern, R., & Lenzo, K. …Oh, A. (1999). Creating natural dialogs in the Carnegie Mellon communicator system. In *Proceedings of the Conference Eurospeech* (Vol. 4, pp. 1531-1534).

Russel, M., & Moore, R. (1985). Explicit modeling of state occupancy in hidden Markov models for automatic speech recognition. In *Proceedings of the International Conference on Acoustic, Speech, and Signal Processing* (pp. 2376-2379).

Russell, J. A. (1980). A circumplex model of affect. *Journal of Personality and Social Psychology*, 39(6), 1161–1178. doi:10.1037/h0077714

Sacks, H., Schegloff, E. A., & Jefferson, G. (1974). A simplest systematics for the organization of turn-taking for conversation. *Language, 50*(4), 697–735. doi:10.2307/412243

Salber, D., & Coutaz, J. (1993). Applying the wizard of oz technique to the study of multimodal systems. In *Proceedings of the Selected papers from the Third International Conference on Human-Computer Interaction* (pp. 219-230).

Salovey, P., & Mayer, J. D. (1990). Emotional intelligence. *Imagination, Cognition and Personality, 9*, 185–211.

Salvucci, D. D., & Lee, F. J. (2003). Simple cognitive modelling in a complex cognitive architecture. In *Proceedings of the ACM/SIGCHI Conference on Human Factors in Computing Systems* (pp. 265-272).

Samudravijaya, K. (2001). Hindi speech recognition. *Journal of Acoustical Society of India, 29*(1), 385–393.

Samuel, M., Gómez-García-Bermejo, J., & Zalama, E. (2010). A realistic, virtual head for human–computer interaction. *Interacting with Computers, 22*, 176–192. doi:10.1016/j.intcom.2009.12.002

Sarikaya, R., & Hansen, J. H. L. (2000). High resolution speech feature parametrization for monophone-based stressed speech recognition. *IEEE Signal Processing Letters, 7*(7), 182–185. doi:10.1109/97.847363

Sarma, A., & Palmer, D. (2004). Context-based speech recognition error detection and correction. In *Proceedings of the Human Language Technology Conference North American Chapter of the Association for Computational Linguistics Annual Meeting: Short Papers* (pp. 85-88).

Saz, O., Lleida, E., & Miguel, A. (2009a). Combination of acoustic and lexical speaker adaptation for disordered speech recognition. In *Proceedings of the Conference InterSpeech* (pp. 554-547).

Saz, O., Miguel, A., Lleida, E., Ortega, A., & Buera, L. (2005). *Study of time and frequency variability in pathological speech and error reduction methods for automatic speech recognition.* Saragossa, Spain: Aragon Institute of Technology (I3A), University of Zaragozas.

Saz, O., Yin, S. C., Lleida, E., Rose, R., Vaquero, C., & Rodríguez, W. R. (2009b). Tools and technologies for computer-aided speech and language therapy. *Speech Communication, 51*(10), 948–967. doi:10.1016/j.specom.2009.04.006

Schatzmann, J., Georgila, K., & Young, S. (2005). Quantitative evaluation of user simulation techniques for spoken dialogue systems. In *Proceedings of the 6th SIGdial Workshop on Discourse and Dialogue.*

Schatzmann, J., Thomson, B., Weilhammer, K., Ye, H., & Young, S. (2007). Agenda-based user simulation for bootstrapping a POMDP dialogue system. In *Proceedings of the North American Chapter of the Association for Computational Linguistics on Human Language Technologies* (pp. 149-152).

Schnabel, M. A., Kvan, T., Kruijff, E., & Donath, D. (2001). The first virtual environment design studio. In *Proceedings of the Conference on Education and Research in Computer Aided Architectural Design in Europe* (pp.394-400).

Schöning, J., Krüger, A., & Müller, H. J. (2006). Interaction of mobile camera devices with physical maps. In *Adjunct Proceedings of the Fourth International Conference on Pervasive Computing* (pp. 121-124).

Schöning, J., Rohs, M., Kratz, S., Löchtefeld, M., & Kruger, A. (2009). Map torchlight: a mobile augmented reality camera projector unit. In *Proceedings of the 27th International Conference on Extended Abstracts on Human Factors in Computing Systems* (pp. 3841-3846). New York, NY: ACM.

Schrage, M. (2003). *Serious play: how the world's best companies simulate to innovate.* Cambridge, MA: Harvard Business School Press.

Schroeder, M. (2006). Fractions: Continued, Egyptian and Farey. In Schroeder, M. (Ed.), *Number theory in science and communication: With applications in cryptography, physics, digital information, computing, and self-similarity (Springer Series in Information Sciences)* (*Vol. 7*). New York, NY: Springer.

Schuller, B., Batliner, A., Steidl, S., & Seppi, D. (2011). Recognising realistic emotions and affect in speech: State of the art and lessons learnt from the first challenge. *Speech Communication, 53*, 1062–1087. doi:10.1016/j.specom.2011.01.011

Schultz, T., & Kirchhoff, K. (2006). *Multilingual speech processing*. Amsterdam, The Netherlands: Elsevier.

Scipioni, M., Gerosa, M., Giuliani, D., Noth, E., & Maier, A. (2009). Intelligibility assessment in children with cleft lip and palate in Italian and German. In *Proceedings of the International Conference InterSpeech*, Brighton, UK (pp. 967-970).

Sebe, N., Sun, Y., Bakker, E., Lew, M. S., Cohen, I., & Huang, T. S. (2004). Towards authentic emotion recognition. In *Proceedings of the IEEE Conference on Systems, Man and Cybernetics* (pp. 623-628).

Segan, J., & Kumar, S. (1999). Shadow gestures: 3D hand pose estimation using a single camera. In *Proceedings of the IEEE Conference on Computer Vision and Pattern Recognition* (pp. 479-485).

Seneff, S. (1989). TINA: A probabilistic syntactic parser for speech understanding systems. In *Proceedings of ACL Workshop on Speech and Natural Language* (pp. 168-178).

Seneff, S., Adler, M., Glass, J., Sherry, B., Hazen, T., Wang, C., & Wu, T. (2007). Exploiting context information in spoken dialogue interaction with mobile devices. In *Proceedings of the International Workshop on Improved Mobile User Experience* (pp. 1-11).

Seneff, S., Hurley, E., Lau, R., Pao, C., Schmid, P., & Zue, V. (1998). Galaxy-II: A reference architecture for conversational system development. In *Proceedings of the International Conference on Spoken Language Processing* (pp. 931-934).

Serna, A., Pigot, H., & Rialle, V. (2007). Modeling the progression of Alzheimer's disease for cognitive assistance in smart homes. *User Modeling and User-Adapted Interaction, 17*, 415–438. doi:10.1007/s11257-007-9032-y

Seron, F., Baldassarri, S., & Cerezo, E. (2006). MaxinePPT: Using 3D virtual characters for natural interaction. In *Proceedings of the 2nd International Workshop on Ubiquitous Computing and Ambient Intelligence* (pp. 241-250).

Sha, F., & Saul, L. K. (2007). Large margin hidden Markov models for automatic speech recognition. In Scholkopf, B., Platt, J., & Hoffman, T. (Eds.), *Advances in neural information processing systems* (pp. 1249-1256). Cambridge, MA: MIT Press.

Shamaie, A., Hai, W., & Sutherland, A. (2011). *Hand gesture recognition for HCI*. Retrieved from http://www.ercim.eu/publication/Ercim News/enw46/shamaie.html

Sharma, A., Shrotriya, M. C., Farooq, O., & Abbasi, Z. A. (2008). Hybrid wavelet based LPC features for Hindi speech recognition. *International Journal of Information and Communication Technology, 1*, 373–381. doi:10.1504/IJICT.2008.024008

Sharp. (2010). *Sharp chronology*. Retrieved January 10, 2011, from http://www.sharp-world.com/corporate/info/his/chronology/p14.html

Sharvit, D., Chan, J., Tek, H., & Kimia, B. (1998). Symmetry based indexing of image databases. *Journal of Visual Communication and Image Representation, 9*(4), 366–380. doi:10.1006/jvci.1998.0396

Shimada, N., Shirai, Y., Kuno, Y., & Miura, J. (1998) Hand gesture estimation and model refinement using monocular camera-ambiguity limitation by inequality constraints. In *Proceedings of the 3rd IEEE International Conference on Automatic Face and Gesture Recognition* (pp. 268-273).

Shimura, M. (1973). Fuzzy sets concept in rank ordering objects. *Journal of Mathematical Analysis and Applications, 43*, 717–733. doi:10.1016/0022-247X(73)90287-4

Shin-ichi, K., Shimodaira, H., Nitta, T., Nishimoto, T., Nakamura, S., & Itou, K. ...Sagayama, S. (2003). Galatea: Open-source software for developing anthropomorphic spoken dialog agents. In H. Prendinger & M. Ishizuka (Eds.), *Life-like characters: Tools, affective functions, and applications* (pp. 187-212). Berlin, Germany: Springer-Verlag.

Shirley, P., & Tuchman, A. A. (1990). Polygonal approximation to direct scalar volume rendering. *SIGGRAPH Computer Graphics, 24*(5), 63–70. doi:10.1145/99308.99322

Shrotriya, N., Verma, R., Gupta, S. K., & Agrawal, S. S. (1996). Durational characteristics of Hindi consonant clusters. In *Proceedings of the International Conference on Spoken Language Processing* (pp. 2427-2430).

Siemans. (2004). *Pictures of the future*. Retrieved January 10, 2011, from http://www.siemens.com/innovation/en/publikationen/publications_pof/pof_fall_2004/research_cooperation.htm

Siler, W., & Buckley, J. J. (2005). *Fuzzy expert systems and fuzzy reasoning*. New York, NY: John Wiley & Sons.

Silsbee, P., & Bovik, A. (1996). Computer lip reading for improved accuracy in automatic speech recognition. *IEEE Transactions on Speech and Audio Processing*, *4*(5), 337–351. doi:10.1109/89.536928

Smith, G., & Marsden, G. (2010). Image recognition techniques for use in a mobile public interactive display. In *Proceedings of the Annual Southern Africa Telecommunication Networks and Applications Conference* (pp. 345-355).

Smith, R. W., Hipp, D. R., & Biermann, A. W. (1995). An architecture for voice dialog systems based on Prolog-style theorem-proving. *Computational Linguistics*, *21*, 281–320.

Solomon, R. C. (1993). *The passions: Emotions and the meaning of life*. Cambridge, MA: Hackett.

Spink, A. (2002). A user centered approach to evaluating human interaction with Web search engines: an exploratory study. *Information Processing & Management*, *38*(3), 410–426. doi:10.1016/S0306-4573(01)00036-X

Srivastava, A., Vaidya, D., Singh, M., Singh, P., & Tiwary, U. S. (2011, August 29-31). A cognitive interactive framework for multi-document summarizer. In *Proceedings of the Third International Conference on Intelligent Human Computer Interaction*, Prague, Czech Republic.

Stahl, G., Koschmann, T., & Suthers, D. (2006). Computer-supported collaborative learning: An historical perspective. In Sawyer, R. K. (Ed.), *Cambridge handbook of the learning sciences* (pp. 409–426). Cambridge, UK: Cambridge University Press.

Stash, N. (2007). *Incorporating cognitive/learning styles in a general-purpose adaptive hypermedia system*. Eindhoven, The Netherlands: Technische Universiteit Eindhoven, Proefschrift. Retrieved November 18, 2010, from http://alexandria.tue.nl/extra2/200710975.pdf

Stathacopoulou, R., Grigoriadou, M., Samarakou, M., & Mitropoulos, D. (2007). Monitoring student's action and using teacher's expertise in implementing and evaluating the neural networked-based fuzzy diagnostic model. *Expert Systems with Applications*, *32*, 955–975. doi:10.1016/j.eswa.2006.02.023

Stent, A., Dowding, J., Gawron, J. M., Bratt, E., & Moore, R. (1999). The CommandTalk spoken dialogue system. In *Proceedings of the Association for Computational Linguistics* (pp. 183-190).

Stephanidis, C., Paramythis, A., Sfyrakis, M., Stergiou, A., Maou, N., & Leventis, A. …Karagiannidis C. (1998). Adaptable and adaptive user interfaces for disabled users in the AVANTI Project. In S. Trigila, A. Mullery, M. Campolargo, H. Vanderstraeten, & M. Mampaey (Eds.), *Proceedings of the 5th International Conference on Intelligence in Services and Networks* (LNCS 1430, pp. 153-166).

Stephanidis, C., & Constantinou, P. (2003). Designing human computer interfaces for quadriplegic people. *ACM Transactions on Computer-Human Interaction*, *10*(2), 87–118. doi:10.1145/772047.772049

Stern, A. (2003). Creating emotional relationships with virtual characters. In Trappl, R., Petta, P., & Payr, S. (Eds.), *Emotions in humans and artifacts* (pp. 333–362). Cambridge, MA: MIT Press.

Stibler, K., & Denny, J. (2001). A three-tiered evaluation approach for interactive spoken dialogue systems. In *Proceedings of the First International Conference on Human Language Technology Research* (pp. 1-5).

Stolcke, A., Coccaro, N., Bates, R., Taylor, P., Ess-Dykema, C. V., & Ries, K. (2000). Dialogue act modelling for automatic tagging and recognition of conversational speech. *Computational Linguistics*, *26*(3), 339–373. doi:10.1162/089120100561737

Stork, D. G., & Hennecke, M. E. (1996). Speech reading: An overview of image processing, feature extraction, sensory integration and pattern recognition techniques. In *Proceedings of the 2nd International Conference on Automatic Face and Gesture Recognition* (pp. 16-26).

Stork, D. G., Wolff, G., & Levine, E. (1992). Neural network lipreading system for improved speech recognition. In *Proceedings of the International Joint Conference on Neural Networks* (pp. 285-295).

Strauss, P., & Minker, W. (2010). *Proactive spoken dialogue interaction in multi-party environments*. New York, NY: Springer. doi:10.1007/978-1-4419-5992-8

Strutt, J. W. (Lord Rayleigh). (1945). *The theory of sound* (2nd ed.). New York, NY: Dover.

Strutt, J. W. (1904). (Lord Rayleigh). (1904). On the acoustic shadow of a sphere. *Philosophical Transactions of the Royal Society of London. Series A: Mathematical and Physical Sciences, 203*, 87–97.

Su, H., Wu, C. H., & Tsai, P. J. (2008). Automatic assessment of articulation disorders using confident unit-based model adaptation. In *Proceedings of the International Conference on Speech, Acoustics and Signal Processing* (pp. 4513-4526).

Su, L. T., & Chen, H. (1999). Evaluation of Web search engines by undergraduate students. In *Proceedings of the 62nd American Society for Information Science*, Washington, DC (Vol. 36, pp. 98-114).

Suendermann, D., Evanini, K., Liscombe, J., Hunter, P., Dayanidhi, K., & Pieraccini, R. (2009). From rule-based to statistical grammar: Continuous improvement of large scale spoken dialog system. In *Proceedings of the IEEE International Conference on Acoustics, Speech and Signal Processing* (pp. 4713-4716).

Sun, R., & Peterson, T. (1996). Learning in reactive sequential decision tasks: The CLARION Model. In *Proceedings of the IEEE International Conference on Neural Networks* (Vol. 2, pp. 1073-1078).

Sun, R. (2006). The CLARION cognitive architecture: Extending cognitive modeling to social simulation. In Sun, R. (Ed.), *Cognition and multi-agent interaction*. New York, NY: Cambridge University Press. doi:10.1017/CBO9780511610721.005

Sun, R. (2007). The importance of cognitive architectures: An analysis based on CLARION. *Journal of Experimental & Theoretical Artificial Intelligence, 19*(2), 159–193. doi:10.1080/09528130701191560

Sun, R., & Zhang, X. (2004). Top-down versus bottom-up learning in cognitive skill acquisition. *Cognitive Systems Research, 5*(1), 63–89. doi:10.1016/j.cogsys.2003.07.001

Sun, R., Zhang, X., & Mathews, R. (2006). Modeling meta-cognition in a cognitive architecture. *Cognitive Systems Research, 7*(4), 327–338. doi:10.1016/j.cogsys.2005.09.001

Sun, R., Zhang, X., Slusarz, P., & Mathews, R. (2007). The interaction of implicit learning, explicit hypothesis testing learning, and implicit-to-explicit knowledge extraction. *Neural Networks, 20*(1), 34–47. doi:10.1016/j.neunet.2006.07.002

Susi, T., & Ziemke, T. (2001). Social cognition, artefacts, and stigmergy: A comparative analysis of theoretical frameworks for the understanding of artefact-mediated collaborative activity. *Cognitive Systems Research, 2*(4), 273–290. doi:10.1016/S1389-0417(01)00053-5

Suwa, M., Purcell, T., & Gero, J. (1998). Macroscopic analysis of design processes based on a scheme for coding designer's cognitive actions. *Design Studies, 19*(4), 455–483. doi:10.1016/S0142-694X(98)00016-7

Suwa, M., & Tversky, B. (1997). What do architects and students perceive in their design sketches? A protocol analysis. *Design Studies, 18*(4), 385–403. doi:10.1016/S0142-694X(97)00008-2

Suzuki, N., & Tsuda, K. (2006a). Automatic emoticon generation method for web community. In *Proceedings of the IADIS International Conference on Web Based Communities* (pp. 331-334).

Suzuki, N., & Tsuda, K. (2006b). Express emoticons choice method for smooth communication of e-business. In B. Gabrys, R. J. Howlett, & L. C. Jain (Eds.), *Proceedings of the 10th International Conference on Knowledge-Based Intelligent Information and Engineering Systems* (LNCS 4252, pp. 296-302).

Taatgen, N. A., & Anderson, J. R. (2009). The past, present, and future of cognitive architectures. *Topics in Cognitive Science, 2*(4), 1–12.

Taatgen, N., Lebiere, C., & Anderson, J. (2006). Modeling paradigms in ACT-R. In Sun, R. (Ed.), *Cognition and multi-agent interaction: From cognitive modeling to social simulation* (pp. 29–52). Cambridge, UK: Cambridge University Press.

Takagi, T., & Sugeno, M. (1985). Fuzzy identification of systems and its applications to modelling and control. *IEEE Transactions on Systems, Man, and Cybernetics*, *15*, 116–132.

Takami, K., Yamashita, R., Tani, K., Honma, Y., & Goto, S. (2009). Deducing a user's state of mind from analysis of the pictographic characters and emoticons used in mobile phone emails for personal content delivery services. *International Journal on Advances in Telecommunications*, *2*(1), 37–46.

Tambe, M., Johnson, W. L., Jones, R. M., Koss, F., Laird, J. E., Rosenbloom, P. S., & Schwamb, K. (1995). Intelligent agents for interactive simulation environments. *AI Magazine*, *16*(1).

Tan, B. K., & Lim, T. Y. (2009). Place-making in online virtual environment: The case of Second Life. In *Proceedings of the CAAD Futures Conference on Joining Languages Cultures and Visions* (pp. 31-32).

Tanaka, Y., Takamura, H., & Okumura, M. (2005, January 9-12). Extraction and classification of facemarks with kernel methods. In *Proceedings of the 10th International Conference on Intelligent User Interfaces*, San Diego, CA.

Tan, C. J., & Gan, W. S. (1998). User-defined spectral manipulation of the HRTF for improved localization in 3D sound systems. *Electronics Letters*, *34*(25), 2387–2389. doi:10.1049/el:19981629

Teh, C.-H., & Chin, R. T. (1989). On the detection of dominant points on digital curves. *IEEE Transactions on Pattern Analysis and Machine Intelligence*, *2*(8), 859–872. doi:10.1109/34.31447

Theune, M. (2003). *Natural language generation for dialog: system survey*. Twente, The Netherlands: University of Twente.

Thomas, M. (1994). *Finger Mouse: A freehand computer pointing interface* (Unpublished doctoral dissertation). The University of Illinois, Chicago, IL.

Tollinger, I., Lewis, R. L., McCurdy, M., Tollinger, P., Vera, A., Howes, A., & Pelton, L. (2005). Supporting efficient development of cognitive models at multiple skill levels: Exploring recent advances in constraint-based modeling. In *Proceedings of the ACM/SIGCHI Conference on Human Factors in Computing Systems* (pp. 411-420).

Tomes, A., Oates, C., & Armstrong, P. (1998). Talking design: Negotiating the verbal-visual translation. *Design Studies*, *19*, 127–142. doi:10.1016/S0142-694X(97)00027-6

Traum, D., & Rickel, J. (2002, July 15-19). Embodied agents for multi-party dialogue in immersive virtual worlds. In *Proceedings of the First international Joint Conference on Autonomous Agents and Multiagent Systems: Part 2*, Bologna, Italy (pp. 766-773).

Trentin, E., & Gori, M. (2001). A survey of hybrid ANN/HMM models for automatic speech recognition. *Neurocomputing*, *37*, 91–126. doi:10.1016/S0925-2312(00)00308-8

Triantafillou, E., Pomportsis, A., & Demetriadis, S. (2003). The design and the formative evaluation of an adaptive educational system based on cognitive styles. *Computers & Education*, *41*, 87–103. doi:10.1016/S0360-1315(03)00031-9

TRINDI Consortium. (2001). *Task Oriented Instructional Dialogue Book Draft*. Retrieved from http://www.ling.gu.se/projekt/trindi/book.ps

Truchon, M. (1998). *An extension of the condorcet criterion and Kemeny Orders*. Montreal, QC, Canada: Centre de Recherche en Economie et Finance Appliquees.

Truong, H. L., Dustdar, S., Baggio, D., Corlosquet, S., Dorn, C., Giuliani, G., & Gombotz, R. (2008). inContext: A pervasive and collaborative working environment for emerging team forms. In *Proceedings of the International Symposium on Applications and the Internet* (pp. 118-125).

Truong, H. L., & Dustdar, S. (2009). A survey on context-aware web service systems. *International Journal of Web Information Systems*, *5*(1), 5–31. doi:10.1108/17440080910947295

Urban, C. (2001). *PECS: A reference model for human-like agents* (Tech. Rep. No. FS-01-02) (pp. 206-216). Palo Alto, CA: AAAI.

Utsumi, A., & Ohya, J. (1999). Multiple-hand-gesture tracking using multiple cameras. In *Proceedings of the IEEE Conference on Computer Vision and Pattern Recognition* (pp. 473-478).

Van de Burgt, S. P., Andernach, T., Kloosterman, H., Bos, R., & Nijholt, A. (1996). Building dialogue systems that sell. In *Proceedings of the NLP and Industrial Applications Conference* (pp. 41-46).

van den Bosch, A., & Daelemans, W. (1993). Data-oriented methods for grapheme-to-phoneme conversion. In *Proceedings of the Sixth Conference on European Chapter of the Association for Computational Linguistics* (pp. 45-53).

Vaquero, C., Saz, O., Lleida, E., & Rodríguez, W. R. (2008b). E-inclusion technologies for the speech handicapped. In *Proceedings of the International Conference on Speech, Acoustics and Signal Processing* (pp. 4509-4512).

Vaquero, C., Saz, O., Rodríguez, W. R., & Lleida, E. (2008a). *Human language technologies for speech therapy in Spanish language* (pp. 129–132). Zaragoza, Spain: University of Zaragoza.

Vargas, M. F. (1986). *Louder than words: An introduction to nonverbal communication.* Ames, IO: Iowa State University Press.

Verma, A., Faruquie, T., Neti, C., Basu, S., & Senior, A. (1999). Late integration in audio-visual continuous speech recognition. In *Proceedings of the Automatic Speech Recognition and Understanding Workshop* (pp. 71-77).

Ververidis, D., & Kotropoulos, C. (2006). Emotional speech recognition: resources, features and methods. *Speech Communication, 48,* 1162–1181. doi:10.1016/j.specom.2006.04.003

Vijayalakshmi, P., Nagarajan, T., & Reddy, M. R. (2009). Assessment of articulatory and velopharyngeal subsystems of dysarthric speech. *Biomedical Soft Computing and Human Sciences, 14*(2), 87–94.

Vladimir, I., Rajeev, S., & Thomas, S. (1993). *Visual interpretation of hand gestures for HCI: A review.* Chicago, IL: The University of Illinois.

Vogt, C. C., & Cottrell, G. W. (1999). Fusion via a linear combination of scores. *Information Retrieval, 1*(3), 151–173. doi:10.1023/A:1009980820262

Vogt, T., André, E., & Johannes, W. (2008). Automatic recognition of emotions from speech: A review of the literature and recommendations for practical realisation. In Peter, C., & Beale, R. (Eds.), *Affect and emotion in human-computer interaction* (pp. 75–91). Berlin, Germany: Springer-Verlag. doi:10.1007/978-3-540-85099-1_7

Vygotsky, L. S. (1978). *Mind and society.* Cambridge, MA: Harvard University Press.

Wagner, D., & Schmalstieg, D. (2003). First steps towards handheld augmented reality. In *Proceedings of the Seventh IEEE International Symposium on Wearable Computers* (pp. 127-135). Washington, DC: IEEE Computer Society.

Wagner, R. A., & Fischer, M. J. (1974). The string-to-string correction problem. *Journal of the ACM, 21*(1), 168–173. doi:10.1145/321796.321811

Wahlster, W. (2001). SmartKom: Multimodal dialogues with mobile Web users. In *Proceedings of the International Cyber Assist Symposium* (pp. 33-40).

Wahlster, W. (2003) Towards symmetric multimodality: Fusion and fission of speech, gesture, and facial expression. In *Proceedings of the 26th German Conference on Artificial Intelligence* (pp. 1-18).

Wahlster, W. (Ed.). (2006). *SmartKom: Foundations of multimodal dialogue systems.* New York, NY: Springer. doi:10.1007/3-540-36678-4

Walker, M., Langkilde, I., Wright, J., Gorin, A., & Litman, D. (2000). Learning to predict problematic situations in a spoken dialogue system: experiments with How May I Help You? In *Proceedings of the North American Chapter of the Association for Computational Linguistics* (pp. 210-217).

Walker, M., Litman, D., Kamm, C., & Abella, A. (1997). PARADISE: a general framework for evaluating spoken dialog agents. In *Proceedings of the 35th Annual Meeting of the Association of Computational Linguistics* (pp. 271-280).

Walker, M., Passonneau, R., & Boland, J. (2001). Quantitative and qualitative evaluation of the DARPA communicator spoken dialogue systems. In *Proceedings of the 39th Annual Meeting on Association for Computational Linguistics* (pp. 515-522).

Walker, W., Lamere, P., & Kwok, P. (2002). *FreeTTS: A performance case study*. Santa Clara, CA: Sun Microsystems.

Wall, K., & Danielsson, P.-E. (1984). A fast sequential method for polygonal approximation of digitized curves. *Computer Vision Graphics and Image Processing, 28*, 220–227. doi:10.1016/S0734-189X(84)80023-7

Walsh, P., & Meade, J. (2003). Speech enabled e-learning for adult literacy tutoring. In *Proceedings of the International Conference on Advanced Learning Technologies* (pp. 17-21).

Wang, H. C. (2008). Modeling idea generation sequences using hidden Markov models. In *Proceedings of the Annual Meeting of the Cognitive Science Society* (pp. 107-112).

Wang, J., & Canny, J. (2006). TinyMotion: camera phone based interaction methods. In *Proceedings of the CHI Extended Abstracts on Human Factors in Computing Systems* (pp. 339-344). New York, NY: ACM.

Wang, J., Zhai, S., & Canny, J. (2006). Camera phone based motion sensing: interaction techniques, applications and performance study. In *Proceedings of the 19th Annual ACM Symposium on User Interface Software and Technology* (pp. 101-110). New York, NY: ACM.

Wang, Y.-Y., Yu, D., Ju, Y.-C., & Acero, A. (2008). An introduction to voice search. *IEEE Signal Processing Magazine, 25*(3), 29–38.

Ward, W., & Issar, S. (1994). Recent improvements in the CMU spoken language understanding system. In *Proceedings of the ACL Workshop on Human Language Technology* (pp. 213-216).

Watkins, A. J. (1978). Psychoacoustical aspects of synthesized vertical locale cues. *The Journal of the Acoustical Society of America, 63*(4), 1152–1165. doi:10.1121/1.381823

Wei, X., & Rudnicky, A. (2000). Task-based dialogue management using an agenda. In *Proceedings of the ANLP/NAACL Workshop on Conversational Systems* (pp. 42-47).

Weng, F., Varges, S., Raghunathan, B., Ratiu, F., Pon-Barry, H., & Lathrop, B. …Prieto, R. (2006). CHAT: A conversational helper for automotive tasks. In *Proceedings of the International Conference on Spoken Language Processing* (pp. 1061-1064).

Wenzel, E. M., Arruda, M., Kistler, D. J., & Wightman, F. L. (1993). Localization using nonindividualized head-related transfer functions. *The Journal of the Acoustical Society of America, 94*, 111–123. doi:10.1121/1.407089

Westerman, W., Elias, J. G., & Hedge, A. (2001). A multi touch: A new tactile 2-D gesture interface for HCI. In *Proceedings of the Human Factors and Ergonomics Society Annual Meeting* (Vol. 45, pp. 632-636).

Wikipedia. (n.d.). *Cognitive architectures*. Retrieved July 1, 2007, from http://en.wikipedia.org/wiki/Cognitive_architecture

Wilks, Y. (2006). *Artificial companions as a new kind of interface to the future internet* (Tech. Rep. No. 13). Oxford, UK: Oxford Internet Institute.

Wilks, Y., Catizone, R., Worgan, S., & Turunen, M. (2011). Some background on dialogue management and conversational speech for dialogue systems. *Computer Speech & Language, 25*(2), 128–139. doi:10.1016/j.csl.2010.03.001

Williams, J. D., & Young, S. (2007). Partially observable Markov decision processes for spoken dialog systems. *Computer Speech & Language, 21*, 393–422. doi:10.1016/j.csl.2006.06.008

Williams, J. J., & Katsaggelos, A. K. (2002). An HMM-based speech-to-video synthesizer. *IEEE Transactions on Neural Networks. Special Issue on Intelligent Multimedia, 13*(4), 900–915.

Williams, J., & Young, S. (2007). Partially observable Markov decision processes for spoken dialog systems. *Computer Speech & Language, 21*(2), 393–422. doi:10.1016/j.csl.2006.06.008

Wisniewski, M., Jozkowiak, W. K., SmoŁka, E., & Suszynski, E. (2010). Improved approach to automatic detection of speech disorders based on the HMM approach. *Journal of Medical Informatics and Technologies*, 1-8.

Witkin, H. A., Moore, C. A., Goodenough, D. R., & Cox, P. W. (1977). Field-dependent and field independent cognitive styles and their educational implications. *Review of Educational Research, 47,* 164.

Wojtowicz, J. (1994). *Virtual design studio.* Hong Kong: Hong Kong University Press.

Wolf, A. (2004). Emotional expression online: Gender differences in emoticon use. *Cyberpsychology & Behavior, 3*(5), 827–833. doi:10.1089/10949310050191809

Woodland, P., Gales, M., Pye, D., & Young, S. (1997). Broadcast news transcription using HTK. In *Proceedings of the IEEE International Conference on Acoustics, Speech, and Signal Processing*, Munich, Germany (Vol. 2, 719-722).

Woodworth, R. S., & Schlosberg, H. (1962). *Experimental psychology.* New York, NY: Holt, Rinehard and Winston.

Wren, C., Azarbayejani, A., Darrell, T., & Pentland, A. P. (1997). Pfinder: Real-time tracking of the human body. *IEEE Transactions on Pattern Analysis and Machine Intelligence, 19*(7), 780–785. doi:10.1109/34.598236

Wright, P., Fields, R., & Harrison, M. (2000). Analyzing human-computer interaction as distributed cognition: The resources model. *Human Computer Interaction Journal, 51*(1), 1–41. doi:10.1207/S15327051HCI1501_01

Wu, A., Shah, M., & Lobo, N. (2000). A virtual 3D blackboard: 3D finger tracking using single camera. In *Proceedings of the Fourth International IEEE Conference on Automatic Face and Gesture Recognition*, Grenoble, France (pp. 536-543).

Wu, Y., Lin, J. Y., & Huang, T. S. (2001). Capturing natural hand articulation. In *Proceedings of the IEEE International Conference on Computer Vision* (Vol. 2, pp. 426-432).

Xiao, H., Reid, D., Marriott, A., & Gulland, E. K. (2005). An adaptive personality model for ECAs. In J. Tao, T. Tan, & R. W. Picard (Eds.), *Proceedings of the First International Conference on Affective Computing and Intelligent Interaction* (LNCS 3784, pp. 637-645).

Xing, J., Wang, W., Zhao, W., & Huang, J. (2009). A novel multi-touch human-computer-interface based on binocular stereo vision. In *Proceedings of the International Symposium on Intelligent Ubiquitous Computing and Education* (pp. 319-323).

Xu, Z., John, D., & Boucouvalas, A. C. (2008). Fuzzy logic usage in emotion communication of human machine interaction. In Sugumaran, V. (Ed.), *Intelligent information technologies: Concepts, methodologies, tools, and applications* (pp. 147–163). Hershey, PA: IGI Global. doi:10.4018/978-1-59140-562-7.ch036

Yager, R. R. (1988). On ordered weighted averaging aggregation operators in multicriteria decision making. *IEEE Transactions on Systems, Man, and Cybernetics, 18*(1), 183–190. doi:10.1109/21.87068

Yamada, T., Tsuchiya, S., Kuroiwa, S., & Ren, F. (2007). Classification of facemarks using n-gram. In *Proceedings of the International Conference on NLP and Knowledge Engineering* (pp. 322-327).

Yang, C., Hsin-Yih Lin, K., & Chen, H.-H. (2007). Building emotion lexicon from weblog corpora. In *Proceedings of the ACL Demo and Poster Sessions* (pp. 133-136).

Yang, J., & Waibel, A. (1996). A real-time face tracker. In *Proceedings of the 3rd IEEE Workshop on Applications of Computer Vision* (pp. 142-147).

Yao, Y. (2007) Granular computing: Past, present and future. In *Proceedings of the IEEE International Conference on Granular Computing* (pp. 72-77).

Yao, Y. Y., & Sai, Y. (2001). Mining ordering rules using rough set theory. *Bulletin of International Rough Set Society, 5,* 99–106.

Yin, P. Y. (2003). Ant colony search algorithms for optimal polygonal approximation of plane curves. *Pattern Recognition, 36,* 1783–1797. doi:10.1016/S0031-3203(02)00321-7

Yin, P. Y. (2004). A discrete particle swarm algorithm for optimal polygonal approximation of digital curves. *Journal of Visual Communication and Image Representation, 15*(2), 241–260. doi:10.1016/j.jvcir.2003.12.001

Yin, S. C., Rose, R., Saz, O., & Lleida, E. (2008). *Verifying pronunciation accuracy from speakers with neuromuscular disorders. Zaragoza, Spain: NSERC Program and the national project TIN. Ziogas, E., & Kotropoulos, C. (2006). Detection of vocal fold paralysis and edema using linear discriminant classifiers* (pp. 1–11). Brussels, Belgium: European Union MUSCLE Network.

Yoskowitz, A. (2010). *Nexus One with Android 2.2 had strong performance gains*. Retrieved June 1, 2011, from http://www.afterdawn.com/news/article.cfm/2010/05/12/nexus_one_with_android_2_2_has_strong_performance_gains

You, K. H., & Wang, H. C. (1999). Robust features for noisy speech recognition based on temporal trajectory filtering of short-time autocorrelation sequences. *Speech Communication, 28*, 13–24. doi:10.1016/S0167-6393(99)00004-7

Young, R. M., Green, T. R. G., & Simon, T. (1989). Programmable user models for predictive evaluation of interface designs. In *Proceedings of the ACM/SIGCHI Conference on Human Factors in Computing Systems* (pp. 15-19).

Young, S., Evermann, G., Gales, M., Hain, T., Kershaw, D., & Liu, X. …Woodland, P. (2009). *The HTK book*. Cambridge, MA: Microsoft Corporation and Cambridge University Engineering Department.

Young, S., Kershaw, D., Odell, J., Ollason, D., Valtchev, V., & Woodland, P. (2011). *The HTK book*. Retrieved from http://htk.eng.cam.ac.uk

Young, S. (1996). A review of large vocabulary continuous speech recognition. *IEEE Signal Processing Magazine, 13*, 45–57. doi:10.1109/79.536824

Young, S., Kershaw, D., Odell, J., Ollason, D., Valtchev, V., & Woodland, P. (2000). *The HTK book*. Redmond, WA: Microsoft Corporation.

Yuan, W., & Zhang, W. (2010). A novel hand-gesture recognition method based on finger state projection for control of robotic hands. In H. Liu, H. Ding, Z. Xiong, & X. Zhu (Eds.), *Proceedings of the Third International Conference on Intelligent Robotics and Applications* (LNCS 6425, pp. 671-682).

Yuasa, M., Saito, K., & Mukawa, N. (2006). Emoticons convey emotions without cognition of faces: an fMRI study. In *Proceedings of the CHI Extended Abstracts on Human factors in Computing Systems* (pp. 1565-1570).

Yuhas, B. P., Goldstein, M. H., & Sejnowski, T. J. (1989). Integration of acoustic and visual speech signals using neural networks. *IEEE Communications Magazine*, 65–71. doi:10.1109/35.41402

Yu, S.-Z. (2010). Hidden semi-Markov models. *Artificial Intelligence, 174*, 215–243. doi:10.1016/j.artint.2009.11.011

Zadeh, L. (1975a). The concept of a linguistic variable and its applications to approximate reasoning. *Information Sciences, 8*(Part 1), 199–249. doi:10.1016/0020-0255(75)90036-5

Zadeh, L. (1975b). The concept of a linguistic variable and its applications to approximate reasoning. *Information Sciences, 8*(Part 2), 301–357. doi:10.1016/0020-0255(75)90046-8

Zadeh, L. (1975c). The concept of a linguistic variable and its applications to approximate reasoning. *Information Sciences, 9*(Part 3), 43–80. doi:10.1016/0020-0255(75)90017-1

Zadeh, L. (1979). Fuzzy sets and information granularity. In Gupta, N., Ragade, R., & Yager, R. (Eds.), *Advances in fuzzy set theory and applications* (pp. 3–18). Amsterdam, The Netherlands: North-Holland.

Zadeh, L. (1997). Towards a theory of fuzzy information granulation and its centrality in human reasoning and fuzzy logic. *Fuzzy Sets and Systems, 19*, 111–127. doi:10.1016/S0165-0114(97)00077-8

Zadeh, L. (2008). Is there a need for fuzzy logic? *Information Sciences, 178*, 2751–2779. doi:10.1016/j.ins.2008.02.012

Zahn, C., & Roskies, R. (1972). Fourier descriptors for plane closed curves. *IEEE Transactions on Computers, 21*(3), 269–281. doi:10.1109/TC.1972.5008949

Zhang, X., & Mersereau, R. M. (2000). Lip feature extraction towards an automatic speech reading system. In *Proceedings of the International Conference on Image Processing* (Vol. 3, pp. 226-229).

Zhu, Z., & He, K. (2008). A novel approach of emotion recognition based on selective ensemble. In *Proceedings of the 3rd International Conference on Intelligent Systems and Knowledge Engineering* (pp. 695-698).

Ziemke, T. (2002). Introduction to the special issue on situated and embodied cognition. *Cognitive Systems Research, 3*(3), 271–274. doi:10.1016/S1389-0417(02)00068-2

Zimmerman, H.-J. (2001). *Fuzzy set theory and its applications*. Boston, MA: Kluwer Academic. doi:10.1007/978-94-010-0646-0

Zue, V., Seneff, S., Glass, J., Polifroni, J., Pao, C., Hazen, T., & Hetherington, L. (2000). Jupiter: a telephone-based conversatioinal interface for weather information. *IEEE Transactions on Speech and Audio Processing, 8*, 85–96. doi:10.1109/89.817460

About the Contributors

Uma Shanker Tiwary is currently professor at Indian Institute of Information Technology, Allahabad, India. He has completed his B. Tech. and Ph.D. in Electronics Engineering from Institute of Technology, B.H.U., Varanasi, India in 1983 and 1991 respectively. He has experience of teaching and research experience of more than 23 years in the area of Computer Science and Information Technology with special interest in Computer Vision, Image Processing, Speech and Language Processing, Human Computer Interaction and Information Extraction and Retrieval. He has co-authored a book on 'Natural Language and Information Retrieval' (Oxford University Press, 2007) and has edited several Proceedings of the International Conferences on 'Intelligent Human Computer Interaction (Springer, 2009 and 2010)' and was publication Chair of 'Wireless Communication and Sensor Networks (IEEE Xplore, 2006, 2007 and 2008)'. His research work on the application of Wavelet Transform in Medical and Vision problems and Information Retrieval has been cited extensively. He was associated with the research work in the Mechatronics Dept. of Gwangju Institute of Science and Technology, Gwangju, South Korea and with "Anglabharti' project at Dept. of Computer Science and Engg. IIT Kanpur, India. He has delivered lectures, chaired many sessions at IEEE International Conferences and visited many labs in India and abroad, including U.S., South Korea, South Africa, China, Singapore, Thailand. He is the Fellow of IETE and Senior Member of IEEE.

Tanveer J. Siddiqui is currently Assistant Professor at University of Allahabad, India. She did M.Sc. and Ph.D. in Computer Science from University of Allahabad. She has experience of teaching and research of more than 10 years in the area of Computer Science and Information Technology with special interest in Natural Language Processing, Human Computer Interaction and Information Extraction and Retrieval. She worked at IIIT Allahabad as Assistant Professor during 2007-2010 and has been associated with Center of Cognitive and Behavioral Science, University of Allahabad as guest faculty. She has co-authored a book on 'Natural Language and Information Retrieval' (Oxford University Press, 2008) and has edited two Proceedings of the International Conferences on Intelligent Human Computer Interaction (Springer, 2009 and 2010).

* * *

Nieves Ábalos is a M. S. and Ph.D. student in Computer Science at University of Granada, Spain. She has also a B. S. in Computer Science from this University. Her research interests and activities have been related to speech technologies and include dialogue systems, multimodal systems and ambient intelligence among others. She is currently participating in several research projects related to these areas. She is a member of SEPLN (Spanish Society on Natural Language Processing).

R. K. Aggarwal was born in India and obtained his B. Tech. degree from Computer Science Department of KNIT, Sultanpur in 1990. Then he joined the Department of Computer Engineering, National Institute of Technology, Kurukshetra, as a Lecturer and Associate Professor during 1990 and 2007 respectively. He completed his M. Tech. in 2006 and presently pursuing Ph.D. from the same institute. He has published more than 29 research papers in reputed journals and conferences. He is in the reviewer panel for International Journal of Speech Technology, Springer Publication. His research interests include speech processing, soft computing, statistical pattern recognition, machine learning, and science and spirituality.

Rashid Ali is with the Department of Computer Engineering, A.M.U. Aligarh, India. Rashid Ali did his B.Tech. and M.Tech. from A.M.U. Aligarh in 1999 and 2001 respectively. He obtained his PhD in Computer Engineering in February 2010 from A.M.U. Aligarh. Rashid Ali joined the department of Computer Engineering, A.M.U. Aligarh as a Lecturer in Computer Engineering in the year 2002. He is member of IEEE, U.S.A. and its Computational Intelligence Society He is also member of IACSIT, Singapore and life member of Computer Society of India and IETE, India. His current areas of research interests include Web-Searching, Web-Mining, Rough-Set based Applications, Genetic Algorithms, Artificial Neural Networks, Parallel Algorithms, and Image Retrieval Techniques.

Kenji Araki received the BE, ME, and Ph.D. degrees in electronics engineering from Hokkaido University, Sapporo, Japan, in 1982, 1985, and 1988, respectively. In April 1988, he joined Hokkai-Gakuen University, Sapporo, Japan, where he was a professor. He joined Hokkaido University in 1998 as an associate professor in the Division of Electronics and Information Engineering and became a professor in 2002. Presently, he is a professor in the Division of Media and Network Technologies at Hokkaido University. His research interests include natural language processing, spoken dialogue processing, machine translation, and language acquisition. He is a member of the AAAI, the IEEE, the JSAI, the IPSJ, the IEICE, and the JCSS.

Halima Bahi received her Ph.D. degree in Computer Science Department from University of Annaba in 2005. She is currently an associate professor in the department of Computer Science in university of Annaba-Algeria. Her research interests include Speech Recognition, Audio mining, Computer Assisted Pronunciation Teaching. She is responsible of the National Research Project no. 50/TIC/2011, dedicated to Automatic Detection of Dyslexia in Young Pupils.

Armando Barreto is a professor in the Electrical & Computer Engineering Department of Florida International University, in Miami, Florida. Dr. Barreto received his B.S. (Electrical Engineering) degree from The National Autonomous University of Mexico (Mexico City), his M.S. (Electrical Engineering) degree from Florida International University (Miami, Florida) and his Ph.D. (Electrical Engineering) Degree from The University of Florida (Gainesville, Florida). He is the director of the FIU Digital Signal Processing (DSP) Laboratory, where he conducts research on DSP applications to different fields, including Human-Computer Interaction (HCI). Some examples of his DSP-HCI efforts are: Customization of sound spatialization, custom pre-compensation of display images and hands-free cursor control approaches based on processing of the electromyogram of the computer user.

M. M. Sufyan Beg is with the Department of Computer Engineering, J.M.I. New Delhi, India. He did his B. Tech from A.M.U. Aligarh in 1992, M.Tech. from I.I.T. Kanpur in 1994 and PhD from I.I.T. Delhi in 2004. He joined the Department of Computer Engineering, J.M.I., New Delhi as Professor in Computer Engineering in the year 2007. Earlier, he served as Lecturer and Reader in Computer Engineering in the department of Computer Engineering, A.M.U. Aligarh. He also served as a post doctorate fellow at University of California at Berkeley. He is Senior Member of IEEE, USA and its Computational Intelligence Society. He is also Life Member of Computer Society of India, System Society of India and IETE, India. His current areas of research interests include High Performance Data Mining, Web Mining and Searching, Fuzzy Logic and Systems, Genetic Algorithms, Question Answering Systems and Natural Language Processing.

Partha Bhowmick graduated from the Indian Institute of Technology, Kharagpur, India, and received his Master's and Ph.D. from the Indian Statistical Institute, Kolkata, India. He is currently an Assistant Professor in Computer Science and Engineering Department, Indian Institute of Technology, Kharagpur, India. His primary research area is digital geometry, with applications to low-level image processing, approximate pattern matching, computer graphics, document image processing and analysis, shape analysis, and biometrics. He has published more than 60 research papers in international journals, edited volumes, and refereed conference proceedings, and holds 4 US patents.

Pradipta Biswas is a Research Associate at the Engineering Design Centre and Trinity Hall of University of Cambridge. His research aims to make interfaces of modern digital devices accessible to elderly users and people with different ranges of abilities. In particular, he works on developing user models that help to reflect problems faced by people with different range of abilities in using interactive systems. He has published more than 30 journal and conference papers in Human Computer Interaction and Assistive Technology. He has a Ph.D. in Computer Science from University of Cambridge. He was awarded a Gates-Cambridge Scholarship in 2006. He previously undertook a first degree in Information Technology at the University of Kalyani and a master degree at the Indian Institute of Technology, Kharagpur. He is a working group coordinator of the International Telecommunication Union's (ITU) focus group on Audio Visual Media Accessibility, committee member of British Standardization Institute, and member of the EU task force on Standardization of User Models, Higher Education Academy, British Computer Society and Royal Society of Medicine.

Zoraida Callejas is Assistant Professor in the Department of Languages and Computer Systems at the Technical School of Computer Science and Telecommunications of the University of Granada (Spain). She completed a PhD in Computer Science at University of Granada in 2008 and has been a visiting researcher in University of Ulster (Belfast, UK), Technical University of Liberec (Liberec, Czech Republic) University of Trento (Trento, Italy), and Technical University of Berlin (Berlin, Germany). Her research activities have been mostly related to speech technologies and in particular to the investigation of dialogue systems. Her results have been published in several international journals and conferences. She has participated in numerous research projects, and is a member of several research associations focused on speech processing and human-computer interaction.

Keith Cheverst is a Senior Lecturer with Lancaster University's School of Computing and Communications. His research over the last decade has focused on exploring the obdurate problems associated with the user-centred design of interactive systems (typically systems that utilise mobile and/or ubicomp technologies) in complex or semi-wild settings and the deployment and longitudinal study of these systems in order to gain insights into issues of user adoption and appropriation. He has been involved in mobile/ubicomp research for over 15 years and has published in excess of 130 research articles.

Shekharjeet Datta received B.Sc. degree from the University of Calcutta and M.Sc. and Ph.D. degrees in Computer science from the University of London. He spent twenty years in industrial research related to information technology and advanced signal processing at the research and Advanced Development Centre, International Computers Ltd, where he worked as a Senior Research Consultant. Since joining Loughborough University in 1987 he has continued to work on speech processing and extended his research activities to include cursive script recognition and bioacoustics. He has authored and co-authored over 90 papers in refereed academic journals and international conference proceedings, and over 40 articles and reports in other publication categories, including editorship of a book and workshop proceedings. He is a Fellow of IETE, India, Member of IEE, UK, British Machine Vision Association, the Society of the Study of Artificial Intelligence, and Simulation of Behaviour and the British Computer Society.

Mayank Dave obtained the M.Tech. degree in Computer Science and Technology from IIT Roorkee, India in 1991 and Ph.D. from the same institute in 2002. He is presently working as Associate Professor in Department of Computer Engineering at NIT Kurukshetra, India with more than 19 years experience of academic and administrative affairs in the institute. He is presently heading Department of Computer Engineering and Department of Computer Applications. He has published approximately 60 research papers in various International / National journals and conferences. He has coordinated several projects and training programs for students and faculty. He has delivered number of expert lectures and keynote addresses on different topics. He has guided four Ph.D.s and several M. Tech. dissertations. His research interests include Peer-to-Peer Computing, Pervasive Computing, Wireless Sensor Networks and Database Systems.

Pawel Dybala was born in Ostrow Wielkopolski, Poland in 1981. He received his MA in Japanese Studies from the Jagiellonian University in Krakow, Poland in 2006, and Ph.D. in Information Science and Technology from Hokkaido University, Japan in 2011. Currently he is a director and general project manager at Kotoken Language Laboratory in Krakow. His research interests include natural language processing, dialogue processing, humor processing, HCI, and information retrieval.

Gonzalo Espejo obtained the Degree in Computer Science in 2009 and the Master Degree in Software Development in 2011 from the University of Granada. He is currently a Ph.D. student in this University, where he has worked in several projects concerned with spoken and multimodal dialogue systems. His main research interests include spoken and multimodal systems as well as ambient intelligence. He has attended several workshops related to natural language processing and dialogue systems. He is a member of SEPLN (Spanish Society on Natural Language Processing).

Omar Farooq was born in Uttar Pradesh, India. He obtained B.Sc. Engineering and M.Sc. Engineering degrees from Z.H. College of Engineering and Technology AMU, Aligarh, India, in 1991 and1993, respectively. He joined the Department of Electronics Engineering at AMU, Aligarh, as a lecturer in 1992, and is currently working as Associate Professor. In 1999, he was awarded Commonwealth Scholarship for doing Ph.D. at Loughborough University, UK, and in 2007-08 UKIERI Postdoctoral Fellow at Loughborough University, UK in the area of speech recognition. His area of research interests also includes wavelet-based signal processing and encryption techniques. He is a Fellow of IETE and ASI, India and member of IEEE, SSI, India and ISTE, India, and has got about 90 publications in Journals and refereed conferences.

David Griol obtained his Ph.D. degree in Computer Science from the Technical University of València (Spain) in 2007. He has also a B.S. in Telecommunication Science from this University. He is currently professor at the Department of Computer Science in the Carlos III University of Madrid (Spain). He has participated in several European and Spanish projects related to natural language processing and dialogue systems. His research activities are mostly related to the development of statistical methodologies for the design of spoken dialogue systems. His research interests include dialogue management/optimization/simulation, corpus-based methodologies, user modeling, adaptation and evaluation of spoken dialogue systems and machine learning approaches. Before starting his Ph.D. study, he worked as a network engineer in Motorola. He is a member of ISCA (International Speech Communication Association), IEEE (Institute of Electrical and Electronics Engineers), and AEPIA (Spanish Association of Artificial Intelligence).

Navarun Gupta received his Ph.D. from Florida International University in Miami. He has two master's degrees – one in Physics from Georgia State University and another in Electrical Engineering from Mercer University. Currently, Dr. Gupta is an Associate Professor of Electrical Engineering at University of Bridgeport. He is also the Associate Department Chair in the Department of Electrical Engineering at the University. Dr. Gupta's research interests lie in nanotechnology, signal processing, and its applications in audio and bio signals.

Hung-Pin Hsu is a researcher at National Chiao Tung University. He was trained as an Active Architect, and studied his Master and Ph.D. in the field of human-computer interaction in the Graduate Institute of Architecture at National Chiao Tung University. He also has a Master of Science degree in the interactive media lab under the Department of Computer and Communication Engineering at Ming Chuan University. Most of the Hsu's research and publish topics are twofold firstly around design communication analysis methodology in both individual and collaborative design processes and secondly around the user experience design and evaluation in the interactive field.

Ilham Huseyinov received his B.Sc. and M.Sc. degree in electrical and electronic engineering from Azerbaijan Polytechnic Institute in 1984. After graduating he worked as a scientific fellow and an engineer in Russia. He received his PhD. degree in computer science and control theory from the Institute of Cybernetics of Azerbaijan Academy of Sciences in 1995. His current research interests cover fuzzy logic, decision making under uncertainty, web-based adaptive systems, multimodal human computer interface, and human factors. He has published a number of publications in the leading scientific journals and international conferences. During postdoctoral period he has got two grants: 1) USA Education Department, Regional Scholar Exchange Research Program, (2000) and 2) TUBITAK, NATO-PC Advanced Postdoctoral Fellowship Program (2001). Currently he is affiliated with European University of Lefke and holds the position of Assistant Professor at the Computer Engineering Faculty. He gives lectures in the field of computer and electrical engineering.

Ramón Delgado López-Cózar is Professor at the Faculty of Computer Science and Telecommunications of the University of Granada (Spain). His main research interests in the last 15 years include spoken and multimodal dialogue systems, focusing on speech processing and dialogue management. He has coordinated several research projects, has published a number of journal and conference papers, and has been invited speaker at several scientific events addressing these topics. In 2005 he published the book "Spoken, Multilingual and Multimodal Dialogue Systems: Development and Assessment" (Wiley). Recently he has co-edited the book "Human-Centric Interfaces for Ambient Intelligence" (Elsevier Academic Press, 2010), in which he has coordinated the section concerning speech processing and dialogue management. He is a member of ISCA (International Speech Communication Association), FoLLI (Association for Logic, Language and Information), AIPO (Spanish Society on Human-Computer Interaction) and SEPLN (Spanish Society on Natural Language Processing).

Jacek Maciejewski studied for the MA degree in computer science at the University of Adam Mickiewicz, Poznan, Poland. He was awarded a scholarship to Hokkaido University, Japan, for the period 2008-2010. During his scholarship, he participated in research activities at the Graduate School of Information Science and Technology, Hokkaido University, Japan. His research interests include software engineering, natural language processing, Web mining, and information retrieval.

Jose Manuel Molina is Full Professor at the Carlos III University of Madrid (Spain) and director of the Department of Computer Science. Previously he has been director of the Ph.D. Program in Computer science and Technology of this University. He obtained Ph.D. and B.S. degrees in Telecommunication Science from the Technical University of Madrid. He is currently the director of the research group of Applied Artificial Intelligence (http://www.giaa.inf.uc3m.es). His research areas are focused on the application of Artificial intelligence in multi-agent systems, fuzzy logic, evolutionary computation, artificial vision, multi-sensor systems, signal processing, context-aware systems and user-centered applications to access information and services. He is author of more than 40 contributions in international journals with impact factor, more than 150 papers in International Conferences, and 16 books.

Andrew Molineux is a Ph.D. student in the School of Computing and Communications at Lancaster University. His research involves exploring how GPS enabled smart-phones can support the capture, geo-reference and subsequent display of situated You-Are-Here maps. This involves creating interactions that will enable users to successfully geo-reference You-Are-Here maps accurately, potentially with no data connectivity, whilst in the field. His research interests focus on HCI centred mobile interaction techniques, pedestrian navigation and digital map interactions.

Yoshio Momouchi was born in 1942 in Hokkaido, Japan. He obtained a master's degree and a doctorate in engineering from Hokkaido University. He was a member of the Division of Information Engineering in Graduate School at Hokkaido University from 1973 to 1988. Since 1988 he has been a professor in the faculty of engineering at Hokkai-Gakuen University. He fulfilled duties of Dean of Graduate School of Engineering at Hokkai-Gakuen University in years 2005-2008. He specializes in intelligent information processing, computational linguistics and machine translation. He is a member of the IPSJ, the ANLP, the ACL, the MLSJ, the JCSS, and the JSAI.

Armin Mustafa received her B.E. degree with honors from Institute of Engineering and Technology, Indore (2004-08) in Electronics and went on to do M.Tech (2008-10) in Signal processing from Indian Institute of Technology, Kanpur where her research on "Gesture recognition in Dynamic Environment" has been patented along with co-author of this book. Currently she is working as Senior Software Engineer in Research and Development at Samsung, Bangalore. Her areas of interest are Computer vision, Signal processing specifically image and video processing. Armin is recipient of award of "Best M.Tech. thesis in Computer science and Electrical Engineering (2010)" and "Best hardware design for Paper gadgets (2010)" both from IIT, Kanpur.

Khaled Necibi is Ph.D. student in university of Annaba, he obtained his M.Sc. from computer Science Deprtment in Universtity of Annaba in 2010. His research interests include speech and language disorders.

Sanjoy Pratihar received his B.Tech. in Computer Science and Engineering from North Eastern Hill University, Shilong, India in 2002, and received his M.E. in Computer Science and Engineering from Bengal Engineering and Science University, Shibpur, India in 2007. He served as a lecturer in the Department of Computer Science and Engineering, University Institute of Technology, The University of Burdwan, Burdwan, India from 2003 to 2005 and again from 2007 to 2011. Currently he is a Ph.D. scholar in the Department of Computer Science and Engineering, Indian Institute of Technology, Kharagpur, India. His research interests include digital geometry, document image processing, graphics analysis, and intelligent human-computer interaction. He has published 7 research papers in edited volumes and refereed conference proceedings.

Michal Ptaszynski was born in Wroclaw, Poland in 1981. He received the MA degree from the University of Adam Mickiewicz, Poznan, Poland, in 2006, and PhD in Information Science and Technology from Hokkaido University, Japan in 2011. At the moment he is a JSPS Post-doctoral Research Fellow at the High-Tech research Center, Hokkai-Gakuen University, Japan. His research interests include natural language processing, dialogue processing, affect analysis, sentiment analysis, HCI, and information retrieval. He is a member of the ACL, the AAAI, the IEEE, the HUMAINE, the AAR, the SOFT, the JSAI, and the ANLP.

Rafal Rzepka received the MA degree from the University of Adam Mickiewicz, Poznan, Poland, in 1999, and the Ph.D. degree from Hokkaido University, Japan, in 2004. Currently, he is an assistant professor in the Graduate School of Information Science and Technology at Hokkaido University. His research interests include natural language processing, Web mining, common sense retrieval, dialogue processing, language acquisition, affect analysis, and sentiment analysis. He is a member of the AAAI, the ACL, the JSAI, the IPSJ, the IEICE, the JCSS, and the ANLP.

Toufik Sari received his M.Sc. and Ph.D. degrees in Computer Science from Badji Mokhtar – Annaba University in 2000 and 2007, respectively. He is currently an associate professor in the Department of Computer Science and Information Engineering at Badji Mokhtar – Annaba University, Algeria. His research interests include Pattern Recognition, Handwriting Analysis and Recognition, Document Retrieval and Neural Networks.

K. S. Venkatesh completed his B.E. in Electronics from BMS Engg. College, Bangalore University, in 1987 and his M.Tech (1987-89) in Communications and Ph.D.(1989-95) in Signal processing from Indian Institute of Technology, Kanpur. His areas of interest are Generalized Signal and System Theory, image/video processing with applications in machine vision, visual navigation, Robotics and human-computer interfaces. He worked as Assistant Professor in Indian Institute of Technology, Guwahati (1995-99) and is in IIT Kanpur since 1999.

Index

A

Acoustic Model 101, 103, 105-106, 109, 116, 119, 126, 138, 153-154, 268, 319

Action-Centered Subsystem (ACS) 32

Adaptive Control of Thought – Rational(ACT – R) 28

Affective Computing 259, 265, 272-273, 284, 287, 289-290

affinity diagram 48-49, 51

Amyotrophic Lateral Sclerosis (ALS) 312

Artificial Intelligence (AI) 5, 128, 235

artificial neural networks (ANNs) 138

ARToolKit 309

Audio visual speech recognition 149-150, 154, 163

augmented Farey table 172, 174, 176-177, 180

Augmented Reality 23, 195, 293-294, 296-297, 299-301, 304-307, 309

Automatic Railway Information Systems in Europe (ARISE) 134

automatic speech recognition (ASR) 101, 137, 149, 265, 290, 310, 322

AVANTI project 7, 19

B

binary information table (BIT) 227

Binaural 81-85, 87, 95, 97, 99-100

Borda's method 214, 216, 218, 229-231

bottom-up learning 33, 38

C

CLARION 4, 22, 32-39, 41

Cleft Lip and Palate 313-314, 320, 323

Cognitive Interaction 42-43

Cognitive Styles 64, 67-68, 77-79

collaborative HCI (CHCI) 36

COMPANION project 133

Computer Assisted Pronunciation Teaching (CAPT) 322

Computer Supported Cooperative Work (CSCW) 43

Concha 90, 93, 100

Connectionist Learning with Adaptive Rule Induction ON-line (CLARION) 32

Context Information 112, 270-271, 285, 288, 290

Contour detection 191, 206

D

Design Behavior Modeling 50

Dialogue Management 132, 134, 136-140, 148, 265, 270, 275, 278, 282, 288-290

Dialogue Management (DM) 137, 265, 290

disabled users 8-9, 19, 285

discrete cosine transform (DCT) 113, 159, 161, 164, 321

Discriminative Techniques 101-102, 110, 126

Drag 3, 207-208

dual representational structure 32

Dynamic background subtraction 191-192

E

EASE tool 7

Embodied Conversational Agents (ECA) 129

Emoticons 234-260

Executive – Process Interactive Control (EPIC) 29

Exercises de mathmatique 175